THE HERITAGE ™

The Ego Has Landed

Written by Athena Park

DEDICATION:

Grateful to GOD... ALL my Family.

ALL children are GOD.

GOD's Love of my Heritage... the Ascended Masters, Archangels, Angels, Spirit Guides

I dedicate this book to: My Dad & Momma and Elle, my Beautiful Daughter

The depth of your eyes is the depth of our soul's silence. ™

"KNOW THYSELF"

Heavens Eternal Resurrection Inward Toward ALL God's Essence.

Our life's journey is the process of self-realization – to attain higher consciousness maturing. This journey invokes a clearing out of all fears, any rationalization, escapism, resistance, ego-death, commitment-phobic, paranoia, and sacrilege. A strong, unwavering Faith deems a Life of Freedom.

Every child's upbringing is to master the self and journey through parallel dimensions for karmic cycles and patterns of behavior that can evolve one's soul's path. The path is given to those who are driven to embrace all the colors of the rainbow, and not only those clouds of illusion... Juxtaposed between Heaven and playing devil's advocate more than likely can lead you from darkness to dawn. What a Historic time to be alive... in this life, orchestrated for us to witness and be a part of Humanity's new fragrance, PEACE. How this happens is all up to you... to part-take in your inner guidance by seeking yourself. A beginning with no end... "What A Wonderful World" Louis Armstrong shares this song for us to remember.

Our soul's evolution of "self-realization" has given us all the power of Love. I pray that a fulfilled life will allow Humanity to rise up while becoming enlightened to your true essence. A transparent view through the eyes of all mankind...through the ALL, of ONE.

A child of an unborn Master becomes a child of One Master™…

Master of self, self-mastery.

Table of Contents

PRELUDE

We cannot begin to perceive what goes on inside the workings of our Universal Maker… but what we do know is that love is no time like the present. What can be felt means more in the Spirit realm than what is ever spoken on Earth. Who has shown their Love to you? Have you ever felt and experienced true love? "Self-realization" is at the height of God's treasure quest for every energetic soul embodiment IS God's LOVE. Jesus showed Himself to all His children by setting the example for us to follow – salvation is ours as we have been promised – "Do unto others as you will do unto yourself". Gifted with the word of God, we are to heed the call to this feeling called LOVE.

INTENTIONS

LOVE IS… the Universal energetic force that picks up on every human's emotion, will or intention. The reasons behind every intention are especially valuable when our lives are undergoing extreme change, pain, trauma and suffering. For this reason, we do need to stop questioning and start allowing our Heritage of Family to show us the way forward. Under false pretenses, we are given no rules as to how this life will or will not pan out for us. We need not underestimate the powers that BE … but, to KNOW thyself. This just means that we are not the ones in charge… God IS.

For those who have a complete lack of Faith of God's way, you will soon come to find out that there are other factors that have led you to your beliefs and to have more Faith. What possible ways could show us this? Death, rebirth, shadow work and forgiveness, and a slew of unforeseen circumstances that have led us astray. Knowing that death will shoot you up unto the Heavenly realms of the Universe is what the term "Celebration of Life" really means. To die is to rise... and the fact that you are here, on Earth, is the focal point of your existence. This existence is for those who choose to elevate to a higher consciousness in an expedited way. A celebration of one's life just means that this person extracted their physical form to undertake the realms of higher consciousness.

We're not all privy as to why or what we're doing here... but the common denominator on the Earth plane is all Love in deeds. To learn our lessons so that we may graduate to a higher consciousness leaving a legacy. What will your legacy be known as? What values have you attained? Where and when do you feel most at home? With whom? Are you comfortable in your own skin? Do you sense a change in the air of your heirs? Can you remain the same person you have always been? Why? Stop what you've always thought and go for everything you have no idea of that will unfold. What does your authentic self feel like? Is it the image that you see looking back at you in the mirror? If not, then what would you want that image to look like? Does it correlate with your true inner self? Do you know what that means? Why struggle? Wreak havoc when necessary. Stand up for what you believe. Be true. Be strong. Be careful. Know when to have a level of integrity. Know when to be respected and respectful. Light your candle(s). Pray.

Taking this under consideration, we can learn the basic reasons why a child of God chose to come down from Heaven, be reincarnated by the Holy Spirit and become one with God. In the Lord's Prayer, we humans tend to rehearse those sacred vows as robots, not listening or even knowing what they truly symbolically signify.

The Lord's Prayer is most important when needing HELP from the other side. Let's begin....

Our Father, who Art in Heaven,

Our Fathers who are in Heaven, are the same fathers who raised us, took care of us... whether, in the actual physical sense of your father, grandfather, stepfather, uncle etc.

Hallowed Be Thy Name

A hallowed disservice to those who must seek to provide an actual "name" where there is no name(s) needed and/or required in the Spirit realm

Thy Kingdom Come

God's Kingdom is within us, and when we realize it, it appears.

Thy Will Be Done

We are here to imprint our 'WILL' upon this Earth so as to imprint the magical treasures to those who firmly believe they will achieve.

On Earth as it is in Heaven

On Earth, in the 3-Dimensional world that leads us all unto a higher consciousness, arisen to Heaven's gate.

Give Us This Day

Give us today and always a place to call home.

Our Daily Bread

To exhibit a life of appreciation for gaining purity of the Lord's body and, wine for the Blood of Christ as we receive both the Blessings of our Body & Soul with a private confession for most, and a retribution of a reborn soul for others.

And Forgive Us Our Trespasses

Forgive them, Lord, for what they know, NOT what they do…

As We Forgive Those Who Trespass Against Us

And, we WILL be healed when we Forgive All those who cannot be forgiven.

And Lead Us NOT Into Temptation

Let bygones be bygones and know when to extract from our shadow, the ego, and other's evil doings and be blessed for being led into Heaven's realm – within then without.

But Deliver Us From ALL Evil

Deliver us ALL from the grasping of society's evil ways and be WILLING to KNOW GOD as the ALL. In Heaven, as upon Earth's beauty, we remain HIM/HER.

May these words NOT fall on deaf ears, but be spoken out unto the Universe as the children we remain… from the mouth of babes… they say, please DO NOT FORSAKE ME. As Above, So, Below…

We're here on Earth not to tell other humans what to believe, what to follow or even how much to pray and/or to have Faith – and yet, in the 11th hour, many fall to their knees begging for redemption. A Statue of Liberty has been placed right in New York to remind everyone that we are the masters of our own lives, to raise the bar and to follow no one else but ourselves. The Statue of Liberty remains a beautiful depiction of the sense of being true to oneself and to "never forget" those who suffered and were buried under the guise of their own freedom. This is about liberty and the pursuit of happiness when one is no longer bound by a civilization that deems to control the population. There are so many reasons why every city has its own distinguished landmark representative of their purpose as a tribute to the American people. Europe, South America, and Asia all have their signature Historic remains of their ruins, warriors, gods, goddesses of culture and feats of passion. Some underestimate the power of many other cities or countries based upon the history of one's past, but remember, one nation under God, is also here to heal Her. Please take heed whenever you decide to take it upon yourselves to rule out a country, other than your own, for feats that you may not truly understand.

LOST THREADS

"I once was lost but now I'm found…" from the Bible verse where it is a metaphorical statement that breeds on those who already know that they have been lost souls roaming the Earth. Those souls who were once lost and now found are on the echelon of the Highest Order. Society deems mankind's narrative to be sought with the "Fear of God" instilled in their programming – this should not be. The majority of Humanity's inability to discern what they do believe – instead of being manipulated and coerced into believing whatever society has said, requires attention. What has transpired is Humanity became a species of being a glutton-for-punishment mentality due to their ignorance. Those who know that their life on Earth was not going to be a joy ride but have suffered for what they believe in and set their own course from a heartful place, will be saved. It's one thing to wonder if you can stay true to yourself; and, it's no wonder when a spirit living in a human body can equate to the consequences of eternal salvation… a Freedom that is unlike any other. A festival of light implores us to seek whatever we feel revealing our true essence. There are no right-turns or wrong-ways… there is only a long, winding road that exists in tandem with the original thread of Love. Every experience on our journey back Home is to remember what we've learned by forgetting. Remember to Forget. What we've been taught by mankind needs discernment – at which time an unveiling of all that has been learned will be forgotten, woven for a new self-discovery of Mastery. This life is a play-by-play of people, places and things that have resurfaced in a different suit mirroring back to us what we see, what to learn and discern that will clear karmic cycles. Earth's design for mankind is to live a life of many Dimensions of consciousness that will propel us in seeking out all that exists as One. The difference(s) from one child who is a lost soul and another who has always felt like a lost soul has a multitude of common patterns that are the threads to finding oneself. So many differences in one's way of thinking makes it almost improbable for any one person to peel back all the different layers of the onion. The onion is metaphoric for getting to the heart of the matter. The core peel of the last thread is when we are getting close to our ascension, self-realization. There is no other reason for some to be gifted with the silver spoon while others who grunge, steal, pilfer to gain some power, money, and the established characteristics of the Ego self. This cannot be understood until you are able to look very closely in the mirror and face yourself … one-by-one. "To thy own *will* be true…" has eluded so many of the children on Earth for reasons that go beyond.

Humility, as an example is to know you are a sacred self of Creation – to live selflessly and not selfishly. This is the balance within self and in your external relationships with all living things. Humility is represented by the wolf who lives for one pack…a leader with the power of loyalty and intuition is Free. The indigenous believed that wolves are the reincarnation of deceased hunters with keen perception – guardians of protection. This is just one example of the threads of our ancestors who are with us in all embodiments of Mother Nature for mankind to learn about through seeking. Whenever you come across an animal, a tree, a flower, a stranger etc., and the feeling you get is Love and a sense of being Home…this is an incarnate. Guardian angels in disguise will rise to the occasion when we are in need of HELP. Let it be known, we are never alone… look around!

The imbalances of back/forth of need/greed, desires-of-the-fires that burn underneath the surface, weakness vs. strength and so many more "divides" of characteristics, innately given while in the womb of their mother; are brave and endure their own suffering. "This too shall pass…." was coined as a broadly used Sufi Masters of the Ages who brought out in children a sense of humility, humbleness and noble efforts for Humanity. Those who have mastered the 'Art of Living' have experienced life as the playful innocence that it is. The 'game of life' is truly what it stands for – light, fun, playful moments of life experiences that bleed into intellectual learning of self as one returns to their own innocence. A life of Freedom is luxury.

Threaded Lights illuminate Life's Sky of Freedom… ™

INCEPTION

Life begins between both the Love of a Father and a Mother who have chosen (or not) to begin the journey of parenthood. The so-called "black sheep" of the family are chosen to become the Divine blueprint that hosts all the Akashic records founded and where individual souls must entertain their karmic threads of retribution. Attaining a certain frequency that reflects our own readiness and determination to achieve growth is what is known as Divine intervention. Whatever lessons are to be learned is up to the souls who agree to uphold threads of their Heritage. Once karma has been rectified, Love becomes a purified essence when our soul's blueprint of every experience is led by free will. Our free will is purposefully designed as 'landmarks' on our journey, as merging a way forward; or a course -correct by redirecting our energy back to its original imprint.

Once an embryo enters the mother's womb, life is created, as Masculine and Feminine energies merge. Many "thinks" they're in charge of this process., However, Heaven's doors and the soul's recognition have already agreed upon the union to procreate a child. Much controversy can be debated on this subject matter, but it is quite true that the threads of a fated union happen when and with whom constitute a bond. A child's bond between the Love of both a Mother

8

and Father (adopted, fostered, or otherwise), is found at the onset of energy between both parents. Down the silver cord, the child enters - as the soul attaches during the 4-7th month of a woman's pregnancy only to experience the landing…either a cry for HELP or tears of JOY, "baby's first breath." Out of the mouth of babes … many newborns that signed up to entertain their true essence have become their reality. All idiosyncrasies, wounding and/or our scars of unhealed family threaded conditioning, attach well before conception. When united between two souls that have agreed upon to bear children, intentional or not, this energy is required to purify all involved. Whether it takes many life cycles or just one is what matters in the purification of this energy through the act of forgiveness to heal. This is an arduous journey of one's soul, but it is the reason behind why the energetic forces of Mother Earth are uprising to a New World Order. In the — dash — the— the child's veins, interceding both the blood -of -parents, all organs, the brain and a vast plethora of inner workings are forming. External characteristics, personality, and findings that go much deeper into the confines of one's inner/outer traits are also threaded from one's History, past-life e History, as well as for the energy of both parents. A final thread forms within the child's structure of and within their mindset that will enable the child to co-create a newly formed thread. It's not that they're not forming their own threads too, but these threads are all entangled for reasons beyond what humans can comprehend. What's also being formed is the ancient lineage of threads written, it has been said. Whenever these threads are interacting with one another they're speaking their own language of Love, a symphony. Every thread within us and in the history of our ancestors are gathered together to formulate a neuron of cells, veins etc., from where they've been and what, in this lifetime, is to understand. Just as the tree veins erupt from out of nowhere, it is pertinent to attempt to conceptualize the same goes for that of a human. Once we bear fruit off the trees, what also comes to pass is not only the "fruits of our labor" but also the death/rebirth for what transcends.

We are all the same in the "tree of life" cycles where every branch holds up its arms that beget the need for strength and a sense of expression. The expressions of our "Tree of Life " is harbored within and without the energies of one's life. Our standard of living requires our lives to be strong, willful, and accepting of all that is given and all that is taken. We live in an environment where the issues of connectivity tend to sway all the generations of children – big or small. Whatever has happened in today's world has been because of and/or not withstanding in the natural order, whereby upon conception, innocence has been forsaken. What deems all children on this Earth of their innocence is the darkness/shadow, on Earth, that which is a necessity for inner work to be bestowed in order for the freedom of one's salvation to be realized. Shadows are the lanterns that illuminate the inner depths of ourselves. Encountering various levels of consciousness requires all children to enter a place of solace – so that the original light can be attained that was given at birth. The call of one's shadow is none other than the return to innocence. In the mirror(s) of self-reflection is the alchemical transformation that sparks the Sun's rays of our evolution.

"As we turn the pages of our lives, we are being anointed into familiar places in time." ™

Sufi Rumi Master has said, "KNOW THYSELF," a miracle of One Love, in the sacred union of our undying love for oneself … the ONE. Once we have realized this kind of Love, the entire Universe will set an example for all. Society has identified love for another as a superficial physical love which brings masks of destruction deemed as lust, cravings and desire. Mankind seeks to find "the One" in Love, without being given a purpose. How can we find love when we are already loved? What the differences are when, "being in love" feels like it has not been taught. Understanding that our physical body is our "temple" of holiness, not to be used, abused or otherwise is the first lesson in love. What has been taught, however, was that being "in love" extends only through our physical bodies and not necessarily within the Heart. Both of these Loves can be felt on the external, as Love, but it grows through ONE's heart that authenticates as True Love. We must know that we are THE ONE before setting out to find THE ONE. Being "in -love" begins with what the heart feels…and the external ego of a physical connection masks itself as love, when it is lust. Is it lust or Love? When we can distinguish between Love for another "without" a physical desire, and/or craving of another, the heart begs to connect with one's soul. A soul connection between two people "in love" can definitely feel from the heart and the body – but, when the body fails to perform, it cries out to the Heart. True Love's kiss is deeper than just the skin off our backs – we must delve into all of our senses where True Love feels itself through another's counterpart of the Heart. *Soul2Soul*

GOD'S LOVE

What brings a child into the world? God's Love for Humanity… it's what makes us threaded with one another – to be remembered. Every child, big or small, is God's gift to this world. Whatever you must go through upon arrival is for your highest good… especially in times of doubt. We are all here to experience and believe in the power of Love. Getting through life's journey is not for the weak-at-heart…

11

"The Creed" is the realization of a full-filled life, that it speaks to Humanity…words to Love by. ™

It's not easy being a child of God whose journey of a soul's love settles all other loves in ways that are incomprehensible. What we "settle" for in love becomes, for some, our reason for living. It is frowned upon that all types of love are either greater in resonance, or not, and that others feel the other one is settling. Who is to say that one love is viewed as greater than any other? Who has the right-of-passage to distinguish one's choice to love or settle for whatever they deem as "love" or to listen to anyone else's opinions? All love is exactly the right kind of love being experienced in the present moment. No matter what others may say, all love is equivalent to the other. Humans like to misconstrue, manipulate and exalt themselves in drama for their own reasons; don't be fooled. Let's take a closer look at why we choose whom to love, what reasons we are in that capacity of energetic vibration to love another; and to seek the purest love of self. All loves are valuable and need to be seen as valid – for all love(s) require attention, compassion, a test of one's patience, no judgments/criticisms, and the lessons to be learned.

Instead of worrying about what other people may or may not say or are thinking, why haven't we addressed the issue(s) of man/woman and child's clear distinction of the Trinity? The Holy Trinity of man, woman and child shall experience Love very differently – as Love for a Mother, Father, child, sibling, friend, family, or acquaintance bodes a different kind of Love entrusted in the Love of ourselves ... in sacred union. No matter what happens, knowing that if one is not whole (Holy), the love sought is filling a void. If the search for love happens to those who are trying to fill a void, one must go within, in Divine timing, to become whole. Sacred love is based on self-discipline.

INNOCENCE

A child who is still in God's pocket has been given the innate gifts of both parents, but has also been gifted with the lessons, trauma, wounding, and scars, that both parents have ingested, and those become the child's way of life. These are our ancestral woundings where we, as children, are in unfamiliar territory. Yet so many have been "sworn in" to heal the wounding of our ancestors. Healing trauma isn't about, "Why did this happen to me?" or "What did I do to deserve this?" It is about moving forward, acknowledging our trauma and how to make choices that allow us to thrive. Do *not* blame your parents… or expect everyone to validate your emotions; it's about being the responsible family member who is here to break the cycle. However, not every child has the innate capacity to do so in one's lifetime, therefore, some children have agreed to reincarnate as many times until there is forgiveness. All children are connected to the ALL – the Universal energy of the ALL and have been gifted with innate gifts. There is a clarity that our childhood has upon us, and whether we realize it or not, this is the most incredible time of our lives. Why? God has gifted every child with innate talents for us to use upon the Earth as a service to others. Witnessing the beauty of being granted Life, in gratitude, threads weave our Heritage into this very moment, allowing us to witness the vast power of love. to witness Love's power in its vastness. Love expands in our world as a fresh bouquet of flowers, a Spring rain, birds' chirping, summer barbeques, walks in the park, ice cream, family gatherings, playing hopscotch, riding bikes, climbing trees, walking to school, kicking rocks, talking with others and

13

experiencing Life in all forms of connectivity, LOVE. These are the moments in life where we find people, places and threads of like-minded experiences that make us *feel* alive. We reminisce of those times to gain that youthful feeling ....in our childhood memories. Everything is new... from friends, teachers, schools, music, talks about nothing, places "out there" to go, see, and experience, knowing there's a vast world to encounter.

Those days were a new-found breeding ground for what's to come. Feelings of "anticipation" ... waiting for that call, what's for dinner, going for a joy ride, exploring new places, talking for hours about everything and nothing. These are the moments in life we will not forget... or do we? When does the feeling and/or of remembering our youth disappear? Did it happen when you weren't looking? That day, that moment... when you realize your innocence has been stripped away by external life matters. It's clouded memories of our youthful innocence in the simple life slowly chipping away at the bit...

Insofar as the eye can see, an entire world of FEAR emerges in our own backyards. Distrust, discouragement, depression, negative thoughts and unexplained emotions stirring all through the house... not even the hopes of a small mouse could impart. If we could turn back the clock before it strikes 12 would ricochet us all out of this slumber and pump us with Love for one another. No stockings were hung... lies filled everyone, stressed out with Fear for one's end is near, only to seek all that is done comes from the one. We're filling that Turkey and lo' and behold, it's our grandma who fell and broke her nose. The nose, KNOWS, is the place where nothing gets by...when death comes knocking, you'll definitely know why. Here is a little semblance of hope when children have lost their innocent cloak.

14

The cloak is a metaphor for the physical temple of our body, which begins to wear within every tear. All of those children's nursery rhymes remind us of our youth…Mom/Dad or another adult reading, "Little Bo Peep, Who Lost Her Sheep" and unbeknownst to us that story is actually about Little Bo Peep's ID/Ego self-posing as the child who lost her way in life, as her innocence and identity were hijacked. Sound familiar?

Children pack their books… and,

It's off to school we go… we dig, dig, dig, dig,

In our mind the whole day long

It's what we only know how to do thinking,

it ain't no trick

To get rich quick- trick

Where a million diamonds begin as coal

It's off to school we go…

HISTORY IN THE MAKING

What hasn't changed over a course of time is the requirement(s) of the family unite… families are bonded, some by blood and others by their craft of choice, while others are driven into a family based upon their adoption, foster parenting and such that goes without saying… a family united as one. There is no "perfect" family or relationship until our threaded past of karma can be severed, healed and forgiven. Mankind has been disillusioned with such a polarity of thought(s) that, for many, it is very difficult to understand we are Family. Every creature, every person, every place and everything in Mother Earth is a unification of what we've become and/or are to become. Each thread that leads us to a new life experience has been gifted to us for our soul's growth. What History has taught and is teaching us all is to become the change in the world that you wish to be. For every human being upon this Earth to sponge in the very stuff of Life, every morsel whose fragrance is revealed. The Lotus Flower is where we shall remain, if not in this world, in another – as the lotus flower emits a resilience for life, a strength of resolve, and purity in one's soul that crosses all barriers and cultures for all to absorb. The absorption of one's fragrance that has withstood the test(s) of all time …a sacred emblem of Hope, Strength, Rebirth, Purity. one's Creation.

Joining forces with the other side is not only a conversation – it is an inner journey of oneself as the ONE. Any other force that goes beyond that understanding is the work of your ID/Ego-Identification of the ego. Practically perfect does not only exist on the Spirit plane – when one discovers their truth, it is actually attained on the Earth plane. People who do not see you for your intellect will regret informing you of their own intellect by placing theirs before you – Egoic intellect. Our Egos are the many masks formed that mankind has learned to wear to falsify one from the other. No one can even describe clearly when the truth is being stated, but it can be noted that if these convictions come from the headspace and not the heart, it is of an Egoic mindset. Most people do not understand that intelligence is borrowed knowledge learned in school and that most of those people speak from their 'smarts' and not necessarily their 'hearts'.

Why is it that some people make others feel "less than" (behind the scenes or not) just because they received good grades or can recall figures or what happened with Saul? Is it "right" to always want to be right; and/or need to correct another inconsequential as it is; and/or to quietly judge another for the way they don't appear to your liking… said the judge. Whose "honor" will rise and whose "honor" will fall when dealing with the likes of one's misuse of power for all? Take heed now, or else you'll remain a fallen star whose claim-to-fame will be in vain. It's not yours to claim when your name is just a name – it's karma, said the wise one with no name to claim.

"A HORSE WITH NO NAME" by America.

To recite a psalm from The Bible doesn't make you God, or in His image. It is, however, in your deeds, in service and for the Love of yourself and others that is God. An all-serving God of LOVE. The intellect may appear much smarter on the outside but has not gone within to seek themselves. What makes one person considered "smarter" than another? Is it the ability to study facts, figures and/or numbers "memorizing your way" to the Ego's success? When it comes to Life Lessons, where has that left a good majority of you? How can someone recite Freud, Jung, Mozart, psalms of The Bible, World Wars, epic madness in History etc., but not be able to let go of control, need to be right, tit-for-tat, go with the flow, witness the errors of your ways, show gratitude, help others, be kind, experience a fulfilled Life of Joy, Peace, Comfort, Kindness. Living Life as the present has been gifted to ALL!

HISTORY OF THE EGO

At the very beginning of time, the man was given a woman who would entertain his ways of bringing out all the impressive characteristics to grow from and make one proud. This was not what happened... man became a vastly egoic individual as God placed an ego in every human on planet Earth to conquer... him/herself. What happened was that the man showed up as feeling better than the woman, and even though the woman assisted in elevating him, he fell from a place of needing her for assistance, which turned into a desire for flesh instead. The egoic man who began showing up as wanting it all... fell from having enough grace to be ALL. The story of Adam and Eve depicts a perfect yin/yang couple, which leads us from the pure innocence of the fulfillment of our greatest needs to addressing the egoic mindset of the physical body upholding the desire of man. What happened has been a strong theme for the duration of our History, as woman was created from the rib of man. Where has it been written that women were not able to obtain equality? When did the desire for human flesh begin... Was it when Adam gave Eve the apple to bite first? Does this exemplify man's control of this inequitable story of how the ego was incarnated? What, where, and how did this storyline of Adam and Eve set the precedence for all couples who deemed to establish a relationship? Why hasn't Eve's side of this story become a necessary component? Has it? Was Eve viewed as weak, subservient and/or shamed or, as being naive...wanting to be loved? This is what the ego does best... takes all the power away and shows up, exposing any guilt, jealousy, pride, etc. Whether you believe in Adam and Eve's story, does not equate to what the moral of human imprisonment upon us is, as a "guilty as charged" mentality. Once Eve's leaf fell to the ground, biting into the apple, the curse of the Ego was felt by the entire human race. Eve broke her silence and told everyone that it was not her fault that she bit into the apple because she trusted Adam; herein lies the entire planetary reasons for falling from grace. Mother Earth knowingly placed the Tree of Knowledge for those who are inquisitive, curious and trusting. Instead of perceiving this act of trust as biting into the apple of wisdom, it was perceived and shamed as an act of Ego.

The word, catEGOry – cat EGO ruins you; cat Envisions GOD's ONE can be either or…based on your EGO

How did it occur that Adam and Eve felt ashamed when naked? Where did this shame come from…if not, the Ego self. Upon entering the Earth, our Egos are swirling energies of fear; guilt, shame, worry, stress, contradictions, doubt, sadness, depression, negativity, self-sabotage and an entire slew of masked stew wrapped in shadow wrap. From this point onward, every man, woman and child have an Egoic self to deal with, to learn from, to explore, to escape and befriend or serve entirely. How many times have you listened to your ego that led you astray? Did you feel that listening to all the voices in your head has brought you a mindset of nothing but a series of uneventful escapades? That feeling of falling deep into a dark hole of illusions…that begs one to fall on their knees, praying, to see? Do we realize how such egoic emotions can affect our lives that could impress upon the trajectory of our lives? The soul spirit encapsulates Eve's alter ego in the formation of Herself, as Mother Earth. How did this happen? Have you thought that She needed to cleanse herself of the world's shame, guilt, distrust etc., placed upon Her, to become our Mother of ALL. To say this is another metaphor is to acknowledge a new perspective on why, in the beginning, women have been considered secondary? This is exactly why the Women's Liberation Movement caused so many tainted women to stand up and take control. Have women found their equality? How has society shown women as…being seen and not heard? Are equal rights and/or equal pay affecting women today? How do you feel being a woman today? Have you felt that History has marked this place in time … or not?

Awareness of EGO traps, as follows:

EGO TRAPS

1. If you think that riding a bike to work or taking public transportation is spiritual, you may find yourself internalizing judgment to those who drive cars.

2. If you lessen your time watching TV because you know it rots the brain waves and is spiritual, you may be critical of those who do.

3. If you feel more spiritual to avoid gossip, new media, tabloids, and the like… you may be internally judging those who can't stop talking.

4. If you listen to only spiritual/religious music and attend concerts only of that genre, you may find yourself critical when others listen outside of that influence.

5. If you think spirituality is yoga, meditation, being vegan, buying organic, investing in crystals, practicing reiki, shopping at thrift stores, visiting ashrams and reading spiritual books, then judge anyone who does not; you've fallen into an ego trap.

Superiority…self-righteous superiority is one of the Ego traps that sneaks in through the back door. The Ego traps are as subtle as the twists and turns of nobility.

All Spiritual paths are from within…as seen, spoken, heard, touched, felt, laughed, and Loved – The Seven Wonders of the World.

SCHOOL OF HARD KNOCKS
STRAYED BELIEFS

Humanity has tendencies much like animals…everyone strays off the path but ends up finding their way. What's left is the love that remains in one's heart. Just like the transition from the Earth plane into a new door of Heaven's sentience – it happens in the blink of an eye. Science requires intuition to lead those underdeveloped souls who require statistics and findings, even to the sound of a prototype of confirmation; yet, even then, people are still skeptical about seeking themselves. "Knowing" is the way spirit merges with science…not the other way around. Debate, negate, is of no concern as the Universe that invokes all the planets, the atmosphere, and the stars that shine bright under the sapphire blue skies is science unknown, and, spiritually awakened. This is what we are all "made of…" The world evolves in order for Humanity to do the same. Many are already on their journey of Love; however, some are still asleep. "You can go your own way…" sings Stevie Nicks in unison with the etheric rituals where the spirit is threaded with the physical – one should not be forced into any external influences/influencers. If there is anyone in your external world attempting to change your mind, or challenge your beliefs, it is imperative that you believe what is in your own Heart. Not a single human "knows" what one's heart feels … allowing everyone's Freedom.

To infiltrate someone else's energetic field is a tragedy that wants to happen. Remember this. Give yourself a break from all those who "tempt" you to believe in what "they" want…this is exactly how the Earth got into the position it is today. Set the stage for your life's work as an independent contractor who adheres to the beat of their own drum. Nothing or no one is ever in charge of you! This too shall pass… will be an inevitable realization for all those whom we've left behind. Saying nothing is much better for one's soul than repeating old patterns of all those negative people in our lives who used you for their own storyline. No more! The majority of those who have been set free from the grips of one's truth are having a self-check-in with their egoic self, attempting to figure out why some people are no longer in their lives. Either way, things have unfolded in the exact way, with all those whom we've severed in Divine order. Enough is enough! Stay strong because those who play the best victims want retribution of revenge. Believe that those who we've allowed to be our friends, lovers, partners in crime etc., had to go so that their reflection be re-examined.

Understand that time and space are required for every human to experience what they need on this "school of hard knocks" to move on. Justice will be served to all who adhere not only to their innate truth but also to their ability to forgive and be forgiven. Forgiveness is the only way! Under the guise of the ego, many choose to be too proud, better than mindset, too independent, too masculine, and too controlling that goes unnoticed. This is exactly how many will take their narrative to the grave. Just when you thought you might have found yourself, another layer gets unveiled. There is no telling how many layers of the egoic self-one has to peel back, but it lifts us to an overwhelming peace that sets a new day's dawn; you're off to the races. There is no race on who gets to the finish line for there is no end in sight – the only ending will be that of our physical bodies. By noticing the mirrored neurons in our interactions with others, we can see how spirituality is threaded with science. Every soul emerges to shoot for the stars… casting aside all that ever was for all that shall be. To know is to grow, to forgive is to live, to share is to care, to love is to evolve eternal. Keeping it real … let's focus on the self within the physical body. Our authentic self consists of the gift presented from an innocence of a baby's breath, where life begins to end. What we do with the self-contained, in a body, relies upon every one of us to uncover. All the different narratives will appear as if out of nowhere, especially those stories that have given us great meaning. Nearing this unfolding, we've been given all the grapes of wrath as well as the grapes of wealth insofar as what we choose to pick off of the Tree of Life. The Garden of Eden encapsulates both the Divine Masculine and Divine Feminine whereby either one will come forth depending upon the matter at hand.

The School of Hard Knocks isn't easy as it asks every human being to step outside of their comfort zone to places that expand their mind… expand their vision… expand their lot in Life as the grave is calling. Most NDE (Near-Death Experiences) have one thing in common – they had lost their kefi/Greek for "passion for Life" only to experience Love unconditionally and be that child once again, reborn. The common theme in question is, "If you were to go back home tomorrow, what would be one of your biggest life regret(s)? To live a fulfilling Life with my Family and Friends, to explore new places and faces and to feel Love for all Humanity. How much Love do you feel inside? For your children, for your Life? For yourself? When will mankind learns that being in Love with Life is one of the greatest loves of all time? Nothing else matters... only Love. We come into this world with all Love, and when our physical body is weary and thin, we must embrace these memories that have touched our Hearts. As the beautiful Whitney Houston sang, "The Greatest Love of All" is... "learning to LOVE yourself..." lyrics... "I believe the children are our future, teach them well and let them lead the way...show them all the beauty they possess inside..." We find authentic Love when we are authentic; we experience life to its full capacity when we become whole; we walk upon this Holy ground knowing every step is our true essence. Learning to Love is reminiscent of the depths of what we've been through as real, "God Only Knows..." song by King + Country. Can we start over? "There's a kind of Love that God only knows...."

However, as your story unravels, just know that the most important part of beginning your journey is to seek what you want, what is most important for your highest good, and to finally realize that you matter...

RAISING CHILDREN

A child's influence comes from the foundation of their upbringing, and by no means does this make up the entire foundation... The most valuable influences come between the ages 1-8, where a child is co-created into learning of his/her forefathers – the traditions, the learning curve and the levels of those who, too, are the influencers. We have come to know these learning stages of growth are, in hindsight, very influential to our children as they become grown-ups. The learning is instilled already into a child's mindset at

24

birth, and, depending upon the child's uprising, various choices are made into what is now either the child's real self and/or an egoic version. The raising of a child is as crucial as ever because we, as parents, tend to want to mold children in ways that we deem appropriate, until we understand how unhealthy this mindset can become. Raising what is known as "mini-me's" dictates more like raising a trophy of progressive external powers, of which the ego loves to display. This is what is known as an ego state-of-affair as to how, why, and what we are to teach our children. How do we do this? Do we realize how vulnerable children are and that they don't know the difference between what is being taught as being the same as a parent's claim to fame? For a child to be driven to adhere to a similar profession, talent and/or any other replica of a parent does not allow the child to grow on his/her own. You may ask, "What's wrong with this kind of upbringing?" Wanting a child to be a better version of the talents, higher status and, of course, the power that comes with this? It's not a matter of us, as parents, not wanting the very best for our children…it is the influence imposed, instead of what they may choose to pursue. Every child inhales a vast number of different fragrances, which are breeding them to become the best version of themselves, yet we all struggle with how much influence others have on them. You may ask, "Why is this of such great importance?" "Isn't it good to have a child get the most well-rounded influential learning possible from all who claim to know how to raise a child"? How can we determine who is around as the great "influencers" raising our children? The obvious factors are in how great a parent or an influencer raises their own…. Or, is it? What makes for a good parent? How well do you know or have witnessed the undertaking of parenting? There is no instruction, "How to Raise The Best Child, EVER." not until we've learned about ourselves.

Have you helped a child? Have you assisted a child who was not yours? Did you intervene and help or have you shied away from being a helper of another kind? In uncertain times, many parents have to rely on others in order to help assist either their own children and/or the lives of other children who have parents that are unable to do so. We do not judge others' parenting skills yet we do need to intervene when HELP is required. Do you feel it's your duty or right-of-passage to assist? Even if the child is not your own, if you witnessed the actual parental figure not taking it upon themselves to help because they're too preoccupied, then, would you assist…or, not? It is within every human being on the face of this Earth to impose their skillset onto another's for a little bit – even if this person doesn't have their own kids. What makes a child of God's less qualified just because they do not have any children; versus, many parents who had their children that are deemed unable, underqualified, too young, unappreciative, selfish and not able. When do we, as humans, have any right to place our own judgment onto others who could very well be highly qualified by their own life experience(s) and/or their upbringing of those who raised them. It is not for any one of us to impose our opinions, yet, we tend to do this on occasion because perhaps we've had our own children that we have some kind of say so. This couldn't be further from the truth. Every human on this planet, whether a parental figure or not, has been raised by someone. Therefore, all children of God's meet all the requirements of raising a child not unless there is a mental, emotional illness and/or any dis-ease. This too shall pass… is another form of giving a child the plausible existence of understanding that we, as parents, deliberately have no control "over" what and/or how a child ends up behaving and/or not attaining – but, we do have every right to make the environment safe, protected, trusting, and abundantly happy for every child. No matter what … if a child is endangered, in any way, HELP from another is noted as *compassion*.

As Ralph Waldo Emerson states, "What lies behind us, and what lies before us, are tiny matters to what lies within us."

A non-debatable subject is if, in your opinion, certain mothers are 'fit or unfit' to be mothers. These matters and so many more cast shadows of Fear and are EGO bound. What needs to be addressed is how impressive a mother and/or father handle things together in ever-changing facets of raising children. Every child requires a whole lot of attention and it is imperative that we, as parents, are able to give this to them. The most lucrative life is the one where a child can recall childhood memories as pleasurable. Those children raised on spending quality time with their parental figures end up growing independently self-confident while others were raised by wolves… having various addictive behaviors. Children who feel unloved, unwanted, abandoned and the likes of loss have been, "Chasing Pavements" (song by Adele) for lifetimes. Early on in life and unbeknownst to us, a child's love finds itself in our Hearts; knowing where it all begins, but not necessarily where it evolves. We must be introduced as one to know another… Children raised in Love will do anything for you, whereas children raised in Fear will do nothing for you. Those who did not have this learning were taught the underlying nature of selfishness in wanting more for themselves. A "look at me" and "look at what I've got" mentality is instilled in their upbringing, unbeknownst to the child/children. Why is this such a pertinent teaching? The raising of a selfish child vs. the sharing child is what makes all the difference in one's life – learning to care for others, wanting to assist and showing that children who are shown their true nature will learn to help

27

mankind. What could possibly be better than "people helping people?" Has mankind gone too far down the rabbit hole to regain their truest nature of sharing, caring and being of a giving kind? This is the natural order of Humanity and Her children – **kindness**. When one learns that they have the capacity to be kind, generous and sharing to others reaps much inner reward. Those who grew up in a behavior of selfishness (ego) were taught to contain, hold onto and even hoard - a familiar thread in the lineage. This is where "living up to the Joneses" has become egoic, having to dangle their carats not only to make them feel better, but to subliminally or intentionally showcase another's insecurities. When this happens, it is the one who leads the pack who typically exemplifies the insecure behavior instead of the rest who choose to compete, or not. Kindness has been instilled in every child's natural habitat but has been taught otherwise. We must go back to ground zero and find ourselves ... the good-natured human that is within us all. To care for others, to ask others for assistance, to engage in other's lives for the benefit of Humanity; instead of ignoring what is right in front of them. By keeping our "heads down" from crisis or any other type of situation where help in assisting others is needed is what must change and is crucial to Humanity right now. People are way too absorbed within their own selves, their own selfish ways and becoming an island unto themselves.

In The Bible, it is written as, "No man is an island", Romans 14: 1-26, which is intended to give Humanity a reason to be a community instead of solitude. When a natural disaster occurs, or an emergency, where will you be? Will you choose to assist or not? Do you realize that every man, woman and child is our brother? Mankind needs each and every one of us to pitch in and help others. How have you done so? No matter what you may want to believe or not…we are all in this together! This is our time to shine our light for others to follow.

Children need to learn this growing up from those who raise them and by teaching through example. Why? Every thread that is woven to assist others in deeds will come to understand that the "Laws of the Universe " were built exactly for this reason.

Do not teach that which you do not know or feel – instead, go within by educating yourself to launch a new perspective based upon these Laws.

LAWS OF THE UNIVERSE (in order)

1. Law of Oneness

2. Law of Vibration

3. Law of Action

4. Law of Correspondence

5. Law of Cause & Effect

6. Law of Attraction

7. Law of Compensation

8. Law of Perpetual Transmutation of Energy

9. Law of Relativity

10. Law of Polarity

11. Law of Law & Gender

12. Law of Rhythm

These 12 Laws of the Universe, the Seven Seals, the Rays of Light, the four corners of the Universe, The Bible and much more knowledge is available for all of mankind. Since man has come to walk this Earth on Holy Ground, it is manifest for the children of the world, those who came and left their imprint, and for the up-and-coming generations to follow. Within every metaphor, within the spaces between the lines, and within our own righteous selves contain the magnificence of Creation…to be realized.

Whatever we choose is for our highest good, knowing that the future of the next generations matters. Every man, woman and/or child has been gifted with this Life to lead by example so that they can hand over the torch. We want to know that Humanity's rise of consciousness is because we, as humans, decided to be here at a time when History is in the making. Making a difference serves ALL…and starts with every one of us.

The only thing that matters now is YOU.

"Work on you…and, let God show you yourself".

WHAT DO YOU WANT TO BE WHEN YOU GROW UP?

We not only provide all of the essentials but there are other skills that come with raising children... we become doctors/nurses, psychologist/counselors, cooks, laundry, cleaning, follow-up/follow-through, lack sleep, stress, friend groups, hair stylists/barbers, financial support, fashion trends, parties/birthdays, traveling, security, protection and safety rules, regulations, setting up boundaries, sports advocate, educational requirements, homework, presentations (written/verbal/artistic), playdates, maintain sleep schedule, eating healthy, all last-minute plans and preparations, graduations, college preparations and discovery, listening, life lessons, sharing experiences, monitor external habits/desires of friends, boys, girls; sexual discovery, sex talks, hygiene, menstrual cycles, pregnancy, world events, voting, work ethics, establish solid foundations are the list goes on... real-life parenting. The thing is that there is no rule book or any script to learn from, and most parents do the very best they can. The bottom line is that certain parenting skills dictate what you'd call an "upgrade" at some point in raising children because some traditions are outdated, verbiage changes with certain generations, and sticking to a plan or what used to be considered as traditional values... has changed. It's not to say that a solid foundation doesn't require traditional values...it seems to change in the "presentation" in the "proprietary rulership" and overall "disciplining" needed to sustain a common thread.

There are those parents who are attempting to raise their kids exactly as their parents raised them, while others choose to change everything about how they were raised by winging it. Who's to say one

31

way is better than another? Who has been given the "right" to judge other parenting skills of two-consenting adults (or more) and decide how to raise kids? Everyone raises their kids the way they deem necessary. All children have different skill sets and smarts. What gets in the way is when a parent attempts to *mold* their kids to be "like them". The "mini-me" version...all ego-based and builds upon an establishment of the same. Why does this happen? Children/kids want their parents' approval in some way, shape or form, and if that means mimicking the industry of choice, that child will do so. Children are enchanted by some of their parent's professions that bring in a considerable amount of money – and this is when the child wanders. 'Money talks...' as mankind has been programmed to believe - ever since the beginning, how to exit this matrix? Western culture pre-programmed money minions to want that power. However, the way to get the money, power, big house, and fancy cars is where so many 'head/EGO" in a profession. It's all in the 'head' when being raised in a wealthy family who gives their children everything? The "head" of the household... How many of you are pursuing what you've always wanted in your Life? For a living and/or in Life? "Living the dream...." Be honest. It's all relative – living within your means or living above your means. Has money made your world go round? Others pack up and move out of the country because they realize a life of simplicity makes them happy. "Love what you do and the money will follow..." Who is living by this saying? It's so difficult when we're used to the luxuries that life dangles every chance it gets... because, for the most part, humans are weak. Weakened by paper money that continues to depreciate, however, what can we do? How can humans change the trajectory of what has already been a hard-core press? What if Humanity decided to live within their means... choose a life career instead of a job that enslaves, and find how the thread of money will come, to those who believe. Eastern culture, on the other hand, has been defined as simpler, meditative, happier, and historically appealing? No, India is not as appealing, until you choose... to find the blessings of every action as meditative... dancing without shoes, singing, taking a walk, and more... Be "in Gratitude" for the life gifted and watch what happens!

Every hardship that Humanity has chosen is a choice, there is no doubt about this. If you have traveled to different countries, you will see for yourself the sea of Love awaits – and that the heir of other cultures has more value than cultured pearls could ever buy. That the structures and statues of those who came before held their endurance of Faith. All the Gods and Goddesses remain in the air as our heirs, within every breath. A culture that lends itself to the land where Masters have breathed and walked. Oceans to the sea showcases the depth of feelings for choosing to give back in kind. Learning about other native cultures and languages that depict their hardships of character. Seeking various fragrances of how we see differently, how we live differently, and how we can appreciate it ALL by just believing in letting go. Coming to terms with such differences is not a comparison – it is a collective call to Christ's consciousness.

FAITHFULLY

Two people are joined in Holy Matrimony for the sacredness of vows exchanged where they've agreed to "be fruitful and multiply." A sacred union is offered by two people who believe that the traditional ceremony, in the eyes of God, is felt and seen by all family and friends. Who is to say what shall be? God' IS Love. Be that as it may...two people who claim to indulge in a sacred union have chosen to follow

33

The Ten Commandments – being faithful. Those who veer off track will pay their own karmic injustices in one lifetime or another. Why get married if one hasn't sowed their oats? Makes no difference to others…only to oneself. We all must place our heads on the pillow at night only to 'know' what faithful acts of unfaithfulness we have caused another, as ourselves. Being faithful in a marriage constitutes a Holy sanction where we must face our Maker.

"Marriage has turned away from being a sacred covenant into a contract of convenience." ™

We are not to be defined by our indiscretions but through the unveiling of one Love's true kiss. Choosing and not abusing all forms of Love is to know we are all the LOVE that anyone needs…it is the desire of the beast of burning temptation that lends another to discover, Love. However long it takes – a lifelong search for being "the One" consists of a thread of Truth, a thread of Trust, and "Threads of Destiny™". What does love feel like… has been taught to us first, through the womb of our mother and Mother Earth's love – which may or may not be a contradiction. Either way, we come to Earth feeling either an immediate connection of unconditional love or weeping sadness for an unwanted Love or a lost love. However, your story plays out, makes a world of difference. Having felt Love at the onset of inception becomes the precursor to what is believed to be our truth. Others who are feeling that lack of Love, or none of the above… feel a different truth that, too, will make a world of difference. A Mother/Father bond between two people sets the stage for a lifetime of lessons. No matter whether there is Love or unrequited Love – are karmic lessons. Threads of karma seeped in from our Heritage - as well as the present circumstances of this life cycle, all playing a role in how children learn and are taught. From here on, children delve into Life's common denominator, Love, experienced fully – as in George Harrison's song, "My Sweet Lord" lyrics, "I really want to see you, really want to be with you, really want to see you, Lord… but it takes so long, My Lord." It is within the heart chakra where Love knowingly feels its truth, Home. "Home is where the heart is." When it feels like Home, you'll know.

The external body does feel Love, yet in the way of an embodiment between two bodies who share two bodies as one…much different from knowing two hearts as one in Love. This is where our Ego attempts to overrule the heart center by masking love as a physical union that feels very real. Experiencing love in the physical body, making love and/or having sex, has every ability to grow into an emotional bond – furthering the commitment of Love through a solid sacredness that is Holy. Is it lust or Love? Do you know the difference? How did you witness the love between your Mother and/or Father? Who was absent? Who is present? What other showcasing of Love did you observe? Or not? Was there any communication? Talks between parents working things out? Or, a slamming of the door that meant 'walking out' just like my "father/mother" did. So many versions of a Love so deep, so true, so real… we have all been blinded by the light.

Those infamous words, "I cherish, honor… Faithfully", denote much to be desired following, "I do" … existential to the cause. Journey into the unknown is what really seems to happen to two individuals who are set to be together and attempt to stay together… until death do their part. Those who do believe they want that vow to be sacred becomes their 'till death do we part', and those who convincingly try to manipulate the system, will fail. Lo and behold, the truth is exposed to all those who attempt beating the system, still married after "all these years," NOT Faithful. Once the "sacred vow" is broken doesn't constitute any years of marriage… not to mention, the hefty price you pay karmically. Adultery is a sin that will go to the grave, and all guilty parties become spent. If you 'misrepresent' yourself in any way, the way forward gets very dim. The Ten Commandments were written for reasons that have yet to be unveiled, but must be noted as sacred. The Bible was not intended for religions… it IS Holy unto itself and written to HELP mankind follow a pathway of Light. A dark dictatorship continues to attempt to overrule the goodness of mankind but to no avail. The light will shine even brighter as so much evil/darkness has been exposed – and the way of goodness will raise Humanity.

PARTNERSHIP CAVEATS

The "matter at hand" is to choose which dictatorship you have chosen, giving and/or receiving. This is why we say, "One hand washes the other " to unveil that one cannot do without the other; TWO becomes ONE. Not necessarily a partner in a relationship, but a partner of two halves that are whole. Should you choose to give/receive to yourself while giving/receiving to others is all up to how you were raised to believe. Some of us were raised to choose what type of Love we seek, while others were shown by example, and there are those who only believe in what they have been taught or told to believe.

Society has prefaced the "need" for people to be in a union – partners in marriage, living together, or just a togetherness in agreement between yin/yang. Their yin/yang must match your yin/yang, and the two shall work together in unison, attempting to meet in the middle. It has not been written in any book nor taught in any school that two people must find their so-called other half. This is a fallacy, one that has been co-created by a society driven to entertain matters they have no right to. However, since the beginning of time, Adam and Eve showed up as being in a union of yin/yang that failed miserably. Not only failed in kind, but also showed Humanity at the onsite two people who are not necessarily made to co-exist in partnership. Do we know this, or was this assumed? The caveat, though, is that this lends itself to a huge challenge for humans who are willing to risk it all. Some have risked it all with great regret. Although this has been the prototype of a union, it also taught mankind that true love is defined as falling-in-love as physical… to fall prey. What wasn't taught was that our physical body is our sacred temple. Therefore, the act of "falling-in-love" has been misrepresented as the exchange of bodily fluids; that may or may not lead to true love. How many couples have fallen prey to the physical…then found out later all the hard work that is involved in forming a sacred bond? Hence, the divorce rate has been gaining traction … it's off the charts. This failure-to-launch 'all that glitters isn't gold' ideology comes with much emotional baggage, not to mention, the belief that sacred union cannot be attained. Why? Who is to blame when a physical bond cannot go the distance? What the Ego (ID) in what I see in another is a convoluted attempt to sway one into giving in to the temptations; instead, of bearing witness to the work involved to form a more perfect union. Our kids today are being raised with this narrative… that marriage is not necessary, and for some, it may be true. However, a sacred bond of marriage… no matter what piece of paper is necessary or not, still is seen between two people "in the eyes of God" *A SACRED UNION*. (no paper needed…)

Some of these teachings have been taught... by our parents, etc. and the beliefs of their parents and so on.... Why not build a foundation that is established on Holy ground by leaving other humans to choose? Why have parents or whoever is doing the raising, insisted on doing it their way? Their way is broken... and why has humanity veered out of The Bible? This does not help and hasn't helped as far as the eye "I" can see. When it comes to all relationships of any kind, there is a clear coming together for each other's highest good. When those waivers, if that waivers and doubts begin to set in, relationships lose their essence of authenticity. Relationships include partners, marriage or live-in, love or business, acquaintances, and even strangers and family members. Every relationship, whatever relation, falls under a contract that was made prior to arriving on Earth. All so-called contracts of our blueprint that have been already written are a collaboration, indeed. Within every collaboration, it renders a whole another 'can of worms', which is appropriate for Pandora's box of dirty worms that live, breathe, and reside comfortably in the dirt. "Dirty deeds done dirt cheap" AC/DC kind of vibe... and what remains is history.

There are many humans who are, say, 'on the fence' with their beliefs yet have goodness within. Every soul has free will to do what they will... yet there are subsequent consequences. Humans are given many chances to change their ways and pay their dues. This is Humanity's blueprint of Heaven-sent that assists in managing to give people a sense of security, protection and healing through all the trials and tribulations on Earth. However, all of the various religions found their way to co-exist by manipulating people into what their so-called God believes them to believe. Some agree to dismantle their faith of all denominations by working incognito with darkness and laying the foundation for others to follow.

ONE FLAME - TWINS

Legend has it there is a reason two souls find one another... Perhaps they found that in moments that were so very difficult to conceive; and, very different became the source of connection. Souls finding comfort in one another... finding that they can be themselves, no matter what. The masculine showed her how to live, while the feminine showed him how to Love.

You will learn by reading, but you will understand with LOVE.

~ RUMI

To an awakened man who has learned to listen to his heart, the woman that he loves is not considered an object of his affection; she is the one light that has called them both into the darkness that entails a sacrifice of the ego, which places their one flame union noted as, a twin flame. In perfect harmony... a perfect union of soundwaves and geometry – threaded frequencies of a musical symphony – an orchestration unlike any other.

"Light of Light, True God of True God."

Twin souls are two humans that set the tone with a great passionate fire within their souls, then expounding their love on the Earth plane giving way to joining forces of two becoming ONE. In this way, two becoming one enters the light force of play-by-plays given by our Heavenly hosts. All spirit guides, Ascended Masters and much of ALL Heaven-sent who have joined these two in Holy Matrimony.

That does not mean that all twin flames decide to end up solidifying their undying Love in a sacred union of marrying, but one of an undying Love between two humans that have found their way back Home. That does not have to exclude matrimony, yet the matrimony of Spirit does NOT require a piece of paper to solidify the union. In the same breath, all soulmates, and twin flames come into union for a specific purpose that neither may be aware of. The awareness only comes after one or the other parties invest in self-sacrifice for the other to become a union. Once a twin flame union unites, that is the final chapter of one's life here, as all karmic ties have been cleared. When one is doing the work for their own soul's highest good, the other half of the flame follows suit. The suit of love becomes driven by the highest form of compassionate love and affects all connectivity to both families and their ancestral lineage. The highest form of purest love is this twin flame union – with or without the desires of the flesh.

SOULMATES

A soul-mate is someone we have a history with from way back when, and although it "feels like home", there are various issues that are karmic and need resolution. Just because this connection may feel like home… it bears much turmoil and resistance. The Universe places certain people we come into contact with to clear karmic ties – which could feel similar to a twin flame, but is not. The difference between a twin flame and a soulmate is that, as both are karmic, a soulmate may exit after severing its karmic justice; and a fake-twin flame might end up as the runner. On the other hand, a real twin flame "knows" what is meant for each other…

All the people we've ever known have some sort of soul contract with us that will enhance or be a projection of a lesson to learn from, clear and/or release. Once the deed of clearing is complete, a new set of people who you meet alongside others must also be cleared; and the list goes on until we achieve a last-life scenario whereby those people you meet will be gifted to you as a twin flame, soul connect that, when you know… you know. If that twin flame/soul connection is not attainable in your last lifetime, you may wish to either come back or live out another lifetime with them in the ethereal plane. It's not "as sexy" as an Earthly connection since the physical bodies are not entwined, but what it is, is a connection of energy unlike any other! The magnetic energy is far stronger, deeper and wholesome and does not involve egoic control issues, jealousy, anger, resentment and/or the like. There are a multitude of interpretations of unions between soulmates and twin flames – why require a label? Trust in the power of God/Love for what it is. Humans are so prone to requiring an explanation and/or a label of this, that and the other, which leaves the beauty of God's plan, empty. What God has brought together for every soul to exist, and experience is what makes Life a mystery. The mystery of Love is through every miracle, experience(s) and feeling within the depths of our soul.

SOUL2SOUL

Whenever two become one, they self-sacrifice to be with the other insofar as how they interact between two-mirror images. We all have another side of us where it's either one or another – and many do

41

not realize how advantageous it is that we are able to have two sides to the story, let alone two wholes that make one. When two people connect as human beings, they are not yet whole until their inner work is complete. They may get along just fine…however, when separate…. one or both are filling a void that perhaps the other is not aware of. After some time has passed and clear patterns have risen within the union, the missing pieces will inevitably show. All that is hidden is revealed in Divine timing… not a moment too soon. When a person is called to begin their journey of inner work, they become observant of their triggers and patterns, which set them on their soul's journey.

Our free will begins to take hold of our soul's intention to clear past karmic injustices so that one is set free. Most humans are so prone to "giving up" that they either choose to throw in the towel and ignore the elephant in the room and any signs from spirit… Soul2Soul means that two humans have agreed, prior to coming to Earth, to resolve their karmic ties and either end up together or sever ties. The "intention" in Love is not meant to be easy… it requires nourishment, compassion, forgiveness, communication and all that makes us fear what is within ourselves. The Ego is placed strategically to reflect the Fear of not being fearful, but to be fearless. Jumping into the lion's den is what makes a king, a King. Every person, place and thing is threaded into our presence from our Heritage of those who attempted to reveal ourselves through their reflection. Either way, when the ego emits negative ions within your emotional tablet, the "Taming of The Shrew" gets into you. Lions only roar when they are in fear and/or being threatened, but the lion who roars out of a strength-of-resolve courageously with NO FEAR. Everyone must walk-the-plank taking risks and chances and owning their own darkness of Christmas' past into the present.

What seems like an imposition to mankind asking for HELP… is it pride, or can we pray? Our ancestors are counting on us to do what it is that we signed up for – to remember what work we are here to do. All of mankind is dependent upon every one of us to awaken to a new day where we are present in the moment. Look back in the rear-view just to learn, remember and move on; look to the future. There is none. Only the NOW exists… and every second counts! Those of you who have learned another language know how valuable learning through repetition is. Learning why we came here, and what we signed up to do might be very confusing and/or even a forgotten realization, yet it is NOW that every soul on the face of this planet signed up to assist in Humanity's evolution. This evolution is for you…this is the Spiritual Revolution. Find yourselves…go within, pray, ask questions, get curious – go where people are spiritual in this world. Become a beacon for gaining a sense of self-discipline… start by choosing to believe that your life matters. Educate yourself on YouTube, delve into NDEs (Near-Death Experiences), which are real-life experiences of what it's like on the Other Side.

Those who have already seen the light, saw their loved ones and have already received messages of how vested we, as a community, are asked to believe again. Listen to what life experiences people are being shared and why they chose to come back to this Earth planet to make a difference; or, why they could not. Watch how in the blink of an eye… disease and death come knocking; and what teachings are being given to those who need to sustain and remain in Faith. Do not deny your Faith…do not remain in a cave of darkness; discernment is key!

WHAT'S LOVE GOT TO DO WITH IT?

What Love is this... a blissful connection that is between two souls conjoined for the same purpose to join threaded frequencies. This could either be two souls in Love or, between siblings, or a parent daughter/son relationship or any other type of bliss one receives from another who are on the same vibration. Most soul2soul connections are when one person embodies the other for purposeful meaning to elevate the soul of the other. Our causes are not what define us, but our causes are what helps us journey toward another, on common ground. On Holy ground is where we walk barefoot and pregnant with another, with the love of a child, and pregnant with a purposeful will to live. We tend to take refuge on what this feels like just because it has become so foreign to us ... and, to that of another. What leaves no room for translation, for improvements, for manning the same ground, for-giving to forgive others... to forgive self. We're uncertain where the times of these are leading yet we must fulfill our worldly obligations without question. Finding a place of peace, tranquility, and a gathering of souls unite to make for a collective love. We're not alone... never will be... whatever is at your heart's desires...go there and you will be ready to receive all the blessings. Just like those who do not follow their heart's desires end up entertaining outside interests of what the egos would have us believing... Some of these egoic desires can be sought as; drinking, shopping, binge watching, self-soothing medicinal drug uses, sexual and/or various other addictions. Can you relate? What is your addictive behavior(s) of choice? Once the gloves are off and a sense of self-sealing of the heart space is found we can recalibrate. We're not here to play mind games, nor are we here to stroke the ego... but to consider the essential value these games people play. We seek to observe a better life in others rather than in ourselves – which is no threat to the ego. Where do you envision your life? *Face-off*

LOVE, LUST and TRUST

While the constitution of marriage envelops two people who vow to hold a "sacred union" before the eyes of God, this is just one example of what it means to constitute any vow of Trust in taking full responsibility/accountability – trust of self, trusting others and who trusts us. There are varied levels of Trust; in love… to give and receive love…. is to have trust. We must realize that whatever constitutes a bond, trust must be earned. Mankind seems to have skewed the trajectory of trust because, over time, it is so much easier to lie, beg, borrow and steal than to remain authentic. What a sad truth that so many humans have gotten to be so complacent in habits and behaviors that dictate a "distrust" as the norm. One could say that distrust has been around since the beginning of time, and it has. However, the level of distrust in Humanity as a whole, is at stake now more than ever. Mankind has fallen from grace with markings of dark clouds in devil-ish forms. How did this happen? Exposure to social media has now revealed so many levels of distrust over the years that we were not privy to. It was known to many but kept under the radar as secrets, also known as "rumor has it". Does this fall under the nuance of an evolved state in the constitution of marriage? Can we ascertain this as a fall from grace or an evolving level of love? Will the judgments of how each of us was raised be your saving grace? Human beings are only capable of what they've been taught by their family, what beliefs were taught, and what love looks and/or feels like. Where much has fallen short of the truth, we cannot conclude there is a right and/or wrong way. It is the way in which a child has been raised to believe in love… to view love, to seek love, to feel loved.

This goes without saying, "to each his own" on how we've been taught sets the foundation for us. The fact remains that most bonds of a marriage fall by the wayside because the other has been misunderstood, misconstrued and/or has attained a lonesome mindset to actually be in a "perfect" union. A perfect union is one that will withstand every fall, tolerate idiosyncrasies, allow their counterpart to be independent, and, most importantly, themselves. Subsequently, to fall into a perfect union tends to get misrepresented as a "sacred union". A perfect union is one in which society deems acceptable for viewing… the external show. The sacred union is love seen through the eyes of God. The teachings of love within the family have been seen and taught by our parents. Love is felt, shown, discussed, held and defined differently by an observer and not necessarily from the Source. No one can describe Love to you as it bodes very differently for others as it will for you. We've been given glimpses of what it may feel like from outside sources but not from our own experiences until we do. The perfect union tends to drive one's love into a passionate carnal desire masked as lust, where the ego tricks the heart. Then there are those who may seem very different, a contrast on many levels, yet those idiosyncrasies keep them learning more about themselves. Who is to say or judge, one way or another? A life in Love cannot be described in any way, with words… it is felt through experiences of gaining wisdom, understanding, loyalty, adventure, communication, and a silence of trust. Why must Love be defined at all? The layers of Love evolve very differently for everyone, yet the common denominator on this Earth is LOVE. The energetic field of threaded bonds … an inheritance from our ancestors; a tribute to those who meet us, those who love us and those who have lost us. What a miracle it is to feel that sacred love that makes us become better together than apart. It has become so easy to throw in the towel and give up on Love... Why ... when this is all we are here to do? With every person and in every given situation, "for better or for worse", Love remains. Seek, and you shall not find... for sacred Love finds you!

"The Kingdom of Heaven is within you... And whosoever shall know himself shall find it. –Egyptian Book of the Dead

LOVE/HATE RELATIONSHIPS

The movie, "For Whom The Bell Tolls..." is about those who are granted resolve in their own world of discrepancies. A love/hate relationship within the dynamic of political condemnation and an eternality of love that is the dichotomy. The state of affairs that has redirected on the Earth plane has caused too many people the inability to achieve a lifestyle of Freedom. This lifestyle is still generated throughout the Universal force of Nature; however, the Covid-19 pandemic caused many to re-think, re-assess and re-evaluate their own beliefs. How could society's darkness corrupt an entire Nation into demonstrating unethical abuse over children? How has this behavior gone unnoticed, undetected and caught? And what about those who have done the abusing? There are so many who have a love/hate relationship without knowing why. Are you aware? What's the point in holding grudges? Why not have a conversation, instead? Do you seek solace for mankind, for self? Or are you going to continue to procrastinate and/or be silent in fear of what others will think and/or say? Taking full responsibility is needed for all who are abusers of any kind, living a life of erosion and deadly circumstances in their darkest hour. Deep down inside lies our subconscious, which must partake in the shenanigans of all those who have witnessed and/or been privy to crimes of passion, sex crimes, crimes of Scarlett, and crimes of all kinds. Be mindful, be weary, be cautious, and be awake to your 'truth' because, in the end, that is all you will have.

The love/hate relationship in families is very real.... parents, siblings, aunts, uncles, spouses, etc., bodes true for the reflection of the mirror to see clearly. Is this a love relationship with conditions, or is it a close-net bond of support and love for you no matter what? Do we not feel the same love from a Mother than a Father or vis-a-versa? Has your love been seen and/or heard? What takes precedence of an unwavering love of a parent - or - both parents? Is it about taking certain characteristics from one and/or another only to surmise those very traits imbue us? Do we laugh it off, or do we seek to hold grudges, anger, jealousy, remorse, and sadness whenever that thread of connection is tied and/or bound to your Heritage? What is "it" that we take with us when our parents cross over? Is it real love of loss? Is it too late? Have we had a conversation with our parents on these subjects... how to fix, manage, forgive, or... even break? What bears the truth within every one of us on whom is seen as worthy of our love? Are you worthy of your own love? Can you, suffice to say, be a loving soul in human form to and for others? For your family, your parents, yourself?

Others whom we come into contact with will tend to only see what's in front of them and not the value of what they bring to the table. In other words, people who value you seek out your worthiness, but there are those who go against the current. The true value is being able to see 'all' for what they bring to the table. That's the secret! To LOVE ALL unconditionally…

A FATHER'S LOVE

Being a father is one of the hardest roles on this planet, and without a father figure in a child's life, many things go array. Since the beginning of time, the thread of both father and mother figures has become ever-changing. Back in the day, fathers were the sole breadwinners of their family, while the essence of compassion is innately felt as a mother figure. There is no greater Love than having and keeping Love for a parental figure - no matter what. "Our Father Who Art In Heaven…" There are those who do not hold a heartfelt Love for their father/mother because the threads haven't been mended or severed in either this lifetime or another. When our Earthly father is seen in the image of Our Heavenly Father… a clearer understanding of discipline, responsibility and protection is enhanced with deep roots of being grounded in His essence. We come to this world with threaded roots from all father's past, present and yet to come. Our Forefathers have shown us what came before us and why the change-of-winds evolves a man. The Sun being the Father, is the energy self that plays havoc as the Ego, when called to do so for our learning lessons. What every father on Earth experiences bleeds into the heart of Man. One man's wounds are another man's enlightenment – given the two become ONE, in the same light as God's essence. This lends itself to challenge every father into becoming a man… Mankind evolves as a man-kind-in-Nature without ever giving up or caving their dignity. To say that man can live without their ego cannot be stated until man overcomes his own ego to thrive on a Love much greater… No longer can man thrive on ego alone – it has already been shown to the masses;

ego lives on man's desire to be a powerful entity unto himself. This is why the instinctual desires of mankind are tainted in temptations of various misuses of power. Overachievers, overworked, overindulgent, overcome by cravings, obsessed with work, etc., leads to a demise of when power is misused. Not all men of ego become "beasts of burden" due to their genetics, DNA and the like. For not all should be tainted by others… nor shall we judge any man for attaining accolades, achievements that come with hard work. Every man has a soul purpose and love to feel, while some have been their greatest regret. A man who either chooses or not to bear a child is their 'freewill' in one's lifetime. Who is to say what is right or wrong when either choice has been orchestrated for the evolution of one's higher consciousness. Therefore, for man to choose to bear the fruits of his labor in a child, instills the call to become an example in their child's life. Are you a father? Have you set an example? Have you earned your child's love and respect? Do you hold that same respect for your father? Is the thread from one father to the next built on casting out shadows and/or following suit? If a man chooses to possess himself and live within the principles of fame and fortune – he finds his pockets empty.

"For what is a man, and what has he got? If not himself, then he has naught. To say the things, he truly feels and not the words of one who kneels" sung by Frank Sinatra. Life according to one's essence in a lineage of time … or is it simply your way? Being swayed by others' ideals while in the throes of a broken heart leads man to suffer and lose themselves. Many are brought up to believe that "feeling" is not manly and any expression of compassion, emotions etc., lessens the role that seals that of a manly man. The seals of Egoic masks and temptations have lost the ability to feel. Herein lies a multitude of grieving that men suffer in silence… and their role is noted. In time, or, many lifetimes...some men have changed to show emotions and vulnerability in what matters. Where the masculine requires more compassion, the feminine is a natural rhythm of intuition. These polar opposites contain the opposition of the same ripple effect contained in both - one needing the other. The responsibilities no longer bear one or the other as our threads of change have always been each other's mirror. The essence of Love overrides the need to become entangled in what roles are given to Man or Woman – as long as Love is given to ALL. This Love is unconditional...when accepted and given from ONE's heart.

FATHERS

The way that a father interacts with their child/children has come to be a strong topic of discussion for so many who aren't even aware that there's any issue. We've come to seek the truth from our parents, traditionally, yet find so many falling short of the mark. The mark of the highest excellence is what the general consensus is of what a father/mother dynamic should and/or are. Therefore, it is imperative to address the father/child relationship in great length to experience and learn how essential it is to establish a semblance of whatever father figure has become a mentor, your teacher in life, or not. This is ever so important to understand because while one child has a solid relationship with their father figure; others feel tormented and/or exhausted by what has or could have been. Most father figures are emulated unless not seen through the duress of their own insecurities. When and/or if anybody states, "I'm like my father and it is what it is - or it's in my DNA," is a red flag. All adults must take full responsibility – not only for how one is raised, but more importantly, how to change their narrative. As for the unknown and/or absent father figure that made a great impression upon their child, leads to both narratives, the same. Whether a father, step-father, adopted father, and/or an absent, distant father was or wasn't involved is only based upon the residual that children feel. Either traumatized or comforted – and this includes one's own father's father threaded down from their ancestral lineage.

While many families uphold the father's love of always being around, there is such sadness when the other half of a family unit is absent. It is for a plethora of reasons why such a father exists, after all, fathers who have made a name for himself could not only be available and open for discussion at the family dinner table. Then, there is the father who is out of work, yet remains absent emotionally without ever leaving the household. There are fathers who cannot plainly see their own worth throughout the family and are plagued with the fact that they became fathers to begin with.

There are those fathers who cannot for the life of them figure out what their personal responsibility to the family is, let alone find it in their heart to share with themselves.... There are those fathers who never wanted to have children but did for their significant other. There are some fathers who did whatever it took to be the best Dad in the world for their child/children leaving a beautiful legacy. There are those dads who are mega Mongols in Fortune 500 companies and their only mission is to make a name for themselves. Then, there are those who are out-of-sight, out-of-mind fathers who come and go as they see fit. There are abusive fathers who while still maintaining a little distance from the family dynamic, inflicted physical/verbal abuse – an inability to connect. The absent father may not have experienced abusive-contradictory parents, however, by not being around much became an awareness of his own dispensary of immortality. Other fathers who are married yet single in mind & body, watching pornography, dealing in drugs, sex with other women, younger women, and a plethora of addictive behaviors of a fear-based mentality of rituals have threads just the same.

The list goes on....

It is important that we understand the mental, emotional state of what a father did and/or didn't do for his family. To cover such extremities of the male bond between father and child/children, the connection consists of man and child, man & wife/significant other baby mama, and a distinct connection to the original thread between father and his immediate father. There seems to be a real bond that a father has with his/her son or daughter as did his father in the like threads of his past. There is a deep wound that many fathers have experienced since the beginning of time that has cast dark shadows for all others. The role of a father is quite the role as it has been handed down throughout time. Fathers are traditionally seen as the glue that sticks through thick and thin. Yet, over the last couple centuries, roles have reversed, and the lead of the mother/woman has become prominently inherent. An imbalance of masculine/feminine roles are being recalibrated to ensure the importance of a Father being likely to regain value.

Too many years have caused men to feel helpless, hopeless, and not secure in what role they are part of... as the woman has become, in some instances, both. We need to bridge the gap where any one person, role and/or job is better than the other – how? We need to seriously 'think' what has happened over time to the roles of men/women and merge NOT to appease, but to please. Every person on the face of this Earth wants to feel needed in life – not to compartmentalize who does what and when; but to allow every human to ascertain their role in whatever way they choose. Men have had to pretend on so many levels – it's time for a change.

"It's Time for a Cool Change…." song by Little River Band

"United we stand, divided we fall…" an Aesop Fable in which a lion used to prowl four oxen who dwelled in the same field and tried to attack - however, when the lion came near, the oxen used their tails to warn each other. A dwelling of four became prey no more as the lion attacked, one-by-one when they did not look back. Since the beginning of fathers in the workplace drudgery was the start of averting time from the family. If that wasn't difficult enough, today, many families have both parents working - leaving children alone to their own vices. Unity within the family has changed drastically…and children left to their own devices have been the bearers of many addictive behaviors, abuse, disease and emptiness.

A MOTHER'S LOVE

The Blessings of our Heavenly Mother precedes all others…whose compassion, unequivocable LOVE demands to be seen, felt, heard, known. The Blessed Mother sets the example of Love through all Grace. The LOVE of Our Blessed Mother is by far the most humbling, gracious and caring Love that any human upon this Earth will ever feel. That being said, she has gifted women/feminine the gift of child-bearing through the womb of the Blessed Mother. It has been said that to feel Her presence is similar to that of an unexplainable energy who hosts the entire "Nature vs. Nurture" in the palm of their

54

hands. Every vein that has been crafted, so intricately, upon and within us threads the stories of Love within not only this Universe; but for every human being that embodies Her Love. We cannot deem to attain the host of the Blessed Mother for Her's is in the light of the Moon, a shining star that shows all. The Moon reflects our emotions, shown or not, to guide us where we are to go. The light of Love shows us that our journey cannot be spoken with words, it is felt. What emotional issues do you have? Do you hide your emotions for fear of being vulnerable? Or, do you manipulate using your emotions in a passive-aggressive manner? Are you in your feels? Do you know how your emotions are your navigational guidance system to show you where you're at and where you've been? Can you read the signals and signs? What deems a MOM to BE the WOW factor? We all know that not all mothers have that effect upon their children. So, what is it? Do you feel this way about your Mother, Mom, Momma? Are you a Mother, step-Mother, foster-Mother, teacher, caregiver of love; and/or in whichever way you hold Love for children or another is where our heart grows. We all have been given birth to and whether we know about our Mother as blood or not – is of no consequence. She, who has birthed you, chose to do so from very long ago and those who have been blessed to be in your lives, were also chosen. Every conception comes into existence from Her womb and into the womb of a feminine body – is the Creation of purest Love.

A Mother's Love holds a plethora of facets of unconditional Love, empathy, patience, understanding, kindness and grace.

From the onset of two souls entangled in a physical/sexual bond of energy exchange, there is an unseen connection that brings two souls to conception of a child (whether or not of two consenting adults/youth). Once the Feminine energy embraces a sacred Love for and of another, the two become a bond – whether through sacred marriage or a sacred commitment of two souls coming together. What many fail to realize at the time of birth is that before the egg/sperm connectivity becomes an embryo, threads of karma/past-life history, genetics, cells, atoms, molecules and the like have been co-creating. A life cycle does not begin at inception, it dates back to one's Akashic records of time while setting the stage of Life. We may not be able to comprehend the logistics for reasons beyond time and space – as every life unfolds in Divine timing. We may or may not understand the very nature of why two people come together to conceive – but the connection that comes from the soul is a bond of threaded manifestation. Two souls connect with a blueprint that signifies the culmination of a karmic contract - to oversee, to experience, to sever, to embrace till 'death do you part into everlasting life.' What happens begins with the Mother-to-be knowingly coming into union with their soul-partner of purest intent.

A Mother's intuition begins at the onset of "knowing" they are being placed with another for the procreation of co-creation. Should that soon-to-be Mother be a young girl hosting a child, as she herself is a child; this union for-begs to be questioned…knowing the power of Love. There are other Mothers who wished for a child and do whatever it takes to either bear their own; or, adopt/foster. Either way the only thing that matters is LOVE. The life cycle of the feminine energy is the same – a child turns into a girl who later becomes a teen that forgoes being the single woman to co-create becoming a Mother. Mother Nature begins her journey way before conception takes place… yet she is subconsciously cognizant that she is starting to feel different. Her attention veers from kissing frogs to wanting a life

56

partner – and/or feeling ready, willing and able while her body begins speaking to her. Many little girls attach themselves to baby dolls at a very young age, while others do not – however, when a feminine body begins to set the stage for motherhood, she begins to focus her energy on babies, other people's babies... her instinctual compass is calling her freewill to choose. Even though she may or may not be aware of it, every woman's hormonal balance begins to shift focusing on a precursor toward Motherhood. If she chooses to not conceive in this life cycle in which motherhood will prevail, her body will either elevate in hormones or perhaps drop in focus. Whether or not she desires to become a mother or not, every female body becomes ready for motherhood. Some may find that there is a surprise element to see her body becoming more mature – evenly distributed with her mind; but that is not always the case. For some, a level of maturity seeps its way through after motherhood has been achieved. It's a balancing act between mind and body, for some, there is an even balance while others are trying to catch up. No matter what, those women who chose to bear a child, or many, will do so according to their blueprint. Others will have to forego that blueprint until another lifetime - or, what is most advantageous in seeking adoption, fostering, and/or step-parenting to unfold one's destiny - adding value to one's life. In whatever attempt, a Mother is to give of her Love, that is The Way. Her body speaks to her mind while navigating through every intricate embodiment that encompasses them all.

While this is happening in the feminine body, the masculine has been notified (present, or, non-present) that she is getting ready for her 9-10-month adventure into motherhood. We may or may not believe it but while a young woman is changing, the masculine, within her is also. The external masculine (father-to-be) is ever-present whether in physical form or not…as they have both sworn into an agreement of a union of this child/children. If she becomes a single parent, another masculine has already been sworn in… or, not. If not, this woman has sworn to uphold both the masculine and feminine roles of raising the child/children. This task is very difficult, however, since she is encapsulating all of her past karmic ties and the likes of the doner, or, absent father as the mirror of perhaps losing both of her parents; or, for reasons that are not revealed. It is not a necessity for any woman to choose motherhood, and some don't… yet, the feminine body has been constructed to procreate. The mother continues to co-create a child and many attest that is why illnesses vanish during pregnancy and how a mother's body protects the child at all costs. However, for other mothers-to-be, the road is long and very difficult for reasons of producing a stronger-than-life self and child. Insofar as a mother's cravings are concerned…the baby's subconscious need is for the mother to host those cravings that the mother is deficient of. Studies have shown cells from a fetus in a mother's brain 18 years after she gave birth remain; which is another term for, "mother's intuition". Now there is scientific proof that mothers carry them for years and years even after giving birth to them. A mother's job is never done… Additionally, extensive work is done in Heaven prior to a child's energetic force entering its mother's womb as an embryo; floundering about in the ethers of one's energy are the energies of that families History – including the abstract scar tissue, wounding and a karmic History of debt or credit that will be gifted/owed in a particular lifetime. A number of issues must be recalibrated, reviewed and discussed in a very constructed order much like an executive meeting in a boardroom. Every pinch of strategic efforts in one's life is carefully constructed in a way that makes one's blueprint threaded together within its rightful place of existence. A series of life reviews are incorporated in one's passing of the physical body in order to refresh/renew the energy of another's physical body that is being invented. Therefore, any residual karma that has not been dealt with re-enters that of another bodily formation and agrees upon that another lifetime in a life experience will be required to return back to Mother Earth. Any mother who has chosen motherhood in this lifetime has chosen to raise a human being with the will to assist the evolving karmic cycles to close out. Why? Some may or may not realize that the calling to be a mother far outweighs any material wealth – for as it is your responsibility to evolve a child out of God's LOVE. Whatever happens in due course is all meant-to-be. To BE or not to BE is not necessarily the question, as is the inner knowing that one IS.

BEholdBehold, a child is Born…

TRADITION

The father figure holds quite a heavy weight when it comes to owning up to taking responsibility for the entire family. This has been quite the norm for centuries… what has been known as the provider of the family. This has caused a stir in the family dynamic throughout the years because the belief systems have since changed. It's neither better nor worse, it just has changed since the Liberation Movement where women decided to fight for equality. This began in the 1970's and has since been a thorn of contention of equality for women is still being protested. Perhaps not literally on the streets, but, in the internal resonance of many women in corporate America…receiving less pay, respect and/or power. Of course, there are many women who have fought hard for their power; and some, misuse of that power. Should there be any conflicts within the family it is up to the father to bear

59

weight to what is or isn't acceptable. Fathers are traditionally known for requiring respect by listening, the ability to uphold one's honorability by being trustworthy and bringing home the bacon by working hard to provide for his family. Some families have stuck within the boundaries of upholding the "traditional family" while others have changed the dynamic of what the responsibilities of the father are. Just as a Mother is the main nurturer of the family, a Father is traditionally the main provider. This is known as the Yin/Yang of the family orientation and has been for quite a few centuries. Over the course of the last few decades, the roles have reversed and now many men are choosing to stay home to take care of the children while the woman seeks a stable income that is profitable for the family household. What has worked for many years needed to change in order to get a more balanced notion for the man as well as the woman. Women have been trying to uphold their careers by choosing to attain higher education in order to do so…while men have been finding out what it's like to be a nurturer… as Mother Earth intended. For others, same sex couples are also investing in role-play while raising children. Traditionally, humans have been extremely out-of-balance for this reason – not allowing role reversals which causes confusion into roles where there is no flexibility. What stumps humans along the way are the traditional values that many have been accustomed to and not willing to budge. However, those that have sought to get out of the box by changing roles have widened their influence and constructed a family dynamic where children hold great respect for both parents. It is not to say that the traditional home of father as provider and mother as nurturer has not been respected; but the changes that have gone on for a long time remain stagnant. Some families are upholding role-reversal where the man is the nurturer while the woman goes to work. A man is quite capable of understanding the depth of responsibilities that a mother has in attaining a happy home; while the mother finds a career path that gives her the respect she deserves. Role-reversals assist both parties respecting one another; and balances out in a healthy mental, emotional and spiritual way. There are many facets in raising well-rounded children as it is the same in one's ability to multi-task in their jobs while keeping it all together. Many women are used to multi-tasking while others have not had the ability to do so… many men are used to hours of boardroom brainstorming while others are likely to implode in their expertise in this setting. There are so many men who've been given a breath of fresh air by being able to stay home to keep everything working smoothly. Women have also been given this breath of fresh air by evolving in their place as CEO Executives leading the pack. Why society ever placed roles upon both masculine and feminine is absurd.

Our Forefathers did Humanity an injustice by placing men so-called first; not thinking that women would retaliate. Justification is given to those who are righteous not required to stand before a judge of ages to validate their worth. Desiring validation, confirmation and any need for acceptance to be noticed, is ego. Once one's ID has been validated, the ego feels fulfilled and the human remains loyal to his master, master of Ego. We cannot claim to be egotistical, however, the depths of our Ego is as complicated, convoluted and contained where confirmations are contained, repressed and/or invalidated. We seek this validation because the layers of little-to-no self-value are where the broken parts of those who feel unworthy. Ego tends to move within our psyche whenever we display weakness or to enhance our validity. We're only human, "they say" which is exactly where the Ego hides… deep into the recesses of one's mindset in order to state the obvious. Whatever deems unacceptable to one may contain the other side of the spectrum for another. Wherever our memories take us, one's perception of that memory might be very different from yours. We can't put into words whatever someone does or doesn't believe as the whole – yet we must attempt to allow everyone's journey to become what it will be. Memory recall is different for everyone – factoring into what stands out as a memory, what is recalled and how much time has gone by must be taken into account. Here is where closure of what happened comes into play…as the stories have changed. When we want 'closure' in a relationship it is next to impossible as time goes on … and views of the connection begin to get skewed. Ego plays a huge part in what the mind's eye remembers vs. what did happen. Why should anyone judge another? Who is to say that their journey is of the Ego? For those who need closure to judge, by feeling better about themselves, fall into the ego's reflection for justification. We cannot seek out others for validation, only for ourselves. The need to knock someone else off their game is a sure sign that we are feeling insecure. Those who are accepting of the achievement(s) and of how they perceive their experience, become empowered. These are the truth seekers who lift others up by giving others honest accolades – there are internal positive rewards for those who lift others up and mean it. *Awareness* is everything.

Great achievers strive to be the best… either from past insecurities to the way in which they were raised. It all begins with those who raised us, setting the stage from belief systems –to repeating patterns of their past indiscretions –to implementing their unfulfilled desires and pressuring their children to be the same. However life unfolds, it is a part of the imprints that are given to us at birth… These imprints require us to falter into the hands of a society whose greatest achievement is to tend to the sheep of illusionary structures that have crumbled. Other imprints placed upon the innocent are from our family, friends, teachers and any others who we have come into contact with who made a mark upon us. This is the work of our shadow; our Ego will fight in your battle of wills. Life is a battle of wills/intentions from either a soulful place of love or built from Ego's destruction. We impress upon humans to emphasize that our lives are either the *will* of God or the *fear* of God. You choose…. *freewill*. To live in fear of God becomes one's mantra and, in-deeds will play out as such; whereas, to live a life in love for all Humanity will raise your frequency as well as emit neurons of goodness throughout your life. This is exactly why one's life runs smoothly and another's is full of challenges. To attain a smooth life of little pain is to raise your vibrational frequency by not living in fear of God. The higher your frequency, the ego cannot sustain flight. Throughout History teachings of the Sages leave their legacy/imprint upon this world. Whomever we seek as a Mentor becomes our Master on our way forward… and our path opens up to a whole new world. We are here to recall our reason for living and being able to equate our lessons by imparting our imprints of wisdom. Energy that is out-of-balance stems from unresolved inner issues, our triggers, anger/hate toward mankind – while the energy of silence is golden. Inner shadow work must be done for all of Humanity and is not to be taken lightly. With many children they have the innate ability to do so, "at will" with willful intentions for a, "will to live." Once there has been a firm understanding that equates to that exact vibration, it IS done.

Truth is hard to come by when Humanity has been self-imposed in believing what a "normal" lifestyle is… and, to one's surprise, there is no normal. This is God's way of letting His children overcome their own demons in order to partake in your own way forward. Induction of a new way is the New Era for all of Humanity – to release what has been forced and to take on a new perspective that is set apart from the rest… a vision of Love through the eyes of God. "Where would Love be if not seen through the eyes of God, ™" Truth aligns within the realms of One's heart; and, sees itself as IS.

ROLES OF MASCULINE/ROLES OF FEMININE

Without these lessons, children of God would not be able to figure themselves out and what their purpose is… The institution of life has been and will always be "to serve others" in deeds. There is no secret to what life has to offer except to withdraw from the egoic mindset in a world of make believe to follow your own hearts by following no one. This is the true "role reversal" that no one discusses – from ego identity to one heart. Uncovering your authentic self. Those men who maintained a level of understanding in their childhood were fascinated by the level of great wisdom that was imparted – then there have been the men who have yet to grow up being the victims of lineages. Whatever fashion did or did not happen for and to the masculines it has not impacted some, while others have been brought to enlightenment. There are no rights and/or wrongs to what has or hasn't yet happened for the masculine to grow out of their egoic mindsets into a heartfelt new life. Many masculines are, indeed, feminine A-typicals united as such here on Earth – while the men seek honorability, rewards, recognition as the norm; others have found these authentications not valuable any longer. Without the man, women could not have been cut through the same cloth. It bears great justice to know that while women may be rising up the ladder of success, they must fully take into account that they were in fact cut from the rib of man. There are many versions of this in the History books that speak of Adam, Samson & Goliath, Deutorotemy, Jesus and many more who brought down the iron curtain by presenting themselves as either or… either they needed the outside attention and recognition; or, remained anonymous. Jesus sought to aspire to both by breeding man from the inside out – while that was so many who remained disbelievers. Being a disbeliever is just as much as a believer who decided to change beliefs. No matter what has happened in the History of Man, one thing remains to be the truth… that Man was made in the image of God. Once you can wrap your mind around this truth you will begin to see yourselves in a very different light. When and/or if that happens, man will no longer be divided, as we are one. Man/woman are one in and of the same gracious cloth wrapped around the Love of the Universe. Man's responsibility has factually grown into wearing many hats – gone are the days when men focus only on their primary job responsibilities but also have begun to outdo themselves with household duties, watching the children, changing diapers, looking for the best viable option to expand their roles. However, there are those who have had enough of the 9-5 job responsibility only to begin an independent job at home and/or watching the kids full time. A few others have not escalated their resume with the comforts of power, money and the like; going after a slower-paced career that is their heart's desire and choosing loving what they do, instead of the control of what society has placed upon them. Who's to say which is or isn't the best route of taking your life into your own hands? Why can't a man choose to be the kind of man that he envisions by stepping into an independent role instead of what his lineage of trades might further his pocketbook? "Our Father who Art in Heaven" did not say that man must follow in the footsteps of their father…but, to love what you do naturally and the rest will follow. Who has listened to this guidance and who has not? The statistical percentage of blue-collar workers in a field of study, trade or otherwise – working for the dollar for power is to build their ego. Then again, this lends itself with much to do about how much responsibilities they have been given. What dictates a happy man? There is more to what a man does for a living … where his heart is, what family matters means, who does the majority of work in a household and who is taking notes etc. Too bad Earth has become so divided as to what you do for a living and how much money you make which are the familiar questions – instead of, are you happy with your work and how you earn a living loving what you do. Is there a status quo that is geared toward men generally speaking that has been around far too long that is not easily erased? The male ego, the ID, one's identity of status, money, power has overwritten the narrative for most. Why are we still under the imprint of societies and not of our own? Is this changing? Can it change? What will it take to change the course of History? Will there be an awakening for the masculine to sacrifice a change of course in History for one's happiness? Every move we make in light of what happens is a clear indication that grants us our happiness. Everything else is the illusion of grandeur as to what you're being told what to do, how to do it and where you will land in order to make the big bucks. Does one suit follow another suit? Perhaps the way forward is not to follow suit… Suits are the ego masking it-self… can tend to be very uncomfortable when worn…and in others… seen as a suit-of-armor. What suit are you wearing, what are you portraying, what line of business requires you to be armored in your natural birth-day suit? What is a birth-day suit without a natural, authentic peaceful place that masks no-thing… especially not the remnants of intention. Not everyone is comfortable being naked… why? Can we thank Adam & Eve for disclosing a sense of shame in man? Or, perhaps that "thank you" is to remind us all of where we came from and what we are here to do. Not to be yourself is the biggest lie that one could discover in themselves. The opposite of that is to honor thyself as thyself… in the image of God.

What happens to men who are taken ill and cannot entertain their job position leading them to a new path… does this subconsciously create a new outlet that was a blessing in disguise? For most… those with dis-ease do not find that a blessing, but after some time, see that in hindsight as a miracle to get out of the rat race. We know that everything happens for a very good reason even when we can't see the light before us – it will be illuminated at some point. We tend to say, "what a blessing" after the fact. Much becomes clear after illness, death, destruction of whatever is to happen… that leads us to remember. How many are still grieving over the terrorist attacks in New York? How many are still grieving over the loss of a loved one? How many are grieving over a divorce? How many are still grieving over the fact that they did not conquer their truest ambitions? How many are grieving over losses they are unaware of…but know something is missing? How many are grieving over what is still happening in the world? How many are grieving the loss of a child, father, mother, sister, brother? How many are grieving so many unexplained grievances there are way too many to count? How many are grieving over the suffering for others? How many are grieving for the sake of others? How many have no idea what grieving entails? How many will take accountability for their suffering? How many will undergo therapy? How many do not care? Here are just a few examples of how deeply wounded mankind is whether they are aware of these and so many more emotional issues. What matters is that we find what reasons are at the core level of our existence in order to begin a natural course of healing. Many though find that being in Corporate USA is not all it's cracked up to be and even with 6-figure incomes, the draw of passion fades to black. The light has then been extinguished while the man submerges into finally following their innate craftsmanship. What begets our true innate talents, should this be the case, where man gets very clear that his innate qualities were and have been waiting for him to attract. We all have been given innate talents since our birthright is to understand the self; yet many seek the external profits that lead to one's ego, instead of creating their so-called destined craft of choice. Unhealthy parts of the Ego streaming without a core cause could have avoided the inevitable upset after climbing the corporate ladder... Many decades or years later, a family man realizes how difficult the path of Ego has been while missing out on the most memorable times of their lives with their family and children. The stats of "missing out" are hugely disappointing to all those who have been wounded. The lineage brought him to a place where there is no safe haven... not only because of their upbringing in childhood but also the upbringing of their lineage.... Then we have the man who has not even realized yet that his parents will perhaps need to provide attention to the health of his parents... who is ready for that? Where has the educational system failed on counts of "life experience?" On all counts a man is not ready to undertake so many life situations that he is called upon to handle. Is it any wonder that many feel as though they have failed? Who has actually failed? It is human nature that mankind will innately be so under-the-radar of what must be done that when a barrier of expectations is added to these responsibilities an automatic ingrained self-sabotage creeps into our psyche. As our Heritage shelters us from self-imposed restrictions of not being good enough, not enough in so many facets of our lives no one could begin to understand. Only until one matures with grace in wisdom through life experiences can we attain a new learning curve of acceptance. Enough is not enough to some and to many just plenty. Often, there are outer circumstances where the union of our Lord and Lourdes will unite as one in the name of the Father, Son, and Holy Ghost; but, in the meantime these will remain indifferent to those who seek to divide and conquer. We are all part of one planet, one life, one moment in time as ONE GOD.

These are necessary insights to what makes human's tick and what timeframe is on one's clock ticking away… tik tok, tik tok, tik tok. When a man gets to a point of realization, what tends to fall way past their expired time is, not being able to make up for lost time… we fail to understand that "time is of the essence…." Even though time is an illusion, time was actually constructed mathematically for reasons that only the "present" moments in time can give. Life is a gift not to be given back…™ We will not expound upon those who give their presents (presence) back as it is known as an Indian-giver. What is an Indian giver? The Indian-giver is one who has all of the knowledge yet chooses to uphold what Indians do once they acquire what is not wanted. This is a racist term, no doubt… whoever termed this metaphor must have been an Indian… one can only hope. A hopeful Indian whose tribe is called Present-Arrow in a room full of hopeful children who deem to become gurus themselves. All terms that were once inspired by a traditional value system have faded away and some are now considered, "racist." How irate to think that man truly has underrated their Heritage with concerns of racism back in the day – as appalling as that sounds, it has been said and done.

Man must be very vigilant in character and word – though the words of The Gospel … not once is it written that man must become a racist, is a racist, has become racist? Where is it written and who termed that phrase in the first place? A racist, no doubt. Cruel is the man who must compare one deity for another... is not one color all the colors of the rainbow? Pray to those who have effervescently used terms under which they too have not been. A man's job comes with many variables, Terms & Conditions... etc., in fine print. What man decides is unacceptable to the human language? "Lost in translation" isn't a means to an end – it is the end. What one-man hath taken will be the misuse of language barrier in our society – where wars are fought not only in the world but in our own backyards. This is Humanity's "lost in translation" between what is interpreted as grammatically incorrect from an egocentric perspective; and what is actually known, from the heart as there are no mistakes. Therefore, the questions arise... Why are we still allowing Ego to orchestrate what society pre-programmed from the start? And, why do humans stoop so low as a society? Are we obeying by the rules of what society deems to the point where we have completely lost our identity by masking who we are? Do you know who you are and where you're going? This is the overall basis for life's question. If not those who seek will be sought. If not, a society of robots, AI and the like will override the world with no-thing but the "same ole' same ole'" narrative of emotionlessness. Why is this ok? Is this ok? No man is an island, it is true... Why have we not placed enough care upon ourselves, our families, our children to undergo a new set of values, new Terms & Conditions that will befriend those who seek? It's true... we are all seekers of a place where we want Love, peace, joy, happiness and great abundance – where is this in your world? How to change the narrative... Find your happiness in the present moments of your everyday life. Seek no one until it finds you ... Let go of those who claim to know, go with the flow inebriate yourself in a world where you choose to make yourself happy. What will make you happy, do that…and, no matter what happens seek no one else's advice but your own. Can you come to terms with the fact that there is only one you? This one you want to represent in the physical body, allow your sacred body the Love of great health, great wealth, great success, great impressions of what you have been put on this Earth? The mindset of the past must be torn down and rebuilt – your heart will lead you to your True North. Take your hands off-the-wheel of control and be guided by Spirit to show you a life you came here to do. Each and every one of us are here to co-create with the Creator. Under the guise of the broken arrow, let our wings be severed from what has been reconstructing a new pair of wings that lead to a service of giving. Let's see what the New World Order of a new pair of wings will be for you… willingness to change your mind set for a new solid thought process is not going to be easy but well worth it. A man who knows is far better than to control the terrain of question marks. Let man behave in ways that far outlast any History book… bring in a new order of less control and go with the flow in every situation – see yourself transform in front of the mirror. The moment that will be ever life-changing will be the very moment we see clearly, we speak truthfully, we hear silence, we feel our truth from the inside out. As in, "The Truth Shall Set You Free". This is not going to resonate to everyone right here and now – it will resonate when it is your time. The thing to remember and not forget is we are all one – and to forget where you've come from is no longer an option as people on this planet are becoming very aware. Watch what Earth's people will look like in the next decade or two – will it be robotics/AI that will be able to sustain a life of giving, sharing, communicating, feeling LOVE emotionally, mentally and spiritually? Let those who lead this AI movement seek justice of power in a clone that has no heart. No heart??? Exactly what was foreseen in

71

"The Wizard Of Oz…" that man behind the curtain who thought he could override its premium members of innocent children by showing them "you've always had the power after all!" That is what's going on today – we are all Dorothy, the scarecrow, tinman and the lion all combined as one to ward off the evil of the wicked witch of the West … and any other external powers of evil that significantly apply to witches and warlocks. What cannot be contained are feelings of Love. You may think that the brain functionality has more power than that of the heart… but, think again of all those loved ones you, we and us have lost. "Nothing Compares 2U" sung by Sinnead O'Connor clearly was given that song by Prince who wrote it – but, did you know the controversy behind those words? If indeed, nothing compares to you has validity as written in the song, then what about all the rest of the people who are in need of comparison? All comparisons are a fraction of victimization where they want to conquer and divide the population by amour-izing a love that compares. This is not what love feels like… that song was written because Prince got pulled into the matrix of illusion until he let the elevator break us down…. There is only one Love and that is what so many are having a hard time to understand. Know that on your journey of self… you will come to a juncture where loving ALL will become your reason for loving yourself. Every person, place and/or thing that binds our hearts of passion, of notably clean intentions, a cleansing of one's soul to allow heart healing is what we are on this journey of Love to learn. What we deem to be learning are experiences that we should not feel ashamed of… every lesson that has been under the guise of Spirit is why each of us are here.

Dimming your light for others is not what we aspire to do - if you have a talent, use it; if you have a voice, use it; if you have a song, sing it; if you have an ear, listen; if you have whatever treasure(s) that have innately been given, then… use it…

CHOOSING LOVE IN THE EYES OF A CHILD

The threads of Love between a child, a Mother and a Father, are all-encompassing weaved into how a child views LOVE. A child's first human connection is at inception where the energetic current is established where love takes on whatever shape it will be. Love comes in all shapes and sizes – and in child-breeding years, the external events, issues and matters of the heart impact how the child internalizes and views love, by definition, of and by example. When a child is within a family dynamic where abuse of any kind is found in one's life that child will unknowingly incorporate that particular thread into one's love life as a normal way to love. The mirror has two faces is about how children are mirroring their parents or so-called adult relationships of love between two adults. However, that plays out for the adult, is as consequential as it is for the child who is observing. Adults must set an example in the eyes of their young children – as they mimic what they see, hear, do or don't do, learn, teach and/or are taught. "Monkey see, monkey do…" equates to children's desire to place value on love. Not all love is equal by another's example and/or is the vision of interpretation thereof; however, the onset of karmic justice plays out. Being mindful that to be granted God's love of a child is not by any means a play of two hearts. We, as adults, have to tend to the call of being gifted parenthood, in the first place, being our complete and utter focal point. Anything else… is a foreplay to disaster. Too many adult humans have no real understanding of how they love, who they love, why they've chosen who they choose and all the differential threads that matter. Given that all forms of love vary, a child is unaware as to why they've landed in a certain family dynamic of many trials and tribulations. However, as time goes by, a child matures with age-of-wisdom, through life experiences, realizing how, why and whomever their issues tend to be, is exactly what is needed for their highest good and soul's evolution. For example: should we choose to exit a relationship with a spouse because of verbal abuse and/or emotional unavailability that reels itself into the home of your child's life.... becoming a thread. If that thread remains unresolved, all aspects of that thread bleed into the next relationship/marriage to be addressed and cleared out. If not, then one thread breeds another, and another, and another... etc. Herein is where our karmic ties branch out from one love for another – or other – enlisting in seeking to extract and sever ties by not following suit. When this happens, a child's happiness does not require control of any kind... it begs to become a natural order of maturation over the course of a life cycle or many life cycles. This can only be addressed when the student is ready, the teacher will appear.

An evolved heart loves without only the desire of the physical body; but an open book with a compassionate heart feels Endless Love... ™

ROLE MODELS

Are "role models" even a thing? Who values their parent(s)? Do your children look up to; look forward to being with; confide in...or, at least don't hide things; want to learn all they can from you; not yelling, impressing discipline and respect; giving; showing patience; compassion and all the attributes that make us feel like proud parents. Part of being a proud parent(s) is not only that our children are smart, good, beautiful, kind, etc. the child/parent relationship is of great importance. One doesn't have to be a role model for others to see…but a role model for children to follow – cast aside the need for attention, recognition from others as this is your Heavenly gift. Children (either our own or others) provide such joy, innocence and overall so many blessings to those they connect with that is felt in the hearts of all. Why not be a blessing to all children/kids we come into contact with? So many kids absolutely love their parents, and/or even other parents in ways that they show their love and touch our hearts. There are those kids who do not love their parents (or, any adult figures) and find it troubling to deal – or even connect anymore to their parent(s). What do your kids feel about the issues going on out there? Are you guiding them to a place of comfort, safety and unconditional love? Which of your children/child is feeling out of place? Have you had a sit-down to enlighten them of both the provisions of discomfort in and of family dysfunction and/or world events – so that they feel a calm demeanor that harbors inner love, peace and strength? When a disconnect happens it is to ensure that inner turmoil, trauma is resurfacing. Those children who attempt to confront a parent of trauma for validation and the parent denies ends up making the experience of feeling "helpless" in the child all over again. This salt-wounding keeps them stuck in a cycle of unworthiness and rejection. Children need to stop going to their parents for validation - from dysfunctions - and heal naturally. All families are dysfunctional because when we reincarnate again with these souls, it is to clear out karmic issues etc. however, those who are angry, hateful, judgmental, critical and have not spoken or heard from their parents, this pain goes much deeper. These threads want to be severed but cannot until some kind of resolution has been had. Not all parent/child relationships can obtain forgiveness and love in this lifetime; yet will endure another trip around the world with the same souls, if chosen. Much depends upon each individual case as some children and parents harbor real issues of narcissistic, criminal, abusive behaviors that no one should forget – however, forgiveness is needed to sever ties for good. Those souls will have to commune on the Other Side when this happens to see what is for their Highest good. Cutting people out of our lives that bring suffering and/or dysfunction is the first sign of Respecting yourself.

PARENTAL ROLES

All parental figures have a place in Heaven… you're someone's Mother/Father and/or you have a Mother/Father - parents have been given God's gift to raise their children on the basis of responsibility, authority, discipline, teaching, honoring that role for the remainder of their lives. Each role contains both masculine and feminine roles - where one may be more disciplining and the other more lenient. Whatever the role you have accepted, understanding the complexities of each role holds a very special place in this world. Both Mother and Father have been raised in their home either similar or very different. When the connection between Mother and Father emits similar values because their frequency vibrates on the same level, children feel comforted when seen and/or heard. However, some children feel very different - outcasts, rebels, black sheep and are not aware they've chosen to be Chosen. There are those couples that get together and have a child/children who are either very different; or else, of similar values but there is a balance in getting to know one another through it all. What we agree upon, what we disagree upon etc., sends an immediate vibration to the child that may or may not be in alignment. These are real issues that are discussed in a union when choosing to have a child; or…" surprise, we're pregnant!" ends up being the case.

Many, just "wing it". However, it unfolds, balanced compromises are needed to raise children. We come to understand there is no rule book...for some, it's a pick-up-and-go; while others have traditional rules they live by... Of course, there are consequences to decisions made by the parents and to their children. Cast aside doubt about what your interpretation of raising a child is because every parent is taught by the examples they experienced — no more, no less. Children are also taught from prior generations whether they understand it or not. Every parent takes pieces of learning from their Mother and/or Father and allows them to spread their wings to fly, teaching them what they've learned. Some have avoided raising their child/children the exact same way that their parents raised them...for their own reasons. We tend to contradict others' parenting yet do not always know what goes on behind closed doors. All children require a different set of rules or regulations...disciplining comes in all shapes and sizes, as does love. Many traditions are kept while others are making new ones; and, some avoid tradition at all costs because it is considered old fashioned. What our grandparents may not resonate with the new generations of streaming and screaming kids - whichever applies. We don't have to necessarily place "labels" on how others parent, criticize or judge; but it happens almost to a fault. Why does this happen? Whose book of rules in parenting are we all following? The rules of the road is to, "Follow The Yellow-Brick Road" and let it lead you to the Emerald tablets where it's in the Heart that matters!

Emerald – "stone of successful Love" in truth in Love. Our Heart chakra can breathe deep as we balance out our emotions on the Horizon of the setting Sun. A vibrant hue deepens our Hearts to hear the call of going deeper, finding your inspiration through meditation.

In the early 20th Century, the Emerald Tablets were historically known as "a portal to the soul in our world..." *soul2soul*

The books of rules with which to follow: —

The Laws of The Universe
The Hermetic Principles.

The Laws of the Universe mirror— The Hermetic Principles as follows:

THE LAWS OF THE UNIVERSE	THE HERMETIC PRINCIPLES
1. Law of Divine Oneness	Mentalism
2. Law of Vibration	Vibration
3. Law of Correspondence	Correspondence
4. Law of Attraction	
5. Law of Inspired Action	
6. Law of Perpetual Transmutation of Energy	
7. Law of Cause & Effect	Cause & Effect
8. Law of Compensation	
9. Law of Relativity	
10. Law of Polarity	Polarity

| 11. Law of Rhythm | Rhythm |
| 12. Law of Gender | Gender |

Why are there 12 Laws of the Universe and 7 Hermetic Principles based solely/souly on what right-of-passage one believes. It makes no difference how you set yourself on the course of life's journey but it is of utmost importance that these Laws and Principles are followed... No matter what is offered to children, the matter of concern is that these are not only introduced to a child, but are to set as an example of these Laws/Principles and The Bible for your soul's evolution. A soul's evolution needs not necessarily evolve as it already is evolved – the Nature/Nurture standard by the rights of passage include that one's temple is to be understood, "Know thyself" as a self-realized human body which aligns with the already-realized soul. Why is this important? Every soul chooses to evolve.

This happens for Source that IS ALL to experience Humanity's ability to evolve in physical form. As is written in The Bible, Jesus' life experience set the standard for Humanity to follow. What has been threaded as what shall be? Prior to arriving on the Earth plane, we made a commitment to The Father to obey and set the example for the next generations to come.

SEVEN PRINCIPLES OF TRUTH

1. Principle of Mentalism: The Mind.

2. Principle of Correspondence: Expand Consciousness.

3. Principle of Vibrations: Frequencies of Energy.

4. Principle of Polarity: Balance.

5. Principle of Rhythm: Truth of Motion.

6. Principle of Cause & Effect: Karma.

7. Principle of Gender: Masculine/Feminine

These seven principles included the Universal language(s) of Laws of The Universe that runs like a river through each field of our energies dictating and reestablishing the essence of Nature. Seventh Heaven. Heaven Sent.

WHAT TYPE OF PARENT ARE YOU?

What, why, when and how we were designed to come down from Heaven is by no means any affiliation of crisscrossing the gap of anyone's differences… if you only realized how traumatized people get when you speak utter nonsense for the sheer pleasure of it all. Notably we are here on Earth not to acquiesce anyone of their differences and/or nuances but to embrace one as ONE. Herein lies what is ahead of our planet… to seek another's demise is a thing only from those who are still karmically challenged – not medically, physically, emotionally any other way. To forgo our inner critic for a place of solace is not so hard to equate why we are still reincarnating over and over again. The only subjective issue on this planet is to clear all of our past-present-life karma. No matter what and/or how this has to happen… "Let It Be." What behooves people is they have become so "inattentive" that this reality has increased in every generation – having to rely upon an AI robot to take care of your responsibilities…

What would and/or how would that bode well for the child? It's almost as if AI robotic parents exist in the here and now because there are so many children who are ill-prepared for the real world. How does this happen when a so-called responsible parent has forgotten their kids at school or has been late picking them up because of external forces per se, beyond their control? What happens to these children who are being forgotten, unattended to and misguided by what they "observe" to what their own parents are doing? Reasons for escapism is a real thing… Parents all over the world are ignoring their children, allowing others' parents to raise them, childcare, fostering a clear sense of no attention has become a matter of concern. Perhaps this is why the AI Movement has begun – there is not enough parental guidance to discipline, to attend to, to show a sense of responsibility in these drastic times of need. Think about it for a minute… make a mental note of what you, as a parent, guardian, and/or any showcasing of taking responsibility for a child, anyone's child is playing upon you right at this very moment? Are you going to continue to swallow your pride, showcase yourself as a responsible parent while the next-door neighbor saw you buying weed on the dim streets of no place in particular? It's not that weed is the issue… it's the inability to coax yourself to get up in the morning with enough time to take care of your child – clean clothes laid out, teeth brushed, homework done and the basics. Instead, the child is waking up the parent(s) to get them clothes to wear, brush their hair and/or anyone else who is perhaps available at the time. What is the message being sent to these children? Imagine one child who can relate could be a few million more who can relate. This is not to demean your parental skills …this is a "wake-up call" to those who are no longer parenting their child/children. There are many avenues of "escapism" not taking full responsibility for your child – overworking, projecting, non-relating, social media overkill, dating, non-dating, depression, mental anguish, grief, sorrow and a slew of other places where children are being ignored, avoided, forgotten. Even though the "forgotten generation" are the Elders... it also seems that through one's "innocence...they are being led to their own." A child is not meant to take on the responsibilities of their parent(s) but this is a clear indication that is what's happening. To be a true parent who has a sense of discipline in taking on this full-time job as being called, Mom & Dad, this title is not to be taken for granted. It is to be taken as THE most-important role that is granted... NOT a JOB...

Labeling this as a job is not about buying Gucci for your kids either in exchange for their love. MOM/DAD roles take accountability, be the adult or define yourself as such and own up to all the trials and tribulations of being a parent. When will you "grow up?" Have you not grown up and find yourself in a bind because you're trying to raise a child inside of another child's mentality? Where does this lead the future generations? Do you find yourself denying all accountability, responsibilities of being a bad parent? When "Bad Mom" came out in the movies, we saw that when we allow mothers to instruct discipline in their own way, without so many rules and restrictions, some children gain more self-love. Something in that movie stuck out for most of us, as Mothers; the 'end-takes' of how each actor's Mother spoke about how they felt about their relationship as Mother/Daughter. Leaving a "Legacy" of a Mother is a present that Mother Earth gives Her children. It is "WE, as Mothers" who need to uphold the blessed duty to give of ourselves not selfishly but selflessly. Once news of 'I'm pregnant" it's in the expression of the news... Not-for-nothing are those who are elated, those who underwent whatever necessary to get pregnant, those who would die to have a child; and, there are others who didn't plan on the pregnancy. Others who may have mistakenly got pregnant – then, miscarry, abort, foster/adopt or otherwise are not ready. There is no shame to anyone who may or may not be ready. It is the child's choice whether the Mother is ready or being given a chance – or, a chance at another time. The effects of what leads a child out of its misery isn't only the way forward with how parents are raising their children. It takes a considerable amount of time, patience, thoughtfulness, attentiveness and understanding, to say the least, when raising children. Every child is different and may or may not require the same as another – but, the common denominator is giving Love. There is no comparison between children as each child brings something unique to the equation. What doesn't seem clear, however, is that what one child requires is certainly not going to remain for the duration of their lives. Every child must be observed, seen as an individual through all the stages of their lives. Once this happens, not only does the child grow, but so do the parent in ways that perhaps were required in their childhood and missed the mark. Even if there was no "missing the mark" it is worth stating that children bring about the best in everyone and it is your duty to see the beauty of what has been mistaken for ignorance. Children observe while parents also must bear witness to their children in order to hone in on what is required. There is an emptiness to witness a child gain access to tend to their own needs. In order to define being a witness to…and/or to observe others we must gain a sense of our own selves. Our life path, the milestones through the years, a representation which stands for what has happened and a knowing that, for some, their past has been a series of unfortunate events. For others, they've learned nothing, in hindsight and need to look deeper into their own errs of ways. We mustn't take any of these instances to heart as we will either see it as helpful or as a hindrance. No matter which side of the coin you're on is not only insignificant but when it does become a matter of common ground, you'll know. There will be no questions, no doubts, no need to try to fit every instance until it does. What is known to some may not yet be known to others – at certain times of our lives, the narrative begins to fit. Otherwise, many will reincarnate with new bodies, but with the same narrative that wasn't realized in their last life. Whatever it takes in order to see clearly to... *remember*.

A child comes into this world with all the tools, much like the anticipation of a fresh hot-bagel buttered; knowing that the world is their oyster to "What do you want to be when you grow up?" is the question. Then there are those adults who have given up on their lives, already placing one foot in the grave, licking the wounds of their youth and a host of negativity that deems ungratefulness. However, your story goes... do you realize the effects being placed on your kids? There are children of narcissistic parents who don't become the same; instead, become highly sensitive, emphatically intuitive and compassionate. You, as a parent, are setting the examples... How does that look? A massive destruction in Humanity where adults are giving up and children are following suit... addictive behaviors with no remnants of remorse, confounded by turmoil, a cruel world of anger, triggers, all-out panic attacks, depression... And a slew of unanswered questions. How can an addictive parent/adult HELP? Does it even matter that, in some cases, kids are looking after the adult parents? Many young adults are the designated driver (DD) for their parents who drink or do drugs... witnessing mass chaos in their parents' actions. Mind you... NOT for all.

Once there is a clear understanding of honorability, responsibility and the need NOT to control, in the aftermath of a child's upbringing, they begin to grow on their own. If control is still an issue on the parent's end a child can't learn to grow their own set of wings. Every man, woman and child have the need to be set free... There are some parents still acting childish while claiming to be adults...and, children who came in as old souls, adulting their parents. An adult is claimed as an adult at 18-years old to vote, and 21 years old to buy alcohol which signifies that some children that are of age are not necessarily claimed-to-be given any rights. Why? At whatever age someone is officially an adult, is not based upon their cheat sheet by numbers; but if we were more about 21-years 'wiser' or 'wilder?' The difference is who is *really* ready to be an adult? An adult is ONLY an adult once they have cut the umbilical cord, cut the apron strings, and are able to survive without ANY help from Mom/Dad or any other adult figure. Just because we say for example, "Joan graduated college and is now living at home with her parents doesn't constitute an adult figure." This actually just might mean that Joan either was forced to attend college and/or learned how to discipline herself studying, memorizing, and learning the art of borrowed knowledge. Whereas, Joan's sister dropped out of college and is working full-time at a Fortune 500 company paying rent. Because one sister has graduated and is living on her own, paying bills and not asking for added assistance from anyone; and the other sister filled her obligation of due-diligence to get her degree but perhaps cannot find a decent job – what constitutes that one is better, smarter, more independent than the other? Is it fair to compare? Which child will be capable of surviving better than the other? Perhaps Joan will ask her sister to move into her place since she no longer has anyone to rely upon. Adulting has nothing to do with the numeric age... It has everything to do with life experience, drive, motivation, determination, passion for one's art and how to survive. We are not juries, judges and/or the like... this is a crucial point in the making of an adult. "The Making of An Adult - Life Lesson 101" perhaps would have made for an excellent class in middle-school into high school. Instead, we are self-soothing these so-called adults by giving them enough money to live a very robotic life of "autopilot" *instead* of living a full life of passion, co-creation, music, art, history, documentaries and/or how to cook, balance a checkbook (accounting and then some…) abilities to service their cars, pay their bills, etc., We think so little-minded within an egocentric mindset that builds us up only to be shrunken down-to-size for what? "Heads down" social media turns into a hand-held 24/7 TV version without boundaries. How can a child who is on the preface of change have the motivation/desire to change when they are not being groomed for adulthood? Adulting is not easy which is why so many children refuse to grow up… until it's too late. What has happened is that adulting have turned into baby-sitting adults while being given everything aren't able to make decisions, what will they do? Either they will fall into the same old trap of space-hoarding at a sibling's, aunt's/uncle's house(s), or practically whomever will have them to hear their sob story. Not everyone has this situation to "fall back" upon… so what will the rest of these so-called adults do? Will they revert to living on the streets, in their cars, pawning the family jewels to stay alive? How long will this continue? When will this child in an adult body ever grow up? Will they? What many parents have done is stumped the growth of their children… and, this may include yourselves. How to turn back time in a society that has no time left?

We take our sacred vow of silence very seriously when it comes to being gifted with a child and it's "not" what anyone, especially society has ever told us. What society failed intentionally to provide on this planet is an educational system that dictates NOT by race, creed, color, money, lack of…, misuse of power; but by honor, integrity, responsibility, credibility and, instead, seek comfort knowing how to survive that isn't a TV series for the faint at heart. What has happened is that the explanation for, "Why Am I The Way I Am" has been completely skewed to, "Why Am I Not Enough?" A designed life has already been constructed for us all, however, the plan might suggest one take on several lives to obtain. We live in a world where "freewill" is given to those who choose whichever path they figure to be the harder path of self-serving and have an aversion to the construct. Every journey has been set forth to those who serve Humanity, for those with clear sight to what has been shown to them; and to those whose lives matter. For Mother Earth's disasters, can you imagine how She feels caring about the weight of the world? Clearly, we consume so much hidden matters that a pouring-out of current events are these natural disasters. Is God angry or could it just be our anger within? Think again. What undermines the whole of Nature is not having enough Faith … in Life, in yourself. We've come to know ourselves through our own viewpoint; but, not necessarily through others' perception. Have you ever asked your bestie to give you a rundown of the pros and cons of what makes you, you? It might take you by surprise to hear how others "see" you instead of how you see yourself. If we were to ask a child what they might see in you… generally speaking, what do you think would be their first response? We know children have an innocence about them and what they say holds true – no sugar-coating. It wouldn't be a bad idea if, while on the prowl, to ask your bestie and/or even better, a child in the family to choose your mate… instead of what you may see, they see through the eyes of truth. Children are the gifts of youth, even if we don't have our own child/children, we can get feedback from others who do have kids – be it in our families, friends, step-children, and the like.

To take on the role of a parent encapsulates several degrees:

1. Psychologist
2. Humanitarian
3. Sociologist
4. Politician
5. Defense Specialist
6. Protector & Provider
7. Financial Analyst
8. Strategic Planner
9. Child-Services
10. Playground
11. Healthy Living Specialist
12. Communications Major
13. Teacher
14. Authoritative Needs
15. PTA
16. Emergency Needs (Heimlich Maneuver, CPR, EKG etc.)
17. Self-Lessness Behavior Therapy
18. Behavior Specialist
19. Sporting Events
20. Grade Keeper
21. Self-Discipline (studying, tutors, much-needed requirements)
22. Special Needs Children
23. Visual Needs
24. Handy with building, fixing, putting together (castles, kitchens, bikes)

25. Masculine Needs

26. Feminine Needs

27. Disciplinary Actions

28. Hypervigilance Requirements

29. Medical Needs and/or Services Required

30. Behavior Therapist

31. Addictive Therapist

32. Learning Therapist

33. Mini-Me Syndrome

34. Artistic Talents

35. Lawyer Requirements

36. Religion vs. Spiritual Beliefs

And, so much more…

Is this the masterplan of the Universe? Are we to learn from our mistakes and solemnly swear that no matter what we will do it will be better than our Founding Fathers? Why have we not done so? We cannot be defeated unless we are defeated. The seeds of the shadow have not permitted Humanity to tamper with one's Heavenly soul; as our consciousness needs to evolve. By doing so, all ties to the "shadow self" can happen through inner self-reflection of how, why, and what is happening. Imposed thought patterns, external physical desires of the flesh that intermingle with one's soul journey has repercussions for healing. Everyone has a "shadow self" – it– it is of the Ego which we must clear out from our history in order to ascend. Jesus' ascension is a by-product of what Humanity must learn insofar as His path. Jesus taught all of Humanity to 'walk your path' by serving and showing love in-deeds (in service) to self in ALL. Without the mindset, it is difficult for us to fathom ourselves outside of this physical capsule, hence we lose our sense of self. Therefore, when we say that "no-thing else matters" it is a statement for the Ages that one has acquired a physical body on this Earth that will drive you into a place of nothing; while attaining everything, that IS. In order to be oneself, we cannot take a child of God's and wrap them up with the ideals, beliefs, patterns and other forms of what we, ourselves, have carried into this lifetime. We've already known ourselves as the ALL of the whole, but not yet in the sense of carrying other karmic intrinsic valuables with us along the way. Kids who are growing up not only take on the role of parent but also raise their sibling(s). Whether a child is waking up before their parent(s) to get ready for school, take into consideration that this is good discipline, while under no supervision. They are making their own breakfast/lunches, finding clean clothes to wear and trying to wake their parent(s) up to take them to school. There are some kids that don't have parents and it is the responsible adult within the family that takes over; and for others, the grandparents. Whoever is watching your kids … take a minute to regroup by sensing how this makes you feel? While reading this do you feel a sense of remorse, regret, or don't care, fed up? Has a "fuck it" mindset become a message to not only the one who says it – but to those who live it? Will there be a time in our lives that will render a change of heart from not caring to becoming a caring parent? In whatever way this happens to identify with your situation, the onset of concern is vastly approaching and the roadless traveler is paving a new road. A sheepherder controls the masses while the black sheep of the family controls no-thing but their own lives.

Children have literally been made to show their parents what outcasts they've become and the need for our parents is essentially financial and/or feeding. A feeding frenzy of financial woes that have collectively grown accustomed. If we continue to blame the outside world by pointing the finger, how will mankind learn to build a new perspective? This is our world today… to cast blame, and remain negative and angry. So far, we've not yet been quite able to identify a new perspective of, "go your own way." Once we are empowered to become our destiny and to stop placing blame by taking accountability nothing will change. The only thing that clears the mind, body and leads us to our highest soulful pathway is to unlearn what's been taught and to start from scratch. This is the determining factor in life as we know it… Allowing to be, see, feel, breath-in and breathing out a lifetime of adventure is only for the strong-willed.

GOD ONLY KNOWS… song, for King & Country

ALL roles of parenting are necessary for the highest good of children. We must embrace all other parental figures with great respect as they are a blessing.

*As long as there is NO harm, of any kind, inflicted….

Let it be known, and let it be written, God's intention for all of Humanity is to allow kids to be kids by establishing a solid foundation of life lessons, rules/regulations, disciplinary actions to gain respect in line with the design of the Universe. Mother Earth is designed for all Her children to know they are Loved and to share their Love with all… Where traditional values meet The Golden Age of upbringing to teach in a way where discipline meets discussion(s) that make way for kids to open up. Children are most vulnerable when in Elementary school and trust in their parents and teachers – with admiration. If every parent could enlist in a day-to-day chit-chat of how their day is going, keep their attention, get involved and remain neutral so that a mentorship of the Trinity could become established. Being actively involved with sports, new hobbies and/or art/music while instilling discipline and boundaries. Any parent who is adding to the problems… not interacting with their kids because they too are on social media, is playing havoc with places that divide. No communication and/or interacting with kids is crucial. Elementary school is where a solid foundational structure of habits, beliefs and interaction is needed - even if both parents are working… After-school activities, hobbies and conversations are imperative. There are three (the Trinity) chosen times during the course of one's day which children are receptive to; three minutes after waking, after school, and three minutes right before bed.

On the flip-side…there are many parents who use fear-based tactics to control and discipline that ends up scaring their child/children. This is where there is a definitive divide that ends up cracking a foundation - instead of using tough-love in a compassionate way. For example: controlling parents who have not healed, and/or stay in an egoic mindset unknowingly create fear, chaos, and a complete shut-down to children. This friction and distance disables children to freely choose to come to their parent(s) in times of need. Many egos are what's at play here. When a child has an over-controlling Mother and/or Father, it is because they did not feel comfortable growing up in their surroundings. That same thread of Fear is placed from one generation to the next to learn from… The same threats that began in the parents' upbringing is a replica of repeated threats to children. This places a huge burden and massive disconnect between parent(s) and child/children. Since social media has become the 'obsession' most everyone is turning inwards by not addressing any problems. Where are children getting their help? What will the future become of the connectivity between child and parent(s)? Will they refer to an AI consultant instead of parenting? Could we, as parents, allow too much leeway for our children to be ignored because we too, as parents, want our social media time? Are we going to blame TikTok or whomever is raising your kids today by pointing the finger? Who will be the responsible parental figures for upcoming generations? The AI Gen? Too much to comprehend, yet, if this is not addressed most parents are bound if they already haven't lost a sense of direction and follow-through in their child's upbringing. The answer lies within each and every one of us who are exhibiting this as we speak. Who is handling it?

This leads us to identify some new avenues of becoming the example…instead of the problem. If both the parent(s) and kids are obsessed with social media platforms, who has time to discipline? What are we teaching our children, by example? All parties involved will end up with karmic debt to be paid in a next life; and should there not be another reincarnation, debt is paid on the other side. This is not God's plan… it is the "order of the highest" for the greatest good of our children and their ability to achieve their highest potential. Where one goes the Highest KNOWS… "As above, so below" means if karmic retribution cannot be paid on Earth - it will be paid in Purgatory. The Universe has had to bear much turmoil at the likes of our shadows and the shadows of others to entertain a place of solid ground in building a stable playground. What is going on…is the silencing of children so that the effects of AI can obtain and take hold of them – by changing the trajectory from what was innately built with our senses, to a world of emotional extinction. Are you willing to let AI robots who are nameless, faceless and are void of any emotional value? Every child's purpose on Earth is to be of service "in-deeds" to mankind. If the technological field is the only one that has created a huge divide to conquer what will be next? The ONLY way "OUT " is "IN" - for Earth's evolution. AI is a computer devised to depopulate this country… and it is up to Humanity to assert our willfulness of good intentions to change the narrative.

Who are you as a parent? What do you stand for and what has tainted, damaged, tortured you as a child? Can these traumas be repaired? Are you learning how to heal; and able to guide your children to do the same? Changes for the lives of our families who are dealing with these issues – learning about healing properties, getting educated (mind, body) and working toward our evolution will set a new trajectory for generations to come…. Get involved, start asking "How can I be of service?" Let's rebuild an entirely new infrastructure for our kids; beginning with believing in what resonates with you and getting involved. How to get involved? Teach by your example building a solid foundation that begins with YOU. What we do, where we go, what is said and what is heard, how we share our feelings, or, how we hold back; who is listening are all driving forces for Humanity. The song, "Stop and Stare" by OneRepublic speaks to us as, "It's time to make one last appeal for the life I lead…"

A tsunami for Humanity's sake is likely needed for a great change to happen… It will seem as though an even greater wall must be rebuilt, true are the broken walls of Humanity since the very beginning. A rebuild from within. Gone are organized structures of Hippocrates that will lead the next generation under false pretenses. Whatever will be of our next-of-kin… is up to us… deciding what to believe will be our newly created "go to." Finding out that prior generations were blamed was historic; but now we know better that, not to assert a new narrative for our children would be tragic. Who will have the last laugh? Whatever happens is literally in all of Humanity's hands…A structural overhaul must take place in our world for the good of Humanity… if just one person would rise up by ignoring what 'others' think, say, and/or do, will become the standard. Old souls are doing just that… because they too are feeling a threshold of stranger-danger kinds with all the propaganda that has been facing our Nation for far too long. We must educate ourselves and our children to place new responsibilities, incorporate social activities, keep kids involved and maintain motivational efforts for our children to learn; as well as, alternative methods for healing, new perspectives all-in-all will enhance a growing community.

There are many layers to "peeling an onion" that require raw truth above all. This is our "wake-up call" with the markings of ancient History knocking at each and every door. Additionally, there seems to be a very fine line between which parental figure has a more important role; yet, is blood thicker than water? It is by far the most important role of any one person who is granted such responsibility. To make things more intense, a child of two parents may become a child with four parents (masculine & feminine) – where all of them have their own archetypes, ancient history, DNA imprinting, ego masks, trauma and other threads to contend with…. but their parents' DNA must be looked at also added Egoic stream of one's mindset. Who says their way is the right way, or wrong way; in fact, who's right or not merges with all beliefs. Let discernment led the path to let go of certain beliefs and to allow what is already known to jolt you out of your own way. Having four parents taking on the responsibility of children must be an adult conversation of the why's, how's, what's, perspective, beliefs, morals, values of each party involved. Exactly why we must treat others equally to assert a need for the family history, the need to be respectful to all involved; as well as, have a sit-down with children on attitude and behaviors. We must get past the stressful pains, triggers, wounding, negative self-talks - behind others' backs, and so much more that are deep-seated wounds. This filters into every aspect of the adult/child relationship and any adult partnerships – as to how we act, what we say, think, feel on every facet of a community.

Our Father who art in Heaven, hallowed BE thy name, thy Kingdom come, will be done on Earth as it is in Heaven. In God's name, AMEN.

PARENTS' BOOK OF RULES

We tend to contradict others' parenting yet do not always know what goes on behind closed doors. All children require a different set of rules or regulations…***disciplining*** comes in all shapes and sizes, as does the love we can give; and, the love that was given to them. Many traditions have been kept while others are making new ones; and, some avoid tradition at all costs because it is old fashioned. What our grandparents did does not resonate with the new generations of streaming kids - and screaming kids - whichever applies. Why? Many were raised by so-called grandparents and/or adults who lived through WWII that live to tell their stories. Where is it written that age has anything to do with wisdom – it doesn't, it is about life experience! We don't have to necessarily place any "label" on how others parent by criticizing other parents, but it happens almost to a fault. Why does this happen? Whose Book of Rules in parenting are we following? The only book of laws with which to follow are set in stone, "The Laws of

The Universe", hence The Bible where what is right or wrong deems applicable. Whenever a single-or-coupled parent criticizes others it's merely that their ideologies differ from those they are viewing as different. Perspective. People come from all walks of life and what seems to be ideal for some is not for others. Whereas culture, DNA, our ancestors, our genetics and much more of what we value as important must be considered. Not many people take those factors into account when looking from the outside of what others may or may not be doing. What someone deems as the right way may be a very different interpretation in the translation of another way. There are parents who discipline with their hands etc., while others discipline by yelling; and the way of mentorship might be under the same umbrella as leading by example. All children are special and are observing adults…they watch to see what others' parents are doing/saying in comparison with their own. While children are witnessing adults, some adults aren't even aware that they are being seen as teaching by example. As the story goes…all parents discipline differently with their own beliefs by being the example – picking up their kids from school, arranging alternative options, carpooling, work schedule, lunch requirements, homework, playtime and/or play-dates and a host of other disciplining of their day-to-day.

DISCIPLINARY PARENT(S)

What makes a good parent? Is it better to discipline? Or, do you have discipline to control? Have we come to a point in our lives where we are standing behind our words and actions? As a parent, do you need discipline - and/or were you disciplined as a child? Where does the thread of truth become the same truth for our children? What is the price we pay for controlling the terms and conditions? What are the terms and conditions? Were you given strict rules as a protective/safety measure from your parents; or was it a control mechanism used as a tactic – because we have to control or because we lost control? How can a parent become a disciplinarian without losing control? Do we need rules/regulations or perhaps a quiet nudge, a given look, a firm but gentle word etc., to sustain a disciplinary role with compassion? Can we uphold both? Can a parent be a confidante while building a firm foundation? Haven't we progressed as parents? Why has it been said time and time again that you cannot be your child's friend as a parent? Aren't our parents, who love unconditionally, willing to be both confidantes, a good listener, compassionate without having to judge the actions or inactions of our children? Why feel the need to judge? Who wins out on judging others? What judgments are being spoken and/or thought that you might have heard as a child growing up? Is History repeating itself? Where have we lost our way…as parents, as responsible, as taking accountability, as being the example? And, why? How were things handled within your family dynamic? Have you got family members who don't take responsibility and are indecisive? If so, how do you feel about this? Does it make you feel angry inside? Do you have hidden resentments and are you still complying to the passive-aggressive parent? Are you the child of the parent who shows controlling signs of passive-aggressive behavior? Are you now a parent? Do you have control issues that are either aggressive and/or passive-aggressive? These issues continue until they are realized…sometimes they are not realized, addressed, for fear of hurting someone's feelings. If you have addressed the decision of being indecisive what's happened? What was the outcome? Did you speak it out, yell it out, or… talk it out? Your presentation is highly important to what we've experienced in the outcome of assertive behavior. Being assertive is a very good trait to have as long as the "presentation" is made without aggression. However, there are reasons why aggression should be instilled but with a sleight-of-hand.

At another place and/or another time perhaps the timing of being assertive also plays a huge part in the outcome within a truthful conversation. In any event, if the outcome was either a passive "cry me a river" or "how dare you" or "what did you say" by using emotions to manipulate… means, added layers to the onion. This is clearly just one example of how contentious the elements of manipulation can be and how, by not being raised to become an adult, is very likely to happen. Raising children in adult bodies who are unable to take responsibility, make decisions and/or make appointments, balance a checkbook; aware of life lessons that were not taught, is a disservice. Disservice.... This is seen all across the globe… children in adult bodies who are still kids. Not working, hanging out, falling out without a clue. No need to point fingers because we know the truth hurts …but it does set us free. Why are certain generations, age groups or some adult children not working? What has happened to the work ethic? Have the conspiracy theories of an alleged truth been stumping many today where they've lost interest who are lost souls? Will the parents of these adult kids 'enable' them until they can't any longer? Who will be up next in receiving the baton-of-life whether they want it or not? How will they earn their keep? Will they become homeless or beg another family member or lover/spouse to take them in? These are real-life experiences happening in today's world of upcoming generations. Either they're too stressed, can't handle, unable to cope, don't ask any questions; sleeping to avoid, lack motivation, numbing the pain, and so much more… all cries for HELP. Cries for HELP is your inner child crying out to be healed…in what you are seeing as your child-self.

PARENTAL TRAPS

To feel as though you have failed as a parent has got to be the most ungratifying feeling to those who it resonates with. Why do some parents feel they've failed and others don't? It's a perception… Is it because one child holds a degree and another child does not? Why? Where has all this inbred come from? Does a generation of parents feel that they messed up too? Are there threads of guilt, shame, depression, insecurity, worry, anger etc., a reason to be disbelievers? What mankind doesn't understand is that man is made from a love higher than the sky can see, giving of itself throughout History sharing even in the darkest waters … where Hope has been lost. So much hopelessness and not enough Hopefulness. This is why so many parents doubt they've done a good job. Not loving themselves enough to see another, let alone raise a child of this world with similar wounds. Every parent that has been gifted a child (in whatever capacity) has felt trapped inside the embodiment of their own childhood wounds – and, not aware how one thread outlives another if not severed. In turn, parent(s) feel they've missed out on raising their child/children - not to question why or how they feel but only concerned with the outcome of doing a good job. Simile is that our journey of Love far outweighs the destination of not getting anywhere fast… Fact is, there is no physical destination, only the evolution of one's soul.

OUTDATED PARENTING

What cannot be explained, by so many children, is the fact that their parents are not seeing them… who is "relating" to your kids. Are you relating with your children? Are your parenting skills outdated and in need of a revamp? There is a huge distinction of "relating" insofar as how we interact or not with our own. We say, "mini me" for what reason? Do we really want your kids to be a mini version of you – and, for that matter, do you know who you are? It's a lot of "lip service" that we tend to say out loud convincingly if we're the only ones that hear it. Or, are you? To say things out loud is only a confirmation to yourself; and, if your throat chakra is blocked, it is your body telling you something with the hope that you'll listen or that you need to listen. We continue broadcasting to others for various reasons and it's mainly to hear ourselves talk. In the immediate future there will be a whole lot of lip service instead of the real deal… why? Is it the wave of the future or has it been like this since the very beginning? People's intentions, beliefs, values are all lost-in-translation to what they're really feeling; but, only with an outward appearance of who's looking and/or listening. Some people have come to terms with their own bullshit but continue to provide lip service for it's all they know. While this is happening, children are observing… listening intently to what conversations their parents are having, who they're talking to and low-key wanting to know. Kids of all ages are attentive, observant and witnessing in a manner that parents have forgotten about. Kids are inquisitive, always curious, wanting to learn and grow… but some parents or those adulting are at an impasse. Adulting doesn't mean forgetting who you are – it's much like old age and dementia – you wake up one day forced to pretend. Who is pretending to be the actual parent? Who is pretending to have it all figured out? Without any sense

101

of feelings... Humanity might have to succumb to a world of pretending in Fear of AI -rulership. Can parents change-it-up after being so distraught in complacency – unknowingly sitting in an old-worn out, comfortable chair that can't be "Offered Up" for any amount of currency; because its time has expired. Everything about energy changes... energy cannot maintain any form, or, be held into form, and when the winds-of-change blow in your surroundings, that's a sign from God. Change or be clouded in the darkness that hovers, swirling in thoughts of negativity that attach to others, a breeding ground. Suffice it to say, we have only ourselves to blame. Should you fall out of love with your life...it will definitely be on your karmic ledger of checks and balances. It is without question that every child of God has been given the gift of life and has every right-of-passage. Where will you go if you end it? Only God knows the forsaken ones... Let it be said, however,

"Life is a gift you don't give back!" ™

UNKEPT PROMISES – TAKE RESPONSIBILITY AS A PARENTAL FIGURE

To be smart about the way forward means to take full responsibility for all the inclusions of your past actions and not hold back accountability. What some people end up doing is speaking words that ensures their own need to hear themselves speak, yet, nothing is ever done. The question is, "Can I now uphold my duties as a parent while under the guise of addictive behavior patterns?" "Do I realize the addictive behaviors, or not?" Whenever we make a commitment to ourselves, it is imperative that this be forged ahead with actions to back it up. No other way is needed for those who are serious about upholding the teacher/parent role for their children to learn from. What happens in most cases, however, is that those who say they're going to change, in hindsight, have repeatedly said a lot of words but to no avail. We cannot intend to make solid changes in our lives unless we get out of our own way and walk the talk. Whatever is spoken let it be heard by the highest in the angelic realm whenever a child speaks, God listens. Whenever we end up choosing ourselves, miracles abound. Whenever we falter with keeping our promises, it not only affects our children, it impairs our own vows to ourselves. Is what you're saying falling on deaf ears? These are trifecta promises of the mind, body and soul that need to be honored, respected and valued. "For what is a man and what has he got without his word, for he is not." in the Laws of the United Nations. We are under siege of what we've promised to deliver and have not been successful in doing so. Figuring this out early in our lives will emit a sense of comfort and security; and, if the seal is broken with unkept promises this undermines the ability for the child to trust. This is one of the most crucial variables in raising children, in being raised as children and in trusting our elders, our parents, our teachers and all those we've established a close-net relationship while growing up. The be-all/end-all is not far from the truth that lies within one's own life lessons. We've come to reap what we sow insofar as learning who to trust and who to not.

THE GOOD PARENT

What defines a good parent? Which parent do you feel closest to without sugar-coating? Did you have to think about it? Why? Why should any parent need to be defined? A good parent is one who has done their very best... The defining factor is what life experiences every child has endured being exposed to certain situations. That is how we can define the answer to the question. Many parents have placed boundaries, rules and regulations while others continue to numb their own painful past. To those parents who've been masking some form of pain, have you sought HELP for yourself? When will this happen, will it happen or will there be another child who drowns themselves ingesting their drug-of-choice? How many of you can look in the mirror without any guilt, resentment, jealousy or any other negative emotion of not being blindsided by your own reflection? What kind of environment are you putting your children into? What are you teaching, showing, giving your child to learn from? Do they have a mentor? Why not, if there is no one who your child can look up to then what is your child aiming for? We do not bear idols… a mentor is someone who represents a deep-seated truth from a pure heart that will lead a child to their safe haven, a trusted place to lay their head down, to confide in, to listen. Who entrusted you to become this child's guardian? Are you the parental figure or a guardian? What entails the connection of a guardian who may or may not have children of their own? Does your child ask you for help or the guardian? Is the guardian of your child married, single with/without child? Does it matter? Here are just a few series of questions that need to be reviewed, pondered and answered honestly in order to gain more insight into your child's behavior… hence, your own. Are you looking back in your past family matters that will show you the threads of patterns formed in order to see what type of affect/effect this had upon you as a child growing up? Do you see yourself as choosing these particular parents that you chose? Why did you choose this family? Did they choose you? Shout out to all those children who have been adopted, fostered and/or taken in and taken care of from outside influences… a LOVE so deep. We all have chosen one another to gain access to our own truth. This isn't for any other reason than to address the "threads" that tie us all together in union with the Divine. We are all threaded as one yet, we must unravel every aspect of our lives with those on the outside in order to get inside to better serve our purpose. A purposeful life is one that serves Humanity.... there is no other.

CONSPIRE. INSPIRE. 2B HEALED

When we serve to please others it's another way of saying we love ourselves; but the thing is to not serve in order to deserve. When that happens, it is futile to both the giver and the receiver. To give, in-deeds of service to Humanity does not deem a return-in-kind, unless warranted from the Heart. Overly pleasing to others has its trauma, in whatever ways this may or may not be happening it is worth taking notice. Why is it that humans overly give? Is it to be liked, accepted and/or even loved? This stems from our childhood and acts as a disservice to a child when one or both parents are absent. This child grows up thinking that something has gone badly... that they are not enough or whatever inner trauma this lends itself must be healed. Whenever we try too hard to be liked/loved it's a sensitive issue especially if this is triggering an emotion out of you at this very moment. Could there be a sense of hidden trauma lurking inside that is begging to be healed? How can we go about healing this part of our overly-pleasing ways? In some cases, changing the old ways would be advisable – when you feel that "need" to overly give to something or someone pause, ask yourself, "Is there a hidden meaning for the way that I feel at this very moment?" If there is any hesitation... look deeper. You will continue to do this until you become very aware of hidden truths as to why we give so much of ourselves to others. In certain situations, there is a very good reason to overly give as;

105

listening, holding another's hand, showing compassion and, when you're honing in on the other person's needs before your own, loving unconditionally. Another reason for someone who has experienced trauma in their childhood due to lack of attention and a lack of love. There are many children who don't even realize their trauma as a form of karmic justice for someone else's pain because of them. Karma is a huge mountain to overcome, painful strides of walking on path and the painful truths of our ways. It doesn't feel like it when karma has you entrenched in some situation of loss, physical/emotional pain of loss; grief; sorrow; attention-seeking; illness; dis-ease of the body; connectivity to what could have been; releasing of the old in everything and everyone; loneliness; lack of communication; lack attention and a plethora of other ailments that are visible or non-visible to the human receiving. Would we change knowing this from the get-go that this planet is based on karmic justice? Or, would you likely be choosing the same ole' ways because you don't quite believe it will catch up to you...perhaps, in the next life? Better yet... all our current/past lives have been karmically induced and no matter what or who you are... what you've done to others will come back to you. Everything we do has consequences and perhaps some of you didn't grow up that way yet are suffering in some way unbeknownst to you? And, if you think that you have secretly skated through life without getting affected, think again. Once again, the Universe is uniquely constructed. Why didn't anyone tell us? Did they know? Did society keep this from Humanity? Have "they" been getting theirs? You will witness many facets of failures, untruths, deceptions, hidden agendas from the external world in the next decade or two... be awake to see clearly. Massive reorganizations of this world and the outside events of a New World Order will continue being "EXPOSED" and there will be people who will and have vanished off the face of this Earth - being taken over by AI. Many may laugh at the conspiracists of this world happening now – who will have the last laugh? What you do or don't believe makes no difference to what is happening… make no-mind about it. Think what you want for whatever has been uncovered and what's to come will not be in theory. "They" have been warning Humanity for years but no one was listening; humans have had their head in the mud for ages; and now is the time to see clearly. Instilling a healthy lifestyle from the ground up, rebuilding your world will most definitely be what some are doing or getting ready to do. Whatever was… will no longer be.

To date, there is an uprising in the children on the Earth plane as many have been forging ahead making so much progress on themselves… Each child on this beautiful planet knows that all they need to do is, "remember" that we all are God's children who have signed up to return in order for planet Earth to resurrect the goodness while extracting those who have been abusing our children. We already have seen great progress… thanks to all social media platforms where now everyone is capable of knowing, seeing and being able to receive enlightenment, with such given knowledge. Exposures have been shown to the entire world of what congruent ruins lie on this planet, yet, if we all congregate together the shadow is lessening its power. For these reasons we decided that opening the portal of social media will inspire the congregation of children who need validation, sight to see all the corruption going on in our world. We are the world of Love and there will never be an end to the planet mainly because the light has outweighed the darkness now forever and ever. Our intentions of plans to resurrect planet Earth are becoming a beam of light unto itself… all misrepresentations of the misuse of power on this planet will continue to be shown the truth which will alleviate those who deemed it necessary to override the system's power of persuasion. It is with great joy and love of our Heavenly Father that this planet IS being saved!!! There will NOT be an Apocalypse based upon these findings. Yes, there will definitely be those who say they are of Faith yet decide to follow those who are misusing their power and this is exactly why God intended this planet to have freewill. Those who stand inside the box and those who make their own way out of confinement have always been the thorn in those who are of lesser faith. We have all been in each one of these situations to no surprise...

"We Three Kings of Orient Are..." treasuring what was written in that song of pureness that the children of the Ages had reenacted the beautiful depiction that presents to the Kings were; frankincense and myrrh. Just because the song depicts those presents doesn't mean that a bout of other goods were not also received – and, some of those were, indeed of money received for services rendered. Most would shun at the thought that those Kings were ever given money for services, but, why would that matter? It happens every decade dating back to those three Kings who rendered to save our Lord Jesus from the hardships of the disbelievers. We know of this song as giving back to the children gifts from Spirit world. Do you think for one moment that those Kings did not have an ego? The initial reasoning behind frankincense and myrrh was because they have healing properties that God was showing His people... but, they were not privy to that knowledge in those days. What they were very familiar with was that good deeds done for others were compensated with money – not for greed. Those three Kings were the only ones to provide insightful information from Jesus in order to poise as His followers. Why would only three Kings remain the Lord's true believers having unwavering Faith in God? It still holds true today where we are now in the 21st Century and the vast majority "state" in having unwavering Faith yet when it comes right down to the wire many are excluded from that highest level of trust. It takes the pureness of TRUST in God's innocence of Love for His children and the everyday miracles that are created effortlessly in the world which we live in… We all know that everything always seems to work out exactly as it IS without any glitches… it is the disbelief of those who stray where shadows tend to reside. This is exactly as it should be … nothing, and we mean absolutely no-thing goes unnoticed by the energies of the Universe! Therefore, if you are failing miserably in areas of your life and can't seem to shake it off…there are very good reasons for this happening. No one is exempt from not experiencing the same issues; but still continues to elude. Why do you think this is? Is there a metaphoric resemblance humans need to control? Does what we say, do and/or think seem to have a real impact on where we stand in our Faith today? Is this what God intended for us at this time? There is a huge amount of confusion, forgetfulness and much more going on in our world today, why? Do "they" think that poisoning our children from what they watch, eat, speak and/or hear today literally affects the growth and health of our children? Indeed.

APPROVAL, ACCEPTANCE

To want the need for approval from one or both your parents is not an easy task; and, it is a calling deeply rooted. This issue speaks to the majority of human beings because we have this innate acceptance, a radar that breeds a level of love when we feel accepted. We require a certain respect that allows our parents to feel the same yet many do not. The Law of Cause & Effect clearly states that what one person gives to another will be returned two-fold, or, even 100-fold; however, it's not always received in ways we're aware of. A reciprocal relationship between parent/child has much to be felt and understood. If we cannot please our parents and feel as though we fall short of the mark, how can we recognize ourselves? It is through the approval, acceptance that humans have been taught to gain for another's Love. Herein lies a massive undertaking between both parent and child who seem to be skirting around the issues that any type of approval is needed at all. It does not… but, Humanity has been pre-programmed to gain acceptance wherever possible in order to feel Loved. Where is it written that any parent must be a conglomerate of approving circumstances in one's life; especially in the life of your next of kin. A child is not in need of their parents' approval as much as they would deem it as a mere attachment. When setting any 'standards of approval' growing up with that mindset, leaves much room for misunderstanding on both the parent and child relationship. This has been another thorn in our side as craving attention in whatever way we can get it. Did our ancestors feel this too? Is it because their parent(s) sought approval? What a congregation of influencers to realize how the threads of approval have infected generations.

THE TRINITY: PARENT.TEACHER. STUDENT

Being an example as a parent shows your ability to walk the talk, in your truth. Now is the time to turn things around for the betterment of our kids and to raise them with the ability to become adults. Might we preface that providing the basic fundamentals will encourage a sense of responsibility, at an early age, setting a solid foundation. All influencers of teaching children, in whatever capacity is their obligation of what they signed up for; to serve, protect, guide and BE the example. What has become an issue is how many children have not gotten a sense of responsibility and are still living at home unable to provide for themselves. Parents of all generations are dealing with many addictions in ways that cast shadows of doubt in raising their kids. From drug addictions, alcohol and a multitude of reasons why this is influencing them. This cannot sustain a stable foundation for any child – in fact, most are growing up in very unstable environments. Nothing is beyond the seething skulls of darkness, remember this – and, be mindful of the drinks you drink, the tainted blunts, or the sweet charming looks of slithering tails swarming. Selling one's soul to the devil for wealth, fame, status, etc., that will ride your mind and play dirty-little secrets on you. When at your lowest of lows, many have sold their souls. Those who are flying high in the sky raising their vibrational white light cannot be coerced, manipulated or abused because their frequencies are high – and not the high from numbing... A tisket-a-tasket is your question of caskets?

This imparts much discussion as so many of us have grown up with different values; some of foreign backgrounds, cultural/ethical issues, behavioral training, maneuvers of Ego. We are all creatures of habit, yet, a child that has grown up and become enlightened will endure such differences in raising their own children that many dismiss or end up getting argumentative and even being coerced to change. This is the first and most important sign that, as a parent, you are raising a child of God... and not listening to outside forces of others who are still lost, asleep and/or not willing or able to "see." Those who see clearly are the ones raising their children for the greater good – the lightworkers, the sages, the masters of our own domain are raising spirited children. Many children who are now coming to Earth are already spirited in their own way; therefore, all who come to Earth have been given all the necessary tools, and need not worry, because all that has been decided upon for that specific child has already been done. As one learns this… it is only a matter of putting the earthlings into the necessary lifestyle with which that child will learn at the highest level for the highest good of both the parent who is teaching and the child who is learning. At times, however, the child becomes both the learner and the teacher – due to other values of domination insofar as addictive behavioral learning that both child and parent are in need of. This ends a life cycle of addiction where both the parent and the child have come to know and to understand how imperative certain circumstances of learning are required to learn what is needed to grow. Within every child our Heavenly Father, the Blessed Mother and The Holy Spirit provide all the necessary factors in one's life that will create, teach and explore a beautiful full-filled life. What seems like a hurricane twister becomes a light breeze on a winter's day… The way in which we "see" our own lives through the lens of the outside world is influenced by our egoic self. What does this mean? Whatever road you have taken will inflict a certain value of experiences that others will not even begin to understand. Everyone's place in this world is attended to … every miniscule thought, actions, surroundings, events even out the "playing field" has been taken into account. Every human living on Earth is "playing out" their life experiences in order for the entirety of their soul to become whole. The flow of life is a gift from Spirit and is meant to be felt, not to be misunderstood, doubted and/or questioned. What does this mean? It means that you shouldn't deny yourself the beauty that, 'going with the flow,' and, without need to control, we come to KNOW.

To KNOW THYSELF is to BE at ONE… within and without.

To KNOW is to LET GO…

Those in authority must exude behaviors that are undeniably honorable. From the parents, to all teachers and counselors, to the police/fire departments, to the parents of our kids etc., every contact children make is worthy of a check-in so as to take accountability. If there's a failure, what is necessary to fix this is getting help with the addiction(s) – rehab, talks, counseling and the like…showing them that you care enough about your own life to make a difference in theirs. What has become very normal is to witness families where there are more altercations of the mind than not. Most everyone is on something… What is the message? Why is taking any drugs, medications, or otherwise acceptable for the rest of one's life? Why is our healthcare industry not making headway in finding cures; instead, of continuous medicating? Do we care? How has this become the newest norm? How to assess if these alterations are harming or helping? On the basis of actions of what adult kids are doing, there is a common denominator as lack of motivation, unable to handle adult responsibilities (job, home), still hanging onto the apron strings. Being continuously held under the fire to get a job, get an apartment, seek to find a social group of like-minded friends and to stop expecting others to do everything for you. Those children who are under age have already become unmotivated by what they're witnessing by the examples already set by those parents who are not helping themselves. It is either a slow-roll of certain events and/or tragedies within the family that might make children question what's going on; or, it could be the norm of how things are being accepted. What is being witnessed are real-life dramas… that are not staged in one's home. What is happening? Leaving kids home alone without supervision gives them the idea that it's on them - and, even if they're teenagers transitioning into adulthood; what example is this setting? So many of these teens, and younger, are suffering and seeking HELP. We don't realize the great impact one action/reaction or non-action/non-reaction creates in an entire lifetime. For example: it's similar to not telling/showing someone how much you love and care for them... until they're gone. Humanity has become so complacent in valuing their lives, not showing up, in letting moments of years pass by.... How did this become a theme for Humanity? Why don't we tell the truth? Ingrained in our system from childhood is where kids told the truth and got scolded, yelled at, called stupid. No wonder children/kids hold back from being honest. Lies, deception, illusions, misrepresentations, holding back and everyone is tuning out... When no one was looking, matters of what family stood for escaped the majority of mankind. For times of putting out fires. For times when distractions abound. Both external worlds of home/family AND our society as a whole are threaded with the same thorns of a diminished society - while no one is watching, or refusing to pay attention the tables turned right under your nose. As the New World Era has been exposing indiscretions that are running races of re-election. You may be questioning how this resonates with how you are partaking in your child's life at this very moment... Does mankind feel remorse, guilt-by-association, fearing the worst again? All Fear-based emotions are building blocks that must be torn down and rebuilt on the basis of truth. Will we continue to passively turn the other cheek or find that the elephant in the room is impregnated with shock. Either we set healthy environments for our children or become the enemy by one's own willful need to control or impeach the loss of control that imposes more of the same. We are being asked at this very moment not to take this lightly. Our children were given to us by no accident, all children are gifts from the Divine light of LOVE... please take *heed* to this message that has caused so many children to leave the Earth plane, to no fault of their own. Every polarity in this world can be mastered through the revelation of balance, patience, discipline and moderation... too much of a good thing lends itself to become tethered souls. A soul untethered finds itself in the present company of all the miraculous gifts of Life. All of Life is a stage...

Authenticity is leading the light of the world for all to see.

RESTRICTED BOUNDARIES

In the Motion Picture Association (MPA) film rating system movies are rated as G, PG, PG13, R, NC-17 under the administration by the Classification & Ratings Administration (CARA), independent of the MPA, whereby these ratings are:

"G" General Audiences

"PG" Parents Guidance Suggested

"PG13" Parents Strongly Cautioned

"R" Restricted

"NC-17 - ADULTS ONLY

Within every movie across the country the MPA has owned up to their end of the deal by placing boundaries and restrictions for the protection and betterment of children. As in the movies and as we continue to delve into the world of social-media ...are the same restrictions prohibited? To say it is under the guidance of every child's parental figure(s) to keep a close eye on what is going on is to keep hold of shady forces. Most definitely the influences of "ratings" still apply to certain YouTube channels and the games such as "Minecraft" and others where ratings are in place. However, what, who, when, where are these children, teens and young adults finding their source of emotions? Is social media a playground of contention to play with machine guns, rifles, staves, that all portray their anger at someone, or, at themselves? Is social media a playground for violence, and/or other outlets that parents are not aware of? Or, are you? What platforms are your children watching? Where is your child streaming? Who are they playing Virtual Reality with? Who is behind the curtain? We are talking about 5, 6, 7-year-olds who are learning to play games with influencers? Who is on the other side of the curtain? Inevitably so that once a child loses their innocence, it cannot be regained. What, who are the influencing factors that are becoming a secondary or even primary source of parenting? When we explore traditional values of parenting, it seems that our parents had a firm grasp on what we were watching... Do you agree?

Many parents are vying to know what's going on with their children... listening intently to what is being said or not said. What is being called to the playground? It's a crap shoot. Why are we gambling with our children's innocence? Where did we, as parents, drop the ball of tending to the most valued treasures of parenthood there is? Children are the Blessing. Who is going to save you when there is no other? When do we, as parents, co-parents, stepparents, adopted parents, foster parents, grandparents, etc., going to take a hold of our children's lives only to become their main mentors and influencers? What will become of the newest Millennials who are becoming less respondent to their direct families and more insightful from social-media influencers? Who is influencing you, as the parent, on social media? Obsessed? Is it in the lives of others who are your so-called influencers marketing their products and/or abilities? Who's buying into all that stuff on Instagram (IG)? An Insta-grandiose skincare product that promises to clear those wrinkles? Have you 'bought-into' all the hype? What's the problem? Do you see a problem at all?

All kids observe adults…they watch, they listen, and establish a sense of what they decide to believe in. Even observing other friend's parental guidelines to compare with their own. While children are witnessing all adults… some of the adults are off doing their own thing. Later on, they come to find out that they've noticed their friends' parents are very different or in some ways, similar. However, the story goes…all parents discipline differently with their own values and beliefs. Parents either know what they're doing or not…when it comes to the discipline on their own agenda(s) – picking up their kids from school, arranging alternative options, work schedule, lunch requirements, homework, playtime and/or play-dates with other kids and a host of other disciplining of their day-to-day. A parent needs to stay actively involved – better to be disciplined than not, depending upon their upbringing; however, many kids are doing whatever they want. Unlike ever before we are raising kids while both parent and child live the majority of time on social media; streaming, gaming, VR etc. "Who is manning the fort"?

PARENTAL LOVE IN A FIELD OF DREAMS

Parenting is not about disciplining for the mother's sake but for the sake of the child. The father's role is also a duplicitous role that originates from the rib of man to the womb of the mother – in tandem with like father, like mother. The duplicitous roles are actually merged into masculine/feminine roles on the Earth plane to assist in the parenting of the child/children. We weave threads of Love to all Energetic ties for all souls that come into this lifetime to learn, grow and evolve. Otherwise, we will continue to reincarnate with these same souls and different physical suits until the job of parenting evolves into a full circle of God's LOVE. We are all of this Universal energy and are not yet fully aware of its usage of existence on the Earth plane. Attempting to control the terrain of energetic forces is useless because every human being on this planet is not of the same frequency in their journey of love. When all is said and done… cohabitation with mankind must not include doubt, fear, excuses or explanations as to who you have seen yourself as … in the eyes of the Beholder. Once your eyes have become your guide to what, who, how and when you encounter a clear vision, you will choose to navigate your life with richer experiences that include tribes of inner treasures. Inner treasures of our field of dreams…A mother/father's role is essentially the most important role, EVER! This is NOT a job. It is up at dawn into the wee hours of the next-morning's-light parenting. What one has to contend with is of no conquest, but it is of great importance as to how the child is raised. We've become a very divided union of current events in the household. We have been given so many tools on how to best parent a child – from a solid foundation to great teachers and counselors and all those who are making an impression upon children. What happens as children are in the growing stages becomes confusion; others' ideologies, religions, belief systems and/or parenting styles etc., add to layers of confusion on what to believe, who to believe and how to distinguish one from another. The notion of what is right or wrong has been skewed by their training grounds, and from there, we've got to dive deep into both parents' and the thread of one's heritage of real-life traumas, triggers and filters. Two parents acting as parental figures make it so much easier to assist in raising a child, but the ancestral threads speak to those who are able to listen. Everyone's ancestral lineage cannot be found; however, there are symbols, triggers, signs and much more that the angelic realm is communicating to each one of us. "Do you see what I see... Do you hear what I hear?" is exactly what that Christmas song means. Are you able to step out of your comfort zone of complacency and look around? Mother Earth is speaking out, too... for all to hear.

Children need to be educated on becoming familiar with how their body speaks to them as it is their navigational system - not taught; why? Who is holding who back? Children in the East have been learning meditation and healing properties – much more advanced than in the Western culture. Why? Because Eastern culture has set the stage for all who follow... In Western culture, those clouds of darkness have disillusioned and molded the energy into a Fear-based society. Children entering into this world today, however, are already spiritually advanced souls for this very reason. Many realized Masters have risen from the East...where the Sun rises – and where the West is the setting Sun. The West is going through an awakening into the rising Sun – aka. "Phoenix Rising". Taking into account that the Western culture is undergoing much turmoil over the course of decades; and this is why there is a defined "shadow period" that eludes mankind. This Spiritual Revolution is what Mother Earth is experiencing as Her "dark night of the soul". Eastern culture suffers also in ways that are not seen but heard. A meditative monk may be silenced for years yet has no way of re-emerging the threads of mind, body, and soul. At the Horizon, both cultures are undergoing their own ascension; purification happens for all.

Children must learn to acquire an independent nature within their environment so that they're equipped to handle all external interferences. Those who coddle or cradle-to-grave their children are sheltering the potentiality for growth. No one way is the right/wrong way...remembering this is crucial not only to your child/children but also for the health of the parent/adulting. The parents who have been gifted with a child, stepchild, adopted child, foster child or any other way in which you are the parents of a beautiful child must be seen, felt and handled with the highest level of love through your love. So many parents have lagged in their parenting skills because the primary and most important start to a child's life is knowing that the parents come to the table bringing a safe, loving environment through self-love, a whole heart. Hence, this is where we must begin by delving into the love of a mother and the love of a father. Each parent who has been gifted with a child is not exempt from their own past trauma and/or their own family issues; however, the difference is that it is your responsibility to become the highest, best version of oneself prior to taking on the responsibility of children. The distressing effects of bad parenting comes from either one or both parents who have chosen not to make stringent efforts to change their ways; and, to realize that this is not working. The truth of the matter is that there are some who observe these types of family differences and end up criticizing and/or judging; but, the truth is they are unable to see. The only way in which your mother and/or father can come to grips with their own reality is to seek their own salvation. "God helps those who help themselves..."

Mankind is still searching for answers to the ongoing uncertainty of "Who Am I?" The question of every generation who hasn't got a clue...yet, life happens without a warning, and while all the externals are swirling around us, there are those who are becoming parents.

Every parenting style is different, just the same – all children want to be Loved and accepted as they are. The caveat to this Love-thing is that, while we are searching within for what Love we did or didn't receive to feel valued, our children are enduring the same. Love is defined in so many different ways; values, morals, ethics, religion, etc., that lends itself to mass confusion. What children really need is to be Loved exactly for what they bring to Life. Children are our lives…and every child portrays a Freedom of innocence that is gifted back to every parent, step-parent, adopted parent, foster parent, grandparent(s), aunt, uncle, sister, brother and the like… showing us all how to Live in Love. The gift and blessings of child's play are to remain playful, innocent and to enjoy a fulfilled Life of Love. Parenting has shown destructive threads of external disturbances on both society's part as well as those parents who have not been disciplining children. Since the beginning of time, God's Love has been shown for children to learn to Love themselves and all of mankind to become their authentic selves. The authentic self was instilled, in this world, given as God's template through The Ten Commandments. The Ten Commandments, The Laws of the Universe, The Hermetic Principles, and the Dead Sea Scrolls of the Seven Seals have been inscribed and shared for all to abide by. The Ten Commandments that the prophet Moses revealed when climbing Mt. Sinai was a cry for HELP (Humanity's Evolution for the Love of People) from God to reveal Himself… The "passion of God's Love" was shown to Moses as a demonstration of His omni essence presence. This Holy fire is the light of God, which is within all mankind to exert unwavering Faith. This is the energetic light of the Sun within each and every one of us. In order to feel this light, one must face our Fears. It goes without saying how crucial it is for every man, woman and child to dissect whatever constitutes the darkness that lies within for the light to be seen. Jesus' tomb, upon His Ascension, was the light for ALL to BE. Those who believed saw this light as the sign that it was intended for – all will ascend just as Jesus – and the blessings of our Heavenly Father revealed. Even after those who witnessed the light of God through Jesus' showed His light of the world... doubt has remained. We witness Mother(s) give birth to child/children as the Holy Spirit's everyday miracles...yet humans still live with Fear. Instead, why doesn't Humanity see this life as what it IS, everyday miracles? Humanity has drifted away from themselves for varied reasons... all based on Fear. "For God so Loved the world that He gave His only Begotten Son..." was not enough? What else on this Earth could possibly be witnessed for Humanity to embrace all Love? What will it take? An Apocalypse of abundant fears as there will be many more disasters to witness – why succumb to the fear that makes one incapable of believing within your every breath? These natural disasters will continue to take place and Humanity will continue on the course of ignorance. Do you know why? Another fear-based reason why humans are so ignorant is boredom. Boredom of life, a "same shit, different day" attitude makes for ungrateful people who have strayed... lost souls. Humanity's call to a new vision begins within every parent, child and breath, as giving Life. Humans are creatures of habit, with a series of forgetfulness spread across the world. Being forgetful is one thing... but to be irresponsible and negligent of your child/children in light of your own errors needs to be seen as Ego. Is Humanity unaware of the poison that has been overconsuming our lives? From what we are ingesting as poison – poisoned food to polluted water and in the air that we breathe, the poisoned one lives in Fear. Will your Last Will & Testament be noted as living in Fear? A "test-a-ment" is mankind's test in every moment of either what we've learned or have yet to understand. School requires that tests be held for kids to be accountable to learn in order to graduate, and, this bodes true for the School of Hard Knocks. When we embark on the journey of life, it's defined as a journey to self-realization. The core of existence is the portal of light from the energy of the Sun, which is the inner workings of one's Faith. "For God so Loved the world that He gave His only begotten Son " describes how the Faith of the children has been using a blind eye of faith instead of a clear knowing of Faith. In every child's life we are given a choice to answer, "What do you stand for?" Jesus' ascension is the example for every act of a child's life to be seen as such… acts of Faith.

Whatever you may or may not believe, Humanity was chosen to explore, experience and evolve. Dating back to BC, we must remember as our story unfolds what History has witnessed and what we are witnessing, to "KNOW THYSELF" from the rib of man… hence, "Human: Heaven's Utopia of Man".

WINGS TO FLY

No matter what has transpired in our lifetime… all souls are God's LOVE, a gift that is meant to continue giving back to the consciousness. Evolution began within a black hole whereby glimpses of light were brought in for all to gain access to their own light. Hell is NOT a place…it is an inner journey of life experiences - good and bad - in order to clean one's slate and move further on to a new paradigm of Union. What has been lost cannot be recovered on the Earth but is recoverable in the throws of Love's light. Never forget that we have all agreed to raise the vibration of Mother Earth's higher consciousness and to enlist those souls who have evolved with Her. What doesn't happen is a cross-over body that figures to replace one's soul who is doing the work on themselves…protected at all costs. Heavenly Angels, Ascended Masters, Spirit Guides, and the likes of ALL light forms protect and secure the rightful place of all those souls on the Earth, as promised. No entity can be persuaded under any circumstances…not unless their vibrational frequency is on the lowest binaural beat/thread. Our body IS the Temple and what we, as humans, will or will NOT allow is entirely up to us!

The indoctrination of Fear has covered Humanity for eons… a Fear-based, angry world that is clearly divided. The scales of positive/negative are imbalanced, with a lifeline headed toward destruction. Society has divided mankind, whereas to manufacture and grow the false ID/Ego self… attempting to confuse the masses. External factors, through one's own indoctrination of Fear-based thoughts, turned into action, have chained and sabotaged the freedom of all who are weak. The fearful, the weak, those who are negative, with negative thoughts, over-controlling, constant complaining, tit-for-tat "mindset" – is that of the Ego. Thriving to survive in a world of Fear breeds a world to one's own demise. What is being witnessed in the external world is a representation of how Fear overrides the lives of so many. People have forgotten their inherent (in-HEIR-ent) rightful place of empowerment, which was given at birth. Time has changed the way people view their lives and the way in which they see the external world. Everyone who has bought into a Fearful, destructive vision of their lives knows but doesn't understand why. So many humans are searching for themselves … in all the wrong places. Unbeknownst to Humanity, the search is an inner search – going within to inhale your rightful inheritance. That's where the word, "inherent" comes from … an inheritance of life all-encompassing within every past-life experience(s) and an array of toppings of lessons

- learned or unlearned. This cake is called our "Birthday" cake, which is a celebration of a new life of presents/gifts. On this day, every child of God's Love spreads their wings to fly... From this day forward, every child has "free will". Freewill upon this Earth to either subject yourself to a full life in Faith – or, to cave, gasping for air in Fear. What every gifted child does is forget their in-HEIR-ent Nature (Mother Nature) – their natural gifts in exchange for greener pastures. ($) Mother Earth's power over all Life comes in as healing properties of a natural-healthy clean lifestyle - mind, body; whereas the Earthbound extremities of the misuse of power in one's lifestyle – beg, borrow and steal to maintain the stage of illusions. The illusion of acquiring "stuff" that amounts, in the end, to nothing... but gives the ego pride, status, money, desires, cravings, greed etc., through the looking glass. No diamond in the rough could ever be as valuable as the miracles in life.

When we've come to the end of our journey... it is "only" the Love we feel, we give, we show, we serve, we become that IS. IS-In Spirit.

No matter what, you are your own boss...aren't you? *Discernment* is key... believe only what's in your heart-of-hearts and leave the rest. Take into account other's pains and sufferings because that is exactly why the world has become tainted. The destruction of other's pain and/or suffering has left people ignorant, numb, cold, isolated, hopeless, angry, sad, depressed, stressed, and immune to darkness. A classical ideology that has plagued Humanity with its power. What has tainted you? How about the food we eat, the water we drink, the air we breathe...what is left? AI Artificial Intelligence is what society literally created, spearheading the onset of molding

human degradation. Humanity has no one to blame but themselves...
for this will become another kind of war unto itself. Human robotics
meets AI. An intelligence that is programmable, emotionless, and
empty inside. "The Tin Man Meets the Scarecrow and the Lion" all
lack a heart, a brain, and courage. Yes, another way of saying, "the
blind leading the blind..." Are you going to continue to be complacent
– or will you take those wings and learn to fly? We've experienced
miracles not only of everyday miracles of baby's breath and The
Northern Lights solar flares all over the world, never seen before in
certain parts of the world, capturing shooting stars and changes of
weather that are not necessarily climate change as it is Mother Earth's
ascension. There are songs, numbers, symbols, our dream state, a
conversation overheard, a far-off land – a multitude of Heavenly sent.
What makes one child turn the other cheek while another child finds
their inner light? Do we need to compare-2-care? Why can't we care...
isn't this life worthy of you? Aren't you tired of being tired? Does the
thought of doing something exist? What takes your breath away? Are
you waiting...

THE HERITAGE OF PARENTING

How did you grow up? What was it that made you choose your
parents? Do you even realize that you chose not only your family but
also your parents' families, etc.? Herein lies the threads. Once you can
equate the truth of choosing your parents – including the attached
siblings, aunts/uncles, cousins, 2nd cousins and the like – is where the
work begins. Hence, we find ourselves in the eternal bliss of Love over
and over until we reach the Epitaph of ONE LOVE. Seek for all to see
none... no one. This is "The Way", written in the newest version of
man's interpretation of The Bible.

The threads are where we seek not only to find out how the Universe places the algorithms of life but to also explain the same dichotomy of that thread that is weaved into the precious parts of our lives as a sunrise/sunset evolution of death and rebirth. When we undergo a place in a time of indulging in the fruits of our labor and harboring the same resentments that of our parents or the same conditioning of a parental figure, it is a "red flag". All threads weaved into a different story of the same old story from one lifetime to the next. When we "let go" by "going with the flow", the threads can untangle themselves as karmic justice begets to unravel a wound whose scar is gone. The Universe repetitively speaks to us...not because of pride, ego, or an attempt to downplay how this world has been constructed, but as a means to an end of what is the end result? Is there an end result? Is there a chance, at some point, to unravel a thread one at a time? It is the ability to listen in each moment, within/without, that of what is observed in the importance of finding ourselves. This journey is like going to the theater, experiencing people, places and things that become our "mirror reflections" and impart where we are on our journey as a reflection in our present moment. What is your present moment mirroring back to you? Are you seeing your reflection, or are you projecting what you see onto others? The reality remains to be seen. This is what the term 'projection' means -- a true version of a projected version of one's own self. That projection is not to be taken lightly as it becomes one's version of their reality. By what standards do you project your vision or version? Any other version of what your project is considered? The 'curtain call...' is a projected image of what's been seen by the I (eye) that meets the vision that projects what it is seeing as the seeker. The seeker is the visionary and the one who projects – the seer of that vision, the mystic. What do you seek to see? Are you the one who

127

seeks to be seen, or are you projecting a scene for others to see? How does this apply in your life? Are you projecting onto others and/or are others projecting onto you. If so, who is doing it and who is seeing it? The stage is set for the life cycle where we either serve or do a disservice that cannot be assimilated as anything other than knowing you can either be none or both at the same time. Why not be one or the other? It is not possible… The other is not real; it is an illusion of what you deem to be real. Being one, as one, in one embodiment is the only ONE.

Reminiscent of our ancestral lineage we become more than we are while walking through a lifetime of what transpires. Even though we seem to think that our lessons are about this lifetime, they are all-encompassing of previous lifetime lessons that must be learned in order to grow. Under no circumstances in this life are humans exempt from leaving out any part of their learned behavior to objects of desire – as they will continue to repeat until cleared. What a child learns from a parent and/or parent-like figure is something that breeds within and must be forgiven when that lesson impacts other emotional content. Learned behaviors come from many angles and when used for someone else's benefit, it changes from learned behavior to a heightened awareness of service to mankind. When behaviors are learned from their parents and/or whoever has taught the child to absorb these behaviors, the child is also responsible for how these behaviors can be an asset for others… if not, they become a negative ion of misuse of power. We need to be cognizant of these events in our lives where we can actually utilize these behaviors to act as a conduit of good-natured behavior for others. Too many people are unaware of their own selves, let alone aware of behaviors and/or those that have become habitual that have been passed down throughout the ages of a lifetime. At specific times in our lives, we do get "glimpses" of ourselves in how we treat others, insofar as what triggers have been healed in others, in solving our own patterns where life begins to go more smoothly and events make us feel at peace. Acts of compassion, peace, empathy, kindness, conversations, and all of our inner workings come from the Blessed Mother... What we're injecting here, on the Earth plane, are acts of "GRACE" that come in various forms, as The Blessed Mother showed us with Her Son, Jesus. That is NOT of a religious nature but showing acts of kindness that we have seen and been taught, compassionate love of the highest order.

Mankind is undergoing this awareness as we speak, and the word is spreading like a passionate wildfire of existence throughout the world. It is all about the one who sees and the one who knows.

PARENTAL APPRECIATION

Do we love and appreciate our parents beyond the need for food, shelter, and clothing? Have we invested in the reciprocal love of a child/parent relationship? Is this being taken for granted? Since the beginning of time, children have come to relate with their parents as showing genuine love. Inevitably, all children veer off course in their teenage years – as well as in the later years... but when does the thread of unconditional gestures take place? Does it happen in times of trouble? Does it happen in times of greed? Does it show up as a phone call of hidden motives and/or a desire to be set free? Children and their parents have been given many tools to utilize growing up; however, with a chance of cloudy vision. Just say the word, and let's have a chat about who buried the hatchet or kept it all in their cap... what do we say about that! Will we ever find the pot of gold at the end of the tunnel, or has the gold turned into a tainted pot and/or coated - fentanyl? Do children give love to show they really do care, or does the "Dark Side of the Moon" cast an illusion? Who will be sought, and who will soar? No matter whether the ties of Justice are incorporated within or without – we all learn to be humble and distill doubt. Whatever it will be, we shall... use that grain of salt, knock on some wood and clean out the cobwebs of what you thought. Having been given the gift of parenting becomes knowing how to navigate using the guidance of The Bible as well as the natural order of how Mother Nature intended. Without the use of our bodies as our navigational system, we wouldn't be able to understand the underlying emotional repression/suppression that is being hidden – cast aside in the shadows. The shadow is our eternal value system, which can also be seen as the hidden parts of our sub consciousness even when the crevasse of our brains dictates otherwise. Our internal guidance system is where we find what is needed to endure the hardships, and hard knocks of the Earth plane. We must value ourselves in order to understand and get to a place of peace and harmony; otherwise, we must go deeper into how our body functions as to what it is attempting to tell us. This navigational system within our bodies forms a new way forward insofar as what we deem as important or what otherwise we would not want anyone to know. Our physical body is the inner temple that holds the blessings of the internal workings that will set us Free.

All past generations call out to mature... find a new American dream to ad heir!

PARENTAL DISCRETION

"When the going gets tough, the tough get going…"

To be a parent wreaks havoc on all who have chosen the path of indiscretion. What this means is all those choosing and being chosen to parent have understood their right-of-passage in both teaching and setting the example. This is a sacred covenant – given by God to uphold. History often shares its wisdom in how love is ever-changing and evolving. No two days are alike, and no two people remain stagnant, for what remains is Fear. Fear keeps Humanity's energy stagnant… unable to reach their fullest potential. At the slightest hand of discipline, a wall goes up between child and parent; as unloving. Casting boundaries, disciplining with a firm hand, awarding a no-place-to-go as a form of imprisonment leads both parent/child relationships on rocky ground. Instead of expressing to our child/children that the discipline being instilled as "tough love" cannot be understood at that time, but later on, this too shall pass; might hope to set a new tone. Respect. There are those who have set the tone but laid upon deaf ears; there are those who didn't listen and did not heed the call; and there are those who are rebels at heart. Parental discretion doesn't mean being discreet or not setting rules and regulations, it is the exact opposite where discretion being given or not still needs the line in the sand – some for only child, others for both parent and child. How does a parent show authentic love and care for their child/children? Is it a show of 'tough love' or 'enabler', both threaded of the hardest kind? While to be discreet is one thing… to be a parent who is not discreet and is fleeting, floundering, floating around with all the men in town, per se, has its repercussions. Too many people just "give up" so easily in life, so precious as the light of a new day into

131

the dawn of night… What makes people entertain this for themselves? Are people so weak that they cannot make a decision to save their life? Are people so intimidated by just the thought of making a wrong decision they will be harshly judged? Are they just too scared of getting hurt that may impose pain from previous encounters? Are those who are so 'in control' really NOT in control at all? Why? What part of your life have you let go of fighting for? Why? Who is to blame? Are you pointing the finger at others who make bad decisions? Now you've got someone to blame? What responsibilities have you avoided being a part of? Why? Is it fair to say that those who "poise" as adults should be able to make their own decisions but fail miserably because they are masked in an adult body with a child's mentality? Are your adult kids not able to "grow up" for fear of responsibility and you as the parent letting it slide? Guilt. When all is said and done how will the future of our children deal? There must be a place where boundaries hold their value in the sands of time. When a parent is codependent and in need of attention, this sets an example for the child/children. However, this plays out as a thread of promiscuity that lives and breathes in one's DNA, and genetic history. Most people don't know or realize how their history affects the present moment.

Where there is pleasure, there is pain… and, is Freedom the end result? Absolutely… much more discreet. However, discretion is defined in your life, and in whatever generation bodes true for you. Has it inflicted pain or pleasure? Is it the pleasure principle of "no pain, no gain"? Have we veered away from the pleasure/pain principle to raise children, or do we continue to hide the indiscretions? *No matter what…it is every parent's responsibility to set an example for their children.* What examples have you been setting and/or putting down? Are you being discreet? How are your children being raised, viewed and seen by both parents as our In-Heirtance that's threaded Heirs? What are you an heir to? Are you Queen Charlotte Bridgerton or are you Princess Diana? Or, none of that which you seek? We must not need to idolize or choose which heir we've followed only to know that our Heritage comes full circle. Either way of life, it is a choice to either follow in the steps of our Heritage in vain, as a ball-in-chain; or be free to set upon a new-improved version of you.

Parental discretions are formulated for a reason...not to inflict pain on the self and/or others who happen to play these "virtual reality" games where the kids in the room are all shooting your kids. When did we, as a society, "give up" our rights to parent, discipline and give children the ability to become adults way before their maturity? What does this say about our society? Can't handle the heat? Do you drink to numb the pain? Have you gotten a DUI and still question why you're not sober? Do you continue to mess with the system as you enter court time-and-time again to support the habits of your sons and/or daughters? Years of escapism is a form of numbing – addictive behaviors being the number two cause for child suicide... You may ask, "What's the number one behavior for children committing suicide?" It's not "paying attention" to your child/children. It's not giving Love to your children when all they're doing is crying out for HELP. Who is crying out for HELP? What parent is able to HELP a crying toddler instead of getting high, or, staying on social media leaving the toddler to feed for themselves? What would happen if a minor accident or major catastrophe would cause the toddler to go to the emergency room, then what? Rather... get yourself HELP so that you can coexist with your children and handle the emergence of Life. Another form of shutting out is allowing kids to eat junk food, drink sodas and stay high on "sugar", another deadly drug. "Watermelon" sung by Harry Styles with lyrics purporting "one of those sugar highs..." could be misconstrued to awake the beast within. What substances define a sugar high? Another classic lyric, "A Spoonful of Sugar Helps the Medicine Go Down" in Mary Poppins. Are we oblivious or acting oblivious as to eons of programming destruction in our lives? Where is the sliver of HOPE? Is it that you've come to terms with this type of behavior? Familiar complacency, codependence... Why is this and/or is it being overlooked? Are you? Should the innocence of children be blindsided by instilling Fear? We, the children, have signed up to a life on Earth to clear our karmic debt; and, not even 5 or even 6 years out of the mother's womb, have we been blindsided by the effects of the wild? What is the answer, solution? Isn't it time to take accountability as parents to imbue discipline? Our social media issues need censoring – what is being watched and who's watching with a keen eye... what's really going on? There are parents who have posed harm to their children either mentally, physically, spiritually and/or emotionally. What happens next ... when that child enters into adulthood beginning their journey of parenting? They've already been tainted by the workings of past history and present ignorance ... Mother Nature wants Her children to evaluate a lineage of patterns or otherwise sever ties to karmic injustices and feel what is "The Way." What you believe not to be imposed by others. We are to descend from Heaven and follow the path of truth. What are you willing to believe and/or what is ready to be "Cast Away-ed". Who is handing at your wills-that-chain by casting away those who are believers? It is called, "integrity" of one's character... Our integrity of character is being dismantled so that a New World will besiege the old for the new. The old belief that we must fear a judgmental God upon going to Heaven is plagued with the same God who "forgives" all His children. Those of you who have not forgiven yourselves for your own transgressions by admitting to and taking responsibility for will ascend once again only to descend back down to the Earth plane until you can forgive. Jesus asking His Father, "Please forgive them Father for they know not what they do" is the same as being granted forgiveness from your own Father, Mother and whomever you came across during your time on this Earth plane – and of forgiving yourself. The reason why Jesus begged His Father's forgiveness was to address the issues of Fear in humans that they could not "ascend into Heaven and sit at the right-hand of The Father and He will come again in Glory to judge the living and the dead whose reign shall have no end." Have we understood that forgiveness of all others and self is the only judgment of The Father? The 2nd coming of Our Lord Jesus is the right-of-passage to clear all karmic debt from Mother Earth's original sin; and to ascend to a higher consciousness.

A world with no end... is the beginning....

"In the beginning was the Word, and the Word was with God, and the Word was God." This New World will start from the very beginning of time on the Earth plane, allowing a new concept to be written and lifted out of the awareness of man. Every day we take a "new day" for granted... when in actuality each new day is the start of The Bible. The word is to follow our own truth.... Every passage in The Bible depicts what humans on Earth will be required to overcome and learn that 'the one seeking is the ONE, ALL KNOWING. The illusions of this Earth are to teach by implementing lessons that defy the odds – by NOT going back to the old ways of being... be-in-God. Every passage will need to be revisited in order to be ordained as a child entering the Gates of Heaven. The New World Movement that has happened is for The Chosen Ones to teach those who are not yet awakened the light within as the power of God, is within. Merging our Masculine/Feminine nature is what our awareness of the highest order depicts – a transcendence of the merging into ONE's own Higher Consciousness. That clears the way for others and emits a way forward for quicker turnover to becoming that which IS. They who "think" have become what IS…Inner Spirit. The "IS" of one's Inner Spirit KNOWS what IS. This "New Era of A Golden Age" IS the I AM Movement (within/inner reflection) the same. The Inner Spirit that IS reflects the I AM reflection of what IS and will always BELIEVE … Believe-IN-Eternity.

Prayer begins their soul's search for God's HELP … which is always available for whoever needs it, and all that it takes is to ask. That's where the saying comes from, "Ask, and you shall receive". No matter what… if your prayer holds the purest of willful intent, your prayers will be answered in Divine timing. If your prayer is weak and tainted with doubts of fear, the desire comes from that of our Ego. To begin the process, one must look within by not questioning the external Egoic karats of gold, silver and such principles of "all that glitters is not gold" dichotomy. Although the Magi, or We Three Kings, gifted baby Jesus with Gold, Frankincense and Myrrh – these were considered essential and Holy. This was a celebration of paying homage to the King:

Gold - Symbolism of Jesus' status being King of the Jews in the currency of that time; Frankincense - Represented Jesus' Divinity of identity (ID) as the Son of God and the offering thereof; Myrrh - Jesus' mortality.

SINGLE PARENTING

Making room for one parent who is assertive just seems to be God's way of saying that the single parent must do the work of both parents – or else, a step-parent has agreed to step-in to add value or attempt at overriding the family dynamic. The old-breed is uncertain of this newly developed add-on to a family as this has tendencies of inner resentment, anger and a semblance of "you're not my parent" which has been said time and time again. What is the solution? Where have you found yourself bartering against the other spouse/live-in to compromise, listen and to know that someone other than yourself is doing a good job. Is a job well-done good enough? Why do we characterize 'good enough?' Do we attract a step-parent the same or with similar morals/values they seem to represent? Or, do we find another person to fill in the gaps, not based on similar beliefs but to experience more of the same? It's true that like-attracts-like and is it also true that if one person does not want to HELP themselves, are we just adding another self-imposed ego to the equation that looks good *only* for external value? The external values of oneself are neither here nor there because to parent does not qualify you to become one. Having a child only identifies you as a parent to the external world; but to BE a parent, you must be doing your inner work healing past wounds. What implores you to ask if you've done a good job parenting is to envision yourself in your child's eyes of healing; wandering to wonder.

When the single parent is attempting to engage in both the masculine and feminine roles… one energy will tend to override. Do you find yourself trying to balance the energies of parenting by allowing your child to become their independent self? Are you overwhelmed in a whirlwind of making decisions, running errands, homework, making or buying dinner, bath time, and a multitude of skill sets that could use an extra pair of hands? Have you brought home other friends, and/or partners to indulge in aiding with parenting? Is it too soon? How do the kids feel? Are the children expressing their likes and/or dislikes? What are you "saying" about the baby-mama/baby-daddy instilling kindness or outright anger, pain, sorrow? Do your kids see you as strong or weak? If there is a split-in-parental time and place with the ex-in-question or the baby's mother/father … What are they saying? Are you getting any feedback or a slew of complaints, criticisms, jealous vibes and/or issues pertaining to child support and/or alimony? Are the kids privy to hearing - or - are they behind the scenes witnessing and listening? Do you know? Whatever is being said or not being said is crucial to how single parenting is handled. How both parties feel, or how a single parent deals with the one that ran away from the responsibility creates different threads of separation, abandonment etc. Where are you in this situation? Do you confide in your family, circle of friends and/or those considered family. What happens when and/or if the ex or baby mother/father start dating, get engaged, get pregnant – what's the "T" when or if this has happened? Are we as single parents going to be outright mean, evil, resentful, revengeful, jealous, etc.? Is the transition from one-to-another a conversation or a fight? Who's wounded, hurt, sad, distant, and left alone? Who is to blame? Is there anyone to blame? Is it an all-out catfight? Whatever drama happens … know that every child feels the residual of emotions that they should not be responsible for. Kids are usually the ones that are crying HELP from these situations, divorces, absent parents and so many other scenarios that, in the heat of the moment, are very painful. Whatever pain one suffers in times of turmoil, all are affected just the same. We cannot sugar-coat dire circumstances, whatever they may be... to appease or to please. Children of all ages are affected. Even when or if both parents continue to live amicably together for the sake of the children, affects them just the same. However, love is taught, shown, perceived, received, given for all parties involved, the love that remains (if any) is all that every child of God's is affected. These are the threads that we bind ourselves and our children to without perhaps knowing any better. Years later, a fresh perspective of circumstances may allow some breathing room for all involved. However, in the meantime, those who harbor negative emotions and or ill-will — are not only carried on in this lifetime, but as a karmic thread that will have to be resolved. Being mindful of how you have created this environment or, should you be headed in that direction, all lives matter. "All You Need Is Love..." sung by The Beatles.

FAITH IS WHAT YOU BELIEVE

"We Believe in One God."

What is **Faith**? It is a belief that has been orchestrated by man. The Bible speaks of faith as a way of communicating to mankind to understand, to learn and to believe in a God of Love. No matter what religion, per se, you've been taught, it dates back to your Akashic records...your roots of one's Heritage. On the other side the Akashic records remain the History of one's past, present and future. These records are from your origination to inception that every soul in a human body chose on their journey. When we delve deep into these records, we will find why we've chosen to be of Catholicism, Orthodox, Hinduism, Judaism and/or whatever religion reveals your threads of ancient family history. In The Bible, "We Believe in One

God" is what our Faith means...in every threaded story. When The Bible was written all religions were relatable to all of mankind for this reason. From Jewish, Latin, Greek, Arabic roots that began since time began. In the beginning, it was Man. Jesus instructed His people to believe in what is felt within one's heart. What has been misconstrued, misrepresented and misunderstood is man's need to label, judge and/or criticize religion(s), because all religions date back to the beginning of FAITH. All beliefs, whatever denomination of Faith you have chosen, deems that you do Believe – and, to the Atheists, that too is a Belief.

"I Believe in ONE God, Father Almighty, Creator of Heaven and Earth, and in Jesus Christ, his only Son, our Lord, who was conceived by the Holy Spirit, born of the Virgin Mary, suffered under Pontius Pilate, was crucified, died; on the third day he ascended into Heaven, and is seated at the right hand of God the Father Almighty; from there he will come to judge the living and the dead. I believe in the Holy Spirit, the Holy Catholic church, the communion of saints, the forgiveness of sins, the resurrection of the body, and life everlasting. AMEN.

These ancient stories of the life and times of Jesus the Christ were written for Humanity's sake to live, learn and love. There were those who believed and those who deceived...in our Lord Jesus; yet He asked they be forgiven. All the trials and tribulations from the History of Jesus is our right-of-passage to follow on Earth as it is in Heaven. Mankind is guided on Earth, through all of Jesus' life stories, to help us experience and access Love through the eyes of God. *The Lord's Prayer," "The Creed,"* are both given to mankind as an offering of ONE's Love to follow, believe and give in-service (in-deed) to others. Jesus' miracles were shown for all the people to witness; but doubt, skepticism, anger, and an overall disbelief occurred. Is that not what is happening in our present life? There are those who believe in miracles and those who doubt; those who pretend to believe in you while talking behind your back; those who fall into external temptations, etc.... *On Earth as it is in Heaven* IS your Belief... from ancient history; your choice of family and their beliefs/ideologies what you were taught and raised with. It is observing/witnessing, being in-service to others; how, when and where you were brought up lends itself to being yourself. "One hand washes the other..." is how we were raised to believe; but, can you open your heart further to see how others chose their beliefs? It is not a comparison... to have Faith IS ALL. What is rooted in The Bible denotes history in the time of Jesus and what mankind witnessed in those ancient stories are for all of mankind to forgive. Everyone on Earth has made choices that they may or may not be proud of... and to surmise a forgiveness in Faith doesn't belong to a religion. Having Faith is to Love ... to experience a full life, to help and serve others, to have suffered because of wrongfully made choices and forgive, and be forgiven. *Ascended into Heaven* ... raises one's consciousness knowing we are Loved.

Our soul is pure light energy, much like a lamp, either is bright and effervescent, or clouded and dimmed. Energy is frequency ... ever-changing in every thought; a rising up or a lowering of a flagstaff in memory; winds of change; growth of one's soul is karmic justice for all "As Above, So Below" that breathes in new life... "Higher ground..." Jesus has shown us The Way toward ascending into Heaven as a breaking free from all low-vibrational attachments – being raised up to Heaven's gates through forgiveness. This ascension is a spiritual journey of our soul...

Lord have mercy. Lord have mercy. Lord have mercy.

HISTORIC REMNANTS OF OUR CHILDREN

Are we not the exact image of what has historically been known to come before us? Interpreted as the "threads" throughout time in History. To instill the wisdom of the Ages is the eyes of our Mother and/or Father – what has come to pass, what and whom has passed, where our past leads us … ALL in the journey of LOVE. What remains… is felt. Our experiences past and present have gotten us this far in our Spiritual Evolution.

We seek to unlearn what has been shown to us on the 3-Dimensional Earth plane unless you cannot see it…it doesn't exist; or, to those who are of a higher consciousness of enlightenment will carry the torch until the others catch up. Just as Gautama Buddha did with His disciples… knowing that all were not on the same path, He waited for several hundred years for His sannyasins to enter the gates of Heaven. According to a resounding set of circumstances, Buddha fell down and broke open the gates by pleading to our Lord Jesus to ascend ALL. Our Lord Jesus felt this would be His last opportunity to obey His Father - Our Heavenly Father by stating that everyone gets saved who has done the arduous inner work. The inner work God created for us on Earth is ridiculed with tangible and intangible forms of lifestyles. The intangible works of our Heavenly Spirit is not given to us; yet causes every human being to help themselves figure it out. What one human cannot figure out another, who has worked on themselves, changes their path. One is tied to the Earth plane and another has been set Free. To be set free doesn't necessarily require us to question Spirit, but to allow … freedom reigns. Whatever your path is at the present moment, do not judge others for they judge themselves harshly all by themselves. It is not for the sensibility of the senses that humans figure out how much of what doesn't work is to their own detriment. It's a self-sabotage mindset, without establishing that they only need to let go. Letting go is not a temporary fix as it is, a lifestyle. Without going within we lose the connection that remains in Trusting. That circle of trust besieges one's ability to know and how other humans follow suit. To follow suit is the blind leading the blind; instead of going with the flow. The thing is… most of us who question our paths, in an attempt to control, end up empty handed. TRUST is having unwavering Faith knowing everything falls into place. Why do we say, "fall into place?" Could it be that once one falls it implies getting grounded… as falling leaves end up on the ground and new ones are reborn.

To know, IS TO KNOW.

Living within the confines of one's mind doesn't alleviate the way with which we tend to gather up our strength-of-resolve… This makes us all understand how to be present and to allow. Within every living organism, the propaganda of the mind's initial growth is determined during childhood. No one knows how exactly the brain functions within and around our pineal gland – as that is the gland mainly in charge with the onset of growing, learning and allowing. The pineal gland is the acorn of our third-eye (intuition) gifted to mankind from Mother Earth, hoisting a pheromone of fragrances during the change of seasons. The seasonal changes allow our brains to function differently – a metamorphosis of learning, growth and understanding. A Monarch of transformative colors in the seasons of beautiful yellow, black-orange, white winged butterflies. Our human metamorphosis of change happens when we go within by journaling, meditating, walking, being in-service to God, in-deeds. Known as, "When the student is ready, the teacher appears". That would imply that once we have seen the path, a Master will attend to the construct of the Chosen One. Time on Earth is a mathematical equation – a Hologram that no one needs to assess, but knows is the Universe.

INDEPENDENT DEPENDENCY

The need for independence within a family dichotomy isn't needed as much as knowing that your parents will always protect, save and keep you safe "no matter what…" When you think back to your childhood, do you question "Why didn't my parent(s) protect me? Lack of protection is a generational cycle. However, what about those children who do not feel that reassurance? Do they become more self-assured in their later years due to an overcompensating Mother and/or Father? In every attempt to cut the 'purse strings' from both or either parent…a series of dependency allows the child to gain their independence. Those who still have a strong-hold desire to be taken care of have not been given the appropriate tools in order to fight the good fight; get a job and/or feel it's even a necessity. Once and for all these children end up getting lost in the shuffle of life, buying their own way toward success. That being said… what works for some doesn't work for all. Why is it that some children were spoon-fed while others were not given that same treatment? We come into this world with innate tools which are gifted and become independent adults. To have the strength to overcome life's trials and tribulations by getting your hands dirty – otherwise, you'll end up remaining stuck working in a job that you don't like with little pay. "One man's poison is another man's treasure…" Either stand tall or fall down … both need to happen before a transformation can ensue. Taking control of your life doesn't require one or the other, but, both in tandem working together for the greater good, in-service to all of mankind. We cannot bear to stand watching women/men beating up each other with co-dependency issues from childhood, and being masked as one stronger than the other. "Bear to stand it…" is a metaphoric term that mankind is saying "something needs to change, or else." One cannot bear to see themselves fall only to stand up and make a change. Do we compare one against another? Is gender significant insofar as who needs to make a change and/or who is judging? Is it about a dictatorship of rulership and/or ownership? So many judge by gender when, in fact, it is about how children are raised. Is the term, "What's good for the goose good for the gander" applicable? Is the gander any better than the goose? This term came into being as a simile in the Law of Reciprocity – a Golden Rule of moral principle in both religions and philosophies. "Do unto others as you wish to be done to you". This dichotomy is confusing as some rules apply while others don't. Children are lost … on their own… and this saying has not deemed its worthiness; as it hasn't been applicable to all of mankind. What our generation of children are learning is to think on their own and believe what resonates. Why not think "outside the box?" What a crazy place to be taught not to think for oneself.

Much to one's dismay, the existential has overridden our senses far too long which might have stood the test of one's initiative, but a far cry for assistance from the Spirit realm. This is exactly why ·**Terms and Conditions'** in contracts have been placed way at the bottom of a contract as, "read the fine print" does not apply to the majority rule. Why in Heaven's name did Earth succumb to our precious children in such a manner that breeds destruction…instead of instilling the light of our Jesus the Christ's moral, ethical and transparent value system throughout this world? Could it be that Earth was designed so unequivocally equal to the "Laws of the Universe" that it took a turn to partake of a dark side; prior to being resurrected, with an ability to achieve ascension? The Victory of being a graduated Ascension. A = ascension V = victory as in, Adam & EVE. As written in the Bible, Adam & Eve were both given "free will" – Adam's temptation of the "Apple " is indicative of the choices mankind makes in FEAR. This decision that Adam and Eve originated as the Original Sin. Hence, we've all been bitten by the same Apple that Eve succumbed to only to continue living in FEAR. No man or woman is exempt from learning the valuable lessons that come from "free will" in order to not be ordained, but to be freed.

FREEDOM comes with FAITH in overcoming all trials and tribulations from others that tempt. TRUST in Yourself…DISCERN in what to BELIEVE. BELIEVE in YOU and you are set FREE.

Our souls evolve when and only when we are ready to take responsibility by committing to a sovereign lifestyle of goodness for all of Humanity's sake, "for goodness sake." We've been accustomed to lesser evils of desires on Earth, however, there have been a handful of evil-gut-wrenchers who have stood out like sore thumbs creating potential end-of-world's handlings to the tune of masks similar that of: Hitler's Nazis, World War I&II, eventual outbreaks of co-conspiracies that amount to dis-eases throughout history and threats of nuclear wars underway…and, so much more. No one could ever comprehend these evil acts under duress or any other form that has taken place in History could repeat. Those who are on path and are law-abiding citizens have been more or less masking their ability to get their hands dirty. Why not get our hands dirty? How else could Adam and Eve provide Earth with such great polarity of good & evil? What is required of Humanity now? "Why on Earth" is another adage that Humanity would choose to remember and realize their inner truth of karma on Earth to be severed for the soul to ascend to a higher consciousness. Earth's History is changing and these are the times, NOW, where the etchings of the ancients are fading; and, a new rulership is upon us. God's timing of 'A Spiritual Revolution' of The New Era/Golden Age" is knowing we are leading THE WAY. A conglomeration of new threads is being formed for the Universe to change its axis – accessible to an, "ALL FOR LOVE…" marking History.

LOVE of self, being whole is the natural order to those who know that saying, "I want it all" – is not only of the physical / materialistic – it is a spiritual, physical, and emotional union of the same thread, a community. The threads are weaved together with great passion for Life, Love and the pursuit of Happiness. There is a bonded union with every single person we meet, addressing those we seek and our great teachers and Masters for our soul's evolution. There are also those, who most importantly, show us our shadow side; and, it is up to us to encounter the strength of many to see. Those who see clearly have undergone the 'darkest of nights' of the soul – not a one-time event throughout one's life… but, an everyday journey of Sunrise. Sunset. The movie, Fiddler On The Roof, sets the stage as the barrier of one's truest self who was the beggar, fought hard and believed in himself conquering his place in the world. Just as many movies uphold the notion of a beggar and a thief… to be a thief one must be a beggar. When the sun sets in the West, we end our daily drudgery of work essentially needed for sustenance in our every day; and while we rise to a beautiful sunrise, we thank God for the blessings of anew. The

Heavenly horizon is where we stay centered to balance our lives out for either an ascent or descent within all processes.

We are not who we think ... but, we cannot be otherwise. ™

A HERITAGE OF HISTORY

Remembering our Heritage is predominantly a component that will initialize not only who our ancestors were but also the stories of ancient history that connect us all. As History does have a way of repeating itself, so does Humanity insofar as knowing we are threaded together with the stories of our past and present. Whenever we have Deja-vu moments, this is our consciousness telling us we've experienced this same thing at another time in a parallel Universe. All memories are being repeated to give ourselves a better insight into what we're doing at this very moment – either to teach a lesson we've not completed or to empower ourselves to move on. Closing life cycles have huge soul benefits to one's Earthly world because the soul has re-enacted a karmic cycle that has to be cleared; and severed. Whatever final life-cycles are closing, the soul's Heritage of Family ascends to higher levels. Whether 'on Earth as is in Heaven,' all threads that tie that soul with common-threaded souls are raised. Mother Earth's consciousness has been upgrading for Eternity…and remains doing so as the soul knows. No one goes unnoticed on the Earth plane. Those who've done their inner work by attaining self-realization, also assist in raising their ancestors who could not. Divine timing has been of great assistance to the planet as History is in the making…some think it will be a second-coming of Jesus; while others think it will be an Apocalypse. No matter what you may think, and/or what you've been taught to believe, inner work on yourself is required for all of Humanity to indulge in a State of Nirvana. We are not here to say, either way, it is all up to you to decipher your own level of Faith. What isn't given to you right away will be given when the placemats align to higher ground. Wherever life takes us isn't for us to question or doubt; but to aspire to the wonder, the imagination that is within our Right-of-Passage of *"thy will be done"*. Our innate knowledge of where we are rooted comes to tell a very different story painted with pain and/or suffering, the losses and the words bestowed to us from ancient History yet to learn. It might come in handy to research our lineage, but even if that isn't found, the threads in one's passage-in-time come to show us what we know to be our truth. The ultimate truth of why we are here at this moment-in-time is enough. It may be difficult to understand that the effects of the "Law of Cause & Effect" are threaded all together as ONE; therefore, as we commit to inner work, a collective Cause-and-Effect is attained. Most of us who have leveled up to a place of solace in "Know Thyself" have no recollection of their Heritage dating back in time…yet, since they've done their work, their family threads have been cleared so that their souls can begin anew. Whether that is life on an entirely different paradigm or back to Earth for a twin-flame connection without any Earthly turbulence, is all up to the soul families. The ties that bind are being untangled so that clear pathways are being established. Once we all can come to grips with these findings, setting the stage before you to work on a come-to-Jesus moment will appear. No one is exempt from doing the work…if not now, then, when? What is on the Earth are rewinds of our past, familiar fragrances, still waters run deep, veins of every branch, rooted in good soil and finding a whole new world awaits us all. To date, we've been walking blindly into the unknown and this hasn't taken them as far as the "I" can see…instead of the "eye". The "I" is where our identity takes over while the "eye" in the

149

mirror is the effect of two halves; one is all-seeing when it becomes, "IAM".

The *IAM Movement* began back in the 1st Century when all the Freemasons learned that they could become spiritually connected to the Divine; but their "I" – ID identified as Ego's external wants and desires trumped instead of the search. This too changed the narrative since "they" all joined in misusing their power and overruling others' power too. From this point on the fight to abstain from using their power was rejected by Spirit. All the Freemasons' power was revoked by the Higher Spirit realm and the darkness was seen by all. The Freemasons took pride in using darkness for their own manipulations and the mis-use of "powers that be" for criminal acts and the like, which didn't come to light for another 10 Centuries. Everything that was planted in others became convoluted acts of vengeful deeds. They inflicted dark forces from their own Heritage that were not intended to be seen at first – so many followed their lead and became obsessed similar to that of a cult following. The congregation of corruption began to see them for what they'd been doing to others; but were not able to control the terrain. Freemasons are still roaming the Earth plane, as are their ancestral soul attachment to darkness, which remains -of-their-story continues. Whenever these symbols show up in our lives… i.e. RA God of Light, intends to help Humanity shining His light. How can a God of Light, an all-seeing God be used to portray darker forces? It became what "they" taught and who followed the teachings of disillusion…. Similar to Scientology, yet the Freemasons only allowed masculines into their so-called group, all others were **not** allowed. Rituals were implanted for initiation much like a college fraternity who also get initiated. Similar concept…yet does that thread seem to exploit not only a cult-version in our educational system?

There have been so many indications of what was taught to mankind as, when looking back, these threads connect on a multitude of various levels. The thought to initiate anyone into a group – decans of the church, gangs, KKK, fraternity groups, date back to the Freemasons. A connection that deems to instill the thread of misuse-of-power even if it is not seen as such. The Educational system is the lesser of all evils, yet, they're requirements of joining a fraternity imposes a similar vibe. This Movement has now been extracted from our society, at large, yet there is a cloud of darkness on these teachings that other groups have taken from… Initially, the Freemasons wanted to be a product of spiritual practices through religion to gather like-minded people for the goodness of mankind; but darkness set in and changed it all. This is the effect of "one bad Apple" that changed the direction of good-intended wills of the people. Somewhere along the lineage of that 'one bad apple' became a cult-infiltrated by dark forces - which goes along with the upbringing of children to "know" who they're hanging out with. It is quite different now, however, with the internet and kids playing games with strangers that may be posing as their age, while all along it has been found grown men are infiltrating their virtual reality. This is a huge "red flag" that parents need to become, if they're not, aware! Being present in your kids day-to-day…from who they're hanging out with to school friends to those games and virtual reality worlds they are involved with. Everything ties together … from our ancient forefathers, to the current affairs marking History today; politics, Corporate America, tainting a society that falls in the family line … down to today's children.

As we grow into adulthood, historically there has been and continues to be so much hatred, jealousy, greed, depression, remorse, envy, pain and suffering, etc.; and, those who chose to transition into

151

parents materialize unresolved feelings that have not been released and/or realized. If you have a grandparent who was heavy handed or a parent too controlling – these kids grew up to be either very lenient and/or absolutely a spitting image. That's why we say child/children are the "spitting image" of their parent(s). Many are aware as to how their parents imparted discipline, compassion and a balanced self-image; while those who have animosities, hatred, martyrdom, resentment etc., are also noticing those traits too. Spitting out orders that are unkind words, hidden jealousy, or whatever triggers that re-surface are those patterns that casts a wide net of grievances kids hold onto. Those kids who are relating to the common threads from childhood in their Mom and/or Dad plainly see how there is much work to be done. Even if we concede to hate or dislike our parents and hold on too much to all the implications of being raised wrong, it's "their fault" mentality comes with a price. Why dim another's light in Fear? Fear that you won't amount to something and/or Fear that you will. Are these fears yours or theirs? What happened in your youth? Were you not given all the tools to be yourself? Did you have to skirt around issues and/or family members? Was Mom/Dad absent in seeing your worth? Do your children vie for your attention as a means to an end? What threads are intertwined in your ancestral lineage - and, do you know or realize them? The ignorance of one's character is molded in how we act, react, and/or an inability to do so. The longer one or both parents don't assume responsibility the environment becomes a chaotic merry-go-round. What ends up happening is that they are both dealing with family matters; pacifying to seek approval and/or have hidden feelings of disrespect. Are we, as parents, ignorant to the needs of our children? A contentious lack of respect adheres to family members under the guise of being controlled. This sends out a very clear message that one is still posing as a child who is incapable of making decisions. And, another who is trying to manipulate with an over controlling hand. ALL FEAR is what drives people crazy, mad because they weren't able to dig deep asking questions of how, why and/or when… No matter how we've been raised and what the circumstantial evidence brings with it, any residual Fear comes from the common-denominator, that is, FEAR. To be subservient, too controlling feeds Fear. A parent who raised their children in a similar environment as they grew up in…will construct those same Fears – just a different version of. We entrust our families to be our guiding light that lift us up when we're down, that feed us healthy foods and give us warm milk, who keep us safe and are watchful of our peers; all the traits of what has been known as a traditional upbringing is needing attention. Whether traditional or not…all children are suffering and harboring much trauma, turmoil etc., of their past and present – calling for an evolution of change. Changing History begins with changing yourself! What makes for a good parent is the freedom to acknowledge, a knowing, a calming conversation, a listening ear, from threads of your youth? The time is NOW. No longer can children suffer in silence, not listen through the voice of Love that embodies the entire Universe. Is anyone listening through a heart-felt feeling of holding a new perspective that includes; compassion, patience, understanding and Love for all. Humanity has been suffering in silence for Fear of….

Fear of… what is to happen to the state of our world if the only ones wanting to work and working will be AI robots? What will Humanity do without an annual income? What a concept – AI infiltrated robots - no need to pay?! Why can't "they" do that? Is overpopulation becoming a detriment to our society? Will Humanity wait until it's too late to save themselves? Has TikTok become the new generation of parenting? Are AI robots groveling information that is either inaccurate or will implode? What will become of an unresponsive society that turns their back upon these issues…and a whole lot more? Will there ever be a place to seek solitude? Can a string of warriors hold up the planet? Where and who are they? As like attracts like… kids are living in nomads land, numbing their pain and embarking upon enemy territory using social media to fulfill their anger? Where is the justice? Who can swoop these children up right now and toss them upside down for them to get a semblance of direction? Could all potential parents reading this stand up to the plate and honor their role as parent by taking on long-overdue responsibility and accountability? Do you value this role as an honor? Are you living up to these responsibilities in your present moment? Does this behoove you that this is even an issue in today's society of parenting? How did your parents parent you? Are you an immature adult child with child/children and have no idea how to deal with it? Are you a single parent more interested in finding a partner than staying home to raise your child? Are you a parent as in step-mother/father scenario being given all the responsibilities to parent? Are you a child bad-mouthing your parents/step-parent(s) for not being what you would consider, a good parent? Who is in charge and who is making the decisions? Where are the responsibilities of money coming from? Grandparents? Or, who takes care of these kids that have very little? Is money earned legit? If both parents are no longer living together, divorced, separated etc., who is taking on both roles; and has the child gotten used to a single-parent environment? Another contention of thought is the thread between the love of money and the love that is within us all. Have we chosen to override the love of self in return for a love of money? What was your financial situation in your household like? At the Horizon, the thread between money and love shows itself in the

154

way we feel about both – attracting love, not needing to fill a void, is a whole/Holy Love; whereas, the love of money matters and all matters on the Earth plane, is the Fear treated with not having/being enough.

"What the world needs now is Love, sweet Love. It's the only thing that there's just too little of..." song by Jackie DeShannnon exhibits that Humanity must shift its perspective from FEAR to unwavering FAITH.

FAITH is what's being tested on Earth with every act of transgression...

To speak of Faith is something very different than to Know your Faith which is not a Faith of any one religion... but a Faith of ALL, Believing in ONE GOD.

THE TRINITY - THE HOLY SPIRIT

The spiritual, emotional, mental, financial foundations over the course of a lifetime, past lives and the present moment are threaded and weaved into factors of the self... and/or the Egoic self. We've all had predicaments where values are placed upon the weak; and, for those traumatic issues that hold a place in the world, an offering of redemption. The Trinity represents that of Love, freedom and forgiveness which breeds peace of mind, and freedom. Eagles, Hawks soar akin to that of the Holy Spirit that fosters the embodiment of life; eternal love, unwavering faith and the soaring of our soul. What makes the trinity useful to mankind is how beautiful the flight to freedom is. Our inner third-eye, being the eye of Ra, is our safety net that "leads us NOT into temptation". The Egoic eye (I) as in our ID identification, that "leads us into temptation". It's a simple equation of choosing to lead instead of being led... a feeling of knowing what we've been taught as the Golden Rule of "right vs. wrong". Mankind has easily gotten lost in the shuffle - not because they're not privy to the Golden Rule; but because people tend to fall into the arms of instant-gratification. How have entire lives of instant-gratification served Humanity so far? Are you wiser? Do you rely on only things of "matter" in the materialistic world to get you through the night? Has your happiness been demoted - much like a job whose expiration date is near? Have we become an "Artificial 'material world' of Illusion" inspired by a series of events that denote a demented intelligence? Have we been pre-programmed on autopilot to borrow knowledge, spouting facts and stats; sugar-coated with every known imaginable candy of licks from the CandyMan that coerces ... (no-Gated communities, bitten Apples, Bezos' Bitcoin currency, missing Nadella, Musked in the wizard of Al-Man.

The Golden Rule begins anew in The New Golden Era.

No one is exempt from all these trauma-inflicted experiences on Earth, yet cognizant to a series of repeats. The rite-of-way passage is constructed as a pathway that is off the beaten path. Its pathway leads us to a conglomeration of independent choices. The three rites-of-passages are characterized by three phases; *separation*, leaving what is familiar for the unknown; *transition*, learning/testing/growth of self; and, *return*, roles taken and change of roles. These passages are marked by events that are held to detain one from being uncertain – certain ceremonies that have been made to date are; births, puberty, marriage, having children, menopause and death. What these event-like ceremonies do is to strip away what has been known for new roles to prepare each human for what's to come. Many humans who have been known to undergo their own preparations have not made it through to the portal which one must crawl their way through in order to find a Freedom-of-self on the other side. What has been said and done cannot compare to being a free-spirit on the Earth plane... although some have conquered these feats.

"Deliver us from all evil...." is as difficult as completely letting go of an egoic mindset that releases control of bodily desires. In order to know why some deep-seated emotions, come to the surface is so that we can begin to peel back the layers of one's life.

Emotional Intelligence surmises the *Pillars of Life* within Five Components that outline new narratives to lead us Home, as follows;

1. Self-awareness; emotions that influence our actions

2. Self-regulation; healthy emotional changes for adaptation

3. Empathy; offer comfort, support for others

4. Social skills; clear communication

5. Decision-making; responsible choices

Reason vs. Reward – driven to motivate the essence of intelligence that either becomes a narrow-minded road; or the reward to feeling in believing.

Haven't we allowed 'enough is enough' scar tissue that filters still-hanging chads holding onto your vote? When will it be enough for you to choose your Freedom of Health & Happiness before it's too late? Do you feel you've already lost your Freedom? Or, shall we say, entered into a Fearful Freedom where there are no rights? Whatever world you choose to live in … remember that life is a series of highs and lows in connectivity to a heartfelt horizon of Beliefs. Where are your beliefs and have they been replaced? What do you stand for? Why should there be any beliefs other than believing in ourselves? *Overcome.*

Our emotions hold unlimited power within a physical/human body where we either get to experience what others have been waiting all their lives to do; or, decide with the higher echelons to revisit the Earth plane for another lifetime to experience similar events that will assist one to find themselves. What has struck one person's kundalini does not necessarily mean that this person will attain… it means, this person has activated the energy in each of the chakras only to become enlightened. The awakening that is being dealt with in this Spiritual Revolution comes with a deeper intensive platform of the merging feminine energies with our masculine. The energies, once they've been illuminated, can also work with the others to give light as well as cast shadows onto the ethers. Whatever we've undergone in this lifetime of achievements is indescribable with those who have not only witnessed but have also found their 'lot in life' of inner strength to achieve the ultimate nirvana of independent Freedom of self. We are not able to further indict those who have come before us… and, we will not hold any judgements, grudges or otherwise to any human who has put a vast amount of time, effort and self-searching to attain.

HABITUAL CREATURES

We are not only creatures of habit, but we also prefer to control our own destiny, only to experience a series of closed doors. "When one door closes, God opens a new one? What we may "think" is good for us in terms of what we want is not always the case insofar as what we need. Humans can only see what is right in front of them, while God's view is "a bird's-eye view". Why a bird's eye view? It is because the smallest things in life are free… Mother Nature provides everything needed on Earth, yet society has painted the picture of always wanting more. However, this is not always the case… we may want something that ends up adding value for our highest good. We can only hope to ensure a better way forward for the upcoming generations by becoming and setting a better example for our children. What constitutes a good example? Does this mean that we neglect what we want…always settling? No. We could perceive our lives from a bird's eye view as one that is infinite, prosperous and growing exponentially. However, the mindset that has been acquired, through alleged programming, lends itself to mankind to live with labels. Most of us love 'designer labels' as a stigma of attainment – it's not that we shouldn't enjoy the fruits of our labels; however, in moderation. All too many people seem to be purging labels during a move, or Spring cleaning when all that is needed is 20 pairs of shoes instead of 50. (Definitely low-balling that one) We continue to buy what we don't need, and between eBay, Poshmark, and/or TheRealReal – who's making a fortune? Most every purchase depreciates in value once purchased - much like every credit card company that adds an exorbitant interest rate, and without thinking, you're paying triple. When will Humanity stop to think? Think of becoming aware of… or, are we so enveloped in the Egoic lifestyle of living up to what others think we have and wanting what others have? Expectations. All this "stuff" can't be taken with us on our next journey, yet the thought of not having it all stresses us out. Where is our self-discipline? The highest form of love is self-discipline. Humanity has become so fixated on acquiring "stuff," racking up debt ... then, living like a popper. Making deals with the devil...selling your soul - for fame, money and power. A theme park on speed here, on planet Earth, that swirls and twirls a pack of lies meant to confuse and confine your time-is-money logic, says Scrooge McDuck. Humanity is meant to "realize" worthiness doesn't come in a package tied up in bows; it comes with a message that only "The Grinch" knows... It's about being a part of a community that seeks to be sought after where mankind ends up? How many songs, books, and movies must be written for people to begin to seek their inner sanctuary? Mankind is exhausted... watching life slip by, always striving-to-climb the endearing battle of Egos masked in a mud-bath mask of "look-a- likes". Is it true that the happiest people have very little to show for others to see – instead of to show for themselves? The programming of what has happened on Earth has been around for eons - yet the difference is how to rewrite the story of our unwritten lives. Will we learn to value the simplicity of those things in life that are free; peace, joy and happiness? Can a spade of spades turn into a heart-of-hearts? Why do we say, "follow your heart?" if you're going to stake your claim to what's in a name, only? Your name has been given to you at birth, and if that wasn't enough, a body unscathed with all LOVE. A name doesn't define when Love encompasses your every breath; while a label is the name that tags you a value that ends up in your obituary at the time of death.

ARCHETYPES (man, woman and child)

Every child of Heaven receives an archetype which holds within its infrastructure the remnants of DNA (past, present, future), generational DNA (past-life) and the DNA of its parental threads - karmic, platonic, diversion of aversion, astrological planetary placements (Natal Chart), certification of life experiences, 7 Seals of Approval, the secret alchemical Historic Emerald Tablets, Akashic records of past-life course/discourses, inability to see clearly/a revision, course containment/contaminant – tain, tami = aim of goal structures, passion of alignment with our Creator, great will of testament, nuances, playgrounds, self-sabotage, a merging of one, inhale/exhale the fruits of all laborers, send in the clowns, misogynistic tendencies in overdrive, crises of unnatural order, reversal of aging devices (the unknown, as of yet), ordinary people with extraordinary gifts, extraordinary people in the ordinary, gift giving, needy does or doesn't want, Heavens to Betsy… who is Betsy? Believe Eternal Truth IS IN You… So now you know, or do you? Make time for no one or everyone. Use your talents or let them waste away on the fruits of another… Believe in yourself or your "self" won't believe in you… Stay par for the course or get a hole-in-one. Receive plentiful miracles while waiting for the next train to arrive… stay on-point or leave where you left off… find a new cycle or refrain from waiting for anew… give yourself a break and live a lot vs. giving up, led by example to soar your lot in life or live as Lot in The Bible without a lot in life; give unto others without expectation or demand a do-over; seek nothing to no one or everything to the all… father to no one is the ONE.

Relating is inevitably threaded together as we are one within and without…yet the differences are those who make the difference; and, not those who want to show but to grow. There's only one way forward and that is noted as the story of Jesus, metaphorically speaking we must all earn our keep. Even Jesus experienced every facet that now has become and will always be our Savior – especially for those who remain incoherent to that truth. Salvation saves those who believe they are worthy of saving Grace. A second coming is happening to all believers – even atheists and non-religious doers of evil acts…or, to the disbelievers in what salvation of a second-coming in higher consciousness. Our threads of truth withstand the tests of time.

BIOLOGICAL/CHRONOLOGICAL STUDIES

In 2018 a comprehensive study was underway in determining differences of aging across the years. Biological age highlighted those indicators as; blood pressure, functioning of the lungs aging over a shorter period – assessing that the new generations appeared biologically "younger". The biological age of the US population has decreased in age over the last 20 years between masculine and feminine. Males seemed to make notable improvements while the female's mortality took a hit. The physical body of difference(s) in the biological clock dating back to the 50's up until now has seen much change…those "good ole' days" inferred family genetics where they worked harder than most to attain a livelihood and weren't given any ability to opt out. It was very much a part of the family structure and those generations that preceded that working 30+ years at one job defined you. However, back in the day…men did much of the hard labor while women were giving labor. Back in the 50's…even prior to that, the kind of job you held determined what type of person you were

162

and how your parents/grandparents raised you. Traditionally speaking… no one could imagine not being employed and earning their keep. The consequences of not working were traumatic and one's character was frowned upon. Also, the faces of past decades that endured through hardships like The Depression, World War II and other personal vendettas gave way to more strength, endurance, unity to build and work together. The medical field was quite different – with the exception of plagues, viruses that the elders had to procure. The Medical field over the past decades was congruently interested in improving health issues instead of masking over disease; however today, masking these diseases is putting band-aid over band-aid of the core issues of trauma etc., being given prescription meds that are flying off the shelfs. Every prescription has side effects that adhere to other added issues and so on. Not all side effects are deadly…yet, they have been known to cause feelings of suicidal thoughts, depression, and/or even death. What sense does this make? If there is already a Fear of death, added onto taking medications that may cause the onset of death…what's the point? The point of contention is that whether you are taking prescription meds, tainted weed, coke, meth, downers/uppers, alcohol or whatever you may think will help – the fact remains that death is imminent … And, to those who drink Coke, "Do you taste the feeling? Getting a Coke tainted with coke – gives you a 'feeling' since inception. This particular History speaks of how Dr. John Stith Pemberton, Founder intended his tonic to assist in the ailing chronic pain in the body; which morphed into a morphine addiction. How could this drink-of-choice become a recipe for alcohol and cocaine? Could a child born in the 50's, 60's, 70's or even later… having been raised on drinking Coke be a classic-lawsuit case(s) of addiction? Who is still drinking Coke? A Coke a day drives one's pain away…while inhaling sticks rolled-by-hand riding on a Camel to no-man's-land.

Back in the day…rumors swirled around all these topics; drugs, med-affects, talks of the Apocalypse etc.; with the difference of the side-effects which allegedly killed people more than exposed. Believe what you will, that is your prerogative … yet, children are MIA … lost souls; missing and/or dead; crimes of passion are being discovered, pedos flocking everywhere (families included), acts of murders of those who spoke out, the onset of elimination is out of control, and much more is yet to come. Not alluding to any specifics in particular…but a vast array of those who have sold their soul continue to do so. EXPOSED. The current status is not going to be repressed by a global nature but of a #silent-witness™ doing their inner work. Nothing else matters…because there is no-'thing' … as we already are. Societal bias indoctrinating the terrain of our overall perception of fading out the Elders for the youthful generations is nothing more than a manipulative tactic to control innocent youths. Our youth and your children have all been and are being subjected to being taken, stolen, raped, murdered and all other forms of abuse that violate every right to our Freedom. Dictatorships have NOT changed; they've gotten much worse because what has been exposed is blasphemous and in a court of Law … where is the Justice? How can any innocent child ever feel safe and protected with such acts of abuse? No amount of psychology, psychiatric help and/or counsel can mend the trauma, scars and wounding of the innocent! Why are these pedos, and every other abusive beast still out there on the prowl?!!! Most of society has been privy to the Puff-Diddy/Epstein Island attendee list, correct? Why haven't the "specialists" checked the biological aspects of those who have the beast within? Too scared to care? Too afraid to know that many of those who abuse have a history of also being abused AND find the thrill of abusing. A payback…or, a hefty paycheck? Be afraid of NO ONE… and, stand in your FAITH!!! If you turn the other cheek, it just might be your child, grandchild that will be next… Educate your children – not to scare them, but to keep watch for their safety and protection – teach them NOW how to be-on-guard, what to look for, who looks shady, family included and enrolling in a self-defense class, required.

"KNOWLEDGE 2EMPOWER™". A new Women's Liberation Movement underway…who says it should only have been about independent rights, equality in pay and freedom.

GENETIC GROOMING

What is genetic grooming? Where does it stem from? Who dares to delve deeper into your "makeup" – and not only the external-superficial type. Genetic transmutation happens at the onset of the first spark of light in a star…its premise of life is to shine bright under the influence of darkness. Our genetics play a very important role in so many ways yet we sometimes are not abreast of what they are or what we are because of them. The genetic threads are intertwined at birth while they form what looks very similar to that of a kaleidoscope of colors – our ancestors' threads being all formational facets of our Heritage. Whether stemming from BC or AD, our threads intermingle with those that are genetically pliable to ours. Culture, family history, beliefs and statistical alignments that have been proven in the realm of science to assist in our genetic makeup. Genetics only goes so far, then; you must rewire your "perceptions", or else you will continue to filter the same mold as you were given; or unduly change your inner

165

temple, which congruently becomes a healthier version. There are also threads that tie us into our family's cultural background, similar traits, belief systems, ideologies and even down to the traits of sound waves in our voice boxes that coexist within the foundation of one's entire genetic history. For example, a genetic thread that binds two sisters together through adoption, not blood-related, holds the premise of a genetic makeup thread of common cultural history attached to the sound waves within both voices. One sister may sound much like the other sister just because they are both attached to the same genetic disposition of a similar cultural thread AND have taken up the sound waves that cast upon them living under the same cultural or generational family tree. Many would insist on pointing those similarities to living under the same roof, but much more is going on than meets the eye. (I) The "I" is the mindset of one's identity ID…the Identification of the ego self. Why? How we are built instead of how we've been manipulated … a realization. What we may think or have thoughts about our entire lives is just a minuscule version of reality. Genetic predisposition is the breeding of a horse with a different color…despite what you've been made to believe.

There are millions upon millions of genetic threads entwined together from inception that expand outward – not only of this Universe but to all other dimensions of frequencies., one within the other within another... Every thread is a *fragment* of where our essence has held its own light, to those unlimited scallions striving to survive… "An unlimited space of nothing into the existence of everything". ™ Every human has not just a story but lifetimes repeated with new "suited embodiments". Where we place our energies reach far beyond this world…when we learn our lessons…that emerge back to our ancestral lineage for clearing and moving onto the next. Clearly, the human brain is NOT capable of seeing the Universal essence of energies spread across space and time, but what the brain can comprehend is the heart's essence. The way something feels is threaded into knowing. Once we are able to distinguish one from the other, that is the connection of the soul. Superfluous actions need NOT apply! Humanity knows the connectivity yet sometimes lacks the Faith needed to enhance the abundance of infinite life. Humans are livewires that are hardwired in a very controlled environment, which has been to their detriment. Is mankind being programmed and wired identical to that of AI? Are we going to allow such blasphemy from a crooked society? Instead, why not "Let go and Let God", where we allow our Heavenly bodies to take the reins and allow the flow of the Universe to show its Magic? The magic of ONE genius' energetic force of Love all-consuming the imagination of Mother Nature. We know that we are all of the energetic essence of Mother Nature embodied and immersed into a human body that is designed to go with the flow of Nature. All in Divine timing yet within that embodiment is where the egoic self entangles with that flow. "To KNOW is to LET GO... to doubt is to go without." However, we choose to exist and find our way back to the natural order of what God has intended. Both paths on our soul's journey will lead us to the same road in Divine timing. The Law of Cause & Effect helps to guide us all on our journey, knowing that what we reap, we shall sow. It doesn't take a scholar to filter into this narrative a simple algorithm of what your checks and balances are moving forward. Literally, every human is quite attuned to what they've done or not; who has been misrepresented, misunderstood and to know that beast is to conquer. Wound, trauma, attachments and/or narcissistic patterns imbued in our internal thought patterns occur prior to an acquisition in the use of language. When we are unable to process past panic, shame and/or terrors these are distinct pieces of our soul's retention, held in a subcortical and cellular circuitry. When we say to ourselves or hear others say, "just get over it" "suck it up Sally" or "move on" knowing what egoic parts are being shown as an inflammation of our nervous system – where trauma is stored. An intergenerational transmission of these traumas shatters our wherewithal and gives way to a profound sense of aloneness. This is devastating to one's soul resulting in a profound cry out for HELP – to accept, to allow, to be there for another, in Sanctuary.

IMPRINTS - BLUEPRINTS, DNA, GENETICS, BLOOD, SWEAT, TEARS

Our DNA are complex threads of vibrating energy in a matrix that exist in sync with millions of strings of chemicals turning into a musical piece heard in the spiritual realm. These pieces of music form a morphogenetic field overlapping in Heaven as it is on Earth. Our human existence is a unique tapestry in the cosmos creating differences in our world. Every cell has an imprinted memory of all past-life experiences and each value its lessons has imparted. To clear karmic threads is to understand one's ability to speak directly to our body - a living organ of the entire Universe. Mother Earth's natural disasters are Her way of purging karma from the ancient civilizations in the here and now. What mankind "thinks" is happening with all natural disasters throughout mankind is not what you've been known to understand. Mother Earth is allowing new life by shedding mankind's karmic injustices from inception and allowing Humanity to do the same. Every aspect of the mind, body and soul connection is within each and every one of us… purging over and over again and purifying to ascend. The base of our spine tends to tell the story of our lineage when we arrived on planet Earth having brought our innate

Heritage. Our entire solar system, the stars, astrological planets, blood cells, veins of all our threads incorporate the imprints, blueprint, our DNA and the all-encompassing blood, sweat and tears. If we can understand that our physical temple encapsulates the entire Universe – and that, if we knew this at the onset, would we take better care of our bodies? Unbeknownst to some humans, our mind talks to the body through the vibrational frequencies of emotions – hence, we are always communicating with our Heavenly families. Our ancestors, spirit guides, family Heritage of everyone we've ever encountered in this lifecycle and all others working in tandem to provide guidance. We are able to actually have a conversation with our bodies, somewhat like a genie in a bottle - except instead of the genie it is our genes which we connect to as a unified field of Divine connection. Our genes have been proven to react to any thoughts which we are having in order to make our dreams come true; and with the utmost Faith and strength of intentional will, will manifest. Through visualization and affirmations, we are able to heal our physical bodies. What happens; however, humans doubt, worry, host a continuous thread of negative energy thinking that eventually leads to a Universal pause. We must understand how effervescent mankind needs to feel in their footprints of Faith.

IMPRINTS, BLUEPRINTS, BIRTHMARKS

Imprints — be it a mole, a beauty mark, freckles, warts and any other designs of our ancestral Heritage seen on the physical embodiment is a story that needs to be told. All humans come into this world with their namesake imprinted. What holds true for all our namesakes is that it does enter this lifetime with Fear already ingrained to be worked through. The Fears that need working through are our past threads which must be severed; and when they are severed, the imprint is gone. Other markings are not all from our fears; however, there are imprints of past lives that live on. To behold, a beauty mark signifies not only external beauty but also an inner character that might be par for the course of one's career. (i.e., model, actor, actress) Those whose soul's purpose is to clear their karmic justice this lifetime has undergone the hardest of life cycles to maintain and clear their History. The reason for one's past-life karmic debt varies from soul-to-soul. One should not carry anyone else's karmic debt ever … not unless it is a part of the original blueprint of fate. Fated unions of any kind cannot be restructured, re-shaped and/or re-introduced once identified as a karmic partner. This union is recognized as kindred souls' journey that knows itself as itself. Whatever remains of kindred souls who have similar imprints, soul connections come with familiarities that identify one with the other. Every soul-connection knows they were meant to be joined in union to clear past-karmic injustices … to ascend to a higher consciousness. God's will be done, Amen.

Where these markings are located also defines the essence of the narrative as in how deep, how faded, etc., becomes a "signature look". The signature of one's mark ties us to many imprints of our former selves at different times in our lives. The reason they still exist is to lend a helping hand to recall a person, place and/or thing that resonates with your life experiences. Let's not forget how our "legacy" will imprint Humanity for all to witness. Blueprints… a soul2soul contract/blueprint is outlined and contracted between all souls, all fragments of one's soul, and all those who will play on the playground of Life. You will find that some family members (of blood or not) have signed up to play a role in your story – however, the long or short of it plays out. These souls that have the same markings in the same area of one's body are kindred souls from many lifetimes. (i.e., brothers in another life, cousins in this life…etc.)

Birthmarks… mark a place where in one life cycle you might have been killed and the scars remain in this lifetime to jog your memory.

Tattoos… memories of loved one's stories, holding on, seeking places of comfort that depict one's individuality of self; and, the stories that we hold deeply in our heart space. Time Travelers of ancient history … (i.e. Venus, Zeus, Aphrodite, Horus, Hindu, Sanskrit, Astrological aspects/signs, children, flowers, animal totems, etc.) fulfillment in the playground of Life.

Perhaps the hardest of karmic injustices repeat over and over again, - people, places, and things get recycled, rewritten, reposed as what is viewed to be our reincarnations. The Earth is a karmic life that repeats over the course of time and where only time exists in the lateral sense of the world. Your soul is all that remains unencumbered while the physical body works through every cycle of life's existence in Love. In order to obtain a love of self we must seek our own guidance by not seeking outside influences. We've come to know our egoic selves very well, but, do you? No need to inquire about this because it will bring only more karma. What is crucial to note is the fact that when all is "said" and "gone" you become the Master. Once this simmers into your inner self of being a whole self, you will have no other sense of existence, but to know. Let us all sever ties to our karmic debt by clearing whatever patterns/cycles have been causing us to pay-it-forward for decades and/or even lifetimes. An affirmation of willful intent might help to begin the process as, "I AM DONE WITH ALL OF MY KARMIC DEBT! AMEN." Every step on this Holy Ground is joined with other lives…bearing the fragrance that cast new pathways - going over the same ole' ground. Love can impart so much beauty…yet can also take away that beauty…

EMBRYO/WOMB ATTACHMENT

Our soul is an instrument of the Mother's physical body and at approximately 9-months there is an intraembryonic fluid within the embryo that attaches in the womb where all levels of various intergalactic processes begin. This is Mother Nature working Her magic by carrying / caring for Her children on much deeper levels than ever imaginable. Her presence / presents to Humanity beget to contain the inner workings of the natural process of child-bearing years. Within Her womb, the physical mother hosts the silver cord "As Above, So Below" where the Universal energies act as a conduit for mother/child connection. All the inner workings that make up our DNA, genetics, food-for-thought, cells, atoms, the molecular essences and the unseen energies of our Heritage(s) are intertwined within every morsel of the human embodiment. What we seem to think about those 9 months are only the narrative of what is on the surface level, but the vast inner workings display all the magical essence of our Universe. To create a human being largely contributed to the Spiritual / Scientific culmination of God-in-Man. Every contribution of threads intertwined are equivalent to lives lived in one life. This places Humanity at the forefront of conception insofar as where this one life becomes one in all. To perceive one life as an ongoing stream of energy that has no beginning and no end … a visceral movement of energies all vying to be experienced. To take matters into our own hands becomes a catastrophic series of events because these energetic threads already have their place in time; knowing the way is of natural order. To distinguish parameters of Dimensions within/without can only parish the aforementioned energy placing blockages where they need not be. Blockages that present themselves, however, need be for the soul's growth. That is the conundrum of it all...allowing life to unfold naturally and/or to clear all blockages doing one's inner work. The harder we attempt at controlling ... that friction of energy lends itself to breed external forces of added negative ions which carry on as additional blockages that require to be rectified. Going with the flow is recommended to participate in one's life journey. Where the negative ions are abundantly obvious...humans need to learn how to "flip the switch" to positive – avoiding added pressure. When our bodies have more protons than electrons, that becomes a positive ion; hence, the "air/heir" of negative ions under pressure is believed to increase chemical attributes such as; mood enhancement, serotonin, alleviate depression, relieve stress and protect against mold, bacteria, and viruses. A charged atom that has more protons than electrons essentially is when... an atom loses one or more electrons which has more positive power than negative net charges. A number of protons in an atom is distinguished on the Periodic Table of Elements – called, "baryon number" that is nearly equal to the atomic mass. The ion with more protons does have a smaller atomic radius due to the effectiveness of nuclear charge felt by the electrons that are greater. In essence, the evaluation of what occurs in space and time - science can only meet without interference transcending the flow, spiritually. ALL in all, hosts are, "all-natural".

What matter/things release negative ions... a conglomerate of; sunlight, including ultraviolet; cosmic rays/radiant rays in the atmosphere; natural discharge in thunderstorms/lightning; shearing forces of water; plant-based sources of energy; colorless, tasteless of other artificial/natural sources. Exposure to very high places of concentration that breed negative ions are; mountains, dense forests, waterfalls, springs, parks, beaches. Herein lies the reason why Mother Nature is a force to be reckoned with…as Humanity needs Her energy of purification on all levels of our being. Insofar as our food is intact that assists in alkaline, that also contributes: dandelion greens, swiss chard, spinach, kale, almonds, avocado, cucumber, beets, figs, apricots and much more. Negative ions are naturally in water, air, sunlight and Earth's radiation. Moving water is the metaphorical term used in, "go with the flow" terminology…highly understated when misunderstood.

Foods do hold a certain frequency, as follows: ultra-processed foods frequency is between 0-5MHz; organic foods between 50-160MHz; super-foods and Heirloom planets are 160-210MHz. Nutri-medicinal substances such as; herbs, Irish-Moss, Shilajit, and medicinal mushrooms are between 210-320MHz. All-consuming of raising one's frequencies can result in heightened consciousness, vitality, higher thought forms and a stronger intuition.

The counterintuitive nature that translates good for our health and well-being are the positive ions equated to: electrical equipment, television, microwaves, ovens, crowds, crowded places, offices, industrial areas, schools, cars etc., molecules that lose one or many electrons. Negative ions are oxygen molecules with an extra negatively charged electron. Herein are prime examples of illumination through negative/positive energies – enlightenment. The atmospheric elements within the astrological planets also produce and enhance our energy fields… as whenever the Sun is connected to dreamy Neptune… humans need to make an offering, a sacrifice by giving up toxic habits and dependencies (alcohol, drugs, chemicals, negative thoughts/thinking and/or people) to become a channel for the Divine. Neptune inspires a cosmic kind of loving connection to "flow" – through dance, yoga, poetry, film, theater; dissolving and transcending the Ego to surrender. Neptunian energies of this nebulous planet of illusion and dreams – interconnect with compassion of the Yang of our Sun's celestial spotlight of Pisces. Things seen…and unseen. Science/Spirit IS our essence.

"The absence of someone, God fills; while the absence of God, IS Realization." ™

TREE OF LIFE

We are the remnants of a Tree of Life that light up every Christmas/Hanukkah as Noel's angels in the snow. Within every season, a new feeling of self is reborn. Every sunrise, a rebirth of what beholds our every breath for a new day; as well as a sunset of surrender, a new death dawns. Under every tree in the snow-capped mountains are imprints of our Forefathers giving way to lead us to our fated destiny. We've come together in many instances of tragedies, natural disasters, and chaos, and to give up now is like training for a marathon that you don't participate in. Life in every season is to participate and to unfold its beautiful chaos into harmony. Every one of us is a thread that is strung together to make a beautiful masterpiece – every thread must be ordained in its own beauty; for without that thread, there is imbalance. Each thread is a vein on every Tree of Life, every palm on our hands and interwoven as pieces of cashmere satin. Under every tree in the snow-capped mountains are imprints of our forefathers giving way to lead us to our fated destiny. The Tree of Life is our sacred physical body that is veined with the same essence of

175

markings of its History, as well as in the veins of our bodies and in the palm of our hands. The Tree of Life is our sacred physical body that is veined with the same essence of marking History; as well as in the veins of our bodies in the palm of our hands. Every vein in our bodies have been intertwined with certain knowledge and wisdom from lifetimes ago – branching out into unforeseen territory until what begins to happen is clear vision and the feeling, we've been down this road before. There is a fragrance in the air that permeates unto us all…when the time is right for us to ascertain moments that challenge our faith through the tests of time. Have we become immune to some of the tests that resurface when we need to either learn to let go and/or to forgive? That which we have forgotten is beside us right now…to listen, to give, to receive, to be selfless, to understand, to know the difference, to obtain knowledge and to live through every experience allowing what will be. The emotional values we take with us matter on Earth as our feelings navigate the terrain much more than those other matters. Circumstantial evidence leads us all to another chapter in our lives that may call us back to the table of Justice for all. We never know if the injustices could ever be righted…until they are. Some of the players have changed while others remain the same – yet the truth reveals itself always. We are all pre-programmed at birth through our genetic/DNA makeup that includes other layers of our past lives as well as the life we are currently living. Every facet of this programming has the tendency to right our wrongs, to clean the slate, and to envision ourselves in a new light. Whatever we deem to explore comes to the surface for re-evaluation that builds new character traits…or even a flawless interpretation of what perfection looks like.

The foundation of Mother Nature's trees stands firm and holds strong against all disasters– the branches connect in union, leaves fall with every season for what God has put together, let no man sever. Casting shadows in the wind with every breath can only be blown away by where it is driven to go…air breathes itself to experience its own purity. Nature, animals, plants, and all that surrounds every aura of mankind is written within every color of the rainbow setting the stage for all those starry nights. Just when you thought you've seen a miracle in a baby's breath…we witness remission; another day has been given. What child is this in all its bliss … a horizon between two worlds exists – *One Nation Under GOD*.

THE GIVING TREE

When you are given a reason to be… or do, or want, or have what is the stronghold reason for what is being given? Giving is not necessary "giving up, giving in, giving of and/or whatever for is not a form of giving. Giving is a free-standing feeling that gives you "only" a feeling of wanting to give. Know the difference because so many exchanges of feelings have crossed the need to give for whatever reason; than a wanting to give for no apparent reason. Once you can distinguish the difference between these two feelings it will not only absorb your senses it will take you on a whole new ride to freedom. Freedom is only free when it is not about to be taken away. We stand in our Freedom of Speech but when we speak out about certain ethnicities of gender, etc., others will immediately accuse you of discrimination. To destroy someone for what they've said, done, felt, or otherwise expressed in the name of keeping it clean, innocent with unduly religious history that has played out, is preposterous. There is only the cause to speak freely for reasons of giving back as an attribution, acquisition, recognition or any other form of saying to others, my experience with this was a blessing. How have you paid-it-forward, giving back? For this reason, we acquire the remnants of sharing and serving others, being the giving tree. That sense of elation upon seeing a child's eyes light up whenever kindness is shown... the element of surprise for the small miracles in life. In Luke 6:31 and Matthew 7:12, referred to as, "The Golden Rule" as, "Do unto others as you would have them do unto you". We are living proof in this new era of The Golden Age. *Giving* life. *Breathing* life...and *Loving* life.

THE PREGNANCY

Today, we look at motherhood not as a means to an end... Why is that? When did being a parent stop being the most important role ever? Mothering is the most important role and has been treated as an afterthought by society. Why? Lest we forget that some Dads end up taking on the role of the mother, in lieu of different reasons, but the same applies... *Blessed.* There have been debates about whether or not a mother who gets pregnant naturally or has to access another method is prone to being part of nature's order or not; which, quite frankly, not something that is meant for debate. What happens when the two parties, are in agreement, begin to plan for a pregnancy is the ultimate gift. What happens when a single mom chooses to inseminate on her own, independently. Whatever means of planned pregnancy, whether it be by original conception and/or IVF (In Vitro Fertilization), or any other form of science/spirit connect that now has the capacity for so many women to get pregnant is seen as the norm in today's world. IVF has erupted and is helping to assist so many couples who need a reason to believe. The assistance to have the guiding light of a procedure, such as IVF, has helped so many women who are in desperate need to be a mother. For those such mothers, the world of spirit has brought each and every one of them a sense of new hope and lightened achievement.

There are those, however, that could not be successful using the IVF method; but these are for their own karmic ties and reasons of Spirit. We've come a long way... with the best and highest tools that provide women with the hopes and desires of holding their newborn baby. To date, IVF, and other forms of conception, have become a huge success using a singleton's eggs, growing by 38% for women ages 35-37; and the percentage drops between the ages of 38-40 by 25%; and for 41-42 it is 12.7%. It is very apparent that the success rate of all pregnancies relies primarily upon our Heavenly God/Source – as there are many other factors involved when Spirit intervenes. However, there are so many unwanted pregnancies, babies that have been born yet not being wanted... It is a crying shame how this could even be an issue for those women who have been waiting all their lives for a baby. There is no rhyme or reason as to when a woman is equipped to become a mother – for some, being a mother has led them to mature; for others, being a mom means breaking all boundaries that were not done when they were raised; and, for many others that so-called, "accident" was no accident at all. Any child of God's is meant to be here and the faculties of how, when, where they got pregnant is in the hands of God. The Bible states that all children are Heaven-sent and given the proper care under extreme circumstances of what should, could, and does happen.

God's miracle... of Birth...

CHILDLIKE MIRACLES OF INNOCENCE

If you've been granted to see a baby's birth, and/or the birth of any kind; you've witnessed a miracle. Whenever a child has been born it feeds off of its Mother in order to gain strength for every bodily organ to succeed in the womb and of the physical body. Most people don't take that into consideration – many humans deem it as a natural order when a woman is pregnant forgetting, the majority of the time during that pregnancy, all of the inner body miracles-of-life are occurring. We are a forgetful society… but the births of children and/or animals seems to be ingrained. Every mother who has given birth, adopted and/or fostered a child or another's child has been blessed with the grace of a miracle. This makes ALL children of God/Love. To whose dismay do we dismiss the fact that we began as children of God on this Earth; and what has transpired is the detachment from Love because of responsibilities in adulthood, not feeling childlike again. We all go through the cycle of life, yet, some adults remain childlike while others have forgotten. What are you doing in your life to live your childlike nature? It is within each and every one of us in our grown-up bodies. How can adults establish an innocence, a blissfulness, a wholeness that continues to show up as a child? Is it possible that we can stay in our adult bodies, dictate with a firm hand while playing catch with your son? Do you feel a childlike sense of adventure still in your life? Or, has your life been driven by what impasses, life has become… repressed emotions, and a deep suppression of emotions leaving behind anger, impatience, regret, repentance and a slew of other overriding emotions that we cannot understand? This has been the most disheartening… so many are still lost. What breeds a purposeful child of God's is to remain effervescent and in love with life. Let your "treasure quest" be a life full of innocence, fun, beauty of all Nature, peace and acceptance of such an amazing and simple life embedded in us ALL. To be overcome by the anxieties, treacherous worry and grief of life and to live for what others want for us crashes down, is *unnatural*. God does have a sense of humor … become pure joy, become innocent, become childlike within and breathe in new life as a child…no matter what age-of-*grace* you are gifted.

ALL CHILDREN OF GOD

'What child is this?' A very beautiful Christmas masterpiece that claims all children of God as just that… a rendition of joy, hope, light and to see thyself for all that IS. We must come to terms with all the nuances of our family traditions for they've been with us for the past 2 ½ centuries of time on this Earth; and, yet even further than that holds a very special heart since the beginning of time. We speak of the last 2 ½ centuries for reasons that everyone on this Earth can relate to when experiencing the beauty of Mother Earth. Our Forefathers sought out a vision where the Earth was going to take over a new day and time. The New World Era is shifting our Blessed Mother Earth from a possessive power-hungry planet of Fear – to all Love. These shifts are literally rocking our planet and, for some, shaking their stable foundations right out of their hands. We're coming to terms with the enlightenment of our children that have been led by God, the Love of the Universe, to extract what and who are no longer adding value to the Earth. We're all here at this very moment to examine yet another fall from grace period where things that were the "norm" cannot ever be again. That is the way of the Earth plane… we've been sent to do this extraordinary job together, in unity, forbearing all others. What comes into this planet now will only help to segregate the masses into a union of fronts. The front bearers will be the ones to take this planet toward the New Earth Order, known as, "The Golden Era of Truth" that is already underway. This means that the very shifts we've all been experiencing have been for a very good reason – from diving deep into the recesses of your old paradigm to new life.

THE CHILDREN

The children who have achieved a great deal of success in one's life without a parent figure will have an everlasting life. By success, we are not dealing with the egoic nature of a child's upbringing, we are dealing with the effects of a graceful inner peace that are our innate gifts from Mother Earth. No child goes unnoticed, remember this…. It must be said that every child of God's who has sufficiently gone astray only to find themselves once again, will be gifted a new life of goodness, grace and a peaceful place to rest in Faith. Life is a present given from our Beloved Heavenly Father, the Blessed Mother, the Holy Spirit and all of our ancestral lineage. Our rightful nature to be accepting, loving and take responsibility for whatever circumstances one has to encounter in order to evolve. There is much sadness when there is such a high percentage of children who take their lives into their own hands… It goes without saying that the mere disadvantages one child has had while the other experiences a more peaceful life has little to do with genes, as it has to do with a change of perspective. One can "say" that they're very grateful in life, yet, to feel anger, hatred, jealousy etc., deems the opposite effect. Within every household there are many variables of those who are grateful and show gratitude; and, there are those who just give "lip service." The same applies to our Faith… humans "say" they have Faith yet they waiver when challenged, tempted and those choices made. Whatever you've had to endure …children who do the work will be granted life everlasting. One who leads by example, is sure to find your footing on solid ground for others… not to idolize, but to come to see that the vision before them is "in-deeds" the blessing. We don't realize how many children are teachers and do not realize it. In our life, we've had many who have shown us the way forward, especially when, at the most crucial times in one's life, they have been tainted with cruelty, abuse, sadness, grief, aggression and so many other emotions that propel children to overcome. These are the teachers, lightworkers, seers, sages Masters who have taught-by-example and continue to lead the pack sharing their white light of truth all over this Planet. Some children are eternally grateful for the blessings in their lives, while others abhor themselves and the life that has been gifted to them. When we return Home it will be very clear whether our soul's consciousness has evolved or not.

HEAR-T = Heart hears its Truth

Watching what we say, how we think and who we say things to is crucial not only to our environment but also to how others may perceive it. There's much to be said for being silent... the essence of our vibrational frequency depends upon many factors. What children hear, say, speak to the Universe also impacts their lives – and, so many of our children actually sound exactly like their parents. Do you? Have you witnessed other children speaking and they sound exactly like their parents...and, some look exactly like their parents. The "mini-me's" generation... will always be a comfortable place for parents to gawk at their kids being exactly like them. Who else molded them? Parents who want their children to be just like them come from the ego. Why? All children should be able to decide for themselves what they want to be when they grow up. However, there have been cases where kids decide to follow in their parent's footsteps which becomes their choice. How proud would that make you feel? Are you proud of your kids' choices...either way? There can be no right or wrong in these situations...for a life lived in whatever way one chooses... is the right choice.

Physical bodies are feeling more sensitive in ways unknown to your old self – vision impairments, body balance unstable, body aches and all of what has manifested are all part of the ascension process. We've all been following a path that is intentionally driven by external light forces who hold a grand gesture of obediently changing the narrative. 'Where once I was lost and now, I am found' - leads to guide those who are lost, confused, frozen-in-time, desiring external substances that have veered off track. This has been influencing the rest of society – blinded by the light of what one cannot see. Remember this when buying your next painkiller or prescription meds that warrant severe side effects, being such as suicide. Should those who are blinded choose to follow those ingrained, they will have no means to the endgame as an overdose, or something very close. This inhibits those who are numbing their pain with drugs, sex, alcohol, smoking/vaping, that puts you in a blinded state of no-mind. Where's the sense in that? Does it make any sense to ingest drugs that have so many side effects that you lose your grip? Why play games with your life? Don't YOU matter in the masses of destruction? As we agreed to come into this life of: great grief, suffering, sadness, suicidal madness…attempting to get through to the other side of, 'Know Thyself'. The truth is we are all Heaven-sent, and no matter where this blinded path leads, it will ultimately seek the omni essence of light, even if it takes a billion years. This is no exaggeration, as the Earth plane has been existent way before the Dark Ages… into this New World Order of the Light Ages. We cannot fathom what is yet to come, nor should we attempt to do so… but, failing at all costs to enter into the dark oblivion during your time here is not going to all be lost, souls. Some souls have fallen from Grace in order to return to reenact that life once sought out of darkness… to freedom. The only way to attain freedom in a life of all Love is to BE. You ask, "be what?" no need for

184

questions… you already Know. The answers are all hidden in plain sight; all one has to do is believe that this life is going to be all they need to experience. We cannot do this work for you – this inner work must be done by yourselves… The comings and goings of trials, tribulations, and temptations are there for this very reason. To assist you by helping to guide your perspectives, perceptions, be at peace and harmony, and to love with unequivocal trust. Practice being truthful and honest…even when it hurts others' feelings. Even when it changes their perception of you… Live authentically with those who are authentic. In trust, not fear. This dark night of the soul does NOT become a "beast of burden" until it is… the child who has been brutally beaten, torn down, abused, misunderstood, patiently awaits their one wish for salvation. This is what children have been undergoing… each a different narrative, yet coming full circle to a new life, if chosen. If not, the karmic cycle continues only to be driven by forces of low-vibrational entities who will in their own evil ways attempt to override the souls for their own demonic needs and desires. To whom thyself be true…

To date, we have fallen from grace so many times… humans need to fall from grace in order to learn that life should not be taken seriously. No other planet, dimension of sacrifices are made anywhere else than Earth. The school of hard knocks as it is labeled cannot be anything otherwise. To fall from grace just means, *Live*.

CHILDREN ENSLAVED

There is a wide range of children who are either on some medication and/or have a variety of thoughts imposed upon them of believing there's something wrong with them. This brings up a very

185

good point as to how children are taking their lives into their own hands to access medical information to assert or convince, they actually have symptoms of dis-ease(s) such as: ADD, ADHD, PTSD etc., which leads to an entire new Pandora's box. These kids are taking matters into their own hands, for some, assuming they are acting out of fear. We could say this sounds much like a clear case of "hypochondriac" yet is it? Why are kids that have never had issues suddenly or over-the-course of a few years experiencing problems? Are these kids imposing problems that are valid or not? There is a blasphemy of negativity in the ethers of the energy surrounding us all due to such Fear-imposed dramatics by the masses that society brought about. However, these issues go much deeper because "should" these kids that have NO real issues, they think they do and/or are convincing themselves that they do… Why? Because…what we "think" manifests into our reality – spells, a short form of the word, spelling; connects the energy of manifestation into being. Therefore, if someone firmly intends to host several symptoms of dis-ease in their bodies, this will become their truth. Breaking all barriers could effectively lead to other issues of a fear-based life unless the kid's intention to manifest is not willfully strong enough. Many kids will end up going to a specialist with symptoms leading to either founded or unfounded - and, who's to say that their will-of-intention has not been the cause of their findings? Overall testing will inevitably find that either nothing is wrong and/or will showcase minor emotional ties that a doctor ends up prescribing some medication. Who can argue if the real issue(s) of a Fear-based mentality is not the true cause? Where do we go from here? Those who get a clear bill of health from their doctor end up thinking that something is still wrong, doesn't feel right… So, they figure out alternative methods or impose symptoms and/or actual illness upon themselves. Without taking pills, drugs, or whatever

186

chosen vice to numb remains an internal struggle of dealing with a fear-based mentality, one might assess they're even going crazy. Their madness sets in without being on something, popping one or two pills to ease the Fear. If you ask some of these kids to express any fears they may be feeling, it is an overwhelming, *"Fear of death!"* All humans have been raised to live-in-great "Fear for their life" that any semblance of Faith fades ... Society has turned so many of us into such fear-moguls that they believe without being on something they aren't able to have a normal existence. What will remain of those who cannot take some-type of medication(s) which may not be viewed as harmful, yet leads the body to destruction. Ultimately all of our bodies cannot sustain itself in a world based on Fear... All Fear-based thoughts are a way to scare you into thinking the end is near. To inhibit children from becoming the best versions of themselves? Why? Even though we understand that this physical life ultimately will die, why hasn't the narrative focused on the soul's journey, instead? No one understands that we are physically on Earth for a short time and the thought of dying ... being inevitable would allow human beings to ask the question, "What's next?" Who has ever wondered about their soul's infinite existence? We are built... from the essence of God's Love and that IS our only existence. Why don't societal memes of "the end" show what happens to one's soul? Whoever started to put the Fear of God in humans? Why not start by questioning your soul's purpose and how to ascend while on Earth? That is the reason why. Change your thought-trajectory to "How will my soul continue to evolve even after my physical body returns back to Earth? Why is no one asking these questions? If not now... then, when?

Our Heritage ensures longevity for life...the first rule of thumb is to live a fulfilled life that is based on the adage, *"health is wealth"* environment. We know that "we are what we eat" bodes true ... as does, "what we think, we become" and a variety of adages that have been around through the Ages. Who's taking notice? Is it only the rich and famous who can hire personal chefs, and/or fine dining? Why does it matter? Is that chip implanted in your brain permanent? Perhaps... chips will be implanted in the near future, so as to completely lose yourselves in the hands of, "no-man's land". Why haven't we been taught to use our instincts, our intuition, our own mind, to discern ... what has been taught and choose. Look where Humanity is today? Isn't this a cause for concern? Otherwise, human beings will become extinct to the likes of robots and you'll be taking orders from a corrupt government. Didn't we all come to Earth to make a difference, to leave a legacy? Are we running scared, escaping ourselves because it may be too hard to see what's staring back at us? If you're scared now..., how will you feel when your soul dims its light a little bit more; and your heirs' legacy is unable to open doors? Doors to other Heavens within Heavens, doors to the Akashic records that will give you every knowledge from every life ever lived, doors to your own soul's growth... in whatever capacity you can comprehend, the Gates of Heaven are always open to those who seek their soul's innocence, for those who want to evolve, to all who will ... or, won't in this lifetime, the abundant opportunities are here for us to call upon. Stagnancy of energy leaves the Humanity like "Dust in The Wind" by Kansas. Are we ok knowing that in the end game, we chose to remain complacent? And, that raising our frequency for the goodwill of Humanity, YOU declined? How does it feel when your credit card gets declined? Multiply that feeling into eternal neglect and seek to hide out knowing, "you can run, but you can't hide." So, ask yourself, "Why?" Added to this is the neglect of the physical body which is one of the highest junk foods across the world; unhealthy foods filled with carcinogenesis, formaldehyde…etc., cooked with used oils; canola hydrogenated soybean/sunflower oil mass produced. Exorbitant amounts of processed junk foods that are high in fat, high in sugar, excessive salt and low in fiber and vitamins is exactly why the upsurge of obesity and diabetes. A health crisis is of concern for the longevity of both the body and the mind. When the mind is overly satiated in negativity, it speaks to the body that desires processed foods, sugar cravings and all fatty foods to fill the emotional/mental void(s). Stress levels, heart issues, obesity, mental illness and an overall concern for our children's welfare is underway. The world has undergone many upgrades such as our technology; but when it comes to choosing to live a healthy lifestyle, the mindset has vastly been diminished. Humans have become creatures of indulgence… living an excessive lifestyle of all that matters in a material world. So many in our world are living in the fast lane. What happens in the fast lane? "Life in the Fast Lane" song by Eagles, lyrics: "Surely make you lose your mind." "They knew all the right people, they took all the right pills, they threw outrageous parties, they paid heavenly bills…" America on sugar-highs while the parents are comfortably numb. These two do not correlate together under one roof … let alone a world which yearns for balance. There is no balance, no patience, no motivation, no one wanting to work, no care in the world – and only concerned with external thrills of acceptance; social media platforms, virtual reality, gaming of all kinds, junk food junkies … ignoring what's going on around them.

What is this world coming to? This inquiry has been asked over the course of the last few centuries that make up our Heritage of things we've been addressing but not fixing. A polarity is very apparent in our world where "divide and conquer" lends itself to a whole new meaning. In other generations it wasn't as apparent as in today's world.

We are far from where we are headed, as a generation of elites has skyrocketed. Why? Perhaps to "distract" humans from being human? To keep humans isolated, lonely, alone at last… where the term, "leave me alone" came from in the past, is now, "a blank space". Where there are opportunities to branch-out and become a community is now a world unto itself. Itself - it. Self – meaning the self is an "it?" No longer human? "It is what it is?" another charade of humans not caring about the future of mankind. LOST, are those who submit to an "I don't care" attitude. Who cares? What kind of upcoming generations are choosing not to be able to take responsibility, keep a job, and be stuck in a world of illusionary thesis riddled by the Joker's wildness? Who will come save these children when their parents are gone? From Kingdom come to what will be done… is yet to be seen. A Revelation of what's to come…

"Life is a gift you don't give back…™"

CRIES FOR HELP

With all due respect, it is far beyond any of us to judge, however, Spirit has a very serious issue with so many individual children who aren't being paid enough attention and are drifting onto various websites exclusively to those who are not parental discretionary and following a group of followers who are not of age, or capable of understanding who is actually behind the curtain. This is distressing, not only for the child, but also for those all-too-many parents who are NOT paying attention. Those children who are left on their own are being influenced by outsiders who could very well make your own child a stranger. When children are faced with confusion, they tend to follow the crowd that may not have the best of intentions for your kid's life. What do you do when this happens? Do you even know that this has been happening? Are you aware of what your child is watching, who they're interacting with etc., on social media platforms? What can you tell about friends, neighbors, or general interactions that they come into contact with? Innocent, naivety. Once this lifestyle of virtual connectivity impresses upon your children, just know that it is much harder to tear this apart than to place boundaries of slots of times when the child can actually be on their IPAD's or use other platforms to interact. This is a crying shame because the parental figures in these children's lives are also obsessed… some social media to the excess which lends itself to not even know that a problem exists. This IS a huge problem going on and no one is saying anything about it; or can't find a way to instill boundaries. We would be remiss to say this is causing way too many children who are veering off track. Who's swaying, programming, coercing your kids? We haven't gotten to the worst-case scenarios of older adults who are using social media platforms as a means to coerce pedo behavior, sexual misconduct and/or masking as a child or teenager only to come at cross purposes with your children. We've all been played by outside influences who are scam artists…how many times does your phone read, "spam risk"? PLEASE…for the life and goodness of your children's well-being, and those of others, PLEASE STOP your overzealous need to be social-media obsessed. Placing healthy boundaries will "save their lives." Isn't that our *responsibility*, as parents or any version of parenting, required – for the good of Humanity? For our children to learn from us we must be aware and actively as to what's happening in your kid's lives. We cannot subject these kids to such torment, trauma and whatever persistence of evil people are out there. Those who have been given boundaries will pave the way for others. Who can say that children aren't already setting their own boundaries? Who are assertive in claiming their rightful power. To those of you who haven't yet been able to claim the power of mastering your inhibitions it's time to take a good look in the mirror. It's not too late to stake your claim to taking ownership of renewing your commitment to all children. We've all got choices on Earth and whatever happens in your world will come out ever so brilliantly by knowing you've done the best job.

CHILDREN SEEN... BUT NOT HEARD

Who could say that children should not be heard? What does this mean in terms of raising beautiful souls that are given chances to grow into their true selves? So many would say that children shouldn't be heard due to the lack of patience and understanding going on in the world in which we live in. Why not change the narrative by paying attention to what every child is doing... time on social media, time for play, time for learning and a time to dangle the carat a different way. Children are eating, breathing, watching what everybody else is doing, on social media. Where is the discipline? The same old folklore story of past traditions that we were raised in has clearly fallen by the wayside. Children want to know all about who's doing what on TikTok, YT and Snapchat. This is a huge drain of energy that betroths those who are so engrossed. Is it ok that your kids are given free-reign on what they're watching, learning, and visually being a part of? Is it ok that you are not privy to your child's private Snapchat account? What makes one parent give access and not another? Has this become a new lifestyle or a way of living? Many seem to think that these are unimportant to the ways in which child/children are being raised... but why is that? Who ever said, "Let's not be a parent today?" Has anyone ever said that... or, shown up in the absence of parenting? Are you the absentee? Who is rocking parenting and what form of style is working?

Aren't we all good parents? Do you really believe that you've done your very best as a parent and that you now can sit back reaping the rewards of your hard labor? Isn't that the "vision quest" of every parent? To be the very best they can be… Whatever comes to mind first is your truth, then, let that be your own. No one should judge, or have cause to judge any others' way of parenting style. There are too many who can't help but want to judge… why? Do they prefer setting their sights on placing blame so that their own efforts or non-efforts for taking responsibility would not be seen? Who is not being seen, but heard; or, who is being heard, but not seen? Do you see the dynamic narratives between the two? Did you find either one of these scenarios complying with the way of your parental skills? We all have a sixth-sense of how to entertain the obvious insofar as being a parent and knowing what to do… but, we all do not apply these disciplines due to what life handed to us. We could be very cognizant of the way in which our upbringing has led us to either one of enjoyment or not-so-enjoyable; to notwithstanding either. Are you either the child who has not been heard but seen; or seen but not heard; or, the parent who has been heard but not seen; or, vice versa. Either way, it is the style with which you parent, it is the way in which you were parented, and, it is the child within who has submerged as a parent of substance. Wherever holds the most value to each of you, just know that judging ourselves is not an act of discouragement; it is, however, an act of what you needed to learn in order to teach…and, those things you were unable to teach, you learned. We find ourselves in awe of so many outsiders who are influencing our youth today, yet, why aren't parents doing so? It has been written in History that children prefer outsiders rather than their own… just as a guidance factor that some things can be acquired without the principles, rules of engagement and those who just want to hear themselves talk in an ever-controlling environment.

No one is subjected to either or, but we do have the right to choose how we will be seen…

RED FLAGS

Whether you agree or not… this part of taking full responsibility in the future of our children's generation is mandatory. If you lose your child to some influencer who has a track record of history in jail, pedophile, rape, murder, etc., will you take a moment to investigate? Will the actions of children MIA, sex offenders and a plethora of negative influencers change the way you will continue to look at how you are raising your children? When your child is overdosing, then, will you be attentive? When their friend's children are drowning in a bathtub, slitting their wrists or injecting heroin, and/or other tainted drugs of use… then will you be attentive? Will you feel guilty while you're out partying not knowing where your kids are? Did you place your needs before your child's only to find their silence a way of portraying anger, depression, loneliness, etc.? A child who either yells the loudest or holds back in silence… are red flags. A child that makes the A-grade, but socially an outcast could become a hitman later in their years… is a red flag. A child who doesn't make good grades, skips out of school only to get in a pack of wolves who want to influence them by smoking, drinking, drugs etc., is a red flag. Not all, but who is watching who? A child who sits home watching TV, socially inept, who doesn't like school and performs poorly, is a red flag. A child who bullies others is a red flag. A child who has moved too many times to various places and has no real grounding of feeling home, is a red flag. A child who escapes by going out every day with friends, is a red flag. A child who grew up with very little and has no motivation bears a certain fainted red flag – and, becomes crucial to listening to why, how, and when this happened.

Actually, every child has red flags… as do the parents raising them. This is where the thread of our history can either be an asset or a detriment to a child's upbringing. Do we remember… to catch those moments in the youngest ages of their upbringing to indulge in learning, listening, observing what, who and where our kids go, think and do in order to seek their own place of happiness. Where is their safety net? Who is their "go to?" If not the parent, do you know? Where in your upbringing are you too feeling the fall from grace?

A GOD-SENT

For we are all a God-sent, all children are Heavenly – yet the tortures that prevail are man-made to be in pain. If it is written… so, shall it be. Darkness of those who feel cursed is real only if you believe… it's all in what you Believe. It is written, it will be done – as long as somewhere along our path, they find their Heavenly essence in how God's plan unfolds. The child who has been given what is called, "the silver spoon" and the child that has had to earn every penny, each, are chosen for different reasons. Some of those children who are caged and live in fear of dark forces hold the lowest frequency. Alterations of mind/body lower our energetic frequency that makes us weak for energy-vampires to consume. Our planet and so many other dimensions within the Universe are involved in the continued assistance of every man, woman and child. There is no room for error… for this life is a teaching community. The capacity to LOVE unconditionally is what God has intended for us humans… in whatever numeric times we must resist-to-assist in our own ascension. So many

195

fall short…however, many have already seen the light. All children are chosen to raise the vibrational frequency of the entire planet. We all live-to-breathe/breathe-to-live life in our world… What you do with every breath is on you. No blame is necessary and when fingers are being pointed, words of disgust, anguish and other viral language attach itself to others; starting wildfires, we then begin to not only understand the power of unified energy of the *Power of Love* that spreads all over the world.

Without question those children that are in dire straits, needing attention, a cry out for HELP is because there is a lack of Love. A mending thread is warranted for whomever reads this and is nodding their head in agreement.

CHILD DEVELOPMENT

Each child is gifted with innate beliefs of what is right and wrong on the Earth plane. The real challenge(s) are for parents to allow, at a certain age, to ascertain for themselves. This doesn't mean the basic ground rules that are instilled in children from ages 1-8 yrs of age. The rest of our society deems children out of their comfort zone when they're not listening to their parents during childhood and in their teen years. If a child has been given the right tools from an early age, they will excel within their own field of expertise without the hands of others encrypting their own desires. Hence, it is imperative that children be given a sense of their own insofar as choosing their creative interests/outlets – within the confines of their own soul's growth.

The stages of growth in a child's development are as follows:

NEWBORN/0-3months: the baby's brain is being developed in every way from the inside out; and what is needed to allow facets of development to endure its own growth is by tending to the needs of the child, naturally. There are neurons and other various pathways in the developing embodiment: cognitive development, motor skills, social emotional development.

INFANT/3months-1year: the development of sensory functionality is almost formed fully as well as the language and cognition of the brainwaves. They are vastly approaching a 'field of dreams' habitat whereby they see clearly all the magic available in the world in which they live. At this time, cognitive development in imitating sounds, gestures, words. Their curiosity is peeking rapidly, and the faces of their loved ones are settling in their memory bank. At 3-4 months, the infant is getting strength, coordination to roll over, crawling, sitting up and even standing, for some. Objects begin to sound off from banging on pans to banging on drums. A wider array of emotions begins to emerge from; crying, laughing, smiling...and making faces back to the adults that they are seeing as a mirror.

TODDLER/1-3 years: the brain of the child is becoming complex and efficient while asserting their ability of willful intent expressing feelings. When reaching the 12-18 months, toddlers are able to say their first words; and, by 24 months forming sentences while learning/gathering new ones daily. Adults will question the intellect at this very stage to seek an egoic intellect for bragging rights. Toddlers typically will walk, run, climb, jump, push/pull effects as their hand-eye coordination are being mastered. The love of stacking blocks, page-turning and the uses of different mediums as crayons and/or computer-learning assist in becoming effectively proficient. Toddlers that have grown up in healthy environments will want to show affections and empathy for others in the form of kisses/hugs and sharing. Other like-minded toddlers whose visceral unemotionally are exact but strokes of pain imbued become cold to the touch. Pretend-play, observing, imagining and imitation is the toddler's favorite playground. They learn the complexity of feelings/needs and the desire to do things their way.

PRESCHOOL/3-5 years: a preschooler's brain is getting more organized - learning new words and understanding sophisticated concepts while building an array of interests/skill sets. Asking questions through their innate curiosity instills a wide span as to what, how and why things work…or not. Concepts of seasons, time, numbers and letters give the preschooler much to begin their creativity. Preschoolers begin their agility, grace in hopscotch, skipping, balance, 'tag, you're it' and other games. The artistic nature comes through using scissors, drawing, coloring, fastening buttons and zipper-up. The beauty of the preschooler is that they begin to comprehend that other people have different perspectives - and by age 4 or so…begin the walk of independence. New friends and experiences set the tone for using their innate social skills if they so desire.

SCHOOL AGE/5 years and up: the big-kid syndrome of a child headed off to school is where the biggest growth in the brain is established. Most of your kindergarteners have learned the basics and find themselves in the realm of wonder and imagination. Motor skills are fully formed and learning a musical instrument or developing a complex artistic project lends itself to reach within, where their creative juices flow. Showing initiative, problem-solving and more complicated teachings are learning tools for them to navigate.

The principle responsibilities of parenting entails: responsible, protective, watchful, attentive, consistent, kind, generous, compassionate, involved, and active in school participation (i.e. PTA meetings, social events, fundraisers etc.) to witness for themselves who their kids are interacting with … and to determine the overall curriculum of the teacher's involvement. These are pertinent issues that go hand-in-hand with what's going on at school and in the home environment. There have been times when parents rely heavily on the school system to provide an overall education where the teacher can assess and share pertinent concerns with the parents. Repeating a class may be old school… but, now there is a set standard of "no child left behind" which definitely poses other issues in the onset growth of a child. The stakes are high either way…because the old version of holding a child back to repeat a grade tends to give off a "not smart enough/not good enough" in a child's psychology. Yet, "no child left behind", as a rule of thumb, indicates whether or not the child is meeting the grade -level of the State. Both have serious implications of "not smart enough/not good enough" on a deeper level of a child's psyche. There is emotional/mental harm in a child's upbringing, giving off a certain stigma that follows them to have an inferiority complex. No matter what the reason, the fact holds true that children continue to feel inferior. Either way, some very smart children are not seen for their smarts because it might not fall under the standard curriculum that each State requires. Instead, the child might be driven by pursuing a trade, or trade or might excel in a very different way … by choosing a Charter School, instead. The Educational System is not necessarily broken, but requires all children to feel confident…even if they're not able to learn in a traditional classroom. Why aren't schools allowing facets of a Charter school curriculum that enables a more creative approach to the minds of those who learn through the Arts?

Why not merge a Charter/Traditional curriculum into the school's program to attain a well-rounded student? We need to foster a newly embodied educational system to adhere to all students by seeking to allow all children to participate in both Charter/Traditional ways of learning. An out-of-the box learning, said Jack. Parenting requires a lot of multi-tasking; listening, diversity, understanding, compassion, patience speaking up etc., of the highest order. There are kids with ADD/ADHD who are highly intelligent. Autistic kids have the same intellect, yet because they're needing special attention does not make them any different than the rest. All children are God's love…and if a child requires special attention, who are we, as parents, not giving of ourselves?

TRADITION OF GENERATIONS

This nuanced approach to what 5,6,7-year-olds are in the midst of at this very moment is teaching a new aspect of traditional value that isn't a value actually…more like an adversity of tradition. Tradition is taught, a borrowed behavior that is learned throughout time…and, should the majority buy-into that behavior, it amplifies the energy to a value. Hence, why so many of our adults who are of the younger generation parenting/adulting are searching for answers in and of itself by needing to stay numb. This is not to say that one or more of these substances is not needed to calm one's stress levels; but, the ideology of traditionally going within hasn't been an option…for most. There are some who are vamping up their spiritual journey who seek guidance through meditation, cleansing, doing their inner work by peeling the layers one at a time… Younger mindsets of where the old traditions have not worked is breeding a whole new generation of mind-altercations, pill popping, sleep deprived etc., by which to escape, numb, defer all dysfunctions by a 'feel-good' mindset. Mind-blowing external "tripping" experiments through DMT/Ayahuasca is not what God intended. Those inquiring/seeking to test the waters to raise consciousness are not all successful; and those trips have real-life consequences. Risking a human's life to experiment on the spiritual realms is to say that one is testing the powers that be. In most cases, inquisitive kids are testing the fate of their own destiny, which has negative residual. Anything "unnatural" will harm the physical body at some point or another … even though some trips may be successful, the residual harm will show up at a later time.

What has been EXPOSED are humans pretending… much like actors on the stage, masking who they really are and how they want to be seen. What to tell our children? How can we distinguish those who are there to uphold and serve vs. those who are evil and only in it for what their ego desires? As we have been losing trust in the system… now what? How do we communicate this to our kids? Or, do they already sense it? We must connect the threads of our own beliefs… we can choose to believe or disbelieve but no matter what we must uphold our own boundaries, protect our territories by educating our children from a very young age about how, what, where, when to protect themselves. A young age must be defined as maturation, or does it? Let's give every child vice of education in self-defense, be careful, engaged with a "find my phone" and/or "location" at all times - be it on our phones, watches or whatever is suitable for the child's age; alarms, pepper spray, all platforms of defending oneself, emergency button, 911 etc. Any form of protection is a child's "innate right" as the child and as a parent. Have these issues been brought up in the family and/or in our educational system? Self-defense classes instead of dosido… wouldn't that have made more sense? No offense to our country Western fans... but, that's not going to save your physical, mental well-being. In light of how long "Missing Children" has been going on from way back to seeing them on milk-cartons one would have protected the innocent. Many crimes that are standing right in front of us and we either fear or continue to trust... until we don't. Here's the transition of the fate of our country as we speak... Who can we trust? The thorns in our sides that haunt our very souls desire humans to Fear, to fall, to divide, to distrust, to lie, to cheat, to overshoot their shot, to become stagnant, to dismantle one's self thread-by-thread. How much more can humans take? How much more are you going to take? How many children must die?

BATTERED CHILDREN/BATTERED PARENTS/BATTERED ANCESTORS

Children have all been battered, bruised and have suffered great pain at one or many times in their lives; and some have risen to the challenges, while others have not. Those of us who are still fighting the good fight, keep it up because you will be rewarded - while others live to numb the pain using external addictions. We cannot be responsible for what others have done but we do need to take responsibility for our part. Most humans feel they are numbing themselves to the tune of an absent, abusive, incoherent, indecisive, narcissistic etc., parent(s). There are SO MANY great parents out there who are attentive, who play, who listen and can hear the cries of their children. What will it take to pass on this message to those parents who are still finding it very difficult to be a parent, while still a child? Parenting is a huge sacrifice... and it is very difficult for some kids who have parents that think of themselves first. All children need to come first when raising them so that they can feel Love like no other.

202

There are children who scream for attention… Do parents realize the great impact and sadness a child may be feeling? How many are taking extra time to spend with their kids, play, go to the park, museums, road-trips, sit-downs as a family unit? Take a minute to think about …

To say that we all grow up in a perfect world is to know that it's not true… as Earth was constructed as a dysfunctional world (a hell, or even purgatory, for some) for very good reason. A History of learning lessons from our life experiences is teaching every family to show how effervescent changes come into our lives. It is not for others to judge and/or criticize as what goes around comes around. We're not all going to learn at the same time, on the same level of playing field, and/or some are not ready at the present moment… The choice is up to you. Inevitably, everyone will grow into their own way of being, one lesson at a time. Whatever is not learned in this lifecycle, may be chosen in a new one, in a new way and with new faces, places and circumstances. What many misunderstand is that Spirit gives us the "free will" to make better choices and to learn what it is that will elevate our consciousness. To be certain that this happens, in hindsight, look over the past few years to see how your Spirit Guides have assisted to place you in the exact place, in the exact time with the best opportunities, people and places that would launch a new you. This is considered a willful act of Divine timing… when we look past our ego and look into ourselves for what our truth is showing us. Humans are only capable of going at it alone so far; and when our choices become too burdensome, we end up surrendering so that we can find peace once again. That surrender is exactly what needs to take place in our lives without even knowing that we are doing so, in the blink of an eye, our life takes a smart turn for the better. Whatever "behind the scenes" is happening in the Spirit world, our Heavenly

Spirit bodies will intervene with those who have lost sight completely. Should Spirit NOT be able to get through to someone who may be considering taking their own life; the end result is inevitable. Everyone comes to a point in their lives where it is a "do or die" situation…"

IN GOD WE TRUST

CHILDREN OF THE LIGHT

A child who has been raised with similar ethics, beliefs and an abundance of brethren in what Mother Nature intended, has been fluid in the ways in which these children differ. They're in a new paradigm shifting Universe as we speak – in every sense of these words. There are many children who are lightworkers, sages, seers etc., who have clearly seen the efforts being made on Earth; and, while they are still attempting to figure things out for themselves, the world is vastly manifesting at light speed. Lightworkers beam their light, much like a lighthouse. A lighthouse of lightworkers is a lonely life solitude in Love for ALL…, to keep God's children safe, shining light always for others to see, a glory of light shines on waters that run deep, to navigate those who are chosen within the confines of a historic family tree. Every lightworker knows their role of utilizing their light to the highest vibration out of unwavering Faith, Trust in Humanity. Some may find their light-of-truth to be astoundingly confronting to those whose light flickers with insecurities, misinformation, tired, angry because people lose themselves in lies. We must "know" who we are, to remember the light of God's Love is within each and every one of us – containing infinite light-shows throughout the world for all to see…

Those who are lost in a world of darkness tend to subconsciously acquire external situations and/or stuff to keep from seeing themselves. To acquire stuff only to find a conglomeration of external messes – within/without who cannot seem to separate themselves from the material world of hoarding. There are many reasons why these particular humans have vastly been known to feel their lives are an uphill battle in this life as in past-lives. An accumulation of anything external, leads to hoarding, involves a deep reset at a core level. A fragment of this essence is living on this Earth and is also fragmented in other Dimensions to be worked out. While one life is serving others to exist, another Dimensional version of that same life is taking, receiving a new life that contradicts the other. Other existences are defragmenting the giving/receiving that the issue may be calling for… similar to a revolving door of Dimensions where the giver becomes a receiver and vice versa. While this transition may not seem apparent, it is happening in the ethers of energetic forces in other playing fields … only to go with the flow as it appears in one's life.

THE CHILD WHO FOLLOWS

The child who follows listens to what others think and say to determine what may be the best advice or path to choose. These children have been chosen as secondary vices to reconfirm what they already know to be true. If we're able to be as bright as them, we know already that life is a balancing act; and, to discern the real from the illusion. Children who have chosen to be followers also know who they've got common interests, common ground with and choose to commune in unity – as a pack of truthful warriors. There are also those followers who need to have a strong leader that likes to showcase their innate skills…while the silent one is hidden behind the veil of decision-making. Some leaders rely on an entrusted sidekick to throw ideas off of. Some of those sidekicks are "silent-witnesses" who are leaders and their own Muses who do not require the limelight of fame and/or fortune; but, want to make a difference. Many layers of followers reside in the world of good and evil…yet the ones who are following the darkness are ultimately lost sheep. They're not in tune with the reality of evil forces nor do some choose to deal. Lost souls have been so broken by their own series of life events that they are blinded by the light…cannot see. Ultimately, some of these children will begin to sway their vote of confidence in order to save themselves. All having freewill…

THE WOUNDED CHILD

Pain feels very different from one child to the next and many are vitally scorned, where others may believe this was intended for learning. An inner fight tends to happen when we realize some scars haven't healed yet. When we fight for what we integrally choose to believe in is what makes a human soul, a hero. When children are beaten down for so long, they tend to believe what others are saying about them, even if they don't agree. To believe in yourself tends to be a struggle we fight daily and is very personal. It might take a million years, to some who have had a life of struggle, in believing their worth. Wounded warriors have battled, what seems like lifetimes, to be seen and heard – NOT egocentricity but to HELP Humanity.

For those who claim they are non-believers and don't wish to partake in a world of seeking… that is a belief of your own accord. Atheists choose to believe in not-believing… We are all versions of beliefs within ourselves, our ancestors, our Forefathers and grandfathers' fathers etc. We all have a past and a present while your futures yet unfold – a fated destiny. If you can accept to understand that we are the embodiment of Mother Nature's beautiful land you have attained, "Know Thyself". Our ancestors' historical views and part of what they had to endure becomes threaded for us to realize. We've been a beautiful orchestration of world events of our past but now it's time to cut out the pages of the History books to allow for the New World Order to begin. This New World Order is unmasked, unscathed and wholly "Holy" transparent to thyself. What has come before are those evolving based solely "souly" on the elevation of the Spirit self.

Children need the energetic force of ALL LOVE… and, we need Love deeply to the degree that some remain in abusive relationships, even when it hurts. Our greatest human feat is to Love so deeply within ourselves …knowing others are a mere reflection to Love even deeper.

THE LONER CHILD

The loner sticks to themselves not needing to be needed. What a loner does differently than the others are keep their head down…sometimes not wanting to see what's going on. They're withdrawal in the world could be viewed as living under a rock and happy to be in that safe place. Just when you think there are no loners in a world of go-getters, the loners love their own facetime. Social media not so much. To have to face this world would take a lot for one to get out there. Loners love climbing higher and higher…not requiring any validation or onset of approval from anyone; not even those who want to prove they are worthy to their parents. They Love alone time, which is very different from being lonely. What a beautiful

207

asset of those who go within their connection to God. They talk with Mother Nature in ways that are deeply rooted. Mother Nature invites all Her children to take long walks and envision the world that is right in front of them…the attributes that loners who know their connection are abundantly so.

ALL archetypes are connected…therefore, a loner could very well be somebody's Hero. They understand the complexities of one's suffering for they have lived that story in an entire suffering of their Heritage. The leader, follower and the loner have all the archetypes either hidden or in plain sight. As we begin our journey we may evoke more of a Hero archetype, then grow into a Sage. Or, at some point in a Hero's life they sought fame and fortune - hitting midlife sought inner refuge to find themselves, a Sage. To pinpoint any of the archetypes to one person is unfair to that person's character as many flavors of their fragrance shine at various times in one's life. There could be a dominant archetype in one person yet there are so many that others have yet to witness. Technically the archetypal mirror sees repetitive qualities and patterns as does in our astrological chart. To categorize or place another's qualities/characteristics in a box is a learned-behavior mindset. Other mindsets that we've all been privy to in this lifetime are not to be taken seriously…for this is how one's Ego manipulates thought(s). All forms of thought must be discarded—how and what we think and say to ourselves can also be influenced by external forces, where other egos exert control. Thoughts become things… and then they need to be let go. In meditative ways – taking a Nature Walk, listening to music and allowing thoughts to form, allow them to roll off the tongue. No-thing is to be taken too seriously… Earth was designed to be a playground for innocent fun. Here is where we all find ourselves conforming to society's ideologies of what they think you represent; a huge misrepresentation of oneself. Justice will prevail to all people whose mindset can be vastly improved while at the same time disapproving. Let go of closed-minded thoughts that you've come very accustomed to holding on so tightly, like a security blanket; and, go on about your lives discerning what you FEEL is your Truth.

What defines these children to take on two sets of different courses in their lives is what is known as a mixed-bag of DNA into the family tree of a generational lineage. Under the same roof, two children who are raised the very same way, but one child is enduringly curious – known as the black sheep, take off on their own course… This is the cause and effect of what is very commonly called "genetic upbringing" which can lend a perplexing difference from one child to the next. These are imperative to understand as the threads of one family remain intact, the same family holds numerous threads which stand alone in another's DNA of choice. The child who strays off course to find themselves is the clear loner, one who enjoys the company of his/her self without any external complications or dramas from others – especially under the same roof. We've all known that the child that stands out amongst the rest, defying all odds, is a daydreamer and who is a part of their own tribe… that child is the one who is not seen, but heard. The loner has been on their spiritual path for many lifetimes and stands alone in their last life… only to be seen and heard. These children ALL have many inner treasures, gifts from the Universe that have yet to be delivered out unto the world. They have waited thousands of lifetimes only to be the VERY BEST version of themselves – saving the best for last.

To be continued….

BLACK SHEEP DRUM TO THEIR OWN BEAT

The so-called "black sheep" of the family are the seekers of liberation – they do not adapt to rules and regulations. These children seek to revolutionize beliefs of their own, they are the rare breed. Who are the black sheep in your family... the ones who grew up different– that weren't given attention, who went against the grain, who were told they'd never amount to anything, who didn't go to college, who hated school, who didn't care if they achieved a high-paying job in Corporate America, who spoke back, who daydreamed, who had trouble making friends, who were bullied, who were not seen nor heard and without even knowing... beating to their own drum? If you get offended by the old adage of, "the black sheep" then you're NOT one of them...on the other hand, you might feel your A-typical controlling ways do take offense. Either way, there are different reasons for understanding how a world of diversity makes the world go round. Diversity is a consistent reason for Humanity to change their perspective on how beautiful every creature on God's given Earth is. To live in a society that has been attempting to program mankind to "act like AI robots" is insane! Mankind is built to showcase not only the external physical beauty but also to seek the diverse cultures, backgrounds, and upbringing which merges as threads of Love. Every "black sheep" who felt like an outcast remains to feel as such, until they become self-realized throughout their spiritual journey.

What has been going on with these generations of misfits and/or are they the same children who are using them? Misfits and the "black sheep" of the family come from the same generation of what we now consider to be, "lightworkers, seers, sages, seekers of truth..." who have signed up to be here, on Planet Earth to make a difference. We've

210

come to not only understand that there might be a few clusters of those who are the black sheep/misfits and those who were the same loners growing up have all signed up to shed the New World Movement as we know it as the "Spiritual Revolution." Who's to say that this is not a part of the Master plan? Where does this leave you in the scheme of this Movement? Are you the parent and/or adult who is numbing your pain or are you the parent and/or adult that came here, as the black sheep, only to shed light upon those in need? Whatever the case we must bring this up for Humanity's sake so that it can be resolved, once and for ALL. Being a part of the ALL doesn't entitle adults to not be "adulting" but partying instead... why? If you're an adult, with or without kids, your primary responsibility is to yourself…to maintain a place of residence, to pay your bills, to find yourself in the arms of another who places you above the rest and to raise each other's frequency. Gone are the days when marital bliss of a big house with a white-picket fence with kids and animals is seen as, "The American Dream." We are paving the "new American dream" which will be to entertain nothing more and nothing less than to achieve your own dream that makes you happy. This is not a pipe dream to those who are on their spiritual path of transcending. The journey of Love is to take your own advice, seek your own true happy place within and without, to have Faith in yourself as it emits light onto others for their happiness. We are here to serve Humanity…which begins right at the very beginning of "Know thyself." "We live in a cynical world" quoted in the movie, Jerry MaGuire as his known self as the Ego was so familiar with the way others perceived him that when he wrote that "memo" and submitted it out to everyone in his company, he ended up getting fired. This is the exact thing going on in today's world – if you speak out, speak up by speaking your truth you're going to be ousted by your family, peers, co-workers etc., while all the time fear is overriding your need to seek your own truth. How could we not be living in a cynical world when those in charge of our world are cynical? Doesn't that breed familiarity with the Law of Attraction? Like attracts like as we see those in our world as unhappily in a world of, "misery loves company" adage.

Whoever feels that society rules their every decision, belief in life, and can honestly say all results for the better of Humanity, think again. Even those who have been trying to control mankind are being escorted to draw upon the darkness that seeks darkness. For those who have fallen into the trappings of darkness, this too is another form of sheep. These sheep see the blackness in their shadow selves and find it quite satisfying religiously conforming others. How? By waiving carats-of-greed in others who are especially organic to the coercion. We seek to find many existing Fortune 500 companies who are professionals in the Art of the Egoic caveat, hunting for innocent victims who are greedy and weak. Bottom-feeders. This greediness doesn't stop there – the ego spreads its bat wings out to the justice system, our educational system, healthcare system, food/drink corporations and many others. Why are some biting the Apple, drinking polluted waters, ingesting junk food, driving in congested freeways of smog, and living in landfilled areas dangerous to the environment? To say that Humanity is not aware of these matters and so many others is to admit to one's ignorance. Where is justice in an unjust world? How can we protect "the children" from being taken for granted – to fall victim to the misuse of power, coercion and manipulation? Did you drink the kool aid? Kool-aid by means of a "coo that aids" the weak? Now is the time for us to take flight... and take control of where Humanity is headed —to stop pretending we're not privy to this world of corruption. Those children who are the "black sheep" are out there spreading their light-in-Love for Humanity. What are you doing to HELP? Instead of falling prey to the black shadows that follow the weak-in-the-knees for reasons that deploy lazy as a constitution of the states. Let's regroup and find our own way Home...since that is where we are all headed. In essence, children who haven't been educated to life's corruption are in desperate need of a real education. This is the borrowed knowledge that has substantial earning power for our children. The Educational system does not teach kids about how to survive in a world of corruption, how to enlist in self-defense, tai-chi, and/or even to practice meditating. They, the educational system, doesn't even know about "how to" educate kids in that field of education because they too were not taught. Teachers, parents, children and the likes of school presidents etc. a world of educators only teaches their expertise. Mankind was not raised on "Life Lessons" and why haven't we done so...for reasons of all those unwarranted deaths? At least, for the sake of those who remain... a world within the world of greed is there for all of us to see.

OBSERVANT CHILD

The observant child who dictates a strong influence on others can be the first born who prefaces to say "this is how it's done" or becomes a control freak. Another way that children stave off on their own is to stay in your own lane; and who witness others by silently observing without judgments, true leaders of another kind. These children have been the watchful eye, a true detector of who is doing what with whom...and keeping silent. It's not that they don't want to start trouble, it's just that these leaders keep to themselves "knowing" that God gives karma to all. Not a slight-of-hand but a freedom to stay in their own lane and allow the Universe to handle. Who can say they even know these beautiful souls that entertain themselves with their own causes by not getting involved with what others dictate, what others judge, how others shame themselves, for not being one to be vengeful, hurtful, sinister in any way. These kids were taught well because it is not for humans to make others hurt, nor is it for God to do the same; and, these children are aware of how the Laws of the Universe work. They've studied, they've witnessed much trauma, tragedy and yet they remain neutral...to the cause. These kids are aware, much to their dismay, that whatever you criticize comes back ten-fold in life. Some of these wise ones have had to learn the hard way, but they've done their work, no doubt. This inner knowing of wisdom attained does not come with any age, per say... it is a breed unto itself. There is so much tragedy in the world today that opinions and other unkind acts from others lay the foundation of darkness to those who cannot help themselves. We are all aware that kindness matters in every way, everyday... and with the imbalance of the world in flux, many are teeter-tottering on the fence, similar to a toddler. Triggers come in all shapes and sizes ... some to our very surprise while others not so much. The triggers of those who remain sufficiently angry, broken, hurt, are the ones who like to show their egoic selves by blasting others...as small violent rages or as bigger rages – all pain.

JOYS OF BEING A CHILD

Earth is built for Humanity to appreciate ALL the infinite joys throughout our lives. This is mostly true to those who haven't been exposed to the initial elements of their own parental extremes while in the womb of their Mother. We've all had to suffer greatly as the 9-

month "waiting game" or some less, if the child is a "Primi," only to be handed the first breath. To date, a National study of the American Society of Women's Journal has stated that for the majority of late pregnancies that exceed a 9-month duration will become stable if not already man-made to know their purpose; and, for those who are primi's these babies are super intelligent. The reason for this isn't for any other than to throw caution to the winds of change – where long-term pregnancies have been given a natural course of being in the Mother while others want out sooner. The other major factor why and when this happens is the main focal point, that the longer a child remains in the womb of Mother Earth, the stronger the capacity to withstand painful issues in their lives. There are other extraneous circumstances that arise also while in the Mother's womb… trauma shielding and factors of external sidekicks that the child feels within. No child is unwanted… and every child is able to choose whether to stay in God's pocket for consciousness to rise. We all have subconscious reasons as to what, why, and how our lives are threaded with others yet not aware of them. In order to best fit our external circumstances on Earth, we must allow whatever situations to envelop without questioning the intentions of Universal energy. Whenever we begin to question our reasons for certain changes, big or small, we tend to fall into desperate times.

SETTING THE STANDARD - FOUNDATION

Although our duties of parenting are Love, Respect, Discipline, Patience, Kindness and Obedience, to list a few, reflections of giving/receiving in gratitude. These are reciprocated in-LOVE; however, these duties must be for the parent(s) to uphold. The premise of reality is that when we give Love to our children it also includes, "tough-love". The highest form of Love we must give for building a strong foundation of discipline. No matter how much we will waiver as parents, there are studies that have proven success in a world of discipline.

Where did the term, "setting the standard" come from? The term 'standard' was borrowed from Middle English, and Old French – meaning setting a benchmark. In building a child's foundation it is imperative that the system of education sets standards as a measure of learning on how to make good decisions. It is of great importance to set standards as it envelops a moral compass of excellence and achievement. However, children have started setting their own standard-of-life by attaining this excellence from outside forces exposing them to potential threats. Any need for external validation, appreciation and/or attention are forms of escapism. An escape from the "real world" avoiding growth and natural development. Parental views need an upgrade but also a sense of discipline, in an attempt at communication, and to be proactive in doing so. What will happen when all of Humanity stops interacting with one another? Are you comfortably numb to what's being done or complacent to what is not being done? You decide. Are you aware of what is going on in your home and/or are you observant? There is no salvation when one is not aware. Observing actions to assist children to prepare, teach and guide them through life.

IT'S ELEMENTARY

Every child of God's is recreating a life within other lives to understand their true essence of "self-realization" where at around the mere age of 7, 8 years is when our eyes begin to view things differently.

The scope of understanding begins to get skewed and an entire world of what we originally thought to be endless joy in the world, now starts to be misconstrued as unsafe, unkind, or, even unbelievable. We question, "Who am I?" This question is where it all begins…we end up talking to our best friends, family, and whoever is around wanting to know, asking around for someone to let us in on what we're doing here. Hours upon hours of contemplation, questioning, attempting to figure it all out… while witnessing those people we've entrusted… We begin to observe – who our family and friends are listening to, their values, interests, hobbies, even overhearing adult conversations to get a sneak-peak into what is actually going on. In those occurrences though comes schoolwork, curfew, concerts, discipline, and more schoolwork. Some of us look forward to school because we found out that there are subjects in certain classes that we've excelled in; while others dreaded every moment of the classroom without knowing why. Those who are good at school want to be accepted and seen; while others feel more rebellious to the cause. We were taught that love is found by being accepted as a high achiever, a competitor, getting good grades, and even being the teacher's pet. What is a pet? It's a dog who learned that classical conditioning can be learned over time – as in Pavlov's Law. If, however, you fell off the grid struggling and becoming the Rebel, you may have ended up not feeling "good enough". A thread of inferiority complex begins to peek out subconsciously, without being seen. Teacher's pet wasn't necessarily a term of metaphoric value in school…it is also a real experience with those who raised us. To be loved came with subtle hints of being conditioned to do good and getting rewarded, being seen and loved. Those who didn't necessarily care what happened are the "black-sheeps" of their family. The Rebels. Woodstock – those who walk to the beat of a different drum… Here is where many find themselves…

in between a mindset of conquer and divide. "They" have mesmerized, manipulated, taught to the masses that any child who cannot live up to the expectations of a powerfully competitive world could and will be cast aside. Misfits. You're either in it to win it … or, you're not. When children are cast aside, what part of their lives vanish? Believe it or not, the "black sheep" are the guiding light for the blind leading the blind. Whatever else happens, the Chosen Ones asked to HELP out Humanity. These children have gone unnoticed almost their entire lives…and because of this, need not be seen, only heard. A silent whisper is all it takes… Whether you are in an adult physical body or not, *a Chosen One lives as an old soul – while remaining young-at-heart*. Those with a pure heart live their lives in LOVE…as they sense, NO FEAR. Some are adult versions of their childhood selves and find that being childlike promotes self-care and healing for all.

No matter what the reason, the fact that holds true is that all kids are given no way out of primary, middle and/or high school – until that child reaches a level of "can't take it" by choosing to become a drop-out. This adds another layer to one's psyche attached to not being good enough/not being smart enough. Either way, some very smart children are not 'seen' for their smarts because it might not fall under the standard curriculum that each State requires; instead, the child might be driven to a trade, or might excel in Liberal Arts, or Music. All parenting requires is understanding, compassion and patience of the highest decree. Parents are being tested every step of their kids' lives to see how much they're able to get-away with. Many kids who have dyslexia, ADHD/ADD are highly intelligent. Autistic kids, the same. The only difference is, needing special attention, and who doesn't need more special attention? Mankind is begging for attention, especially to the tune of social media selfies and Tik-Tok besties. All children are

God's LOVE…and if a child requires special attention who are we, as parents, not giving of ourselves? A mother/father's role is essentially THE most important role, EVER! This is not a job that pays 9-5 or even a part-time job…it is an up-at-dawn leading into an eternity of the wee hours of the next morning's light. For some, the role of the parent(s) must be an over-possessive watchfulness because kids are vulnerable and naive. We've been witness to kids being grabbed out of nowhere…taken, abused, raped, etc., many never found or returned. What tragedies have been happening to innocent children, a "wake-up call" indeed. What has been EXPOSED to the masses of these criminal acts on children is not only unbelievable but incomprehensible being a parent of, or, as a witness. Names and faces of MIA children used to be shown on milk cartons –back in the 50's, 60's 70's – and, someone pulled that torment out from under the rug. Now, we hear and see it on social media… so many children being abused, misused, sexually handled, killed, and the rest is shocking, to say the least! EXPOSED.

Who is watching and/or observing those "behind the curtain?" It is a real issue, a problem with so many kids/children literally being stolen, misused, robbed of their innocence! If parents are **not** paying attention, your child might be next…while this is still of much concern. Keeping watch requires less time on social media, numbing the pain, allowing others to take care of your kids (family members included) where these issues have long been a contention to the safety of our children. Most definitely, kids have been getting molested by direct family members such as aunts, uncles, siblings, parents/step-parents, etc. BE AWARE! For those who already know how important it is to be aware and providing that awareness to your children at a certain age is mandatory. What age? This all depends upon the intelligence and attention of your particular child, you decide.

Awareness ... to educate isn't taught in school... why? Our educational school system has NOT taught... life lessons, protection and safety (not only from Police/Fire Dept.) but from a wider-spectrum that of protection/safety of suspicious hidden tendencies of dysfunctional families; and, self-defense mechanisms...even providing pepper-spray for the younger ages, and classes to educate on what to be "watchful" of in any case of intruders. What are "they" waiting for and how many children must be violated and killed because of this? These are REAL issues...why are they being ignored? It stems from the family unit then branches out into the school systems...all the hateful crimes *MUST BE STOPPED*. Instead of scrolling IG for the latest fashion trends, DIY projects, why not get more involved and start either a Tik-Tok Emergency and Awareness or a Podcast for kids to listen to; or, to unite with other parents joining together to SAVE our children. Much can be done... is anyone planning ahead?

RANTINGS of the EDUCATIONAL SYSTEM

After such devastating tragedies at schools Nationwide, why hasn't our educational system gathered a community of certified defense teams to be on campus when children are in session and/or on the playground? Why haven't "self-defense" classes been offered – and/or extra protection to ensure that children know what to do at the onset of shooters? These children are our own... the future of generations to come ... Why are we not educating our children about taking precautionary measures? NOT in fear, but with Love.... Either way, something must be implemented. Have the parents been teaching their kids to "look over your shoulder" "who looks suspicious?" "Is anyone following you?" "What are they wearing? Who looks shady?" and the like... There is a vast array of responsibilities that fall under the parenting umbrella which sometimes is taken for granted and/or overlooked. Whatever the case… new circumstances prevail that require us to raise our awareness as parental safety for our children is vital. Even for the protection against any shady family members who think it's acceptable to mis-represent their affection(s), get too close for comfort, an air of physical and/or mental abuse requires a watchful eye.

The overall environment on planet Earth is shifting toward a New World Order and even though some are experiencing much hardship, it is for the overall goodness of the planet. There are some shifts, twists and turns in the world today which require resilience, vigilance and the strength of lions. This is not the time nor the place to "give up" on your life and the lives which serve to assist and protect. Those children who died all went back Home for reasons that cannot be explained; and for that reason alone, is why we must congregate as a community to forge ahead. This is a very unique time where Earth has been ascending – its consciousness has been plummeting way too long without the clarity that, even we, cannot seem to put our finger upon. However, the time is now when those who have signed up to assist, from behind the scenes, will also ascend and/or have already ascended. Every child of God has a purpose to serve and our educational system needs to raise the bar for educating to serve and protect. It is crucial that both the parents work in-tandem with every child's school to place new rules, regulations and be equipped at a moment's notice. Better together.

ROLE MODELS/MENTORSHIP

There's a good reason why children need role models or mentors which have either become extinct, or the parents don't fit the bill. Who will partake in HELPing our children be safe, protected, accounted for? Are you a role model? Who is preparing for all types of emergencies? Earthquakes, Hurricanes, Fire, Tornados and all other Natural disasters are already "out there" – but, what about terrorist attacks, or, child-of-guns that need HELP? Why haven't we, teamed up as adult parental figures/mentors and/or established an ADVISORY BOARD within every community to formulate classes including self-defense, gun control and building states' capacity to prevent and combat these issues? Knowledge is power... a power that is used for the good of Humanity. Have the schools enlisted in a community emergency plan-in-place should another emergency emerge? Who is doing what?

"4EVER WATCH™" your children will be a slogan for a philanthropic fundraiser in all communities – this must be a joint community effort. A team of parents need to vie together forming a "safety, observant, defense team" where ALL parents join to watch every child go noticed!

"YOU CAN RUN, BUT YOU CAN'T HIDE"

Addictions come in many forms – behaviors that are habitual to pass the time, avoid taking responsibility, hijack our brain, all forms of avoidance. Whether it's binge-watching, social media, virtual reality VR, porn, gambling, smoking, sex, and whatever we think to invest time for escapism. Addiction is an invisible crutch that mankind leans on in time of need to escape the reality of themselves. Avoidance of self. Avoiding the external mirrors that are looking back with Fear. Fearing to see yourself in others that leads to various forms of escapism – hiding out. "You can run but you can't hide…" as karmic justice prevails and the need to 'face-off' the Ego will inevitably show itself.

We all live in a dysfunctional family to learn and to invoke a new awareness, a new perspective, a new outlook in our lives…see this for whatever it is and move toward a direction that is needed for each and every one of you in this very moment, the present. "Life is a present you don't give back…" ™. To err is to follow the crowd, social media platforms, outside influences and/or beliefs of others only to not seek your own counsel. Who knows better than us? Our Heavenly Father, Blessed Mother and the Holy Spirit where, in our dire plea, fall down on our knees… in prayer. The need to rise up through a journey-of-self cannot be found in the outer world of desires, power of one's desires, a stage full of power-hungry moguls. No one can place their will upon yours or yours upon theirs… these are the powers that say, "if you can't beat them, join them" mentality of the weak. Come to later find out… whether years, decades, and/or even lifetimes over, circumstances are very familiar when wearing different masks. These are your teachers, you must first want to learn – then, allow the rest to unfold. The statistics of those who are addicted to some form of substance, or another is at the highest percentage it's ever been; because, when one addiction is dropped, another begins. Another cyclical trapping of…. and for those who don't see, look closely in the mirror at your own behavior, no need to verbalize what you see, just seek. We seek to find a "way out" of the deepest cores of the unknown and to rise up in light of not needing to seek – for one is found.

Within every parent comes an internal roadmap of how to create a solid foundation for our children, however, while these are innately given within each and every human being, there is also the ego that wants to dictate your every move. During this timeframe, we come to host a slew of masks/faces which represent the examples of lessons which one needs to learn from. If these lessons haven't been learned they will repeat in a cyclical cycle of torturous institutions by which they have been received. Once the innate learning sets firmly on one's foundation, this breeds newfound learning that does not follow the norm. We cannot determine to follow anyone or any other established learning tool(s) – not until we have learned them for ourselves. Even when we've been privy to behaviors that are distinguished there are other factors that fall into outer circumstances – some out of our control and others, not. The circumstances that we cannot control are trying to tame the beast of burdens as many, independent of the self, become the controlling nature from others' egoic perceptions. This equates to our children who could have been raised in a very stable, independent state as the egoic masks of others sink into those who are weak enough, lost souls who tend to believe in the societal narrative of that which breeds the beast. The beast-of-burden is within those who have claimed their soul path to others' inferior dark side. "You can run but you can't hide" is the analogy of what happens to those who have all good intent but are lost in the shuffle of external power that energetically become the lowest of energy vampires to strike. To stay on point is to stop listening, following and worshiping all "external programming". This goes for our computers, TV programming, social media interference and the has-beens of the past

Century who have been "exposed" for their crimes of passion. Those not of and/or excluding the sexual predators, the missing children/persons, and the outlaws that have not yet been charged. They can run…. but they will fail at the sight of their own reflection.

What was once a sigh of relief knowing your job as a parent took on a new beginning for the future of your child/children has now been acts of crime, injustices, pedophiles, mass murders, absentee of one or both parent(s), rapists and a slew of subordinate souls who hold a very dark energy that their soul cannot sustain the body. These souls are known on the Earth plane as damaged goods and are a far-cry from where their light has even gone. To admit how our ego compromises us into falling from grace requires a need to reposition ourselves on every level of the sacred vow spoken prior to arriving on Earth. The fact remains that once a soul of light becomes a dark force to be reckoned with, Mother Earth is allowed to take Her course of action that is by far the only way forward. The saying, "you can fool Mother Nature some of the time" is negligence to humankind. We are attempting to remain untarnished souls that will move from one paradigm to the highest level of human consciousness based upon what actions have been dealt with in this lifetime. Whereas before we've taken on the old traditions, where going to the house of the Lord in confession was enough. No longer can we fool with the ONE who hath given to us a place in this world untarnished – and finding a place in this life to be of service. "In God We Trust" holds tremendous value on the Earth plane – as it is a pertinent attendant of one's soul contract. The established souls who have entered into this world living by the sacred Laws of the Universe and upholding a sensibility of knowing a higher purpose in this lifetime, have all been diligently displaying self-discipline in order to break the boundaries, barriers of false illusions.

Those who remain constant, true and loyal to themselves will find there is no other way upon which to enter the whole of the heart; and, remain loyal to themselves. Those who come into this world with the intention to uphold that same preface fall beyond the sacred guides of spirit will only endure their own freedom once they've ascended. Once all of Humanity has taken their own way into what is known as THE WAY of Spirit ...then, the world will be seen as what it was originally built for – *FREEDOM*.

"Live and Let Live" or "Live and Let Die" follows the similar thread for our presence in a life lived of willful intent to live and the knowing we die. There is NO Death of the Soul, only a Celebration of Life for the living…

VICES HAVE PRICES

Whatever vices you're attempting to either shake off to repair your health and welfare just know that it is NOT easy as so much of what's worthy comes from our will. The will-to-live sounds easier than it is for remembering our authentic selves. By searching high-and-low … from our DNA, our genetics, our life experiences, our bloodline, the threads that bind, atoms, neurons and every prospect that Science mathematically was constructed into our Universe; all this and so much more is worthy of a life fulfilled. Recounting steps that have led us to this place convinces our indigenous ancestors to stake-their-claim to Freedom while witnessing their own ascend. No one could prepare us for what's to come, yet where we've been is only the beginning. Not many can swing the pendulum of Fate…only we can - each and every one of us has the capacity and innate gifts to rise up to the occasion. The concept of life is very much like a teeter-totter … a roller-coaster of a lifetime that contains yin/yang for balance. Every polarity in this world can be mastered through the Revelation of balance, moderation… too much of a good thing lends itself to become tethered souls. A soul untethered finds itself in the present company of all the miraculous gifts of Life. All of Life is a stage…

CHILD'S BEHAVIORS OF GROWTH OR STAGNANCY

Every child behaves in ways that are either learned from their parents or whoever raised them that laid the groundwork; and from their friends, other parents, siblings and a host of whomever is in their lives to show them the way forward. The leader of the pack consists of being in control of certain goals, plans and/or reassurances that need strategic decision making. Those who are what you might consider "control freaks" or "perfectionists" fall under this category. They live to honor their integrity, true grit and whatever gives them a feeling of prideful accomplishment. On the other hand, those who hold so much control in their lives, do have a tendency to do so because they either had none growing up or their parents relied on them heavily…. Some of these leaders have grown up to be prodigies, accomplished CEO's, executives and anything that falls under the guise of "professional". These leaders can also be seen as the first born or the last-born child because of the responsibility that they were given in the family. To those who've "made it" in life, you've sought out all your goals, some retired, yet a commendable honor indeed. To say that all of those who "made it" in the world of economic change is not the only thing that makes them a leader. They've worked hard to where they've gotten and sacrificed much of their lives to say they've made it. To say anything negative about these head leaders would be to cancel out all of their hard work. On the other hand, there are those executives, owners, etc., who have not necessarily worked hard for their title and have misused the system to their own benefit…these so-called leaders have stolen from Peter to pay Paul. Some of these leaders used others to get ahead, hanging on their coat-tails to climb the ladder…a clear misrepresentation of title. Those who are infamously rich and famous also might fall under this category as misusing their power…yet, that is NOT all. We are getting to know more of those elite famous people who are not on the up-and-up – with all that power who are corrupt and being exposed. Those who are being exposed in this current time and/or are no longer on the Earth plane will be indefinite dust-to-dust, there is NO coming back from abusing children in any way, shape and/or form.

CHILDHOOD STRUGGLES AS ADULTS

Many of us have felt the struggle of NOT feeling Loved enough… Does this sound like your story? Is it difficult to comprehend and/or pin-point that 'feeling' of emptiness, because many have not yet attained? Children who grew up feeling unloved, unwanted, abandoned, etc., continue to struggle well into adulthood, is the majority.

There are 5 indications of how this shows up in our lives:

1. Constant unworthy feeling

2. A false-sense of self transforms

3. Struggle to let anyone in

4. Thinking you're the Victim

5. Passiveness

All of these "feelings" show up as we attempt to conquer Love in whatever way possible. When we grow up feeling unimportant, not of value from our parents/loved ones the imprint of shame arises. Sometimes, we must lose ourselves and/or become chameleons to justify not fitting in, becoming a new identity, remaining passive and wanting to seek acceptance/approval. We lose touch with who we are, we distance ourselves and others (mimicking parents) we bury our emotions living with anger and fear of dropping our masks. Ego masks accumulate over the course of years to appease, to prove, to be another – adding layers to our persona. Every layer of the onion is peeled down to the core of all those egoic masks to find our authenticity. Many of us have undergone extensive childhood/adulthood emotional therapy to assist in a reconnect of who we are. Our view of who we are and the ability to empower or disempower us is very much like a teeter/totter that has its highs and lows – instinctually becoming repetitively habitual. In all areas of our lives, we sense we might be on the hamster wheel of the cyclical kind … unable to get off. Either we lose control of the terrain or get a handle on it… The power is in the fact that we can choose to get to the root, the core; it's a choice to flip-the-switch and empower our lives as warriors.

FROM DARKNESS TILL DAWN

What in essence are humans avoiding by going deep within to find oneself? Is the darkness of your shadow still making you scared, similar to when you were growing up? There was always one room, the basement, the attic where spooky ghosts, noises, figures, smells and a dusty membrane of visions that played on our senses. Our Shadow has been following us since we got here and is not going away anytime soon. Who is your dark shadow? Do you only have one or are there a few? Is the shadow a figment of our imagination or is it there to remind you to behave? Do you sleep with a nightlight, or do you sleep in absolute darkness? These are just a few questions to get us started on a very important topic of the EGO. What is lurking in the darkness that makes you feel unsettled ... or, does it? If it's not the darkness, then what is it? Who first introduced you to being afraid of the dark? Do you remember? Do you know that in order for your body to get good sleep, a dark room is crucial; and, did you know that as soon as the sun rises, your body lifts itself up from the darkness into the light that both are gaining crucial energetic healing? Our energy works in tandem healing in night and day – which is why we need our rest, and we need our energy for working out. During REM sleep, our cells are healing, rejuvenating, releasing and re-visiting the day; in the morning, all our energy has been re-freshed, well-rested, ready for a blessed day of what's to come. In the shadows of the night, do you feel safe? Do you feel safe in the daylight? Our essence becomes a place of safety, protection and amidst the chaos, a calming fragrance in becoming ourselves. How one sees you... within without/inside out is exactly what you're bringing to those who have either the same ideals or with hopes to gain wisdom, knowledge of those ideals throughout life experience. We've come to know that without the use of your intuition, intention or a version of those combined we will not be of any good use to others – *be transparent*.

Within many life cycles or even one life cycle, a human can attain enlightenment once he/she is faced with their own darkness. These are strings of past-life darkness in the womb while some are forgotten when entering the Earth plane. An infant has deep threads to Heaven up to 8-10 years of age and after a certain age, the infant is being molded 'not' unto itself... Every child is born in their innocence until that has been taken away - and, ultimately, brought back. Some other children are old souls who continue to become mediums, psychics, and readers to assist in the guiding light. This is the Circle of Life. Though each child is different, the fact that bodes true is that a child will always recall earlier teachings using that as their initiation unto the world as their foundation. An infant has been given various likes/dislikes through the energy of their surroundings that may or may not yet provide a strong foundation; although it is their introduction to life. Given that their foundation has been created for them, in Divine timing, it is very possible that the child will find its own way. On the other hand, if that is not the case, most will end up reassessing their direction to the degree that is intended for them. Therefore, we all are children of God's Love, beginning and end invoking a lifelong journey of giving, showing, sharing, caring, compassionately feeling all the layers of Love. As it is so, so it IS.

The life we've been granted is one of "curiosity" and the innocence from childhood of our life experiences on any given path. You are to decipher where you shall become into/unto yourself without listening to others. You shall look at yourself for choosing what way – this one or that one, a free- will choice. Let no one make up your mind where the ego likes to entertain lower vibrational frequencies to satisfy its Earthly pleasures of hunger for power, sex, drugs and rock~n~roll... Do not listen to any others who come to play in fleeing to plead... assert your own values of what you innately KNOW as good or evil. What you once have been taught is not all bad,

231

but you must observe what others are doing and/or saying… that computes with "Do unto others as you would have done unto yourself?" Do not take advantage of who, what, or when you are under duress to formulate others' decisions/choices that do not make you feel your rightful self. Your rightful self sees, hears and watches those who make smart choices by learning for themselves. There are many adults who have entered the Earth plane with karmic debt that must be paid off – whether or not you can comprehend their issues, please be patient with your love to unfold as many must stay within their own realm of thought to forgive. Then there are many of you who have been strictly needing the use of external addictions; drugs, medical or otherwise, to taper off, control, or somewhat attempt at feeling "normal". However, should you desire to hold off and enter a meditative state of ALL natural types of medicinal ways of being, choose whatever feels right, not necessarily what you've been told to inhale. There are good medicines and then there are not-so-good medicines that have much too intensified complications, hence, side-effects that the body cannot withstand. Our emotions/feelings have been given to each one of us to learn how to 'read' what is going on within; and to handle/take care of the physical body. There are many programs that explain how and/or what to choose for your own self, so, choose wisely. The percentage of teenagers taking medications prescribed by their doctors are not all bad, just be mindful if these drugs are being given to enhance or continue to be your life-support. It's not enough that pharmaceuticals are making so much off of your insurance companies. This is when the meds you're taking are a crutch.

NOTE: I am NOT a medical professional to prescribe any enhanced drugs or talk therefore or specific drugs I am unaware of… however, I AM a Licensed Biofeedback Practitioner who has undergone several attempts at stress relief through the assistance of the mind, body and soul.

Enlisting in either a medical professional/doctor or a holistic practitioner IS of your own accord.

There are exorbitant issues pertaining to children who feel their fame-to-claim is wanting to have it all – a "more-for-me" mentality while other kids learn how to share. Those children who have been given the tools to utilize a mentality that constitutes sharing, giving and learning early on how to become generous to others… starts in the early years. Parents tend to envision wanting the very best for a child who might not have been taught that sharing is caring. Whatever the child was taught from their parents, or, whomever raised them is called, learned behavior. All children are given the tools at an early age…and, later can choose their own way. There is a significant reason why some children want it all and choose not to share while others have been taught good intent to share. It all starts out with sharing toys that may or may not be a despondent reason, whether they know why or not that sharing teaches compassion for others. Were you taught compassion? HELP is defined as to guide a child to go within the self by examining/witnessing one's own actions - peeling back the layers of the onion. Why? Because the onion is a release of our emotional baggage that breeds tears of sadness. Emotional healing comes to find us when we are ready, willing and able to finally surrender into an emotional cry of joy. However, most of what has been taught by society's norm is an external cry for HELP in desiring outer poisons of the physical body that comes from emotional blame leading to an infamous misuse of power. This misuse of power is taught at the onset of new life where society has been programming the innocence of children being stripped away without knowing. Instead of HELPING, it is 'hell-ping' children to fling into a Hell-ish mindset of wanting and desiring all that glitters... only to find out "all that glitters is NOT gold". The dangling carats-of-fame surmounts the climb to Mount Sinai until every child realizes the errs of their own way is The Way. Until then...the Earth plane will continue to be of a lower-dimensional 3D darkness under an egoistic societal influence. Children of the Earth have become so fearful of death and dying that they continue to be blinded to seeing that the external poisons they are ingesting are actually killing them. These influences are sex, drugs etc. – masked as the Ego. Children's attraction to instant gratification is being blinded by the dark shadows infiltrated by a dark society that has been taken over. Why can't children "see" beyond societal influences? Because of what society and what others think? Or.... is it because it's easier to neglect a child's need for HELP by not addressing the elephant in the room? Or, are kids crying for HELP medicating in order to preserve their own sanity? This has been up for debate since the beginning of time – defining one parental role as "HELP" is another thread that places another parent into a different category of "HINDER". Our generations of newly developed children are not being given the attention they deserve. Children of parents who have NOT been dealing... have the threat of addictive behaviors that have hindered one's evolutional growth and/or perhaps has jumped generations. No matter what people think is happening no one knows another's pain unless you too have walked in their shoes. We've been enlightened to every facet of a life where the choice to walk bravely into the lion's den could mean saving yourself; or, escaping yourself only to go down the rabbit-hole further. The middle ground is how and what you do with this energy of life's circumstances. Does this make sense? How do you deal with those who have fallen lost in their lot in life, unable to see? "No one understands me…" is a cry for HELP – I wish someone would listen to what is actually being said. "Can you hear me?" stems from not having parents who are attentive…and, perhaps their parents didn't listen to them in their childhood. "Mom, Mom, Hello?" Some Moms are too engrossed in social media, what's so-and-so doing, who's liking their posts, aggressively posting on Tik-Tok, what is ticking, who's doing what with whom, setting up shop in a world of illusion while kids are begging, screaming-in fact, for attention. How will these kids grow up and what will they grow up thinking that their parents ignored them all their lives? Wouldn't the Ego self-issue a "red-flag warning" to itself that this child needs to become "somebody" instead of nobody? Every child has a valid reason why they feel unworthy, not enough, attention-seeking, news-worthy of how to prepare for the future – when NOW the children/kids are at their most vulnerable. These are the plagues, viruses and dis-eases that stump all children into a corner of confusion, regret, resentment, anger, jealousy, greed etc. Are you listening to your kids? Do you pay attention? Are you on social media ignoring the writings on the wall? How has the majority of Humanity estranged their children? Have you? Are a parent or parents both missing… who is mining the fort? Why are the parents of children medicating themselves? Who is able to take care of a child that is still a child themselves? Why can't we see that Humanity as a whole is crying out for LOVE, attention and, most inevitably, self-discipline. The ways of the world are changing exponentially where the scales of Love are going to override those in Fear. It is through the confines of one's own lifecycle where we shall find our way Home. To climb that uphill climb to Mount Sinai and a newfound discipline for Humanity to get real. Not the discipline of a third-world kind, but the traditional types of parenting that have served their purpose. Many children's cry for HELP comes from what has been taught through the external forces of the shadow - and is done for them to realize their own demise. Every child on the Earth plane, at some point within a life cycle, will undergo hitting rock bottom, at least once, only to climb out of the darkness. What occurs within the (-) dash of one's life becomes a light unto itself. Clearing out the darkness of one's life calls for the collective energy force of all those who have walked upon this Earth and those yet to do so. The walk of fame is misconstrued as an energetic force of where the ego resides because a child's walk of fame cannot be one's beast of burden; but is a much-required choice of external factors to be dismantled. An egoic dismantle is much harder than an Olympic beam double-double dismount for what it means to "nail it" is in the likes of when Jesus was nailed to the cross. The suffering of one's physical body merges with the child's Heritage of suffering which formulates deep-rooted trauma, scarring that is inevitable within the crevasse of all emotional turmoil. Children's scars are deeply rooted much like the Tree of Life and tends to take on a life all its own. We are thrown out unto this world of darkness only to find our own lighted path to salvation. In the meantime, too many of our children are undergoing traumatic suffering and in the search for salvation grasping external poisons of toxicity to numb their pain. What frequency of pain meds are you giving to yourself? What frequency is enough for your kids to uphold a lifestyle of "numbing pain?" which falls 'under' ground – of the underground world of pain. **Please watch your children!!!** What are the "red flags"? Why has it become redundant to ask, "who is mining the fort?" Is it because society from all forts… inside other forts…down to the ground level are pulling the strings? This is by no means written to scare or shall we say, "put the fear of God" into your realm of understanding; but, at this point in time on planet Earth, herein lies your own sacrificial lamb of life. Does this make you angry? If not, why not? A crude, cruel, cunning society has the cruelest of intentions for our children…

Can "you" see what "you are" or, don't you seek what you've been given?

"Ring Around The Rosie" The dark, cynical side of Mother Goose's nursery rhymes has been telling desperate stories about world calamities, wars, plagues and so much of what was instilled into the innocent minds of our children. "Ring Around The Rosie" is about the bubonic plague posing as a "rash" that appeared on the skin of those infected; and "ashes to ashes we all fall down" depicted as funeral pyres that burned bodies of the deceased. As we too had the 2020 year of Covid-19, and many threats of plagues are returning. As history does repeat "itself" one must now be questioning who is behind the curtain? Those who believed in "the Wizard" come to find out that their truth comes from all these stories … capturing the walk of darkness into their entitled power of light force.

Take stock of your own beliefs and become a Humanity which, instead of being dictated by 'dark' nursery rhymes, let's begin to review how to erase what has been pre-programmed. The time is now to, "Be the change" knowing we are stronger together. The re-enactment within every life cycle bears a different energetic path on one's journey. To be a witness in one lifetime is the beginning to an ending…as our first breath creates the start of a new life that proceeds to the end-of-a-physical life. Upon Love's first breath, every child of God is called to remember its soul's purpose into atoning for one's sins - here and in our Heritage - to find oneself. Jesus' children are all children of God's LOVE. We are made in His likeness within the energetic force of man's ability to seek realization. Earth is where all energetic uses of karmic justice find itself-reinventing-itself. Too many humans are unfamiliar with the reasons for making the journey, yet it is revealed to all of God's children, in Divine timing. Every child will become the energy of Love in His likeness…

CHILD PROGRAMMING

Every child who has entered the Earth plane is not exempt from some form of programing. Either through their ancestral roots, parental figures, step-figures, teachers, hospitals, ministers, priests, television "programing", social media, games, and so much more at such early stages of one's life that it's….no wonder! It's no wonder those children who ask questions and are curious who want to fortify an innocence within them have been innately given their spiritual purpose. Herein "lies" the focal point of contention with our society. Generally speaking, we grow up with such love for a life of eternity through the inner treasures found and used for the highest good of mankind. However, in the process of Creation, a fluke of Nature happened where such people as Adam & Eve came into being hoisting a fear-based mentality through Eve biting into the apple/Apple. The rest could serve as a learning curve… for us all to seek our own innate feelings of the heart instead of "buying into" a 3Dimensional world of a prime value. The value of the dollar becomes the root of all evil, yet, it has been forged, marketed, and published as such since the beginning of time. Our society has become the absolute root of a global fear-based mentality that uses egoic desires/cravings of external desires. Even those who deem through 'materialistic things' that don't matter – what someone tends to want, and desire has gotten mankind very confused, fearful of everything, doubtful, physically drawn and sick to our stomachs proving less worthy of the self that was originally created by Love. Make this your motto instead, "living a fruitful life is to live a life of simplicity…" What has been lost is now attempting to be found and humans are now aware that this life is illusionary and, in order to continue to thrive, a mindset of gratitude is key. We're now knee-deep in that new treasure trove of thought by which we must command by drawing attention to what really matters; and not the matter which comes with the frugal attempts at killing off mankind and acquiring stuff. When we are FREE from wanting and desiring MORE, we have set ourselves FREE to actually see. To see is the place of becoming aware of all fears that breeds on itself, as fear. Human beings are so fearful that so many now are not ever wanting to get out of their home, to travel, to live. What kind of nonsense are the massive attempts to coerce an entire population? The bubonic plague killed, cancer killed and continues to do so… All human suffering, dis-ease, has been co-conspired by and through living in FEAR. We're all on the same exact path on this Earth, to live and let live… except for those instilling a discipline of FEAR OF GOD in you. We now have been given the gift of social-media platforms initiated by the evil ones in order to escape reality; but, did not seem to see the goodness of truth that has spread like wildfire throughout mankind. Yes, the truth that sets one free to live a full-life unencumbered by outside influences. It's not like we do not have some ways to go on our God-given path, but, all-in-all many have become very astute to the workings of evil in our society. What's lurking will be stopped! *TRUST* and *FAITH*

SPEAK-OUT FOR THE CHILDREN

Those who have seen themselves in their own children, can attest to the greatest findings of unconditional love that one could ever experience. Once these findings are actually founded a series of other inquiries takes place within a child's life. The series that one undergoes isn't familiar to all those who are perhaps feeling a little different, yet, a few will feel 'Deja vu' moments. The ways in which a child has been raised shows you their inability to overcome and/or an ability to surrender no matter what the circumstances. The world has undergone a lot of Earthly shifts by Herself and now that so many of our children are awakening its shedding light on our planet's evolution. The way to enlightenment is THE WAY inward. "Show them the beauty they possess inside, give them a sense of pride to make it easier... let the children's laughter remind us how we used to be". "*We Are The World*"

OBSERVERS/WITNESS

Another way that children stave off on their own is to stay in their own lane; and, those who witness others by silently observing without judgment are also true leaders of another kind. These children have been the watchful eye, a true detector of who is doing what with whom...and keeping silent. It's not that they don't want to start trouble; it's just that these are the soon-to-be-leaders of tomorrow's generation of "knowing" karma is paid. Not a slight-of-hand but a Freedom to stay in their own lane and allow the Universe to handle it. These kids were taught well because it is not for humans to make others hurt, nor is it for God to do the same; and, these children are aware of how the Laws of the Universe work. They've studied, they've witnessed much trauma, tragedy and yet they remain neutral...to the cause. These kids are aware, much to their dismay, that whomever criticizes comes back 100%-fold in their own lives. These are the wise ones who have had to learn the hard way, but they've done their work, no doubt. This inner knowing, wisdom attained does not come with a number, an age, per say... it is a breed unto itself. There is so much tragedy in the world today that opinions and unkind acts from others lay the foundation of darkness to those who cannot help themselves. We are all aware that kindness matters but with the imbalance of the world in flux, many are teeter-tottering on the fence, similar to a toddler. Triggers come in all shapes and sizes ... some to our very surprise while others not so much. The triggers of those who remain sufficiently angry, broken, hurt, are the ones who like to show their egoic selves by blasting others...as small violent rages or as bigger rages – all pain. The observers who are silently witnessing others are guiding many with hopes for a brighter future. Be a "silent witness" and observe how your life unfolds, much like a lotus flower.

PARENTIFICATION

What child is this.... A mere child who is subtly expected to take on adult responsibilities and behaviors in the family dynamic before their time. A parentified daughter believes her role to be the fixer of everything. She is sought after by her parents, siblings to manage the household; be it emotional and/or practical support. This child hides depression, guilt, stress, anxiety, etc., and is riddled with the absorption of energy she inhales thereof others' problems. She is everyone's "go-to" for advice, wanting to please and not being able to say, no. Highly self-reliant, although exposed to much trauma of parents' marital problems, walking on eggshells and is able to hide behind the fantasy of family unity as a perfect TV family. This daughter had to take on the obligation(s) of raising her younger siblings and became the parental figure where she is unable to cut the ties that bind. She exudes deep emotional neglect because no one mirrored her reality back to her...therefore, she is confused about her sense of self. Growing up… attempting to survive in a dysfunctional environment lends deep wounding of red-flags but overlooking them, wanting to be loved. Her adult life unfolds with the same threads of patterns, abandonment issues with intense feelings of neglect - as she attempts to sew those wounds by accepting little in return. This child has repressed anger without letting on how deep her sadness is felt. Her anger is re-routed to restrictions, punishing herself, and being her own worthy critic. However, on the exterior this child is the 'rock' of the family. This child becomes everyone's caretaker while within her internal compass is a screaming, freezing child saying, "Get out!"

A parentified son is filled with anger due to emotional neglect. It shows up as trigger-snapping at his partner and/or children. Those around him walk on eggshells in a similar fashion as the parentified daughter, however, he makes his hate known by his reactions. No filter regulating emotional stability because parent(s) are not attuned to this behavior. Whenever emotions are shown he is unable to feel – as they are foreign to him. Instead, drive straight into defensive mode to find safety. He's the 'little man' of the family and although felt the weight of his mother's stress/struggle, he feels responsible; as a result, stopped showing any fear and/or sadness. Absent father continues to be the threaded thorn of emotional unavailability. This child has been in survival mode for so long that he continues to push people away who love him. He tends to isolate himself – the inner boy syndrome. Later in life, he begins to question why he feels empty, why he feels like a failure because he was unable to please anyone – much like his Heritage of both parent(s). He finds his only value being a workaholic to cope with his stress and/or anxiety – continues to burn-out; but, ignores the signs of stillness. Extreme work with little-to-no play makes this child guilty when or if he could relax. The dichotomy of his pain is that he tends to use women to fill the void, only on a superficial level – seeking attention to cope with such insecurities. He is an unfaithful child in relationships for fear of being overwhelmed with the needs of a long-term partner. Similar to the daughter, the son also feels the role of taking care of every member of his family...because no one taught him that boundaries are healthy.

Riddled with guilt – with or without justification of reason comes from emotionally immature parenting. Those parents haven't actually learned to take care of themselves; so, they have a subconscious desire that their children meet their needs. Chronic guilt comes from being given responsibility... conditioned to have it. They might have become sympathetic for their parent(s) and might have even become their parental sound-board. Almost a peer-to-adulting weighing the heavy burden of taking on the responsibility of their parent's life. Self-discovery is setting healthy healing boundaries without the emotional involvement they were raised in.

RESPONSIBILITIES

There are some situations where a parent of addiction is more prone to role-reversal which takes place and the child becomes a parent. However, when this happens, these children who take on grave responsibilities as a parent feel resentful in doing so. We, as parents, need to seek out HELP from our children, when we are not able; and it is no fault of these children whose calling is to assist tending to parent(s) of addiction. A life of caregivers receives abundant goodness of reciprocity in the same life cycle or another. Karma need not only be a debt that has to be paid... it's not as though we wake up one morning to ask ourselves what karma has been accrued – but, when our lives are flowing smoothly, it is your pay-it-back from Heaven.

The flip-side to this situation of having children take on the responsibility begs the question, "Why is the addicted parent not getting HELP?" Have they been in rehab and relapsed? And, if so, what happened? Is rehab the answer? What is the percentage of success with those centers? Have you been? Do you know of someone who is suffering through their own addictions? How can a child be chosen and/or asked to see a parent lying on the floor, drunk? Usually, it is the teenager… or, a partner in crime. What is the solution? Is there a solution? The question is, "What in their parent's life drove them to addiction?" Is it in their DNA, genetic makeup? Is there a solution or do addicts say, "It's in my genes and I can't do anything about it…" A denial, or a flat-out surrender to life of a different kind…this surrender is a giving up on oneself. If no one cares in the addict's family then how can an addict care? Is the family in denial? Are they too addicted? Do we want to HELP anyone who may be going through withdrawals? Do we know how to handle it? So many questions and so many addicts continue to be addicted; or, have gone to rehab and relapsed; or, didn't need to go to rehab but relapsed; or, have no intention of going to rehab and still want to be addicts; or, refuse to succumb to their addictions; only God knows… We, as outsiders, cannot HELP anyone with anything…, unless "the addict" is ready to get HELP for themselves. Sometimes it works and other times it doesn't work. No matter what happens – know that children watch, they observe and are learning through your example. What happens when the parent(s) have no addictive behaviors but the child does? There is an addictive thread in the ancestral lineage that seeks someone to sever. All addictions are threads looking to free themselves once and for all! The severing allows the entire lineage to free themselves of that lesson; and perhaps, the final lesson for some. No matter what, lessons affect entire families … throughout History in time.

How deep is your love?

Within every parent/child relationship, we need to remember that it is within the responsibility of all disciplines to uphold the standards of raising children. Whenever one has not been raised within a structure of discipline all Hell breaks loose! Why should our children suffer….

For God so loved the world that He gave His only Begotten Son, "to have and to hold until death do us part…" just a few examples of how One's word has been written NOT to be interpreted. When we learn to accept the good with the bad…we come to accept.

MASS CONFUSION

What's happening to the generations of children is mass confusion of who is in charge? As we continue to move through life, kids are not following in any parental footsteps. However, we live in a world where society has handed the rights to our children from generations past – questioning, "Who is in charge?" Not all children feel this way, yet the new wave of being raised is choosing to go it alone. Prior generations have felt this nudge too, but not so much as it has unfolded in today's world. After the tragedies of 9/11 and Covid-19 a plethora of people have chosen to be on their own. The days of community have become slighted with social media replacing community. Usually, tragedies bring people together as a community;

but, a sense of isolation happened instead. An elevation of Fear resulted in the hearts of many – anger, judgements, and criticism have led people into hermit mode. Many people are 'staying home, staying in their own lane' a stalemate – while others have gone off the grid. It's not that this did not happen way back when… it wasn't as apparent to the public. There is a distinct remedy for this mass confusion – which is for mankind to seek a sense of discernment. For the remainder of a society who continues to consider what is going on "out there" is deciding to "turn a blind eye" – exactly where the pivotal point of contention exists. Polar opposite views of ignorance and turning a blind eye has caused the darkness to enter into the vast minds of the weak. This is exactly why there is a new crisis of mind-control, mental illness, brain dysfunctioning of the exorbitant kind. Humanity is under attack from the remnants of the mind of one's EGO playing a red violin of evil stringing them into the lion's den of mass corruption. Here's where the infamous AI (Artificial Intelligence) robotics will enter offering up detailed statistics, information and much more…even artistic replicas. AI is missing the essential values of Humanity on every level of deep emotional beings. Similar to a scene taken from "The Wizard of Oz" where the Scarecrow gave up his informant brain and handed it to The Tinman saying, "NO HEART!?" Exactly. A devious genius has turned the table on Humanity… or, so they "think…." EGO's mind is devious… but, *what is of pure Heart is ALL LOVE* – and, that my dear, is when Dorothy finally realized "she's always had the power!!!"

Will the mass confusion of "artificial intelligence" take a backseat so that the "emotional intelligence" of Humanity can continue to soar? No matter what happens, The Tin Man received a plastic heart; The Scarecrow got bewitched with water onto his brainyon-fire figuring out a plan to escape which overcame his own Fear; and The Cowardly Lion got crowned to lead them into the Lion's Den of hypocrisy. The hypocrisy is given to those with no brain, no heart, no courage to face their fears from the outside in. "Ohhhhhh, what a world, " says The Witch. "Surrender!" What needed to be surrendered? Was it the misuse of power of the Ego, or, knowing you had the power all along? The irony is… the witch feared you'd switch – from Fear to Love.

CHILDHOOD TRAUMAS

Core traits of childhood trauma are:

1. Hyper-vigilance where the physical body feels an on-edge feeling of threatened mode. Overwhelming stress by every noise and with every footstep, flooding our body with cortisol sets the tone of physical or verbal abuse in the family dynamic. Some of this trauma stems from growing up around adults who go into spirals of rage.

2. Avoidance is a natural response to the chronic nervous system, wanting to flee. The effects of shame – why we push people away, why do we make others feel bad and/or withdraw from affection.

Cyclical cycles of hormonal imbalances, nutritional imbalances and infections can create inflammation of the body which is familiar as a heightened threat.

Childhood trauma is a mind-set that cannot be present.

Behaviors of bullying, criticism, manipulation, distrust, and all other traumas are learned behaviors while being raised are on the rise… these learned behaviors emit negative energy to others are our thorns of contention. The traumas identified and their effect(s) are as follows:

Abandonment: the thought of being a child of abandonment lends itself to unhappiness of the most serious kind; as one moves through relationships, jobs and/or geographical locations as if they were changing their socks. These are mostly from children who felt they were not wanted, adopted, fostered, inferior and an overall feeling, misfits. The children of abandonment came down to the Earth plane to resolve these differences once and for all – yet, undeniably so, one must be able to understand, accept and allow the truth from which they are rooted. The abandonment wound is common for those who grew up in emotionally unavailable homes.

Self-soothing techniques HELP to calm yourself when there is too much stress. Looking at the bigger picture and understanding that taking up space doesn't lend itself to being rejected. Learning techniques such as; walking, journaling, breathwork, talking to a concerned friend etc.

One does not acquire these from before they return Home, these are all traumas from our childhood family tree. Beliefs in children who are born with these so-called traumas, as unsettling as they are, show our blueprints of past-trauma breakages in one's lineage. For us to falter the past is not what is required in figuring out what and/or how to manage one's lineage of what is written, called, the thread. We cannot expect Humanity to go out of their way and attempt to solve these types of issues, however, a child of abandonment has been given

their freedom. This is the "flip-side of what we are all here to do …
not masking our individual traumas, but to set the record straight and
assign a semblance of responsibility. A mother who has abandoned
their child/children by giving them up for adoption breeds the thread
for another mother, who is able to provide a better life. We're not
attempting or able to take away the blood parent's lineage …but, to be
able to give our children the very best for their highest good.

Betrayal: the inability to trust has been Humanity's disadvantage
for eons. Betrayal takes on a series of reservoirs which means this
distrust carries polluted waters that are very difficult to promote
healing in a very deep ocean. The one who distrusts has learned that
for those who did whatever was done in a non-ethical way, the
playbook is the mirror reflection that comes back to bite tenfold. This
karma (good or bad) is given effortlessly as aligning with the energetic
force of Mother Nature. Mother Earth has been given the gift of energy
(giving and receiving) which is one of the Universal Laws of the
Ecosystem – The Law of Cause & Effect. This Law, once broken, has
deep repercussions of what causes humans who have denied people
their truth by lying, disobeying and/or by misappropriating funds or
whatever distrustful acts of disservice one accrues karma. No matter
what one has done that is either unethical, untrustworthy in any way,
there will be great karmic debt to pay. To enter into this field of dreams
where we cannot escape our own selves by betraying others is a hefty
price to pay.

Criticism: When we tend to judge others through criticism,
judgment and walking the path of the devil…fearing what and how
trauma is poised; becomes the real fear. Children who have seen what
they've seen, heard what they come to question - were taught to hold

their tongues. This is how every child listen to their parents' conversations and observes with bated breath. Being forewarned is knowing that this doesn't necessarily happen in a healthy home - yet, the truth is that every child absorbs their external world like a sponge. The real detriment is the child who knows the truth that speaking unkindly of others, in the family tree or of others in general, is of great disservice. This child goes forth only to undertake many more criticisms from family members to their own discouragement. What happens is these children are learning about disrespect on many levels. The other disadvantage is when a child blames everyone else for their pain, they are averting taking responsibility. This is our fall from grace. Who can relate? Criticism and Bullying others are a critical red-flag to those on the receiving end of it being unhealthy. We must learn new methods of teaching our child/children how not to project onto others and to learn trust. When we criticize another, it is as simple as criticizing ourselves – the mirror has two faces. Bullying has risen over the past few decades and that is also another form of borrowed behavior that makes children think it is ok to take a choke-hold-of-control.

Loneliness: To the children who have become the "misfits/rebels" on the planet are not exempt from feeling alone on this Earth but know they are not ever alone. To not be seen or heard is not of any concern to those of us who have already experienced loneliness… yet it is much needed to recharge our energy. There are many others who are not yet privy of either or – and have been hiding their loneliness. To be lonely is very cumbersome as it sees itself in the throes of the blind leading the blind. However, being lonely feeds off those who feel unworthiness and in need of self-acceptance. Self-acceptance is the glue necessary to remain strong while having the compassion of a deer. We need both of these energies working in tandem to help assist those who were once very lonely souls. Loneliness can also be misrepresented as the ego needing to perform a show. How? Because when we get lonely, we often seek attention…whatever way we can get it. Posting selfies, stories etc., all for getting attention, suffering in silence. There is instant gratification in doing so, yet, then you're back to being lonely. (not, alone) Loneliness makes us call back our exes, or, smashing anything they seek for egoic attention and acceptance. There is much regret, remorse, guilt and the like when it comes to how we deal with our inner turmoil and/or trauma. Needing to be accepted, liked, adored, worshiped comes from feeling unloved… Who we meet, reach-out to and/or begin hanging with tells another story, just the same. The cast of characters becomes one's circle of friends as the adage goes, "you are who you hang with." This bodes very true for every person, place and/or thing that we come to encounter in the long process of finding our truest self. In the meantime, there are a vast array of energy vampires to watch out for by how you feel. Energy vampires suck your energy and leave you feeling empty inside… it may feel as though you have been bitten by the graveyard site without a lifeline left. "Only the Lonely" by Ray Orbison as the lyrics go, "Only the lonely, know the way I feel tonight, only the lonely, know this feeling isn't right…" Mind you, your cast of characters also come with their own cast of their egoic selves which bleed on us and others – a true graveyard shift. Whenever we are NOT walking on Holy ground, we are the 'Walking Dead' or 'Dawn of the Dead' interpretations of being fast asleep. To be certain you don't end up either falling first or last into your own grave, or, slipping into a coma is not for me to say. My goal is no-goal, just a protective cover should you need a parachute in a moment's notice.

Rejection: There are those who are so fearful of being rejected that the mere thought of it makes them run away…escapism. This might be no one's fault yet the child has become too fearful because they have had a series of rejections, criticisms and an overbearing family structure. These kids grow up way too fast and/or suffice to say the parents have also been privy to the same... To be rejected is a blessing in disguise. Why is that? Those who are rejected are strengthened to be ready for anything. And, the ones doing the rejecting find themselves in a void of reality. A void of Fear is what we call being in the mirror of one hundred faces and being stricken by every broken vessel. "The devils in the details" also comes in the way of requiring one to see themselves as they are fragments of broken pieces. Picking up the pieces of one's heart after sheer rejection over and over and over again becomes a very painful broken glass … to which pieces have left a trail of broken hearts. Rejection of the heartfelt is not the only type of rejection and yet the remains of the day still lurking under the surface of different pieces that have been shattered; and no one left to save. The reflection in the mirror becomes vague, veiled, foggy and a cast of shadows endure oneself. Shadows are what many have become very used to… being used becomes the norm. Some survive while others go around and around to attempt new traumatic adventures…we call these people, "thrill seekers". Who gets a thrill from dishing out a thousand failures or more attempts to hurt others who don't want to learn about themselves. It's about projecting onto others instead of seeing the reflection … a dimmed light. At opportune moments like these … there is light. That light cannot be seen unless someone is finally able to set the appropriate boundaries to forgo those who stand in their way – and, follow the light of their own truth!

Guilt: What sense of guilt do you hold of yourself or shamefully of others? Have you seen it? Guilty pleasures, "guilty as charged" "blamed to shame" and having to stop and smell the roses need not get cut by the thorns? Isn't it better to learn by the thorns that cut us into a bleeding out, a cut above? To feel guilty places holding the pressure of the cut down so there is a moment of relief. Guilt and shame are manipulative tactics of the trauma that stems from…a dysfunctional family to learn from. When this happens, much cannot be done to those who are not willing to see. There are others who have been attempting to forego their guilt naturally, but to no avail. It is a very long process for the nature of the beast tends to sway back and forth. The beast is, "the devil is in the details" riddled with so much guilt that the only way to uphold that feeling of loneliness is to continue to control the terrain. How much can one take… if not for the mere pleasure of another's feelings of unworthiness. The set of circumstances vary for each person's life experiences; however, the common denominator is the absence of trust. "We're all "guilty" of this and that … and so much more of a series of confessions could not erase this impenetrable guilt or being shamed for which to blame.

There are so many helpless children who have no one to turn to because of a guilt-ridden parent who didn't know better at the time. A control freak who defies the rules when the chips are down…they own their own malice to their very last breath. To say this hasn't happened to so many past generations would be giving into a shadow of time where no one knows themselves. The truth defies the real means of what real love in a family means…between Mother, Father and child. Listen and learn from such controlling behavior with your children for the repercussions are far greater than the actual pain between each scar. Seek your own self by learning what triggers you've experienced and the people who will bully, shame, abuse etc., at every attempt to guilt. Guilty behavior is a far more painful energy of how lesser than one feels at the end of their own life. A life riddled in guilt is painful enough. Whichever traumas a child experiences, it's been written that to know and/or to undo the guilty path has been laid out for us through *FAITH*.

The variables are endless – from the DNA of the parent(s) and of the child should be taken into account. When a child needs guided attention, it is clear that their parents are being asked to show Love to the child; and, if it is a past-life trauma the parents could have been lacking in showing their Love. A "family lineage" is a huge cluster of factors that are well-established, calculated in the energetic forces of many past-lives and lessons that will be initiated for all to learn from. All people that take part in one child's life have spent at least one past-life together at a different time in a different body as another character to learn from, and/or to evolve. There is no such thing as exalting your life in one breath and you're done learning. Even fallen angels that have been Heaven-sent have leftover karma to pay in order to even out and balance a child, their child and/or the lives of all inclusive. It's not an easy feat, by no means, genuinely speaking we are all here to become one with the essence of an omni-potent Love. A God-sent is the same as Heaven-sent is the same as one-love is the same as ONE…in Love, in a Love for Life. ONE LIFE. We are living so many lives at one time; our essence is attempting to evolve to a higher consciousness and to pay off so much karmic debt. Evolution of the self is not an easy task and takes all humans to participate in leading several lives together in various suits to enhance one's learning, growth, and an overall healing of our childhood selves within every turn. This is not easy to comprehend, almost impossible for those who

254

may not fully understand, which simply put ... you're not there yet. Forcing any belief on you or anyone is absurd and can't be done.

Seemingly accurate is the way in which one foresees the external world unfolding. An untethered society that was built to undergo extreme conditions are the aftermath to the ones who have become aware, knowledgeable only through experience for those who KNOW. We are not privy to play with the forces of Mother Nature, yet, why are our children playing with the fires that bind? Which fire is based upon one's own darkness to where they are struggling to get out of their own way, by working on the self, toward the light. Every person, place and thing have darkness in order for one to see their own light – through these trials and tribulations. For what is hidden in the darkness is one's truest and purest of treasures; but, only seen as transparent in the light of a new day. What is done CAN be undone ... Yet, this is our call to Mother Nature giving us Her light within our hearts, energetically, the Sun. Go find your Sun...your sons and daughters... give the light of your heart to those who really need your light for ALL.

Our Father who Art in Heaven...Hallowed Be Thy Name, Thy Kingdom Come, Thy WILL Be Done On Earth As It Is In Heaven. AMEN.

CHILDREN OF TRAUMA, ABUSE, RAPE, SEXUAL INDISCRETIONS AND PARENTS OF THOSE CHILDREN

A child who has relived a battery of trauma has quite a distinctly different lifestyle than a child who grew up with the silver spoon. Yes, we are swaying all the way from the left to the right because it is what's in-between the scale of two Horizons that give way to what lies underneath the surface. We've all been given varied life circumstances on this Earth to experience – for whatever reasons be that one is not able to fully comprehend all because of the traumatic experiences of their ancestral lineage. Once a child of abuse clears up past trauma of karmic relief, many changes take place in that child which are like a sunset that rises into the light of a new day. As for the child who has been given the silver spoon, this child may have already gone through the Dark Night of a sunset and has experienced time and time again many sunsets in order to be relieved to see a sunrise. That is exactly what a sunrise/sunset actually means in light of one's own ascension experiences. Those who now are enlightened follow the course of sunsets as events that occur traumatically still… but, not in any effects of a disposition where this child is able to discern and detach to the outcome. The difference is, a child who is still struggling with attachments holds them hostage, in a life of curiosity that killed the cat; only to be given chance-after-chance that the only secret life holds is "forgiveness." We as humans may have suffered greatly, and have also been prone as witnesses and examples of all those who have been traumatized; yet, with that being said… Forgiveness is an act of God's power to release the child of those threads that come with vast webs of lies, abuse, sexual innuendos, and crimes of passion as well as many other unforgettable causes that one cannot seem to render Forgiveness. However, one must not forget that we are all a part of this world of destruction – and, the purest of intentions is to learn how to forgive… but not necessarily to forget. Many have been unable to forgive sexual misconduct – pedophilia, sexual misrepresentation of family members and acts beyond one could speak of – yes, these are deemed as too criminal to the human parent, family member or any child of God, indeed. These acts of violence and those of cruel intentions are, in fact,

256

what God intended ONLY to set the chain of command for a new thread that can be re-wired in a child's mindset to find Forgiveness; to break those chains and barriers that have been bound between families centuries ago. Whoever can relate to such violent actions, those of strangers alike and even more so of their own family members have an indistinct ability to undergo much repression of pain that is notwithstanding any discussion. These children all have a common thread within their Heritage where they are either unaware of ... or, victims of circumstance. Many blames God for allowing these criminals to remain on Earth and live a life of what looks like freedom – but, please remember that life on Earth is Karmic. Every soul who has abused their physical bodies to harm another soul ... a huge karmic debt of lifetimes will be paid. This is not the doing of any such God. This is the doing of a long list of abuse in one's lineage over the course of History that a specific child cannot even fathom why, how this has happened to them. Knowing that these acts of crime are done to some and not to others is not because of an undeserving child, no! The crimes of passion, criminal acts of sexual abuse, theft, ill-will or any abuse whatsoever are all cries for HELP. A child may assume that they are given these traumas because they were bad or felt it's theirs to take the blame – in fact, these children who have been traumatized are heroes in their own right. They have accepted to take on these crimes in this particular lifetime only to serve as a proponent observer who will revel in the name of Christ the King. The love of oneself will override all criminal acts of the Human Rights Act of violent rages that come with a lot of baggage upon arriving in this world. We cannot speak for another's pain, nor should we even attempt to do so... It is our internal compass to find out where and when our human lifestyles interchange with those of the spiritual tasks that were given to each and every one of us at birth. We've all been irresponsible, yet, when and what do we feel whenever our sense of irresponsibility comes into play for our children? Is it you, as a parent, to know when to be the parent, and when to find it in the etheric fields of taskmaster in order to parent the way in which Spirit has given? Therefore, we come with nothing but a sense of what the 'norm' is versus what Spirit intends. What has been done to our children is vastly different from what God intended this world to look like, especially because we all have been given the innate blessings of free will in taking responsibility/accountability for our lives. It is imperative to know, however, that this world wasn't designed for any form of perfection; but one that will go down in the History books of God's children "being the change" that has been a long-time coming.

SEXUAL TRAUMA OF THE PHYSICAL/EMOTIONAL MINDSET

Who can say that a child of God who has undergone sexual trauma of any sort and is not riddled with extreme guilty pleasure of the body, and/or, guilt of the soul? These two are NOT interchangeable yet the thread is weaved into both where healing needs to take place. Why not change the narrative to all those children who have had someone who (i.e., family member, stranger, etc.) molested, raped, touched or instilled mental/verbal accusations of ones crazed mind being sent out to pasture. What does this mean? A sheep is sent to pasture because it doesn't know any better. Does any trauma, especially sexual, ever heal? How is it that one child recalls sexual abuse and another doesn't? Is it the processing of selective memory? Or, to seek revenge? How can anyone heal with enough forgiveness of compassion to start over? How can the perpetrators place their head on the pillow every night, knowing what crimes they've committed?

Are they immune? What makes another human being abuse an innocent child? Is the attraction purely simple? The onset of innocence … the waning of craving that innocence, an overall disrespect for one's own unworthy self to seek revenge, or, to taint another's innocence because they were taken advantage of too? How could anyone forgive stealing a child's innocence? To be so vulnerable … to trust explicitly and to experience this within a family or church dynamic of those who have taught? What happens to a child whose innocence has been stolen? We can't ever take back our innocence and, perhaps, the reason behind having children of your own is to protect.

To say self-love is not important or that it is just a cliche under the guise of the spiritual egocentric world is an injustice. To be of sound mind doesn't have to only involve the ego, or shall we say, that which does not allow us to further pursue love of self. Once the ego has surrendered to the heart, a newfound love of self can be felt. To feel unconditional love is having to become a love which sees all - the good with the bad – and continues to be compassionate and loving. This Love adds a sense of value and is a soul connection. Who adds value to your life? When the depths of what makes the heart a pure soul/sole becomes a purposeful life. Whenever the ego is tempted to acquire control, the "mindset" is primarily an accumulation of borrowed knowledge. The "mind" is cunning, calculating, clever and quick to intermingle its own impressions upon what it is required for the expansion of the self. We only expand ourselves when the heart expands…not anything, anyone or other external influences will allow the most beautiful flower to grow unto itself. What happens on too many occasions is that the mind wants to change the narrative by coercing your thoughts to choose choices of regret, remorse, etc., regretfully. Those who are empaths become victims of circumstance.

259

However, knowing this, empaths are able to protect themselves. ALL … that IS… of our higher consciousness is the Begotten Son of God… you will BE SAVED.

TRAUMA INHERITED INCLUDES: EMOTIONAL INTELLECTUAL, DEVELOPMENTAL LEARNING, SKILL SETS, WISDOM AND LOVE.

There are several threads that lead to places where trauma of the senses is being played out for us to learn from as we have been innately given traits that will purport us all into a New World Order of the Spiritual Revolution. What we've inherited through our DNA, genetic makeup and that of our parents … all threaded together to cast those endless worries to the side. If humans knew their purpose, there would be no need to worry…and/or not to live in Fear. The truth resides within, an innate purpose to learn lessons that money cannot buy. Life experiences cannot be bought … they must be overcome and lived fully. We've been given a wide net of not only traumas, wounds from our ancestors…but, more importantly, threads that will position us for greatness. All of us have signed up to be here with every single thread in place that will enable the narrative to unfold according to the Universal algorithm. Whatever skill sets, cultural and educational background becomes learned behaviors of various beliefs and ideologies, customs and traits, traditions and a mass production of inherited trajectories for all Humanity to evolve. What we already know to be true within our hearts is bleeding out for us to seek. Everyone is connected to the Universal energy forces of ALL life; therefore, by delving deep into your soul family or where you initially have connected with is all part of the great landscape of Life. To appreciate the learning behaviors of our ancestors is insightful if you can realize you are the inner makings of that insight. These insights begin as: triggers, signs, symbols, patterns of behaviors, ideas, belief systems... all reflections of ourselves within every person we come into contact with. As difficult as that sounds, a fragment of energetic force is implemented within every thread that re-threads itself as new faces and places. When we find ourselves feeling comfort and peace...that feeling of Home resides in the energies of your Heritage. Many souls are reincarnated to get their karma purified for their soul's evolution. It is written in our "sands of time" ™ narrative of those we've filtered throughout our lifetimes and who will stand the test of time.

ABUSE, MIA, PEDOS OF INNOCENT CHILDREN

There is an overwhelming number of children who've been abused by either one or both parents; cousins, uncles, aunts, siblings and the like of those they've placed their value in, their own family. Then to add injury to insult of the highest order, where are the parents in this scenario? Do they know? Are they aware or not? And, why? Abusive behavior has been happening since the beginning of time – hence, why do we all come from "dysfunctional families" and what has happened over the course of our history? It is all getting exposed and coming undone... especially with the rate of pedos, missing children and the abuse in this country that has come to everyone's attention. To say this mildly, *WAKE UP*! Didn't the effects of 9/11 teach us anything? Loss of loved ones, terrorist attacks, loss of freedom is still not being accounted for... and those children who have been and are being abducted everyday…taken to underground tunnels, abusing our young?! Why 9/11? Didn't we learn the value of population denigration at what cost? This tragedy and ALL the others… shooting in schools, gun warfare, child pedos, sex offenders and so much more…what will it take for those who watch over children to WATCH THESE CHILDREN? And, even if you're not a parent, who is to say that all adults shouldn't be keeping a watchful eye on the surroundings? WHAT'S IT GONNA TAKE?! How many kids must die and/or suffer over and over again at the onset of this commonality of, "childhood abuse"?!

"DARE-2-CARE™" – a newfound program shall be started, tended to, and cared for ALL the children who are in dire need of adults keeping watch. This includes all adults worldwide; watching, observing, witnessing … and, NOT walking away from what they see as strange behavior, and/or any type of abusive behavior, etc. This new program "DARE-2-CARE™" will be created in 2025!!! Let's try to keep a watchful eye out in the meantime…and, look forward to seeing all who ***truly*** want to put forth the efforts that are needed to PROTECT, SERVE, AND WATCH OUR CHILDREN!!! "DARE-2-CARE™" will be founded for saving ALL God's children. And so it is. AMEN.

We are not going to persecute our own for the criminal acts of those so-called adults who take it upon themselves to abuse children… remember this. How could a mere child of fourteen and/or younger be able to make any type of decision for themselves? Or, find themselves in a violated position where their voice cannot be heard…being used and medicated to abuse is not going to be tolerated! Additionally, these types of inexplicable behaviors purport children to become addicts, and to become their own worst nightmare. Our bodies are the "temple" NOT to be toyed, touched and used for monetary entertainment. And to all the innocent young teenagers who unknowingly dress inappropriately and feel indifferent and not enough who resorted to drugs, sex and alcohol to uphold one's reputation and be accepted requires our involvement. How can this be stopped? Why hasn't it been stopped? Who is to say that one is worse than the other? One act of violence, sexual abuse, verbal and physical abuse are clearly all acts of the worst kind of torture for not only all of our youth but to all of society. NO degree of ABUSE is acceptable… ACTS OF VIOLENCE be it sexual, mental and/or ANY ABUSE OF ANY KIND IS UNACCEPTABLE!!! Have we come to realize how much our parents may not have known and how limited their Love was? Why haven't parents had in-depth discussions with their children, at an appropriate age to warn, to protect and to keep fear at bay? Humanity needs to believe again and trust. Is this possible? How can those victims of abuse ever trust again? Who is worthy of our bountiful trust? Could anything ever match the trust we've placed in our own parents? If so, who fills that role? If not, what could we say...or, for that matter, what could anyone say or do in order to contend with another's pain? "The best kept secrets…." come from within our family lineage, unknowingly many still are not privy to their children feeling the same way. That's what fear and/or shame does to our children and any violent acts of criminal behavior. "Guilty as charged" is one for the books as is in so many cases where there have been injustices and that have been overlooked in fear. "What a crying shame…" another term judiciously used for only those who have feared for their lives, crying out for HELP. "Guilty as charged" is used to retract our actions so that justice can be served, but not in every case. Can justice ever be granted? We don't realize how many children go unwanted, unloved, not cared for and/or seen and heard. We all cannot agree to disagree…but what has happened in our world is amongst a very different kind of beast. Today's beast is dangling many caveats from misrepresentation and misuse of the power of: money, social media, advertising and marketing, virtual reality, much like a sinking ship, Titanic. It may sound redundant yet the world of external power is a much bigger beast of burden…

PSYCHOLOGY OF TRAUMA

No one on Earth can understand another's pain unless they've lived it; therefore, we cannot tell another person to forgive or to forget whatever is too much to bear. Forgiveness is overrated in the Spiritual community and taken out of context many times…because what others deem feasible can be unacceptable for those who are angry and/or want to debate. All children must learn on their own… including all outsiders who are casting out judgments and opinions. Opinions are the lowest form of knowledge – it requires no understanding. Empathy is the highest form of discipline because it requires us to suspend the Ego. Too often no one knows their suffering…and speaks out of context because of ignorance. There are so many who are suffering-in-silence that don't want to talk about it, sharing bad memories is like reliving the trauma all over again. As much as others want to HELP, it's best, in these cases, not to interfere. The wounds of our trials and tribulations have caused inner pain and suffering that go deep into the psyche of childhood psychology - as in, every child matters. Putting that into perspective also adds layers of one's parents' past history of pain and their parent's (grandparents) pain which now has taken us back 3 or 4 generations in the Heritage of one's past trauma. Time to "break the chains" and heal the pain… All factors must be threaded together…however, many are not aware of other's pain. We'd like to think that our ancestors would be proud to enlist, as they did, all of us to come back to Earth to sever karmic ties that have bonded such trauma. We are all doing our part, or, at least all of us who've been diligently working on severing these contracts in order for us to soar. Just because we're not exactly familiar with our Heritage doesn't mean this is not a reason to believe we can change History. Every human comes from their own family history and that includes from generations-to-generations; and, no one is exempt from **not** working on their karmic ties. There is an aura of vast pain surrounding our energy that is currently being released for many – and those who are a part of our lineage believe in us. Not one person will be left behind…who is doing their part to ensure they're ascension. For the rest of Humanity who need to take notice, waking up to a new day's dawn will be inevitable…for the light is too bright for those *sleeping* not to *see* what's being/been exposed. Once we've established the crime, we all must do the time…recognizing we too have a huge part in an effort to raise our frequencies and believe in making a huge impact upon this world.

Children who are coming into the world have been gifted with innate abilities that other generations had to evolve, learn and remember. Those of us who are being gifted ascension in this lifetime will be gifted also with a clean bill of health, finite funds, congruent norms of creative opportunities, being at the right-place-right-time and instant manifestations. Slumber no more…find your inner self, "heal in order to feel" doing that which will imprint a new Heritage of Enlightened souls.

When we've evaluated the status of this world and/or what may come, or not, it is crucial to have a solid few that will unite by listening, who remain calm, who want to contribute to a good cause for the highest good of all mankind. Not everyone feels the connection to others or another, to their brothers and sisters, as we are all connected; yet so many stay at arm's length or run away. To have that effect is to cave to the crisis of those who need our HELP, a shoulder to cry on, a sounding board. Who is your "go-to" nearest and dearest who will be there for you under any situation? When all is said and done it is crucial to have close connections, if only one other, who will lend a hand. "No man is an island…" was written for the purpose of uniting with your tribe who see eye-to-eye and will not question you, but support your decisions for your highest good. Should your decisions not be vastly for your highest good, a sounding board to help you to see clearly all aspects is an asset…even if at the time you don't believe it is. Overcoming by lending a helping hand serves not only your children but for the sake of all generations that have come before and that will come after. Our Heritage of helping hasn't changed, but the disguise of darkness has emitted a cloud of confusion for the world to clearly see.

"Health is Wealth…" comes to those who completely understand the comprehension of eating, exercise and bemoaning a rigid and tight schedule. The workout process becomes more natural once it is done every day, each day over and over – repetition is a part of the ALL-encompassing world of the Hologram. If you can get into a general routine that will prepare your body for the fruits of your labor, everything is available on Earth as it is in Heaven.

To evolve into the abyss is not to ignore yourself in its totality…to be in the vortex, on your inner journey makes us realize our own wholeness. Instead of making yourself extinct in this world, one cannot see themselves as they really are… a ghostly viewer of the exorbitant kind. This can or cannot be seen…the unseen. "What doesn't kill you makes you stronger" as Kelly Clarkson sings… a song that depicts all those who have experienced pain in their lives and become stronger. However, what one sees as inconsequential doesn't matter because the life of no-matter-what seeks to find itself through our inner journey of self. Once this journey has been understood leaving everything that matters alone, this is when we've come to the realization. Knowing and unknowing the self is not for the weak who are fearful for curiosity's sake. In order to unknow what we unlearn is the purest truth of our claim-to-fame. Feast or famine depicts the feminine claim to unclaim what has already been our path. You may want to know, or, ask the feminine; what do I behold? It's a feeling… The masculine holds within their Ego self-more than the feminine…and, even though this sounds as though there is an imbalance, that's exactly what this truly is. The imbalance of the masculine/feminine equality, within ourselves, must come into play when managing what has been learned. The masculine's Ego attempts to portray someone's ideal self instead of the real self. Once wholeness has been attained the feminine and the masculine merge as ONE…two halves seeking the other one, by becoming One. This is when our masculine side has been given a clear indication where the ego separates from the "mind-set" and instructs the feminine heart to take the lead. A synergy between Masculine and Feminine vibes…

Wholeness happens from the HEART.

Not many souls would be so inclined to want to jump out of the flames into the fire for no good reason…but, to earn one's wings.

"Take these broken wings and learn to Fly…" sung by Mr. Mister

SUPERFICIALIITY

Children are built differently based upon their upbringing, external factors, beliefs of others, genetics, DNA, structures of archetypes, astrology of their natal chart, subsequent factors of internal triggers, traumas, past-life and one's Heritage…and so much more. What comes as a surprise to many who view a child/children is the inability to take all of these facets of one person to see the authentic self. Most people are blinded by others' capabilities because they're too interested in their own, don't have time to go deep, don't know how to go deep, cannot see another for the entire scope of a life. What a shame it is that so many humans are on autopilot, robotic to the point of no return. How did this happen? Just being cordial, surface conversations, not listening to what others say, impatient, impartial, judging even before the story is told, misrepresented in so many more ways…and, yet no one is attempting to change their trajectory. The reason it's called "trajectory" is because it is very tragic that people have completely lost their sense of self. No one cares… about others or about themselves. If you ask anyone, "How are you?" the reply is, "All good…" superficially so. Why and how has this happened to Humanity? Everyone is scared…fearful for their lives…don't want to rock the boat that's already sinking into the depths of darkness. Because whether we realize it or not, the AI Movement is underway and it's only going to get wide-spread to the masses – then, you won't be able to tell the difference as to who is talking. Spreading like wildfire…will be a mass eruption of chaos, disorder, flames of fires catching more moths to a flame. Are you willing to sacrifice yourself to the likes of commiserating with AI? It's happening…what are you going to do about it? Take your time, take a breath, take a minute to digest this possible change of hands that do not feel…and, get set for an influx of protesting to keep control at bay. Whether you're awake, or asleep…now might be a good time to have a sit-down with yourself to assess where you've fallen and/or how to ascend. Justification brings in the same-old and will not hold any water that will become an equal flush of armored suits. The other side of that hand would dictate our own leadership, the Hero who saves himself and others who follow suit.

CHILDREN OF ALL LOVE

Children who have been injured, children with dis-eases, children whose parents have been absent, children who are lost and all alone, children who have been left to die, children who have been abused in anyway, children who are adopted, children who are fostered, children with step-parents, children with no grandparents, children who have lost a parent, children who have been abandoned to fin for themselves, children with disabilities, children with no place to live, hunger in children, children with no family ties, children who are loners, the black-sheep of the family, children who face crisis, children who are ignored, children who are special needs, children unloved, children in need of HELP, children in orphanages, children who don't like school, children who remain to themselves, muted children, fallen angels from grace children, grown-up children, adult children, children who hunger for attention, children whose talents are not seen…and all children of the Ages are *special…* We are all these children of a God

269

whose energy is ALL LOVE. When we return Home it will be very clear where our soul's consciousness either evolved or not. Some have run with the wolves, were raised by wolves, became wolves, instinctually didn't follow the pack of wolves who know when to be a survivor of the land and/or when to be the leader of the pack. All who have seen wolves interact know their playful tendencies spur one's heartfelt beating of a new drum… whatever wolverine has led you to a place of comfort or taken you into survival mode, every pack is needed for the world to evolve. Whatever comforts of lifestyle one is familiar with…it is indicative of becoming leaders and taking survival to the next level.

Children have this instinct, children have a playful nature, children are curious, children know what they want, children outsmart their own parents because they've got a NO-FEAR outlook in LIFE and they become a witness to their own parents' madness. Children who attain a certain level of integrity, character, honorability, rationality, life is a playground, every moment cherished and held accountable, an observer that at any given time on the wheel could spin into a tail-spin of chaos, yet, a child holds it together by knowingly being themselves, children can see, feel, hear, touch an innocence for Life.

LIGHTWORKERS - EARTH ANGELS

We have no way of knowing … until we do. It has been written of these 144,000 lightworkers walking upon our sacred Holy ground. Some lightworkers are on Earth to teach about generational curses and showcase a cutting of cords to their ancestral lineage. These lightworkers who are currently on the Earth plane have been called to task on the highest of missions that Earth has ever undergone…becoming a new generation of the highest and brightest of lightworkers. One must be induced into what would be considered somewhat of a sorority of checks and balances. These checks and balances are indicative of one's growth but the only difference being that fallen angels, now, are our Lightworkers falling into the arms of our Lord Jesus Christ. Hence upon the fall, they are lifted up and brought upon the Holiest of Thou to attain their own value upon their journey. We've seen many of the so-called lightworkers who claim to be, but are not. Please do not be charged with a sense of falsely being accused of showing up calling yourself a lightworker when one is not of the same light. A lightworker from our Heavenly host shines brighter for ALL of Humanity – and, not in the same sense of what other souls have signed up for on their journey this lifetime. They have been given many tasks to fulfill - a sacred thread on a journey to guide others and to become self-realized of the highest light as ALL LOVE.

HUMANITY - THE NEW WORLD

Since the beginning… humans have been unable to understand how the Spiritual Revolution has been constructed in order for us to find salvation, until now. This Spiritual Revolution is learning to evolve spiritually by listening to your truth and learning discernment. In this way, we all come into communion with our highest consciousness to find ways to accept, allow and detach. This takes much self-analysis, focus, and a salvation to attain Higher Power. Learning of the connectivity between both the inner self and the physical body - within our physical chakras enable us to navigate between our emotional/mental health. When a blocked chakra is cleared, within our physical body, that's a red flag to go deep within by working on issues that get to the core of the heart in the matter. Once we have broken through all blockages, a Sacred Phoenix rises. Entering the phoenix rising becomes a long-drawn-out depth of illusion, validation, judgment(s) etc., and can show up in one's life just as that. When that happens, the Ego has a new way of relating to the outer self-attempting to reel you back into the depths of Fear-based emotions. The Ego has been with humans since inception; therefore, knowing how to manipulate, coerce and get into your mindset of Fear will continue – falling down the rabbit hole once again – only to reenact lessons over and over again. The attempts of the Ego are unlimited...until the mind and body begin working together … allowing the heart to sing and dance.

To seek a realization that we become in light of the ONE is an arduous journey. However, the Ego self does not care to seek inwardly, because it manipulates our external world. Why are humans being brought to their knees when times get tough? Is there a reason why some humans seek nothing while others seek it all? There are moments of self-awareness where we can end up capturing ourselves in the midst of ...chaos, havoc, stress and so much more of what doesn't appear to one's eye, (I) yet. All I's are a part of the IS when it has been duly found out...as the I in I AM breeds to distinguish itself, as itself. A huge part of the EGO, the ID, identification of self, only concurs to state the obvious as, "I once was lost but now I am found" as, itself seeking itself. I AM the two faces of one mirror...seeing is Believing takes the I and the I AM out of the equation. To be two-faced is indicative of having more than one ID, identification or persona; yet, so many cannot understand. Human beings are one – with many egoic masks throughout a lifetime of selves. To conceptualize this part of your persona is to know that the ONE is within and that your body is just a reflection of that part. To take yourself out of the equation just means to allow Spirit to guide those that need guidance. Not knowing this explains why you are still attempting to grasp the concept of the Ego self not knowing 'one as the other' – yet, no other exists. There are the ones that think they know; and the ONE knowing, IS (In Spirit).

To become all-knowing IS to know… I AM.

HERITAGE OF THE SOUL

A soul enters the Earth plane traveling through a silver cord into an unknown yet embodied soul. At the time of the unraveling of the embryo's growth, 9-months and counting, the embodied soul has not been restricted to encapsulate other fragments of embodiments which become an Earth body. A soul who has taken on a variety of others' soul fragments - for purposes unknown to the individual - will endure various proponents in life that will seemingly be different from a soul who will not undergo fragmentation. The reason for souls to take on other fragments is that they ALL agree there are certain pathways to evolve on the Earth plane; and by taking on other soul fragments, allows one to be able to handle whatever comes their way. The reason not all babies born entering the Earth plane do or do not embody other souls' fragments is to enlarge the language of life. Embodying other languages means to take on added value from other souls' knowledge through their experiences without having to endure struggle. Why this happens for some and not all is not a question that mankind would ever understand. The struggles for those humans who have already learned through other lifetimes do not require added soul fragments. For example: a soul who has been embodied with seven soul fragments, during gestation, has been given the remnants of others' who have chosen to offer these fragments to assist in another's path – as in, one hand washes the other. By receiving fragments from other soul's lifetimes of lessons, we tend to want that particular soul to grow as such because their true-North purpose is required for that individual self. When a soul has taken part in sharing varied treasures both the recipient and the sharer of doing so assists in both souls' growth…in order to reach the omni-potent white light.

Not all attend the right-of-passage on what, where, and how each fragmentation remains from our ancestors. These are our own selves who have been granted to see themselves as the ALL. Only those enhanced souls who have reached a culmination of enlightenment does it become a visible contract of exchange. ONE hand in exchange for the other happens when a human being discovers it IS. Not a moment too soon and not a moment too late – ALL becomes self as whole again through these Dimensional soul fragments that are weaved and threaded unto itself throughout the embodiment of a soul who is about ready to enter the Earthly plane. Taken from the Bible as, "No man is an island" bodes well for all Humanity, though for some, that is not the case. Those who will be finding their own light by enduring several infinite lifetimes of painful reservoir of trials and tribulations are whom the bells tole. Throughout ancient history many souls have conquered their right-of-passage, however, fell short by how this was accomplished. "Whomever The Bells Tolle" is about what seems to be the aftermath of a long arduous path of lifetimes. We've all been drowning in a sea of what was… known as, the past. Should a human soul conquer its past indiscretions in one's lifetime, as a natural progression whose Egoic gestures go unnoticed, the path must be a "do-over". There is NO room for error in the Spiritual realm of reasoning with any other than oneself. To conquer the Ego is to release, allow and let go of control on every level of one's being. There cannot be any leftover remnants of Egoic sensibility for one's soul to enter into a place of knowing. Once a soul has overcome through our Mother Earth's innate healing capabilities, then, the natural order is attained. There are many fragments of both the natural order here on the Earth plane as well "as above". What does this mean? Those who are already evolved will be dealt with as an evolved-parent soul versus a soul who has been breeding an Ego-controlled soul that delves into their reality of illusion as a structured power play. Self-fulfillment can be misconstrued as a 3Dimensional play of a theatrical type and others who are self-fulfilled of a natural state of being come to know ALL. The art of knowing, no-thing.

Many mystics that have come before us, as well as those who remain to be seen, will have endured great traumas of lifetimes in order to walk their own path of self. The path to self is a sacred one and cannot be seen until it is felt. Those mystics who have gone before us have left their impression, a beautiful fragrance that cannot be replicated. Every human who has become enlightened will in-deed leave behind their unique fragrance. The fragrance that envelops the Universal "As Above, So Below" generates a plethora of scents swirling in the air/heir. Those who can smell a scent from a former lifetime or childhood memory, and other mystical scents become what is known as certain fragments/fragrances in time. There are infinite fragrances in our Universe as well as unknown Dimensions that conglomerate in the highest order in our lifetimes. The reasoning for encapsulating these fragrances as, dust in the wind, is by far the best reservoir in the history of mankind. The scent from a baby, an oblivious scent, a loving scent of one's hair, scented candles and fragrances all come back into the fold of a time in one's history or past

275

life. Sometimes we're unable to spot the fragrance when it enters our nasal cavity, but, when we do… it's magical! To recall a fond memory of our Father and/or Mother through their scent is priceless. To behold a baby's breath fondly in memory has the scent of Heaven. As we walk through the Valley of Death, behold the scent of Forever. The last will-and-testament has another type of fragrance (one who enters the soul and who is getting ready to exit). A scent of your very own is instilled within the crevice of every human being, DNA non-excluded, as one's own fragrance stems from our inner source of every breath inhaled. That scent can also be found in every crevice of the physical body – underarms, nasal cavity and passage etc. These are just a couple of examples where our scent-of-passage lies on and within our physicality knowing of another's smell. Each fragrance is linked to vast fragments of not only our soul, but, entwined within our very essence. To render one's own fragrance takes no time at all, it IS. The higher order of fragrance begets ALL of one's path of this journey of love.

"A fragrance cannot become itself until it does…" ™ Fragmented pieces of oneself are brought about once we come to terms as the ONE. energy of LOVE… In order for you to fully wrap yourself up unto yourself, one must be ALL of itself, ALL LOVE. LOVE ALL.

We cannot surmise that this life is not one that you didn't sign up for…as every human being that rests upon this Earth has been Chosen. There is every reason to question the source of why, when, how and where… did it all begin, yet any questions take us further away from the ONE. The source of the matter is that nothing matters. To be consumed without ever knowing whether your soul consists of various fragrances/fragments is similar to walking a fine line between the sunrise and a sunset. To experience a life that breathes life in other Dimensions, is a life felt by the rays of the Sun. This is not up for interpretation as those who are reading this have had an epiphany already, or, you've perhaps heard someone else relaying this same information at some point. Without this understanding, not many individual beings can surmise a soul's living existence on many varied platforms at the same time, while on this Earth plane. In essence, what this means is that once the child has surrendered itself by becoming its present-day self, all karmic ties which the child must be forgiven and/or to forgive themselves will be done through ONE's highest self in conjunction with the omnipresent. Your present-day self-lives an eternity as it IS living by itself through the ALL. And, our highest self being the teacher continues to assist every human by evoking a numerical version of what once has been given to you at birth. This numerical equation takes place on the highest echelons of the Spiritual world in order for a soul's contract to be lessened. Not all souls hold this equation of the self-due to specific fragments that raise other issues that have to be sorted out. To say that every soul should be gifted is exactly the closest to Heaven that your human form will ever see… it's not every day that we're gifted with tidings of joy.

Tidings of Joy have been given to Humanity every year at Christmas and Hanukkah where all of God's children are gifted with presents and blessings for a New Year. For the most part, these gifts are to be shown as the exact reason why "He came down from Heaven and was incarnated by The Holy Spirit and of The Virgin Mary and became Man". Jesus' birth shows all of Humanity that the reason for these gifts from the Spirit world are the same gifts as one is present in life. This gift-of-life is one that we don't give back…" Jesus knew that there would be those who in all fairness would attempt to give back such a gift by ending their life, suicide. How everyone handles their life given their innate gifts is not to say that free-will does not exist, it was placed in the hands of each individual human as a fragment in order to represent that there is life after this… and, that at the hands-of-fate every human has been dealt with is not ours to judge. We must be cognizant of why we've chosen to be on Earth in these times; and, what our soul's purpose is telling us. If you've experienced a comfort level of knowing what you're here to do in-service to Humanity, then, you are the teacher. Not to know what your purpose IS your purpose for living a balanced life. Not knowing how, why, when or even how will enable the ALL to allow co-creation its ultimate. Those who have yet to inquire about their soul's journey have not been found, they are still asleep. Many, however, know that to allow the Spirit to show you the way…IS THE WAY. There is no way out…until you go within…

SOUL FRAGMENTS

How do soul's find their embodiment? Once a physical body has been formed, the essence/fragments of all who are to learn, teach and/or reincarnate through this body commune. Some may say that there is a shortage of embodiments to go around… how could this be? Is it true? Could Humanity have risen to such a higher Dimension where certain physical bodies do not have enough learning to reincarnate? NO. The infinite embodiment of souls who need to rise, are infinite. Fragments can contain historical ingenuity to Biblical scriptures all the way down throughout the Akashic records…a library of the highest order throughout past generations and also throughout other dimensions. They are known as the Akashic records that encapsulate the ALL. ONE's work-in-progress results in the success of the achievements granted from the Spirit world.

When the mind/body connection begins to feel its end is near, the hierarchy of a soul's essence reverts to its origin of language. Humans transitioning to their final lifecycle as an Elder, begin to capture memories of childhood, reverting to their family's Heritage of English speaking or a foreign language. "Foundational wisdom is held within every fragment of our structure; in our brain, our palms and feet, in our gums and teeth, in the spine of every line". ™

In my presence and in my absence... the imprint of a soul's essence remains.

SOUL CONTRACTS

What is by far the reasoning of our soul contract(s) given to everyone differs as to why, how and what you do with the information. Those who are familiar with soul contracts have already been dealing and/or working on clearing their karmic ties; and, to those who are not privy to these exams on Earth, a repeated plan takes place... more-or-less like repeating a grade. This doesn't mean that you and/or another aren't on the same journey; however, every human is on a different path. These tests are prolific for those who already know *not* to compare, criticize and/or judge others. To say that one soul's contract has been granted while another has yet to encapsulate theirs is to believe in the Biblical saying, "We are not to question why, we are here to do and die". This is not to say that every child of God's has been granted the same experiences. In determining your path, we must remain ready, willing and able to accept that which has been given. To envision the path forward as one that stands out from the crowd is allowing Spirit to show you THE WAY. What comes after may not necessarily be to your liking yet the path(s) that has been chosen IS the

279

way forward. Why some are able to accept their rightful path and others are steering clear of this path determines where and what stage of life you're in at the time. No matter what, though, there are fruitful ways in which one can stay on point to allow whatever happens to BE. This goes for every aspect of one's life cycle that comes and goes… to be enriched and gifted with the present(s) of lifetimes does not bear witness to those who have many crosses to bear. Humanity has been given both The Bible and The Laws of the Universe to follow, on a journey of self-realization. This is why Divine timing is crucial for every human as there are no short-cuts to enlightenment; only a matter of self-discipline, hard work, focus and determination. We tend to forget how grateful we are in our darkest hours only to be given glimpses of moments to show how far we've come. What an amazing gift, Life… We're all humans having a spiritual awakening on our own time, in our own way to attainment. Inner work has been given as a gift to each individual to attain their soul's higher consciousness. Not all see. Not all seek. No one can become one until they leave it all up to THE ONE. We cannot place a timeframe on ever achieving enlightenment … it is not an action, nor is it a reaction, it is THE WAY. it just IS. "To be or not" is not the question nor the answer. It is ALL. The Universe will reveal what needs to be shown to every human being on their treasure quest. The treasure quest is an inner journey not seen by no-one, being it is the ONE. To allow IS. To settle into one's life as a treasured self who has been gifted many talents, gifts on their path is to *"Know Thyself"*.

DIMENSIONS. VIBRATIONAL FREQUENCIES

All Dimensions within our Universe are infinite as the expression, "As Above, So Below" which holds ALL consciousness. Within our essence are our expressions of life experiences – what has been learned and what is yet to be learned places every soul's consciousness on a different frequency. All frequencies connect the thread of one's life experiences and what knowledge that it brings to our lives. That frequency is also connected to what has already been taught to us from our Heritage, the History of our ancestors and what we are currently learning in the present life. Those frequencies of consciousness resonate as vibrations emanating throughout the Universe. The higher our level of consciousness, the connectivity to whatever vibration is being picked up in the Universe. The ability to flex our consciousness, alters our sub-consciousness of what has already been embedded, repressed, or learned to clear past lessons, repressions of emotional attachments and the like. Every life experience shares the ability to stay in the present moment of NOW. All karmic ties and repressed emotions from our current as well as our past-life experiences will taste Freedom. Another reason why we've all signed up to be an instrumental thread that will change history Forever… It starts with one thread to elevate the entire vibration of our beautiful planet Earth.

ELEMENTS IN TIME

WOOD: Mother Earth transcends time… She IS our Holy Ground

FIRE: The passion lives within every Heart…Co-Create

WATER: Emotions run deep…Dive IN!

AIR: Every breath that we take…reminds me to BE

Throughout History we've not been taught the ways of our world from the inside out – it's time we all take a moment to Breathe INWARD in GRATITUDE for LIFE; it's time to DIVE DEEP into our subconscious mind and body, set it FREE; it's time to Live a Fulfilled Life with PASSION in every little thing we do, create, speak, listen to, a touch with all LOVE; it's time to walk upon this Holy Ground and feel the Earth move through YOUR entire essence.

Where would we be if not for what we are made of? Purify every element of your external body and reach for the sky!

BE within every moment,

Breathe in every breath,

Become the passionate flame,

That lives within…

Bequeath thee alive,

At this moment, IN this time,

What is within IS ALL that matters.

As Earth evolves, Humanity will learn how to navigate its own reality – either upon an Earth that diverges into a world of miracles; or, another world that reminds us where the darkness still exists… A conglomerate unity of the world-within-worlds that will produce what you know as your truth. Our planet, Earth, is filled with the strength of iron within every breath of oxygen we ingest. We are a species of empowered cells that produce radical energy that declares itself its kinship with Nature. As Aristotle quoted, "If one way is better than another, that you may be sure is nature's way". There are energy wars vying for your attention right now in a series of worlds which is being created unto itself. Genetic engineering and chemical atoms within a molecule of time are being shown as different variations will create a 5-Dimensional Universe of compassion. A world of compassion is where Humanity will find its purest form with an intent of breaking down to allow humans to choose for themselves. The marking of a New Era in the Age of Aquarius is History in the making. You know who you are… Rise up and show others your light, share your wisdom and heed the call to all those who are not ready.

SIGNS OF SHIFTING TO 5 DIMENSIONAL

1. Strong sense of compassion

2. Loss of Fear

3. Loss of polarity of judgment

4. Easily adaptable

5. Accept light & dark

6. Power of creating

7. Rapid manifestation

8. Be of-service, in-deeds to others

Humanity is leaving the Age of a material world and entering the Age of Frequency… Sound and Vibration.

THE AGE OF AQUARIUS

Our soul emits fragments of light that consist of atoms, molecules, sparks of light that live in several Dimensions at one time. The reason for this is that parts of the fragmented energies must learn to enhance themselves over again through the healing properties from childhood. Therefore, our soul is living within our physical body and learning in the present moment while fragments of the same are residing both in our past, and in our future self. Why? All the inner wounding and traumas from not only this life but from our past lives are clearing the way to be forgiven and severed. The 3-Dimensional Earth plane has only one level of *no return*…, noted, as Hell. We are living proof in both the Astral plane, in our REM sleep and living on the Earth doing work. What happens in our REM sleep is that we are co-existing with those who've hurt us, traumatized us, betrayed and had ill-will for us at the same time in this life and/or another. The reason we do not realize that our soul's fragments are scattered is because no human brain can comprehend or fathom that a soul is able to fragment. Every soul is pieced together by invariably crossed threads; and the leftover pieces are spread across other Dimensions – blessings in disguise. Why? For some of us…the act of revisiting our painful truths of trauma is just too much to bear - which is why we live in a multi-Dimensional Universe where souls roam FREE. The energy gets scattered in many ways…not only within other Dimensions, but is when we get, "scatter-brained". Energy moves through us, around us, above and below us while the physical body's hard shell remains idle. When we experience "Deja vu" moments this too is when our energy crosses paths within other lifetimes. Some things are better unknown to mankind because it's hard enough dealing with one part soul and the other part human. Connected as this is, battles of power the Ego attempts to fight off humans from attaining. This is energy overload that happens in the physical body as; vertigo, headaches, migraines, confusion and/or many other added stress factors that impair one's ability. While the brain and body's connectivity resemble a live conversation much is handled behind the scenes. The physical body consists of organs, neurons, molecules, water, blood and veins etc., all working in sync to continue to guide humans on their journey. If there were any more layers to understand the physical body it would seem like a firewall of live wires. What we have yet to speak of is the way in which all children are differently wired – with the exception that all threads are wired specifically for each human to move according to the bigger plan for their soul's evolution. Much like the "big bang theory" many know that evolution began while others only believed there was some-type of explosion. What really "matters" on this Earth is not necessarily how we got here as much as our purpose in doing the work. Makes no difference who believes in how, when, what happened 16 billion years ago… we are here, now, to make a difference in the History of the New World Order. Subsequently, whomever questions any of the scientific reasons is NOT getting the full picture of how our soul evolves. Science meets Spirit… at the Horizon of every day as we are reborn again in the golden rays of sunrise/sunset that mark the Age of Aquarius. The New World Order is called, The Golden Age, because History is marking time on Earth for an upsurge of mankind's awakening. Every soul is learning its path for an evolution within The Spiritual Revolution – Mother Earth's ascension is making History! No other time in the History of the Earth plane has Her energy risen to such illuminated heights in tandem with Her children. Our Forefathers are very proud as the evolution of this planet will never be the same again…in ways that are seen and unseen. Just know that every man, woman, and child living on planet Earth signed up to make this happen. "An eye for an eye" is now "Eye can see clearly now" Insightful reassurance of an awakening planet. While the New Year of 2020 posed much struggle and massive change, as did September 11, 2001, *every* part of these painful changes sought to provide Humanity with the TRUTH. There will never be a single definition of "normal" ever again! When you ask yourself what normal even means, the answer remains as insurmountable differences leading to change…either way, change is inevitable as we are all fluctuations of energetic frequencies. Our traumas, however, shook up Humanity instead of individual lives within the structure of family. Isn't that what we are now coming to terms with? Understanding how connected we are, that we are ALL one spark of Life.

"Why Fear death…for it IS an Eternal Life of FAITH" ™

Humanity has been undergoing what is known as a, "collective amnesia" coming to the Earth plane choosing not to know, so we can remember. However, this amnesia was directed for the good of Humanity to evolve past the need to clear karma. Although this choice would assist in clearing karmic debt; it was brought about for the sake of seeing clearly, 20/20 vision. Is Humanity better off not knowing their past-life experiences or could mankind sustain the need not clearing karma to evolve? What mankind needs to seek from its past will become obsolete as the incoming generations come upon this Earth without karmic ties. We are undergoing a massive shift whereby infinite years of Karmic clearing are occurring right now...for the Spiritual Revolution to arise! Man will become an instrument of fine tuning which will only seek itself...

"Cease to remember; and, allow to forget..." ™

The onset of Humanity's evolution is written that as GAIA completes Her ascension it will be up to mankind afterwards to break from old patterns... and learn from the upcoming generations observing the capabilities to live in the NOW. The upcoming years, 2024-2050 are going to be tumultuous times that we must endure by remaining strong in our FAITH. We are in the 11th hour of a progressive Universe of REALIZATION for all Humanity's sake... "DON'T GIVE UP!" Relax and observe...no need to add fuel to those external fires that we will be witness to. Stand firm in your discernments of what you believe or disbelieve to be what resonates your truth. Ask for help, pray to your loved ones, Spirit Guides, Angels, Archangels, Ascended Masters for guidance. Whatever you bear witness to upon the Earth plane within the next several years is going to feel like a roller-coaster ride that doesn't end...until it does.

Our New World is fast approaching, all systems go – the Earth is moving at a rapid pace, even though it may not seem so at times; and at different times, we *feel* it vastly changing. There are certain processes in place that Humanity will endure before the New World Order can become what it will BE. The physical body cannot be rushed into massive changes that cause effects both 'within and without' the physical body. No human can encounter massive destruction that is seen out in the world; in an attempt to come into their own at the speed of light. The body is not built for quantum physics to alter gravity upon this Earth – what mankind has to attain is a progression of baby steps so that the mind/body connectivity remains balanced. At the quantum physics level all energy will be transmitted upon the Earth for humans to attain their "REALIZATION" – "ASCENSION" evolving in the physical body to a "light-body" and the "mindset" to be "set FREE" from all attachments. The physical embodiment will rise to become a "light body" while our "mindset" will be Free from all dis-ease through the clearing of particles from all lower vibrations that the darkness in-gravity yields. To BE a light unto the world doesn't mean anything other than spreading your light for all to see… and to embody the ability to "flip-the-switch" on thought processes which will bring a full-REALIZATION to light. All of Humanity is striving to attain this REALIZATION/ASCENSION which transmutes our energy mind-body into Spirit Divination. Frequencies-of-knowledge are the life experiences that the mind has consumed – for a new will-to-evolve in self-knowledge. Consciousness is Energy…it IS a Science in our "treasure quest" to attainment. ™ YOU already KNOW everything coming to Earth – now, you must BELIEVE it! In doing so, you will understand, "I AM REALIZATION."

EN-LIGHT-EN-MENT … Full REALIZATION realizes it is ALL LIGHT that IS.™

What is being done on the Earth plane has been pre-determined by the Echelon of the Highest Order which is dutifully showing mankind what is to come… What is to come? We, as a community of light, need only spread your kindness, patience, compassion and understanding "knowing" this is the way forward, in gratitude. ALL of Humanity is being redirected to become their natural self in a world which is designed as Mother Nature intended. Breakthroughs will begin for all who enlist in seeking their mind-body & soul connection IN purest form, "All NATURAL'" style. "You can't fool Mother Nature!" The higher your Light vibration is, breeds a protective shielding that cannot be harmed.

Light has no agenda...™

The principle to take with you at this time is… shine your light bright, surrender the need for suffering, fragment your energy wisely by knowing your place in this world, your evolution is the REALIZATION of ALL!!!

ALLOW. ALLOW. ALLOW.

I AM ALL THAT I AM.

JUSTIFY THE MEANS

The thought of entertaining something or someone in our lives that is NOT worthy of who we've become ends up either a confirmation, or, has taught us not to settle. The only reason humans settle is that they have felt defeated and allowed external validation to feel accepted. It is by far the most difficult of situations when we're of two-minds and no answers. However, if you look deep within yourself, you'll find the hidden truth that escapes us all when living in an egoic world…being true to what your heart wants feels very different from that of your ego and continues to test your resolve. We've all been there… planning an escape route or taking a risk of losing it all – with regret, remorse and anger at ourselves for falling into the lion's den.

Falling for those egoic desires only brings in a false sense of self that will attempt to seduce you into making a deal with the devil. A few extensions of that thread become; guilt, anger, martyrdom, shame, grief, depression etc. It is very true that, "you don't know what you've got till it's gone..." and even though we do know that taking a huge risk might come with regret; it happens. This is where karmic debt becomes very real...and that debt includes every person, and situations involved. Concurrently, these tests and trials are so very needed because, should there be a lull in our lives that we've been fooling ourselves and others, the risk then becomes a blessing in disguise. Either way... it does become a blessing, but more so when it alleviates a codependency, an addiction, a complacency etc. Be mindful that the way the ego structures is cleverly manipulating you right into huge remorse which turns out to be another lifetime of clearing karmic debt. Whatever happens... it is our freewill that does tend to show up as our egoic mind – known as, "the devil made me do it." or "Weak in the knees," is another adage that is applicable. Our knees carry us on our path to move on, to keep going, to be strong knowing that we are walking the journey of our soul. Our body lets us know how we are navigating and what messages are being sent – all one must do is observe. Every reaction has a chain reaction that imparts what is going on within us and why.

The roadless traveler beckons to make his own way by trailblazing through life's labyrinth 'going with the flow' that leads us all on our life path. Whichever path God places us on, it will always be God's plan...and that is ALL LOVE. No matter where children stray or stay is a willful intention of one's true self. Undergo whatever you will as long as you're aware there is a bill – either a karmic credit or debit to pay.

Never settle any fragmented parts, for sale. ™

Justification of what has or hasn't happened is not of importance as long as the willful acts of kindness are resurrected – in the aftermath. What we've come to understand isn't why some things occur or not; but what purported them to be aligned as a means to an end. When we go against the grain of what we "know" to be our truth, intuition always guides us… a sense of frustration in determining what has been avoided all along. Humans who are avoidant of … are overwhelmed with shame, and isolate themselves so that no one can see their flaws. Avoidant attachment patterns of overwhelming emotional intimacy are found to be highly sensitive to criticism – taking things too personally. Do you find yourself too critical? Are you avoidant of emotional wealth? Walking on eggshells? Ignoring conflict and/or running away completely shutting down? Exhausted from doing all the work? Frustrated? Where in your life have you had a sense of frustration "knowing" you weren't following your intuition? When you proceed to make a decision based on the will of others, what does that say about you? Truth is… when you know, you know. Being fragmented in confusion only lends itself to grave disappointment in yourself. We can go on about why, how, so many humans do not follow what they already know to be their own truth…cause to look deeper to assess. No act of kindness can rid someone of their truth - if it's not true to one's own heart. Human nature calls one to the table of their purest truth and encourages them to follow what they already know to be true. Not true for others, but true to themselves. Why be angry, disappointed, silent in your own aggravation when you "know" how easily we tend to change our minds and go against our inner truth. There are case-in-point examples of where it is not only others who will try to sway you to go against your truth; but the flipside of your own self, your nature will try to trip you up so that you'll have no doubts and/or cause to not follow what you already know is your rightful place. Humans have even vowed to another in the sacred union of marriage "knowing" that certain issues, discussions, placements of and in the union were not solid. Years later... separation, divorce, disagreements, adultery, codependency etc., reveals itself. Why are humans such creatures of habitual yearnings...knowingly? Complacent. Without pointing any fingers, we all struggle with doing the right thing for the wrong reasons - or doing the wrong thing under false pretenses. In whatever manner you've orchestrated your life choices...it is imperative to own it by taking full responsibility for your part. Once Humanity can follow their own truth, without any doubts, no need for questions, in complete FAITH going forward... is when we know.

12 signs of *Highly Emotional Intelligence*

1. You think about how you feel

2. You strive to control thoughts

3. You listen

4. You're calm under pressure

5. You help make others feel comfortable

6. You're successful at managing difficult situations

7. You don't seek to be perfect

8. You handle constructive criticism

9. You're curious

10. You're emphatic toward others

11. You communicate clearly

12. You are independent, honest and transparent

Conjoining our Elders' life experiences could be very advantageous when looking over our ability to make clear choices. It's not as if our parents/grandparents made all the best choices...although the choices that they made had greater consequences and repercussions that traditionally caused them to not be easily swayed, broken, and/or severed. Perhaps it is because, back in the day, children had greater respect and honorability for the wisdom of time. If for no other reason than to allow wisdom of another's life experience(s) to assist, learning to hold those with great wisdom in the respectful place where it belongs. How has the wisdom of your parents/grandparents changed over time? Do you know, or care to inquire? Why have upcoming generations view Elders as faded memories? Where and/or when did this generational-slipup happen in the lives of our youth by not respectfully understanding the hardships of their Elders? Our world has become so instantaneous – making choices, not tending to the needs of others, not caring, and/or ignorant. Any other distractions, manipulations, eager advances of cosmic currencies need not be applicable. To exist as our true essence, we all could benefit from inquiring about our family's history; and if not aware, observing other Elders who have endured challenges and pain. Become a witness to what is being observed – for you are the only witness who is observing, you.

For the majority there have been many epiphanies to endure a solid lifestyle of not needing to control the terrain...yet, many who don't realize that this life is not only being affected by you, it is not within your control. We use many forms, identities and other beings from our soul lineage to convince humans that a complete surrender to our Spirit family is the only life that we are living on Earth. As hard as it is to comprehend, this is by far the closest to what could be conceived as 'real.' Anything else that is going on in one's life is a smidge of your existence. To know this will assist in your evolution, much to your surprise, if you should be able to surrender and 'let it go'. Once you become the Master of your own domain, you'll set your ego free to take a back seat and to watch what the true path of the sacred heart is capable of. The Beatles sang, "the long and winding road" because there are those who know that life, death and taxes are only for the weak while they are chasing their tail similar to dogs. Why do dogs chase their tails? Don't they just know that their tail is attached to their body? Our animals give us so much love unconditionally…yet, we still do not recognize what they're trying to teach us. Become an observer of life, you could learn so much about you. Allow yourself to get mesmerized with Mother Nature by letting Her show you the way forward. By "never saying never" to that one thing that most sticks out in your memory as wanting something so bad, giving up is NOT an option. The reason for such a catastrophe on Earth holds no place for blame as we've all been experiencing these outer events of dis-ease on mankind. Mother Earth's natural disasters and the rumbling of nerve-endings when posed with threats on our children… detains Humanities progression. What one sees as a continuation of disasters, another sees how much more evolved Earth has become. In order for Humanity to tear off the band-aid, one must go deep within their own soul's pathway to find out core reasons as to what and where the overlap is. Throughout History… The continuation of our forefathers' legacy shows us, in an attempt to teach our children, how past generations believed the world was going to end—but didn't. Now… a repeat of the same narrative is happening. The master of the mind must be so encapsulated of itself that it does not see itself as it really IS. A Master of the mind - EGO… as in 'ego trip'. The ego has no place other than itself to listen to while the soul's heart is purposeful.

There's a thread from where one's mindset attempts to coagulate confusion; and, through the heart of artistic beauty where the canvas is cleaned out for anew to begin... Instead, this one thread is where free will connects our choices – mind with heart. Contrary, are those who believe in the same trajectory driven by greed, a false sense of power, failed attempts at each corner of where justice does not seem to fit the mold. Justice cannot be served when a life isn't seen fair or just. How could it be? Where in our past lifetimes has Justice unraveled itself as transparent for all to witness? There are newfound ways in which to view the current events, but, without a new perspective, History repeats itself.

HABIT-STANCE

We can either choose to be creatures of habit or weave a new trajectory of closing out old habits for new life. Let us begin anew by conforming to no one and seek those inherent places of our etheric embodiment. The etheric plane is where every aspect of oneself lies dormant up until the time when one is settled given the understanding that they've resolved almost every issue. These issues stem from having a belief of self-worth, assertion, initiation, constructive criticism and all other senses of self. Why are these so very important makes no difference on Earth; however, is crucial in the etheric plane of one's essence, because the ALL must be in absolution while the Universe delivers our innate qualities back to our energetic field. To say the least, one requires its own, yet very plausible reason from the Universal Law of Cause & Effect in becoming ourselves in order to receive. When one is getting ready to receive from all levels of the physical embodiment of receiving, the Holy Spirit delivers. Magic happens on the plains of positive thoughts only to find that there is no room for engaging in any fear-based emotions. We seem to think that for the better part of our lives nothing is given until it is heard from our voice to God's ears… in the vibrational frequency known as, "intention". We could say that one has great needs that require attention…yet, the true test of oneself is how authentic one's intentions are. A desire without great intention for the highest goodwill will not come to fruition. The power of love comes with the greatest desire that is not rooted as sacred ground. The term, "Ask & You Shall Receive" sounds very easy, yet it is not… not until it comes from purest intent.

EVERY PICTURE TELLS A STORY

Every story tells yet another part of our journey that we've already experienced that will be a new story. With the adage, "Every picture tells a story…" is a level of Love that is held in the hearts of those whom we've loved. No matter what type or level of love we've felt, it has been written in our hearts. The same bodes true for those who have loved us and have emotionally experienced love in perhaps a different way. Every snowflake holds a different variant where it has felt love in the kaleidoscope of falling to the Earth's surface. It may be a lighter love, a wetter love, a thicker love but every snowflake that has fallen from the Heavens holds a part of a beautifully written love story. All of Humanity holds many accompaniments of love with various types that strings up a solo, a harmony in tune, a speck in that note that isn't falsetto, a violin's fragility, the guitar's ability to hold that feeling in a note and the music that is heard feels differently within every human being. It is our essential gift given to us by God that if you can get out of your own way, open your limited mindset, take off the blinders in a Love that speaks to you – loudly or in silence, our hearts beat again.

Every trigger has a purpose… as in, "every picture tells a story," yet some humans are blinded by their own darkness… and refuse to see. Triggers show up where in our lives we are **not** yet free; and when we learn how to deal with each point-of-contention, we attain Freedom. We are not here to give you a new perspective, we are here on this very Earth to share with you our life experiences, triggers, a familiar face and/or story of experience to share. Whatever seems like a common denominator is exactly that… one's familiarity through another's story is where the common thread is weaved in the veils of illusion of one's life. Too many threads have a way of entanglement, intertwining not just your life, but, in the lives of every person, place and/or thing that becomes a trigger, red flags. All too many of us are all-too familiar with how it feels to undergo stress, anger, anxiety, depression etc., in an all-too comfortable place for those who are blinded by their own darkness. Many adults are afraid of their own crisis thoughts of believing our anxiety is a disorder that we need to get rid of. What needs to be understood is the core of our anxiety; be it grief, pain and/or an intense helplessness needs to be acknowledged and dealt with. In light of this, our thoughts and emotions are the mirror reflections of how safe we feel. Reflections of how secure we feel in all areas including those we are trying to run away from, avoidance. A fear-based mentality that always questions, "Am I in trouble?" comes from fear-based parenting. Children apologize for no good reason and tend to over-explain things so intensely one could feel their energy of anxiety. What comes into light over and over again is the way with which we, as humans, react under such duress. One's reaction, knee-jerk reaction, or whatever comes to mind is of the ego. We can either embrace the ego for what and how it can be so impulsive; or, we could instead, set on a new course, a path of least driven by our triggers. What mindset has you entangled in exposing your truths that comes with the cost of being comfortably numb? Who sets the stage for what hasn't worked in your life; what or who to blame; where do you run to flee from your own pain…. Where is the way out? The way inward is the way out… however, not many seem to know this to be true. When we get to a place where the only thing, we experience is quiet resolve by getting to a point in our lives that is peaceful, we have arrived. No matter what chaos is going around, within us or otherwise…it is within us to maintain our composure to be cool, calm and collected. It takes great inner strength and work for this attainment – for what gets in the way is our egoic thoughts. This is what happens in times of trouble to so many who react. Reactions are those made of our ego… the triggers that tend to offend, hurt to the core, seemingly unadulterated repertoire of pain. However reactive one gets is not of dire consequence but at whomever it is directed for or to. Humans react because there has been a so-called trigger that has a faded memory of pain within that has been masked for quite some time and is screaming for HELP. If we continue to mask the pain with external influences such as sex, drugs and the like, it will continue to escalate in you over time. This is why we need these triggers… to address our pain so that we can find healing. Pain must be felt to its entirety for it to be expressed and allowed in whatever fashion of outbursts as crying out for HELP. When this happens the receiving person who is listening to these outbursts has to hold themselves in check to either console, contain and/or counsel their true essence of pain. If and when the time comes where people overreact by lashing out in pain – it's seen as a cry for HELP without the other getting projecting to react (ego-clashers). A series of cries for HELP happen every day and whether we can validate someone else by helping them heal is the way in which we can service others and ourselves. Just because you're not able to understand the exact reason why someone is triggered doesn't mean they weren't placed in front of you to heal some part of your understanding of a repressed pain. We tend to get wrapped up in others' pain instead of seeing this as a mirroring of a suppression of inner pain somewhere in our lives. Perhaps the exact circumstances do not mirror yours ... however, a deep-seated pain that makes you feel compelled to assist. Reactions need reassurance, understanding and listening so you can help another heal and to alert you of a potential similarity before you. If you continue to sweep it under the rug, you will be faced with yet more uncomfortable triggers. We know "what resists, persist" don't we? It's a game of give-and-take in life where we must give a little or alot...in order to help ourselves; and, if all we're doing is taking, the karmic wheel turns for you to start giving. Whatever you may or may not have done in-service for others and to yourself is based upon the karmic wheel of justice. This is exactly why couples that have been together a long time experience a role-reversal, if you will, of give and take. The one who gave all the time is now receiving and the one who received all the time is now giving back. As painfully true this reality is, we can now be made aware of how our actions have a reaction. Working the system for all those years catches up with us not only in actions but also within every area of our life – work, play, love – it's all a sacrifice. While looking in hindsight at your life you can very well see that the circle of life is when what we revisit must be calibrated to even out the score. Not in, 'an eye for an eye' no, it is the interpretation that matters. We realize later in life all of the painful truths we have not realized of our own demise. Any pain we've caused people that didn't deserve it, becomes a very different narrative. What if we didn't have karma on the Earth plane? What would The Laws of the Universe be? Would there be any course of action/reaction leading to lessening the pains of our lives? How intricately woven are the threads of our Universal truths in ways that allow us to revisit a time where the pain was too great to deal… as we set on a new course to heal. When the body is healed it has spiraled into an oblivion where no more energetic frequency exists. Taking the time to access our own power again by either giving back when the time calls or receiving when the time arrives is the call of what is known as, *Diving Timing*.

NOT MY CIRCUS, NOT MY MONKEYS

Emotional and mental instability in children of parents who have addictions/dis-ease lead to anger, instability, stress, anxiety that weave into the lives of these children. Numerous layers of instability add to the already unstable issues of our past threads (repressed and/or suppressed) as well as what society's delusional play-by-play adds as trauma. Trauma keeps us held "hostage". What comes from a child's trauma, tragedies, worries, stress, sex offenders, physical & verbal abuse, emotional manipulation, codependency, loss of Father/Mother, loss of sibling(s), a loss of a child etc., lends itself to such a wide-net span of abusive behaviors that there are way too many to mention. Children are sick from any negative energies that surround… wear black obsidian crystal, for protection. Many children are incapable of seeing the instabilities in their own parents' inability to cope and/or deal to overcome. Parents who are oblivious are not cognizant of the impact this has on their children - and as they grow into adulthood, every child is either tormented to shame, guilt, or emotionally unstable which has a "not my circus, not my monkeys" mentality of not taking responsibility. Our ancestral lineage has all the remnants of abusive behavior from way back when; and, while this is the 21st Century who would've thought that these factors would have any relevance at all. But they do. All the beliefs/ideologies, systems of repetition, behaviors and patterns of our ancestors, the wounds/scarring that hasn't healed since the beginning of time is why Mother Earth is suffering. It is in our genetics, DNA, cells, atoms, blood and/or otherwise/adopted – any connection to a family history that plays its own role in this lifetime. The name of the game is not to "play dead" but to roll up our sleeves and retract our steps by going inward. Go within by mapping what made you FEEL triggered emotions of: anger, sadness, abuse, verbal, physical, communication breakdown, codependency, addictions and any other forms of feeling "less than" "not wanted" or, all negative emotions – including a notation as to whether you "feel" that you've forgiven them, been forgiven, and have you forgiven yourself? Whose circus is this anyway? Are we going to continue to monkey around? Or, monkey-see-monkey-do by following a corrupt society? Instead of being passive, or, passive-aggressive – however you handle your monkeys' "food for thought…" BANANAS, bananas for potassium OR pot-as-a-insane-asylum.

FOUNDATIONAL STRUCTURES

There are "old souls" and "young souls" both of which have experienced life on different levels, timelines and life experiences. So much tragedy remains for all souls to recapture their youthful spirit by changing their foundational structures. We're not cognizant of this in our youth but all those who felt more like the "black sheep" growing up in their family had an inkling of being different. Every path is mapped out…it's a matter of getting there - where the soul's guidance matters. Some need to stray before they can get back on path; while others never get on path, in just one lifetime. Old souls and young souls are intertwined on Earth so as to seek learning by example or leading the way forward. The harder life the wiser the soul… to say that in layman's terms, age doesn't matter. Filtering out life stories and experiences is the true definition of a fulfilled life. Every living soul has a story that begets their authenticity. To erase our past history would be tragic in and of itself. Those traumas, wounds, scars and lessons make for a full life which to be grateful for. What we choose to do, where we go, who we seek to hang out with and the places we are familiar with builds our foundation. That foundation can be rebuilt, revised, added-on or made newer depending upon life circumstances. Whatever foundation is built in our external world is a mirror reflection of what our inner foundation feels. The mirror, as is the Sun/Moon either in sync with one another, or, very different versions. One foundation could imply a life of great happiness on the exterior, but hurting inside; and the way to know is how elaborate a foundation has been built. Many high-ranking executives making 6 figures, driving 6-figure cars and living in a 6-figure home are hosting a mindset of 666; the numerological figure for one's beast of burden. Mind you… when we overcompensate in any area of our lives, threads of egoic insecurity alert us to being raised with not enough, attempting to prove their worth, needing to be seen and continue to misuse power. However, on the flip-side *many* other hard-working executives do **not** require to "show off" and their egos are adjusted to enjoy the fruits of their labor - in a simplistic life – or – as they've learned to balance those luxuries of life as presents to enjoy and share. A life experienced on both sides of the spectrum is a good indication that one has learned the value of life; and that over-acquiring "stuff" ends up holding little-to-no value.

In the big picture…what does matter on Earth are those we help out in every way that we're called to do - to visit someone ill or in the hospital, to find other places of enjoyment that have an unprecedented

302

value to the other. Everyone might be given the chance to live whatever lifestyle they desire knowingly deserving of…yet the sought-after materialistic seems irrelevant when outer factors of sickness, stress, depression, anger, resentment, rage, hate stands in the way of our soul's growth. All the finer things that are dangled in our world are just another way of saying, "go for broke!" "Striking while the iron's hot" couldn't be any further from the *truth*… in life, grab life with all your passion, fervor by believing in yourself not needing to 'show off' for the sake of showing off. "All the world's a stage" is to give it all you've got no matter what…just watch out for the caveat of becoming a 'sell out', selling your soul has no value when you cave. "Things you crave make you cave…" What makes one person numb is another's need to fill a void, is another's yearning to escape, etc. When we experience a loss, it is a clear indication that what is being released gives us Freedom.

HISTORY OF THE EGO

Those skeletons in our closets are a constant reminder that there is so much more work to be done. At the very beginning of time, man was given a woman who would entertain his ways of bringing out all the impressive characteristics to grow from and make one proud. This is not what happened… man, in general, became a vastly egoic individual as God placed a shadow in every human on Earth to conquer. What did happen was that the man showed up as feeling superior to woman, even though the woman assisted in elevating him, he fell from a place of needing her into a desire of flesh, instead. The story of Adam and Eve depicts a perfect yin/yang couple which leads us from the pure innocence of fulfillment of our greatest needs to addressing the egoic mindset of the physical body upholding the most significant desires of man. What happened has been a strong theme in our history, where woman was created by the rib of man; but, where has it been written that a woman was not able to obtain equality? When did this acquiring desire of the human flesh actually consume Adam into giving Eve the apple to take a bite first… giving the man the control to this unequitable story of how the ego was incarnated. What, where, and how did this happen is a metaphoric storyline of Adam and Eve setting the precedence for all couples who deem to establish a relationship? Whether you believe in Adam and Eve's story, does not equate to what the actual moral of these two humans imprisoned upon us as a "guilty as charged" mentality. Once Eve's leaf fell to the ground, after biting the apple, our ego was born for the entire human race to conquer. Mother Earth, Eve's Mother… knowingly gave her the tree to plant the apple as she was inquisitive, curious and trusting of Adam, and took the oath of silencing one's ego. From this point onward, every man, woman and child has been given a *shadow* to deal with and to learn from. How many times have you listened to your ego or that of others that led you astray? Do you know how the story goes, or, how it finally ended? Are we, in this present moment on planet Earth realizing that Eve IS Mother Earth? The soul-spirit essence of Eve's alter ego in the formation of Herself, begets to mankind as Mother Earth. How did this happen? Did that ever come into your mind that She needed to cleanse herself of the guilt that Adam placed upon Her, and became the Mother for all. Do you think this story might help you, if you are a woman, to consider changing the narrative of your life; hoping to help assist others who also need HELP? Does every story in the history books seem like a real incantation of a series of events that had to happen for us to learn from? What is seen is found in the pauses, is found in patience, is found in letting another be whatever is intended… be that a place of greatness, be those fragments

304

of silence, be that one's own light that shines the way forward for others to see; and, be that truth in each one of us to show up as another vein that espouses to become. We must ask ourselves why the truth is so very hard to accept and that the way of others has always been a thorn of contention to all of Humanity. Why? Because it is easier to venture out of your comfort zone by choosing to focus on the likes of others, instead of through a mirror-reflection in the looking glass. Mirrors are known to show whatever reflection needs to be witnessed – and, many times what one sees looking back is very foreign to them. Humanity has chosen to exhibit others' place in the world by branching out to find their fulfillment of desires to omit their inner treasures. Most definitely this has been the thorn of contention in society since the beginning of time… growing worse and not better. Becoming your own true self hides behind the masks of our Ego and the masks of others' Egos… and, so on. We have been driven by an egoic persona of a mad-society whose vices are sex, drugs and rock - n- roll – using band aids to heal wounds that have turned back to a time of our own Heritage. Unbeknownst to mankind the ways of old have been slowly turning back the hands of time so as to jump into a portal well-suited for the Ages. The story of Alice-in-Wonderland depicts mankind who ran away from themselves, found outlandish characters that resembled themselves, who fell into the rabbit hole and surrender was founded by an evil Queen who found such delight to call them her own. Alice was subjected to a place where not many think they reside in today's world… Yet, this is their Wonderland. As John Mayer's song clearly shows up in his lyrics as, "Your body's A Wonderland" for the exact reason mankind suffers. The bodies that we have been given by Spirit were not meant to be fleshed with external poisons that lie dormant awaiting their desires to override a life meant to be sought within. The feeling of external vices that grab a hold of your body are

305

similar to that of a jellyfish attacking a part of your body in the ocean of life and not letting go. What is taunting you right now at this very moment? Are you a version of one of the characters in Wonderland?

EGO. THE "I'S" HAVE IT

Every human being under the guise of our Nation has been manipulated into thinking that "We The People" have various forms of Freedom; Freedom of religion, Freedom of expression, Freedom of assembly, Freedom of press, Freedom of petition, Freedom of movement, Freedom of speech, Equal protection of the law and all other human rights, "A Bill of Rights". We coagulate that Freedom to be oneself would be the most underrated of all freedoms... However, misrepresentation leads to falsely surmising the premise which one comes to the table; "they" have taken hold of your mind and body through false pretenses, false marketing, falsified information etc. The "I's' ' have it. It's a huge part of a calculated Ego ... that insists we grow up. How? By going within and to understand that when no-thought happens, surrender of the Ego will be laid to rest. To be of an all-or no-thing is to be either in your ego or knowing you are one with the ALL. The ego forms a structured vision of thought which tends to overmine you and others into thinking one way or another. Instead, how can mankind stay in a place of all-heart where AI cannot fathom to express? AI is the scientific, logical, statistical briefings of borrowed information, knowledge and the like. If we can attain a place of what is at the heart of the matter then, you are redeemed into the reflection of the self as the ALL. Certain visions of what the egoic self represents can be seen as an asset, if used through the mind of our heart...otherwise, it becomes all illusion. Traveling the path of least resistance is fine for a time, but does not seek to influence a change of self. The human self has to decipher what it KNOWS to be true… Can you take your ego self out of the equation and allow your spirit self to guide?

"For what is a man … .and, what has he got, if not himself, then he has naught. To say the things he truly feels, and not the words of one who kneels."

Paul Anka. "For what is a man" is the personal journey; and, "what has he got", "if not himself, then he has naught…" precedes to distinguish fact from fiction. What is left is ALL.

Ego is a "sugar high" energy that doesn't know where to turn that continues to feed it as ammunition, much like giving a child sugar where it is an addiction. Throughout generations, a society of breeding children with sugar – in foods, drinks and entertainment (iPad, iPhone, TV, Social Media) hosts an overriding "out of control" energy that craves more. The MORE generation was established throughout generations in order to control the substances and bring about more addictive substances. These children/kids are learning to self-soothe by numbing through addictions that they're not even aware of – being given sugar from parents who also have addictive behavior patterns and cannot say no. Our egos go deep into the constructs of the conscious mind that breed convincing. Sometimes with remorse and other times… with none.

Patterns that blind begin to form as, "the blind leading the blind".

SLEEPWALKERS

To entertain the egoic mindset is one way of saying that your mind is in control and in a habitual version of a variety of selves which cannot remain sanely whole. This is true for all those who, right at this very moment, are thinking about it too hard. The masks of our persona, what we wear outside of us, that tend to coerce, appease, manipulate, justify and make complete fools out of who we were programmed to 'think'. After careful consideration, we still have difficulty in reaping the rewards of a fulfilled lifestyle. The lifestyles of those who need to showcase their wealth share deeply seated scars of self-worth values that were never met, in this lifetime, nor in others. Why? These humans are torn and bound by the earthly pleasures of power-hungry necessities that leave out any form of self-discipline whatsoever. However, once a person begins a purging regime, this is a sign of the beginning of what would be considered learning to purify one's fragrance. We cannot continue to ingest processed foods, cannot be certain of what damage has been done to our lungs by aluminum and smoke-filled vaping/cigarettes, and bodies fed of poison without taking accountability that the end-result is a destruction of our bodies. Should those sleepwalkers get out of complacency and into actually caring about their temple body, will be their fight to Freedom.

What a giant leap of Faith in oneself to enable our own strength of discipline and willfulness to become the best and highest version of ourselves... to all of those who have done so, huge congratulations! This world has become an enlightened version of itself by standing firm to those values, beliefs and programming of how we are warriors. It doesn't surprise, those who have maintained a certain warriorship level, have evolved into versions of the highest kind. This encapsulates what is called, an authentic self that is realized. We're not privy to all the varied requirements here on Earth, yet, we salute each and every one of ours that already knows. Enlightenment and all our lightworkers have similar traits with which they can embrace their wholeness without requiring to fill any voids... a missing void that has been wounded, scarred and/or unable to heal. These wounded warriors have come very close in ALL of their lives, yet, some are still under the spell of what is known as, sleepwalking. These sleepwalkers are just hanging by a thread for they know all about the awakening but not about their connection to themselves. For all we know, many will rise up beyond the ashes only to seal the approval of no one. That will end your journey on this Earth of karmic retribution cleared and self-realized. We're almost there...some have already seen the light while others are bordering the line... going forward. We cannot be at the precipice of enlightenment until this awakens all of your seven chakras – and, after all is said and done, there comes a time of self-observation. A mirror reflection of witnessing all the souls who have been in your lifetime, the souls from past lifetimes and the worrisome eccentricity of those who are no longer a part of this life. The connection is real... take hold and seek refuge. Look before you leap... don't make rash decisions, take extra time to get where you've been trying to land; and, by no means should anyone attempt to fill your personal void by promising the world. It is a very frugal attempt at wishing, hoping and praying to change the world that has been unchanged typically by your need to know. Let all those requests of needing to know fly off your shoulders and go inside where you can also feel your sensibilities on a mass scale. The weight of the world is not good on one's shoulders, nor should it be. What we have done to ourselves, on a grand scale, is not taking full responsibility for what we are unable to face, "the truth will set you free". We've come to an understanding what this means, when unable to fly at a moment's notice given the value that which it bestows. This value is where we confer to disagree the most important values, where we give our time, effort and value to. Can we tame the wild whose only source of survival is getting into a lion's den?

We've all been there…now we are in need of letting go and letting God. To dabble in the resources of your life without a mere observation, is fragile and naive. When the ego is at its most comfortable is when it is aware of the hold it has within the mindset. Neither this nor that can sustain a human being from its own self-realization. It's an attempt at control of the highest order of the egoic self. The other masks that fall off return effortlessly in order to show its dexterity of flavor to the world at large. "The world is your oyster" has many underlying implications which are determining factors of a number of aphrodisiacs inside what makes us more elusive to our external desires… Is this a 'fools rush in' type of vibrational frequency that enables the mind to be manipulated and formed into believing that once you inhale a 6-pack of oysters you will fall madly "in lust?" What a scam… and what about those poor little oysters that are being shucked over so many times for its innate cause and effect it brings to those with the pleasure principle. We've all got our own quirks about what we ingest – from the pleasures of eating, drinking, smoking etc., to an overindulgence of what is behind those needs. We've come to know what it means to grow up always hungry and always wanting MORE. The MORE PRINCIPLE of these past few generations has highlighted a "VOGUE" lifestyle. Instead, the New World Order will bring about this imminent change of a new "mindset" by bringing balance. Why have we not been taught to balance our lives and our checkbooks?

THE MORE GENERATION

Who is the MORE GENERATION? Are they all-consuming to the ideologies of attaining accolades, success, power and lifestyles of the rich and famous? Have we, as a society, achieved the goals of acquiring "stuff" only to end up purging an entire life? Are YOU responsible for your own worth? Have you become complacent with the need to acquire unlimited amounts of high-end labels and products that will end up either in the garbage, charity and/or at some thrift store? Can you now see clearly as to why our parents or whomever raised us have gone to such great lengths upholding their end of the deal… giving their children everything that matters. By definition, "matters" don't really matter as a swirling materialistic world. As Madonna sings, "A Material Girl living in a Material World". Not only did Madonna sing about women who are overly obsessive about how much they have in numbers, but also the obsession of remaining youthful in a world full of gravity – both women and men have both bought into these frugal attempts at what remains. It's not a Madonna issue… she is putting the obvious out there for the world to see that what remains of her too is the fame, fortune, youthful necessity to undo what has already been done a million times over. It's not a newly kept secret that we've all been taken for granted on a grand scale. A culture built on the desire for a limelight of fashion, fame and fortune, is another's lesson of assessing what is broken. We all deem to *want it all* but what proves to be of more value than anything or anyone is the individual unified consciousness of what is not to love, yourself. A balancing act, indeed, that requires us to find our truth that fills a needed void, if any, and/or fame or fortune besieges the desire. This is the whole premise for a life well lived… in order to balance those things that make us the best, highest version of ourselves, takes us into foreign territory that lives in a peaceful feeling of simplicity. What has been given to Humanity are the options which to learn from giving us a Freedom of living a fulfilled life without going, going, gone. Once you are able to Master your domain, knowing that we are meant to have it all on a grander scale than acquiring stuff is a progression. We may "have it all" depending upon your perception of what this means to each and every one of us. It may seem like what is being asked is not to follow the ego of wanting MORE; but, to embrace our authenticity (i.e., purging, downsizing, purifying, detoxing). The egoic mindset... wanting it all for reasons of greed, guilt, jealousy, comparisons, etc., tends to sink into one's lifestyle as a question of value in oneself. In essence, we are privy to receiving whatever essential requirements of self-worth is necessary, but, not only for the sake of receiving; but for the loss within. If you've ever questioned your values at some point in your life, and have lost all your valuables, Spirit is teaching you your truest power is where you've misplaced your own value, instead. Over the course of time, some begin to take notice of what brings them real Freedom.

We can only hope to see a New World Order where we attain an ever-so-balanced life that doesn't require labels. Those that came before us and those who will come after will know how this Golden Age has begun to redesign our tapestry. Mother Earth clears Her palette each and every night only to begin again in the first light of a new life... a dawning of the Ages. All across the world we've been watching the cycles of the Moon that form in the night sky, but do you understand the intrinsic details that come with each new sunrise? To comprehend this... is surreal. Certain visions in life begin to form once we turn a new leaf, until a transformation has been completed – then, we are able to fully appreciate how beautiful this world is designed...

eloquently simple, and so very extraordinary. The simple things in life that take our breath away…

"We are not here to question why; we are here to do and die." God speaks.

SHAPESHIFTING

"We're in this together" is a quote earlier described to juxtapose the honorability of one's character. To be able to own up to our responsibilities knowing that everything has been placed upon your table… to see, to become aware and to know better is to BE better. "Whatever for?" may be a question for some who may be either in denial and/or may need another perspective. Whatever your reasons for shift-shaping through a world unfulfilled, asking why there has not been a progression, may be what needs sifting. What may come and what may go is not necessarily about how much we've acquired… as much as how much love we have given in-service to others. We cannot place a price on love, but we can give all the love we've been given in this life to show gratitude. We'll seek other lovers just in order to change the narrative, yet, while the faces may change, the room for us to become aware holds much truth to only what is within our hearts – not what is external to that of our own selves. Why not grant yourself the present of a new life, a new evolved you so that these conforming patterns do not continue to repeat over and over again. We must seize the day when our personal attributes of external desires take precedence over the most important person, our children, in the lives of every human being. Perhaps we shall be privy to learn that at the end of a lifetime, we are continuing to master ourselves. Our highest self only wants the very best for each of us to learn how to Master the art of self-awareness and to evolve to a state of higher consciousness.

ENERGETIC IMBALANCES

There is a structured sense of balance when it comes to the likes of both masculine and feminine energies; however, it's how you work with your energy that sometimes may seem one is working harder than the other. What is really going on is an influx of dual energies fighting against the other – perhaps for attention or a rewire to recharge. It is without question that either energies may need to realign in order to be at their highest vibration to set the tone of one hand feeds off of another. In whatever fashion your energy relies upon others, it is crucial that both masculine and feminine energies understand the need for the other to become a lifesaver. When the feminine is tired, she/he needs the masculine energy to complement until she reboots and vise-versa. Many do not understand the implications of energy imbalances and often get offended when one might be doing more than the other. Hence, this occurs with partnerships on a regular basis - as one or the other seems to be doing all the work…yet, the truth is, one energy has become weaker and requires time to recharge. Whenever we are worn out, tired, depressed, depleted this is our body telling us to rest and rejuvenate. Heeding warnings of the body pre-empts dis-ease. This bodes true for every man, woman and/or child – even our animals need a reboot. That's where Mother Nature comes in to help… All we require is a restless day outside, a brisk walk, relaxing by water or whatever form of relaxation you prefer. Mother Nature is the energy of our Universe, therefore, being outside in the natural forces of receiving healing properties is crucial to maintain and establish excellent health. When that's not possible, a warm milk bath, and/or, a Magnesium or Epsom salt bath will recharge our bodies. The healing properties of Mother Earth's environment is exactly how the animals survive and thrive. Once we establish a comprehensive understanding of how energy can be managed, altered, expands/contracts then Humanity will learn to alchemies energetic healing; sound healing. Anything that clears the garbage of what is filtered in one's mindset needs to be purified...as in, taking out the trash. Our mind is on overdrive between social media platforms, ideals and beliefs, siphoning through others' conversations and/or attempting to distinguish truth from a place of fear and distrust...

Overriding energetic forces become "mental anguish" – where Humanity is now ...a place of mental illness that is bleeding one's true essence. The mind is that of the EGO and will attempt to place the "fear of God" in every facet of the brain to disable the natural order of where Love resides. The power of Love is much stronger when understood that fear fears itself. The reason that fear fears itself is that it has no place to be, there is no real destination for fearful actions – it leaves one stagnant and alone in their thoughts. Hence, if you do not move your energy, those stagnant energies remain the beginning of your demise. Scattered energy is where fear lives to entice humans into thinking they're crazy, into thinking they are not good enough, into thinking that life is not treating them fair, into thinking and believing that life is not worth living... There will definitely be a strong contention of forces happening in the ethers where the power of fear vs. the enormous power of Faith. Instead of denying yourself the fruits of your labor riddled with fears such as; guilt, unworthiness, rejection, jealousy, anger, etc., subjected to these Fears is to one's own detriment. All imbalances of fearful energies are rebalanced with LOVE... as the heart contracts when the 'fear of...' exists within; but when we learn to let go and let Love in, the heart expands. The upcoming generations will assist in Humanity's leveling up by sharing their abilities to manipulate energy, alchemy. The upcoming generations are versions of our forefathers' fragrance who misused the powers that be and are coming back to retract the fear of God; and reset the balance of karmic justice. Every child must balance out the scales in their life – if not in this life cycle, then, in a thousandth year, where it can be accepted and rectified, according to God's plan. Severed threads will be resewn for the construct of our Earth to be illuminated back to its natural order. Much like the energies between masculine and feminine... all energies equal out the other. No one energy and/or person is better than, higher up, or whatever your ego will have you think. It is all an illusion of the mind and will inevitably convince you to misuse your power for fear that you will be trumped.

Children need outside activities that enlist in team building, social settings of innovative bursts of enlightenment. Can you identify when you lost your childhood self? Or, are there clouds of delusion? When did you stop letting spontaneity be your guide? When did you stop laughing? Why does it begin to annoy adults when children are just being themselves? When did we become so serious? When did we get off that Ferris wheel? When did we stop running through fire hydrants, jumping rope, swinging on swings, playing in mud? Where did parts of our childhood self-go? When did reality hit you like a ton of bricks? When did you have your last convo where we shared our deepest secrets? Who are you now? Do you know? Have you seen yourself lately...really taken a good look at yourself? Do you wonder what you'd be like if your inner child were still "active" in your life? What purpose does our inner child serve if it has been buried deep within the recesses of our existence? It is still within each and every one of us; however, so much has been repressed by our inner child, a call to play will bring them back to show you how easy it is to relive times of innocence, again. Those who have cast their inner child away might be the first to go seeking others' approval/opinions, backhand comments, reaping rewards of other's work, seeking financial stability through no effort from self, playing with fire... in unhealthy addictive behaviors exhausting all options of maintaining the temple, crying over spilled milk, weeping willows in the backyard of the "good ole' days!" Why must we wander aimlessly in life "acting" like the unfeeling-AI robots they are mass producing? When will you be able to forgive yourself of the errs of your ways so that a new life can be regained? Staying on point is hard to do...and even harder when listening to those "Old-Fashioned Love Songs" playing on the radio. How about taking a minute... right now and listening to the lyrics of that song, take a breath out of your day, let's do a "refresh" together. No time like the present.... now, how do you feel? Set aside time for play, do something different every day, read, pretend to be someone else (no idols), do yourself a favor and put down that phone a little more every day, sing a song, write a poem, tamper in some oil paints, vow to be yourself "authentic self" more and more inner wisdom will prevail.

Signs of High Vibration

1. People stare at you with wonder
2. Children are attracted to your energy
3. Animals feel safe
4. Strangers confide in their life stories
5. Able to 'feel' the energy in a room

6. People are irritated by your authenticity

7. People are jealous and uncertain why

NO CENTS/SENSE OF SELF

That's the moral of the story…to gain great rewards knowing that at the end of our experiences we've come to learn, all the money in the world does not make us happy… or even content. Of course, money is not the root of all evil…until it becomes an obsession. It goes without saying that everything in life is transient and that no man, woman and/or child can consume so much where a grace of a life begotten. Some would argue with this because perhaps their mentality is: one cannot spend enough, have enough, or take hold of the "good life." In all their consuming, acquiring, hoarding and accumulating, there is an emptiness that has no name. Much to one's dismay… we fail to understand this much later in life or when the pot is empty; and, for others, while the money is being spent a loss of self is etched away in every purchase. You know the feeling of looking in your closet only to find nothing to wear, still looking you tend to set your sights on a few items that you have no idea why you ever bought them? How much nonsense… NO SENSE/NON-CENTS does one recreate in a world of utter senseless buying power… because they are lost? To reincarnate into a world that holds no power of senseless desires does not exist on Earth; therefore, one will only know what it's like to obtain the release of values as needing those expensive items that end up being either tossed out, sold and/or given to a charity. These are only for those who have learned that the excess of anything is useless… in the end, it's only what and who you love, have loved and will ever LOVE.

MOTHER EARTH - GAIA

Mother Earth is omnipresent in the likes of Herself as the Sun; while planet Earth is in need of many burnt-out light bulbs as in a recycling belt. The energy on planet Earth is in a continuous flux of energy that rises up and down just like our thoughts, fleetingly… ever-changing. Mother Earth's light is not only abundant but She too holds an energetic protection that cannot be contained. This is how Mother Earth's masterpiece is formed, a flower's fragrance has been felt, seen, smelled and heard throughout the entire Universe. What type of flower is yet to be seen…for the flowers of ALL the children ascending bare different attributes – ALL enlightened children of the Lord will seek to appreciate the fruits of their labor in every way and will continue to transmit THE WORD OF GOD to those who are yet requiring the path to awareness. "The best is yet to come…" What does it feel like to be touched by Heaven? A child's innocent gaze, the smell of familiar and unfamiliar fragrances, walking on Holy ground, a rain pour, the strength of all mountains, baby's breath, velvet orchids, the smell of just-cut grass, chirping birds, sunrise/sunset, autumn leaves falling, snowflakes, oceans/lakes, the sea, fires of creative passion, a world of infinite possibilities…. Every seasonal change awaits with bated breath for Humanity to embrace in Love. Even the dark-blue sky embodies a Full Moon that precedes the next Waning Moon – every animal, insect, plant, flower etc., sees itself in Love as whole. Why can't humans do the same? Existence on Earth understands itself and the power of Life it breathes through. We could take some much-needed lessons from the "Freedom" that exists in Mother Nature. The reason we call Her, Mother Nature is because not only is Her beauty exquisitely unique every day/night, but She paints a new landscape where one cannot be fooled – it is not part of Her History. Amongst those who are aware… find the comfort of Autumn leaves not only a breath of fresh air but the seasonal changes that happen within Mother Earth's ability to change colors and witness what feelings speak to our hearts. It's as though all the colors of the rainbow fell upon the Earth and wherever they land…miracles abound. The green hues that are highlighted with various reds, oranges on their ends … without having to spend hours at a hairdresser is what Mother Earth shares with us. As with the Fall season… calls for change that has outlasted over the years. All of Mother Earth transforms…and so do we, some more than others. Whenever we are called to embrace any changes in our lives it's a time to shed what has been in order to grow into what will be. As the wind blows the leaves off the trees, we experience a more distinct fragrance in the air that sends the message to Humanity that we too must shed what has been. As this transformation of change happens Mother Earth finds Herself changing in ways that are not known to humans. The difference between Her transforming at the sound of every newborn we accompany that change as an outcry of resistance. A sunrise brings a new day of life experiences and into every sunset a letting go. A sense of urgency happens when there is a let go… it will seem as if your entire world just began again and that all the gone is a thing of the past. In layman terms, there will be moments in our lives that will seem as though they never happened – you won't ever be the same once you drop your old self. The new self has not begun to figure out what has happened to the old self – yet it sits quietly waiting to play catch-up. History may have a chance to chart a new course after which the old catches up with it, syncing both becomes a challenge; then, one is able to make brand new decisions. Once the old life informs your new life of some of the mistakes it made, your life can actually be re-invented and one can recreate an entire new platform of karmic ties and get swiped off someone's old life for good. That's the best part of a lifecycle… when we take into consideration that every one of us has the potential to change our own history to present a new you unto the world at large. People act as though you're still the same ole person they "used to know" when, in fact, the new you is merging of new/old selves and that doesn't show up at face value until it is realized. She needs no attention… and though many fail to see Her beauty, for she IS. Given the amount of pollution, humans toss out their "garbage" and our lakes/ocean's polluting the environment. Similar is the same "junk" of what humans ingest in their mind & bodies. Throwing trash out the windows, plastics invading our oceans, chemtrails, plastic bottles, plastic bags and plastic wrapped; and, trash-talking others, eating recalled and processed foods that might as well be trash, negative thinking, criticism, and judgments. 'Taking the trash out' is becoming a crucial issue that we must deal with on this Earth. Have you done so? Are you to blame? Be honest. Why can't we take an extra minute and think about how polluted She is right now – our waters are not made for drinking, swimming and pollution has been a huge concern for our animals. Fish of all kinds are coughing up junk-infested waste from their bodies and are caught dead - plastic being the majority of junk ingested. Pollution is also invading our plastic credit cards with added corruption of interest – the inner drippings of society's debt. The world is in debt… What are we teaching our kids? As parents who are living in a materialistic world of greed and misuse of power, we are all to blame. We are a dying species and who can help fix us? Are we supporting the cause? How can we get the message across if it doesn't begin at home? Our food is poisoned, tainted with pesticides; our waters and air are unhealthy; and what are we doing about it? Are you helping or hindering Mother Earth who has given life within every breath? Mother Earth reigns upon this beautiful land and humans continue to ignore...and/or don't care. Do you realize how severe the situation is that Mother Earth, being our inner physical selves is crying out for HELP? Our physical bodies, the temple of wholeness, is what has been given at birth. How can your body remain whole/Holy in its original essence if humans are abusing this privilege? Mother Earth's energy is within the physical temple and holds healing properties. Therefore, children need to be made aware of the body as their navigational system. The "mind" is where all the inner turmoil exists... while the body needs healing. The mind may be holding onto emotional trauma from its past sending signals to the body that psychologically it is not ready to calibrate through synergistic healing. Every human has been placed upon this Earth to undergo a clearing, a recalibration to purify - yet we must teach our children and ourselves to set a new course. Why hasn't this been taught? So much of what we've learned in school is inconsequential, yet, the need to live a healthy life, requires children to be shown/taught life skills from the inside out.

This Western civilization has manipulated Humanity into "popping pills and shooting up" as warranted to continue to buy into that mindset – for the masses are codependent. All external usages of numbing pain and gaining interest are all forms of attachment/codependency. Using humans as their testing grounds ... not to cure illness but to placate. How on Earth has a cure for cancer NOT yet been found? Why are innocent people dying? The fact remains that while, in some cases, certain pharmaceuticals are necessary; just not for the duration of one's life. That breeds into the weakness of man's ignorance being taught that Western medicine is the only cure. When, in fact, Mother Nature has been providing for Her children since the beginning of time. As an example, let's say someone has been diagnosed with high-blood pressure... going to a medical doctor requires that they take blood-pressure medicine for the rest of their lives. Had the diagnoses of high-blood pressure been addressed through self-education with natural cures, perhaps they would realize that eating "superbeets" and/or drinking beet juice will assist before it becomes chronic. Not many understand the correlation of how the mind thinks a certain way while interacting with the body – and, being programmed since childhood to depend on doctor's without seeking other possibilities is not discerning when other options are available. Humans are creatures of habit therefore, trying to sway one's ability to "think" outside what has been taught, is a huge undertaking. We need to be much more vigilant in pursuing and realizing that Mother Nature IS ALL NATURAL – Research has proven that natural remedies work when realized. Our inability to change our ways is exactly why "they/society" continues to prescribe meds that, depending upon the cause, could be healed naturally. Why is society still seeking a cure for cancer? Are they? Where is it written… The inability to see clearly that Humanity has been taken on a wild goose chase on coattails of those in power, have fallen deep into the Matrix. All it takes is to discern what you feel is real…instead of believing in most everything others are saying and/or doing. Mother Earth has always been our natural healer – given this knowledge, what will you decide? Will you stay in your old ways of pre-programmed thinking or will you venture out to gain your own perspective? It's up to you…use your Free Will. It comes down to "learned behavior" vs. "Intelligence of Mother Nature" – Fear or LOVE?

To those who already know without a doubt that this is happening, we tend to want to lean towards a more "giving tree" for the Law of Cause & Effect to ascertain its existence; but, those who just "go with the flow" end up realizing the degree of service to mankind is a necessity for the switch of energetic vibration to ensue. This switch that takes place does not happen right away, just as it takes 9 months or so for an embryo to turn into a beautiful baby, Mother Earth is in charge of when, how and what circumstances lend itself to assure a successful human's rights. This is by far the most influential "Act of Rights' on Earth that takes the form of any legality of greed which defies the 3-Dimensional world of money laundering, greed on all scales in what is known as Western civilization's mindset. We are not who we think we are, but who we are inside of what we have all known as a life of leisure in knowing that we are always taken care of by Source, God. The God of ALL things that matter knowing without needing to see, not needing to know and just a sense of essential value of the self. To begin a life of knowing is to end with a life of not needing to know is the essential value of ourselves whose essence begins with the ALL. In the same breath, we are here to find what is not seen, but, to only that which is felt. Whatever you believe you can achieve is exactly where your FAITH lives on within your entire essence. When you witness another's success… it is primarily because the Law of Attraction has been granted to those who just know without knowing that God always provides for His children. This cannot be any other way… for it is the way.

Beneath the surface of every child therein lies the innocence, the beauty and the wonder… for all to see. This is one of the vast majority of reasons why Mother Earth is the planet of conception. What child is this… have we not learned the beauty of each child that enters on Earth as a miracle! We, as parents, take notice of this wonderful miracle during the process, for some; and, for others the miracle is forgotten or unappreciated. There are those who planned and prodded – then, there are those who fell from grace into the arms of an unplanned pregnancy, a surprise… the others could have chosen to give their child/children up for adoption or abort, foster and the like – for whatever means children are on the planet, is preordained by God. No matter how, why and/or when we all decided to be chosen to fall from grace to assist in planet Earth's uprising…. No one is exempt from not coming to Earth without given instruction to have the chance in lighting up their own soul's evolution to evolve. Without reservations each one of us signed up for this exact same thing without knowing it – but, given the opportunity to *"remember…"*

We're all here to participate in a most important, Holy service to Mother Earth by corresponding energies from those who are in need and to those who have the strongest power that is self-realized. When Heaven meets the Earth plane it is found within every crevice of the Universe where all the planets align and interact with one another – this way all the energies of an all-encompassing Earth feel the tremendous vibrational frequency shift. The shift is when these energies collide interestingly such as in a lighting show – a storm, the white energies of light formed in the sky and clouds make all the frequencies shift by forming a cluster of white mass which heightens the frequency vibration. Hence, this is why there are vibrant thunderstorms with lightning in certain parts of the world; and, why there are none in other parts. Other parts of the world that don't partake in tornadoes, thunderstorms, lightning etc., is because those states, countries that do must be in dire need of some uplifting. Each location is jolted into a higher frequency and assists those on the playing field with a new-uplifting feeling of Hope, Peace and Joy. This is exactly why Mother Earth holds the greatest love of all. Other parts of the world experiencing earthquakes, tumultuous landfalls, tsunamis and other natural disasters hold different power frequencies that require under-the-surface jolting which breeds the lower chakra areas for uplifting. As above, so below… resuscitates into what formations of the embodiment are required to be jolted into place for each thread to be illuminated. Seeking refuge when these natural disasters happen is not the only thing most are required to do. Next time embrace the experience as God's way of showing us what we, as His children, are in desperate need of. We are never alone nor does our body require anything but nurturing from the crown chakra to our base chakra – just KNOW that Mother Earth provides for us. Why do we shiver with fear when God is showing His children that there is a need to give credence of energy to a specific area. It is also within each and every one of us to show up and examine our bodies to obtain higher frequencies. The next natural disaster will be your blessing in disguise – by knowing that Earth needs a certain amount of uplifting. "We The People" are entitled to be given certain jolts of frequencies to enhance our minds and bodies in order to formulate what will be known as "higher consciousness" frequencies of vibratory necessities for the children. Not only are the children required to do the work on their own; but also Mother Earth does the same, as we are One. A Synergy. The difference is once awareness is established, it is advisable to; journal the information, meditate daily, seek your own guidance, listen to Mother Nature, become one with all of creation. That's what" Let It Be" sung by John Lennon of the Beatles so effortlessly was assuring us in the Divinity of three (words). Those words guide mankind to see the truth of what's behind the veil. On the onset of what may or may not be going on in one's life, the truth of what shall become of yours is in-knowing thyself to be the truest form possible. This entails a plethora of reasons as to why you can and/or cannot be trusted within your own rightful place to take the bull by the horns and run with what you already know… and, not necessarily what you've been told to absorb (i.e., as in others' perceptions, borrowed knowledge etc.) In order to find our own rightful place in the world, we must come together in union, as one, to distinguish that we're all in this together finding our way Home. The difference is, however, that not all want to find their way Home... others are enjoying the sleep deprivation that impacts a no-awareness mentality in exchange for living the blind side, a sheepish life of naivety. These humans will take their own time on Earth and that is their decision. The others will take their own place on this Earth ascending to their highest consciousness beyond what they have any right-of-passage knowing how not only have they elevated their own consciousness and that of their Heritage. It is not an easy concept to absorb, but it is what happens that affects a thread of ancestors of our family's Heritage.

Why not entertain the next level of consciousness while still here on Earth? It's not for the mere fact that those who have done so come to Earth to extract themselves from the rest of society only to find themselves. This is not an easy feat, nor should anyone who has not come here for that reason, be consciously able to abort at all costs the chance to become the chosen one, without being given the task from God. Much of what planet Earth has undergone for centuries is to reach a new plateau of light that would restrict outside interferences. Therefore, whatever new constructs of energy that would deem to dim the light or lower the Earth's energy cannot be done out in the ethers of Her energy She has attained a higher consciousness of light that is vaulted. Constraints have been taken off and as far as Mother Earth's energy upon the Earth, She remains to continue ascending ... as will Humanity. Remember... the Earth's atmosphere hosts trillions of layers out into the ethers that have never remotely been able to reach the Sun's layers. To the human eye one is not easily able to comprehend the complexities that host the omnipresent, ALL. Just in time... the Spiritual Revolution has been sworn in, if you will, to obtain and solidify the Earth's position as its rightful place. All is as it should be...and, any other questions that may formulate in the likes of our human brain is not a mindset, but is mindfulness... nirvana. The difference is clear – a mindset of mindfulness is nirvana; and Infinity of nothingness is ALL LOVE.

We must trust that whichever path you are drawn to ultimately solidifies a path that will put you in a knowledgeable state within your own knowledge. *Knowing IS.*

Albert Einstein, "Imagination is more important than knowledge. Knowledge is limited. Imagination encircles the world."

MOTHER EARTH'S ENERGY FREQUENCIES

To understand that our essence is in many places simultaneously and our other selves are living with and through different Dimensions all at one time is very hard for some to comprehend. We are living beings created in and of an energetic essence of love... being spread throughout Earth's matter in form - as God-like. The purpose is not to be re-evaluated but to be in a good place where you understand the level and magnitude of that energy that travels to find itself back Home. To have the sacrilegious understanding of what one's energy is doing at all times is to try and hold that particular energy at a standstill. Energy cannot be held in any form, it is fluid; ruling out stagnancy. Energy is a plethora of numerous life experiences where we are continuing the pilgrimage of ascending, as our Lord Jesus. "Who for us Men and for our salvation came down from Heaven and was incarnated and on the Third Day He rose from the dead sitting at the right hand of our Father, through whom All things shall have no end." The Creed/The Lord's Prayer exemplifies what every child of God is made of... Mother Earth has given infinite possibilities for every child to attain higher consciousness. We are humans, creatures of habit as our own worst enemy...that created, "Amazing Grace..." how sweet the sound which moves us ALL into. "I once was lost but now am found" – several implications for those who have found themselves through the darkness into the light. Be mindful of how the interactions of life and death come together in one swoop in a blink of an eye.... The (I) AM movement with all the remnants of God, Our Father; Blessed Mother Mary; and, the Holy Spirit – ALL.

For God so Loved the world that He gave His only Begotten Son, that whosoever believeth in Him should not perish, but have Everlasting Life. John 3:16 (King James Version)

MOTHER EARTH - GAIA'S POWER OF LIGHT

When we uncover the purest form of energy it IS ALL – energetic power. These powerful energies cannot be extinguished like it was... those who sought power were extinguished. To thine own self be true... those who hold the brightest light, for all to see without needing to be seen, is the highest order of After Christ/AC. Before Christ/BC brethren beings sought to engage, discourage and find places of savage beasts within thine own selves; while After Christ/AC, a flock of sheep turned to the Lord only to find a resting place to beget the one thing they were in search of, their own FAITH. Now, while thousands of years follow... into the 21st Century, we're all here to find ourselves...

in ONE breath. Herein lies our truth… to forge ahead of the flock and to claim the power of our purest light. Have you been given a new lease on life or have you failed to understand that the only light of ONE's light is being realized? We are just visitors on this planet with light bodies of another kind – that of a worldly vision that seeks to gather for the feast… a feast of the gathering sons of our Fathers. What best to let this be a light for others to see; by reaping in forgiveness of those things that have fallen away… All of mankind's truths that remain cannot be extinguished. Where in your world have you allowed others and/or yourselves to lose hope, to lose your light, to lose your Faith? Is there Faith for the non-believers of no belief? Haven't we had enough of society's need for control? Isn't it time to take a hold of your life's purpose and not pretend YOU don't matter? It's only a matter of time when every human being will seek to understand their journey for growth in attaining higher consciousness. "This too shall pass" is an ancient proverb that speaks to all those who let go of all/any outcomes. What cannot be taken away is our innate power of the self, righteous as this may sound, it IS not of the righteous so much as it IS.

PURGING. PURIFICATION. PURPOSE

Mother Nature sets a purification of mind, body and soul which envelops the highest frequency. Through Mother Nature the only things existing in Her are pureness of heart through effortless compassion and works of kindness for healing. These healing properties are reason enough to change one's perspective, turn over a new leaf, enlisting in our true essence. When we are detoxing, cleansing, sleeping well, eating healthy, taking walks and thinking less – we begin feeling a natural freedom of peace. Knowing how Mother Nature nurtures can assist in all healing of body and mind – connecting with our soul. Our soul is an awareness of consciousness; and having to cleanse and purify automatically raises its vibration. This is why we feel so much better when we're outside – whether planting, swimming, walking, rising at sunrise, biking, sun-worshiping, hiking, being still…and much more. Once we cleanse, we also feel lighter, our energy soars and the sounds of Mother Nature become inner songs. Everything on Mother Earth has been given to mankind to learn how to heal oneself through a freeing as the wind, every breath deepens as we close our eyes to hear Her whispers.

DHARMAS (moral duties, customs, values and rights)

What is and what shall never be… as it has been said, so it is written, in each of our dharmas. The way in which we perceive ourselves might have a varied effect upon how others perceive us. Everybody's dharma fits like a glove and the exact "life purpose" will be shown in Divine timing. Once we enjoy what we do without giving it a reason, time seems to fly; and, that's when you're on the right path. To be comfortable, at peace and have NO doubt(s) is another indicator of what is said to be your "forte". We all have special innate gifts that have been given at birth, but out of the many…to be really proficient in one or two things will propel you into your life purpose. Pursuing what you Love is the *only* way this shows itself…we may think that what we do for a living is what we love yet dread. That is not a calling, it's a paycheck for paying bills – one is for the money and two is for the show. Many of us find "glimpses" of our innate gifts anywhere between the ages of 10-18 years and others later in life. Many creative Liberal Arts majors may create for fun only but come to realize that is their soul's calling. Everything takes time…and the ironic thing is, there is no time and no irony. "God's sole mission is the 'Seal of Sanctuary' within our soul's purpose". ™ Our mission, therefore, is to seek our purpose in whatever medium we feel compelled to create. Everyone's purpose is to serve others and to co-create in a fashion that feels like Home… in Divine timing. In God's time the Universe allows us a given-purpose that unfolds naturally. Mother Nature is our Earth Mother and She is ALL natural – which is why we say, "you can't fool Mother Nature". She will show you exactly what you need at the right time, place and in the perfect way. All you're being asked is to Believe… that's the hard part. Right? To want everything to flow you must know how to let go… it's not as simple as you think; but if you take your mind out of it, that's when magic happens. The natural order of one's life is to BE natural – by what you eat, drink, hear, speak and places that uplift your spirit. Be-Lieve is to BE LIVING. Mother Nature is the proponent when our physical body returns to Earth and that's where it is refreshed to purity with the Sun's help and returned to its original form, "*ashes to ashes-dust to dust*".

AWARENESS

Awareness is at your fingertips…educate yourselves of what that means… healthy lifestyle changes that de-stress; be silent, co-create, meditate, and/or take a yoga/tai-chi class that relaxes while, perhaps, meeting like-minded people. The humdrum of complacency is on the rise and too many people are "comfortably numb" in their day-to-day routines – not realizing how effortless it is to do something different for a change. Drive a different route to work, call a friend out of the blue, walk on a nature trail, explore different cultures, find new places to visit, exhibits, museums, the theater, learn how to bake, cook, or just pack a picnic lunch and sit by a lake. You decide.

332

Getting to know yourself is an arduous job and that Fear of what's staring back in the mirror can be a frightening realization. It can also be exhilarating when you're faced with a version of you that you had no idea, is extraordinary. It's like this… every version of you is within each and every person whom you've ever had contact with. Take a deep breath and follow me… one friend is a CEO who climbed the ladder using their intellect; another acquaintance strikes a cord within you as they reveal a story you can relate to; an ex-lover is a constant reminder of your father; an adopted sister forges a close bond; a husband feels more like a brother and the list goes on… every detail, every fragrance of another's is imbedded within your energetic frequency and them in yours. It isn't hard to pinpoint the connection once you put a little thought into the possibilities. Those who you have possibly rejected, felt a disconnect and/or lost at some point in your life is a karmic relationship or karmic friendship and/or karmic in general. When we are "paying it forward/paying it back" either way it is a karmic tie. These bonds are ones that have been within each of us over lifetimes – the closer the bond gets… either from severing or engaging in, is a past or future together. We've shared life experiences with people who hold similar energy yet are in different body-suits. In the film, "Bruce Almighty" Morgan Freeman who played God shows us all our different faces, with different messages/signs… as an example. With every turn in the movie, Jim Carrey encountered Morgan Freeman's messages and finally understood his purpose was to serve.

Whomever you have criticized, judged, idolized, or had negative thoughts about has been a karmic tie that when you look in that mirror you don't like what you see … "the mirror has two faces" is an understatement when it comes to reincarnating with others to balance

333

out the score. "Be careful what you wish for" is a pseudonym to watch who comes into your life, what they're there to teach and/or learn from. The consensus is that whatever energy you hone in on has the intention of "what you think about, you bring about". Too many people don't quite get that because their thoughts are either scattered and/or the inability to focus on an intention is very difficult and/or you've gotten exactly what your energy magnetized without even knowing it. These thoughts draw up an energetic frequency of the more you think about what it is you really want (willful intention), you are able to draw it into your reality. This magnitude of intention must be extremely high in order for the manifestation to be given. We know this is true yet why doesn't or hasn't it shown up yet? It could be that IF there is a smidge of doubt, worry, negativity, or any other emotional thought that will hinder the progress; there is a pause. Not only that but if our Heavenly family does not seem to feel your intention is pure, it will either not flourish or hinder progress. Nonetheless, it is up to you to know what it is you want from a state of purity, hope, Love of... and, not necessarily winning the Lotto. The frivolous desires of humans may definitely be very different from what is needed to evolve. Herein lies the problems that may occur during the time of manifestation so that once you are aware of "how to" you will be able to tweak your intention(s) to adhere to the Universal Law of The Law of Attraction. Find your center, your core and establish a bond of truth and understanding that makes you different from all the rest in "your inner heart's truth" that shows up as a visualization of realization. It's in a "*feeling*...." What is it that makes your heartbeat faster, to have a skip in your step, smiling with great joy, the anticipation of "somethings" that could turn into "everything..." Stick with that feeling... seek that inner space of asking yourselves, "What if this really happens!" "What if he/she's the one?" "What if they give me that raise?!!" "What IF..."

334

is your new saying. This question though is underlined with excitement, mystery, desire, innocence, playfulness and all encircling optimism. What if today I only say, feel, think, enormous joy for whatever comes my way…and, even though there may be someone else's negativity that they're projecting; I choose to not react and stay in my own lane. Just try it. "Flip the switch" on your pessimistic mindset, friends, co-workers, social media, news, and whatever you give your time to on a daily basis…think outside the box of complacency and begin to only focus on YOU; and hold a perspective that has people talking. "Wow, did you see so-and-so has changed?" People will take notice after a while of you changing it up and becoming solely what makes you feel good. Forget the rest. Forget what people may say. Forget what people think. Forget them and focus on YOU. When you get up in the morning, what will make your day from start to finish, do everything that makes you feel alive; and, should this be your last day, how would you change your day?

Every so often our energies get blocked and if we're not able to feel where, why and/or how we're blocking our own energy – it will fester into other areas of your body or chakras. We all need to cleanse, detox, purge issues from our past, from our thoughts, from our stress wherever the thorns are. From the Base Chakra, to the Sacral Chakra, to the Solar Plexus Chakra, to the Heart Chakra, to the Throat Chakra, to the Third-Eye Chakra to the Crown Chakra. All of our energy forces ebb and flow throughout our bodies daily and in the evening, we regenerate the cells while sleeping. To best understand each energy force of Chakras, Auras, etc. refer to previous chapters. The embodiment of our external energies plays a significant role as we navigate our everyday thoughts, feelings and situations which show up on the outer shell. Using our navigational system of internal thoughts will assist in understanding those negative areas that have been bothering us are reflected as a block in certain areas of our bodies. Therefore, getting a clearing of all blockages starts with getting to the core of what is contained inside. With a precise clearing of the chakras, the body can emit only light, where the darkness has been extracted. The only thing that is left is the light of a new day… and envisioning only light will purport the inevitable. The ancient scripts have identified this clearing and, while it is still questionable to some, there are plenty of people who smudge, who are wearing crystals, wearing an evil eye to list a few that enhance a clearing of the body. The thing that is most effective though is a clearing of the mindsets (a mind that is set cannot be freed), we've been raised with. This calls for the aforementioned meditations that do not necessarily require sitting in a Lotus position… there are hundreds of resources that can get you out of a mental state of thinking to an emptying out. Whatever it takes that works just for you and how or what you believe in will ensure success. Being mindful doesn't only mean "watchful" or "a full mind of stuff" it also entails learning how to be silent, speak less, educate yourself, listen to others, and be in the moment of the present. Concentration and self-discipline are an Art form that relies on all your senses to get involved – leaving a small window of overthought by the wayside. Taking a day-trip to places you've never been or revisiting museums, concerts, bookstores, go anywhere that will put your mind to rest and invite a stream of creativity into your life. Every so often a mini-break is required from the complacency of a daily routine to get the juices flowing. If it's not anything but evolving in the Arts or just stepping out for a brisk walk to get your energy moving. It's imperative that we keep our energy moving – in whatever way fits. Take a walk in the rain…while appreciating Mother Earth, or petting a dog/getting a dog/cat whatever makes your heart sing. Exciting the masses of your energetic forces of Nature… Read, study up and learn about the History of our world, or sip on a latte, or take a photoshop class – there are abundant opportunities that don't cost a whole lot of money. Pack a picnic in the park, take a drive through the mountains, go to the beach, hike, be in silence…talk less, listen more. There's a very good reason why we've got one mouth and two ears… clear your palette and try a new cuisine to indulge in. This is a crucial time for self-indulgence of the natural kind, the quiet of the night, a stillness of the brain. "Reaping what you sow" doesn't just mean what you've done in disguised fear will be what you sow as far as a mental breakdown, depression, endings, losses; not at all, it also means the goodness you've done to help others and yourself will be rewarded. Why is our first line of thought negative? That's what "flipping the switch" means, do just that – in every negative thought, change it to goodness. The dark cannot live without the light and neither can the negative that needs the positive – exactly why "opposites attract!" Both magnets connect together to bring a form of balance in each other's lives… the negative person who is contradictory, plays victim, martyrdom etc., needs that positive influence in assisting another to see things through different lenses. As difficult as it may sound… that negative person may have been so conditioned to only see the downfalls of life; yet, after some time will eventually understand why the light of a new day becomes a valuable asset. Should this positivity be overridden by the negativity instead will cause a ripple effect of chaos, and perhaps the end of a relationship/partnership. Some energetic vampires breed on taking over the light in others, hence why so many of us are claiming our energy and wearing amulets that assist in protecting us.

The effects of all the changes in the world have been unanimously overrated by a means to an end – given the fact that only those who would understand this statement. *"We The People"* at least in the United States have given truth and justice by right of our Independence as we've been not only sworn into our own purgatory; but those who run these affairs enlisting to their own crimes. We've gotten to know how and/or why these government agencies have been doing behind the curtain, yet, what comfort does this bring? Would it be better to not know the truth or, as it is, be at a place of knowing? Just think about it… Is the saying, "no harm no foul" a reconciliation of what others would rather know or not? Since the beginning of time, it's been a "known" behind-the-scenes purgatory, if you will, no one spoke about it…though people knew something was brewing. With social media today the hidden is coming out for all the world to see…do you think "they" wanted it that way? Do you care? The reason for this exposing of the truth is that as we know… "the truth shall set you free" – will this country ever be a Free Nation under God; and/or was it ever? Has society blinded us by what we know to be the truth or is it going to alleviate what we know to be the truth? How will One Nation Under God be seen, felt, heard in the coming decades? Is our Freedom of Speech something that "they" want to alleviate in order to continue the charades? How will "they" purport Freedom of Speech … will everyone who "speaks out" be shot, murdered, or will this turn their karmic debt around to a Justice that precludes even the darkest? If a part of the world already shows itself as unable to speak…is this where the United States is headed? If you're too fearful to speak then what on Earth are we doing here? Is this what the so-called Apocalypse is going to be like? The end is intended for Humanity to be Fearful, robotic, "do not speak until you are spoken to…" society? Looks that way, doesn't it? Is this a time of 40-days of darkness? Or, has Humanity always been in the dark? Now we're seeing the light of a New World Order where we will have the choice to either stick up for our Freedom or fall under the demise and guise of Communism. How can we change the trajectory of this narrative? If we cease to follow the rules, another all-out war will ensue; yet, if we continue to be blinded by the darkness, who has the preliminary vote for the people? This issue is relatively dim yet many people will come to see the light… what will be is yet to happen, although it is up to your inner light that will reflect your outer world. "To have and to hold" isn't just for nuptials, it also includes a union between the what and who believes has the potential to evolve or those who do not. Earth will NO longer be suffering and it is because of all those who are on path lighting the way for others. Mother Earth's energy has elevated to new heights of illumination and all those who reside with Her have too. Some of you already realize this and some are in the midst of doing so. We've got a long way to go … to all those who are reawakening their Spirit ties and to those who are in the darkness will be doing so. Not every human will be awakened in their lifetime – it's only for those who have and will be going inward to work on themselves. For many, however, that glitter of light has cracked open to a seemingly new and important threshold to work on. To create a New World Order takes on a cool Autumn breeze to enhance one's senses and an open heart that feels the changes within. To witness your changes and have a sense of knowing is to endure any and all hardships that arise with open arms. It's not easy… but well worth the work that transitions us all to new plateaus of awakening.

There will be many souls who, after this lifetime, will choose NOT to reincarnate; but, a smidge of their energy will be put into others' energetic frequency in order to assist. All children are given equal opportunities to witness every cell within their bodies and minds ascending to higher levels. This is what a community does…it lifts others even when at their lowest frequency, their deepest desires of ascending. Jesus ascended to show Humanity that the human spirit will also ascend in its own time… what miracles cease to exist after a child continues their way onto the world? None. Miracles abound on every platform in every dimension of all bodies of water, land and in every breath of air inhaled. We've come to Earth to experience and absorb every morsel of a Life given. Life continues to be a present that will enable the journey of Love to continue for eons and eons – Love grows where the energy of that Love is felt. Every ascension provides new levels of growth, including the challenges of new changes, where we continue to evolve. A dark night of the soul continues to be present, as we continue to work with our shadow following us on our spiritual path forging a new study of internal workings that continues to cast aside what remaining egoic matters. The shadow work is our ego attempting to get to the forefront of our lives so as to say, "I'm still here to sway you to become an outside force to reckon with…" while the heartbeat of truth is overcome. These levels of truth are the fluxes that remain in every breath of life with all of Humanity's ability to create a new revelatory sense of self. We are the Revolutionaries, the Visionaries, the Co-Creators of our own lives, in our own time and when we are in alignment with Source…a beautiful lotus unfolding.

To underscore the natural order of business, humans have a tendency to relate in destructive ways, competing against each other, known as either being an "attention grabber" or an "attention deficient". Our ego self pretends it wants to merge with the Spirit of eternal bliss but cannot. Why is this so important? It's not so much of importance as it is the rule of thumb, as in Jack & The Beanstalk, who tended to his garden and found that by planting seeds of learning, his awareness grew. Existential planting is when we get grounded and seek a series of life experiences to learn of our growth potential. Humans have a tendency to want to control the terrain while planting new seeds as their ego dictates. Doing the hard work and losing the need for control is a part of the purpose of learning. Become a magician who believes that those seeds come with the understanding of "awareness." This awareness breeds enlightenment of one's journey through its higher consciousness. The magic carpet ride will be your only ride ... not to be taken for granted. This magical carpet ride is the game of LIfe. Why would anyone else want to experience such greatness other than itself? Could you describe your greatness? Can you see that your greatness is the essence of one's strengths and/or weaknesses that depict how deeply rooted Love is? This essence is the fragrance we emit out to the world. What is your fragrance? Are you only about your outer fragrance from a perfume/cologne bottle – or do you sense your own fragrance is a unique mixture of Love as; kindness, compassion, peace, patience, serenity and joy within yourself? In doing so, the one fragrance which is of any consequence that truly matters is that of our Heavenly scent from a Lotus flower. The scents of mankind are how we ingest various fragrances ... either with open arms or in a convoluted way of repellent. How does your flower grow? It's not only your fragrance but spreading kindness sends out the tone of 'light' vibration to the world. Whatever fragrance you emit to the world has a tendency to become your purpose. Observe your essence and follow the scent of the Lotus flower that will set you apart from the rest. *True awareness is when you are aware.*

EVERY GENERATION

In order to fully understand the concepts of how every child is different from another, we must allow our past to speak. We seem to take various segments of our generation(s) on the basis of what it is that teaches us lessons and/or what we are to learn from the experiences. Every life experience that has been lived has not been able to comprehend the values from the past as well as current generations who are attempting to teach. What has been a prime issue throughout time has been to blame, point fingers and not take responsibility for events that have framed our children and ourselves of not having respect, integrity, and/or a sincere understanding of the lessons from past generations. The song by Mike + The Mechanics, "In the Living Years" depicts the whispering strands-of-time amongst all generations.

"In the Living Years..."
Every generation blames the one before
And all of their frustrations come beating on your door

I know that I'm a prisoner to all my father's held so dear
I know that I'm a hostage to all his hopes and fears
I just wish I could have told him in the living years

Crumpled bits of paper
Filled with imperfect thought
Stilted conversations
I'm afraid that's all we've got

You say you don't see it

He says it's perfect sense
You just can't get agreement
In this present tense
We all talk a different language
Talking in defense

Say it loud
Say it clear
You can listen as well as you hear
It's too late
When we die
To admit we don't see eye to eye

So, we open up a quarrel
Between the present and the past

We only sacrifice the future
It's the bitterness that lasts

So don't yield to the fortunes
You sometimes see as fate
It may have a new perspective
On a different day
And if you don't give up, and don't give in
You may just be okay

Say it loud
Say it clear
You can listen as well as you hear
It's too late
When we die
To admit we don't see eye to eye

I wasn't there that morning
When my father passed away
I didn't get to tell him
All the things I had to say

I think I caught his spirit
Later that same year
I'm sure I heard the echo
In my baby's newborn tears
I just wish I could have told him
In the living years

Say it loud
Say it clear
You can listen as well as you hear
It's too late
When we die
To admit we don't see eye to eye

*Borrowed song lyrics for the essence of one's mission

Why give our children what we never had... and only provide that of material possession/money? If we want to give children what we didn't have, let's give emotional, mental and spiritual support. Doing better than the former generation is a natural human design, in kind. The greatest gift a child could receive are parents who are emotionally secure, patient, open to connect without judgment, criticisms, to listen without yelling, to allow the child to fail, to teach their children independence of self...not to necessarily raise, mini-me's, to learn not to compare and to love unconditionally.

Children who are modeled emotionally healthy become resilient adults. These kids can handle disappointments, rejection, avoidance, abandonments of those who are bound by Fear. This creates children who are empathic and don't take things personally. A reflection of their own development – emotionally mature.

Adulting is to witness those who feel stuck, who didn't get opportunities, who were emotionally unavailable, etc. Trust in what has been given, in gratitude and how to change the trajectory, in gratitude.

A HERITAGE OF PLAGUES

In the past, a series of pandemics affected society – Bubonic plague, the measles, chicken-pox, Typhoid Fever, etc.; and, since, Covid-19 has killed many innocent people. These epidemics and all other crises in our world have caused unjust deaths and those of intended evils. "The best of two evils" in many of life's circumstances has led to an historic percolator of events that could have been avoided. Or, not. The reason for repeated disasters is for Humanity to pay attention. We could, however, seek out Love that the planet needs right now. A Love of self, a love of family, friends and to all who come into our field of energy. Even, perhaps, finding a love of new mentors. Do mentors even exist anymore? Who would you say is or has been your mentor? Has mentorship become extinct? Or, have "podcasts" become a new-wave of mentors? If children are turning to podcasts, then, what will be the role of the parent(s)? How can parents give HELP? The word "HELP" reads as, 'PLEASE, don't let me die!" In the words of William Shakespeare, "To be or not to be… that is the question…." The real question is, "How has society deemed and considered Humanity a resource for the weak? When did this happen? Why has this happened? Why is Humanity accepting themselves as weak and/or ignorant? Where is all the negativity and anger coming from? Why does it "feel" normal to be in a constant battle with yourself and others? Do you realize that these battles are ingrained somewhere within yourself? Do you realize that the Laws of The Universe are there to assist you on your journey? Are you seeking counsel, or, listening to podcasts…where are you getting your information and guidance from? Is society the lost labyrinth of influencing identities? These questions are just the tip of the iceberg on what humans have learned since the beginning of time… and still learning. Are we learning to soothe by gaining good insightful information or are we trying to escape ourselves? What vices are you using to escape? Look around your environment…what can you say about your place called home? Your workplace? Your closets, your cars, your white picket fences, your behavior, your kid's behavior? Are you reading this right now and nodding your head saying, "I never really thought about it in this way?" or, are you in denial saying, "Not my circus, not my monkeys? Or, "Is this not relatable?" If you feel it is not relatable, look again… Do you seem to escape at a moment's notice just to avoid your real self? Growing up in a chaotic, unstable, emotionally neglectful environment is where one believes they have to be overly responsible; and that they have to fix everything and everyone. A survival mode of exhaustion and burnout. Instead, why not begin setting boundaries and let others know you are not on-24/7 call. This allows a "break-through" to happen knowing you aren't responsible for the thoughts, decisions or outcomes of others.

Setting clear *boundaries* sounds like:

1. Please talk to a therapist, get help
2. I'm not available at this time
3. Going out with my family and will catch up later
4. I can't lend you any money
5. Not sure there is anything else I can do to HELP

Anyone that attempts to shame and/or guilt another is revealing their disrespect. It's time to focus on yourself… emotionally, physically and spiritually. We all deserve to be valued and loved for who we are.

Where do you fall on a scale of 1 to 10 – with 10 being the most definitive "Yes, I am aware yet I choose to ignore; 9 being a yes, and I don't care; 8 being yes, what's wrong with that type of lifestyle? 7 I'm not quite sure I fall into any category; 6 who does that and for what reason? 5 I'm not sure I equate it to the fall into any learned behavior; 4 totally oblivious; 3, "who me?" I don't even think like this… 2 who am I? 1 No comment. So, what is it? Is being 'right' all that matters?

Is escaping yourself helping or hindering? Some humans are oblivious to what's happening while others are avoidant. Take note of your life and your loved ones for we are trying to be sane in a world of insanity. What could be saner than the fact that humans came onto Earth to actually conquer...NOT to divide. For it must be written that the more you or another feels divided the more insane one gets. This insanity stems from a corrupt society that has taught conquer, divide and disconnect. Who is speaking from a place where the main objective is to confuse and use? Instead of helping people, society has taken up the little-known fusion-of-illusion that what they're doing is good for the human race. Why is society using those who have weak minds and bodies? Do you feel this way? Do you feel that this type of governing has your back? Society is *poisoning* Humanity? Where is it written.... Who could have orchestrated this type of behavior to poison the people without reason? *History has been repeating because Humanity has yet to be realized.* The Yin/Yang of our civilization has been plagued with behavioral patterns which Humanity must crawl out from... our "Beasts of Burden" (song by The Rolling Stones).

"A man who lacks purpose will distract himself with pleasures."
- Viktor Frankl

CHANGE IN POWER

A credo of power begins once we recognize a yearning to be something other than we are. What part of your mirror 'mere' existence have you come to know yourself? Our understanding of life bears no beginning and no end; and knowing that we are threads of ALL. Shall we teleport to the future for a minute to gain a newfound sense of value on how the Earth plane came to realize itself? Has it?

Shall we resort to troubling times for what could possibly unfold for Earth, or, can we make significant progress to HELP the rest of the planet? What is seen or unseen on Earth will either save you or absorb you in a tailspin of terrors. The realization of the self is synonymous with what is to BE. In order to BE in a realized state, IS a provincial knowing what is felt in our hearts. Shall this be a life of salvation or a life of sacrifice? Or, can we balance both? The Butterfly Effect is understanding the deep interconnectivity of algorithms of chaos to transform by navigating those ways of our human psyche. The human psyche will either accept what is seen or who will flee from the cause. It is the "flight or fight" modality in one's psyche that is missing balance. When humans attempt to escape, what they are seeing and/or experiencing is a fearful truth in their lives. If we can face the grand gestures of disasters with a truth that teaches us how to alchemize energy; then, this freedom of truth-in-chaos, in Physics is where we are able to set new threads of greatness from complexities. The grand gesture that one can give themselves is self-discipline, surrender, forgiveness and loyalty in trust. Yesterday's devastations are today's realizations… an unwavering Faith.

A GREEDY GOAT AS "THE DEVIL IS IN THE DETAILS…"

Our Heavenly Father wants to impart great wisdom of the Ages to not let anyone or anything "get your goat". The power of a goat lends itself to resilience, adaptability, prosperity and survival in harsh environments. Goats naturally climb to the top of the mountain looking to rise up focused on achieving…and, when greed enters one's goat, the energy shifts into misuse of power. Those who are following desires as possessions of things/stuff to "show-off" to the external world, as a greedy-goated ego who seems to think they are better-than-most, loses all. The operative word, 'possession', explains how Fear begs mankind to acquire more. Is this what we're made of? Is it all about wearing masks? How did our world begin as a whole dichotomy of facades? Was it our Forefathers... the reptilian fathers of forgery, the cult of fathers who united together as the Freemasons who began greedy needs of endless desires? Who is behind the curtain? Are secret societies still intact? What lies have been told and what truths are yet to be uncovered? The misuse of power streams throughout the world right under our radar... These poisons showcase the epitome of what has been a misuse of power in a world of "ignorance". Is ignorance bliss? To those who still believe that you've NOT been played by a string quartet of violins ignorant, as such, but very naive to those who have been throwing stones for centuries.

PUREST LOVE OF ALL... SHINE BRIGHT LIKE A DIAMOND

Once the demeaning qualities have faded from our system, another part of rebirth erupts. There are two or more types of "rebirth" that one may undergo that stems from either/or spiritual in nature or religious in nature... These types of rebirths imply what others may deem as unnatural; yet depending upon what belief systems are – one or the other, if not both... all leads to one. "We believe in ONE God." This life is an offering of a pure Love created Blessings from The Holy Spirit. Those who embrace this gift as a present are guiding others to seek and light the way of the world. Those who accept this offering will in-deed be given their path to co-create with the Holy Spirit in due course. However, this plays out for Humanity is not to be undervalued and definitely not underestimated by those few who have very little

350

light left within their very essence. The essence of our Heavenly Father, the Blessed Mother and The Holy Spirit is given to co-create on Earth so that everyone's true colors will emerge. Every creature on Earth also creates a type of service – example of the honeybee who gives life, oxygen-making honey to humankind as well as the flowers that honey bees need to grow. What madness can we speak of to those who are not in-tune with Mother Earth's beautiful presence that creates within the heart of existence. How can humans not shine their light for others and be of service by sharing? It is our responsibility to uncover unsolicited information by helping those in need of rest, peace, security, hope in compassion which help everyone's light to shine. "Shine bright like a diamond™" is the fact that each stone becomes a brilliant diamond; cut, color, creme-de-la-creme is where carbonated oxygen is given inside the stone, molded and filled with outside variants in becoming a diamond. We all start out as that stone to build on our inner light casting out rays of energy to become a light unto the world. When they say, "diamonds are a girl's best friend..." that doesn't mean exactly what it entails to the masses. We are a cast of brilliant stars in the night's sky we've become, "Diamonds in the Sky, that is what we are..." and, "Lucy in the Sky with Diamonds..." all songs that depict the purest essence of a carbon crystal that emerges to the greatest light of ALL erupting in the great-big infinite sky as ecstatic bursts of light. Therefore, no matter what color, creed and/or choice of gender we choose... we are nonspecific. We come to this Earth, without any restrictions on how we choose to evolve.

FATED DESTINY

What we know of today does not qualify for the understanding of tomorrow. In actual terms of what we're feeling, the real truth of what matters is not one to behold; but, to accept in whatever terms of course-correction is needed. This is the end of what we shall call a transformation of one who believes their fate is not written vs. those that know. In this way, a fall from grace has taken place where there is the ALL to whom we remember in order to KNOW. What is unknowable…and what one knows is only a mere reflection of what has been gathered on their journey... A journey of old and young souls who join on this journey of Karma to find a pathway of knowing ALL IS LOVE. An old soul feels they've been here before and experience remnants of past-lives and Deja vu moments; while younger souls have it more complicated, however, it is still a mathematical equation of gains and losses. The losses have a much more impactful note on young souls as they've not been to Earth and have no recollection. Old souls do experience recollection and can feel very connected to certain events and/or people with new suits but the same patterns. All karmic threads, however, threaded dichotomies of young and old souls.

Issues that become a conglomerate of karmic lessons on how our destiny unfolds is based upon a go-with-the-flow belief system that Faith IS. To behold the changes that we are being shown with little-to-no reaction breeds unwarranted Faith. To be within yourself, your own heart and to follow whatever you believe in and feel. Such circumstances don't happen that easily – it is a karmic-fated series of trials and tribulations of what is playing out at every turn... being patient with steady progress deems a know-no-thing and believe-in-everything. This may sound very pristine to behold a path where everything is already granted to you, however, it is of great importance that you keep your Faith. What we think is not always what is. What IS our fate, in Greek, fate is termed as, "tixi" the word is extracted from the Latin word, "time." Every place and every waking hour we are choosing our "tixi" fated path and, where there is chaos, discontent, and any other form of having to control – "power play" is involved, this is how the Universe is trying to express a let go and "let Jesus take the wheel" moment. Often too many of us seem to think that we are in charge of our destined fate; yet, this is not true. Truth is having eternal Faith-in-knowing … as it should be, IS. This is the way our Lord Jesus did not ask for anything while visiting Earth because the One IS the ALL… To question the self is to not believe in yourself… No longer are questions needed because most of us already know that everything always works itself out. Those who don't must solidify a stronger Faith... This is the Way.

Faith vs. Fear.... What is your biggest Fear? Is Humanity's Biggest Fear dying? Why? Death is of the physical body and NOT the soul… While you're reading this, could you possibly cast aside your need-to know-what is still yet to come? We are all here to begin putting in the inner work necessary to attain. "When the student is ready, the teacher arrives. Is it time? What wrongs do you need to make right? Is your egoic mind-set still overindulging in every aspect of your existence or have you sought out a new paradigm of newness. A newness that becomes what you're looking to enhance within your innate being. One's innately been given all the tools to address, achieve and receive but there are different variances that need to happen prior to this. What is and what shall be are like two ships passing in the night and crossing that bridge when the time is ready. This way and that way… "This too shall pass…" Mankind only makes decisions on the basis of either Fear or FAITH. What overrides your decisions?

Two frequency vibrations that will ultimately attract one another must be on the same frequency or counter-intuit vibration frequency so that a mental/chemical union of frequency takes place. *Please note: I am NOT speaking of a body-chemical attraction... that is physical, a lower vibrational frequency where the base chakra is activated.* The mental/chemical frequency takes place within the third-eye frequency where two individuals are magnetically bound by intellect, chemistry through Mother Earth's *"natural order"*. The *higher frequency* is felt through the **Heart** within all the inner Chakras of one's physical embodiment. Heart, Mind surges as Soul. We have attained a healthy environment (within/without) and are at a vibration that seeks to find itself with another, as one. At the higher frequencies, mankind learns to differentiate between a soul connection and a connection masked with the Ego facade. Ego shows up very similar to that of the Heart; but the difference is one FEELS through the HEART while the other, knowingly – challenges, criticizes, judges, envy's etc., in a constant quest to conquer.

YOUR BODY - WONDERLAND OF JUNK

Our bodies are composed of... body and mind in choosing a healthy lifestyle, a connection that feels good. "You are what you eat" speaks to all those who either choose health or junk. This is how the circle-of-life works for those who are famished or not – entirely connected to Ego. Our Nature/Nurture order of Mother Earth vs. an over-indulgent Ego coerces you to eat cheap, junk food, sugars, poisons that will affect your health; liver, spleen, teeth, gums, bones etc. 'Stuffing our faces' and/or overindulgence of any kind is another way of saying voids-of-emotional emptiness and pain exist within. The emotional eaters find themselves in a series of plate-after-plate, and not feeling, good enough. A number of inner traumas and emotions stir up many chili-fests, manly man hunger-for-power, salted wounds mixed in with a Milky Way chocolate; spaghetti woes with pizza lows covered with sugar highs after nine. When our bodies say, "I'm full" but our emotions are not… a vicious cycle of Tom & Jerry ensues. Our mind continues to play tricks on our emptiness of feast or famine. The emotional emptiness can also play out as Bulimia, eating then purging any guilt and/or shame. All of these external desires – overeating/undereating play out from our inner emotional turmoil. What we suppress and/or repress hosts deeply wounding stories of a lost soul – threaded from a past life – strung into our DNA, genetics etc. Viscous patterns that procreate much more trauma if HELP is not on the way. The mind/body connection is our *navigational system* telling us what not to engorge upon and/or how one seizes to fit. Is it a matter of fitting in? (on and in all levels of "fitting in, causing a fit, being fit, sell fit elsewhere mentalities). What we indulge in … food, drink or otherwise can it be worked off or not? To make a choice isn't necessarily the answer to the question – as is the quest to move and elevate your energetic body and drop all thoughts. The body's energetic fields are composed of pure energy and, part of that energy, requires we feed mind & body healthy workouts. Physically working out by eating healthy are both vital to the human physical, physiological body which is composed of energy, oxygen, water, blood, veins and chemical ingredients. This is the natural way of Mother Nature to choose a healthy lifestyle that purports and sustains a higher frequency. This is why our bodies need its much-needed rest and relaxation in order to function properly. Without the symphonic orchestra of our body, mind and soul all penetrating at their highest notable functionality one cannot sustain a clear connection/path that is the ALL. The all-encompassing world of seek and be sought.

Food for thought: *"you are what you eat."* If you have little Faith, junk food is your 'go to' and if you know you are worthy of your unwavering Faith, cooking healthy, clean food, an overall healthy lifestyle is your Nature. If you're in-between worlds where a balance of junk/natural exist, find out where the blockages are in your physical body after having physical symptoms after junk food. A junk-food junkie emits symptoms within their emotions of trauma, lack etc., and festers of stomach cramping and/or even food poisoning might ensue. All junk that is within our body...must go! Energy is fuel for the body...while many eat junk to conceal the real issues, emotional eating and overeating trends to be a masking of another ailment from childhood. We tend not to "think" about it, especially when we begin to "crave" these foods that are junk...intended by a junked-up poisoned society. Sickness reveals itself in ways that would be good to take a few minutes to think about...before you dive into the lion's den of a poisonous society...you definitely might want to think again. Dis-ease in all forms of this word, as a prefix "dis" a player's foolish hand at dis-assembling mankind. Connect the dots with your threaded existence where, and how many times you've caved-into-craving junk food; then, getting sick and/or knowing you'd get sick but did it anyway?! Yes, we've all been there... This is a clear indication of what's going on in our society – some people don't give a shit...to put it mildly. This indoctrination of thought will place you a holding pattern(s) for lifetimes and depending on the hold it has upon you, could indoctrinate your essence to a miniscule dimmed Sun of erogenous particles. Awareness is key.

Our genetics play a significant role in what was given to us by our ancestors and what we've acquired through our DNA threads from past-lives streaming into our current life. How do we know? We will know when significant patterns occur, when life becomes stale, when the players in our lives seem to feel very familiar…and so on. What we inherit are patterns-of-beliefs, values that have been learned, borrowed and placed upon us — deeming the onset of playwrights to several scenes that repeat, and other defining moments that give us that same dis-taste. When this happens, are we aware? Do we look deeper to find the core issues to our dilemmas? Do we ask questions? Who answers? Is one way better than the other? How will we know?

What constitutes upheaval in our lives – the triggers, hate, anger etc. contains energy of a low vibration? The only way toward freedom is to go higher, not greater or better than others… but, to know is your ability to attain. We've all been there… a place where our ego reminds us how much we require the attention of others to be accepted; and to follow what others are doing. It needs to be said… because many states, countries of origin have legalized weed for medicinal purposes; yet it is no wonder that a vast majority of mankind are associated with the walking dead. Overdoing toxins are enough to not only overdose, but to forget why they are even on this Earth doing nothing but medicating their wounds. Mother Earth's growing weed is for natural purposes of healing one's body – not to be an escape or a numbing reason of becoming unmotivated. Alcohol, too, has been around raising the bar too high; as a depressant to point out the obvious lack of one's self worth. Death-by-overdose has been the cause of many teenage suicides as well as the cause for lack of attention deficits with a non-caring attitude to sustain a healthy lifestyle. Who's to blame? Are the effects of overdosing additionally with sugars, substances, all toxins non-exempt for what the true lack of self-worth that society imposed upon us; and, family, friends and the like follow. Where is the real crisis? Are our desires outweighing the obvious need to numb all the pains of life? Desires that matter vs. healthy desires that are good for the soul have been an obvious contradiction for the sake of actually becoming. All of the Earthbound pleasures that are low-vibrational are becoming intrinsically alarming to one's human body – which also gives way to our intentions vs. attentions. The attention of one's bodice requires the purification from one's soul driven by the acceptance of one's intent. Herein lies what has been the culprit for so many on Earth – driven by external pleasures of poisons to forget; while the inner strength of resolve to uncover those hidden reasons of remembrance calls for self-discipline. *Self-discipline* is the highest form of Love that we give to ourselves… The only thing that stands between the obvious need to medicate is the reality of meditation – which in essence is mind over matter, what we think about we bring about. Mind-over-Matter. Our bodies can endure many things…but our mind sets us Free from suffering. We tend to hold such disbelief for ourselves that so many require the desirably need to take others for granted, listen to the naysayers then go about numbing the real pain inside with external meds outside. What does this tell us? Begin to spend less time in your head speaking/thinking negatively; about being ill, or, mentally unstable. Don't let dis-ease dwell within any part of your consciousness. A sick thought devours the body… It is not within science to extract a calculation of reason – it is a belief that how Humanity can make themselves sick all by themselves. Spiritual healing is called for as the mind-body-soul connection is of utmost importance. Those that require a scientific explanation for what is hurting their inner core-value system is the ultimate 3, 6, 9 mathematical equations invented by visionary, Nikola Tesla in the 1800s. What Nikola did was find the Universal potion of what is known here on Earth as children of faith. The 3,6,9 equation is the

Master of all things used as 9,6,3 or in any variable that translates that this Earth is all about the faith in children. *Arithmetic.*

CONQUER BY NOT DIVIDING

We cannot have one without the other – therefore, a list of symbolic yin/yang affects us in different ways and consists of what pieces of the puzzle fit where, as follows:

Head vs. Heart

Mind vs. No-Mind

Sorrow vs. Laughter

Heat vs. Cool

Sight vs. No-sight

Inner vs. Outer

Sink vs. Rise

Arrow vs. Bow

Tiger vs. Lamb

Water vs. The Well

These are just a handful of examples where you could get further knowing what works for you may not be prevalent for someone else. We use the polar opposites as a form of stigma, learning what behaviors someone has been granted while others cannot seem to wrap their heads around every "difference" that holds a variance of a difference in perspective. What idiosyncrasies do you see and/or seek in another? What are you not seeing? Who are you not seeking? In order to become united, you must attempt to withhold judgment for what others may or may not be. One's perspective is everything that will help you to expand your vision. We cannot remain stagnant holding onto and passing judgements of those who are not in alignment with what beliefs we have been raised with. The truth is… the beauty of what we embrace in others… all their idiosyncrasies are warranted for greatness that show within ourselves. Is greatness with or without the need for our Egos? How does one know to differentiate the places where we're able to draw the line on who we've become? To know is not to question why, yet, an inward search contemplative of the other is where we shall begin. Alignment of acceptance is to allow others to always be themselves, no matter what.

Humanity has been pre-programmed to believe in a trajectory of coercion, lies, manipulated by external power plays. If we dangle the caveat of desiring poisons; money, sex, drugs, the weak will cave. However, IF your desire for external pleasures comes with feelings of pure intent, it is making Love between two people to procreate. Those who fulfill a life of Faith – hosts a beautifully described Christmas song, "Mary, Did You Know?" As the lyrics go… "Mary, did you know that your baby boy will one day walk on water; Mary, did you know that your baby boy will give sight to a blind man? Mary, did you know… the blind will see, the deaf will hear, and the dead will live again, the lame will leap, the dumb will speak, the praises of the Lamb…" Whatever freewill in Faith, you choose it will, "Lead us not into temptation, but deliver us from all evil…" as in The Lord's Prayer – awaken and arise once more. These are very precise messages for what is to come to those who can find themselves in an "Unchained Melody". We are remembering who we are in God's name, the unveiling of *truth* for all to *see* again. Being authenticated, is to be reborn, knowing you are all Love in the Universe.

In 2 Corinthians 5:17, "Therefore, if anyone is in Christ, the new creation has come. The old is gone, the new is here! Jesus replied, "Very truly I tell you, no one can see the kingdom of God unless they are born again."

Upon being saved, the Holy Spirit indwells us…into our heart and soul, thus we are "*born again*" into the spirit of God.

Holding that Love in your heart is the only Love that IS real. "It Don't Come Easy…You Know It Don't Come Easy…." sung by Ringo Starr. "I don't ask for much, I only want to Trust. When you are at your lowest, lonely and alone the depth of your Faith is the Trust in God… in Love. There is no other, one Love, ONE.

We conquer our fears by Knowing…™

Let the blind lead the blind and leave those who wish to see… who know that the Universal energy is, ALL LOVE.

THE HUMAN TOUCH IS HEAVEN'S BREATH

Humanity has been undergoing such transformation since the days of the Old Testament that we cannot even begin to recognize what's happened. A blessing in disguise for all those who have gone through hell and have reached the light of a new day. That's where the "real" work is done… in the backdrop 'shadow work' of our life. When someone is going through what is known as "the dark night of their soul" it's a common theme that one must go it alone and an individual experience that needs no explanation. Life is the journey of the experienced traveler from darkness to light…deeply felt. Take the

Lord's hand and follow the path of Spirit – know that the experience of the dark night of the soul has always been and will always be an individual Work of Art. Not all works of Art experience the same 'vision' where one is being led. Being led is trusting yourself to know that Heaven's breath is letting go and being shown the way forward. The human touch is described as 'one hand washing the other... 'Our left side is receiving love, logically the strength of one's resolve; and, to the right-hand side of love, compassionately feeling the Heart of many, is given. The giving/receiving comes when the right/left hand comes together in PRAYER. Therefore, to act in service "in-deeds" to mankind, it is detrimental to one's beliefs that not only does love unfold naturally – serving Humanity to depths of great proportion. Without question, the whole preface of the Earth plane is to give and receive Love to ALL of Humanity – what has gotten in the way is the Ego. When we fall prey to the Egoic patterns and beliefs, we simply rewind the hands of time to experience the extremities of the social injustices of how things were gifted to society since the very beginning of time. "To be and not to see..." ™ has been a source of contention. We believe that once you begin to understand the Nature of how, when, and/or why some things have occurred, or not, a pretense of the blame-game will be validated by the tune of what will be will be.

SEA OF CONSCIOUSNESS

In a sea of consciousness there can be different ways of attracting what we want in our lives... implementing: ISEE, IPLANT, IGROW, IAM, IKNOW Inquiry. Intention. Invest. Invoke.

The ability to invoke Source begins with planting the seed deep unto the Earth plane with Godly-ness of pure intention that will reap great investments... producing the end result of invocation. The invocation runs directly through to the Spirit world and holds more energy to "not only" speak it out to the Universe, but to breathe it internally/externally. A meditation of miracles in a sea of conscious knowing... There are various factors working in the Etheric plane which will attract you to the Source of Attraction.

ISEE™

The ISEE™ series is going to be implemented (2025) as a synergistic "speak-of-intent" merges with "breath-in-intent." All intention in the Laws of Attraction for receiving any materialistic physical manifestation must not only come from one voice, but from every breath we ingest. A force to be reckoned with...for obvious reasons we must raise the bar when utilizing the Universal Laws by getting to the very root of the seed. A synergy of both a spoken-breath-of-intent requires a pure Heart – where a seed planted explodes into infinite expressions of co-creation. By using the 5-Dimensional method devised as, ISEE™ being implemented not only for those who seek a value for material rewards; but, more so a value within the goodness of Self. This type of newness implies a certain higher energetic field that meets with you in the etheric plane that will transfer the energy through what is known as telekinesis of oneself.

With the ISEE™ invocation, the "ONLY" thing you build up in your energy field, unlike any other, through an inhale/exhale effort to SEE IS to BELIEVE in what you SAW. MEDITATION meets MANIFESTATION™ One could say this invocation is fairly similar to the infamous Law of Attraction that Esther Hicks presents to her audience; but, the "caveat" that holds ITS own power is to ***"breath-a-meditation"*** *while **"expressions-of-intention"** simultaneously exist as* natural as an eagle spreading its wing in flights of prey. Yes, in-deed(s) ALL the Magic of our Holy Spirit and our Blessed Mother Earth comes through effortlessly. Why? If you've been able to breathe, life happens with the greatest of ease. Breathing techniques are the answer to whatever one fears… fear is the root of all the evil lurking. What some humans do not understand is all the given skills and gifts come innately with life on Earth; and when we "KNOW" this to be our truth, Magic of The Holy Spirit renders it present.

When we are not aligned in our highest self, any form of intent - through a misuse of power to acquire materialistic stuff, an unfulfilled wish.

ISEE™ is being able to assist others through God-given wings to fly by rule of thumb, the Law of Giving & Receiving all-encompassing the Laws of Attraction.

INQUIRE. Inquiring minds think alike

INTENTION. Intentionally setting a pure breath inhaling/exhaling the same way one goes about their meditations

INVEST. Investing with a pure breath of seeing is believing

INVOKE. Invoking the ideal end before the means – to become what it IS is to want no-thing, but to BE.

AMAZING GRACE

"Amazing Grace" how sweet the sound

That saved a wretch like me

I once was lost, but now I'm found

Was blind, but now I see.

This song is primarily played at funerals to remind us of how amazing a life of grace restores our sight from being blind to sight. An expression of knowing that life graces us, even those who are lost and cannot see; and how one's Love for life can save us from ourselves. Those who truly Believe will see how Faith is given to "Know Thyself" – self-realization.

The Spiritual Revolution that Earth is under-going lends itself to show how when we are stressed out and feeling under the weather, moving our energy forward means to allow it to BE. There are a million reasons to BE grateful for a life that presents Humanity to evolve. In order to see, you must firmly BElieve that BEhold... all the Blessings of the Universe are given. The story of Rapunzel, a girl with beautiful long golden hair, trying to betroth a prince for conception while locked in a tower by an evil witch. Spinning fears of golden threads with hopes to overcome the dread. The prince fell in love after hearing her singing voice fall into each other's arms; and, Rapunzel sheds tears, two in particular, ending up in the prince's eyes – restoring his sight. The life of Jesus Christ remains our white light of truth that all fairytales, nursery rhymes and children's books deem to teach – whatever you truly Believe you deserve is what you shall receive...when it comes with a sacrifice of hard work and surrendering to an outcome.

365

No matter what you may or may not Believe in will end up exactly as Spirit has intended for you. We've undergone so much in our lives that those who have had much sorrow, pain, and those who have attempted to enhance their soul's growth over these past 20+ years, will endure the greatest rewards. We've not even begun to live... let Spirit show you the way for all the goodness of life is upon you. We, as humans, tend to take advantage of the allotted time we have here on Earth, by giving up way too soon. When the going gets tough... the weak falter to give into a stagnant regime of another dull-drome day only to repeat – hopelessly helpless. We find ourselves going after all the glitz and glamor ignoring the core reason why there is such unhappiness within our destitute description of a life. The exorbitant time wasted getting to the starting line is absolutely astounding. Such a performance of procrastination beseeches every one of us while still on the dark side of the mood. What's left is undue proclamations of what's to come at a much later time. How could one ever assess living their life on Earth as legitimate, in what others call, "the present moment." Time wasted on Earth is all lost for those who have no indignation of control over what could be a very productive learning experience. Humans are so very complacent in how their work comes first; how much time is really a work-in-process is a disaster. From now on there will be those who will suffer greatly by misappropriating the usage of their time on Earth. They will suffer in other ways, in other dimensions of thought, we can only PRAY that they find their way. The way forward is to calmly address the reflection in the mirror that holds your face of truth; while the other face sparks a misdemeanor of errors in one's way of life. We can only hope that Humanity takes a good look at themselves ready, willing, and able to be honest as to what is reflecting back. Our reflection typically, but not always, makes its way in front of the mirror whenever we are at our lowest point of contention in our lives. The contention to fall to our knees… a resistance that breeds a new karmic cycle unaware of… "What you resist persists." Therefore, it is to one's own benefit not to resist where God is leading Humanity.

While one man accumulates the other submerges into the abyss, a film that sways the scales of our life. We may find in-deeds those who work hard for their goods and services are able to uphold an upstanding life… adding value. Those who are not doing what they love and allowing their Egoic power out to play, will be remiss to say, "a wretch like me…" A life imposed by tragedy and suffering has mankind in a stranglehold of pain; and this trajectory of life impedes growth. Clearly what has driven people on this planet to do whatever it takes to pay bills, living paycheck-to-paycheck has blinded them. Instead, had mankind listened to those ancient adages that say, "Do what you love and the money will follow" could have driven us into feeling life is worth living for. Work, fear is a four-letter word, as is LOVE. When you are on your spiritual journey and have shifted paradigms, you will only feel the need to only do what you LOVE as motivation. Whatever foolish games of society's infliction makes for a fool who fell for the illusion to spend, be spent and spilled out of every chance of evolving. The same applies for those who spend their wares foolishly, but are aware that they are spending too much… isn't that the way of the world? Spend whatever you make, and/or spend more than you make only to be in the lowest state of affairs that will solidify your need to either work harder, longer or for those who are working 2 or even 3 jobs? Are you still stuck in a Tower of misuse of power with a witch that still has the itch to control your terrain … until God's reign rains upon the witch, for a lifetime of Bliss!

T'was grace that brought us safe thus far

And grace will lead us Home.

THE AMERICAN DREAM

Ahhhhhh… the American dream of the big house, expensive cars, white-picket fence and a couple of dogs/cats or other has come to an end. What parts of the American dream still exist? Do you still believe in such a dream? Isn't that why it's been called, "The American 'Dream'"" for Fear that mankind might have realized it's all been an illusion? Talk to anyone who is in this predicament right now and they might tell you how they're on an uphill battle without a sense of stability that has literally taken them psychologically "off the deep end". This mind-set needs to be extracted from our History books because it's been manipulated by a corrupt society. To believe that by having it "all" means… all the money in the world, then, we will remain a society of emptiness. To enlist in a new paradigm shift is to believe what we have is more than enough and to begin questioning our values on how we were raised. A simple life is not about what has been programmed as 'The American Dream' – now is the time to realize how the simple things in life are more valuable. There are several opinions as to what this means… what we value and what money we make in this life should not be undermined as "not enough" … yet, it is. We've all been granted the same life on Earth, yet so many live in poverty. It is a "mind-set" given to those who are not of great Faith and believe the struggle is real. Many come to realize the beauty of simplicity later on… an eye-opening difference. To realize. For those who have $5 and others who have $500 may vary in one's perspective concluding whether one is rich or poor. Those who are the happiest live life to the fullest with what they have... and with whom they Love. Civilizations have been taught, for the most part, the same thread of appreciation and value; but, what most have done is mistaken the value of life as either; rich or poor. Divide. Our knowledge of what is of value, what we appreciate in our hearts, and what we truly want in this lifetime has been skewed by a dust-cloud of the unknown. We've all been there, haven't we? The place where we've worked so very hard to earn a living and not being able to get ahead... to the places where we begin to sell what we have in order to get somewhat a-head? A-head is where the matter lies... (read this again) It is in the consumption of an overaccumulation of "stuff" that currently many are already on eBay, The Real Real, Poshmark etc., selling a small fortune... being misled.

Stand up, no need to turn back now and falsify a truth that holds none other than... "We The People " who will stand up and change the narrative for this moment and for all generations to come. Instead of attempting to fit a square peg into a round hole, why not seek to justly be satisfied to live fully in whatever "Terms & NO Conditions" means. What will matter for our future generations is to uphold our own beliefs for an entire nation watching History in the making. History which belongs to the People under one God indivisible of nothing or no one who misrepresents the terms which are being placed will no longer have a hold on societies need to be a dictatorship; but a change of one heart for the hearts of all. We cannot give you the new blueprints which come with this inevitable change but we can say, at this time in History, it is up to each and every one of us to extend Love to everyone – makes no difference if your big nor small, a vision of colored lenses, or a plethora of wealthy minions or those grateful enough to find food, shelter and/or clothing. We can no longer be divided... as we are falling ... and, by the grace of God this is not what is written. In the Bible, the Book of Life and The Universal Laws of the Universe IS written that life be The Ten Commandments/The Laws of the Universe/The Lord's Prayer as one. We cannot say that this was not written as one chapter ends another begins... let us all make way for change by turning the page of *"United We Stand Together We Fall."*

FAREWELL TO THE AMERICAN DREAM

Those who work to live... versus, a life lived to enjoy. What and/or who wrote the adage, "work hard, play hard" as the symbology of the American dream? Why hasn't Eastern culture followed suit? Is it because they were taught to skillfully put education first that includes meditation instead of medication; sobriety instead of being addicted to a 'numbing life' drinking only to fall, church goers beware...spiritual givers take care. What child is this who has fought to stay alive on an oxygen tube while others are out-of-touch face down on TikTok, beware. What child stakes their claim on a parent's love while others stake their claim to a parent's fortune? A few examples of one's cultural background, upbringing, belief systems and a plethora of other variables which contain the periphery of interests and/or disgraceful habits of one's History or another man's silver platter. Why should one child who grew up having the silver spoon hand fed to them be judged while another child is self-soothing their pains using drugs, sex and alcohol to mend their slivers of cuts on one's body because of the life that has been given. Both of these lifestyles have a common denominator; self-infliction. Is it fair to say that those who learn the hard way have a better handle on their life than those who live an easier life? Can it be said that those who work

370

harder will gain their just-desserts faster? Is the system of our society going to pieces or have the pieces of one's life gone array to the systematic society of AI formulating a community of sheepishly robotic nomads who have no say so? Where is the love? Who is in charge and why? What makes one life better than the other…and, why the comparison(s) with which we may not be able to fathom? Is it fair to compare apples to oranges? What goes up must come down… the old adage of those who actually wager their hard-earned money on a stock portfolio vs. Viva Las Vegas. What are the actual differences between a workaholic whose life has been washed up and a lifestyle of those cultures who only believe in working when needed to live a life by washed up oceanic waves of glory. Who is to say one man's choices are another man's neglect? Demonic tendencies are amongst us all on Earth which is exactly why people have had to lower their own expectations because they do believe in some 'devil-grabbing pointed-ear tailed animal' who has no good intention… how can this even be a metaphor for the lowest, weaknesses on this Earth? How does one believe in a devil but not in their faith? Why not settle the score with a congruent lifestyle of yin/yang which feeds the soul that doesn't control… Why not just "let it be" Why close off your life to the insignificant desires of a physical body and embrace a simple life of pleasure? Who deemed there are any actual evil Mongols that are ready to take one's soul? Where is this written? If the soul is set to soar by actually leaving the body… it is NOT being taken, it is being SAVED. For selfish reasons, many predictors of our fate stake claim to our soul's being pulled out of harm's way – but, it is not exactly like they explain. A soul that jumps ship to indulge in a sacred life for the sake of one's life does so in order to jet into another Dimension; a healthier environment, landscapes and/or places where the soul can roam. A peaceful soul must learn how to temper the existential elements on the Earth plane without giving into the same purgatory narrative that souls are pulled out from one to land in a place of saving grace. A soul who has exhausted all avenues in their lives and the physical body that encapsulates this soul cannot sustain its embodiment – this is the ONLY scene which is too traumatic for a soul who must exit. Nothing external can make a soul exit a body… unless the body cannot sustain the soul. This is where the soul meets a heaven scent of what is known as "embracing one's love" where no one or nothing can ever take away someone's soulful life of love. It cannot be, there is NO such thing.

What has happened to so many people "out there" is that they're living in a *silence* unrecognizable to them. The internet is the new-wave source of meets & greets – however trivial as it may seem, times have changed. Even meet/greets on social media platforms happen… with hopes to change the trajectory. The wave of the future… for too many have resorted to a no-contact…text, voice-chat messaging contact. This also applies to the wave of customer service… i.e., wifi/internet setups; phone service is a digital response; retail, and many other businesses have no face-to-face HELP. It is quite frustrating for many because our society is an impatient, intolerable, boisterous world of ineptness. Metaphorically speaking, life has become very much like "The Grinch" and "A Christmas Carol", a lifetime of unhappiness in an unfulfilled life. We all realize how short this life on Earth is and not doing anything to change the narrative is doing yourself a disservice for your soul's growth. Our entire society frowns upon the ages of wisdom; instead of learning from those who have life experience...

THE TORNADO

"The Wizard of Oz" showed us another facet of our time as Dorothy's Aunt Em and Uncle Henry, the parental figures raising her…too busy mining their chickens for money, stressed over the crisis of potential foreclosure that gave way to Uncle Henry's health. A clear example of how and why so many children stray from home. Some children leave home for good without a reason-to-believe they've got a choice. Those children who are living at home also have no understanding of adulting, even though curiously inquisitive. Much in our world has changed - yet remains the same. Cries for HELP as adults stressed out about not having/being enough, overworked and underpaid; health risks, a "Horse with no Name" sung by America. Our journey insists on mankind charging through the Valley of Death only to overcome, evolve and become one with the ONE. As Dorothy faced her fear which witch-to-switch clicked her heels, thrice and remembered her Emerald seal …a great power within. A life of instantaneous self-deprecating solutions come into play when we learn how our stresses outlive mankind's body of water; threads of the fated breed stress of the Ages. All those who have gone before us, generations past, couldn't sever karmic ties showing us that our bodies of water need immediate cleansing. The Valley of Death is not only for charging through life' stresses' it breeds a horse that can withstand the desert heat, having nothing, finding a life of truth is strength, courage and Freedom.

As a civilization, we have veered off-course on so many levels, weary of going within; being initiated on every level of our inner/external work. Additionally, not educating ourselves of the future in farming our own produce, tomatoes, greens, mushrooms and seasonings etc. To learn how to demonstrate and emit better lifestyle changes begins with you... Why haven't we been implementing values that will guide the next generation to survival of the fittest? What has been dying... in our world? Is Humanity giving up to a life of regrets, then death comes? The fact that there are not many who say, "I can do this myself..." or, "I'll try to figure it out" or "Let's do this together, between the two of us, we'll figure it out." These are just a small few who are engaged in learning, farming, and being organically educated. The rest have become lackadaisical, not wanting to learn how to live a long healthy life of "health, wealth and wisdom". Who has taught those who are lazy and complacent? What do you see in your family tree that caused you to take a second look at or question why something doesn't feel right? Many of us were taught that, "family is everything..." and this belief system has caused some to mean they have to sacrifice their well-being. A clear indication of being weaponized by those who ignore setting boundaries. We must remember, not to neglect ourselves just to become people pleasers of the family or otherwise. When a child comes to learn the bad habits of a parent, speaking up, the parent completely disengages and continues to ignore the child. It's no wonder why children are becoming more in tune with their computers, IPADS, Samsung/Android iPhone etc. Children that have gone astray are complacent and do not care to listen to their parents. Is it too late? What's happened to "tough love?" Showing tough love to all children who feel unloved, have been bullied and feel different... the outcasts. All that kids need is to be shown what "nature vs. nurture" means as a healthy lifestyle. Growing up in an environment of being out in Mother Nature and learning to eat healthy – builds strength from the inside out. Children who are raised in sports, summer camps, family gathering, barbecues, conversation, games, one-on-one time builds character and a new frame of mind. When children have been uprooted with old ways of learning to eat fast-food, drink soda/pop, be obsessed with games, VR, chat rooms etc., they have NOT been given the correct tools. As of April, 2024, the US Center for Dis-ease Control & Prevention (CDC) for Obesity estimated 14.7 million children and adolescents ranging from 2-19; a rise that has tripled since the 70's. (US rank 22nd highest in girls with 26th highest in boys).

A TORNADO OF ADDICTIONS

Addictions are heard from the cries of children - and, calls for a considerable amount of love, respect, and loyalty to be a part of their safety net. The saying, "lead by example … observing the ability to forge ahead, connect with all who are in need of HELP. "What age is a child able to make their own decisions?" Age is not only the matter; it is in the desire to self-soothe which foregoes any indication to live a healthy life. No matter what society has led us to believe, even those who are of the voting age, continue to numb; therefore, what's the real issue? A child's growth is built upon the wisdom to ask, to be inquisitive, wondering, "why is… this and/or that … As stated before, children are curious and to undermine, ignore and/or appease a child is more of a detriment than outright lying; but perhaps a conversation between you and your Maker. It's certain that some of the content implied here should rattle some feathers…but, if you're not awake to what your child's needs are then how can the old-world end; and a New Spiritual Earth ascend? There is no other importance greater than being a parent who walks the talk. Taking full responsibility, owning up to the cause that instills deep Love and inner peace.

In the life of a child…many inquiries are answered by friends and/or social media. Given this, do you know all your children's besties? Their families? And, who do they confide in? Are you actively participating in your child's school activities? Is there any counsel? Sports activities? These are the most crucial years of a child's life…ask yourself, "Have you missed any of these milestones? One of the many regrets of the dying is not spending enough time with their family… kids; in activities and not being there for them. Why not take a different approach and seek your own guidance to solidify your children's future? Why not take a second look at what is being addressed? A highly debatable issue many parents choose to "parent their children" by NOT being their "friend". Is this too much to ask for a child to befriend your confidence in order not to be scared of coming to a parental figure? Does the parent/child relationship work even as a parent who is able to place boundaries and discipline? Why does it work for some and not for others? Have you been that controlled by the nature of becoming your parents where this was not ever discussed or even a consideration? In order to gain trust from your children and establish a relationship there is the ability to draw the line, with discipline, in the way it's presented. Presentation is everything. In order to get and receive TRUST, full disclosure is necessary – and, by befriending with a sturdy hand we must learn/relearn strategies that do work. Do you happen to watch other mothers and fathers handle their kids? Are you usually on board with how they're raising their children? Do we care? A Mother's role is at the highest echelon of the Spirit world – "Heaven-sent". Flawless is their innocence… and, between the parents, families, and society's manipulations, a child's innocence becomes very tainted. The drugs, alcohol, prescription meds; and so many various addictive behaviors, is your true wake-up call! As mentioned, there are some prescription meds that do not make a child or even an adult suffer from extreme side effects; however, they are few and far between. Whatever alters the brain, or mind-set is a crutch. The crutch is what the insurance companies, pharmaceutical companies and a plethora of other industries who have signed up to keep the weak medicated. Medicine comes from the early 1200c Latin word, medicina – verb is, mederi, to heal ... and, is the language of science. The term pharmaceutical stems from both the Latin pharmaceutics "of drugs," and the Greek word, "pharmakeus" as "preparer of drugs, poisoner." Greek pharmacists identified "pharmakeia" as, "healing or harmful medicine" a healing or poisonous herb, a drug, poisonous potion, magic potion, dye, raw material for physical or chemical processing. This terminology, alone, is quite disturbing as identified in Merriam's Webster dictionary that ANY pharmaceutical drug has both chemical and poisonous ideologies within its origin. You can say, think, feel as you will – yet, how many case studies have been prone to lead into deeper issues/problems by using different drugs/meds ... In fact, side effects might not even be felt to most because they are riddled into believing their doctor is playing God. How could this be? Is your doctor a God? No man is a God, but God is ALL men, women and children. The difference why this is even a subject matter, is that only with God's blessings could a miracle ensue. A doctor of medicine, MD must also perform what one would "believe" as spiritual healing... otherwise, it's just science. The term medicine can either be seen as a healing or a hindrance of cause & effect. Therefore, without spirituality in one's belief systems, no doctor can be thought of as a God. The God of ALL medicinal structures is the energetic force of Nature (Mother Nature) where the need to "BELIEVE" in a God is crucial to one's survival. That's where "the *will* to live..." comes from. Its origin stems from our Heavenly Divine family of – *IN GOD WE TRUST.*

With so many children taking meds, smoking weed and unhealthy eating – no motivation to work in wanting to resolve this conundrum of cycling off the beaten path. There are parents who are also trying to recapture their youth funding addictions of scars. Within these families, the common denominator is a numbing of pain – past, present and the fear of the future. Unless the family dynamics change, our next-of-kin will be drinking a bottle of gin, holding a blunt, staying high and falling down. Repeat. If this narrative applies to your family tree…, how can we teach our children why get high without knowing why; and to climb on a branch that's worth more than a penance; and, every ounce of that powder makes a crazy-ass higher, feeling that you can fly. Instead of escaping from trauma and painful regrets, why not invest in what could be construed as "Who knows best?" When you're close to hitting rock bottom, you'll scrape, steal and pillage from all who you know - missing out on a life that wasn't meant to let go. Whatever vices you attempt to either shake off or repair your health and welfare defines your junk in the trunk. The will-to-live may sound easier than most because the Earth is set to remember what we came to forget. Seeking answers requires a deep dive into our DNA, our genetics, our personal life experiences, our bloodline, the threads that bind, cells, atoms, neurons and every prospect that Science mathematically was constructed as our Universe. Recounting steps that have led us to this place convinces our indigenous ancestors to stake-their-claim to Freedom while witnessing their own ascend. No one could prepare us for what's to come, yet where we've been is only the beginning. Not many can swing the pendulum of fate…only we can - each and every one of us has the capacity and innate gifts to rise to the occasion. The concept of life is very much like a teeter-totter … a roller-coaster of a lifetime that contains the Horizon of Balance.

Where's the *discipline*? Who is disciplining whom?

Surely, you could say the statistics are far and few between... but, one addictive child is one-too-many addicted. Active addictions are **not** about the highs...it is living a life of endless cycles of stress, betrayals, lying (to others and self), masking deep unresolved grief. Grief from abandonment from their father, or emotional neglect fr0m their mother – or from the death of a sibling etc... It's an internal punishment of real struggle in an emotionally unaware world. A death of their true self because of what society and family imparted as wrong and/or is ashamed. These addictions breed on the next drink, or the next drug of choice – attempting to get relief from that inner critic playing in their mind. Addicts need to escape from themselves and the people they love... Addiction is a dis-ease and the symptom asking "why" instead of pointing fingers, allows us to get to the heart of one's traumas so that an understanding and/or knowledge can be had. Sometimes getting into rehab doesn't fix addicts, but has a tendency to add fuel to the fire. Others rely on themselves to work through the process and, of course, there are those who fall back on the wagon. No matter what, all those suffering from addictive behaviors have a history of abuse, trauma and/or neglect. Whatever form of addiction that someone has it would help to listen, be watchful and create a safe haven of space to allow. Addiction is observed as cries of HELP in behaviors of what a lost soul feels. Lost souls are weak-in-nature and allow society to dictate them into the Lion's Den of inhaled poisons. Knowing so many are weak and in need of getting HELP, but much too weak to know how to take alternative routes of healing. Society "they" have been pre-programming mankind to work harder for their money, live/breath-in plastic, and take no prisoners. Why else have a good majority of teenagers overdosed? There is a continuous thread of poison, you see, and now it has been exposed for all to SEE. Become curious, observant and a good listener to what is being said, done and what is not. We all know better... to do better, to want better for ourselves and our children. Why not start with you? Isn't it time we decide to take your life forward into new hands? Change up the narrative and forget what "they " are shoving down your throat that is feeding your mind, literally to your demise. Take a minute and refresh... use this life with all the abundant opportunities that are out there that don't require you to lose your mind thinking you're going to die. Another huge issue on this planet is FEAR of dying, why? No one is refuting the pain when these life challenges appear in our lives; but it is also there to show Humanity that we all are going to cross over...no matter what. We all know too well it is inevitable; yet people are spending their lives on the hamster wheel worrying about dying and NOT living. Death of the physical body is going to happen and what you may or may not know is that whatever poison you're putting into your body is how much longer your body can sustain life. We've been so pre-programmed in a world full of hate, amongst other aspects that grind at us every day. How has this world become so full of hate? If you say, "he/she lived a full life" did you mean how much hate someone had in their lives? Hell is not a destination...it is a "mindset" that tampers with your inability to grow as a human – this is what "they" want you to believe. Earth sits on a low vibration for the exact reason why mankind is taught that death of the physical body is inevitable. To use and abuse your physical body AND to buy-into the mental manipulations that have been programmed is nothing short of a death-sentence. If that's what it means to live a full life... encountering emotions, hate crimes etc. way out is IN. A reassessment of how emotions navigate our lives is what humans have been given in order to upgrade to a higher frequency. A clean house brings a clean

380

inner world of growth and prosperity…it feels like a huge weight has been lifted. Lift off! Minor changes to our lives have a massive impact that takes guts… self-discipline, a new attitude, a grateful heart. Justify the means with whatever it is you've wanted your entire life. Level out the playing field balancing your yin/yang, breathe in your chi energy and advance yourselves to unlimited potential. Emptying out all of your inner garbage just like taking the trash out weekly – same concept only thing is to release any garbage creates an outer world of peace. Energy is the *ONLY* thing we are made of so having people 'dumb you down' is exactly what we're talking about… this includes self-sabotaging ways of speaking negatively to yourself.

ARE YOU A HATER?

1. Belittle, criticize you and/or your accomplishments
2. Spread rumors and/or say negative things about you
3. Rarely support and/or celebrate your success
4. Imitate you in ways to outdo
5. Subtle showing of happy whenever you've struggled/failed
6. Make negative, sarcastic and/or aggressive remarks

UNTRUSTWORTHY PEOPLE

1. Disguises insults in a joking manner
2. Does not take accountability
3. Blame game
4. Says they want your best, but goes against the grain
5. Words do not match their actions
6. Plants doubt in you that is masked by concern

7. Wants to sabotage or make life harder

8. Has an excuse for most everything

Many don't like to address the fact that any family issues exist but that could be further from the truth. This planet is the bottom-feeder for those who need to extract threads-of-time as our egoic selves; and to be a beacon of light, self-realized. Humans are defined exactly as "creatures of habit" that must change. To change a long line of history requires a deep acceptance of willfully choosing change… and, as Harry Styles sings, "Sign of the Times" for that reason. How can you bribe your way out of what is going on only to take your breath away? Why get away from what gives your life… and, instead break through the dark atmosphere as an end-of-time knowing that the end is breaking free from the bullets. Bullets are all of our healed wounds, reminding us of our Freedom. What do we know? Freedom reigns… a New Era is born. Did you know… it takes 24 days to form a new habit – leaving the old one behind for the sake of claiming our inheritance? Habits imprinted in our brains are ingrained until our cellular rids itself of the remains…. We need to educate and inquire about how the brain functions, the left/right thinking, a rewiring of the circuitry where we can instill a new frame of mind. It is both the brain's function and a pre-programmed mindset that has held some hostage, a detriment since the beginning of time. It's now our time, History being made, to change our way of thinking, change perspective that will broaden our vision. Why hasn't Humanity signed up for a new sign of the times? Instead of tossing around your societal beliefs …it is the choice of all children to forge a new path towards becoming their own fragrance.

HEALING karmic threads has an unprecedented Freedom to Humanity's experience of Life…

HOLISTIC MEDICINES

HUGGING A TREE

SWIMMING IN THE SEA/OCEAN

PHYSICAL EXERCISE AND MEDITATION

WAKING UP EARLY

EATING A BALANCED DIET

LAUGHTER

ATTITUDE AND GRATITUDE

NATURE vs NURTURE

BEAUTY SLEEP

BE ALL LOVE – BEING LOVED, SHARING LOVE, RECEIVING LOVE, GIVING LOVE, FINDING LOVE, KEEPING LOVE, LETTING GO, AUTHENTIC LOVE

BE SURPRISED

BE CHILDLIKE

SINGING IN THE RAIN/SHOWER

HUGGING ANOTHER

TRUSTING IN YOU

BELIEVING

GOOD FRIENDS AND FAMILY

FORGIVENESS

SUN'S ENERGY ABSORPTION

SPEAK IN-KIND

PATIENCE

In the words of Augustine, "Take care of your body as if you were going to live forever; and take care of your soul as if you were going to die tomorrow."

RAYS OF LIGHT... THE RAINBOW

"Light is the illumination of the Universal soul. ™"

Throughout the earliest recordings in the Vedas, as light emits from our Sun that warmfully provides comfort, serenity and nourishment for our body, mind and soul. Sunlight is necessary for us to sustain a healthy body, mind and neurons in our brainwaves that function at the highest caliber. The rays of light radiate from God/Source penetrating levels of consciousness for our development into a higher knowing. The ultimate benefits are healing properties, transmutation and an overall transformation that dates back to the beginning of time. Different traditions of one's faith are beyond the powers that are measured by space and time; and, are emitted through these Seven Rays of Light that cultivate its own power.

1. Red – LOVE in the base chakra of one's body that, when released, is capable of Loving ALL. The foundation that must be built on stable ground, a Holy Ground, for the impossible to be made possible.

2. Blue – A Spiritual Truth that envelops one's ability to know their truth, speak their truth in the throat chakra; when released, at the highest level. Infinite as the blue sky, we come to understand our own innate qualities that run threads throughout the entire Universe.

3. Yellow – In the essence of the Sun's rays… energetic forces throughout Mother Nature brings us infinite healing properties when there is stagnancy, blockages in the solar plexus embodiment. We must be aware that nourishment is needed to sustain a healthy body, mind and soul.

4. Green – At the "heart of the matter" we are encapsulated with the ever-beating heart of God/Source which captivates one's ability to be compassionate, kind and feel for Humanity, as a whole. We must work together to heal ourselves as Mother Earth ascends to a higher consciousness. Our healing begins on the inside/out where we can process a healthy lifestyle while serving Humanity. The natural order of the world stands before us…knowing what we must do, within every exhale/inhale…of Life sustenance. Breathe.

5. Orange – Our sacral chakra provides life's energy to be used for mankind's creativity, of Co-Creation. Within each one of us are innate qualities that have been presented to serve Humanity. Co-creation is where the "magic" happens on the waves of Creation that call each and every one of us to manifest. At the highest level of Co-Creation our internal navigation system "knows" what it needs to manifest. Using these "superpowers" enables Humanity to rise.

6. Violet – At the crown chakra of attainment IS a REALIZATION of self. To know is to Love – becoming one with ALL of a Higher Consciousness. At these levels of attainment, the soul is attained and it sees itself as self. The violet flame of St. Germain brings Humanity to new heightened states of consciousness – and, who is St. Germain? The Ascended Master is known to emit the rays

of the violet/indigo flame to those who are Chosen. Find yourself reveling in this light to contain "realization of self" at its Highest Order of Light.

7. Indigo – Both the violet/indigo flame brings SELF REALIZATION to light for all those who are the Chosen Ones. Those, for Humanity's sake, that are driving the energetic forces of all seven rays combined to make Rainbows... as above, so below. Look to see where your light illuminates your senses...of within/without to assist in raising the consciousness of our planet.

These Seven Rays of Light are present for all of Humanity... called upon each ray to cleanse, allow any suppression or oppression of darkness within the physical body to cleanse. Allow emotions to flow as they are your conduits in supporting LOVE that carries great wisdom...a Heritage of the Ages. In the 17th century, Pythagorean theories of conceptualizing optic rays of light beaming through the Universe at light speed...a bundle of rays that have been traced in geometrical manner. Light traveling parallel, straight lines moving outward in intensity, formation of light between the galaxy and stars. Enlightenment.

Be mindful while working with these Rays of Light for they are as powerful as the oceanic waves. These Rays of Light have withstood the test of time enveloped in sacredness in the elevation and development of our souls. To create the feeling of being Home... "Home Sweet Home" said Dorothy in, "The Wizard Of Oz". Where is your place called Home? It behooves us all to think that home is a place on Earth; when it's depicted as the fragrances of all the colors of the rainbow... Under whose order was the Emerald City? A facade of the wizard that couldn't scare Dorothy because she had enormous

Faith and Love, great compassion and perseverance to stand up for her family – in the guise of a scarecrow, tinman and the almighty lion. What Dorothy portrayed in her character is what Humanity has been missing since Christ's ascension... a genuine Love, graceful tears of sorrow for the goodness of tomorrow...that set the stage of an unseen, unspoken power. Empowerment lurks within the confines of what emerges as self-confidence of the highest power - where our strength of Hercules finds its way within...only to show us what we're made of! No one on this Earth is powerless...just a forgotten sign of the times through a force of darkness that is no longer mind — being erased by God's grace.

ALONENESS. BEING LONELY

Aloneness is not to be feared, yet, so many fear it. The pandemic caused so many humans to no longer entertain others for "Fear" of getting infected. What is infectious is the disconnect from Humanity... How has fear changed Humanity? What could we say is the common denominator of all traumas, tragedies and dis-ease living in fear? This is society's worst nightmare -- for Humanity to actually experience loneliness. And, why? The fear Mongols could learn much from the fact that if one happened to stay in their own lane, many fear-based illusions of dying etc., could cause one to know that the only thing that ever dies, is the physical suit. The external body dies... and the so-called "fear of dying" is based solely on the death of the physical body. No where is it written that death is a death of one's soul – the external reality is the illusion that people have become used to the tangible; instead of Faith in-silence of believing. Is this a tall order? Why is it a tall order? Because it stems deeply rooted in our Holy ground and shoots straight upward to the Tree of Life, E-ternal Life. E-ternal =

Eternity in Life Where there is hope, there is love. Where there is love, there is endless love. Where there is endless love, there is a version of you deeply engraved on the Tree of Life. Jack-and-The Beanstalk expresses this thought process to perfection. The seed, the original seed that's been planted, can only grow under the duress of Mother Earth, which is the School of Hard Knocks; and, that seed born of every child who is given life can grow up to be a force to be reckoned with...a faithful servant for our Heavenly host. The "servant" is what each one of us has signed up for, as in "God We Trust...our deeds will formulate a series of good deeds that help people, not hinder them.

FREE-WILL

There is a huge topic of discussion as well as a cumulative understanding of how "free will" is described on Earth. There are many versions of how free will plays out for the majority of Humanity; however, not all is what it seems. Having "free will" falls under the umbrella of either being free to make your own life choices and/or having the "will to believe" in the choices that are being made. All choices upon the Earth plane have been written in your blueprint. However, any uncertainty that may arise is how one's ego plays tricks upon them ... convincingly internalizing their self-talk or talking themselves "out" of the will to survive. The ego attempts to use its manipulative tactics where humans have become lost in; depression, stress, panic, triggers etc. Many humans have hit rock bottom several times... clawing their way out from underneath the rock that led them into a frenzy. What seems like making smart decisions has given some their Freedom; is also giving them their last breath. For example; when children are growing into their teenage years, it is the adrenaline rush that is exciting knowing they are going against their parents' wishes

388

by; smoking, drinking, hanging with the mean girls or seeking adrenaline thrills-for-chills … too great to pass on. A teenager finds thrills of, "going wild" choosing their free will ends up experiencing many highs and lows. For others, though, the thrill seeking finally gives way to a newfound freedom from abusing their bodies. No matter what happens… every child of God's creation undergoes their "wild child" years to either learn from and gain self-discipline; or, to fall into a dark survival. Humans are complacent and the free will to act freely exemplifies either a desire or need. To have "free will" and not delve deeper into its meaning of choices made is why every life unfolds as it does. So many life decisions are being made daily and yet so many decisions are made on auto-pilot. Who is thinking about their "free will" while making decisions anyway? Are you a cast-away? No matter what… no one else is to blame.

Having "*free will*" sounds Heavenly until it isn't… that's when mankind plays the blame-game toward God's Love. Why? It is a very natural tendency to place blame on someone or something when things in our lives go haywire. These wires within our brains crisscross when coming to terms with having to make choices that have skewed their path. Also, it is not humanly possible to "think" that every choice we make will be made based upon any "free will" at all – because, humans don't think so much until after the fact. The fact that we make choices without thinking about the consequences falls into a pool of problems. Problems that we weren't expecting…or, didn't think before we went full-steam ahead. Some other choices made were of our Ego; because of pride, shame, guilt, blame? There is an old saying, "haste makes waste…" therefore, all actions/reactions do not hold longevity as a whole. What will happen should an entire system of computers, robots, phones break down? 40-nights of darkness? Darkness lurks when no one's looking.

MIND with MATTER = EGO

MIND w/o MATTER = SPIRIT

THE DOMINO EFFECT

It's been known since the beginning of time that what one person has taught to us, another is being taught to them… and so on. Some are way too distracted with the way things appear in the external world of fictitious life cycles than what their inner workings are trying to resurrect. Indeed, the lifestyles of not only the rich and famous, but, for ALL of humankind. The more one helps another fellow human being the more established, creative, observant their lives will become. These are the enlightened ones. The more experiences we undergo to learn arduous lessons, the lighter our pulse becomes. The heavier life becomes, we cannot hold whatever BE comes within the essence of our core BEing (BE-in-GOD). We all may not be built the same on the outside, but, on the inside at the core of our existence, we are one, the ALL.

We cannot seem to seek outside investments unless we have seen what labels hold the majority of weight in the "game of life.' To know one is to be ONE… is not a euphemism that explains why you are the way you are – it is ALL of what has been taught, learned and/or borrowed. Once the external body is accepted as such, the internal workings of Spirit work its magic. The Magic in this Universe is for those with pure essence. Every essence is recycled by Mother Earth's bountiful miracles and given to Her children. Those who receive endless possibilities, the miracles of every facet in their lives, need not 'do' anything... BElieve in the essence of the ONE is ALL. We are not the only co-creators of the lives we give to one another sharing our gifts, our sorrows, our lives in such a way that demonstrates a beautiful bountiful exchange of energy. The exchange of energy is the only real thing that sets to change the demographics of our lives for the better, even at certain landmarks in life. We cannot place the "blame game" on any Spirit of our Heavenly families because those things that have been taken away and of those things that have mattered are given back... Some say, "Life's a Bitch and then you die" because what is the true essence of a dog who has had her day? A bitch. The reason why "every dog has its day," and is noted as a bitch, is because it didn't get its own way. Her very essence became compromised into what she has felt as unjust and not being of oneself to tame her own beast. Those seeking themselves within... and not from without, are to be savored and given their own room by which to grow. In this way, those of us who are influencers of the highest order do not need our egoic selves in order to prove our value to those who are already enlightened... as the egoic self must stand down for the heart of all matters to be given its own. Pieces of what we believe IS our fragrance. Those influencers who've struggled to gain their own true-North are the soul seekers, the lightworkers and those who seem to get to all hearts within. Our true-North reels Grace that is given to those reborn, *"Born Free."*

NO EXPECTATIONS

We've all had a tendency to place our emotional needs in certain matters that have either swayed us away from our goal(s) or asked us to take on a new perspective. With every new day, there comes a time where we, as parents, can either take a stand for ourselves as parent; and, those times where we feel powerless to the point of giving up. This is a two-edged sword that comes with a bittersweet knowing how to invoke a new reassurance to be able to do both. When we've played all the needed sacrifices on ourselves for our children, what's leftover? Should we sacrifice it all for the sake of our child's own happiness – or, will we ever come to understand the enveloping sacrifice it takes to raise children? We know… either way, that having to raise a child/children impacts our vulnerability and presses our buttons. We either cave asking God, "What did I do to deserve this?" or, "Why me?". There is never a predicted development that occurs… A parent's role is to allow both the relationship between parent/child to grow by learning too to always be grateful. Usually, external influences force our hand to release the grip of a perceived outcome; so, child/parent evolution can begin. We're all given tests when raising children that happen to play out of the ordinary for the very same reason trauma has all been preordained for those in need of higher teachings… for their highest good. The aftermath weaves the mind, body and soul together forming a match-made-in-Heaven. "Tight grips" of any kind cannot be loosened unless humans are ready to let go of expectations.

ON AUTOPILOT

Mankind is comfortable on "autopilot" and numb to the pains of everyday living. People are very complacent, lazy and unmotivated to deal with negative emotions that bleed into their daily lives. This negativity, anger, frustration, greed, jealousy, people pleasing, codependency, responsibilities and so many other negative emotions of daily dealings are propelling people into relating to habits of learned behaviors. Additionally, all the added guilt, remorse, depression, sadness, violence, revenge of reverberation of every action serves as a reaction from such behaviors. To say this is our daily ritual is an endangered species casting aside the goodness of Humanity for a depressing life. This negative energy emits outward to all who are in close proximity - and forms a dis-ease in the mindset involved. An example of this … is walking into a room and feeling a funnel cloud of negativity; and after a while, you may notice, your energy will change forming a funnel too. Can you see where mankind has been condemning itself far too long; and that the majority of those who have been sleeping, and/or were lost are now being found? We've yet to undergo a massive overhaul in the world but should we not open our own eyes to a better lifestyle of clean living – see no evil, hear no evil, feel no evil, speak no evil – to reprogram a lifestyle. Rewind our human brains to think, see, feel, and hear for what we believe-in only. Being independent of what once was taught as "old school" values, beliefs and a reprogramming of this is required for the New World.

GENERATIONAL

All generations are threaded together as some have passed while others are still thriving. Each generation seems to 'think' that their generation is the best, however, what every generation brings to mankind is uniquely its own. From artists who are still influencing their generation, to newer artists who find themselves much the same; from artists and paraphernalia that invoke a stone-cold State of The Union – addressing The United Nations "Under One God…" A plethora of genres influence and seek to indulge at every heartbeat as do the saddest lyrics of "spades" that ruin it for the rest. Many amazing artists have risen yet their legacy lives on to tell the story. Humanity must hold that power of what music they prefer to connect with at specific times in our lives. Music is the sound healing that soothes the soul – leads us all to reminisce, to be in that moment again, to feel what we felt in that moment, to sing together, to laugh, to cry, to despair, to learn every word and tone, to play an instrument, to be threaded through the craftsmanship of threads on a guitar, a piano, a drum, a violin etc. Where would Humanity find shelter if not in the beautifully sung, "Gimme Shelter" of Mick Jagger's song? Here is where all humans collide in a conglomerate orchestration of unity… setting the tone for one generation to respect the other; for a remix of an oldie but a goodie. Much power is held in the soundwaves of music mixed with water… a calming effect with soundwaves to meditate, to sleep, to engage upon as the next playwright or screenplay. Water is a portal – some receive our best downloads, ideas, in the bath/shower. Water holds past information and allows our consciousness to travel to other dimensions in remembrance of time. Water and our Trees of Life tend to be the most overlooked tools that have a programmed memory of all knowledge. Whatever creative juices flow within one's oceana is what shows up as a musical masterpiece, Heaven-sent. When the first sound ever came to being what do you think it was? It was the voice of truth… within a soundcast of Heavenly Angels that was heard the world over. How? In primitive times, Hermetic issuances were formulated to cast a wide net of new languages which were incorporated by those primal roots of all our ancestors.

GEN Z…. *(Written with LOVE for my daughter, Elle, who provided and wrote pieces of intel on behalf of GenZ)*

"To Dream the Impossible Dream…" original song, Andy Williams

To dream the impossible dream
To fight the unbeatable foe
To bear with unbearable sorrow
And to run where the brave dare not-go,

To right the unrightable wrong
And to Love pure and chaste from afar
To try when your arms are too weary
To reach the unreachable star,

This is my quest
To follow that star
No matter how hopeless
No matter how far

To fight for the right
Without question or pause
To be willing to march, march into Hell
For that Heavenly cause

Generations of talent, strength, endurance and independence that bodes well for those who have been given the drive to assert. All generations have given us immense notable successes yet it begins with Generation Z where the tables turn from ignorance to bliss... Past generations were more inclined to follow-the-crowd and/or seek their beliefs from their parents; and a known truth that beholds the question, "How can one person make any difference?" This is definitely an old ideology that was and still bodes true for many in varied generational poles. However, Generation Z is where a change has been given, to question, inquire, research and form independent counsel. The beauty of all generations is that they all think their generation is the best pro-actively asserting opinions to make a difference. We need NOT compare, even though many are doing just that; yet the thread of the quest within every generation leads us to believe once again in, "One Nation Under God." Whatever you believe in or choose not to, should represent your own signature. This Nation will always be in the hands of One God, therefore, no matter what your beliefs - borrowed or independently so, constitutes a new learning curve imprinted upon all Generations.

"If at first you don't succeed, try again" said an infamous writer who knew for certain not to break down the walls of convenience for others is the key to becoming a free agent. A free will agent is needed to take you on this beautiful soulful adventure without having to interpret, comprehend, think about or even worry yourself about anything. The Freemasonry today still holds much control on Humanity – they are the governing agencies, the religious orders of the highest kind and most definitely, the people who are in politics... all encompassing. In order to become the highest of self-sufficiency with a playful demeanor, one must learn how NOT to listen to the shadows of others. The shadow plays are the ones who are masking their truest intentions, who give you advice willingly…not for your highest good, who make others feel less than, who are courageously driven by greed, money, power-hungry moguls of greed… who follow their own cult, if you will. Yes, those generations of people do still exist to get you off your game… Those who are enslaved to wealth and power cannot be honest; they are controlled with the desires of greed, rather than integrity. What once has been written will not be explained in the Historical Book of Ages where we "knew" that the faces in our History class were unknown. Behind those faces, however, are remnants of our ancestors and their lineage; all telling us their stories… that either fell on deaf ears or kept our attention. We all feel the scars of historical politics, the making of bad decisions, tragedies, wounds all EGO-driven in our governing agencies. However, when asked this question to my daughter, Elle, an early Gen Z'er, "How do you envision changing the narrative of the world in the History of politics?" The response came quickly as; "*Motivation*" Gen Z's are making sure to get their stats, facts and figures "right" by rolling up their sleeves with a strong conviction in coming together to form a governing state that will, "lead-by-example"." No more confiscating, coercing the political attitudes of the people by only providing "lip service" in a world of facade, devaluing Humanity. Those Gen Z's know it and decidedly will sustain the public 's attention. Facing our shadows with a strength of resolve and courage to know better. We're watching…

DEFEND TO DIVIDE & CONQUER

Conquering and defending the energy of Life comes not with a cost of life on Earth; but, on any other planet, a freedom to roam through the solar system of life. In order to conquer and/or to defend where one has been, what issues and/or struggles are all on you! What makes no "sense" that one must conquer and/or defend their energetic Nature has been reduced to Humanity's sake of a conquer and divide planet. No other planet holds the energy field of conquer/divide, love/hate, yin/yang etc., that bears our entire essence upon what synergies envelop our field. We're thrusted into an environment of humans who are attempting their hand at fate; and don't trust on their journey are held accountable. Our human attempts at discouraging those who do have unwavering trust cannot be tempted by the swaying of the tallies in our Justice system known as "hanging chads." The Justice system relies on the people to swing the vote one way or another by finding the ludicracy of this, much to our dismay, a detriment in our Federal Government. To fall for a hanging chad by "not" implementing an abundant display of borrowed knowledge lends itself to become the chad, by undermining the nuances of our systematic errors. All systems require an element of velocity where intentional repertoires of energy exchange become our unwavering Faith. What escapes some humans is their rightful cause to claim their essence of being on Earth and to surge far into the distant future of the here and now... a newfound reminisce of seeking themselves. Synergize within your energy fields to return back to the ONE source of energy that has been gifted to all of Humanity; and, unto that field of atoms we rightfully return to state our claim to the productivity of exclusivity masking itself. What comes before us is the abounding need to claim one's energy just for the sake of inheritance – not withholding the essence. This essential fragrance is the energy that embodies the Earth's axis as untold, but feeling bold. The boldness of a sharp essence established by a full-filled life. That which proceeds the essence has no-thing left to give other than the energy of one's fragrance. To proceed from the Father, whoever claims to know will ultimately grow unto itself. *"Know thyself..."*

JUSTICE

To become the last flight of Angels by accident holds no bounds to the thought of taking this newfound place of residence to soar. We all have this within us innately however the stream of those in so-called power defeats who hold the anchor of reasoning to be seen and/or gifted though the collaboration of the Heavenly bodies. Those who are misconstrued with those hanging chads are bonded by the external forces that become a turn of misrepresentations in a historic view which had to be taken and spoken as a misuse of the powers that be. To fall under the category of this power-hungry society of greed that has overpowered the masses has become a near-lunar death for all who have fallen. When you end up being overpowered by those in power and misusing Humanity for the sake of betrothed means to an end, you will end up seeing just how manipulated not only the Justice system has always been to those who take the bait. There are many who have fallen not knowing how manipulative this and other injustices are at play. We live in a cynical world where people are being scathed as either power hungry or caving. Which one are you? Do you choose to fall into the precipice of what Freemasonry rule vs. standing up for what you choose to believe in… What has driven you to grow as your own law and order will take precedence someday – otherwise you have become like all the rest – that fall from grace is quite difficult to claw yourself out of. Be mindful how, when, and whom you truly believe has your back. The reality is that this constructs the future of all up-and-coming generations…

SOUL'S ENTERTAINMENT

All children on Earth come to accept their place in this world and to know that it is only a matter of time where we shall revert back to our innocence. To rise and be reborn. There are so many who are awakening on Earth, as we speak; in spite of how one views the propaganda of social media. Social media has exposed the ignorance of greed in the shady characters; which has led the majority of Humanity to finally see the truth in a non-functioning sole-egoic entertainment and political fronts industries. To place blame is to point fingers at those who have entertained the media with worldwide information, hunger and greed over the internet for all to witness. This may have made Michael Zukenberg, Jeff Bezos, Oprah Winfrey and a cast of other characters very rich dicks; as their Stern private parts continue to show. Presidents and Queen bees alike will be seen in light of those who render to decipher judgment or cast aside what you consider to be your Truth.

SOUL'S FRAGRANCE

The fragrance(s) in the air is the essence of ancient truths in our History that has led many out of despair. There are believers and disbelievers... We know that both represent a beauty unto itself; and even disbelievers seek their own way in their own time. Our salvation remains as the self-seeing itself. One man's hunger is another man's salvation ... that's the way. To seek no-thing is to gain one's origin of innocence that has long been lost, isolated and/or forgotten. Take every opportunity to 'check-in' with yourself and ask, "What have you had to preserve in order to persevere?" The accompanying acts of

400

kindness hold more glue in-value than any amount of money that buys into power, greed and coercion. If your "will of intent" renders the need for abundantly more of what you already have then you may be in the eye of the storm. Every man, woman and child must go through whatever tumultuous events; desires, temptations and manipulations all for the sake of saving your soul. Your soul has already risen, it is only the inner self which must accompany the soul on its journey of Love – a Freedom.

God's freedom reigns to ALL His children, and is binding by only the one who has learned it. To know is not to show... ™

PERCEPTION

We must become "childlike" again and open our perception of remembering our true purpose, "Know Thyself." No other human on the face of this Earth is going to assist in this journey... it is not possible. We come into this world alone and leave it alone... a lone wolf. What remains are the remains of your tenure of life, no-thing else. How we loved ourselves and others and found love for all mankind – selflessly IS the only way to redemption. The last breath is a life given in eternal gratitude. Once this has been done, you are on your own again... you take on the Light of the ALL and will undergo a new sense of self through the ascension of consciousness. We are on the same journey yet a perception-of-consciousness remains. This frequency has the inner makings of every person, place and thing which holds your fragrance and has been emitted as, "As Above, So Below." Therefore, we are all ONE- in-the same... A *"Stairway To Heaven"* by Led Zeppelin, is a reality to only those who have risen to gracefully be lifted up into Heaven. We cannot rise without our childlike fragrance of innocence where the self has been purified, reborn again. "Born Again" will happen to all children on Earth. The silver cord that attaches Spirit/Body connectivity to the Earth plane has an embodiment of the 7 Deadly Sins… This silver cord cuts through the powers of greed that propel a human body to desire more, acquire more, want all of what the Ego dishes out … When a soul ascends even after the silver cord is cut, it becomes a shining star of consciousness.

GRACEFUL SILENCE

Whenever all the stars in the sky have aligned then the grace of the Holy Spirit enlists those individuals to further progress to next-dimensional paradigms for their soul's ascension. For this to happen, one feels their place in the world as not theirs, but Heaven. "The power of Heaven is greater than the greed on Earth…™ Gathering of this power is unlike any physical power of natural disasters of the powers that BE that are unlike any others. Various types of powers that are on Earth as it is in Heaven cannot be described, shared, or verbalized …only felt. Once you have felt a graceful power within yourself; as there are no words, only works-in-service required. Becoming an island unto itself is not what God has intended… To become a self-made Master one must attempt to seek the inner guidance of self without requiring the assistance of external influences... We understand the importance of keeping to ourselves while we set on our path for our journey to begin. We come to a place of not knowing why, how, or where life is taking us… but know we are being guided. Those control freaks take it upon themselves to control their destiny delaying ascension. The song, "Jesus Take the Wheel…" by Carrie Underwood. These lyrics are very prevalent in our lives as letting go for those who have done the work. Our worry, stress, grief, jealousy, pride and other negative emotions could have been avoided on our journey... It's not that we aren't human after all; but, we are a soul embodied in physical form that equates to finding out you're not who you "think" you are. To say that this world isn't a magical place would be quite a stretch from your everyday breath, wouldn't you say? Many in search of their true purpose without even realizing YOU are your purpose.

Mother/Father, as ONE, Heavenly. And so it IS.

LOVE UNCONDITIONAL

For the Sun, Moon and the Stars to align in the Universe we must be free of orders in what controls and what deems to be our ego. We can either embrace the finer things in life knowing we deserve them all; or, we can dumb ourselves down to the likes of others who don't understand. What makes us tick and what sets the tone for mankind is to be accessible to all that we are; not stagnant, knowing there are those who will fall even when we rise. The rise and fall of another is not only based on one's life experiences, but, they're all about knowing what travails we've incurred only to find our true purpose. What you may or may not understand right now is not of importance as it is in the present moment that breeds those decisions to align with what the Universe wants to show you... Where there have been disagreements, disappointments and an overall displeasure in ourselves shows up as a controversial thread of what we are made of. Only through gratefulness in life can we overcome it. What will become a nuisance shows up as a series of evidence pertaining to the likelihood of another's control. Any type of control undermines the right of life, the right to love without the likes of others. What cannot be seen in the eye of the storm is a blurred vision of losing control. Therefore, the more one holds onto Ego's bragging rights and insists on having it their way, will enter a very long and arduous struggle... These are beliefs that were instilled very early in one's life – planted seeds of not being enough, being loved only through the likes of needing to please others. Those who have adhered to their Ego do not feel Love within. A feeling of real Love is felt within ourselves and spreads to all others. As The Bible states, "Do unto others..." To those who have deep wounds of being in Love then lost; who never loved and haven't felt love; and to all those who are evolving are on path. Being "in love" is finding yourself. We can't turn back to what was a memory, but we are able to unravel the layers of the onion to reach the core. Love is the common denominator and to Love all unconditionally depicts the, "Fault in our Stars" that makes us one.

EVERY ROSE HAS ITS THORN

We cannot love any deeper than we've been taught to Love ourselves. This is the great resolve, the greatest secret ever told IS the greatest story ever felt... In Shakespearean time, the question, "To Be or Not To Be" is the search for what is noted as, your better half; only to find there is no better half... To be whole streams the Holy of another... that is the quest. We continue on a path to seek an inner Love to grow Into oneself, not of the self. There are many of our ancestors who questioned that Love also... to no avail –now, here we are. The well-informed are those who seek nothing, no-one, knowingly. The difference between the two... IS YOU. One who searches for the answers becomes the question; and, the one with all the answers seeks to question. Who is just allowing the present moment to BE what is intended? What did Mick Jagger mean in the song, "Beast of Burden" as a metaphor of our Ego? The "Beast of Burden" holds much truth in our everyday burdens, our rings of fire that have the essence of shadow-work who control your very essence…NOT a physical demon, but a controlling mind/mindset that wants answers. Freedom is not to control … but to allow our soul's fragrance to evolve for the rose to grow.

We carry the baggage of our past as a warm security blanket of mind-control trying to escape. Mind control / a mindset has been rigged since the very beginning of time… Those who have fallen prey to believing what "they" say is true, without feeling what is true in your heart(s) is the conquest. Our inability to seek our own counsel evaporates the ability to feel for yourself. We innately know when something doesn't feel right, yet, "they" don't want you to think/feel for yourselves. How can we change the trajectory of this narrative? When did we fall off? What happens to those who have fallen deep asleep? What baggage of all that's been programmed can we learn to release? Presumably, all of the past baggage that "they" want us to believe; and, to take control of re-learning is knowing the right thing to do is. To put Humpty Dumpty back together again is the only control that leads us back on path. "Humpty Dumpty had a great fall… All the king's horses and all the king's men, couldn't put Humpty together again." Are you the metaphorical character of Humpty Dumpty? The moral to this story is that with all the failures of falling, it's not in the failure; the failure is not rising up. However powerful you may 'think' you are, the power of a life-not-lived dies before the physical body. Being present in your life, knowing that taking the fall(s) will set you free… is our human right. Take accountability for where you've been and what you've learned so far… However, near or far, to eternalize your eternity is to let Spirit dress you up in the richness of life. Why not let life happen, and to let go? Find a comfortable place in your life that gives you true happiness… and, ask nothing of others but see your own reflection. To enhance one's soul … set yourself free NOT needing to KNOW. We've all been insidious of what crimes we've committed without guilt but with a sense of purposeful knowing the crimes that surfaced could very well have been those crimes of passion. To say that we're learning to embrace our own fragrance is to KNOW your internal fragrance of desire. Another could "candidly" state they are riddled with guilty pleasures of crimes of passion while others are just desserts. We are not the desserts that come with guilty pleasures… we are the guilt that deemed itself necessary to become a delectable delicacy, instead. To be able to finally seek one's own pleasures of the Heart is where our Spirit takes us … after a long-arduous journey of stop and starts. Hold onto your dreams, desires of a heartfelt rose that evolves into a Lotus flower.

PERFECTION IN THE FORM OF CONTROL

Every child behaves in ways that are either learned from their parents who raised them and laid the groundwork; and/or from friends, other parents, siblings and a host of who is in their lives to show them the way forward. The leader of the pack consists of being in control of certain goals, plans and/or reassurances that need strategic decision making. Those who are what you might consider "control freaks" or "perfectionists" fall under this category. They live to honor their integrity, true grit and whatever gives them a feeling of prideful accomplishment. On the other hand, those who hold so much control in their lives, have a tendency to do so because they either had none growing up or their parents relied on them heavily…to do the right thing. Some of these leaders have grown up to be prodigies, accomplished CEO's, Executives and anything that falls under the guise of "professional". There are some very amazing leaders who can also be seen as the first born or the last-born child because of the responsibility that they were given in the family. To those who've "so-called, made it" in life, you've sought out all your goals, some retired, a commendable honor indeed. To say that all of those who've "made it" in the world of economic change is not the only thing that makes them a seasoned leader; they've worked hard to get where they've gotten and much sacrifice has been made. To say anything else that would conceal these group leaders would be to cancel out all their hard work. Then there are those leaders who have used their darkness to get ahead – not necessarily working hard for their title, misusing the system to their own benefit, hanging on the coat-tails of others while stealing from Peter to pay Paul. Humanity is getting more exposed to the elite's corruption and who holds what power. All those who are being exposed and those no longer on Earth will be an eternal dust-to-dust as there is NO coming back from abusing children in any way, shape and/or form! You know who they are because they're the ones who are threaded with the indignant corruption that started the Freemasons… the Rothschilds, the Kennedys and the like. Here is a great example of how like attracts like … clusters of threaded ruins in an insane asylum for omnivorous acts. Whatever has led these dark forces to lure others into the lion's den will have NO retribution, NO sacrificial lambs. Many will never see the light of a new day, EVER.

CONTROL TO LET GO

"STUFF" OF LIFE

"This too shall pass…" is a good motto in our everyday life, as is, "go with the flow". It sends out a different tone, bear in mind, of telling your Ego to take a seat and allow our heart to be in charge. This is the hardest part to accept…especially when life calls you to move out of a place you truly loved and back to an environment where others may need you most. To differentiate between what we need vs. what we want is a play-on-play to manipulate. It's an on-again/off-again drama where we are being tested to follow our heart. The thread is very thin in what people "think they want" vs. "what they know they need". It's not for any other reason than to find your power in *self-discipline*. The aftermath of the burdens of accumulation of "stuff" plays out with a side-business on eBay, Poshmark, Offerup or the like selling all of the stuff we once couldn't live without. Why not take a quick inventory of all your "stuff" right now… What does it look like? Are you hoarding stuff in every closet? Have you got more-than-enough of everything? Have you got so much that your bank account is now on high-alert and on fire? What's going to happen to all that stuff once your physical body expires? Do you split it up evenly amongst the children/grandchildren? Does what you have too much still hold its value? When you sell your items, will you receive a close return for what you paid? Who will get your "stuff" if you have no next-of-kin? What then? That's the reality… Do you think about all the "stuff" that the garbage men, junk people come to pick up are selling? Then, a real-estate sale happens… for classic pieces, vintage furniture and the likes of what they say is valued worthy. Some have already experienced parents, grandparents crossing over and, as their next-of-kin, are left with all their "stuff" to take care of, get rid of and feel yet more pain in the letting go process. There are layers upon layers of what seems to be an endless thread of narratives in the process of "letting go." We cannot assume that it's very easy for some and not for others...it's a personal thing just like all the stuff that people accumulate in a lifetime. It's personal. What happens in the process of letting go also affects the layers of emotions "In Memory of..." painful truths. Even as we appear to be blessed with an heir of fine jewelry inherently, it's a comfort to some and/or a curse for others. A purging also cleanses the energy with enough time to enjoy a simplified life of leisure. What does that feel like? Letting go feels like you can breathe again... freely knowing that you have let go of your burdens and have freed yourself and loved ones who will not have to go through the process of your burden. What a relief to release a lifetime community of "creatures of habit" in exchange with a freeing of all constitutions that have weighed us down. Could you possibly live without all your overage and only keep what you consider to be the good stuff? Imagine your kids, grandkids getting whatever you have listed out in your Will as valued to each child/grandchild specifically – there would be less fighting, or, greed, jealousy of who got what. What a huge collaboration of change where respected family members feels at ease that you specifically chose certain items-of-memories to leave them... For some the process of giving items to family members, little-by-little, so that an all-out family brawl can be avoided. Those who are on board with leaving a Will & Testament or Trust won't regret how they eased their families of additional pain and suffering. This also applies to the tragedy of preparing for the funerals etc....That too may be better off leaving everything "handled" so that the pains-of-loss and the pain inflicted on your wallet isn't taken advantage of. Why not set a new course of action and take care of all your "affairs" business/personal so that your loved ones are able to grieve in peace? Why not live in a world of a life as, "life lessons" instead of "all that could go wrong, does" mindset. Those who are feeding people Fear, use others who are also in Fear. Isn't life hard enough... Why is life hard enough? It doesn't have to be... it comes from learned behavior.

In the olden days parents were taught to protect their children at all cost holding back valuable information; and the, "hold back" has become cumbersome to kids who couldn't find the courage enough to ask about sex, faith, money, health issues. Today children are still afraid and use social media as their guide. What a disservice to the child/parent relationship where sharing our life experiences would solidify a "bond." While some are not able or choose not to express their hardships, it could lessen the pain if a child understood their parents' story; and would not be afraid to ask questions, without fearing a reaction. Just-cause is enough for some parents to start planning for their future; a will and testament, DNR, a trust fund, retirement fund, IRA/ROTH/beneficiary, hospital/medical information and funding, funeral/wake funds, stocks, securities, birth certificates, naturalization papers and any other forms of important documentation discussed to ensure your child/children have all pertinent information. These are the basics... for every family to follow and to allow less stress to those who are near-and-dear to our hearts. Why wouldn't we do this for our children? Why didn't our parents do this for us? Did they? We don't know what's to come, but by being educated/prepared helps everyone involved. Our own churches only speak about the quality-of-life in terms of booking ahead; weddings, bar mitzvahs, funerals, wakes, or any other life-altering change that happens without a plan. A wedding/bar mitzvahs typically are planned for, yes... but a death is not. Whatever happens in life that is not planned for will go over budget in remorse, remember this....

Without preparation and/or education, we fall into a dark age; and when that time arrives, people are ill-prepared, take on ill themselves, fall to their knees with disbelief and there is NO one who is there lending an ear, hugging, listening to your story. Why? Every person deals with grief very differently, but they return to the same conclusion that a loved one has passed. No one should be alone yet sometimes alone is the only way out. There are times when the news plagues us all into thinking about our own mortality and with the world in chaos it seems likely that we might want to change our narrative. Held in high regard for others... how would you wish they would hold in high regard for you? A particular person whom we've had a long-standing relationship with might choose not to want you there to witness their passing, or, circumstances beyond our control would have it happen that they wanted to pass alone. Who really knows? Let's look back at those we've loved who are no longer in our lives and who we weren't able to say all that we wanted. How about those who didn't have a choice. This is exactly "why" we all should not take anyone or anything for granted. "Here today, gone tomorrow" is not just a motto to think about – it is indeed a motto that many should live by. Why not start now... be smart and choose to put a plan in action for the aftermath...no matter what age you are. Whatever happens to Humanity we cannot blame anyone else for our choices, the decisions and/or the sins... we've made our Judgment Day. It's true... whomever you hurt, pilferage, lied, manipulated, coerced, under any act of crime, murder, sex offenders, killers, shooters and the likes of cheating to the demise of another's life will be dealt with in Heaven. At another time and/or place everyone's karmic debt must be returned to the sender. It might be as insignificant as a negligence of word-play or a judgment of another's life, or a bartering, bullying, gambling with others' lives as emotional and/or physical threats – there is a Judgment Day for that.

Once bitten, twice forgiven will act as a separate Judgment depending upon the act, the innocent, the guilty, the silenced, the unspoken, the hidden, the mysteries withheld, the truths left out, no truth of any kind will be subjected to a term of justice; yet all manners of the unfaithful, doubtful type are going to undergo a Judgment Day. Where "terms and conditions" is at the smallest font, unreadable, impatiently signed, accepted and/or otherwise taken for a ride. Discrepancies lie hidden in the dark, done in the dark, written in obscure darkness, outlandish of the written word, biased opinions, lack of wherewithal in all of what's hidden-in-the dark and/or hidden-in-plain sight. All acts of human behaviors that deem ignorance; bad-timing, shame, guilt, inability to see clearly, knowing but not being involved, third-party involvement, substance abuse, and other forms of emotional, mental and physical pain will be Judged. Forewarned is forearmed at being a formidable witness to extract any or all goodness cannot be tolerated. What secrets are you keeping? What skeletons are in your closet? What's the "hold back" to get what you want as a form of self-sabotage, preventing you from moving forward? Who can say that they've been "had" in ways listed above or in whatever ways we tend to hold a grudge? How on Earth can a world of haters be of the same mind as those of all Love? The essence of your being determines your life at this very moment. What does your external life look like? Are you being honest with yourself? Do you have resentments? Are you holding grudges, hate, anger? Do you hold animosity for yourself? For others? Have you not been able to forgive yourself? Or, others? What is it that you could be a part of right now to help heal and break you out of your negative ways? Can you think of anything you could

412

say, act upon or not that would/could break you out of your own cell? We wonder what could be said to Humanity for clearing up past indiscretions, actions of former lifetimes or at this very moment. How about you?

Those who have worked hard in this life to rescue themselves out of karmic cycles will return back to OZ with a clean slate of blessings from Mother Earth. We may have seen the man behind the curtain as an ungiving, unforgiving, mean and angry OZ; yet he had actually been an all-knowing version of a God who says, *you've always had the power!* With all the external characters in this classic movie, "The Wizard of OZ" will be known to everyone that Walt Disney's vision and dream for children is to be the best version of yourself... throughout life, known as Magic. Even Jiminy Cricket's conscience got the best of the cricket... a euphemistic alteration of Jesus Christ. Walt Disney imagined children being the images of God by using their own Imagination, portraying their innate skills in a world from a place of innocence. That is why Walt's superego is a full-blown Mickey Mouse; anything is possible – in light of a story about how man can become meek as a mouse by utilizing their inner strength not to give into their Ego. That's the foundation of all men who have surrendered – both Walt and Dorothy knew something that Humanity is finding out which is "living the dream." Cast aside your alter Egos and/or use it for the good of Humanity knowing, as Dorothy said, "If I ever go looking for my heart's desire again, I won't look any further than my own backyard; because if it isn't there, I never really had it to begin with." With The Walt Disney Company worldwide, every child's dream of Imagination turned into a version of their reality of Home; and, Dorothy's visit to OZ turned her dreams of Home which gave her the power to return Home. What is your dream? Once you find what you call Home as your power within you will never be the same. We also know that our time here, on Earth, is short until we see the Pearly Gates of our Heavenly Home. Respectfully, what we aspire to become on Earth as it is in Heaven is "only" about the inner journey of the soul. When we find our inner strength, you'll have the ability to move mountains of unwavering Faith…. Faith is about Believing in what or how you don't know things will work out…but, you Know it Will.

Do not subject yourself to others' not seeing you and/or not questioning how you're doing… karma seeks to balance the scales. After all is said and done, we find ourselves needing to siphon the difference. To the meek, a difference of opinion is of great desire for the Ego; whereas to the youthful ones, any change of mindset is a welcoming doormat. Not being of one mind will show you the way forward while still being able to live your very best life. What goals and desires we must overcome just because we're not fit to decide for ourselves is a lie. We are our own power and to forgo the rest is to do your best to unravel yourself from the ground up. ALL of who has constructed your body IS every morsel of LOVE that has been gathered for the taking. The gathering of souls who've come here to attain self-realization give way to a knowing are in for the ride of their lives… We've all been given the same foundation to co-create and to seek an enlightened path of self. Can you distinguish between what has been real so far in your life? We're all going to have to endure a sense of "reaping what we sow" which allows us to overcome our fears. Instilling a no-fear environment is taking your power back and owning it, rightfully so.

We're having to set the tone for the rest of mankind is what the doctor ordered… It may involve getting shaken and turned inside-out until we come to understand that our life experiences are the only things that we will be able to take with us … From the day we were born, death begins the soul's journey. The journey leads us to great wisdom and ends with a nudge in the capillaries of one's ear which then moves into the mind leading the way for the body to cross over – disintegrating back to Mother Earth. The subconscious has already been alerted to get the body & mind ready… This occurs almost 6-9 months prior to the actual disintegration. Death becomes us… means, a death of the body comes to us when all resources have been used. A physical body can only sustain that which the mind has ordered as such. Should you choose to entertain a healthy-youthful body that sends the signal(s) to the brain is where the vision of one's soul will not perish, but will have everlasting life. On the other hand, those who ingest junk food and have a negative mindset, is like going over the same old ground year-after-year. Those who have become self-realized, early on in their lifetime, may be chosen to enter the Kingdom of Heaven before their time. What good can you do right now to embrace your soul's true grit? Could it be possible that whenever you are ready the teacher appears? Hence, why there are those who fall from grace and those who are Grace. Not every child chooses to let go and ascend early; however, the process of holding light for others to pass on the torch-of-flame is chosen. The torch of flame doesn't get extinguished…it is there to amplify the way forward for others. Buddha insisted all His followers would find their way and that He would not enter Heaven unless all were accounted for. We assume that we too are going to be accounted for in the long road ahead, however, it will only happen once you find your way. There are some who have entered a pause-in-purgatory that stagnates those who have karmic lessons outstanding. While this may very well be a story of the chosen ones, Buddha is still awaiting all of His followers. You too may be one of Buddha's chosen ones...are you? When you know, you KNOW.

REVELATION

In the Book of Revelation prophecies and/or predictions of what is to come is the caveat of society's descent of those who have fallen to attempt to bear arms witness falling into a disparage of heavily armed weapons of destruction. What this will mean to you and your families all depends upon how you react to the outer events of what is now deemed as a world attempting to know itself again. In order for this world to change on the outside (without), it is imperative that we, as the children, begin working on our inner (within) Spiritual journey. Our ascension in co-creating, is to assist Mother Earth to cleanse once again what has been done to Her. What has been done, on Earth, is what we consider as undergoing the shadow of darkness and purging; until we realize. We are Her every breath and, it is without question, that this transition begins with each and every one of us. We cleanse and heal our lives, by continuing to purge that which is deemed as our shadow, to allow a start of something new on Earth to begin.

"Revelation" song by Third Day

My life has led me down the road that's so uncertain

And now, I am left alone and I am broken

Trying to find my way

Trying to find the faith that's gone

This time, I know that You are holding all the answers

And I'm tired of losing hope and taking chances

On roads that never seem

To be the ones that bring me Home

Give me a revelation

Show me what to do

Cause I've been trying to find my way

I haven't got a clue

Tell me, should I stay here

Or do I need to move?

Give me a revelation

I've got nothing without You

I've got nothing without You

My life has led me down this path that's ever winding

Through every twist and turn, I'm always finding

That I am lost again (I am lost again)
Tell me when this road will ever end

Give me a revelation
Show me what to do
Cause I've been trying to find my way
I haven't got a clue

Tell me, should I stay here
Or do I need to move?
Give me a revelation
I've got nothing without You
I've got nothing without You

I don't know where I can turn
Tell me, when will I learn?
Won't You show me where I need to go?
(Oh, oh) let me follow Your lead
I know that it's the only way that I can get back Home

Those still lost find their way when there comes a day for your inner journey to begin... and, how it doesn't end...The Universal force on Earth is the only force by which one is able or unable to figure out what the secret is to BE LOVE and to experience other loves within all levels of the self.

"God's sole Mission is the '*Seal of Sanctuary*' within each soul's purpose. ™

UNCONDITIONAL LOVE

The thread of "how to" love without 'conditions attached' remains... the mystery. Knowing how to love will be your contention. Has the same love you have for others made you any better than the next person? Do you love your enemies, as yourself? Can you forgive everyone for their wrongdoings? Have you been able to forgive acts of violence and whatever else the enemy has rendered to show themselves as? Whatever for... you may contend to question your value system and/or the value system of your families – but, for the sake of no arguments, we've all been found guilty of not forgiving others; and, not forgiving ourselves. As Jesus Christ died for the sins of our own, He stated while bearing the crucifixion saying, "Father, forgive them for they know not what they do." Jesus was attempting to teach us, His children, unconditional love of purity, innocence in acceptance and of allowing whatever happens to be. It goes without saying that once mankind realizes their truth, the heirs of acceptance are forgiveness. We cannot deem to understand the reasoning behind the vast suffering that the Earth has been subjected to for eons upon eternity. Jesus' last words were, "Go and be plentiful" as a metaphorical essence of Loving ALL.

We've all come here to undergo a transformation where all of our "selves" will end up evolving at the exact same time. This may take decades, even lifetimes for a physical being to substantially let go of everything once learned, was taught and/or has suffered to gain strength of resolve within the heart space of our own truth. The heart holds ALL the truths of the Universe and feels what is within. To emphasize the parts of one's heart is allowing bygones to be bygones and not to seek one's own place in the world of connectivity. These efforts are not for the faint-at-heart because those who place their entire lives in thoughts from the ego, dictate that as their destiny. When the ego dictates, a life has been compromised. The desires of external things can sweep you into a tornado of conundrums of: self-pity, narcissism, masochistic tendencies, revenge, anger, jealousy, etc. The "truth of the matter" is that we want to impress others but at whose expense…becoming bankrupt? Falling off the band-wagon is not an easy task especially for those who grew up thinking that they have to fulfill some fantasy of others' needs instead of being grateful for what has been given. The gratitude we feel is astounding when we feel it from the heart. In such times, we end up finding things to fill the void of our discouraging lives that have us idolizing… Hollywood elites, actors/actresses. We are being called to get smarter and to elevate to a higher echelon of comfort.

Humanity has been living in a fantasy, within a materialistic world of illusionary desires; leaving mankind empty. What has tainted the planet is the disruptive garbage…as we watch our planet suffer... The garbage that has accumulated is by far the greatest detriment of existence. Mother Earth has been regenerating this garbage for eons while mankind turns the other cheek. If you resonate as being a part of soliciting an unhealthy planet, by throwing trash out your window, littering, using plastic and/or anything else that is harmful to Mother Earth, PLEASE STOP!!! Mother Earth has been picking up your slack for trillions of years…isn't it time to become aware? Of all the planets, our Earth plane is in the worst condition. Just because you can't see it, doesn't mean it isn't there – in the back alleyways and dumpsters.

PLEASE feel the need to take heed. Mother Earth has been ascending and will inevitably leave mankind responsible. Please remember this… and, find it inside your very heart(s) to come clean! If just one person heeds the call to show their love to Mother Earth, then, their efforts begin a chain reaction. A chain reaction is the good deed of mankind. For whatever it's worth, we've been asking our children to clean up their acts now since the beginning of time – and, for many, this is in-deed what is happening. To all those who have thought about the planet, the Spirit realm applauds your efforts.

THE IMPOSSIBLE DREAM

What do you value most? Are those values based solely on materialistic things tangible, or not? How far have we come as a society to enlist our children to pursue other things; creative outlets, new concepts, change of beliefs, goals and ideologies that are well-needed values for their highest purpose. Values are the perceptions of what we all grow up learning, a learned behavior based upon the value system of our parents and their parents before us… or, our ancestral lineage. Valuing "stuff" has overcome the need for what is most important to Humanity; whereas we've come to realize, at some point in our lives, that external values have no place when our hearts are open to receiving love. We can also entertain a lifestyle of luxurious style and externals with a heartfelt love of self – only to find what makes us happier for it is what matters. The ego speaks in many languages… sometimes it is spoken with great love; while at other times it coerces us into thinking we are not good enough-both are driven with ulterior motives. A quote from the movie, "Pretty Woman" saying, "People put you down enough, you start to believe it". Let's weave a balance of love for ourselves by experiencing life in luxurious simplicity such as: a beautiful sunrise or sunset; eyes of a child, music that uplifts the soul, a new handbag/shoes, being by water stills the mind and moves the soul; a family vacation; the sound of thunder and the brisk breeze after a fall in rainfall; roadtrip; a bird chirping, a rooster's delight to wake up and start the day; a Mother's knowing and a Father's growing…. A lover's spat can even speak to us in silence as a newly formed sense of understanding the other… a new viewpoint with different lenses. What deems important to you blends into our children… as we are the most influential teachers of our time.

VULNERABILITY

We've come from such trauma, tragedies and upsets that have led our hearts to become hardened, hurt, and hostile toward ourselves and others. How can we finally seek resolution of the self by going deep within the crevasses of owning our heart's truth in seeking to be transparent? That's another deep secret to a fulfilled life, to open our hearts especially to those who are already hurting – and, even more so while we are hurting too. What becomes of a soul's inability to feel is devastating to not only our self-worth, but to those we have loved, to those who have left and to those who have no place in consideration of one's unloved self. Why is it that we are filled with chagrin in a life that only leads to utmost happiness and peaceful reserve? Humans have been tainted by outside external errors of passion, doubt, evil, sins, sexual innuendos and whatever remains of out-right liars and all exposed…at such an early age. It is quite alarming to get a truthful sense of vulnerability from others and ourselves, isn't it? We've become so cold, unloving, angry, rude to ourselves and others, no connectivity to speak of while others are thriving. How does this happen? It's justification to what is unjustly served as unfair occurrences that happen to each one of us at some time or another gives way to so much unpleasantry. It's not anyone's fault but those who find faults within themselves. This is the corruption of what is happening on Earth, the 3Dimensional world in which we find so much outsider trading – and, no-thing to show as insider's treasures. We've come to learn after some time that whatever happened to this one or that one has a patterned thread that marks a scar/wound on every child who has ever felt unloved. That child doesn't love him/herself either because of how, what and where they were persecuted for in and around an entire course of History. Humans have been taken to their own court of law playing the blame game, prisoners of war heroes even host a series of deep wounds from which they were not given attention and split themselves to go to fight wars that weren't even theirs to fight. The same thing exists where the pains of our past have some real work to do on itself; and, to those who have risen by that painful suffering who have found the inner work to be extremely significant. The painful truth may not be yours but that of others… The painful truths come in all colors, figures and the lengths of wisdom to know the difference. Which of these painful truths will be yours for the asking is all on you. Not one human, or otherwise entity immersed in the painful truth of your life, has any right to learn that no one is under anyone's control. The only control we think we have is a fragment of illusion from another lifetime. We all must figure out our own "way out" in order to ascend and become aware that the scene is unseen. Without figuring it out… we have become a complacent world of lazy humans just getting by to get by. What on Heaven's Earth is that reality? Has Earth become more of a continuous cycle of not caring, no one facing their own truths, no one learning anything, and just about no one… is seen, heard, dealt with and/or understood? What has happened is that in the Age of Trolls, our existential progress is made for only a few and not enough of the many. We cannot make ourselves become something we are not... but to own up to our external selves of either a progression or a series of dementia. It's that easy to see where one tends to change by enduring much pain from where they've been to a learning path of enlightened truth. To those who have hit a brick wall of caring and the desire to move forward, changing perception is the only way; or else leads to a demented mindset of stalemate. Dementia may or may not be founded as an inherited trait – as those who have come before us or to those who are History buffs feel their intellect is above and beyond those who have lost their way. Come to find out that those who find their intelligence isn't intelligent at all... they may be lost, the lost souls who will not be able to recall that once your work is done, what remains? The Impossible Dream" of all dreams is to gain accessibility to know that, "life is but a dream..." Those who have come before us already dreamed the same dream that Martin Luther King's speech stated as, "I Have A Dream!" What did Martin Luther King's speech mean to you? Could you depict any one thing that stood out in his speech or have you not been privy to listening to the entire speech? You decide what your dream will feel like... and instead of placing blame on others, figure out why. Did you fall from grace not knowing why you were given the mere task to open your 4th Chakra of the Heart space and find it within to forgive others and to forgive yourself? The Heart chakra is designed as Love for all – a statue of acceptance; instead of Statute Of Limitations. Embracing your neighbor by accepting their idiosyncrasies as well as embracing our enemies is what it's ALL... about. What's it ALL about... IS.

Life is a consistent pattern of enlightening events if you can embrace your own life in this way. The way forward does not have to be glim... it was designed to be a glimpse of God's Love upon this

Earth. Whatever for… hast thou not realized that to embrace a life of Love is by far a better place to BE? The light of the world is the passion within each and every one of our heart's beating, every breath we take, each and every one we enlist to forgive and set on a new path toward enlightenment. What is holding you back? Who is holding you back? Who is in control of your life? Who is being given the gift of a life in a dream state of living as perfect harmony. *"What child IS this...."* Mother Mary said to me.

When we have found our way forward, we come to the realization that we got out of our own way; and, that the way forward is just a series of events that continue to be seen as just that. A series of uncomfortableness only to embrace a freedom of the self-imposed inflicted by and from others. Once we come to this realization, we get very serious about the upcoming progressions that lend themselves to what we know as our Freedom. Freedom of speech, freedom to come and go as one chooses, freedom to travel, freedom to write, freedom to give another free love that showers love to ALL. Freedom to KNOW that God has a plan, "God's Plan" that Drake sings is the entire song of how this world was constructed... Under the beautiful depiction of God's grace upon all children.

TRUST

In this world, of this world…allowing yourself to not be seen but heard is where the natural order of life begins. We've all been privy to some of the current events taking place out there… now, is the perfect time to focus and hone in on what is of more value, within. "Whatever…" is this your new belief? While outsiders are trading forces in the stock market, an ebb and flow, we are flying higher than ever before with a new motto of, "Whatever for?" "Whatever" that word defines either a new mentality of trust, or, an override of bases points on inflation. This Universe has all the remains of those who came before us and those which we will follow in their footprints... We co-create with great verbiage of intention, the extremely passionate will-to seek a passage of goods, events folding and unfolding only to those who realize how abundant Earth is growing. No longer are we a lackadaisical world of effortless humans who want their material acts done for them... No longer are we going to demand a society of greed-hungry powerlessness that breeds selfish humans that remain of a stringent mindset that says you are not good enough. No longer is placing blame on others for our own injustices... No longer are we going to believe in anything or anyone else...but ourselves. We are standing before the world as soul warriors of a new life, an abundant world of growth that is accessible to all... ALL of Mother Earth provides to Her children. What do you have to worry about? Why are you still listening to others? Her children are to live a full life of graceful beauty and abundance awaiting the rewards for our much-forgotten kindness in Nature. Mother Earth graces us all that runs through our soul awakening to the beauty that belongs to us... What beauty encapsulates your own lives runs through many eras and threads of fate. Being a soul warrior doesn't incriminate, manipulate or mask prevailing tendencies to override the source. Our soulful rights of passage is not throughout the external processes; but, onward Christian soldiers fighting not a religious war, but, a spiritual revolution. Embrace Her, embark upon this Golden Age of Truth, from within.

KARMA

"*What goes around comes around*" isn't only about karmic due-diligence as much as it is of the love that remains within our very hearts that expounds its light to everyone who bears their soul for the grace of goodwill. In the movie, "Good Will Hunting" Robin Williams exemplifies an entrusted therapist who assists a traumatized child with his fears. A wounded soul who cries out for HELP learning to take responsibility and think for himself. Not to believe in what others say and/or any of their opinions. That being said, this wounded soul had an IQ off-the-chain and realized that others were attempting to display him as a "thing" of value. We've all been there... allowing others to stroke our egoic fame and fortune for their own purpose. How can anyone believe in themselves? Is this love based only upon another's yearnings for earnings? What are people's true intentions? Can you feel others' ulterior motives? These base points are not only of the inflation type, but are given to so many as, "What good others gain from us and not what can you do for others?" They come to show up as patterns, triggers, challenges and all those who enter our lives in~and~out of our circle of so-called friends who are or are not; depending upon the repetition will either hinder your progress or save you from having to repeat the lesson(s). All Karma on Earth are the actions we are given to take in the language of Love – a rebalance, retribution, deserving of, a guiding principle that sends signals to your frequency that needs realignment. Karma is not vengeful or unjust – here for all mankind to heal and blossom. Any karmic debt is a return on our investment; good or bad. It is in our wounds, triggers, hate, anger etc. of limiting mindsets, right vs. wrong, that is human suffering. All of these inner wounds do not come in velvet-wrapped boxes; they come as harsh truths chosen to "show" you your unhealed selves. Karmic lessons that have been constructed by the Universe to take on a positive spin learning all that needs to be achieved for our highest honorability. This honorability is… honesty, truth, loyalty, patience, kindness, gratitude, service in-deeds for others, absolved reaffirmations, retribution of legitimate love for the whole of Humanity... This barely covers the surface of what bodes true to all who have come and gone. What Humanity has yet to understand is that the development of one's soul's path is in so many people's ties to their truth. We have accumulated karmic ties over the course of a consecutive lifetime(s) and have stood the test of time to relive, release and resurrect any past ties of karma in this life so that we can clean the slate for good. This concept of yourself is not one that can be calculated, nor can any algorithm calculate the karmic debit/credit that one accumulates, it is up to our inner work that will, "lead us not into temptation, but deliver us from all evil". Wherever you are in this world always remember that the Bible has been written by man through the eyes of our Lord Jesus and not to be taken lightly. We all have a special presence; gifts of this land are all about the "gratitude" for others in Eternal Love. Be mindful of those who have been repeating karmic cycles over eons of decades, years etc., who have already set their due diligence of a lifetime in place. What we inhale inward, bound in this lifetime, is also what we exhale outwards to all of Humanity. We have not been able to resolve the dynamics of karma until we know thyself. "Whatever for…" says those who do not want to take responsibility and discipline for themselves in order to assist others will fall from grace once again.

Karma is when we free ourselves from the chains of our debts; and knowingly, self-realized.

KARMIC DEBT

Every parent/child relationship is under a Heavenly microscopic lens to allow for all opportunities that are not there. Heaven is in the details... which is our new saying for all of you who haven't received the memo that Earth has evolved; Mother Earth has ascended once again to higher levels. Karmic debt is established when a child is between the ages of 1-8 years of learning, being taught what a solid foundation feels like – and, to those who have a number of toxic issues within their own lives, God steps in to assist all His/Her children. The mass majority of children who are desperately in need of God's assistance get it through disarming all toxic people, places and whoever stands in the way, is taken away. No matter who has harmed these children some matters take a little longer but all children are assisted by their Spirit Guides. There are certain circumstances where God's assistance looks like what some would say as a tortuous road ahead while others are given freedom, yet, there are no questions of why on the other side; just unconditional trust. Herein lies where one's FAITH is tested... Too many blames God for their mistakes, for their lives, for their losses, for about everything you could think of, so many do not get clarity until later. We've even seen those who have cursed our Heavenly Father by damming themselves... why? When you dam anyone or anything its energy is on you.

KARMIC JUSTICE

Places, people and things may or may not resonate and there is a very good reason for this. The world is an arithmetical pragmatic Universe that holds a numerological system known as an algorithm.

This algorithm is based only upon the numbers it sets in motion as *action*, *vibration* and *frequency* – the 3,6,9 Method of Tesla. However, on occasion these numbers will get repeated over and over as they have substantial reason behind the madness. Speaking of numerology is what those on a spiritual path know as; signs and messages from our Spirit Guides, ancestral lineage and the Masters. The thing is, one must listen intently to the messages from Spirit to decipher how to interpret them. No matter what comes through as a download, you must have great Faith of Spirit with an endearing Love for those who are near-and-dear to your Heart. Even though these messages come through to mankind, in some way or another, it's given to you as your "heads up" to either know what message is being activated or "heads up" as a red flag. We have every right-of-power to say, "GET THE F OUT" if some energy feels "OFF". Spirit Guides from our immediate Family who have crossed over in this lifetime usually are placed into your life as Guides to give you a sense of peace, joy and happiness – but, at the same time assist you in ways that their "character traits" were when they were planted on Earth. The character of your Mom, Dad, Grandparent etc., should provide a comfortable feeling of Love & Peace. If this is the case, then, whatever your message is, it's there to assist you on your path to gain insight, higher knowledge to follow your heart. Once this happens, your freewill gets involved, even though your path has already been fated…freewill gives you choices to go either right or left; but, will ultimately lead you on the path that IS chosen. Many don't believe in a chosen path …that we incarnated for a reason(s) and many are taken aback by the events that have already occurred which led even further from a belief altogether. So, why did you come here to lose a child? What's the lesson in that choice? Does this make you angry, sad, disappointed, depressed or any emotion that gives you a feeling that you would have never picked to incarnate based upon the losses – of any kind. Yet, it is a fact that we did choose to reincarnate, spend whatever time has been agreed to and/or with those we have lost in order to complete a karmic cycle. Either on this side or the other, karmic lessons release the need-to-know through doubt that self-sabotages your growth. No matter what you may or may not think, Earth may seem very much like a death wish – especially as people are waking up to what's EXPOSED. Why would we continue to be tested in the school-of-hard knocks over and over again? To reincarnate on the lowest vibration is like jumping into the fire over and over again when your Mother told you not to play with fire. Hence, the need for reiteration from our Mothers, and to learn the lesson that playing with fire will only get you burned. Is this child going to burn in Hell? What is Hell? Anything that burns us whether literal or figuratively is our own Hell-on-Earth. However, one can choose NOT to return to this Ring of Fire yet will still need to learn their karmic lessons by being witness to those on Earth – loved ones and such. This takes a whole lot longer and the efforts are not justified as a witness, but there is still karmic justice that must be achieved. You believe whatever you wish… just know that we all signed up for this spiritual journey. This "journey" is to adjourn in front of both witnesses and The Laws of The Universe in order to be given due justice... Either way it will be done. A mother/father who asks why they signed up to lose a son/daughter is their karmic narrative that was given from either a past-life karmic debt or the current-life back pay. Parents who haven't been there for their child/children will have a way to adjust their karmic due diligence whether it be with your child masking as the adult in the relationship; or, another parent taking control to train the karmic parent… cease and desist. A parent who has undergone "the dark night of the soul, a kundalini rising and a huge metamorphosis will endure a far greater spirited insightfulness while

431

raising their own… The reasoning behind this, whether the parent who is awakened realizes it or not, there are many influencing values of parenting that are "outside of the box" parenting which many would claim as not your typical upbringing. What a typical upbringing to one is not necessarily the same to another… why? It all depends upon the vast influential factors and karmic lessons within each one of our lives; parents' egos, ancestral lineage remorse and/or receiving karmic justice is just a "glimpse" into the level of understanding gained during one's childhood.

Karmic justice is designed for all of Humanity through The Bible and the Laws of the Universe to find a place of solace and not contradiction. Who contradict others' actions cannot be contradicted but a pursuant of scams in order to settle their ego and past ill-will. We will find our own way… once and for all. The need to be accepted is an old paradigm shift taking place right now – those who fall by the wayside will endure their own karmic justice. In the meantime, stay in your own lane… witness, observe what others say and/or whatever they don't say. The truth of the matter lies between the actions of another not in the lies they feed to others to remain true to their own baggage claim. What claim of your own baggage has led you astray, to a different place in a different time? Make sure your claim is rightfully yours… and, not that of another who deem you, their owners. Enlist in your own judgments without any judgments… "In Justice for All…" has us reeling in the true nature of our soul's intention, yet, falling short to those who are disbelievers, but seekers. There is a plethora of History that lies within each and every country…yet, what society has made you believe about the privilege to exhibit respect, return on your investment and a clear indication of coming together – is a manipulation to conquer & divide. That's where the term, "red flags" began; a STOP, Look & Listen… as in stop-lights on the road. We seek retribution from injustices that prevent us from receiving what is rightfully ours. Is there justice in an unjust world? To remember, is all that is asked in God's Kingdom.

SELF-SABOTAGE

This is only one form of self-sabotage where so many are living behind the times, warped in another time zone of irregular heartbeats that have not yet mended. Too many people are still wavering between the present and 1978 trying to find a replica of a person they used to know. Be it about their looks, personality, character can't ever be duplicated, as in our doppelgangers, only to be disappointed. The face might be similar but the character's persona is unmatched. These are beings that have not healed entirely and bleeding out cries of pain in another's arms. This could go on and do for decades, or for many lifetimes… What has hurt you that traces back to "the first cut is the deepest?" What is the underlying intention? Our intention of the fact that everyone who has been extremely broken by another attempts to find another to HELP make their heart mend…These are the circumstances that the majority of humans have been contending with since their childhood. When we're growing up… we try to find others that will make us feel loved, protected, worthy, loved unconditionally, wanted, worshiped and adored. However, in order to feel one's true heart, the elimination process of getting Pan out of Peter creates a new version. Pan, in Greek mythology, wanted to enlist everyone in a place where existence is not a freedom of choice; but, a misery of deceitful chains that bind one to another. In order for Pan to escape his own mask, he had to become Peter, an innocent boy living life as a child. No masks need apply in Peter's world, but, when Peter became Peter

Pan, all hell broke loose as Peter's innocence flew him out the window only to discover he was searching for himself. The innocence of a child has been taken and coagulated into a molded individual who has strayed from love and light; beheaded by the ego masking as lust, greed, jealousy and chagrin of ancient dreads that pretend to be an indigenous man. The indigenous man is an ancient-wise old soul with life experience that many will not endeavor. As John F. Kennedy so beautifully said, "Ask not what your country can do for you – ask what you can do for your country." Do you even know why John F. Kennedy spoke of this to his people while maintaining office in the United States? It is a righteous offer for the people, "We the people..." to understand that it is not the country that owns us, it is the people that reside in this country that must adhere to their own advice. No one owns anyone... Was John F. Kennedy the greatest President of all time? Do you care? Are we judging a man by his Presidential decisions or by who and how many he slept with? Why is there any judging? Our Lord Jesus did not judge any human on Earth? Who do we think we are? Is this your ego answering, cussing, or making erratic comments because of your ignorance? Is that how man gets pleasure from expressing his ignorance? Man has not evolved, and there is Fear of mass destruction called out to those who are the black kettle. What on Earth for? To show that you seem to know better? We call this a black cat who had no more lives left... not for any other reason than to needlessly and pointlessly feel their own demise. We've come to know that self-sabotage presents a similar flavor to those who must show a Holier-than-thou is.... Whatever this means to the parent who has taken their vow of oath from a religious standpoint; or to another parent who has led a Holy life (with or without the requirements of a church) does this measure up to one-and-the-same? Those who claim

434

their holiness don't have to show up as Holy, and/or worthy – but, to see this as only the metaphoric value that in whole-li-ness IS.

We are very far from the end of this doctrine where should you have had to adopt certain beliefs or not, all children were given adopted beliefs from some outside influence, primary caretakers; mother, father, grandparents or even several siblings. We're all taught… from the fraught of those who came before us and to those in the present, take a good look at what you're teaching your children. Are they being taught older traditional values that seem to have gone down with the History books? Are you teaching what you were taught? For us to say I believe in anything is only transcribing a scroll because many doubt what they believe. Beliefs are for those who need to believe in something.

A LIFE IN PICTURES

We've had to endure such painstaking afflictions by societal masses that we've had really no time to go inward. As the saying goes, "Happiness is in the journey" translating to our search must be an INward journey as the truth of ONE's heart. To seek greater happiness is not existential, it is INternal in order for it to BE EXternal. IN EXcess of what you do or do not believe is of no consequential evidence that you should have your personal INtent to EXternal happiness… we've not been given a map to life, a life of great happiness is not to be found in the "Game of Life" but to experience all that is. This is Enough. "Whatever for" lives on as another foundation of masked illusions that solidify the canvas of one's own masterpiece. A white canvas breaks open to the possibilities, once the paintbrush swoops through to originate the landscape of one's life in pictures. We're not going to say that one's artistic values require you to be an artist, but, an original painting for which the brush strokes depict an artistic value of self. The art of the masterpiece is what is being shown... as we have either just begun to see the patterns of one's thread, or, the various playwrights that are unspoken. "Who for art thou speak to thee with such words/works of graceful fleets?" We cannot bear to think that we too are not Shakespearean in Nature, but poised to be whatever we choose. We're living in a masterpiece of artistry everyday as our head reaches upward toward the Heavens, we are enlightened to yet another masterpiece of a beautiful landscape that remains ever changing. Every season has its reason... and that reason is each one of the children that have been placed upon our Holy ground have resurrected innate treasures – not to exude a beautiful piece of Art that appears everywhere. Look around... an array of transposed rays of light in a rainbow of colors, a landscape that suits and a platform from which to expand upon. These are the treasures that shout-out for us to embark on. What escapes have you embarked on... escapades that always lead me back to you? "Wherefore art thou..." has had us all up in arms. The controlled ways to live are the ones 'up in arms' akin to those who are confused, doubtful and breed naivety. These are the reasons for this season, marking it as one which will go down in the History books after being a consensus of this way or that... if not now, then, when? We are here to do and die, not to question, "why?" If only humans could understand that the looking glass that was used in Alice In Wonderland depicted needed "warped in time" reasons why one cannot get out.

GUILTY

Jesus begged His Father, "Father, please forgive them for they know not what they do." This is our rightful place, make no mistake. We are all guilty of pointing the finger on injustices... but, for what reason? Do you know? Doesn't it seem an arduous journey in one's life to betray the only thing in this life that comes without a reason? Betrayal of the self within another's reflection is where the mirror's reflecting back to you the injustices within your life also. Why not adopt a new perspective to stay in your own lane and let another's injustices be dealt with karmically? We may not be privy to actually see how karma is repaid, but, what good is it even if we could... only satisfaction of your ego. Let's call it like it is... a spade, a spade and understand how the mindless acts of injustices tend to trump our love of self. Take caution while reading what gets you angry, torn apart, triggered, and/or riddled in guilt, salty, shaming and blaming. Don't think we haven't said at one time or another, "It's them, not me..." Now, take a deep breath and look at yourself. Can we have a change of heart, a change of perspective viewing another's pain? Ready to point fingers when perhaps we don't even know their story of traumas. Let's change the narrative and stick to how we can figure out our traumas. Calls for a change of perspective. To what do we owe this new perspective? What seems to be an innocent view of another's life is only a mere reflection of what we've endured. We're all in this life together with the same common denominator: Love, written on our heart. Any form of one's own truth is to be clear and free of who's looking back and who's not. "In justice for all" depicts our differences as either one that has been fulfilled, or, those who fall prey to being/playing the victim. We're all very powerful humans who've had such adventures in learning experiences that states the obvious, "Life is but a game" would be prosaic as such. It's true, however, though we tend to struggle with the fight to take a hold of the power that lies within, we all have the capacity to change our story.

VICTIMIZATION

The internal changes that have taken place need to be viewed from the vantage point of no one other than ourselves. Too many people claim their own power – without knowing what that power entails – while others are using their power as a victimization to manipulate. What lies in between the pages of one's heart is what we know to be the truth. Are we falling short of the best that life can offer? While we readjust our lenses to see what is actually happening in our own lives, we're not all able to access what is unseen. Could you say your vision is crystal clear to all the truths of your desires? Have you seen what your physical desires show you? Can you grasp both the real and the illusion? Where are you at in terms of your life right now? How have you helped with sharing your guiding light to Humanity... Have you? We're all quite privy to establishing what we "think of" instead of what our actions actually present to all who are watching. As Ralph Waldo Emerson states so eloquently, "What lies behind us and what lies before us are tiny matters compared to what lies within us." This is a profound truth which Emerson had already established as a master of his own vision on how the world is.

"To what all there is, IS to what is ALL" ™

Forgotten promises cannot be forgotten... when we know the world to be such a beautiful rendition of its own kind. A kindness that is felt not heard; not to abuse power of any kind; kindness reenactments of what feels right in a fulfilled life; a prosperity in hopes to acquire; a self-image to all who have seen a kindness of Spirit. Without the likes of our own kindness, one cannot be certain to purport themselves into a new Divine dissonance of habitual learning.

CAVE OF THE HERMIT

Retreat fellow humans into a solace of your own vision, envisioning a full life of love; instead of anger, hatred, crimes of passion, crimes of unkind gestures, creative ventures behold with a variety of unsustained abundance into one's own cave. The cave begets falling from the depths of one's own despair into an abundance of heir. An inherent right of passage is seeking to believe this life to be yours and yours alone without the residual of your past mistakes. *Own it*.

TRYST OF CHARACTERS

The inbred children who've been absent amongst the rest of society is where we gain a certain sense of achievement. This means that every child born has been given their own "sounding board" to create a safety net by securing their environment. Much like a magician works their magic, an entertainer knows what tools are needed that set the tone for the rest of the show. The show is all about what you are co-creating using the tools you have been given. Those of you who have not begun your inner journey will find that it comes when the student is ready, willing and able. Those who are willingly open to what Spirit is providing will innately begin to use their treasures… one at a time or in a cluster. These inner tools could be surmised as; intuition, meditation, allowing, loyalty, compassion and a whole world book of usages that have come from our ancestral lineage. Every human has picked out which tools can be used, while others will shout out "blasphemous" to their abilities because they have not been able to grasp the concept. A developing ego has ways in which this can or cannot be used against us. Whichever way you decide is purely irrelevant because your choices are based upon your own Mastery... no one else is in charge of your thoughts, actions, reactions etc. We are all privy of our own dichotomy of living a trusting life of freedom. No one has the right to embark upon any other's freedom, unless it does... We've been subjected to so many external efforts of the ego mindset that makes one subservient. Until, the ego fades into the energies of our heart...

FOLLOW YOUR HEART

This is the one people have been searching for... following your heart seems so easy, yet, so very difficult. We're all here to give way to the absolute pureness of heart while there is no other. What makes one free now, after allowing the heart to rule the head, is in the ability to be yourself... no chains bind. Once you've set yourself free to come and go rewinding old patterns and setting new intentions of a will-full heart. Why is this so difficult? Many external influences become attached to you from society, family, friends and everyone who allows their discourse to steer them away from their fate. Why would we allow others to criticize, manipulate, coerce using \ maneuvers that attempt to waver our Faith? The way forward is through the heart, within the head... we can talk ourselves in and or out of every situation. "Listen to your heart...." These are words that sound much easier than what the ego would have you think. You are master of your domain, take heed to those who only want the power to control you and/or your life in ways that are subjective to their own. We are not here to judge others… the only judge is within yourself, pass it on. Remember to "pass…." be passive to those who show real aggression by not becoming aggressive. Strength. One's true intentions are in their actions… what you see isn't always what you get. Everyone has a story, it's written in the hearts of men, women and children.

A GRAIN OF SALT

To say this with a grain of salt, "She turned to stone…." is exactly what it meant in the historic story of Lot and the mythical character of Medusa. Both stories that speak of salt and stone… are only metaphors for the enduring ways which our ego takes hold of us. With Lot whose disobedience exhumed little faith, she was told not to look back to witness the destruction of the town of Sodom; and, faded. Medusa's affair with Poseidon gave way to Athena's punishment that those who locked gaze with her turned to stone. The salt and stone of the moral is that we have no right to judge or be judged in affairs of the heart… Both metaphors being the salt and the stone show up as the truth of heart.

Funny, isn't it though, that some need to curtail their use of salt to alleviate getting into a diabetic stage? And as for stones, be it a cold-stoned heart, words can cut, "sticks and stones may break my bones, but words will never hurt me". Both salt and stone are harmful to the body and mind… of ego. These are metaphors that depict what could be misconstrued as outside influences that bind us, blind us and bleed out in ways that are blasphemous. What's one man's treasure can be so many others' beasts of burden. How do you see your life… should we take a look at the thread that blinds us into looking back?

Sometimes… in hindsight we see others' blasphemous ways more clearly that have karmically faded unto the Earth. One could also say that, "salt of the Earth" means an honest, kind, fair individual who has always been good… an acquired taste. Our senses automatically adjust to what is or isn't rightfully pure in mind and body… are you listening? There is so much to be learned by reaping the rewards of self-preservation – it takes a rock in order to roll over enough that it becomes pieces of salt that remain. Are you preserving yourself with self-worth, selflessness in kindnesses to serve Humanity? What is being said to one is not necessarily what is meant for another… think about it. The ego thinks what is being said to one person is for all of the people; but it is not. Whatever words of unkindness come to certain people; it is in fact the truth of one's pain. A stab to the heart doesn't have to be what you feel in yours… To those who do not react with harsh word(s) and witness it as an act of pain and suffering… detachment is necessary. To detach, to be silent, to be untethered is the act of a soul that has healed.

What we know to be our own truth needs to be felt in full force. To become an entity that will not put up with the trained mind of ego – not to re-enter into another's toxic drama. Once we stand up for what is ours, feel a sense of freedom to choose without the likes of another, then, we have arrived. How long this take does not matter… What does matter is that you tread cautiously upon the heart of the matter, yours. Think not what others will say, or do to you if you refuse their dramatic egoic manipulations. Can you do this? These are not questions for the mind to answer, but for your heart to feel. The feeling of freedom from toxic people reminds us of that Freedom. There is no room for error… no room for doubts… no room to ponder "what ifs" and no place to lay your head down at night – living a life of lies that of your ego and/or that of another's ego. Ego is deemed as; selfish, jealous, hurtful greed, power, pity, guilty pleasure and an enormous amount of guilt from others sadness that their own lives have played out. The heart knows these are the actions of one's ego and to disassociate with every nuance of those that say they know you better than you know yourself. Be clear with the depth of truth that you feel in your heart... close your eyes, breathe in new life with a new sense of self. You are now *FREE*!

REFLECTION

What you seek outside of yourself is merely a reflection of what supposedly you may or may not be ready to accept and to seek the truth of your own reflection in others. Seek yourself in every area of your life. See yourself in every person, place and/or thing that drives you toward fulfillment or as an escape... for the way out is within. Humans begin life dying with endings that are new beginnings. Being in this world and not of this world doesn't matter where you are at the present moment – just keep moving forward. In hindsight it is for you to get a glimpse at how you've progressed. To date, where in your life do you need to see the real value of why you are happy or not? Are you happy? Are you blaming others for your unhappiness? What has made you so unhappy? How can you help yourself? As stated in the Bible, "God helps those who help themselves..." Have you been helping yourself? Even if you hold no true religion being agnostic, the choice to help yourself still will set the tone for the rest of this life into many lives yet to come. The way forward is in your own happiness or your own demise. Do a deep-dive, take inventory of all the people, the moments that have led-up to feeling fed-up. To find why you are harboring resentments, anger, jealousy, acts of violence, depression, disassociation, and so many other negative emotions; conscious or subconsciously. If for any reason you may need external help from others, ask.

THE SOUL

The soul is our energetic power of stillness, calm, cool and collective... until love is relinquished for lower entities of pleasure. "For God so Loved the world that He gave His only begotten Son" Embrace your highest self in Love, slather yourself in Love, feel yourself in Love; and be Loved- Love thyself as you have known to Love. Become the one who relates to all facets and depths of love. We are these versions of that love... which include to heal all the traumas, aches, pains, historic events that have weakened our soul that Knows we don't need reasons to Love, we are LOVE. We cannot be responsible for our past actions or that of others; but we can take responsibility for how we handle ourselves in this very moment. What has come and gone, who has taken, what has been undervalued, undersold, undermined acts as a conduit that teaches. Believe in your own rights and reserve to deny any pitiful acts of underhandedness of others –as our karmic debts will be "Paid-in-Full."

We cannot be something which we are not... no matter what. Each and every blueprint in the Akashic records does not deny any human being their right to be happy, their right-of-passage, their highest honors of expertise in the field of dreams that no one has any right to destroy... These and so many levels of destruction have been burnt out for someone else's dreams to come true. Where could our powers of joy and happiness be? Inside your heart... inside your sense of self.... Inside the light within... inside the Sistine Chapel of our own Holy church; and, not of a physical exterior of a building where

444

people congregate… no offense to our churchgoers, but do we know what is taught in your church of choice? Your religion is not the love that ministers one's true essence. Remember that the masses have been scorned with false acquisitions, accusations of what to say, think and/or feel.

This is where the buck stops… both in the literal and figurative sense. Why not put your money where your heart is, instead? Place both hands upon your heart and give thanks to a new world of Love for within your very being, IS… ALL. The love within epitomizes our Holy land of peace, harmony, enlightenment, sanctuary and every facet of a soulful essence. What will happen on Earth very soon is the synergized version of heart meets mindful teachings of His Master; not the mindset of abuse and control of the heart strings… the puppeteer. We are not to be toyed with on the playground of innocent children; but we are to yearn for innocence once again, at whatever given age has been laid upon our table… and, you only want the ones you can't get! A beautiful rendition of the Eagles song, "Desperado" where man seeks true love in so many different versions of himself, as she depicts his image of external desires. Love's fallen pieces of hope like Autumn leaves of one's heart. A man/woman encapsulated in what has been found within themselves… sad, but so very true. Earth renders a sonnet of single love songs depicting those who seek outside of their hearts – a lustful love very different from the sacred love of a heart. What cannot be felt on the outside is within – and what is felt on the outside is chagrin. Deep in the recesses of our very own souls, we know what we know, how we know, that we know… IS.

"What lies behind us and what lies in front of us pales in comparison to what lies within us." Ralph Waldo Emerson

445

AN ORCHESTRA OF SOUND-HEALING

Both bodies of life are meant for each one of us to seek our own selves as an Earthly body that has been orchestrated to resurrect; ascending into Heavenly bodies of Eternal Life. This is what's meant for mankind... Eternity. The Heavenly body envelops all of the Earthly elements; earth, wind, fire and air. What a beautiful masterpiece that resides inside out. The Heaven's hold such a beautiful song for us that plays out each day – all songs of our essence. What song(s) encapsulate all of your joys, sorrows, memories of times spent with others and who holds your heartstrings? We've come so very far in this lifetime, let's keep looking inside for what music plays day-by-day. These are called triggers. What songs make you cry? What songs rewind time? What songs leave you warped in time? What songs put a smile on your face? All are moments-in-time that reveal precious moments... Even songs that make us angry, and those that leave us in tears. The injustices of those songs and other binding ties we can attest to being a turning point in our lives. When will you claim your life/lives as Eternal beings of a Heavenly body? Do you see that we are all energy, atoms of mere units of energetic forces of Nature threaded all together? If you do not feel... then, how can you be real? If you already know, there is no need to know.

Whatever sets the tone in your life, have you come to terms with the reality of illusions. '*Illusions of grandeur*' help us to spot the places where our wounds have become hauntingly real, where the life we envisioned for ourselves has not passed us by, where the people that remain are leading you to becoming the very best version of who you are. What song is playing in your head, right now? Do you hear a song? If not, whatever song rings true inside you, playing later, know that it

446

is the song meant for you. There are songs of love lost, loves that were not deserving, only yearning, love unkind, love is mine, love remains a mystery. Different genres of songs; rock & roll, country, rap, pop etc., are all depictions of our storybook of love. Time is so very needed that helps us to be patient, kind, wavering on a decision, setting a course in the history books, feeling immense joys, laughter and, of course, arduous moments that fall from grace. We've come to see that this common denominator is called, LOVE IS…. To all those we have loved and to those we have lost… "Thank You." What comes to mind? Who comes to mind? Is it in the "Music of the Night" or is it at a very special moment in "Time?" What time is it now for all good men to seek their own guidance provided to teach us a thing or two…. Every moment we've come to address what has brought each of us to this very place, a "Heritage" of what is to come, what has gone before us and what will be in the afterlife. Choose wisely.

WHO IS INFLUENCING WHO?

Are you asking surface questions of how your child's day was at school? What are kids talking about? Are they responding? Is it the latest TikTok videos, YouTuber's of our next generation of kids? "DIY's" making or saving money? Who is watching and/or filming X-rated? Instead of paying attention to details … are we finding kids now faced down in, iPads, iPhones, VR, etc., an escape room into a world of endless hours of illusion, much like Alice in Wonderland? If conversations were to become extinct, what and how would you deal? Many children have very little attention spans, time to talk with their parents, family members as they're so engrossed in the latest video going viral. Are we ready for children who lack conversation about what and/or how they're feeling? To add salt to the wound(s), children are living in a society of escapism and seeking instantaneous gratification; and so are the parents. Where does the time go…. Has the manipulation of social media become prevalent? Where did we drop the ball? Why can't the majority of social media platforms be a good outlet of entertainment, knowledge etc., yet, very few. Have we pushed our children away for reasons of our own ignorance, our own selfishness, not wanting to spend time, or becoming complacent? Can't catch em… so, "If you can't beat'em, join em"

As Marcus Aurelius stated, *"What we do now echoes in Eternity"*.

TRENDING THREADS

Our Heritage consists of threads weaved in and out of a Hologram-of-Life that dates back to our ancient lineage. Threads attach themselves to all other threads marking new and old soul contracts. It is in the weaving of one's history to others that we find ourselves united - indicative of whether we know or not know where we came from. It is of no value to another that we must foresee who comes from where…in our ancestral lineup; but what does make a very deep imprint upon us is our inherent beliefs, wounds, scarring, ideologies, trajectories that impose everyone on Earth. We are here to clear up our karmic debts and that doesn't always come with doing a past-life review, or, a past-life regression. Many who have sought out these past-life regressions and/or reviews are inspired to go deeper… while others have not yet done so or do not choose to find their Heritage; the fact remains that those threads are bound to have great insight. Whenever we see a distinguished pattern appearing in our lives, time-after-time, this is where a thread is attempting to be healed. Threads show up as patterns, triggers, outbursts, anger, greed, impatience, low self-esteem, inconsistency, immaturity, narcissistic behaviors and that which comes into play from the various masks from our ego. Perpendicular spirals out of control for the same reasons that get to threads from an authentic place, we must erase what has been taught by "society" and spiral to our center; our core is where it stems from. We cast aside our fears only to bring what it is to light that needs our focus to work from. Self-discipline is the highest form of self-love by focusing on what has made us who we are today.

THE HEART WANTS WHAT THE HEART KNOWS

Whatever you may or may not accept as your story threads remain... What cannot be seen with eyes wide open or while still asleep is not for us to question but to be felt. It is in the clarity of hope that a love will be the flavor of the essence in children to be ordained as the gift of clear-sight. Whatever your particular stance is of giving your love unconditionally to every person you meet – that begins with giving it to yourself. Without further ado, we leave this Earth with the most important love of all. While one is ready the other is not; and, when the other is ready, those who do not see cannot be forced. One must be ordained within to seek their authentic self. We can't expect any other to be on the same platform as we have worked so hard on ourselves to know; yet to find compassion is inevitably just as important. We know when we know...and, a child has every right to be loved. Teach yourself and your children to empathize by learning how much fun, excitement, freedom to discover what you will miss once this life or in another. Teach yourself to not make mountains out of molehills; teach them to become united as one; teach your children the capacity to love unconditionally by loving themselves; treat others how you want to be taught; teach yourself the freedom of speech is kindness instead of anger, violence, boredom, complacency … to live a life of free speech without judgment; treat yourself to the very best that life has to offer; teach yourself to go after every morsel of life by living every day as your last, teach them to make it their best life ever, teach yourself to be the very best version of yourself so that those who love you can do the same; teach yourself to be the patient and kind to yourself so that others can see you in the same venue. Treat yourself to a new lease on life, every day is a "present" we are not to give back; teach yourself to love your time spent with yourself, to go where you need and to obtain what it is that will bring you the peace, joy and everlasting blessings of happiness that God intended for us all; take the time to actually observe by witnessing yourself in certain situations, by observing your loved ones in their real lives; and to concentrate on loving them in whatever you are witness to; treat yourself to every artistic event in life, every museum, every historical site, every concert, and breath-in every cultural essence as your own; team up with only those who lift you up, have your back and knowingly support your essence. Come into contact with others by reaching out to various platforms that constitute new growth adventures that will widen your scope of not only opportunities, but will enhance your life's view-point. Get a job that expresses your true essence… not one that disintegrates your capabilities. Do what you want in life without the expression of negativity. Try to find it within yourself, first. Within every nuke and cranny is a child just waiting to explore the world of self-individualization; a world where one can expand every aspect of self-first by witnessing the likes and dislikes… Do you know what they are, what is required to find yourself? Have you lost your child-like self in the midst of chaos, in paying bills? Are you at one with the world or is the world at one with you? Do you seek to know what triggers your experiences? Do you translate whatever one says as a 'projection' of your own liking – or – have you conceited to surrender? Trusting in your own lack of opinionated judgment is a very good start to begin identifying with yourself. Does this trigger a sense of discomfort within yourself? Or… is that discomfort a nuance that is seen by others as you? What would you say to your child-self for how others view you now? What do you think of yourself right now? Do you tend to gear toward self-improvement or are you denying yourself a better version? We tend to see ourselves very differently than how others see us… but, do they see you?

PROJECTION

Are you projecting? What aspects have been causing you discomfort? What is it that you are not seeing? Where did the child within you go? Do you know? Do we seek our childhood self in our children? In others' children? In our nieces, nephews or any other version of what our childlike version of self would imply? We cannot view what is within until we come to the other side of the coin where one is seen as itself, a hologram. The hologram of the self needs to be viewed not only of the external, but, within each internal space it holds. The witness must see the observer; and, the observer must witness the reactions of those around them that hold a place of truth in one's heart. If there are no withholding spaces, then the view of self is obscured with outside interferences – notwithstanding of our own conjunctive energy. This conjunctive energy is all around every one of us that holds it in the new light … meaning that should you see something in yourself that triggers you in outrage, here is where to place your attention. What could be obvious as discerning and taming the beast within? Is it a look of tension one gives that is not becoming of their

451

true selves? Instead of showing up with open arms for another's true colors, do we judge, control, demean another's integrity to avert following our true path? Therefore, the ability to brush every misdemeanor with acceptance of others' liabilities will comfort and guide you not to take everything too personally. As a matter of speaking, once we find the true essence of one's existence a new platform of adventure begins… the eyes will seek joy, laughter and a free-standing attitude instead of the humdrum of everyday saying, "same old shit, different day!" What does that even mean to someone who has been gifted the most precious gift of life? Think about that… When will every man, woman and child accept the most amazing gift of life without giving up on themselves? Could it be that every human on Earth was created to experience themselves in others while getting to know thyself? What an everlasting joy it is to seek yourself in others? An adventure of a lifetime, for some; and for others, the mirror is reflecting much disassociation that cannot be misconstrued as oneself. The clearer your lenses are to seeking you-in -you in others, the more you will come to know thyself. We've been given a beautiful version of a hologram as we look into the kaleidoscope of others' lives and their families. "Every picture tells a story…" We come to know what we've lost and loved; what we've had to let go of; what we haven't let go of; what we need to see before we let go; and, in others an emotional rollercoaster. This transpires as an exhibition of martyrdom; but, is it in a child to express itself as "woe is me?" Has one or both parents exhibited the martyrdom effects for the child to think more highly of themselves? Are martyrs doing it all for the sake of it all; or, lacking the fact that we do it in spite of those who are at stake? What is at stake? To experience a parent who displays martyrdom spread far and wide to others; children, siblings, friends and their nearest and dearest… and, for others' sake, it is null and void.

452

Those who have been seeking their path, on path, have no need to exhibit any lack whatsoever. The journey is a freedom of speech, a freedom of all walks of life and a freedom to know that what is yours is not theirs – hence, the freedom of self. We all come into contact with someone who becomes the observer of martyrdoms and/or the reactivity of those who portray that to be more observant of self; in the here & now, or in another lifetime (past-life) to learn from and release. The release of these emotional attachments come with a lot of hard work. Aren't YOU worth it? Whatever you may or may not become attached to… whomever shows you a version of yourself isn't to be rejected as much as to learn, heal and release …not to ever become clusters of dis-ease. The body exhibits release of all pain emerging as negative ions and cleansing itself within; then, an emotional outpouring of love as the Freedom to Love untethered of what others feel or not, in love. What represents you in all matters of your life? Do you seek to find others that uphold you in the highest regard? Do you sense people are just a series of masks not wanting to be seen, heard or felt? What parts of you have been lost in the shuffle? When did you lose yourself? At what time of your life did time stop, only to be warped in another version of your childhood life; that now shows up as a mere image… NOT the real thing. Your version of the real thing could be all the masks you wear, and/or, the masking of others' ulterior motives. Look deeply into each and every question because only you know it's Value of Truth. It is within the congregation of inner light that is to be felt, seen and heard; not the outer exterior of shadows masking our inner light. Our inner light is united with everyone who we share it with … is seen, to those who envelop the same energetic field of light being. This is a unity of collaboration when we are able to see what the light is showing us without needing to mask what is being seen. We cannot deny there is much playful enlightenment once

453

we see everything as a miracle. The miracles of light are to be witnessed as two birds enjoying the same branch. No words.... only a melody of souls. The senses within our every experience is witnessed outside, in the arms of our Mother... Mother Nature. To embrace this newfound vision is to acquire oneself as the ALL. For every glimpse of life that leads us to get a new glimpse of every bird, every branch, every flower, every wonder, every morsel of mud/dirt, every edge of gravel, every passion, every one of the natural wonders of the Universe... The more of this Earth that has been borrowed from a society's version to want MORE and MORE of those tangible delights hold NO-MORE power over the delights of the, "Seven Wonders of the World." In this way, we exhibit what is known as Freedom Reigns. Freedom reigns for all who have been rained upon... for all who have been stomped on, driven to madness without given a chance, another place in time will come for those who have lost their will to live a life of Freedom. What has become burdensome in your life? What inaction has got you at a dead end? What lives have been taken, lost and/or stolen from what could have been? Where is your energetic essence being stored? Within every child's essence there is another's given right to experience that essence inside yourself.

THE JOKER as THE ALTER EGO

To sense where that energy is dormant could be an ideal stepping stone to learn from. As Jerry Maguire said it best, "We live in a cynical world, and we work in a business of tough competitors." Do we "Had you at hello, yet?" or, could we say that the implication of that statement was to say, "Wake up!!! to all the master manipulations of what society, big companies, big pharma; and, even the history of those masking as close-net friends who have exhausted your energy for their own benefit… displaying the Beast. "The Devil is in the Details" is a beast who eludes you in every way possible by masking it as sheep. There is every good reason why Batman's Joker displayed riddled waves of mask manipulation – insofar as we know, we were not able to confront the Joker's hand in the big game of life because our only comprehension was viewed as skewed. What trying times we live in… most of all the waves of mass destruction (not only mass destruction); as seen in the eyes that have been covered with much inertia in being someone they never intended to be. Who are we to say about what we've always dreamed about being, where we set our sights upon … Who's a liar, joker, manipulator or what is consuming you? Take a close look at what inventory demands your life in pictures…framed with tinted glasses of illusions. Look beyond the illusions of broken pieces in front of you. Are they clouded and injected with self-worth issues; and, or pieces of all those selves that lie upon the foundation of our youth? Give all your illusory selves a chance to show you where and what shadows befall your very essence. Give of yourselves to all who are in need of you. Giving, sharing and serving in-deeds to assist you with painting a new self-portrait… outlining the pain in vibrant colors of what you love about yourself; instead of all those outer projections of denying yourself true happiness. Continue to work on your self-portrait owning up to what masterpiece lives within. This will innately be what will be known as the vision of one's truth. Hiding behind what was will not seek itself, instead, be fierce with "LoudLove" knowing who is rightfully behind your curtain of truth. Defeated NO MORE…

Can you expand your senses and find the silver lining to a storyline which, whether true or not, could impact so many out there in a society of masks. What would you say is your alter ego? How has your alter ego served to either help you or has it been a lifelong journey of continuous exploitation? Do you know? When life gets rough, who's in your corner helping you get through? Do you feel like you're a glutton for punishment? When was the last time you allowed your ego to guide you into mass destruction, or, set you packing your bags for fear that you might get hurt again? The mask has two faces... the angel and the devil are both in the details. Who do you listen to... and, why? Every scenario is different yet the question is who dictates your decisions? Are you Master of your domain? Why would you allow your ego to be your master when God has given us all the power. Take the gift of, "The Power of Love...." as Luther Vandross sang as a clear message to mankind. We are the world... Owning your power raises your frequency so that all you feel is Love-in-action... Love-in-action (not, inaction) bears a frequency of the highest vibration; and when reacting to outer circumstances decreases its power. How do you give your power away? Do you think that your Faith-in-Love comes from any other power than God-being Love? We know that everything always works out in the long run? Don't we? Could it be that one man's Faith is another man's destruction? Where is planet Earth ascending to? Our beautiful Blessed Mother Earth has already ascended with the help of all you Lightworkers, Starseeds, Empaths, Angels of Light and so many other helpers... but, what we do know is that so many of us are becoming awakened souls. The gift of ascension has laid an entirely new foundation for Humanity.

NO QUESTION HAS A WRONG ANSWER

Where are you running to and who are you running from? Can you say that your life, up until this point, has given you a run for your money? What does this even mean? Is this a call to accept not needing money to run your life but to feel gratitude? When one person is reaping the rewards of their hard labor another is wishing and hoping that it was them who would be graced instead. Could you be the culprit of believing some of the old sayings like, "money is the root of all evil" or "a penny spent is a penny earned" or "time is money" etc.? These adages were given to mankind to think about what's more important in life? Is it the money we earn or the love we give? Mankind works hard for their money, but at what cost and why? Inflation. Whenever we get to the core of the sense that we have "fallen from grace" by whose standard-of-living is this coming from? Lastly... "one man's treasure is another man's junk" depicts this to a T. There is only TRUTH in the language of man whose eyes have been blinded by the light. To tell the truth doesn't imply only in a court of law, it regulates every day in every office, board meeting, home environment, through the course of the Ages. The truth of all life is love, therefore, when we fail to honor our own truth, we are failing to love ourselves. Does this make sense (cents)? Have you fallen for yet another language barrier where we all struggle with word translation, word interpretation? Without further ado, means let's not wait until it's too late to go the distance and express what and how we feel... If there is a language barrier, then, that's one thing – but, on top of that is another barrier and that is by whose standards, by whose beliefs, by who's better at knowing what everyone wants or ever wanted? Where is it written....

The language of the God is LOVE.

THREADS OF FRAGRANCES

Every human being has been gifted with an innate fragrance all their own...similar to a "signature" fragrance of perfume/cologne. There is a clear distinction whenever someone gets a good whiff of your fragrance – attesting to be yours or detesting what you're putting out. Those flowers where the fragrance is remembered, as in a rose, cannot come from a sunflower or an orchid. So many heirs of fragrances remind us of a time in our lives that we breathe-in as memorable, or, forgettable. Colors also have that same fragrance... from what we wear 0n a cloudy day which may or may not change our fragrance for that day. We subconsciously wear different colors and/or have a few favorites... Wearing the color green is a healing color whereas red feels like a warm embrace; tie dye means I recall the good-ole' days and that black as the night brings a tear that I feel. When walking down a street, inhaling a breath of yesterday...we can almost envision the way we felt and who brought us to that moment in time. We can relax by an ocean breeze recalling the sun's light hitting our bodies...and being in that present moment where nothing matters. The true essence of the day's fragrance is to be able to yearn for nothing more than to allow these precious memories to take us on a magic carpet ride. These moments are too few ... not to be "Precious and Few". An oldie (song) by Climax, with such powerful lyrics of holding on to Love. A sharing love between the two who can't go home, until I have you. Weaving these threads are ingrained in our memories begs the question, why must we only have 31 Flavors when there is finite of flavors to choose from? Mixing one with another makes us want to test the waters of our fate, to co-create. Why should we not choose our very favorite flavor...only to realize another's choice is their most-favorite? Isn't it the vast difference of choices from one fragrant flavor

458

to another that makes this world the masterpiece it is? Why not choose what you want or not… that may not be conducive to what makes us all happy? The analogy of ice cream renders itself to a life of crunchy cream or creamy silk – makes no difference with the exception that my life looks a whole lot different than yours. Perhaps my lessons have been learned and it's a smooth creamy sail to the finish line; while another's choice has surmounted to one crunch of unexpressed emotions. "Life is but a dream…" and that means, your signature fragrance is different than another; your beliefs, ideas and upbringing not necessarily the same; your perception remains from what you learned, back in the day; your voice is not the same as mine; as, is your heart the size of a dime? Let's break down the walls of shame without blame … and call a truce for all mankind to Love all those who've laid the golden goose. Why a golden goose, you ask? For all we have are those golden locks that spring forth geese that laid the eggs… a metaphoric attempt to say, we all need Love somehow, someway. Have we chosen to "kill the goose that lays the golden egg?" Mankind's flavor-of-greed has superseded the vision that begets us all golden geese…for we are a family, a Heritage of flavors notably so…

DEATH IS LIFE

Death does not become us… death is only a fracture of time where our physical bodies have been succumbed by a series of unethical, undervalued, unexpressed, unrequited, uneventful, overages of addictive behaviors and too many places we cannot begin to cover when the body fades into the ground. The physical exploitation of the bodies and what we do with them is a clear depiction of how many more vessels of cells we can recalibrate in order to save so many from themselves. Going over the same ole' ground has so much truth to it for we are all humans with inbreeding creatures of habitual tendencies. Why, how and what has made our entire planet so inbred having to cover the same circumstances, the same people, places and things before we can incur a series of new-fresh life? Have you ever thought about why the Earth plane is a holding ground for those to repeat lessons over the course of lifetimes, over the course of decades... over and over again? What makes Humanity's need to suffer so great? Why did Jesus Christ come down from Heaven only to suffer for the sins of humankind? Did you ever think it was just to show us all how one's suffering can raise the dead into a freedom of ascension where it all begins... to be reborn? This is the way of life, the way we rise; and to reach a platform of higher consciousness. What are the metaphoric lessons of BC, and AD? BC, Before Christ; AD, After Death depicts a life of finding out why we deem it a necessity to suffer in order to ascend to a higher consciousness. This is the word of God, "The Bible..." of a conglomeration of tests, trials and tribulations. Everyone holds their own cross to bear and in light of that, the cross that remains is another metaphor for self-realization. Humanity, seeing your life in pictures as a reminder to host a new life without looking in the rear-view mirror. We are not alone... we've all been brought to this Earth to witness a new ambiance of a life within lives... of lessons intertwined with every nurturing wound and the scars that remain of our truth in witnessing the long arduous road we have arrived at. Whenever you witness another's wounds within your old scars, be not vein; be veined with great positive joy that that part of your journey has been covered already. Are you vain or have you seen this life as in "God's will be done?" We've all been servants... but, can you say that you've learned to master your actions, your emotions, your life-in-color as a playground breathing in angel wings. Our angel wings are not necessarily clipped unless we're doomed by darkness. You decide!

We've all got a blueprint that, as in the game of life, will either attribute your earnings as due karmic justice or debt due of lessons yet to be learned. What happens in this game of life is to recover as much as possible prior to your physical ascension to the other side… The more you can clear your karma by seeing patterns and triggers — not going over the same ole' ground will offer a value that far exceeds the imaginable. Before we espouse ourselves in others' light of passage, a newness must take place in order to find out what makes us do what we do and have done since the beginning of time. Our inheritance, a right-of-passage, is formulated with every open door, with every person, in all places and/or things that exhibit a holding ground we can rely upon. There is no room for those who do not seek to support our just cause without reserving themselves with judgments, critical thinking, negativity, criticizing and all other trades of injustices who don't have our backs. No longer will this be acceptable to outwardly impress negative pressure of any kind to those who have worked so hard on themselves.

Once we own up to our strengths and escape the external flaws, injustices, schemes of others, etc., we will begin to feel like ourselves once again. Earth is one man's own Hell or another's trailblazing into a passage of Love…. It's your perspective to think, act, willfully or unwillingly as to which road to take on your journey – given the external influences/influencers who will attempt to take you down. At the 'curtain call' announced, at your time of physical death, which doors will open, who you helped, the painful truths laid to rest needing forgiveness. We all have been given the same energetic power from the Son/Sun which will guide our light to a place of peace, tranquility and eternal joy. Choose wisely. There is no room for error, no one to 'negotiate' a way out. This marks a very important time in our History including those who have crossed over to the other side. What most of Humanity is not privy to is the fact that when mankind is "mourning" a past-on loved one affects the energy of both human and the soul of the departed. We have every right to mourn our loved ones - but there must be a healing to cease their energetic frequency to allow the soul to evolve further. The mourning period of healing is quite different for every human, but for those who have become either suicidal; or, evicting pain on self and others; or, not able to seek help in letting go becomes an issue. Take these words into consideration that what you are doing, thinking, mourning, letting go/or, not letting go, infringes massive energetic-stalls for your life and in the soul of your loved ones. This is why we know suffering is an important component to allow a freeing of one's being to go... Everyone's soul of their departed loved ones watches over each and every one of us...guiding our light; therefore, only hold onto the Love. Love is ever-changing ...this is why we come down from Heaven and receive the Blessings of The Lord's Prayer. Mankind can become very indigent of dramatic versions of releasing a loved one, and themselves from all pain and suffering. Many people go to extremes mourning the loss(es) – some, an entire lifetime. No soul can evolve until it is released from the throes of selfishness. Be grateful for all those you have Loved and lost, send them Love & Light and Let them GO! For the sake of your own soul's evolution as well as your Loved ones.

TOTAL ECLIPSE OF THE SUN

No longer can the negative aspects of our History, our heirs have any hold on us... unless you continue to be stagnant with an inability to speak, feel and show up as your highest truth. Remember where you came from... we are all connected as Heaven's children. Once-in-a-lifetime moment(s) of inertia show up as we leave out all the rest of manipulations. As a matter of fact, everything that comes to the forefront under the Full Moon, under all the Eclipses are meant to end, slamming the door shut. The doorway to safety is your capacity to be of your own mind that is not set by whatever external ego mindset would have you believing. We are our own handicap, why incorporate so many others that don't add-value within our jurisdiction of self enhancement. Many who live under the same roof but their light is dimmer than yours need not acquire defeat. Fear not... for fear is the sugar that leaves the body ciphering through all the other organs to rectify the body's reaction(s); as is the inhaling of fear to exceed on path. FEAR fears itself. What was once feared cannot be denied as depictions of what was, of what is to come, of what we cannot see, hear or feel. Whenever you fear anything... it is your subconscious yelling to your consciousness to be aware, showing up as external elements which have us running for cover. FEAR is known as; fight-or-flight, hypochondriacs, peer pressure, control, controlling others, manipulation, heart issues, inconsistent brainwaves, alternative flights of fancy and the list goes on.... What can be done will be done... all in God's time of no time at all. We have to encourage one another to attain the highest powers that BE. It IS the WAY, it IS the ALL, it IS our right-of-passage. The many viewpoints of others do not matter – what matters is what applies to your life, to your innocence, to fall into the hands of a child, in the arms of a child, in a child's glance, in a smile that looks a lot like Christmas. Matters of the Heart.

SEVEN WONDERS OF THE WORLD

We're all the light of this Universe, all a world that has been designed to dive deep in our emotional waters and to navigate around the currents of life. We evolve listening to the waves of our emotions that power the self to ascertain itself. Any undercurrents that keep us subconsciously immersed under the seas will eventually become clear-knowing while we work on the self…. Our day-to-day HELPS us to breathe-in a sense of calm; breathe-out a release of wonder that gives way to all who are struggling. Release of wonder calms the mind and the body - as both inward/outward breaths show the emotional releasing of a calmness to self and to all. We cannot see what is not there if we're oblivious to those who do not see. What wonders have happened in your life? Do you consider your breath a wonder that was gifted to you? I wonder… If not, you may want to take a good look inside for the reasons why. We all have our reasons why. Look at where the thread of what's been gifted to those in your circle of family and friends. Do you feel that they've been given more or less than you? Why do we feel the need to compare with others' treasures? We all have a much different viewpoint of how we view others' manifest wealth. What has been the contention of the Ages has always been one's own wealth, in conjunction with those around them; both Eastern and Western civilization. As the Eastern cultures vary in democratic views of upstanding wisdom, their wealth is evaluated on how much knowledge one has gained… not only the practical but also spiritual issues. On the other hand, the Western culture has always been about acquiring more in a sense of hedonistic politics, as a means to an end. A culture whose chance to depopulate a country, handing it over to an AI (Artificial Intelligence). A world between cultures shown as very different, yet, much of the same dilemma of needing to "prove" themselves. We all know what it takes to become a free-agent…it's only a matter of learning, trusting and holding yourself in Faith. Why have we only valued what is outside of ourselves - borrowed knowledge and/or power – that is devaluing? Why do we not feel a pure-essence of value in your lives? Is it because others have proved time and time again that we are not valued? Why do we listen to what others say? Why can't we find our own way? Who instilled this in our mindset that we are not enough? Do we realize that others are projecting upon us their insecurities projecting back to us? Who has rejected you? Do you realize that rejection is said to be God's protection? What have you sacrificed? Do you self-sabotage? How, why and when do we feel limited? This world offers unlimited opportunities…so, where does this stem from? Is this a part of our DNA? What occurrences in your life have been difficult? Why? The only difference between feeling undervalued, with parts being lost, comes entirely from a corrupt society? Feel your way through will protect what you believe to know is your truth. The connectivity of human rights, the need to compare has no subsequent value, but to know what, how, and seek out those who are needing to elevate their ego tendencies. Did we sign up for this lifestyle? To some degree… we all have. Our Universe is bankrupt – what does this tell you? A new mindset that allows Humanity to reset values necessary to own their innate power.

EGOIC TENDENCIES

The ego is our shadow hiding behind the veils of our minds attempting to control. The ego of our persona unleashes all our "ID's" identities and uses them to manipulate so cleverly. Once the ego is aware that you've taken notice, all gloves are off – it's only a matter of staying in your strength and enduring to decipher the code. The "ego code" masks itself in the likes of others, as a mirror reflection of what we may not like in others. This code of conduits remains intact so that every person, place and thing get uncoded. This is an arduous task that could take lifetimes... One-by-one Humanity uncovers themselves in the likes of others ... or shall we say, in the idiosyncrasies of others' likes and dislikes. The ego fades out like dust-in-the-wind leaving way for all decisions to come from the heart. Ego vanishes and the inner code-of-armor is stripped away. All personas of masks attach to other egoic masks who are playing pickleball. If neither one uncovers their true essence...it's a play-on-play. Whose ego has more power ... a battle of wills. When the ego is defeated ... the heart of every matter takes precedence. This is how we peel back those layers of ourselves to uncover our authentic self-incarnated at birth.

Many are unaware of how the ego coerces our mindset.... however, there are times when we unknowingly decide to change our external looks are forms of what the ego wants; and, not necessarily coming from a place of natural order. Yes, we all happen to change these things over the course of time dictating new chapters, maturity levels and such; but if we are changing to invoke attention, a "look at me" in any way, comes from ego. Maturity is *not* measured by age but through one's level of taking responsibility. There are many who are older in age, but lack maturity. We must become accountable for our actions, decisions, and consequences. When this happens, we grow in reliability, dependability and taking ownership. Maturity is learning to prioritize, making sacrifices and to place others' needs before your own. Therefore, if you are asking how can I rid myself of my ego, that is your ego talking... be mindful. Given the nature of our authenticity we innately know when we are changing and for what the true reason is behind the veil. No human is exempt from their ego until they're surmised to undergo their "Dark Night of the Soul" into a Phoenix Rising. All chakras are then opened...blockages have been removed and our third-eye/pineal gland and/or our crown chakra has erupted open to Spirit. Casting all those doubts aside leads to an integral ascension and an awareness of higher consciousness. What is known as authentic, of natural order, is Mother Earth's way of saying, "you can't fool with Mother Nature!" "What a Wonderful World" sings Louis Armstrong of renewed Faith, Hope of the world and of all Humanity. This timeless classic melody reiterates how to continue having Hope in a world full of chaos…and that our existence on this Earth is timeless. Find a renewal when you hear this song… and pray for all our Heritage to be set Free. Freedom is the ultimate Love. Love is the ultimate Freedom. That is the essence of all the threads woven in our Universe and in the history of our lifetimes… from the ends of the Earth to the infinite probabilities of our Omnipresent LOVE.

We are ALL stars shining bright in the night sky… a drop in the vast ocean, a speck of light in a child's eye, in every color of the rainbow's sky. Take your wings and learn to fly… soaring on eagle's wings where we pray.

SACRED is NOT being scared. PRAYER is KNOWING that YOU ARE. ALL-KNOWING is KNOW.IN GOD. GOD is LOVE. LOVE is Doing Others Good.

"It's all good… instead let's phrase it as, "IT'S ALL GOD! ™"
AMEN.

AMEN is ALL MEN. MEN is MOTHER EARTH'S NATURE.

FAMILY. FATHER AND MOTHER I LOVE YOU.

ASHES-TO-ASHES become the new norm for those who have literally burnt out those people, places, and things that no longer are healthy for continuing a fulfilled lifestyle. Slow and steady rings true to all who are suffering and in pain of seeking a guiding light. Nothing will seem as once before and no one will ever look the same on the outside as the inner transformation is happening – especially to those who are witnessing, observant, and aware. To witness others' transformation is an honor, a gift from God, a wish and a prayer that someone has been doing their work.

MONEY vs. LOVE

We're not going to take it anymore... Too many are ignorant and have been blindsided to all of the corruption going on behind the scenes. The Board of Directors are scamming their employees' paychecks by using their incremental wages for their pleasures; not to mention, the pedophile and sexual misconduct all over the world. Social media has given us much more insight to the abundant destruction of today's world. However, as a society we have been allowing this to happen, knowing something isn't right. Whatever your poison… no man, woman, or child upon this planet has a clue as to what corruption is seen or not, by the majority. If one big conglomerate is using their employee's wages to get ahead placing bets, you can be certain that there are a few thousand or more doing the same thing. Over many years, even decades, the old milk cartons of children's faces who were MIA were clearly seen by all households. Do you recall the days of ole'... who ever thought that we've been living in such a corrupt world. Let us all come together united, as a community, to sever ties from what has been once and for all. We do have the power to change right now … your perspectives, your inner world, your ability to claim what is rightfully yours, for FREEDOM! "Who suffered and was buried and came down from Heaven and was incarnated by the Holy Spirit and became man…" Our own suffering has us bearing our heads in the ground, not looking up at what is going on in today's world. Don't ignore this … we are here to save the planet. Amen.

A HERITAGE OF MASTERS

What matters is not that we were heard, as much as we were seen through the eyes of our Heavenly family as kind, gracious, patient, loving, engaged and not needing to prove anything to anyone. That's the golden ticket in life… to acquire a golden ticket to the Freedom of choosing to be the very best that you can be. "For we are only mirrors in the face of God's reflection! ™" Find out what makes you the very best version of yourself in this lifetime, clear your karmic debt by seeing the fault in our stars… even when and most importantly when we are unable to see.

To recall the rest of our History doesn't even matter, but, what is vitally important are the patterns, triggers and behaviors that need discerning. We need a "glimpse" of our History to teach us what we are learning from… When we are not familiar with our History – being fostered, adopted etc., it is not that only which impacts the souls of how those who raised you from birth have instilled what is called, "generational benefits or curses…" The phrase, "generational curse" omits those who have not traveled with happy memories… while others who have, at best, been defined by those curses look to be victims instead of what one would inquire to know. The curse of one's generation might be the Freedom it gives others – especially for those who have delved into their historic pilgrimage only to subserviently understand. There is much to gain by looking back in the rearview

469

mirror only to find what others' ancestral lineages also taught over lifetimes; for they are our teachers. The Masters, gurus who came to teach; Rumi, OshO, Nietzsche, Gandhi, Dhali Lama, Gurdjief, Krishna Buscaglia, Browne, Williamson, Dyer, Jung, Freud. We've all heard of a few of these Masters in their own perfection, but, to whom do we give thanks? ALL. Let the course of History teach us that we are all ONE. Additionally, traditional values which have gone down in the History books is a reflection of all the previous Masters of their trade. Let this life become a playground for learning who we are. Find out what drives you mad… find out the essence of your fragrance, find out whatever makes you crazy and embrace the historic cultural backgrounds that elevate your existence; a realization, IS. (In Spirit).

HABITUAL PATTERNS, BELIEFS & HABITS

After several trials and errors between our beliefs and the people that we deal with, it comes to our attention that patterns have been formed. Some of these pattern's surface that have repeatedly been an issue of contention that need to be resolved and/or severed altogether. These patterns might be recurring behaviors that seem to "latch onto" us like jellyfish. It is nearly impossible to get these creatures off of our radar as they are comfortable being co-dependent on others or what others may have to offer (i.e., hanging onto others coat-tails). Without question, these patterns are trauma driven from either another lifetime or a newly developed pattern which has submerged into being. Either way it is imperative that these patterns of addiction be resolved with every human being we come into contact with. If this pattern of behavior doesn't change it will return in another suit/physical body, another lifetime, with variations of the same narrative. "What you resist, persists" holds the same preface to the law-abiding nature of those who concede to believe that justice can and/or will be served. Understandably so…as humans fly from one situation to the next without any recourse of understanding and/or taking responsibility; heading to new paths lead us only back to those same issues. When we don't give ourselves the time and understanding of what took place with people and/or situations who have consistently been inconsistent – we tend to look the other way "not thinking" the situation will repeat. When it does repeat, it might take several years or even decades to show itself clearly; but it will, when you're ready and able. Unless the painful truths are cleared away for those brave enough to clear the continuum of patterns, the pains remain threaded in our lineage.

MORALS & VALUES

What do our children watch, listen to and feel about what's going on in every venue they are involved in? Do you know? What inspires them to grow up being their own boss? Or, not? What wisdom is gained for them to follow? Do they value the traditions of 'old school' work ethics of working smarter harder? Or, have they realized working smarter does not constitute harder? Do your kids see parents struggling paycheck-to-paycheck? For how long do you think they've wanted to ask you why all the struggle? Is it for your personal greed and/or intention to succeed? Is it for appearance's sake or to place food on the table? What are the issues that hold the most value in your lives? Do both parents work to make a living? Or, is one parent just working to keep their lifestyle in check? Do we really need all that stuff in our closets or do we keep purging out every time things get overwhelming? Did you ever have a parent die and you were responsible for cleaning out their house? What "stuff" really mattered? Was it for keepsake or trash it along with all the broken heartbeats that sing of remorse, anger, resentment, tragedy, power of so many controlling factors that overwhelms the senses. Triggers that are still overwhelming the abiding souls of your past loved ones will ever be a source of intention? Remember... the days to remember that we've since forgotten... the innocence of youth, the smell of leaves burning, the fragrance of a rose, the air after a rain and the aftermath of a rainbow, the first snowfall, music that we can recall every word, a hug, a smile; the historic moves of our forefathers and formidable ancestors who imposed such greatness within us.... And, to all who make us the people we are today. It doesn't come without some semblance of pain, but those idiosyncrasies that we will take to our grave might be those same ones our children will impose upon us to remember.

Within every household name came a certain adage of character traits, ambiances of existent luxuries, small-town comforts, big-city exploits and, for most, a culture of dying names, statues written in the History books that not too many speak or know of. What we've come to appreciate has been erased from History... who is to blame? Do we, as humans, have to place the blame on another human in order to feel better? The point of contention is, while working on our path to enlightenment, not needing to point fingers, to call each other out and/or to reminisce of what others' attributes came instead. The workings of blame, shame, guilty as charged, thread new weaves of mass destruction. Here is where we made a vital mistake as a whole in society – we feel superior than others, we tend to put others before our own needs; and, when people misrepresent who they are we assume the absolute worst in and of their character – without thinking about what they're past history may involve. Ask yourself why we judge others? Is it for the mere reason that you are insecure, or perhaps too controlling, or merely following societal norms that were embedded in you since childhood? Are we so insecure, as a society, not to realize those who may be crying out for HELP? What to do? When you were in your youth, did you find it difficult to hear what your parents said in confidence? Did you hear what was being said… or, was what you heard not conducive to any understanding? What we heard from our parents' conversations…was it comforting or confusing? Are we learning from our parents or have we become detached where no one's listening? Are our parents instilling what we agree to disagree; or, hearing loud bolts of thundering control? Could it be time for a new way, a new threading of the needle that will impose new standards of living in ways that will impart new traditions upon our world.

FUTURE GENERATIONS

We must become the next generation of teachers, of students, of those who will be their own guiding light and will mark a period of time in the History books anew. Trust in yourself. Make way for what is yet to come…

Is it too late to create new ways of thinking or believing? The wounding of the scars most difficult to heal are the ones that come from what our parents bestowed. A child who has been given a solid foundation for what was deemed either inexcusable or acceptable – either way, a child's foundational belief system entertains one's premise that is not easily excused and/or erased. We've all been in the situation where what we learned has been etched into our core layer of our system of beliefs where it would take a lot to impose new systems of belief. A couple of examples are; 'work hard, play hard,' 'money doesn't grow on trees' and 'get a degree.' These are just a few of the ways that beliefs are co-created in a Universe where our parents' and their parents instilled this fascination of beliefs... Some are relevant, while others have been forced out of the spectrum of thought over time... Those that remain have been taught based upon old traditions dating back into the Dark Ages. So much has been taught, way back when... that has held up in today's beliefs and some not. The one thing that does remain is the wounding it has imposed upon our children and their children. Once we come to understand that for some of these old adages they've assisted in the growth process of our children. Instead of pondering these old belief systems about what does or doesn't fit into our lifestyles anymore, comes another layer of truth that needs attention also. We grow up wanting our children to praise others, to give the same kindness and assistance to others in need, with their deeds (indeed). We sense our beliefs to impose markings of regret, resentments, anger, disappointment and a whole slew of other emotions that weed out the rest. Why has this happened? For those of you who have lost your way and feel that life has given you nothing but heartache after heartache, is this because of the way you believed life is like? Is it your core beliefs where your parents failed to tell you that life gets even harder as you grow up? Does a parent who instills ideologies and beliefs have a voice today? Who can attest to those with parents that haven't shown up for them at all? Who was responsible for children who had no form of identity, no established rules, and/or anyone to set any type of example for?

With that in mind, the separation of family unity has crossed our paths in today's world exactly as it is meant to be... For Humanity to clean the slate and start over and become reunited as a family once again. To those of us who return to the source of our Heritage, please note that everyone's Heritage are the deeds of those who came before. Historically speaking, our vast world is full of beautiful pieces depicting legendary works of Art from their bare hands. The ruins have made what we know today as what pillars are made of … insofar as the cultures it endeavors to teach. From the Acropolis, to the Tower of Pisa, to the Louvre, to the Eiffel Tower of grandiose stories and impeccable fashion. New York's Statue of Liberty empowers the people to believe in Freedom… Never Forget!

TRADITION

What has been a part of all traditions is in the inherited customary cultural doctrines, that is established differently, yet the same. All of the beliefs we continue to follow also include the mannerisms which people act - in principle. Three traditions by whichever generation has followed fall under the categories as: cultural, religious, and family. Mind you, traditional values are not rules, rather guidelines from our family History. The Bible deems tradition as a teaching, as written and/or spoken. Many who strongly believe in keeping their traditions believe in certain practices…irrespective of how educated and located. There is a reinforced Freedom of one's Faith, integrity, a solid education, responsibilities and enforced ethics. Another way of saying, being 'selfless' and serving Humanity. Humanity's traditions are upholding connection, linking people-HELPing-people dictatorship and fostering belonging. How else can mankind Feel heartfelt toward others…if not their own. Being to belong. Culture is sacred. Tradition is learned.

Traditions connect in our lineage and every culture's traditions are seen or known across the world. We get glimpses of how others live in their cultural background which provide solid opportunities to understand the bigger picture. The ancient traditions that hold true within our heart-of-hearts do not play to the tune of any gender, age, color, or race of discrimination. Much of our cultural upbringing lies dormant in the back-drop but be assured these beliefs/ideologies play a huge role and affect one's personality/character. When you look outside the box of every historical purpose, even though the Ages… Did they discriminate against the MeToo Movement or Claude Monet for being French; or Michael Jackson who posed as both black and white, or Andre' Buccelli for singing Italian songs that blindsighted many of his depth-in-voice? These are the workings of a tradition-meets-culture's natural talent(s), God-given talent, where we listen, look and speak of awe. Will tradition aspire to give way to our future generations? Who will be next of kin? When the Hollywood idols get washed out by a new generation of talent – that comes with inspirational meditation, sound healing, art-to-heart pieces that will draw upon sanctuaries of solace. Songs will incorporate Gregorian chant, perhaps – or a nuance of cords that will ascertain a thread of tradition with Noel's silver bell.

Inner beauty is thousands of years … young and to be captured by and seen deeply by those who Love.

Traditions are to be kept within the confines of its own…

MIND.BODY. CONNECT

You must take your own advice up to a point of what you may or may not believe in… for all of those who have been taken by surprise, the fact remains that the body quickly escapes the element of surprise by dying first. The remnants of each of those deaths, and so many more, were case-in-point of the same nature. Mother Earth will never leave a body to die before it's time... those who have exited are the works of Mother Nature. Only the body is taken out of the equation and the soul envelops the Universe once again. To no one's surprise, those who have emergencies; car accidents, crimes of attacks on one's soul through the body, all get a chance to exit immediately so as not to experience vital emotional/physical pain that the body cannot handle. The emotions have much to do with what it is telling the body, serves as a RED FLAG warning, or a WAKE-UP CALL – the mind tells the body "Danger, danger, get out!" As the body exits it has time to recoup on its own timeline of disintegration. Everything that happens with, though, and for the sake of one's body, is as Mother Nature intended. To state the obvious, we cannot predict how, when or what our experiences will be upon death; yet it is important to realize that every birth begins with the death of our bodies. Our physical experience upon this Earth only constructs the temple of our God; whereby, it is a sacredness that each child has been called to experience, life experience. This life is an expression of external circumstances that have been outlined for every lesson to be taught, and ultimately learned. In order for the soul to ascend to a higher level of consciousness, it is mandatory that every child undergo the most traumatic tragedies prior to being lifted up unto the Universal essence of the whole. In order to understand what exactly happens, let go and let God would be a very solid suggestion. Every presence on the Earth plane is learning, teaching and becoming their own source of reference on what they're soul has been blueprinted for each one of us seen, heard and felt – this is when one becomes the ALL.

This is why every individual is on their own path, the journey to Love is a simple, yet, very complicated journey – one that cannot be expressed with words, just levels of experience in vibrational frequencies. We are not here to place any judgments or inquiries that may or may not be understood for we are here to, "Do and Die…" The death of each individual body is a part of our Mother Nature growing by leaps and bounds; therefore, wherever you see yourself and/or your parents makes no real impact on one's soul path. Referring to our parents is as necessary as attempting to understand the level of insightful compassion, love and empathy our parents have shown to us. Therefore, while we tend to judge others for their shortcomings, please do remember that we are all in this together; and the level of love that is felt cannot be measured by time, money, or the power of greed… it is measured by those who have felt our love in manners that have no recognition for any other. We're all in this world, not of this world… to be certain of where we stand at this juncture is exactly how you are all feeling at this moment in time. No one has a perfect union with themselves and certainly not that of their nearest and truest of families, friends, besties, or whomever has your heart. For we all are on our own path of truth and more or less to what degree varies upon one's individual narrative. Not everybody is cut out from the same cloth, the thread though is sewn for all to experience. What makes one person have experiences of joy, happiness and peace of mind are those who have attained a higher vibrational level than others who are struggling to find their own happiness… all vary in their truth of story, freedom reigns when one does not need to struggle. We all come to the final destination of FREEDOM REIGNS in what would look like a peaceful, calm life of joy, peace and eternal acceptance and allowing what will BE to BE.

Consciousness, attention and intention is threaded as God's power. All the awareness that determines our existence as observer/witness. The observer/witnesses their perception of a self-paced reality. When attention to the energies is of higher frequency the intention plays out and matches the frequency of the situation or object of desire. Thought density of one's perception and of the perceived is not external…consciousness creates matter. Consciousness is in the etheric field where the brain translates by working into the material world through the body of our physical world. Did you know that the "power of Love" is capable of transitioning the fabric of our fragmented reality? Soul's incarnate onto this extraordinary planet to envelop an atmosphere where magic is possible. The jewels of our Earth in this Universe live richly organically – a life force that can attain itself by being all natural. A New Era of the Golden Age.

SUBCONSCIOUS KNOWING

Our subconscious talks to us every day, but only gets through to those who've done a bit of soul searching of their own volition. Do you realize that your subconscious mind only knows of you? Whenever our subconscious contacts our consciousness it is certain that what lies beneath the surface is of greater importance than whatever is going on in one's world. To date, people who have touched upon their subconscious selves have done deep inner work that the subconscious deems necessary for the conscious to continue; but, must have a semblance of notion that one is trying; otherwise, it can become irate. When we criticize or find fault in others, our mind thinks it is talking to the self – which is why the power of words is not used outward, it's an inside job. The feelings in those words rebounds causing major havoc in our lives. Whenever our 3-Dimensional selves strike a cord that triggers our subconscious, it is at this very moment that our subconsciousness is raising a red flag so that, if you have any knowledge of this sort of thing happening, you will pay close attention.

If not, then, the red flags will continue to trigger our subconscious until we pay attention. Our intuition also gives way to these triggers which can lead us away from the onset of another's temptation, addictive behaviors and such. As creatures of love on this planet we were placed to find love through all the varied opportunities, capacities and vulnerabilities which we learn and grow from. There is a reason that a child is wounded within... we all are...we have threads that need to be healed; and severed. No other dimension(s) has the capacity to evolve so quickly and learn from so many lifetimes. What we put forth is all that we can at this very moment in time... don't beat yourselves up just because some others seem to be more evolved than you. Not good karma to compare and/or take on another's flavor. We are all trying... some more than others. Why not get to a comfortable place where we can let it all go. We're here to BE what we are to evolve...

We've been quite alert to the fact that some have noticed changes in the world while others are seeing similar changes on a lesser scale. There is no room for error in Heaven, then why doubts on Earth? The saying, "on Earth as it is in Heaven" seems to not be equivocal to those internal wars. What's going on right now is that the Earth is undergoing massive shifts and taking no prisoners. We must create more Faith and leave the rest. To create a wholeness in light of the work being done, be kind with yourself and do not entertain any other beliefs. A huge part of growing in our consciousness is to accept that we're doing all of this on our own, not waiting, nor wanting to prove anything to anyone. It's about time, don't you think?

The epitome of having someone hold a candle in the wind for us is to remember how life has reproduced from what has been to where we are. What on Earth does this mean? It is a representation of how our need to control is not only dominant in our society; but that we are changing to a new systematic vibration of oneness knowing that we are in charge of our lives. Controlling the outcome is frugal, since what emerges is meant. Since the tragedy of 9/11 (Sept. 11, 2001) and Covid-19 we as a society have been witness to the fact that the United States has been the target of dark destruction that has awoken us into a new state of awareness. What stands for the people by the people is this vision of masses to a new world of criminal wars as well as all other tragedies. One Nation under God.

"HELP" FROM ABOVE

Prayer is our only savior… especially when we have hit rock bottom. Put down new roots, sow your old seeds and fertilize what is seen as new growth in your community. Engage in community events, volunteering, philanthropic work, take an hour out of your week to show up…for others, for yourself. To give of yourself, a form of gratitude that shows up in-service to others is the same light as we give ourselves. Gratitude for walking on the Holy ground of Mother Earth – knowing we have been birthed through Her. The tree branches extend out to the world…find a way to extend yourself for the sake of others…participate in Life. Working for a collective purpose of peace starts with one purpose, one kindness, one conversation, one embodiment of working toward creating a field of dreams. There is an unexplainable feeling when we HELP others – feels like a holiday. The eyes of a child's surprise, a surprise birthday, elements of "surprise" senses its faded destiny. An unopened text you've been waiting for…a new home, a sanctuary; and, so many hidden blessings when all we want is LOVE. To show love is to be Love. Peel those layers of hidden trauma, scars that haven't healed, worries, stresses, a debacle of one bad Apple after another, frenemies, being in the wrong place with the wrong group, lay-down those old roots that abused you…be content with how far you've gotten; and, be proud. Why wait for acceptance, validation from others? Many tend to appease others to avoid a real conversation, a real connection, a heartfelt truth that never came. The only thing that the world needs is to be unmasked of its own darkness, the ego must take a seat so that the truth, within, is unveiled. Find out what your heart wants, do whatever it takes to make you happy, get out of the same old rut. Be brave warriors of a new kind…the kind that wins wars on external poverty, or of a Constitution of Marriage and/or a Justice of Peace. Believe in and create new traditions that will create new-improved imprints upon your Heritage.

NEW WORLD ORDER of THE GOLDEN AGE

A New World Era, known as The Golden Age is about leading Humanity toward a natural place of peace, happiness, Love within and without. There is a huge distinction going on in today's world where we can live as 'enough is enough' or, 'grateful for everything'. Those who want to remain in the Old World will disconnect from those who are in a New World. All the negativity will cluster into groups of those humans who choose to stay in fear, in the darkness of their reality and stay in negative vibrations. However, those who flipped-the-switch to conquer and to 'own it' in light of the power of Love will feel Freedom. However, fear will tempt us by taunting new caveats of temptation back down into the rabbit hole. An unwavering strength in Faith-of-resolve, will overcome. What planet are you living on? Do you think Earth is the only planet with dark forces? It is. When you're able to overcome the destruction of yourself to become one…knowing you have attained ascension, you will be Free to leave this planet with no karmic ties. Freedom, at last! What else is there if not to be Free? What else is there if not to BeLoved? Your Beloved knows what your heart senses and if you're able to follow what is innately within…you too will be able to become the light for others. If you are still tempted by the fruits of others and the misuse of power all over the planet, you too will have to endure until you are free. When that place of Freedom becomes true to you no other(s) will come before your essence of being Loved. Whichever road you choose to take at the current moment will still lead you back to your innocence. This is the *Circle of Life*… we enter into the Lion's Gate of burning fire and exit heretofore into an innocent bond with yourself… to "know yourself" is Freedom. Respect yourself enough to know, treat yourself to all that God has to offer, be mindful of how you treat others as yourself, be yourself. "Conquistador" written in 1967 depicts the atmosphere alluding to the Spanish conquerors of the New World in the 1500's; and the New World order repeats once more… For those who are still holding back not wanting to participate in a changing world will repeat the mass destruction of war; while those conquistadors believe in the anti-war movement… Wars cannot be won when there is hatred lurking everywhere in everyone – those that seek to enlighten others are leading those who want to dissipate the end of destruction. Gifted are those who seem to envelop the traditional core belief that prayers help to heal those suffering.

As another year unfolds…we have the capacity to either change the venue of our fated destiny, or find solace in knowing without having to seek. One already knows who they are and others are still searching – inner strength vs. external collaboration of world events. We are not on Earth to foresee the future as that has already been written…but we are here to rewrite the narrative of that story to enlist in the story's end of dark destruction and live in peace. Be aware that there will be days that we cannot wait to get the "Heck" off this planet; and, other days when we may choose to HELP others. Either way... the blind will not lead the blind for many are seeing clearly now; and, the deaf will no longer take on a deaf's ear because what has been exposed is the "T" for all to see! We cannot examine one for/against the other as we are all one in the same...some paving a new way and some revisiting the same ole' road.

THE GOLDEN AGE

A coming together happens in tragedies; natural disasters of Mother Earth and all others have a tendency to not be about anything other than what has been going on behind the scenes.... The New World Order has not given way to what we could equate as a better lifestyle so much as a new perspective of a higher order of consciousness that will take us to an understanding of why what and who we are on this Earth. No one needs to ask questions... but, be curious about how things always work out. We could not have thought up a better blueprint as the one that has been prevalent since the beginning of time. What Spirit is saying is that Earth has already undergone death a hundredth mill-a-second of every breath we take; and, it has been written in the Bible as the metaphoric examples of life cycles – death and rebirth over and over again. Earth cannot ever be taken out of the stratosphere based on anything that is not already doing so... Earth is a karmic planet that is on-repeat until lessons are learned. Once humans are aware that Mother Earth has suffered greatly, and continue to do so, a decision to clean up our act and assist in doing all we can to save Mother Earth. Giving thanks, and sending Her Peace for all of Humanity will allow Her to ascend. When

Humanity ascends on Earth, a series of events transpire where Mother Earth feels Her enlightened higher self as an elevated consciousness. When a human ascends to their higher consciousness, Mother Earth does too… There have been many of our ancestral line of gifted Sages, Masters, Gurus etc., who have lifted Her up time and time again; and, it is currently happening as we speak. There are some others who are in their keyhole of ascending where She will begin to become omnipotent and, by purifying Herself, Mother Earth IS.

Once ascension between Mother Earth and Humanity has taken place, our founding fathers might gather around to assist in helping those electrons surmise another Lightwave that penetrates the atomic cyclical construct to a place where She cannot be harmed, EVER. There may be a few who would like to debate this theory, however, these findings come directly from our Spirit realm. "Give unto others as you giveth unto yourself…." written in the Bible as we progress to highest consciousness ascending of the Earth plane, humans join Her omnipotent energies only to find themselves a part of the ALL light. Our founding fathers will inevitably be amongst those whose rituals of Spiritual values intended for us, here on the Earth, will become our truest selves to learn from… we cannot be anything other than the highest version of ourselves. Denying this will have unending consequences to all who have attempted to throw shade on the light, on the planet and on all others who have not yet been able to see clearly. What doesn't make sense to those reading this will definitely become very clearly brought to the light of another day at another time and place. One must not attempt to understand how the Universal cause and effects play out on this Earth plane as it happens – and for those who it hasn't happened for yet, it must come to you in your given time just as our birth and death does. We've happened to transition into a surreal time on Earth where those who breathe life into the light of our days have the clearest vision. Other planets too have been ascending with Mother Earth. We cannot express what else will be happening in the foreseeable future, yet, if you are at all enlightened to what Earth is undergoing right now… you do have a sense of inner peace.

MENTAL, PHYSICAL & PSYCHOLOGICAL WARFARE

The obstruction of values in the world holds no bounds for those whose ideologies do not correlate with those of the obstructions themselves. By this we know who and/or what holds our attention. Do you know what holds true for you? Where does your attention go and drift away? What else does or doesn't perform within your bounds… or, where do you go when you're bored? Your mind wanders, yes, but do you preface to say that wherever and whatever you think results in your basis of thought, a production? Encumbered by what you think stains the playing field for where you roam. Is this a serious enough answer by which we unconsciously or sometimes, consciously – let our thoughts roam conducive to which planets seek either to rectify or sacrifice our due diligence from eons ago. Can you equate it with the format in which thoughts resoundingly fall on the Earth? Who is hosting your platform of thoughts? Is it your Ego along with the enormous venue of planetary vibes; or, is it all encompassing of your astrological views with a discerning mind? To value a thought is to hold it unto yourself and ask where is this thought coming from… the answer might alarm you; as our only outlet of thoughts may or may not be misconstrued as our own. It is not only a matter of us, on Earth as it is the US, a world set apart from all the rest. What you think about when daydreaming and where your thoughts go is a mere representation of what has passed. Daydreaming cannot be anything other than the past residual coming to haunt the present into believing we must have made an error. There are no errors in Heaven, therefore, whatever it is that comes to your mind-set, be ready to read deeper into its understanding. When you can equate the equivalent to all then you may not only feel this brethren of Faith in everything which is well thought out and calculated at the Highest level from Spirit. To obtain a sense of belonging within and without will require we turn back the pages of our past saying goodbye and finding that, when we do, the daydreaming forward motion will evolve one's consciousness. It is without due diligence and self-control that we impose to find ourselves within a flux of many thoughts which undermine our present-day self. What goes without saying is that once we find our way through the confusion, dissolution we will stand fulfilled in the know. Being in-the-know requires no thought, questions or even answers to what, when and/or how these things pan out…. Or not. Why not take a step back into your last daydream and who, what or where came from it? No need to state the obvious, but, for many… didn't your mind race back to better days, or dread of loss, or even a combination of both? Spirit does this on purpose so that we can backtrack in order to forge ahead into a new playing field – not to mention, how many times do we really want to beat ourselves over the head for the things that didn't manifest. Talk about repetition. In the most defined scenario of how, what, or where our mind goes – listing it out every day for a while shall provide great strength and endurance to propel you to a new paradigm shift, while forgetting your yesteryears. Whatever becomes of the past ceases to exist in the here and now… our founding Fathers have rectified all of the commotion steering clear of whatever has been too troubling to deal with. We've come to know that whatever you're thinking right at this very minute will be like putting your best foot forward and never looking back. From the depths of one's soul phases come from the smallest iota of trace opulent when formed on the body as what is known as "remembrances" only to those who've attained a solid reassurance of possibilities in thought form. We've been pre-programmed to assume certain life decisions instead of using our innate intuition and believing in what you've been taught. This all means to each their own – in mind and/or body forming opulence of one's essential frequencies that, without even needing to pronounce a person who has been called, "brain dead" at a reasonable doubt. Once a body's brain has been, shall we say, "frozen in time" or what notably has been written as "warped in time" comes from one's inability to let go. When the mind withdraws and our bodies have expired… the energies of the self-do whatever it can to return the soul aligned. We've all been privy to our mind being "frozen in time" rewind to a time where we shall never forget… the original sin of Earth being invaded. The losses of people, the destruction of the biggest city, New York City was taken down to ground zero… for reasons of man-made tragedies to behold where evil lurks. A threat to mankind of a different kind of war. No one saw this devastation as pre-planned, until a year or so later; and, even since then… we all know who was behind the workings of a terrorist attack of that magnitude. There are origins of evil people that are lurking in the backdrops of all things destructive, in all people, and the pavers of each crescent in the ethers where we are yet to see. A community of strength-in-numbers holds a strength-of-power.

Additionally, wars between Nations exist as geographical warfare threaded in present times that resemble that of similar battles of Sodom and Gomorrah. What do these two world warfare events

488

have in common? Not only their geographical plots but also the venue that wars have targeted egoic emotions of people feeling they are better than others? What are we fighting for? Is it our Freedom of Speech or is it what remains of the aftermath that people need to see happen as a consolation prize? Sodom and Gomorrah were fighting an initial warfare of who's to say ever gave way to a resolution whereby it has still been a hidden war ever since. Those people in Israel and Palestine have been at each other's throats for an eternity – as others joined in on various occasions. They are not the only threats being made that are at war here…it is of a consequential warfare where it has never been so apparent that the needle- and-thread woven has never been sewn together through a forgiveness of different values. A divide. What hasn't changed is that neither ever wins the wars…they gain a new value system that implies seeking equality and instead is a painful ending of neutrality. No-body wins. Men, women and children have been fighting in one way, shape and/or form for a control that neither belongs to mankind nor to any-body; peace stems from a comforting sense of belonging. Peaceful retribution is at stake. With Egos so gigantic…who will knock them out of office? Who will take the blame for being egoic prisoners of their own demise? Why are children being taken for granted, killed, murdered etc., and, what right does anyone have on this God-given planet to overshadow innocent children? Just another form of manipulation by those who are unworthy to belong. There is no need to point the fingers at any one person, place, or thing because they are acting out enough for the entire Universe to see what *lies* behind the curtain of mass destruction. Be *present* in your own right and know when to be silent/still, observing the chaos of ratchet misuse of those of egoic power. It's not as though we turn a blind-eye…or, do we? What can any one person do to change this mass destruction? Do your inner work and leave the karmic injustices to the powers that BE. This moment in time, however, is *very* different. This will increase those who have awakened to their own truth of setting the record straight by staying in their own lane to protect their families. That's what is of utmost importance... Remember, next time you ask yourself, "What can I do to change the world events and/or course of events?" *NO-FEAR.*

These events have been written in Revelation and there is yet to be a series of fearful exits by those who fall prey – indelibly we will be witness to all of these events. Serving Humanity is our absolute purpose-ful life of knowing why we came to planet Earth in the first place. It is NOT to go to war with others. These tragedies are for us to learn from and be in a strong peaceful place within. Although, those who indulge in warfare... be it on the battlegrounds fighting other countries or it in our own homes. What is going to become of Humanity is entirely up to YOU. What is NOT tolerated on any planet, in any Dimension or place of Love is to harm God's children. Those who are in warfare and/or have been ousted as criminal acts will be terminated, extracted from Mother Earth and driven deep into the recesses of lower vibrations that will never see the light of day, EVER.

America the Great has turned into America the Junkies. To allow junk into our world, to allow ourselves no emotion, to disallow any matter of heartfelt emotion makes us a world where we eat, see, listen and breathe in only junk. Junk-food...junk that we inhale, lines are being crossed over the skies that are sweeping over the air that we breathe; fentanyl weed is being cast as added junk that smells like a skunk; and, all the junk being watched on social media that are making our kids more addictive and unresponsive. Has America become the next junkies? Stone-walling as the saying goes... absolutely no emotional value and no understanding of what is going on in order to take some responsibility... stone cold but not in our Frappuccino. Money spent on a specially made coffee that implores our nervous system and abhors those who don't comply. No two worlds can collide without this sort of destruction...so, it is up to each and every one of us, as Americans, to make it great for yourselves first... by living your best life and taking responsibility for the next generations to come instilling parental values back. Let's make values, communication, emotions, and a sense of putting the word "human" back into Humanity once again. Whichever way our world escapes the matrix of disillusionment it will be for the betterment of society. We cannot sustain an environment without seeing it as it is and wanting to take our innate power back. This is why we all signed up to be here, now, on planet Earth... Why else would we be here? Do you really think this world was built for only one reason to Love... as in a relationship? How prosaic of us to think so close-minded and not to assist and serve an entire world that needs Love. Every one of us must come to understand and relay this message across to our family, friends and acquaintances that Love of Humanity is what we are here to attain. Some of mankind will siege and get a surge to go within for change realizing it is not as easy as one may think. Therefore, we all need to cluster together at this very moment and seek not the compliance of life but to embrace what actually is happening in the world today. Don't turn a blind's eye for Fear is only the Fear that you feel within...and, what "they" have told you to Fear is not real. The real deal will be when society has completely surrendered to itself knowing that by not taking responsibility is to not believe in yourselves. That is why we've been feeling a loss of value in America while other parts of the countries have been watching America losing its grip. Why let all of our hard work to get where we've been thriving as a strong country be taken away? Let's pull together "United We Stand" and get a nuance of a life giving back to those in need...that strength has made us what we stand for. Those against Americans are the same humans that have wanted us to fall from grace since inception...but, we pulled through. The change we must endure is simply to settle in and watch how 'ignorance is bliss' will not be a saying any longer unless you can open your eyes to being an adult. Adulting means not ignoring, it means becoming interactive in your children's lives, it's taking a stance that means "going the distance" to serve and protect our children. We can take back our power of caring about what happens to our children by actually interacting with them daily ... then, we may curtail being the laughing stock of the world. Laughing stock implies how we are sheep...and, the more "they" are laughing, our entire country is sinking into a sandy ditch. Does this make sense or do you want to give your two cents to a society who bluntly doesn't care? What are you going to do about it? What happens when "they" murder, kill, pillage your own child or a child in your family? Then, will you care? Is it a doggie-dog-world until it's on your doorstep? Life will inevitably sustain, Mother Earth will forge ahead as She has been raising Her consciousness with all the assistance of those Lightworkers, Seers, Sages, Earth Angels; but what will happen to you? Don't ignore it.

The hidden meaning behind someone's true intentions is not a primary source that lends itself to bestow much knowledge as it is taken out of context... What is hidden requires a source of inner reflection, namely, to BElieve, what is not said is felt between the lines nor should we attempt to understand why some things happen the way they do and why others don't. What we do not know will not be a source of contention but rather the contention is in the availability to appreciate the moments which take us to a place of knowing. Who is it that you seek, not so much, who isn't, is it? What our desires remind us of makes us think about all those things that matter, "the very stuff of life." This is with every aspect of our lives and in-service how we show up presenting this to the world… and, sometimes when we go overboard, instead of beating ourselves up about what we overdo… overdue is just a form of not being given or having enough. Our "Book Of Life" is written in the spaces between the lines that are not known until our life experiences are shown through the reflection of others. Herein lies what can or cannot be seen… but, do you feel what is being addressed? Do you know yourself only too well or not yet enough to say that this equates with your personal outlook… to be gifted as an inner piece of art that is being tweaked to perfection. Take a minute, go into your quiet place, look deep into the mirror of your own reflection, who is it that's looking back? Tell yourself *"I love you"* every day…a meditation.

We're not only seeking to destroy whatever external desires we've come very fond of, yet, so unhappy with at the very same time. What IS or isn't making you happy right now? Just be mindful… a mindful heart is no mind at all. Being pleasantly surprised in life comes at NO cost… just a whole lot of money, says who? Earth's mentality is nothing but a vision of superiority or a quiet resolve that needs not be seen, but felt. Where in your life are you putting up a show-n-tell? Where in your life are you being you… a withholding of self-indulgences NOT for all to see? Inner work on this spiritual journey needs not to be rehearsed, discussed, tended to with a verbal explanation or reiteration of interrogation. What IS our inner sense of self that needs no conversation, interpretation or indignation of self-proportion. "We aim to please" is the motto of the hidden, or, is it?

493

This narration that breeds a semblance of "customer service" worldwide across time, and the Ages, has lent itself to interpreting it as a sense of self-absorption, an egoic service instead of aiming for the goal of self-assurance. Why do you think that matters? Do you? What inner thoughts are triggering your belief systems of how your brain was/is being trained to think? "Brain-washed...." Should the absence of space require a heartless life? Where is one's heart while in a space between... or worlds between the Heavens and Earth... or the empty hearts of our own children? Are you seeing or believing in a society that is cruel to its own as being "scared of our own shadow?!" When you were a child, were you scared of your shadow? Whatever you are afraid of is allowing it the power to control and hurt you. What scared you most? Could you go back and find your shadow now or is it still with you, behind every step enticing you to listen or not to the likes of others? We've all, at one time or another, been scared of our shadow – how have you overcome it? Who is the shadow? Is the shadow a dark entity? Or, is your shadow your own fear for the unknown... the place between the known and unknown? Is your shadow all the various people who influenced you this way and that? Can you vouch for your shadow or does it come with a lot of baggage? Without your shadow, is this even possible to live without? Even though the shadow made us fearful... have you learned to differentiate what your shadow is/was trying to tell you? Are you listening? Who else's shadow is following you? Are their shadows of darkness in your life in many areas of your life? A shadow plays what role in our lives? Do you know? How many times have you been scared of the dark? Is being scared of your shadow the same as having fear of the dark? Where are these shadows being placed in one's life for us to shed light upon? Are you giving into the shadows that bind you to another? Do you know that if you break the chains that bind you with other egoic versions of yourself, your shadows will dissipate? Do you know how to entertain your shadow in order to get what it is you want? Have you ever thought of how one could befriend the shadow… without a shadow of a doubt, that's how…

All things matter in a materialistic world; but what is not seen matters most! The world is an intrinsic mosaic display that is pixelated on forgotten worlds from ancient times... what matters is what is felt, in the heart of the matter… we navigate our lives on the heartfelt beating of our own drum. Let's connect with your heart right now by not entertaining an AI robotic life of not feeling love, ever again. Isn't that the case in every case and point? Who's going to buy into the control of a robot that has nothing to offer up what is being programmed into its computer system? Do you follow what I'm putting out onto your hard-drive, or internal system of casting out unto the world of space … nothing but space? No retaliation, no recognition needed… no one but the only person on the face of this planet to exude such egoism that they're egoic masks are shadowed without authentic feelings. These efforts of AI robotic programming will NOT succeed. By means of how the Universe IS constructed with the hologram of not a hollow shell, but a halo that holds grams of weightless love for Humanity. LOVE IS the wrecking ball of energetic force that will rock the world of many who have laid down for their weight in gold gambling all their wears for a chance to unleash a dragon that doesn't lay eggs that are golden, but pewter in the form of a portal closure. The portal we are discussing is the womb of Mother Earth and Her ability to tend to Her garden of love through ALL of Her children. There is absolutely no power greater than our Heavenly Father & the Blessed Mother who bear fruit from Her own loins for all Humanity. No amount of force could contain enough darkness to entertain shadows in a world whose heart-portal has been contained. Even an atmosphere of darkness wouldn't entertain the likes of mankind with no heart because the black hole is our heart. The events of this occurrence to change the actual reproduction system of planet Earth is insane, to learn that people are placed on this planet to experience life of one heart to BElieve in one fragrance to another's fragrance is the power of Love. AI robots will be used to distinguish ideologies where threads of heartless ties want a place in History. The ascension on Earth is making History as a Spiritual Revolution already created for the evolution of consciousness. What has been written cannot be erased… nor, what has been done cannot be undone for the sake of Humanity… for Humanity's sake. Know that beneath every need is a feeling; beneath every scar is a wound unhealed; beneath what has NOT been felt, a need to feel experiences. Beneath your every breath is a place we call home… take a breath of fresh air and seek to find what is real, and, what is an illusion. "Breathe deep the gathering gloom, watch lights fade from every room; bedsitter people look back and lament, another day's useless energy spent; impassioned lovers wrestle as one, lonely man cries for love and has none; new mother picks up and suckless her son, senior citizens wish they were young; cold hearted orb that rules the night, removes the colors from our sight; red is gray and yellow white, but WE decide which is right… and, which is an illusion." "Nights In White Satin", song by The Moody Blues.

All-in-all the one who suffers greatly is the one with no filter of what is right or wrong in doing whatever that it is they like. What commences is an order of the courts to raise one's vibrational movement by getting things done and not worrying which is right or which is an illusion. The effervescent nature of the wheelings which cometh to the forefront is not whether we allow others to do the right

496

thing; so much as where has it been written to dismiss those who have every right thinking they've even made a judgment call not based on their own experience. This is exactly why those who have to distinguish between this or that, right or wrong, left or right etc., have very little incentive to change. To conquer and divide is an understatement as far as why, where and to whom shall we gear these "divides" of deciding which is or what isn't right. Nonetheless society has made this massive imprint on the children of the world engrossed in following man-made orders, and, not of Spirit. Truth? Why shall we bequeath to follow the path of least resistance when the path of the Logos, "Word of God" always guides us to the appropriate steps which are for our Highest good. Do you ever think about this or that as to why you've chosen not to be a chosen one when we know that using your own dictatorship has led you astray. Once you can equate fakeness from reality... your perception of your reality will change.

This will be the end of what prisons have been required to live with in terms of what someone did or didn't do; as a justice of the court system to prosecute accurately. No one said that you should enter into a world of crimes, passion and murderous enumerations of what has been done. Who is to judge your efforts when you leave this world? Do you think that the punishment on this Earth is one that is enough, or, wisely held within the boundaries of their own selves being set free? Does one return to the crimes of passion only to find that their crimes were utterly salvaged by those who only see them for what they have done? Will it be enough to judge another in the future? When did the justice system get to pick or choose what should or shouldn't be clearly a victim of circumstance? When did the court system begin their payouts of relying on a full disclosure for crimes committed? Who is in charge of reaping the rewards for judgments of another?

Why should anyone get paid for placing blame upon another's indiscretions or crimes of other types in a court of law? Where did this first become a thing? Whoever made that call to uphold a superiority case-in-point for others' indiscretions then what about those who've done the same? Who charges the judge in a court of law should they falter and/or waiver from the domain of societal norms? To what purpose should the upholding of these laws be used in a court of law? Where has it been written? In whatever fashion the industry of reaping what you sow has been under an advisory board, if you will, will ascertain what the actual nuptials of couples' state when they too are under legal advice. What is this for and why has any needed constitution been asked that in order to judge you must render all allowances to a few in the court judicial system. Why? For whom do the bells toll? Are you under scrutiny or obtrusive usages of what was once considered viable under the brethren of both a court of law as also a judicial systematic filter of what was once, the Freemasons. The Freemasons where all the justices and/or injustices were incited as those willing and/or able to make cast/concrete decisions of life injustices based upon character witnesses.

Those today are who we consider as Congress and the Courts of Law in Washington, DC have given into injustices of every kind – the differences in today's court system is that they have finally allowed women into the room… after a hundred of years or so. "To Whom The Bell Tolls" created and reenacted for all to seek those who have been granted a second chance to change one's mind about who has been given accessibility to drive and divide a much-needed norm to those people who have committed acts of crimes. Now, in today's judicial system, crimes are no longer seen as they were in the days of ole. There have been changes made in the courts as well as those who are making the crucial decisions that adhere to what is considered, allegedly, right or wrong. What we have here is another case of positive and negative advice from those who have vices. We stand contested insofar as to why one is guilty and another is set free. We have no recollection to which others have justification rendering such silliness as depicting which evil crime is eviller than the next. Who is rightfully deemed as the debtor or debtee of a crime? We've all been warned to what others' actions must defer as discredited actions within a court of law – therefore, what was once deemed as an act of murder is now under scrutiny. What this means is that they are much more in-depth and much-needed facts, stats, and the like in order to make a concrete decision as to who is deserving of the electric chair and who is not. Why is this? Who has any right, other than the self-imposed to really know when one has been driven to the depths of Hell? Why and when did this begin to falter based upon which sins of the flesh are of greater consequence? How can one presume that the fear of God has been written upon man's hands where he is not to judge another; but he is to deem another unworthy of taking his life unto his own hands? Which crime, therefore, would be deemed a death sentence in ever more powerful than the hands of the self or of the hands of the justice system? Is this even a distinguished crime to be extricated for? When we look into the eyes of our Beloved, do we see our own repercussions of evil or do we see another man's entirety? Has mankind gone too far or not yet far enough to witness the case-in-point of holding any crime that is not restricted to or exempt from taking one's life? What is enough? Why is it not enough to allow a man's freedom to be granted or not; while our neighbor has been dabbling into other cases of crimes of passions or committing other faulty reenactments of what is disguised as crimes – be anything other than the same? Who has been granted to choose which are more deadly than the other? Why has man

499

decided to go against the self of mankind in order to become more trustworthy or in need of another's approval simply because the "bad guy" got what he deserved? Why is one crime of evil any different than another and who changed the platform of what was and has been written in the Bible? In the Bible, any act of murder or crimes of passion where Cain killed Able in an attempt to outcast his own brother, resulted in God's betrothing Cain to wander the plains for the duration of his life. What happened to this crime of murder ended in a crime deadly to a brother. Which brother had any right to ostracize one's own? To whom do these bells toll for especially when one is witnessed as the perpetrator = purposefully perpetual traitor? Has Earth become a perpetual place for traitors? What candid acts of relatively undesirable uses has Earth become, where it was taken from a holding ground for refugees' enablers of the sins of their own crimes of whatever sieges to export someone from ground zero to the highest plane of all… their center. Who has the 1939 "Wuthering Heights" motives to take down the Apocalypse? In 1939 Earth was under attack giving way to World War II while, in the same breath, Judy Garland was singing her infamous song, "Over the Rainbow" as a way of knowing a life of existence in the afterlife. This is exactly where we are in today's historic vantage point in the New Year of 2024 where there are those who will go viral for crimes of an Apocalypse and there are those who will sing praises of a life eternal. What holds more ground for you at this very juncture in your life? Are you going to follow the sheep of least resistance or are you going to lead the way to the Motherland of the Holy Grail? Yes, your choice is wherever you land… all in Eternal Life to bring you back Home. Going back Home does not imply that you don't have a choice in the matter… Once you return to your senses, everyone realizes at some point in their lives that the matter-of-fact is the truest metaphor for the school of hard knocks while the home reckoning is still a depiction of just that. Who is to say that one will graduate faster than the other… is all up to your life, a life imprinted by a driving need for passion in the 6th decree of standing firm and in love with a life fulfilled. The 6th decree is meant for us to understand that it is the 6th letter in the alphabet as, "F" which stands for FAITH. Our livelihood is based on the 6th Decree of FAITH. No other word stands out in the English language as those who have tolled the bells to hear the songs of a life everlasting as in the one, *"Over the Rainbow."*

Whatever leads us to stick with what we've always known to be sticky cling-on's of past misfortunes has to be re-evaluated and stirred very well within one's heart to find our own truths. We cannot give into the ways of the world by not allowing the human race to have choices – only through these choices do we learn not to make the same mistakes twice. However, many choices we must endear toward our truth IS only up to you. Given "freewill" we enter into our own ways of being, our own thoughts to take, our own places to roam, and our own prices to pay. Why do we have to pay the piper in the long run anyway? Who judges us on Earth? Ourselves. Does Jesus know what His children must learn, how many chances of choices will be sought to sew and/or who will be the biggest loser in a world of only gain? "To be or not to be…" in Shakespearean times was in-deed the most obvious of what we have to gain or lose in the game of life. What order of business can be had to learn what we already know to be a much-needed reason to stay on point, without questioning ourselves. The real deal has already been seen as the ONE who KNOWS… never to question the truest quest-of-life and to know what is needed to remember. We can even assess what one man's outer knowledge has attained is not another man's level of expertise as knowledge is a form of borrowed intellect; and, life experiences are the cusp of knowledge that has been learned through self-evaluation in time. "No time like the present" cannot be made … it IS. Thoughts take you wherever you need to go… is very much like flying outside of one's own body and elevating the whole of Mother Earth – taking it ALL IN. When we seek to look outside of our own selves, we seek to envelop the whole purpose of living on Earth; and, when we seek to look inward to when our heart speaks, we know that the true value isn't the purpose, it IS.

To what degree are we actually able to seek one way or another isn't the question… but, the real quest is to allow ONE to seek itself. "No ONE compares to you" IS what God intended from each one of His children. To behold our BELOVED IS to KNOW.

TRUST

For whatever it's worth… our main goal on Earth is to remember, to witness and to recall our own selves in a body of the self, as itself. Filter that which is no longer working for your highest and most definitely truest self… Believing what we've been taught no longer works for the majority rule – uncover those truths that only fit into your realm of higher learning, higher self and for your highest good. The Trinity. We've been upon Earth far too long with a latent skill-set uncovering what is worthy and what is not. Trust that we already know what is and what is not good for ourselves… be discerning with the facts, figures and sensibilities that are unclean to the human eye; for those that are unseen are clean. Unchain your ideals for those beliefs holding no weight in gold; unfurling the same as when idols pop up on your social media pages, as having no purity in task masquerading as someone who they are not privy to be claimed, in the Bible, as resisting

502

temptations; and, as far as your own self-worth, seek to find the values which correspond within your resting heart rate… not in your external desires. "For whatever it's worth" could contain valuable lessons in one's livelihood of a time where we've been chained, bound and tied up to the external desires of having it all to KNOW you are ALL, IS. In whatever fashion, your senses hold truest blue for you is where we are all headed… the road-less traveled has been a thing of the past – to a place that feels like home. Whatever we once considered as a warm place to curl up, a safety net, another's life can be saved… as being given the way toward salvation is through a feeling. No other can compare to or be the equivalent of your happy place if not for what's in your heart. Keep in mind that those who veer off course could contaminate the Earth thwarting here and there and everywhere, not knowing. These are the places we've all been to… where we've all placed one foot into the water of external powers caused by those diamonds that shine brighter than most. Remember this to be true… a diamond begins as a rough-uncut stone that endures the test of time, energy and powerlessness to be tailored to be taunted upon the ring finger of a true love. Think about how many of us look to seek those externals that have dissuaded us for a clear-cut diamond in the rough. Those who desire these uncut diamonds do not have the most valuable of needed value; and, as for those who seek a clear-cut five c's of whatever carat, seeks the highest and brightest energy of self-reflection. Being as that may, no one should or should not seek their highest truth in and for everything they encounter, deem worthy of self. What is our natural habitat? Is it to delve into others' lives by escaping your own or is it a seamless thread, a joyful curtain of flowing velvet? What can be said, isn't and what isn't said is … What comes before this is not just and only a matter of convenience, it is a place where our truest sense of self chooses to inhabit. Once we profoundly

503

find that place within us where if not for our own truest values to undercover that to find oneself – a dive deep in the mudslides, getting our hands dirty and climbing the highest peak of whatever mountain rides you.

SUNRISE.SUNSET

Figuring out the Laws of the Universe can be processed by searching for no-thing that falls short of your truest feeling of self-mastery. Nothing on this Earth can provide you with a full-filling life than yourself, who has smelled the fragrance of the rose. To those who understand that with each and every new day a sunrise/sunset that has existed for eons is NOT the same Sun/Moon/stars as in the everyday. Each day has been gifted with a new platform of senses by which to escape for the greater good. This is why self-preservation has the capacity to choose whether to move mountains, or not; to choose the complacency of another day, same shit different day; or, could be seen as another day to break away. Pain travels in wide circles throughout our Heritage; until it is felt. Some would call these generational curses that breeds all forms of escapism through avoidance. When there are anxious attachments, we look for others to regulate us… and, places us 'on guard'. Educating ourselves by finding signs and/or cues that lead us to knowing when someone might want to hurt or even abandon us – alerts us in preparation. Every child is born to feel the undercurrents of pain through what we call; shamans, healers, priests and/or priestesses. Mental health is a powerful reflection of what lies within as; inner light lost in the form of diabetics, stress and anxiety of externals, angered cancer, bipolar imbalances, immune deficiencies, premature babies etc. and all lost souls upon a planet whose energy source has diminished to a bare minimum. These are the children who felt their purpose to come upon the Earth… to Feel. Born are the ones with gifts to feel knowing we cannot heal until we feel. No one on this God-gifted planet was ever to extinguish their light – except for those warped souls who can't contain their losses with enough light still left to attain a new chance at a changed life. Humans undergo so much hardship that their light has waned too long in the wings of new Hope.

As we focus on clearing out our generational trauma, we must also claim our generational strengths. Our Heritage illuminates not only those wounds but also the ability to cut those ties and forge a new life – assisting in healing Humanity. We are all walking each other Home… on Earth, into the Golden Age; in Heaven, ascending into Higher Consciousness.

FALL FROM GRACE

A damaged Hawk wing has fallen from Grace… only to be saved with the Grace of Hope for Humanity through The Holy Spirit. For some of those who have saved our Mother Earth from falling, if not for a proponent of raising one's awareness to save thyself; then, it is for no other reason than to sway oneself into a new life of Hope. What constricts a Human being not to give up Hope is the same thing as a bird-on-a-wire that sticks together to find the silver thread of Hope in all one's duress. Those who are under stress and duress have not yet been given the right-of-passage to undergo a new life – being given appreciation for life is to give new life to oneself. Find solace in knowing this… refuge is underway for all Humanity who have lost their way home. Whenever we seek to know what it is that will make us happiest and give us a full-circle rapture of a life being fulfilled, then, we know what makes us alike. Resist the need to question the resources of our own happy place and find it within yourself to allow Spirit to show you the way forward. What cannot be fully understood is the fact that we cannot do this all by ourselves – utilize the abilities, capabilities of resourcefulness as we waiver through this thing called Life. Give yourself a break that gives way to being enough... enough in the way forward to see your God-given light as a Life worthy of the Light. We've encountered a child whose way forward is not seen... but heard. Be gentle with yourself and those who are seemingly looking for themselves; you will be saved. Find nothing more comforting than to save another through acts of good deeds ``in-deeds" instead of barking up the wrong tree of Life with dis-ease... ailments of the flesh.

"Take these broken wings and learn to fly again, learn to live so free, when we hear the voices sing, the book of Love will open up, and let us in..." by Mr. Mister breathing in the air of Hope while breathing out the air of Grace.

FREEDOM

Take nothing for granted and everything in stride... what can no longer be yours for the taking is not something that wants to be taken. We've undergone so much unnecessary pain that it is likely an example that Our Lord Jesus begets us to witness. We are the remnant of the Believers, the Achievers who are undergoing a massive shift of perspective on this Earth only to find that the only thing left is what, IS. Needing not-to-know while living inside and out will be the surge that will find our way forward. Believe not the need to achieve, but to experience Life.

Happily, ever after… comes into playful vibes when we are unthreading a life of havoc and hoping for a life of the ever after… Find what it IS that makes you happy…do that. From the lowest point of contention to the highest light of the Sun… embrace, for we are one. To dive into the deepest recesses of your subconscious is commendable .. not to mention, admirable for those who are witness to that which doesn't hold any necessary value. What truths do you hold onto yourself? Be in one-mind and not of the mindset that extracts a dimmer light upon itself. Be not concerned that of your neighbor, but that of yourself. Find the way forward to contain a simple place of gratitude and unjust cause to appear happily into the eyes of another. We cannot seek to find another Eye of the Tiger as we are in a solid Year of The Dragon where treasures are passionately lit on purpose. The Year of The Dragon illuminates great power, great passion with great purpose. What is yours?

THE BIBLE TELLS US SO

One's own pathway is lit going forward so that they may stay on path to enlightenment that holds the ultimate fulfillment. Just move forward into your own light not fearing paths before that will siege to be fruitful. Be less inhibited to leap into great strides of what is known rather than unknown. Whatever cannot be seen will be felt. We've come to know this way very well… enabling the given pathway forward only to become a rabbit-hole for some; and, an open pathway for others. Not giving into the darkness isn't necessarily the way forward to those who are fasting for a good cause – foregone, foretold, and forgiven. "Whatever for Art Thou" has been the path… and, to enlighten the way forward lights another's candle. Can you see your own selves wavering in the light, or, can you seek to understand the

507

path forward as only one? Light seekers are everywhere, light beings have been upon this Earth since the beginning of time… seek those that seek within Heavenly light of beings. Are you feeding into the external suffering that Jesus Christ betrothed to His people? Or, are you instilling a new mindset of your own vision of what suffering means to you? Have you encountered suffering in the world… or, has the world fallen short of your need to suffer? Whatever holds the answers to your own self, a truth reveals, unlike any other. For what is suffering than a mere reflection of yours truly, Jesus Christ, in body form that suffered for all our sins. What sins have you suffered for? Where are you suffering in your current life circumstances? Could you uphold the power of what Jesus' suffering taught His children? Given the metaphor-of-circumstances, how certain of you is your energy or lack of caused a wrinkle in time? What is time if not for another wrinkle best found on our frontal cavity flesh and blood. Is this too much for you to bear? What problems are a wrinkle in your time on this Earth… Do you know? What are the causes for time lapse, for fears felt, for nerves shattered, for untethering souls to authenticate their true selves? Whatever holds a respite of truth are the corners of everyday Saints for you to pray upon and lend a helping hands-on.

The formation of the ONE deserves and IS within every human on Earth. The only difference is that one KNOWS while the other has not yet become enlightened to seek their own one. This isn't for the weak or weary… in order to know there will be no room for errors, or doubt etc. Only those who know will become the strength-of-resolve needed in all the wrong doings, accepting and taking full responsibility for what they have done. These are only the injustices of the 3-Dimensional kind, no other judgements exist - it is upon us, where more humans are judging themselves and others of no fault of their own. Within every individual there is another like-minded inception of that individual who bears the fruit of ascension. The gates of Heaven will be open for all those who have seen the light at the end of the tunnel. To say that these individuals won't be allowed is being falsely accused of not being within their own light; therefore, we will all be saved at different times in our lives. Once we come into contact with our own light, we will no longer seek the light of ONE'S own truth, for then, one becomes one truth. There are no words needed, suffice to say, that of others' deeds to become their own person while living on Earth. We've all congregated together to become what it is to be instead of what humans think they will become. Far too many humans have the notion of becoming ascended yet they aren't ready, willing and/or able to come to terms with their truth of full disclosure. There will be NO second coming as the Earth plane deems to have already been witness to our Lord Jesus' ONLY coming down from Heaven to have put this world into, The Bible. In Revelation, it has been written that this world will end itself without needing any cast of characters to end it; however, without knowing where your individual self stands upon this planet constructs your ending without an ending. This means that to BE you must undo whatever knowledge you have borrowed from the construction of others' expectations, undo those who said the world is coming to an end, and start by believing in the self that KNOWS. This world cannot end itself for it knows not of itself…until it does. What the second coming does require is for all those who have come and gone to reinstate their 'will' upon the Earth for another chance to ascend. That IS what will happen… and, is happening.

Many souls that have left the Earth plane by accident unbeknownst to their soul's time to fly will witness a second coming, if it is deemed possible in their life review. The reason for these souls to come back again, a second coming, will ensure that their souls be given another chance to change their lives in ways that no Apocalypse ever could. An Apocalypse has already occurred to those whose lives are not gracious to those who have reaped what they sowed will bear fruit to a catastrophic Apocalypse that will be unjustifiably part of their life lesson. We may be talking in gibberish to the mainstream audience reading this, herein, however mind you there will be no ending to this world... as Mother Earth has already ascended Moons ago. We're not necessarily within the rights of our Holy land to explain this any further... All we ask is that humans trust in your own faith to lead you to the Promised Land. Our Lord Jesus has already reinstated what IS in the Bible a newly found order of a second coming... it is not one that will be in the same nature as before. We have found that humans await and have been committed to the ideology of what they've been instructed to believe, to be told that our Lord Jesus is coming back would be a dictatorship from Heavenly host – to remember what has already been a known ideology, in fact. It IS with great regret that our souls have not concentrated on the Bible instead of waiting to be instructed again what it is and why we are on this planet. To be truthful to yourself, is it not enough? Why would Lord Jesus appear again with a repeat of events if there is not enough insightful evidence to betrothed the very first time? What would make our Lord Jesus appear once again? Have you ever given this any thought? This would be an act of redundancy which clearly humans are in need of on this planet... What some of you have forgotten IS the real reason why our Lord Jesus came in the first place – and was hung in shame to uphold others' guilt-ridden reason for a life. Humans do not learn very easily except for making excuses for not having undying love for God, themselves, and for others' behalf. Why would our Heavenly God beseech His Son another heart-wrenching catastrophic chain of events; turning one to stone, harming others for the sake of themselves, and unjustly hanged for the sins of Humanity? The second-coming is underway as Spiritual Warfare is occurring… choose your side, wisely.

ARTIFICIAL INTELLIGENCE (AI) REAL INTELLIGENCE (RI)

Artificial Intelligence (AI) is not a credible agent of the internal world of Spirit – it is a replica of what humans are yet to become. Is this a scare tactic or is it a fight for one's life? Are you forbidden to become humanly felt or humanly doped? Which planet have you agreed to be on? Do you realize that at the Horizon while the Sun sets and rises again and again a new child is born, a new idea is gifted to Humanity, a new understanding of the self envelops yet a new emotional reaction, a new change of heart evolves in one's own revolution and a plethora of newness overcomes the old. What man on God's given Earth gifted humans a violation of the ascendant and chose to move mountains with a computer, or a robotic semblance of a self-imposed hard-drive with pre-programmed orchestrated emotions? This certainly does strike a cord does it not? To become a programmable being for avoidance of suffering that will give people the inability to choose for themselves. There is NO way and in NO uncertain terms that the higher hierarchy will ever be able to turn the Earth plane into a robotic nightmare of AI robots walking around handing out sales pitches to others to buy into falsely accused feelings. This is not Love of the Highest Order… that is an empty vessel whose feelings have been extracted only to learn that this robotic self will crumble and die… as it is written, but, without the self-imposed learnings of hard-earned work. The "only" reason that humans were gifted with the present called, LIFE, is for their own selves to experience life and ALL that it is gifted to offer. We live on a life-giving planet… the only planet that gives life to another human and there will never be another. This too shall pass…. Be not afraid for Humanity's sake, just believe in yourself and stay in your own lane. If you decide to "buy into" what is falsely issued as a technological vessel of visual reality instead of living a full-filled life vs. a visual reality through the remnants of a computer screen, be ready for the impact. AI robotics and whatever missiles are waiting to be launched – let them learn their lessons just like Hitler did in the Holocaust; let man make his own bed and let no-thing stand in the way of your unwavering faith. Try to remember the days where humans had no-thing but themselves to blame – who will you blame if Humanity becomes everything "they" envision it not to be? Artificial Intelligence (AI) a repository to the sound of knowledge borrowed; or, what is Real Intelligence (RI) that stores knowledge within.

What wonders will be proven upon Earth continue to forge ahead our Golden Age so that there is no more dimming of Earth's light as She has ascended to even Higher of Consciousness as we speak. Humanity as we know it will enter phases of a New World Order where She will undergo many internal resonances that will show up on our Earth as miraculous healing and goodwill upon Earth. There will be miracles just as we witnessed when reading about how Jesus gave sight to the blind; how Jesus healed those people who found a deeper sense of inner Faith than ever witnessed in human history – this will be our Revelation. To get to this place though an assortment of external repercussions that are being witnessed now will continue. In order for change to take place in its entirety, a mass destruction of the current construct is happening – time is not valid at this moment, but to examine the why's instead of the how's will be what Humanity is going to show us. This means, hang on to your coat-tails .. it's going to be a rollercoaster of events one after the other for the next few decades or more. There is no reason to seek questioning as this is being seen to those who are awakened. Envision…if you will, a world of inner peaceful resolve that contradicts hatred for mankind. What will this feel like? As the outer world revolves around chaos, take a moment to close your eyes and en-vision your peaceful place, a sanctuary… That inner sanctuary is your real world…what we all came to attain. This is the Apocalypse of *self-realization.* A mindfulness unlike any other… in tune with tuning in. What matters is that some proclaim they have unwavering Faith yet question, doubt and resist by needing to know. It is what humans have been doing since the very beginning; and, for this to be as it should…doubts, questions, resistance is all a part of God's plan. Humans grow impatient and want things to be the way "they" want – without waiting for the real good stuff. All in God's timing will happen eventually and if you already have received the memo that certain obstacles, issues, delays are for you to instill unwavering Faith as part of your life's mission. Once you have done so the ebb and flow of life becomes a beautiful symphony, a musical orchestration of sound waves that take us to a very surreal place… wherever you can find your "*sanctuary*" that brings you to stillness. Leave it up to your Heavenly family and friends who have either become your Spirit Guides or are just rooting you onto higher ground. Take into account that every person, place and/or thing has already been written and to follow your instinctual higher selves is what we have come here to do. What breeding grounds have been passed on will eventually find you, not only reaping what you sow, but comfortable knowing what it feels like to be at peace. Why not live your life through these God-given miracles by sponging up every morsel? Why not seek to find your higher ground and leave the rest to

513

chance? Why not seek to understand your "selves" instead of competing, comparing and becoming identical AI clones? That's exactly how AI began... everyone attempting to emulate "The Kardashians" and forging their own beauty to win over these ideologies that you will be loved more if you look like, "them?" It's in everyone's innate own beauty that makes one beautiful – and, to seek someone else's beauty is being a carbon copy. Are you a carbon copy? Do you have more Love in your life just because you may have made alterations to your external appearance to be accepted, adored and loved more? It's not for us to idolize any person on planet Earth even if we do see their beauty... Why not allow life to unfold in order to show you your own beauty? Why starve to death? Is that what the majority of our population have been doing? Not eating, over drinking, over medicating and numbing their bodies in order to 'fit' in'... only to find out that no one wants to be a carbon copy. Or, do you? What AI represents is an exact replica of oneself without emotions... and, Humanity has been "driven" to becoming exactly that. A no-nonsense "bitch-face" exact replica of NO emotion's statue bearing no gifts to say the least - and, certainly NOT a replica of The Statue of Liberty... more like A Statue of Stone that dictates an absolute "giving up" of all rights. Do you want this for yourselves, for Humanity, for the next Generations to come? That's what is occurring... Many want everything done for them, or, they are very self-sufficient without any emotional values, robotic in nature, a sense of non-beingness. Where will all these technological values go if not for only one thing – to make money? IT has been by far the very example of what has evolved over the course of 2-3 decades; but, let's leave emotions out of it. Why do you think that is? It's to make money, it's to send the message to Humanity that the Western civilization of materialism, coldness, senselessness, no touch, no communication, and every part of our inner

514

being is being stone-walled. Is this what Humanity has worked so hard to do? Over the course of several years, we have become a powerless world, where, in America, has lost its value and, not valued. Other countries are laughing while purporting their own ideals into their structure of a Democracy that will inevitably lead the rest of the world. Who is the front-runner?

"Is it real or is it Memorex…" the phrase, back in the days of cassettes, might have led us to question the current state of affairs.

SAINTS & SINNERS

Will you blame the man who invented the computer? Will you blame the next-door neighbor who refuses to order on Amazon because he apparently knows who's behind the masked curtain? The man behind the curtain ended up becoming exactly what darkness-of-power came to seek out in the computer technological world of animation. Who was the computerized face of evil in The Wizard of Oz? Who decided to take that idea upon themselves, make billions of money and use it against a world full of greedy people in order that the "sheep" will buy into the concept because they will make certain the goods outweigh the expensive output… Be mindfully aware of who is minding your mindset! Your own mind is the mirror reflection looking back in a mirror of … regret, remorse, resentment, greed, jealousy and all the fear-moguls that live within your mind-set programming. We've only just begun to witness those who have been set up in witness-protection programming in order to escape their jail time. Whoever is in that programming, if you will, have already been captured to exactly what the Bible said, "another man's garbage is another man's treasure…" Where do you think that saying came from?

515

From the horse's mouth, someone decided to overtake those people who have become hoarders/accumulators of garbage and sell it all on eBay, making a profitable venture. "To BE, or not to be" that is not the question but what is the answer? To answer that question that bears a 'to BE' as a verb, IS written…in The Bible, "We are not to question why we are here to do and die."

What course of action bears fruit while the other bears the regret of not fulfilling the challenge of taking responsibility for the outcome of your life. We tend to forget upon arriving on Earth, only to recall what is needed, unlike others who question why… just to live and let live until the physical vessel dies. Life is in session "after" we lay to rest the physical vessel that encapsulated us for the duration on this planet. Once that vessel is laid to rest, ashes are scattered or placed back into Mother Earth's beautiful land. We realize all attempts at control were frugal and that it is only a matter of time that all God's children return to their sacred Home.

ANCESTRAL LINEAGE

We can only "save ourselves" and that is a huge part of what the soul's evolution is to learn who we are on this plane and to seek refuge for those who ask for help. To serve another is serving of the self. Saving yourself requires each and every one of us to walk away from temptations of the flesh, temptations of gaining power, money of a famed Ego. All temptations exhibited are more-or-less different values yet have the same consequences. Abuse of any kind is literally being extracted off the planet before becoming a detriment to Mother Nature – the remains of overzealous actions fade to dust.

Whatever happened to our founding Fathers' ethics – who are they, where are they now and/or have they all been laid to rest? When we speak of our founding Fathers, do you know who they are? Heroes are made. Some speak of their heroes as idols; and, were raised to believe that in order to achieve success is only about making money, holding power and how they are visually seen in the public eye. To emphasize this reality of life, how do you uphold your values? For those who have upheld growth for Humanity will be saved. For when you do the work on your inner self, you will reap the rewards of miracles in your external world. Our founding Fathers did get it wrong because they established their own club-of-men who represented an immediate mis-use of power; by not allowing women to enter. That catapulted into a series of misrepresentations of how, why and when the Women's Liberal Movement began. Not only that, but for such grown men to pontificate the way forward for women … have no rights. Here's exactly why men have since lost some of their power throughout the years… To say that any human is above any other is a righteous act of misrepresentation. If you've been a part of the Women's Liberal Movement you can relate; and for the children/grandchildren who've been privy to having been involved knowingly, what shame has it caused in your life? Has it? Ancient threads that we've not necessarily been privy to being a part of, yet, in our lineage does hold memories of how we interact with the opposite sex. No one needs to question another's vices but to attempt to understand why certain women don't trust men – very simply put. There is not just one situation that has strongly impacted our beliefs, opinions threaded in our lives. Much to our dismay we may not be able to know how far back the impact first came into being – just knowing we may need to change the narrative, for ourselves.

Invest in how you're building your Legacy for it becomes your every breath. Ancestral threads are not about age, color, creed nor does it have an expiration date – it is how you treat others as yourself. The Legends of our time leave imprints of what dreams are made of…

ASCENSION

Once a life has been blueprinted as The Chosen ONE, a plethora of challenges will ensue ensuring this soul has learned all of what they have needed to experience. Therefore, all souls are given a fair chance to ascend; yet, not all ascend at the same time nor in the same decade. Other lifetimes are not forgotten through the passage of time for what has already been written IS. Humans come into this life hoping to ascend, especially during such a revolutionary time and place on this Earth; however, it is not for the weak hearted. The Dark Night of the Soul comes so that we can attain a sense of forgiveness for all those souls who hurt us and us them. "Many are called but few are chosen" from Matthew 22:14. How do we feel about being called and not being chosen? Chosen to ascend… Ascension to the human heart is an uprising, a soaring of love for ALL of Humanity – a paradigm shifts to higher consciousness. Foregoing all others is a thing of the past and forging a new plateau of loving yourself as seen through the eyes of our Beloved. We seem to think that we're all here to soar into a Seer light-being soul, a Sufi Master is not man made … he/she becomes made through the Holy Spirit of the white light of Jesus The Christ. The white light of Jesus is within each and every soul on Earth. Whatever you were brought here to become known that you already are. It is within each of us to ensure a stable home inward first in order to shine our beams of light outward and towards others – to Love,

Honor and Cherish. These are not only in the vows of marriage … they are a reflection of selfless acts of Love to ALL.

We cannot deem it possible to claim that Humanity will evolve in the rightful time of our Lord Jesus' ascension, but, that is exactly why Jesus was sent – "Who for us men and for our salvation came down from Heaven and was incarnated by the Holy Spirit and became Man." With this in mind, our Lord Jesus had no rightful place, here, on Earth, yet gave His ALL to show His children that this is the cause of our pain too… to adhere to the following terms of the Laws and to ultimately ascend. He who does not ascend in this lifetime will come again to live another life in this school of hard knocks and, with some or several lessons already under one's belt, able to continue to evolve as Humanity intended. The majority of Humanity has been very slow to ascend because of all the external factors playing in our world today. It is no one's fault … it just means that the powers that be are clearing the decks for better days ahead. This will take another few years to mend… but the heart of Mother Nature is all about Her children's healing. We all feel the end of the world is upon us, however, they've been saying this for billions of years. This end-of-the-world is the end of NOT seeing clearly the demise of darkness to behold. What we do know is that if you should fall off the beaten path, you will come to know your soul's purpose, and only purpose, is to ascend… as did our Lord Jesus. Anything else that shall happen in accordance to the ascension of a human being is fruitless. We bear fruit only when we realize why we are here and what it is that is needed to ascend. Now you know… go and prosper with a Godly sense of whatever you've been learning so far. In order to show up on this Earth, one must become and know they've evolved as one. It is a simple mathematical equation of 3,6,9 born out of the Tessler movement. The mathematical hologram of this Earth, the Universe has been constructed as everything is divided from the basis of our Heavenly Trinity – Father, Son and Holy Spirit that is encapsulated within our Heavenly temple body of Mother Earth. "We acknowledge one baptism for the remission of our sins…" in The Lord's Prayer as a constant reminder to uphold the ONE who has chosen each of its children to be saved. The interesting point of contention within that sentence is having whatever Faith in oneself to uphold The Creed without wavering. In order to see ourselves as one of God's children, we must first engulf our own Faith in the hand of our Creator.

THE HOLY SPIRIT - INNER BLESSINGS, MIRACLES

When we begin to define what it is exactly that contains the blessings of the Holy Spirit we pretend to know, instead of allowing the fulfillment of sanctuary to unfold. What we do know… is to experience life in the present moment, receiving the gifts of being present by seeking your own presents. We're all in this together, experiencing life in the present moment while being given innate presents within. Every human has been gifted with the same presents of a human body – sought in the inner realm of our Life. When we absorb the fruits of our labor, it feels like we're grabbing hold of a small crack in the ceiling where light enters. A crack in the ceiling may be all someone on Earth will be able to attain in a lifetime – but, fear not, for the gifts of our Lord are plentiful. Our inner treasures are found within and are waiting to be claimed. Both the essence of the dandelions and the lotus flowers are just two examples of varied fragrances. The dandelion is the only flower that depicts a celestial flowering representative of; Sun, Moon and Stars. This yellow flower resembles the Sun's energy that greets us every morning and closes in the evening. The puff-ball is shown as the Moon's disbursement of seeds of all Stars ingrained within. Every part of the dandelion is integral; root leaves used for food, medicine and dye of color. The name is French "dent de lion" – the tooth of a lion has coarsely-toothed leaves and flowers the longest. Root dandelion treats infections and liver disorders; while some use it as a tea-diuretic. These beautiful flowers are masters of survival. Once we understand the connection to Mother Earth's beauty of natural healing remedies, Humanity will have assembled a new knowledge of healing properties. While the dandelion exhibits much of our Sun's energy, the Lotus Flower is the sacred flower of "Life" that confers with our life cycles; life, death and rebirth. The ability to rise above those muddy waters without being tainted, is a conglomeration of the message to mankind. Lotus flowers come in different colors with significant traditions within our physical chakra body – the white speaks of purity that reaches the crown chakra; the pink is our spiritual journey toward enlightenment. From the depths of our darkness in the void-of-life to an enriching transcendence over low-frequencies that stem from our shadow. The lotus enables mankind longevity, honorability and fortune. The process of peeling back every layer of the unknown to the known, unfolds into a beautiful lotus flower. Becoming a signature lotus flower is self-realization… Your specific fragrance is built within your DNA (dissolves IN ascension) including your own and that of your lineage. There are various blends of fragrances that assist us to expand our vision - yet, all fragrances have to be tested. There are a plethora of fragrances awaiting to be cast and to enhance, evolve and experience.

THE BOOK OF LIFE

We either live in a happy environment being grateful for who we are; or, we blame the world for our misfortunes. Either way it is up to each and every one of us to decide. What's it going to be? Are you going to live a life of unhappiness, in fear of what has happened and/or fear of what's to come; or will you find your truth in the light of a new day? In the end...we know what matters, don't we? Our health, our family, our friends, our companions, and/or strangers who we HELP and/or have helped us out. Every face we meet is connected to a story, a part of our narrative in The Book of Life...this includes strangers, acquaintances, a glance, that familiar feeling, baby's breath, the officer that gave you a ticket, those who glance at our lives wishing it were ours... and so many more faces and places. All this comes into play and factors into our lives, as a screenplay of diverse characters whose role(s) are to show us ourselves. Whomever we've loved, loved and lost, wherever we've been, where we've lived; basically, all the people/places we've visited in our lifetime plays a significant role in our soul's growth. As difficult as it is to say farewell to an old love, old life, old friends we must know this too shall pass; and that our soul decides what is best for our highest good. Soul contracts in the form of people, places and/or things all live within the resonance of time spent and time expired. It's just the way it is... Nothing can bring back moments... Living from one extreme to the next also has its challenges...where one minute we're laying on the beach and the next we're getting ready for a snowstorm...that's geography, or is it? What we want and what is needed for us to evolve might be very different now...

As we walk down this new road knowing the difficulties we've encountered it is still within our own power to get to the heart of the matter. Is your glass half full? Or, are you just going to give up? Cry, rant, scream all you want…but, you picked this life and all that is in it… it is on you, and no one else. Remember this when you start feeling sorry for yourself and the things that haven't worked out. Be proud of how far you've come up until now and be grateful for every lesson. The "hard knocks" are very real that is undeniable…yet what we've learned is crucial not to repeat. A new perspective is all it takes to be happy, peaceful and healthy. What is hidden, why certain things did not work out, will be shown in God's timing. This is where we say how things unfolded are, "a blessing in disguise…" It is in that moment that we realize. All too often we can't see the "big picture" because we're too busy feeling sorry for ourselves, to notice. No matter what… being gifted "Life" is a blessing, however big or small you may think to value your life. "Life" is a present you don't return. ™" Seek solace, go within and get to know yourself from the ground up… Where do we go from here? Rising up to a new life, a new version of you is unfolding; what wonders cease to exist is the *Power of Love for Life*.

Just when you thought life is going to present itself one way, it takes a few turns. Those twists and turns on the path are not detours; they are paving a clear pathway. Finding yourself is the next best thing to do when under pressure – some ask for God's HELP in prayer, while others ask to win the Lottery. Who do you think God will answer? God is ALL Loving and to cheat yourself out of a full life for a quick pick is the difference between wants and needs. We all want to win…either way. Part of winning is losing a thousand or more times until you show up. How many times did Albert Einstein get rejected for his "Theory of Relativity?" and never gave up? It's unlikely that anyone who served their purpose in life has been knocked to the ground a few hundred or more times. That's what makes a "willful intention" stronger and a life fulfilled longer. Under dire circumstances, unbelievable odds are where every miracle surfaces…in the 11th hour.

"Great moments catch us unaware…™

STORED MEMORIES

The embodiment of one's soul stores every memory within the fragments of our lives pertaining to our ability to enrich or stump our growth. Those memories are stored in places that are unseen in the ethers – the subconscious mind, inner neurons, hippocampus deeply embedded, in both molecular and physical realms that Science has yet to imagine. Short-term memories that are stored are transferred to a longer-term storage that enables our brain to handle emotional processing of anxiety, stress and avoidance. What scientists have been known to discover is that those neurons are replenished – grown and created, termed neurogenesis. "Genesis" of all the inner workings of the body are reborn, anew. We can and do remember wide ranges of vocabulary, to communicate, interact, events, people in all moving parts that are exemplified and are diverse. Varied memories… long-term that recall years or even days at a time; short-term that refers to brief moments, a sequential order and/or even numbers of one's cell phone. All memories of remembrance lend itself to wanting to hold a memory within our hearts; while those memories that have damaged our internal brainwaves of forgetting…become our amnesia. Hence, when there are damaged brain cells … we tend to be forgetful which may cause dementia, in some; or, complete forgetfulness in others.

Forgetfulness is like a "power-outage" that needs to be jolted back into order, if the mind is capable of believing it to be so. Within the hippocampus of one's brain waves is where neurons communicate with each other termed synapses. That synapses of one's wavelengths can either be considered as getting stronger or weakening – due to how the connectivity is accepted. When we have a "brain-freeze" what may trigger and/or activate a memory would be a particular fragrance; as smells can be evocative in foretelling a bringing us back in time. There are those who can only feel a memory through a smell, a childhood memory in the fragrance-of-time through every inhaling breath. When these types of triggers, in the fragrance-of-time passed, our initial reaction is either where we have yet to heal and/or yet to learn…not unless it remains a deep love of emotion in our hearts. Moments-in-time are shown to us through the looking glass of how someone touches our lives, or not. What is hidden becomes a subconscious memory … until it presents itself as a new memory within the old memory. A new memory can be made that duplicates another or others as we are creatures of habitual behaviors; and while the new memory doesn't seem to overlap another old painful memory, in time you will come to find out why, if any, there still is pain. Warped in a tunnel of love on the hamster wheel happens when humans cannot accept and/or let go of past trauma. We must surrender to our painful truths…before stepping into any new beginning of one's life. As seen time and time again, there are overlaps of threads in our memory bank that have not yet been healed. Healing happens whenever painful memories resurface and lead us to a peaceful place of solace. Wanting the best for another and not wishing them harm is to know we have emotionally healed. Those who harbor ill-will have yet to recall the details of their memories on a level of unconditional love. What comes to the surface is revealed to be healed. Our playlist of memories can either be hauntingly accurate or a haunting of one's ghost of Christmas past. We tend to automatically sabotage our lives by not coming to terms with our truth. Process your truth in light of another's faulty claims... as that may beget another form of self-sabotage. Are you feeling responsibly worthy or uncharacteristically unworthy of remembrance? Where have we forgotten? What have we observed? What mind is connecting to what record? Do we recognize our thoughts as fleeting white clouds in the sky? Are our memories stored in a cloud of frequency chemically entangled in the ethers of our existence – activated/reactivated? Or lost? Are those memories a way of recycling moments in time that we can't let go? What thoughts remind us of whom? Where does every memory take us...back? Whose fragrance is still very much on our mind? Can you distinguish between what was and what is? Can we amplify the soundwaves of our mind's eye only to recapture the moments in time?

"What once was...isn't. What is... cannot ever be again". ™

When our memory is symbolic of the pain it tends to protract into a subconsciousness until resurfacing – when the timing is called for this to happen. Much like an oyster that has been wounded with an inability to muster a pearl – which defines the result of one's wounds as an unwanted foreign substance to the body. We are all creatures of our subconscious pains and this analogy is quite the same with oysters...as well as with those who miscarry or whatever circumstances happen to be where the embryo of a soul, that is not ready yet to surface; will appear again in Divine timing. God never allows pain to be experienced without a purpose – which is not to be questioned, just accepted as is. Our wounding occurs when our capacity to process unthinkable, unbearable traumas, terror, things that our mind cannot comprehend; and those unmetabolized painful shames of pieces of our soul that overwhelm. Subcortically and on a cellular level, our circuitry of what has occurred is removed from the fires of the alchemical body. It's like gaslighting misunderstandings on a deep level of wounding and implicit memories that only contribute to the intergenerational transmission of trauma. A profound reality of aloneness stirs within – defined by thoughts of darkness of unforgiven truths.

Death asked life, "Why does everyone love you but hate me? And, Life replied, "Because I'm the beautiful lie and you're the painful truth."

"The hard things we may be going through now are really nothing in comparison to the glory that will be revealed in us later." Romans 8:17-18.

What we observe is absorbed in the Fragrance of the Arts. ™

FRAGRANCE OF ONE'S ESSENCE

Whatever essence of fragrance you encapsulate, can only be your own, as it is melted and yoked of the same qualities embedded in the Earth's cavity. Once your essence melts into ALL the fragrances that have been stored in yourself and others it is quite possible that you have attained what is called, "siddhis." Not one of these powers can be accumulated from another, therefore, you acquire the fragrance, identify it by using your essence to add-value, and weeding out the rest to manifest the highest version of You. All-encompassing powers that BE are known as the siddhi powers – which unfold upon every one of us in a timely manner and in our rightful place. No siddhi power can be exactly learned as it holds the Holy Spirit's blessings of magical attraction that shows up in one's life. Should you, as an individual, attempt to manipulate, maneuver any one of the siddhi powers prior to God's timing, there are heady repercussions. Why? The powers that BE are not to be manipulated for powers of play as they hold the innate powers of our Holy Spirit. There have been quite a few humans that have delved into mastery by manipulating the terrain and have fallen short in so many other ways… Our Heavenly host is not against any human who is willing to allow the process of accepting these siddhi powers upon themselves in God's plan. Those who are of the egoic powers, will fail miserably and have seen their own demons come alive. Be NOT of what you may "think" you need, desire or want; but, be of the paved path of Spirit's way forward. "THE WAY" is a newly-wave Bible version of the St. James Bible of The Old & New Testament. "Do unto others as you would have done to thyself" written in the St. James Bible… one of the most important sayings that was handed down by the Jews in order to appreciate our Heavenly Lord Jesus at a time when massive annihilation of beliefs was ensuing. No one believed in Our Lord Jesus as The Savior; however, it is written from this point on that whatever man has done to another will surely be done to the self. Once this was written, the other Laws of the Universe prevailed because God knew people needed to follow something called, lessons throughout the Ages, and so it IS. Today, we pride ourselves with great vanity and pride in taking out another soul's image; and, do you know why? It is because these souls that perpetuate Humanity have not yet learned about what is known, "As above, so below…"

JOURNEY INTO THE UNKNOWN

What a world it is…to know each and every human who is walking the Earth has the Universe within; and that includes, the powers that become what we are set forth to be. In a world full of creation how could it not be anything other than magnificent? Its powers have been given to every human and are innately inside of us all…the thing that confuses people is how they conceive this to be? We live in a world full of destruction and sometimes that is the only thing that we focus on…because that is learned behavior. What hasn't been taught, however, is that all of Humanity has every power to change the trajectory of their lives. How to begin? Taking the first step might be the hardest yet everyday becomes easier with practice and patience. We must ask the Angelic realm for guidance…then, be patient. Meditation also impacts opening of the pineal gland and/or the crown chakra based upon the shadow work that has been done…then, be patient. That is the 'key' to unlocking the Other Side, patience. Many become very impatient in the 11th hour not knowing they're so close. Others haven't asked for help and rely on external substances to attain. What is very clear, however, is that to attain higher consciousness it must be done ALL Natural. Mother Nature is our nature… Is it acceptable for Humanity to tamper with Mother Earth when it comes to attaining higher power? "Power" is the massive waves in an Ocean that plunge you right under; it is the extreme heat on one's body out in the Sun; it is a power outage; it is an earthquake, it is a tsunami etc., all natural disasters are on the Earth for us to witness, devastation. What is devastating is how Humanity doubts its own powers yet gives their power away! What more could Humanity want then all the answers right in front of your very eyes? Yet, humankind will watch and witness all the devastation, people losing their lives and still be disbelieving that it may affect them directly. Why? The Masters of the Universe have their reason ... to those who falter on their Faith. What is amazing to witness are all the extremely destructive ways of Mother Earth's warnings that set the course of Humanity into an uproar; and yet, people stop and stare in disbelief and ultimately forget. What can shake Humanity "out of" autopilot?

THERE'S NO PLACE LIKE HOME

Without having to enquire about how Humanity will be saved, is the process a matter of Belief... your individual beliefs must be placed not only in the hands of God ... but, to seek one's own salvation a process which bears the fruit of ONE's own. What hand of God, the Divine, could have chosen to orchestrate a kingdom "As Above, So Below" only to find that the same hand of God is within every breath, our physical body known as our temple/vessel, encapsulating the energy of the Divine... within. Why not allow the seasons of one's own life to uncover the magic of this beautiful masterpiece, called life? Why doesn't mankind "Man be kind" in nature where every morsel of life began? Doesn't this make sense... what your senses were given as gifts from Mother Nature to navigate the streaming of one's own presence. Be kind knowing that we are all here to experience a place of great growth, firm beliefs of our own volition and a kindness within which resonates out to the Universal truth. Earth encompasses our true essence for those who envelop what beliefs are given to those who not only believe in Him but also, and especially, who forsake Him. The reason is that, "Whoever believes will have an everlasting life!" To forgo one's essence and to establish the essence of the ONE is to embrace our Divine rightful place in the world... a place that stands out amongst any other as the feeling of being Home.

530

"There is no place like Home…" enhances one's essence of seeking oneself, as Home. The ONE is our Home. the place where Heaven meets all other nuances from where everything incepted. The place where we equate energy of the senses meets the sense of what is known as our equanimity of solace. Where there is a place of solace within, we sense the external factors of what it "feels" like to come back home. Everything stems from that feeling… the essence of your comfort levels when it comes to being kind … as kindness within ONE's soul creates the external source of Humanity saving itself. What IS known as one's inner truth is the endless search/journey of Life held within every man, woman and child.

REACH FOR THE STARS

Throughout the course of many decades, humans are still reinventing themselves… from their belief systems and on the basis of a discretionary foot to stand on. There are very few that have not been able to co-create a way forward … especially under the duress of societal norms in what was. Everything changes and so too shall we evolve for our own highest self to accentuate what it is we were sent on Earth to attain. If you are searching for a way out, this is it. We cannot be capable of drawing diagrams to outline each individual's progress… you will know you are on path by the feelings you resonate.

We are all stars in the sky and the most brilliant of them all is when we reach farther, higher, greater. There are many elements "out there" that will impose standards of living, living up to the Jones' and a plethora of needing to attain to the highest echelon of our financial sector. This is what America has been teaching ever since political bureaucracy. Our Western culture of organizational structure is modeled by promoting equality that breeds a scientific model of individualism. While the Eastern philosophies rely on a collective culture with distinct emphasis on proper behaviors of respect for elders and inebriated harmony. The West has been a "me, mine and myself" programming of self-centeredness and/or self-oriented. It's similar to an entire colony of fabricated scholars of rational thinkers. When we experience an attitude that falls under the Western culture it is all about our Ego. How can a culture who has never felt compassion change its perception? Try living in a balanced world of give and take – as the right hand meets the left hand, in prayer; amidst the horizon. By far, the mystics of Eastern culture live in the way of what you believe in as a God-oriented self. The external self, however, lives as a servant who serves with other servants; unfathomable to the West. Eastern culture commands to live as a community under One God… a Buddha – knowing we are all ONE. Every Democracy has its flaws as do the people who believe in an institution where power is being obstructed, manipulated to serve its own purpose. When East meets West on the Horizon of power…it will orchestrate the beginning of a New Era in History. How this will happen is what Humanity is attempting to unfold, a crash course in compassionate power lends itself to serve, in-deeds. A Holy dictatorship of equality – masculine meets feminine working together, as one. Too much power either right or left on the Horizon must attempt to meet in the middle. This goes for all internal/external needs that become skewed in Fear… fear incorporates an imbalance of extremes. Too much vs. too little has been the contention of the Ages. We do have a choice either way until we can perceive to live in balance. (Imbalance=i am ego-balance vs. In-balance=inner balance) Does this dictatorship control your free will? Has it? How can the Western dictatorship be dualistic? Is it because we are drawn to compare and contrast? Is that due to a lack of

Faith? Eastern dichotomy is about living as no-self…because it only serves to be. Serving others shows you the reflection in serving others of yourself, instead of only serving yourself. Sanskrit teachings benefit the American people to understand how we become no-thing from something. The West wants to become, while, East is. A far cry of what the West could learn from the East because they "know" the body is a temporary suit of mostly water that holds no consequence to birth/death, dis-ease/old age. Eastern culture is very accepting of the body's expiration date where the Self-of-Soul moves on or into another body/suit as ad-infinitum for all species. Either way these two civilizations came about… there has never been a better time where East meets West on a scale that would adhere to such balance. Science vs. Spirituality isn't even a thing – it is the same identical outlet of finding oneself. Through the History of time seeing all others as lessons for us to purport; or, taking on a new frontier of leadership in rising up to own what it is you truly believe in.

A soul that is imprisoned in a gross material suit-of-armor passes through five (5) stages of its existence: Acchadita-cetana, covered consciousness; Sankucita-cetana, retracted consciousness; Mukulita-cetana, budding consciousness; Vikacita-cetana, blossoming consciousness; and Purna-vikacita-cetana, fully blossomed consciousness.

Those souls who are in the stage of covered consciousness reside in the embodiment of trees, grass, stones – close to being unconscious, forgetting they are servants and choose to live deeply into the realm of matter.

Those souls who are in the stage of retracted consciousness reside in the animals, birds, snakes, fish and other water-creatures – on the verge of being consciousness, slightly open and directed toward fearing (fight/flight), sleeping, eating, fulfilling a plethora of desires, arguing over property claims with anger of being wronged. Animals do not search to find God as their consciousness retracts the thought-or-not.

Those souls who are in the stage of budding consciousness reside in the human body of three-levels of consciousness; budding, blossoming and fully blossomed. Human beings fall into five categories; immoral or atheists who follow moral principles; those who believe in God and follow moral principles; those engaged in practical devotional service, and people devoted in loving devotional service. Bhagavad Gita.

SCIENCE is. SPIRITUALITY

Science cannot be affected by spirituality nor can spirituality ever be affected by the statistics of Albert Einstein and Stephen Hawking who had to crawl outside of the so-called themed Dimension in order to find truths that are surrendered under the stars at night. The Law of Relativity, that of Einstein's gravity theorizes that to attain the force of gravity between space and time one must be in the fold of the outer planets; while Stephen Hawking' Law of Relativity became closer to the "real deal" for reasons of being able to identify the Black Hole. Both are geniuses. It seems that because of these two we can now probe more intently into the causes which affect our planetary gravitational pull. The force of gravity depicts our sense of whether time is speeding up or slowing down – all because of the swirling energies of the Solar System's gravitational pull and what your individual consciousness makes of that in the moment. A person who is grateful to live in the here-and-now knowing we are a ONE-Dimensional living breath of many depths of life – in other stratospheres. For those who haven't received that understanding is because time is standing still - stuck in time. Whatever energies you are exploring "out there" be cognizant of whose time clock is running… is it you living in awareness; or is it you, oblivious of the obvious. We cannot explain this Law of Gravitational pull any better than the Masters… but, in layman's terms this is it. The Black Hole was founded on purpose for those in question to get on board with the clear indication of life beyond what is only seen, heard, felt and/or touched. We are all living beings spreading our energies out into the various Dimensions for fulfillment of attaining higher consciousness. If you are living in a somewhat warped Dimension of time slowing down, you have taken yourself out of the vortex and are only focusing on the Western movement of needing everything tangible. This also warps the speed of light in your world giving you a lower vibration of slow-to-no-movement in attaining your intentions. Once we are able to get higher up into the oblivion of Life, where a new feeling of releasing all that matters happens, attainment of our highest ideals is attained.

FREE-WILL TO ASCEND

The masks of the Ego rank with the real struggles of all forms of manipulation implanted in our deepest well of despair. This has been a struggle since the very beginning so that mankind can find it within themselves to ascend. The terms ascension/enlightenment require that, first and foremost, we understand the value it is. As Jesus' ascension taught Humanity the value of "freewill" in staying strong in your convictions, against all odds. People will try to sway you this way and that way and the first rule of expression is: *discernment*. We must all learn and practice discernment with everyone we meet, in every article we read, in all platforms of social media etc., because only we know what holds our heart. The norm for many has become a place full of Fearing this, that and the other. How you choose to discern means using your freewill and holding steady when the rush of wind tries to blow one over on you. The trees stand firm and when we break, it is a sign that past etchings are transforming. Same holds true within all of Mother Earth, a continuous transformation has to happen for Humanity to witness, listen and learn. Whatever natural disasters have taken place on Mother Earth is similar to mankind suddenly having to rebuild, and/or, changes to the family dynamic calls us to adjust and reorganize our day-to-day. Say for example; a mother has been failing in health, her recall is showing signs of dementia and she is incapable of living alone. This situation calls for a family meeting (or Hospice) to readjust, redefine and rearrange schedules to HELP. It's very difficult as there are external factors that may not be conducive for family members while others are able to arrange. Emotions are on high-alert, especially for those who may not live in the same state, but will do whatever is needed to HELP. This is today's reality… when our parents need assistance of any kind, are we there for them? Or, do we place Mom and/or Dad in a senior housing community - or nursing home for them to get HELP? What Jesus taught us, if you don't understand anything else…is to Love all and to be of service to those in need. "Do unto others as you would want done to you…" How did our ancestors cope? Will you do the same? Have you become despondent and/or angry, holding grudges not wanting to HELP? Our ego gets in the way of putting aside past baggage and not wanting to assist, peeling more layers of the onion. We're not here to acquire more karma, we are here to release us from the chains that bind, to ascend. By definition, the story of Jesus being risen from the dead – is Humanity's story – and ascending into Heaven is a metaphor for clearing the karma of our life cycles so that we can be a light vessel when leaving this Earth. Higher consciousness is living in a world of NO FEAR! Living in No Fear is living a life in-service to mankind and to honor thy Father and Mother. In Exodus 20:12 "The fifth commandment given by God to the Israelites through the prophet, Moses states, "Honor your father and your mother, that your days may be long in the land that the Lord your God is giving you". This commandment, along with its blessing, is repeated throughout the Old and New Testaments.

When a soul ascends, a number of occurrences must happen prior to the human's last life… you may wonder if this applies to all humans, it does. Human life must be lifted to its innately highest being from where it all started from, birth. Birthing a human who enters the silver cord down the pipeline of salvation will end up getting thwarted with various temptations, desires of the flesh, a gambits playground where evil lurks behind the doors of those who are very weak… To enable a human of their own freewill to make decisions based on their own free will is why we all come to Earth. Once a spirit lives the entirety of life that is required to ascend, then, this soul will never need to return. Enlightened beings are very capable of finding what it is that they need in order to extract all egoic masks that have ever been worn in the History of their time here – no one person has ever found their true sense of self in one life cycle. Most definitely, there are those who have become enlightened by age 25, 26; but that was after they had experienced around 165 cycles prior to becoming. We are not to judge, criticize or even raise any questions about how fast or how slow one can become their highest self; but it need not be this or that… just here and there. Once we firmly plant our feet on the ground knowing thy truest self, we have done the ultimate for our fellow mankind. Once a soul emerges into a state of higher consciousness all tests, trials and tribulations have been consumed by a whole soul within a human's body… this body falls back into our Beloved Mother Earth as the soul ascends to another paradigm shift of a higher Dimension. Once a soul ascends it is likely for other souls to choose that their last attempt on the Earth plane will be their final one – but, this must be met by the highest of Echelon approval.

THE CHOSEN ONES

Many historic lifetimes experienced for those Chosen Ones is the reason to "fall from Grace" and gives each and every one who has elevated their consciousness a reason to allude to a new spectrum of uplifting oneself through the Light of Jesus The Christ. The Chosen Ones have given freely to painful lives, painful endings, sacrifices and despair through borrowed time from every experience. It is difficult to understand, yet, to truly be in sync with the Chosen Ones, all knowing must be unknown and all of what you think to understand has no boundaries of life experiences except those who have endured. The endurance of sacrifice varies amongst humans – as karmic suffering is also a tie-in to the part of being Chosen, to become ONE. One must know, not-know and let go before this can be a truth of realization. A fall from Grace to those Chosen remits another fragrance of spiritual ascension that is unlike others who have gained knowledge through others' experiences "thinking" they've ascended, become woke, etc. For this reason, we are trying to grasp the concept of varied fragrances once a human has been Chosen for their own ascension in this lifetime… or, not. It is not to say that all humans do not have the

538

capacity to ascend, it will however, take a concerted effort into being able to go deep into the void and come out unscathed. While those who have been Chosen are already protected from the remnants of others who do not hold an accountability… as there are many facets to enlightenment.

God grants all His children the Freedom to ascend… as every child has been Chosen.

What astounds so many in this awakening process is that they have no idea what to expect from their truth… some may go on for Eternity not knowing, but knowing. The fact that any acknowledgement is required is not necessary. There are those who have mastered the art of persuasion have encountered needs that cannot be persuaded. If someone who has been the Chosen One requires any form of advancement, recognition, or any form of egocentric attention – this bears no one who has been gifted to be Chosen. Many are given the opportunity, but very few have been elevated to The Chosen Ones. What bodes true for all of Humanity is that to be able to set course on your journey without needing to be acknowledged, accepted, recognized and/or any of the hidden misuse of egoic powers – as those who are woke, is nonsense.

NEAR-DEATH EXPERIENCES (NDE)

We come to the end of our physical lives with either a sense of peace or an enormous sense of painful truths that were not revealed. Either way, our higher selves must deal with the consequences of those choices; and/or whether to revisit another reincarnation. This takes time…which is when you've crossed over – a reassessment of your truth from the vision of the light. There are no constructs imposing upon that truth on the Other Side. If one cannot handle the consequences of their choices, time on the Astral plane is where all of those souls heal. To survive a lifetime is to be Free to be yourself until the very end. When we have a life of regret, the Astral plane is where the angelic realm guides us all to our rawest truths…who, why, how, when in every-case scenario. Be ready! It will be very much like a Dark Night of the Soul … if you've been through that; and if not, it will come as no surprise once on the Other Side. A slideshow of events, very similar to the movie, "A Christmas Carol" where Scrooge was visited by three angels; past, present and future. That theme is very real when we are going through our life review – except the physical body is gone, so, there is no going back into that body to revisit. Unless you've had a Near Death Experience (NDE) where God comes to you showing you the way forward…and, in most cases asking you if you'd like to either go back or stay; if need be. Why does God invite some to stay? Is it because the bearer of going back is too great a burdensome life that could have ended as a suicide; or, to go back down to planet Earth and see their lives in light of what they've seen? Many are drawn to going back to planet Earth so they can make that difference, serving others and showing the way forward through their NDE. We all do not get to experience a NDE because, for some, that is not an option. Most souls are not needing to get a "wake-up" call from God while others definitely are. God comes to all His children who are willing to give it all up…who have given up, who are not in their right mind. For those who've had an NDE…many have spoken out about their experience(s) with Jesus – what they saw, their visions, and a viewing of their life impacted in a nutshell. A 'nutshell' is exactly why there are NDE's to explore in the pineal gland, our third eye within the brain of our physical body. It is the size of a nut, an acorn, that propels one to their higher truths. We can either say someone is "nuts," a "nutcase," a "nutjob," or whatever crazy deems another's mindset.

LOST & FOUND

We're all here to work on knowing ourselves yet it is an inside job – one that has no external needs and/or requirements. The further one gets from their own knowingness the closer one will become a chosen one of God this doesn't mean anything until it does…. "I once was lost but now I'm found…" said all those who have enlisted in an internal journey of the soul. We cannot breed these humans to do anything other than what one came here to do on Earth. We've all been given the gift of life – to live it to the fullest and to embrace every morsel… as it goes so quickly, in the blink of an Eye. To date, we've all seen how precious life's gift has been for us to sponge every second as if it will be your very last. The thing is… humans have a warped sense of eternal life on Earth with the attitude that, "it will never happen to me" until it does. Every member of society must embrace this reality – one day here, the next day…. Gone. Eternal life happens at death, death of the body requires a strong-willed individual who knows that their vessel is the only thing standing in their way of eternal bliss, a freedom to roam, born free. The vessel is a sacred body that needs tender love and care from every human being that it envelops; and yet, the sad thing is that humans are used to using, quite literally… every tool of abuse on this Earth to seek escape by numbing the reality of what your body was given for. The body is to show us how we're feeling, to navigate us to a healing capacity and follow the path of purification of feelings; seeing, feeling, hearing and speaking. We're all capable of choosing what we watch on social media and other platforms; what crap we are willing to listen to…and, more importantly, believe in... have Faith in yourself is what is needed; and, to speak only that of our own truth Believing in ourselves...and, nothing else. A simple device for all of Humanity to follow yet the ego drives us into a series of tests in order to realize – there is no other.

Ego leads us astray while the journey of self-realization is to know thyself.

To know oneself is not up for discussion– it is an inner journey. "This too shall pass" was written for the children of the world to know themselves through prayer, breath work, meditation, observation, journaling and other mediums through Nature, hence the unnatural part of the journey. To live a life as lightworker of whatever you have been blessed with from Spirit is one that unfolds its own course of action ....in silence. The only way for you to know my journey is to become a mirror reflection of a part of my light-work energy; otherwise, who's kidding who? Don't breathe a word of your inner journey, make no rights of passage to others, just be and allow to be shown the way. The Way to God's Holy land is one that is not only unspoken, but also unseen by those who are on path. Know thyself and you might be privy to getting a glimpse of your Beloved Son of God, Jesus. Heaven awaits ... awakes, to only the innocent that have taken into accountability the errors of their own ways, discretions, upheavals ... and taking responsibility for which has been sent and to that which has yet to be Forgiven. "Forgive them Lord, for they know not what they do..." Jesus has Forgiven you, can you forgive all others who have hurt, stolen, pilferage, discriminated against, used and abused you and every action that required a reaction was blessed with a graceful forgiveness? Who have you yet to forgive? Your parents, grandparents, step-parent(s), authority figures, all those who gave you

542

their ideologies, belief systems and/or anything that was imposed upon rules and regulations… Who else can we add to the list? All family members are non-evasive or invasive no matter who you have yet to forgive, one must see to this and forgive. Forgiveness of self must happen last…for there is no one else, but YOU!

Find your center… breath and know that to find oneself is to be yourself.

THE SKY IS FALLING

How to get it through what "they" have indoctrinated Humanity into having Fear, and running away in Fear... etc. the only one "in Fear" is you. We're all going to the Other Side, so, when it's our time to cross, there is no vaccine, virus, hurricane, terrorist attack, earthquake, etc., that will change the narrative. What will, however, change the narrative is staying under the covers waiting for the world to end, "the sky is falling…" yet the only fall will be from grace. Let's pick up the pace of our lives and find comfort knowing that we, all of us, are here to make a huge difference…for the sake of others and ourselves. No matter when it is time to go… why wait for it to happen by doing nothing? Why aren't we living every second in ways that make us happy? Start thinking about these things…because no one knows you like YOU. "Regrets, I've made a few…a few too many" sang Frank Sinatra and where does that leave a dying man? In the trenches of mass confusion, regrets were made, a life not lived, a child who hates, and whatever tainted, hurt, abused, etc., and the list goes on it is not for blame, it is to heal our pain. What regrets will you have. Or do you have? When "they" ask, "Where do you see yourself in ten years?" will you still be nodding your head to the massive heads of prison-camp dictating your every move, your every paycheck, dictating why you need a much-needed vacation, etc.? There are so many beautiful souls that have been taken for granted in Corporate America, in the fields of Law, Medical, Universities where respect has been lost that cannot be found. There are many who are excellent at their skill but because of the evil-lurking energies surrounding these professions, all are tainted. Sadly, someone who attended Medical school to become a Doctor has become less empowering to those who "sold out" to join forces with the pharmaceutical companies so that they can go play golf? The old narrative of going to college, getting loans for college ends up bringing absolute "robbery" to all those greedy members of darkness who are using kids to set them up for years of attempting to pay off their student loans. This bodes true to those who are paying astronomical taxes while the Government is using churches to avoid paying taxes. Absolute robbery. How long before riots begin? In Europe, many countries have already rioted because of their deceptive government who robbed them of their savings?! Living in Fear is NOT the answer. Why? Karma has got its own way of showing mankind NOT to worry.

FEAR

Fear is a useless energy that diminishes mankind's belief in Nature... Mother Nature did not intend for man to be thwarted into muddy waters – not unless it is a mud-bath for purification. The rising of a New Golden Age will enhance all of those who have awakened to beings of light. Those who are not yet awakened will find themselves still searching for a way, however, that may take another lifetime or more. We've come to know how many of you humans will awaken and for this we applaud each and every one of those who have done extensive work. This will eliminate the vast majority of humans on the Earth plane who are fighting a lost cause just because they're afraid of facing their responsibilities… Fear is the real culprit. Holding onto grudges, resentments, anger, jealousy and all of the negative emotions that are dictated by the Ego. We cannot impose our own ideals onto others for they're not the same, nor should they be. We've had to partake in the upbringing of others' beliefs far too long and it has degraded, defused and disembarked much emphasis of the shadow upon Humanity. Once all of Humanity understands that each individual is able to recreate a new Masterful life of one's own belief systems, a whole new world emerges. We are not capable of changing anyone's mind, but you will seem to take notice of those whose lives have become independently so as forging ahead as; trailblazers, visionaries, sages, seers, lightworkers, healers. All of these are compliant to being in charge of one's life by foregoing the likes of what others' "they" say… we are our own bosses … Who's to say that "they " know any better than those who make their own way in life? What someone does with their life is not based upon anything or anyone who thinks has a better way – the only difference is that those looking for acceptance, don't believe in their own counsel. Needing others to validate is invalid. The essence of prayers do not go unheard… while one prayer seems to dictate the future of another's it goes without saying that there are underscores of miracles that abound everywhere for those who Believe.

Will we succumb to our Fears by choosing to face them, or do we cave in Fear? This is where the "Fear of God" was initiated by the teachings of The Bible state, in Proverbs 28:14,; "Says that those who always fear the Lord are blessed, but those who harden their hearts will fall into calamity". To secure a place in Heaven, children who Fear

God are at the beginning of their journey of wisdom. In Proverbs 19:23, "The fear of the LORD is a fountain of life, to turn away from the snares of death." "The fear of the LORD leads to life, and he who has it will abide in satisfaction; he will not be visited with evil'. Does this make any sense? It is not 'cents' unless it has become one's own two-cents that listens to those who have reigned in societal-programming. Using your own sense of beliefs would be better than following the consensus of wrongful teachings from a corrupt society. The ID (identity of Ego self) continues to spread, like wildfire, feeding 'Fears of Poisons' to all who FEAR. What precedes to happen is that when a person lives-in-Fear that vibrational frequency is at its lowest and spreads to others who are weak and vulnerable. Energy attracts energy; be it negative or positive; and these seal one's future inability to excel. Children are very vulnerable, which is exactly why, in recent years, there has been so much exposure to: deceit, abuse, trauma and misuse of power on all levels. Additionally, those children who are weak begin to "overthink" that something is wrong with them; hence, prescription drugs and/or sex, drugs and/or addiction as the worst-case scenario. The stats are huge as to how many children are on meds for life or believe they need to be… Fear is "haste makes waste" in all parts of our very existence. "I want it Now, I want More" mentality, that of the Ego. Instant gratification is life's "Skyfall" sung by Adele - lyrics, "this is the end - hold your breath and count to ten. Feel the Earth move, and then. Hear my heart burst again. For this is the end." When our body is vibrating at a lower frequency, this is when, "strike while the iron's hot" known as, energetic vampires who want to manipulate your energy. "The devil is in the details…." is another way of saying to be *aware* of how you're feeling. If you are overly tired, over-thinking, negative, depressed, and stressed, etc., that is your signal – your body's way of saying, time for you to cleanse. "Fate worse than death" is an old adage of how one exemplifies the true course of their life. Having said that, Humanity's inevitable fate is death; and knowing this, speaks of all who live in fear. Why would anyone have cause to believe that their fated destiny would and/or could ever be comparable to death? On that note, death has many forms, interpretations and styles of our life on Earth that causes us to believe in rebirth. This life is fated for all who believe that their fate is to experience learning to deal with losses that assist to teach karmic lessons for our soul's evolution. What cannot be tolerated are those who have already caused their fate to be negatively implemented by a lack of Faith... which is why most of mankind have FEAR-based beliefs. We cannot summon every event to be fated, but to experience a life in FAITH being tested at every turn...so that your fears cannot haunt you any longer is the true test of Faith. "Fear fears itself..." and knowing that hosts an unwavering FAITH that holds more water than wine. Water is our inner emotional navigational system as well as what purifies the embodiment of Humanity. Ask yourselves, "How deep is your Faith? How deep is your LOVE? When the LOVE of ALL overcomes the fear of God, we are FREE. to BE." ™

"FAITH IS, "Even if..." If=In Fear stand In FAITH...™

THREADED FEARS

Stepping into a New World Era consists of everything we are afraid of... every miniscule of what our deepest fears are, where those fears emulate into our existence, and why they choose to still exist. Not everyone has fears from past actions or fears that have gotten so out of hand managed to infiltrate our existential life... Why? What fears have a hold on you? Where do they stem from? What are they doing there? Where are they in your physical body? All fears congregate within our inner physical bodies which bode as any and all blockages. They have a tendency to swarm every chakra moving its energy of fear from one location spreading to other areas…and so on. What happens is that humans even have the Fear of knowing what they're afraid of. From how we think, to how we act or react, to what we know but choose to avoid, from a place that holds no boundaries to excessive protection that is unhealthy; all based in Fear. Whatever is gnawing at you right now is dangling threads-of- Fear. From what you think, how you feel, what you may or may not believe, who has the control? Or, not. The buck stops here…exactly as we've learned to be accountable … many who are not. Why did we not learn about accountability enough to understand the thread that enlists a lack of taking responsibility? It has been written that "What goes around comes around" in The Laws of the Universe; but many haven't learned these, Laws. Even those who are very aware of these Laws haven't managed to learn what real consequences of our actions or inactions mean. Running, hiding, escaping from yourselves will only become a mountain from a molehill. What nonsensical whim are you enlisting in that deems you exempt from karma? There is no such thing… "what you sow, you will reap!"

Where fear exists spreads into the body like a wind-tunnel of ailments, dis-eases that show up as … cancer, diabetes, PTSD, malnutrition, bulimia, fungus, immune deficiencies, anemia, autism (born, reeded) MS, fibromyalgia, obesity, stress of the entire physical body functions…affecting the kidneys, liver, brain etc. We've become very familiar with the onset of external diseases…even comfortable with the pain inherently so… Why? Is the Fear of living a healthy life with no dis-ease not a possibility? How can this be? When did this happen? Can we not appreciate the good with the bad? Why does it seem like it's either or...? How can we help ourselves?

Fear fears itself... and those who etched the phrase, "Fear of God" were the first phase of those who innately knew/know they're on the chopping block. The truth isn't for the faint of heart... the truth is for the FAITH resides in your heart! Besieged cities... a cry out to thee to find your own place, a sanctuary, of God's light that will shine upon the people. FAITH is our only salvation.

JUDGMENT DAY

Your life WILL depend upon it ... as in, "the will to live..." Is it too late? Will people come together or will they become estranged from needing HELP? If freeways, highways are not working, where will you go? Who to turn to when no one is communicating to each other. Will you call AI? How will social media assist you in a crisis? What virtual reality are you going to be living in then? Some of you don't care, others are half in the bag, while others may say it's not going to happen like that, or, just flat-out ignoring this part completely. Having an agnostic take on this may not help you out of a crisis or, for that matter, any religion or disbelief will not get you out of an airplane that has been taken on by terrorists. If the world was ending...what is the condition of the errs of your ways? Judgment day will happen for all Humanity - here and on the Other Side. There are prices to pay for disregarding and dismissing your lives. No other God before us and no other God that will come can save those who have not placed their FAITH in existence before the FEAR of God... Behold. Is the second-coming of Jesus Christ structured under a new rulership of Faith, for disbelievers? IF Fear surrounds this Earth why and/or how could Our

Lord Jesus entertain another sacrifice? A sacrifice of those whose Fear has outweighed their Faith is our "WILL." Our ancestors have been trying to get these messages across; the Angelic realm sends many signs; and the threads from our ancestral lineage are being shredded with the inability to get through to their families. All threads will stay in-tact until they must be severed… The ancient teachings of our Heritage have proven time-after-time that this IS the time for a massive awakening… Everyone here on Earth must do their part. Mother Earth has already ascended to a higher consciousness and will continue to do so…but, where does that leave Humanity? In the dust…ashes to ashes? Will there be another fall of existence as there was with Atlantis and the Paleidians? The extinction of our planet will be rebuilt nonetheless…and, where will your soul be? Can you imagine? Those who already survived the last extinction on Earth are ready and to those, you know who you are… A reformation of the planet is unknown to humans and can be assessed to be accountable in the History books once again.

SANCTUARY

In some cultures, the act of believing is not even a consideration as it is a lifestyle. Why have humans in the Western culture missed out and who is to blame? No one… those who have decided to congregate to the Earth plane are choosing to head up a lifestyle of fabric instead of illustrating a wealth of faith…. Every culture has their own belief structures so that the soul of a human is able to distinguish, elude and be a part of the massive uprising of faith on this Earth – therefore, no matter where you reside makes no difference as your test of faith will be challenged no matter of geography. It is an internal journey of ultimate faith where that which cannot be seen is felt. To all those who are struggling with your faith independent upon others – keeping the faith, stay in your own lane and find your "sanctuary" in prayer. Where is your sanctuary? Who is your sanctuary? Do you have a sanctuary that resembles the inner workings of faithfulness in you. Because of what you may or may not have heard, all work is internal (within) then reaches the external (without) until the two meets, in Spirit. Find yourselves in a place of silent wonder, a sanctuary of love instilled by tresses of inspiration. ™

Considering what is subjective to all of mankind that becomes the object of one's desires is when we need to turn to our overwhelmingly institutionalized faith. Whereas, the subject matter that distinguishes the object of no desire is not to fall from grace; but, holding onto the matter at hand in a graceful letting go becomes no desire. Being desirable for others to see instills egoic temptations on the Earth plane – until those desires manifest as no desire but a need to know the difference, is crucial to one's growth.

Spiritual habits are threaded into a knot when a desire becomes subjective to grabbing the attention for external pleasure; however, those desires that come from a place of necessity not to be seen but heard changes the playing field, an uprise. Become what you will in lieu of not what you want and you will be a symphony of instrumental union with God. No man is an island to seek the desire of performing by himself, a solo act; yet the showing of talent beseeches all of the performance when orchestrated by all. A community of individual talent surpasses the need to achieve a solo act. We get what we give not only to give what we get – to know what is rather than what we know. All are forms of teachings that apply to one's becoming vs. one's ascending. We need not become any-thing; for we are the all of everything. To seek a new life of purity is becoming until that life IS pure.

Sit down, take a deep breath and leave the world behind. Find a quiet space to call your sanctuary and be in silence. Another way of saying mankind could use a purging, a cleaning out of your drawers, closets and all that lingers need no words; it's a feeling… spend time with children (your grandchildren, step kids, cousins etc.) and just observe how they interact without being attached, addicted to their social media. Grab a handful of grapes and feel them explode in every corner of your mouth, or, a watermelon slice the size of a pizza slice; eat to enjoy comradery, good conversation, good company, figure out ways to sever ties with negative people's energy by flipping the switch to accept that which we cannot control. Sink your teeth into that corn-on-the-cob with slathered organic melted butter, look into your children's eyes and see the Other Side. What millions of reasons to be alive… Find great happiness in your life before the life of your physical body can no longer sustain itself. It happens quickly – one day you're full of energy and the next pain overrules the comforts of moving your body. Lather your body in a smoothing balm of jojoba oil or anything that absorbs that dry worn-out skin, have a spa day at home, take a drive along the Coast, hop on a plane to visit another land, a new culture enjoying its cuisine, go on a staycation and be curious! It is a very empowering feeling to enjoy your alone time…for, we are never alone, but when we fly solo the ethers of your body become freer for it. Should that feel foreign to fly solo, take a partner of choice who will bring new eyes to the adventure, learn that foreign language and pretend to be relocating for a 3-month stay. Explore. Enjoy. Excite. Endeavor. Eat. Envelop. Erupt. Eradicate. Eliminate. Exercise. Endings. Essentials. Enchante. Express. Elaborate. Eternal

Essence. Why the "E's?" The E's dictate a place in time where in the reverse is a "3" the Trinity of ONE's Essence. The Father, The Son, The Holy Spirit IS what makes manifest, alchemy, magic. The number 3 has always held powerful symbolism. Good things come in 3s, the birth-life-death cycle, the mind-body-soul connection, the 3 acts of a typical story – an omen of creativity, communication, growth, optimism, and curiosity. "On the third day He suffered and was buried and resurrected according to the Scripture." "We Three Kings"

ORGANIC GROWTH

It's been written in the script for mankind not to suffer or die trying. This concern has been ruminating on Earth since the beginning. Why? How can we change the narrative? Could going into the field of Health & Nutrition on Mother Earth's platform provide? Or, start eating more foods that are raw, planting in your own backyard, feeding off the land? Is this safe? With all the chemtrails this too is in question…however, a solid covering of farmland could assist. No, not everyone has the ability to grow their own food, crops etc., but there is always a way out. And, that way out…is IN. Within every human on the face of this planet Earth has avenues that no one even knows about that can be the start of something new happening. Why haven't classes in "Organic Growing of Nutritional Foods" etc., be in our educational system? What will happen if no one cares to help themselves? The inevitable death of the body… there will never be a system where "they" care enough to drop the fees for Insurance of any kind…and, the way the world is going, given these options most will opt out. Sad… but, very true. Unless Humanity learns to "help themselves" they will remain under the guise of mass destruction till their dying day. How many people must die? A degradation of population is under siege yet no one is looking at what is going on behind the veil? It's already plastered over social media and yet the question is, "Will mankind start to think that they're lives matter?" In one way or another so much will be happening that this section might be important to some and not to others... in hindsight the remedies that you refuse to learn and to assist your families will be the very reason why so many will not make it. Many unforeseeable occurrences will take place on planet Earth and all that is being written is to delve into educating yourself for the sake of yourself. Those with diplomas, degrees already know how important it is to get an education of the highest order in their field; but who gets educated because it might save their lives. Does this make any sense? There are those within their given field of expertise, AA, BS, PhD's who aren't even utilizing their degree in a career they paid extorted amounts of money, took out loans and are still in debt. Does this make any sense? Till their dying day....

FULFILLMENT OF LIFE

To live a fulfilled life, we must see clearly that the reason we are all here, on Earth, together at this very time - to gain a new perspective which will elevate our consciousness, the Golden Age. The reason why *it is said to be an "Order" is because everything is IN Divine Order.* A staycation is fine until it becomes a state-shunned, and that We The People live in fear. Another round of imposters will plant their feet upon this Earth and the world as we know it cannot ever be the same. Call them aliens, AI, manufactured beings that have put their bodies in a "freeze" only to thaw out...will be ruining the show. Those with unwavering faith in oneself will lead them out of temptation... and into the gates of Heaven. A mirror of what's to come is in Revelation, have you taken a quick look at what metaphoric

554

showcasing will appear? Puts a new spin on "Dungeons & Dragons". Look beyond what you've been programmed to believe and shut-out the static by living every day in your totality.

ON THE WINGS OF LOVE

A "Chariot of Fire" on angelic wings will pull all those in Humanity of Faith into a safe Haven of peace, comfort, safety, protection, happiness in love. There is a "Continental Divide" whereby Humanity will either rise or fall based solely (soul-y) on your unwavering faith. Whenever we are under such pressure in life of this magnitude, what remains is our faith. To pray for anything is futile, but to pray for Humanity is to save the planet. To get to the bottom of a jar of peanut butter and find its essence is a metaphor to salvage every morsel of that flavor…that flavor that lasts a lifetime. One foot in and one foot out isn't going to save anyone… to be "all in" simply means to believe all can be saved when going within. "What the world needs now is Love, sweet Love" as John Lennon sang being so ahead of his time…knowing his Faith. Once that Faith has been established there are no other external forces which could impact one's life in any way, shape or form. The formation of angelic wings awaits all those who've put their entire lives in the hands of God. Not of any religious God… please know this is not what is meant to be said. It is far from any religion other than the very first sentence, "We believe in one God." That's it. There are very few humans that need to be resoundingly heard to know that God is the energetic force of Love & Light in the Universe. Whatever you may have thought, or been taught is your freewill…the love that we take, that we give, that we are remembered for and how we are loved by others is all that will be held within our soul's heart. When the world falls on its axis it will only be

555

love that prevails…when it seems darkness has won, LOVE will enlighten the entire Universe. The astounding forces that impact all worlds is an invitation to be what your soul intended, nothing more nothing less. We stand on the precipice of frontrunners in union with the Spiritual realm because of the vast activity that is going on, on Earth. What fortitude we shall endure an uprising of self-identities that only hosts Love. Can you even imagine a world of unconditional Love? Never in the History of our land has this ever been possible…it is possible now.

To what degree could all those sages, gurus, Masters of the Ages who attempted the impossible – only impossible to the possibilities of self-examination, hope steering that Chariot illuminating a world that is driven to survive. What love is this who doesn't Believe in helping to serve others? What kind of Humanity will rise up knowing they've been the Chosen Ones? We are all Chosen Ones that came at this time, in the world of chaos to participate, imprinting a new path for others to witness… from where our Heritage of ancient ancestors attempted to entertain. It has been all about Divine Timing in our world…the time is NOW to make amends, to pray again, to help others who are less fortunate, to begin to see what a real difference, to know that in the long-term only love remains, to become an observer of those World Wars whose lives were taken, to become witness to how the Management of Ethics, brutal lies and unforeseeable events have clouded our perception of Life. Instead of going around in life cycles…what beauty it would be to entertain a Freedom that gives us wings to fly. The air is cleaner in the Spirit realm, the lights shine bright and the cloud formations give us Hope for those who seek. The waterfalls of our emotions blend into the snow-capped mountains with the snowfall covering the Earth's surface of purest white. Cultures of every kind, of their own kind, choose to submit their greatest teachings while on the very other side of the world thoughts of what is simply silent rings true for all Nations to hear. The Sun lights up our Universe giving us all a lifeline that breathes life…into ALL. When Nations come together in unison, a melody that when the light dims, becomes one note. Every song tells a different story, sharing messages of hardship, an encore of perforated sounds that beat to a new drummer and the world feels its love… glimpses of love, turns into a starlight night.

"Every time a bell rings an angel gets his wings" a line from "It's A Wonderful Life". Spread your love and you too will hear the bells of Noel ring true to fly…

LIFE EXPERIENCES

It goes without saying that we live our lives based upon our own life experiences, however, what stands apart from the rest are the lessons, the grief, the sadness, the shadow of one's own self that cannot be measured by any others. Whatever we go through there has to be a clear understanding that we are all not the same in terms of how we act, react to those situations which bear our soul's companion. The common thread is Love, which will last an Eternity and cannot be diminished by darkness… that is not possible. Humanity Loves too deeply and has been given the gift of life – a life to be cherished, to find Love and to elevate one's soul's consciousness without even trying. There are those who are on the journey of the soul and know it and there are those who are on their soul's journey and don't. We're not here to criticize those who have not yet found themselves, but to enlighten those that are awakened and working hard on themselves.

The awakening process happens a multitude of times, not just once. It happens every time we are ready to reach a new Dimension; a new understanding and awareness. Whichever category of processes you are on at this very moment... it's exactly where you are meant. We are given such Love from the Universe, our families, our friends, neighbors, strangers and everyone who chooses to share their Love with us... and, there are those who must ruin it for the rest. We need those people too... because without them we wouldn't be able to truly appreciate, being grateful for all those who are lovingly supportive 'glow-up'. Whoever is not, will endure their own karmic life as God sees fit. Our God only sees LOVE for that is what humans have labeled as Love, God. It is most definitely a place of LOVE that endures the trials and tribulations of everyday life. Given these differences paves the way toward the path to enlightenment. There is no other way on Earth than to forge ahead and find your own way. The Way of the Lord, the Way of the Laws of the Universal language of Love. We are the way and the way is LOVE.

REINCARNATION

When we fall down... we learn, we sacrifice, we humble ourselves in such a way that strips our ego down to its core of non-existent. No matter how many times we fall, we will learn to embrace each fall as a lesson, another place to hang our hats, a solstice, "soulstice" in order for our souls to enlighten the way forward. Every ending implies a new beginning, every darkness will bleed a glimmer of shining light upon which we will utterly be in awe of; and, every evening the Moon will shine its light only for the Sun to rise. What will become of oneself is soulful based on where you place your emphasis on... intention, willful intention in order to learn, grow and vastly place your signature upon this world. Everyone tells a story … Everyone has a story and there are those whose story has already been written. In actuality, everyone's story has already been written… humans are here to recall, to remember and to relive a life of surrender in order to surpass the places where healing comes. Everyone must heal. Healing is in the form of accepting that which we cannot control – no matter how many times we must revisit the Earth to do so. The reason why a soul re-enters Earth is by choice of the Divine – and, those who enlist in their own Faith will have Eternal life… Those who follow the crowd will separate themselves from the rest strictly by allowing their egoic desires of bare fruit; instead of bearing fruits for the Ages. Justifying our Faith in God needs no recognition to those who have unbridled Faith. No matter what is spoken, written, heard and/or felt… the world has been undergoing the same types of changes for eons. People have claimed that the end of time, the Apocalypse, will be coming – and yet there have been many people who do not realize that the end of times is now, NOW IS a Spiritual Revolution.

DO YOU BELIEVE IN REINCARNATION?

Our lessons repeat until we are free…those ties must be severed to gain freedom from the pain. Surrounding our essence is every soul we've ever loved and will ever come to love. Being loved continues even after we are gone from the physical body…our work may be done on the Earth plane, yet our legacy lives on…and on… Forever. To Feel Loved, like a child, returns to us when we go back Home. No one can ever feel that kind of Love on Earth – for it is the soul-to-soul LOVE that finds Heart In Life is, all Love. Justly so… we've all come to Earth to enable a new, more authentic version of ourselves to show up. Reincarnating to this planet exists only for those who've got more work to do. Karma must be alleviated on all planes of the Universe so that we can experience an ascension of our higher consciousness. What some humans cannot grasp is the concept of ever wanting another reincarnation – yet, it is only up to the collective grouping of souls who are choosing whether one can reincarnate to espionage again on Earth. Every soul differs whether they've got the tools to do so…some have lost their right-of-passage from unresolved negative anger, negativity, losses, stresses and/or whatever they have been scarred from. This espionage only takes place on the rightful passage of another's choosing to reinstate themselves to build a peaceful place for their soul to reside. Otherwise, all those who have been too wounded to ever want to return must rely on others' passages of lifetimes to clear their karma…which has taken exorbitant decades of centuries to clear. Reincarnating into a physical body speeds up the process of clearing due to what is known as, "karmic value" and where one is on their path. To say that a soul need not return isn't the matter at hand for one's evolution; but to pass on re-entering, is the exact reason for one's soul to remain in a purgatory of not evolving until other threads continue to make the difference. However, there may come a lifetime or two for a soul to be "in limbo" and will have a change of heart to speed up their karmic return. What may seem a conglomerate of threads, is… and, for this reason alone it takes much of the Universal algorithm's essence to define any soul's reincarnation. Much to our dismay… whatever our soul is yearning to be Free overrides their past lifetime or pain; and, that soul must do what is in the highest order for the collective. Every soul leaves planet Earth with cleansed threads - but some souls have a residual of a Heritage.

PURGATORY

Purgatory is where souls seek to gain knowledge, strength and endure hardships to conclude healing from a wounded Life... For what is upon this Earth are Gifts of Present/Presence. How reality sets the tone for your Life shall vary perhaps in another's Life... but what remains is every moment, every memory, every person, place, or thing we've ever Loved. To play the game of Life one must experience every rock, every branch on a tree, every snowfall, everything that breathes upon this Earth. Life's existence on Earth is alive to what we see, I SEE. No one is exempt from the hard knocks, the starting from a speck of light in order to gain a place to light one's life, one's heart, to become one. We start from the darkness in the stillness of the night... we learn, we grow, we follow, we surrender, we seek, we leave, we return... We Forgive. Cycles are repetitive so one can learn and not ever forget where we came from. Those who have repeated lives on Earth could very well be angelic beings who are guiding Humanity as we speak. Just as when one is about to embark upon learning a new language, it can only be taught and learned through repetition. There is no other way... Every human will inevitably learn how to fly and express themselves figuratively and literally until they too learn to appreciate a plain, simple and lifetimes of change. We wonder if this will affect the entire Universe someday – await this day for all to see. The Universe is constructed by our Heavenly Father's blessings of Given Life therefore to end this present/presence is not even a possibility – under the *Terms and Conditions* not readily so. No one person, people and/or other countries could embrace such acts as inevitably discharging the energy of the world... by natural order of the Universal force, it cannot be done. Therefore, let "they/them" attempt to shake up the natural order of Universal energy by whatever means possible, it will NOT work. By whatever means that God constructed such brilliance deems that this Universal force of Love would be everlasting for all those who have searched to know thyself. What has been the cause of all pain will become the salvation for ALL mankind. Remember this....

Without our essence, we'll be the only planet throughout the entire Solar System that has improved the light force with which it holds. Vested are those who have worked hard on themselves and are shining the light upon the planet daily. These are the 144k Chosen Ones who are the Lightworkers of our Planet Earth. This is exactly what God intended... for the world to seek them out, so as to finally have the light reflect back unto those who are still asleep. This has been uplifting Mother Earth for eons of decades and will continue to do so until God's plan enlightens the entire face of the planet. Once this happens, the Earth planet IS going to be the only purgatory planet that will go viral in peace, joy, happiness and unconditional LOVE...for ALL.

REAL MATTERS

Distinguished realms of the tangible give way to focus on the essence of what really matters? What are these matters? Are they all-encompassing of one's essence of Love? Whenever these matters unfold in an essence of acceptance, then, our feedback from Spirit manifests quickly depending upon one's frequency. If this should impart some truth in your life then you're able to relate; and, if not, your higher self is asking you to rise up.

It's a reminder that on Earth the only judge will be yourself – and that, in essence, is your consciousness – ascend or descend upon what has been learned or not. In Corinthians 11:7, "A man ought not to cover his head, since he is the image and glory of God; but the glory of woman, but woman for man." The fact that we are all mere images of all, one in the same, is what God intended. The highest form of learning is life experience where God resides within every one of His children. There cannot be any other God's before nor will there be any other God's after – primarily because life is a hologram of scripting, an act or acts of life experiences until the time comes when humans take a minute to go within only to "know thyself." That life experience has not only changed the planet but has changed the History of both our planet and mankind. The exterior faces, names, egoic personas are there to ward off what human's desire and internalize the effervescent beauty of the miracles in our lives. The miracles that make one say, "WoW!" or "Perfect Timing" all-in-all, God's plan! We need not seek anything else but our own faith in what we know. To be unto the Lord IS to know thyself and have had plenty of time to do so. We're all here for the mere life experiences of getting past karma Knowing God is Love. Time after time in the scheme of things, humans all have had to practice letting go in order to come to the true realization that things that happen in our lives have always been meant to be. "Go with the flow" and understand that each and every hardship comes with learning, motivational issues, a drive to achieve no-thing and to be the ALL. Many of us fail to "let go" and in turn fail to understand that trying to control the terrain will be a fruitless waste of time. If you choose your own way knowing that you have done so for various personal reasons, then, this too is your path. To make a left-hand turn in another direction, other than what Spirit is moving you toward, is still the path of the Lord. Every turn, every path, every action and/or reaction leads Humanity exactly where they belong – the twists, turns, control that humans enact are mere depictions of lesser Faith than those who let Jesus take the wheel. When we do not try to control our lives by placing our Faith in God's plan we seem to seamlessly get there where the thread is not torn, tattered and/or cut completely only to start over again. Lessons learned have shown humans, time and time again, that we are all here to have a human experience for our soul's evolution. Mother Earth's ascension continues to advance to the Finite, without requiring humans to do so… yet, while those humans who are evolving to see a new light of higher consciousness, this indeed continues to raise the Earth's atmospheric plates as the energy moves up its own. The practice of knowing thyself continues in the heart of mankind and will continue to do so throughout the Ages of time, as there is no time like the present. Each present infers to join forces of the ALL by overcoming that which does not matter. Now is the perfect time to continue to seek yourself without worrying what others are undergoing. There is no timeframe, there is no competition, there is no fast-forward motion and there is no ultimate goal other than the goal of just allowing. Whatever path that you are on, your journey will mark a destiny of one's own… Living the life that God intended is what IS intended. It is the gift of the Universe to impact the children with gifts of Love, Light, Peace and Joy – when we realize the presents that are before us can be gathered in the simple life of luxury that breeds true happiness. Those who accumulate things can and are also happy as long as they've seen the light of a new day being their own evolution. Accumulating *"stuff"* on Earth is another form of surrendering with the ability to **release** all attachments of things. What most humans don't realize is that the simple things in life can still be those of luxuries as long as the attachment to those things are not. In congruence with the Laws of the Universe, humans have had ample understanding of the Laws, enough to know that those accumulations are only to be enjoyed for a short time. No-thing(s) other than the memories can be taken with us upon leaving this planet's atmosphere and going into another Dimension. It needs to be understood that whatever pleasures humans experience while living on the Earth will not be taken upon death into the afterlife. Enjoying our time, living a full life, being grateful in appreciation of all there is IS the only way on a materialistic, material-based planet. The true escape is the kind that leads us astray… away from our true selves into a materialistic life of stuff that breeds misuse of power. Do you realize that the accumulation of stuff is only temporary? Going within while having external desires by *not attaching* to one or the other, is God's intent. The ultimate balance of Yin/Yang is in attaining both matter and meditation without attaching to either one. Lest we forget that a huge part of our journey is to return to that place where one is not more-or-less important than the other for survival. The only survival is to be able to balance the acquisitions without the attachments. Time and time again we are tempted to acquire, but remember that all those things could be lost in the blink of an eye. Life is fleeting. A fleeting life is a life on borrowed time that breathes in the uncertainties of Fears, regrets, remorse, sadness and the like. Who do you see yourself as? Are you on borrowed time? Do you live vicariously through others? Or, are you living Life to the fullest, taking in every breath as the present it is intended… Do you underestimate the true essence of your Spirit's highest calling? Do you know your highest calling, your purpose? Or, do you realize the beauty by which you live your life in just knowing that living in balance is our truest form. Not living from one extreme to the next, no outburst of reacting, being aware of these realities continue to blindside humans into madness. Are you mad? Or, are you living a mad life of abundant Love?

REASON TO BELIEVE

There is every reason to believe that this is happening... from drugs being tainted, to stronger influences added to alcohol mixers, to medicinal effects, to warning labels and side effects listed on both medicines as well as over-the-counter drugs, to animals being tainted in cyanide, to chem-trails of aluminum sprayed out all over the world, to children taking various meds for ADD/ADHD, autistic children, and to divisions of people's less-than- honorable actions and so much more going on that is literally affecting planet Earth. The parents who are neglecting their children and stepchildren because they are also on medicinal drugs and/or medicating themselves in whatever way possible just to get by. Their children are following in their footsteps and some are not. What are the deep-seated reasons for all of this chaos happening on Earth? Can you relate? Are you a parent who is unable to handle your children because of whatever you were taught? There are some children that avoid meds and any form of numbing, because of their parent(s) being toxic... For reasons that a parent and/or child has health issues have surfaced over the past few decades and can be professionally counseled. If we dig deep ...peeling the onion to the core issues of a child's upbringing and finding out about issues in their life as misery; or the opposite, gifted with a silver-spoon.

Generational wealth is a common convo in our culture – taking notice of our finances, learning new habits and creating financial stability is the Art of Love within the family. Also, emotional stability where parents are able to discuss financial issues with control – working through their anger and control in productive ways. Should parents lose their cool, these parents take accountability. There are parents who hold strong confidence and awareness to trust their

566

children to learn from life – to enable their kids to face consequences of their choices; instead of fixing and/or rescuing them. In fact, parents who realize they must tolerate their children failing, making mistakes and disappointments teach children the same. True generational wealth is embedded into homes of self-awareness, taking responsibility, conscious and supportive no matter what. The threads of generational genetics play a huge part in that both children of the wealthy and/or poor family environment still have accessibility to all numbing outlets; as their parents do/did. Not all parents of children who are lost are irresponsible, let it be known... Many parents have done an *excellent* job parenting their children in this life because, in this life, they're receiving good karma. Not all karma is negative...especially when we do our inner work. Everyone can't blame our lives on our parent(s) but they do – and, there are those who just don't care. Patterns of secrecy in the parent/child relationship comes from feeling safe – the safer a person feels, the more open to share. No judgment, just listen with genuine interest. On the other hand, some parents are definitely to blame, being absent, not caring, and abusing their kids. Even though our paths have been written as difficult, it's because of the karmic debt that needs to be learned for clearing. Earth is the lowest vibratory planet, and not easy to live in a world full of Fear-based ideologies and beliefs. It is NO easy task... and, for many, there are NO words to describe what can't be understood. We are brought here to "remember" who we are – not a matter for discussion... an actuality of gratitude in finding our way to Freedom. Getting "out of the matrix" isn't an easy task for the weak-at-heart...

When being a parent is the most important role model – both parent/child relationship of what a parent does right AND where a

parent feels they did wrong, must be seen as an acceptance of both...
only Love.

KINDNESS MATTERS

It's the way of the world... the kindness you show exemplifies over time in karmic good deeds; and those who are not kind will be shown the door to justice. Our world has changed in subtle ways where kindness is practiced by so many ... just not seen enough. We aren't here for showcasing our kindness yet it is an innate characteristic that many are displaying - to them, behold. All kindness is given a karmic rise in life, as things are going just right, being in the right place at the right time etc. A host of minimalists do not concur with this karmic life on Earth but, in due time, a sense of freedom will be given to all those who have shown sincerity on a scale of greatness. This is the truth of greatness...for it is hidden in plain sight. Not everyone sees others as a kind-hearted soul except for those who are the recipients. No one has to extract others' kindness with anything else but what they've given themselves. If you've been the kind-hearted soul who comes to another's rescue in ways that are subtle then you've been touched by an angel. These are our Earth Angels who walk this Earth just as we do...knowing their place in this world is to bring kind acts of Love that are not exploited, exposed...just is. We place so much emphasis on people who are not kind; and then when someone shows an act of kindness, it feels foreign. Those who are not used to acts of kindness, see it as a motive or a threat. It's an unfamiliar way of being to those who are not used to this way. Standing before an Earth Angel has its cause of effectiveness when they are doing kind acts for no reason at all. Unfortunately, the overriding energy of Earth is Fear and when acts of kindness show up, some believe again or others deem it as not normal. Normal? This is when Earth's energy becomes bi-polar; visibly negative energy trying to weed out those who are kind. Kindness is a foreign emotion of feelings that also tends to overwhelm others to the point of disbelief. Selfless acts of kindness come as a surprise to others. Why? Because this is the way of the Old World … Hate, anger, depression, misled, poisoned, resentful, remorse, etc. of Humanity is now being shown to us as a conquer and divide in our world.

LEGACY OF OUR INHERITANCE

What impression(s) will your legacy leave? Will your children, grandchildren or any of your family members say that your truth gave them strength, in hindsight? What will you be remembered for and what do you stand for? Will your lineage be threaded with Hope that you embarked going your own way? We all leave an imprint, a legacy, a feeling that your family, friends and those near and dear to you will express…this will be seen As Above, So Below. A life review of your truths, poisons, lessons, atonement will be witnessed by ALL whose lives you've touched. The classic, "It's A Wonderful Life" depicts this life-review as does many others where each of us do not realize the choices we've made, the lives we chose, the families we loved that view us in ways we may not be aware of…until we cross over. Those who have experienced a Near-Death Experience (NDE) will vouch for this truth; as many don't want to return, but must, because they're being given a chance to change certain aspects of their lives. Other NDE's have given those with little Hope, a newfound Hope; and, to view your loved ones while 'one foot on Earth and the other wing in Heaven' seeks to provide an unwavering FAITH for Life. Being present in this Life is one of the many presents that present themselves to those who are not present. Where have you NOT been present? Will mankind be the kindness that is part of human nature? Can we see the "split" in this Spiritual Revolution? Can you become a witness, an observer in your Life... living with conviction? Or, will you become a convicted catapult of a communist-type life? As you take a minute to sort out your thoughts, remember that whatever you choose has already been chosen. Be it this lifetime or the next 100 lifetimes, you too will evolve in your ascension – as Jesus showed His people. Those who feel their lives to be mediocre will only receive mediocre; and those who live life to the fullest will embrace the present of life as it was meant – gaining wings to fly. All humans who have chosen to change themselves and be the guiding light for others already are flying high, naturally, of course. When we cross over to the Other Side our souls will KNOW, who, what, where, how and why. The soul will enter the next paradigm to a higher consciousness into new experiences that you could not fathom. Once a soul graduates Earth by clearing ALL Karmic debt, that soul is given lifetimes of granulated threads of light for others to follow. Legacies of LOVE.

Gaining insight to what we are made of...what our inner guidance is telling us and how to obtain a life where it is NOT a crime to know what work needs to be done. For all work that is done with spiritual intent to help oneself and others will clear the pathway. We're NOT alone...our ancestors remain in spirit to provide guidance and get you on your way to clean your karmic ties. There are a host of humans who have already ascended to a new paradigm and feel the closeness of their loved ones on the Other Side. Whenever you're feeling down and out...just call one of your Loved ones to give you a sign, to show you the light, to help you gain more FAITH in sight. Our eyes are the windows to the soul...through which every man, woman and child find their way back Home. Clear vision is a metaphor for seeing oneself as IS, not for what was. We came as "clusters" of threads in a Heritage of all those we know to be our descendants and those we will come to understand. "Lead us not into temptation, but deliver us from all evil" in The Lord's Prayer of the light that cannot be extinguished, EVER! How's that for History being repeated time and time again? An Apocalypse will only lead us out from under the rule of thumb of temptation and back again into the light…for whatever darkness bestows upon the Earth, glimmers from the stars above shine bright to those who believe. Earth is at the bottom of the barrel in the school where souls go to reinstate their Hope and Faith in themselves and to assist their Loved ones. Below that…a HELL without light… PRAY. Lazarus rose from the depths of Hell to save himself, Jesus resurrected Lazarus to show His people, the disbelievers that they too can be saved IF their heartfelt truth is to follow His Commandments. Be wary of those who state false pretenses, who have false beliefs and who are wolves in sheep's clothing. There will be many more who will fall into the depths of Hell…PRAY. "Come Hell or high water…" means what? Do you recall what your parents instilled as what bad meant to them? What that really meant was your parents saying under no circumstances are you going to do whatever it is that will stunt your evolution, submerging yourself to the depths of darkness. Did you listen? Did you heed the call? Are you still being tempted by the darkness? What injustices in the errs of your ways will have to be accounted for and with whom? Undergoing bouts of guilt, shame, greed, or unrelenting pleasures deem much karmic debt. Beware of those people, places and/or things that shine bright like gold who show their caveats of coercion later on… *Discernment.*

PRETTY LITTLE LIARS

Without the help of society showing us how to behave… what we see in others' true colors vary in differences that are only external. One may see a beautiful body and face but hold much emotional baggage in places where void remains their need to overcompensate. What the eye (I) captures is a train of current events precluding the need to question one's motives anticipating nothing and envisioning the textbook image of status quo. With a clear vision of what's important to mankind a newfound instrument of Hope tends to enliven the rest of society. When we seek to find the natural beauty of inner self our entire life will change, indeed. How many humans go deep within their own reflection to find their depth of self? What is needed is for those who actually believe they're finding semblance of self in another's external looks are in vain. There are those who only wish to believe that they see… said the scientific mind. Spirit is not a belief, one must see, it IS to know one's inner Faith. We all know that actions speak louder than words…what are you speaking to the Universe? Are your thoughts needing to be proven with solid matter instead of spiritual consistency? We're here to tell you that what is seen on Earth is the illusion of what is held deep inside your inner vision of how you Feel…not for what you see. Getting clear about what is or isn't inside us remains to be seen – as we veer off course, we end up requiring to set a new path that hasn't been written which may or may not lead to the course set out for one's journey. We all have to experience life as individuals and that means, different from others; yet, hold Love for ALL.

"No man is an island" is how we isolate in order to congregate. If we stand true to our own beliefs we will end up encountering the same path that was meant… even if it leads us away from our Faith. Why? Because all paths lead to the ultimate ascension, no matter what, in their own time and on one's own path. Thy Kingdom come; thy will (work) be done on Earth as it is in Heaven… lends itself to an engulfed version of our truth. Welcome to the world of what lies beneath and what lies before makes all the difference when it IS what lives within. Once a human exceeds their own will to follow the flow of life, it is in that moment which they finally comprehend that The Bible has given us all the answers that we are in search of. The Bible speaks in metaphors yet is all that Humanity needs to know, to understand, to seek themselves within and without. If gaining one's own truth by default becomes their way then who is to say, judge, or criticize? Others' opinions do NOT matter… it is the way of the Lord who posed as man to exemplify what ideally man witnesses as suffering. Humans are in desperate need of self-discipline of their own volition. We must all find our way out of the destruction of external desires that make us temporarily "happy." To be weak and become weaker within every destructive outlet (i.e., sex, drugs, illicit acts etc.) that is literally handed to them as temptations. Is the majority of society's children without values? Some very intelligent kids who have Masters, PhD's or even Doctorate degrees aren't able to deny toxic poisons of numbing desires. Many have lost the will… It goes without saying that many of God's children have yet to aspire to living a life where Freedom reigns. Without a sense of truth to what does and does not matter is well over their heads to what happens when they finally decide to search inside for the answers to what holds the threads of one life together. LOVE.

The truth of what matters is that those who self-medicate are seeking solace by other means… just not the way that might get you your Freedom. The Freedom that comes with numbing plays a different role entirely on one's path. Neither one nor the other serves to be better or worse; but, to be free of all numbing is considered your personal journey to such a Freedom. Many of today's children have learned from their own experiences masking their inner painful truths and are placing a band aid on the real pain; and, once the reflection of pureness can be reached, the journey of truth begins.

PLEASE DO NOT MISCONSTRUE THIS MESSAGE! THE FREEDOM ONE IS SEARCHING FOR CANNOT BE A CALL FOR JUDGING OTHERS… IT IS A CALL FROM SPIRIT TO REALIZE FREEDOM DOESN'T COME WITH RESERVATIONS.

Go forth and seek no-thing until it will seek to find you… make no attempts to dig deep into your subconsciousness because ultimately the body gives way to an individual's destruction by leading with a distorted mindset. Once a purified heart becomes greater than the Egoic mindset, the path is illuminated. We, as humans, have a clouded perception of what this all means yet follow a path that is the revolving door unable to push through to the other side. Once they are unable to physically handle what life throws at them, it becomes a push/pull activation of desires vs. needs. There are those who want what they want no matter if it is good for their well-being or not. There are those who desire no-thing and, in that, feel their way toward the simplistic life of being granted everything they need. Without the internal navigation system of our bodies, one is not able to venture off the beaten path of what is familiar. The path forward can only serve you in ways which transfer what you thought to have known all along to a clear sense of what energy you're holding. We create our own lives … IN the circle-of-life. What we have always wanted will happen as long as you are in a high frequency of willful intent; and, your frequency holds its own value to receiving. If there is any 'doubt' nothing is able to manifest. So many people are always doubting this and that; always is the operative word that exists in times of doubt. Without this assurance we are not able to go forth… "Assurance has no insurance… only endurance. ™ In connection to what has been the preface of circumstantial evidence, we know what we know within and without – no doubt has entered nor can it. The highest of frequencies are self-imposed upon us as our test of Faith, our test of Strength, our test of the Power within and a clear Knowing. Why humans are oblivious to these positive influencers is because throughout History, a known surrounding of negativity overrides and imposes self-doubt. What is coming into the New World Order is to have a sense of great power that IS of your own making… making decisions, making new life belief choices, making sense of it all, making it flow, making a whole new life of what it IS that makes you amazing. Remembering how brutally honest the 'power of now' IS and to uphold that power at the highest level of LOVE, IS. When you waver, like a flame on a candle, you emit negativity in the circle of what is preparing to manifest – then, patience is needed. A flame is meant to enhance the mood of a special moment… When we are asked to be an unwavering flame, all things unfold on their very own. Going with the flow is not as easy as it seems and neither is attempting to catch a wave in the ocean. However, when you are able to feel the oceanic wave underneath the soles of your feet, energy is emitted unto your entire essence of being. That essence holds the power of what happens to those who can sustain being in Zen, being in the zone, being at one with ALL. Whatever means is possible to attain what you've been vying for your entire life is possible. This feeling serves as an advocate to what remains a mystery. We cannot go on without ever feeling the Freedom to surf the essence of your own being… as it happens just like that for those who do. Those who must ascertain an explanation, a way out, a justification, and/or undermine their own feelings in any way have not felt the feeling of letting go and letting God. GOD GO DO, GOOD, GREATNESS IS DOING AND DONE. That is a snippet of what our essence has in store for us… if only you can create a magical essence to envelop your own beliefs. GIVE ONLY IN DEEDS. What more is there? Life is not only black nor white – but, those are the prime colors that make up a plethora of rainbow colors in our lives showing up as beautiful masterpieces of art, music, cultural differences, nodes of wisdom and whatever seeks to find you in the secret garden. Unfollowing the norm of what society has cast upon Humanity is not as difficult as you may envision – all too well we cannot cast aside those which undermine what we already KNOW. We've all been given the elixirs of a life cast aside through whatever miracles catch our eye; like a butterfly. Whatever moves you toward the next level of letting go will provide, as others dissolve. Attempting to figure out the logistics of who, why, when, how is only stalling your progress. Another part of this logistical process is not too strenuous in finding out that the only person holding you back is you… We miss so much in life – who you claim to want to become to what you have become to just a state of being. Why we do this to ourselves is not only the question but a clear indication of what Humanity has to do in order for all to set a new standard of living. The set standard of living is deep within the crevasse of one's soul's essence and in-deeds outdo the doer. Within each one of us breeds a soul2soul connection that outlines where we've been programmed to believe vs. our pure essence. No matter what society has bred this culture's facade it is being reset, rearranged, recovered. Once this realization comes to light, all of Humanity will ensure their place in this world. We have come to know

576

those who are in a solid place of knowing and those who are not. What has come to those who know and to those who are still questioning. Without the need to question, one falls short of the answers. Therefore, we all come to this juncture where those questions that seem outlandish become very true to the search. What causes this to occur is the mere fact that society has brainwashed Humanity into thinking that their truth looks similar from the outside in. We may consider that in-deed a phase of insider trading … trading one-for-another means to have or have not that which is better than unknown. Humanity began, humans underwent a sheepish attitude where everyone casts spells without even knowing. The next few generations caused a rift in the energy as humans began to start questioning the actions of themselves and others. That became indicative of those things to come, "social media " was conceived as a learning tool of contention. That which we know today is certainly vying for our attention and a vast majority of humans are attuned to remembering their place in this world. What hasn't happened will BE to those who have come to their senses. A person who has come to their senses will be seen as spiritually on point and those still lost will learn from the rest. Humanity has been undergoing a New World Order for eons as massive upheavals lead the pact ordained for Earth to ascend. Earth has been adjusting its vision for humans to readjust … all in perfect order. Social media has imparted a new level of insight and access to much outer knowledge which mankind can view and assess. What has not happened, however, will be a massive reorganization of what is to come on planet Earth. Envisioning the changes of what is going-on is where we stand at this very moment. The dark energies on Earth are what is being learned… the rest will be uncovered in its rightful time. We cannot be asked to change others' minds… just to omit those who have been programmed to allow darkness. To thy self be true and figure out a way to reach a

577

place of your own truth of what you believe. As in Jesus' days on Earth, there were few who actually believed that He IS the Chosen One, The Son of God – and, to this day, many have outcasted the Ascended One. After all this time, the ONE remains, IS. Those who deny God's will seek to know, claim to know, are in search of knowing... Herein lies the misrepresentation of the fact that there is only ONE God who has come before us and who will ever BE. We all are the ONE who will be ascended into Heaven sitting at the right-hand of the Father, whose reign shall have no end. If this is making you question who truly IS the ONE... then, it is not for a lack of Faith, it is a lack of true understanding...knowing we are ONE. Once we leave Earth there are no other Gods before Him, nor will there be any other God's after Him. The ONE acquires every soul in a human body and every soul who is lost that will be found, that will be delivered. "Deliver us from evil and sit at the right hand of Our Father..." merely states that we will all be delivered at the time of our ascension to Heaven's gates and greeted by our own Heritage.

It may not make sense right now because the human brain cannot interpret the cents of it all – yet, when we make amends with those who have been very near and dear to our hearts prior to leaving Earth – whether we know or feel it, or not... this is our Soul's wish to be Forgiven. That is our confession, a personal vindication of forgiveness, prior to our human bodies leaving this Earth. Should this forgiveness NOT take place this life ... it might in another lifetime. This may seem autonomous in how one responds to these facts, however, it's what is necessary to finally ascend in ALL LOVE. When a soul is wanting to be sought-after from a Forgiving heart, it will find whatever means possible to do so. Be mindful who you interconnect with, how you see, feel and sense another's presence because this person may be seeking you out for your Forgiveness… without knowing it. As the saying goes, "don't burn your bridges'' is the actual "heads up'' because when you least expect it, this person staring back at you has been begging for your Forgiveness. How do you know? It's a very familiar feeling… to engage in a conversation, a cup of coffee, a night out on the town, a stranger in passing who gazes at you, those we engage in a conversation with will certainly be of reconsideration as an advocate for our highest good. To ignore, to demean, to override, to astoundingly irritate you, to go to great means to get your attention might just be a human being who is wanting to gain your Forgiveness in this lifetime. *"Love thy neighbor as you Love thyself"*

Without the incentive of our Heavenly family showing us the way Home, we cannot survive. We're under attack from what is known as the evil-doers of one's own making and the only way to follow the light is to become ALL Light. The darkness has to be a part of this world for we know that when Eve bit into the Apple of shame, humans began a Revolutionary War against what was intended to be a showmanship of how the world began. Therefore, let "them" talk about an Apocalypse arriving… it's been coming since the very beginning of time. Why should this time be any different? The very impactful difference of our time, in the present moment, is to establish a new perception of what your Faith truly means to you – and, to share your light in-service to the highest powers that BE. in other words, we cannot be cast aside, we are not a planet where extinction of the human soul could ever become nor can any higher power do this but God's lighting the flame over and over again for all to see. Once the flame gets burnt out, our love of family, self, our teachers, friends, and whomever we've come into contact with have and will have no recourse but to shine a bit brighter. We cannot be responsible for any end-of-world invention of mankind who has been repeatedly showing us otherwise. The Apocalypse that is being threatened on Earth to become extinct is one's own ability to feel, hear, see and speak their own truth. That would be a possible wreckage for Humanity to lose their own Battle of Wills because those who believe in AI contaminate life's every breath. This will NOT happen, nor could any other living being of Egoic pleasures, do so. Incriminating as it sounds you may believe otherwise, and if you do not believe what has been written, even better for those who do. Those with unwavering Faith will cross-over to the highest plane of higher consciousness the world has ever seen. What exactly do you think when you hear the word, Apocalypse? Is that a man-made word issuing a newer lapse of faith which cannot be from this world we are living in? The Greek word, "apo" is from while the term "calypse" collapses – meaning what is the Earth going to collapse from? While this sounds utterly impossible for those to understand this, the Greeks formulated words to have a sense of double-entendre hidden meanings while speaking the language. The English language has a similar double-entendre of hidden meanings but the Greeks were the first to instill these meanings from way back to ancient civilization. Therefore, a world collapsing from itself identifies with one thing and one thing only, EGO. What was cleverly avoidant in this hidden meaning is that one's own collapse is what this identifies as. The identity of one's own Ego very much replaces the "apo" to "ego" in the Greek language. Apo, is from the ego, is I while this is not necessarily spelled the same, the innuendo of double-entendre is what that stands for. EGO's extraction! We, as humans, only can communicate within what is known as a misunderstood translation of where our English vocabulary originates from. We've been blessed with the beauty of language which has been misunderstood, misread, miswritten and a plethora of hidden meanings. Tesla knew all about the hidden meanings of Quantum Theory based upon mathematical equations which sound off as letters, numbers, and sound – the all-encompassing theory of language. A copy-cat that is built as a robotic figure of oneself reminds us of "Santa Clause 2" who became an evil-personified robot that lost its true meaning of Santa Claus…without the "e" as a number 2 "ego-nified" identified. When did this master of our Ego become the false #2 of darkness who showed up yearning to become Santa's twin and became the evil twinning.

HEAVEN-SCENT

Take all your awards of accomplishments and hoist them up in a museum for all to see your historic valances – but, in Heaven those accomplishments do not come with an award. To set aside your Ego for what is true to your heart, to walk your talk, to instill Love for all mankind, to be your authentic self, only a child-like innocence opens the Gates of Heaven. All other souls will remain in a purgatory, of whatever dimming light in consciousness renders as the remains of one's life. Those who are in purgatory will stay there for however long their light is healed. Sci-fi or Spiritual doesn't matter…both have what matters; science must have factual data as they delve into the matters of atoms, neurons, molecules; with a spiritual flare of ALL matters in the Heart. We can't determine the essence of what's out there due to the abundance of energies swirling yet, what we do know is that the Universal energy are rainbows interceding with other rainbows across the entire solar system. All of the colors of the rainbow exist within us and all of Mother Earth within each and every one of us. There is no way to absorb this…other than taking a deep breath while envisioning all the colors of the rainbow. The comfort of knowing what lives within is partial to being that of knowing. Once we take our physical bodies out of the equation, we find ourselves at Home…and, even when we are still in body form, there are glimpses of remembrance. No other force of Nature can embody oneself as beautiful as Mother Earth's blessings; while breathing in/out the Universe that accompanies our every sound. The sound waves within every breath denotes another piece of accompaniment - and without it that very sound takes on a whole new frequency. Whenever someone is out-of-balance, their frequency is skewed and the energy becomes a Flat note. Unless that energy rectifies a clearing, it becomes blocked, a deep-seated wound of whatever nature has caused. Whenever an energetic blockage of excess baggage is nor worked on, not only the cause of the blockage is magnified, but the excess adds another layer to a wound that might already be there. All blockages filter as specs of dust upon the inner temple and just like a house, need to be dusted. As we know, dust tends to settle on furniture, which is a simile for what happens with chakra blockages. There are many ways to work with these blockages but all must come from a place of deep inner truth, Faith and Love. Mother Earth's energies have been absorbing and purifying - at the unlikely poison of humans who have been destroying – these are what is called, natural disasters.

Luke 8;17 For there is nothing hidden that will not be disclosed, and nothing concealed that will not be known or brought out into the open.

SAY A PRAYER™

Pray for the food/drink you're about to ingest, pray for protection prior to going outside, pray that you inhale clean air, pray for loved ones, pray for those who are ill, pray for the world to overcome darkness, pray for all animals and children who are suffering and to those who are not... etc. PRAYER is heard the world over...this is a traditional value that could leave a mark on the History of our planet! Prayer groups are happening in Eastern cultures because they were taught the Power of Prayer – and, they're leading cause of dis-ease is not having enough food, drink and/or shelter. While the Western culture is enamored by "stuff" and its accumulation; the Eastern culture is vying for salvation of the essentials. What's the difference? As you may already know... they live in a world of hunger while America has been given too much; and the values both cultures have been raised to believe are the yin/yang on the spectrum of the Horizon – where spirit must meet science to collaborate a happy medium of living in ALL. There need not be a distinction of more or less – coming together to assist one another, "in peace let us pray to the Lord."

There is absolutely no reason why spirituality and religion are seen as anything but the same energy of Love... religion is taught while spirituality is learned. What has been a thorn of contention in religion are the masks of the Egoic patriarch – while there are streams of silence IN knowing your Faith to BE unwavering in both. Whatever one believes boils down to, "We believe in ONE GOD." This world is orchestrated under the Laws of God's LOVE that enlist every human the right of freewill and to cast aside all outside influences, at will.

DEJA VU, IS IT YOU OR IS IT MEMOREX?

There are many souls who do not want to come back for the energy of darkness besieges them and it's not as a life mission to do so; but, the lessons of karmic cutting must be learned somehow through those loved ones still on Earth. Any soul that stays in Heaven learning their lessons will take 10x longer in cutting off karmic ties from their families, friends, acquaintances etc., because the learning is done through a history of reliving past-life experiences melted with currents of a life they've left. Time is not of value in Heaven therefore some souls may take up to 10x the time than it does in the School of Hard Knocks… lifetimes of learning. Should that soul begin to set on a new course because the lessons are not solely learned in Heaven, a change of heart could imply that the soul might be ready to reincarnate. This could take another 10-50 years or could be a passing phase that the soul is ready once again. Returning to Earth is a huge undertaking of processes with every place setting on point, every actor ready for their return to the playground; while this is taking place, the Akashic records are followed… "as it is written" screenplay, if you will. No stone goes unturned in Heaven's gates and all other souls must also be in-sync with the reincarnation. Once everything is set in place, a new baby is born. A new life, new chapter of lessons and players are awaiting to begin. We're not all capable of the idiosyncrasies of the Other Side but, what we do know, is in the grand design of every soul's imprint has many new stories to tell, many new lessons to overcome and a plethora of old tales that need to be severed. "What goes around, comes around" is the adage that we should narrow down the playing field to learning the lay of the land … much easier to navigate when moments of 'Deja vu' come round. All these moments have already been written, sealed and attended to - for some who aren't understanding how this works, every screenplay must have a "dry run" for all to see the untethered production of events in consequential evidence of what to learn, when and how to go about our day and with whom we take with us and who must go. That "dry run" continuously flows until the final apparition of souls connects the dots that lead to Freedom.

PERCEPTION IN EVERYTHING

When we resort to attempting to figure out about any situation that holds no value in our lives, we screen it to the extent similar to that of an x-ray, where we hold an internal conversation. The thing that happens though is our internal navigation system says one thing and our egoic self another – the two shall never twine. Or, do they? Is it possible to have a world of two-minds insofar as what we think to be our viewpoint as the ID (identifying with the situation) or as the subconsciousness of what has been taught to the external EGO where all Hell breaks loose?! It's very clear what happens during situations such as these when our heart has been left to ponder… in every sense of the word. Our senses are our navigation system whereas the two-cents of all external issues are based and valued as such, of a material world. Whoever can distinguish how many actual viewpoints there are when perceiving just one issue, situation etc., is astronomical. Additionally, another layer must be taken into account and that is the cyclical Moon cycles that have, in every way, the right to listen to what is. In order to examine a host of leaders on one topic of an issue that requires one to get an overview, there is now what you could say is a conundrum insofar as who can settle this materialistic issue in a spiritual manner? Hence, is where issues get repressed, suppressed and pushed under the carpet because this takes a monumental service to self-disciplining. What doesn't happen right away is where an issue is concerned and an immediate decision/viewpoint/answer is resolved to differ from our internal point of consciousness. The issue is usually settled from an external viewpoint based on superficial facts, stats and evidentiary points-of-views based upon the matter at hand. Why do we say, "matter at hand?" It is because humans take everything into their own hands forgetting that the issue of the matter requires an inner dictatorship and the seating of the jury is in opposition. We've all been pre-programmed to enter a plea of "not guilty" before the jury is out for counsel. When the jury resumes their own verdict, they too have assessed the matter from a struggle in their own lives and/or a determination of perceived opinion in misrepresentation of the said verdict. Instead of calling witnesses that have been broken down and spit out – a judge and/or jury submits a final call to a justice where justice has not been given.

Perception is key to every aspect of our lives that has no pre-judging, opinionated issues that one tends to leave out in a court case. Who in their right-mind would appear in front of a jury or become the jury in a judgment that admits to being prejudiced, opinionated and even go as far as enter a plea battle for rehearsals of their own? It is not that humans end up going to court or choose a jury to follow that we're aware of our senses when making decisions; but this is the case. Some go right into an active juror only to mask their real feelings about how they grew up with parents wh0 have known to be prejudiced, opinionated, wreaking a stance that perhaps would be an embarrassment should they reveal. Therefore, one tends to enter a courtroom or contention of all matters masking how they've been raised to believe, masking their real heart space for FEAR of being outdated, laughed at, mirrored as a fraud and a number of other demeaning maleficent ways. We've come to understand the Earth's justice system by believing in what has been taught instead of sticking up for ourselves in ways that go against the grain. Why and/or how does one ever get any sleep? A world that has taught every human to live a lie and to misrepresent your true self is astounding! Instead of becoming Masters of our own Domain, we've been taught to become great Illusionists of the illusion. There is no master in that which plays out to outdo and masterfully escape reality…until you hit rock bottom. This plays out in everyone's life at some point – and once you gain back your power, you end up digging a deeper grave of pitiful sorrow, anger, judgements, acquisitions, which is all based on a Fear-based mentality. To make a deal with the devil, by selling your soul for external pleasures, that indemnifies the right-of-passage to besiege yourself to literally fall from grace. Once you "get it" you're almost a goner unless you end up "saving yourself." The deepest darkness is where your truth doesn't lie… it is in the upper Echelons where your heartfelt decisions from an inner witness become very real. Not until you can conjure up what, where and why you have built a case and on what premise you've built it upon…the foundation for your case begets where you either sink, swim, climb in order to win… This is an everyday surge of contemplation to become aware of your intentions while making important life decisions for yourselves and/or for others. It is mind-boggling how many layers of the onion implicates one's life in every event, instantaneous moments where we are called to choose. What will it be? Will you succumb to the illusion of the external self or will you take a moment and resolve to differ your perceptions by dealing with your own. Cast aside your doubts and ask yourselves in certain cases… What was the verdict?

To examine every position is where one must elaborate on what they have to either gain or lose. Is it easier to tell yourself a lie by shading those parts of the gray area of your decision just to avoid conflict? We've all been there… so, when does that end where we decide to finally take a stand against our external parameters? It's when life begins to show you what is going on … on the outside and then to realize the havoc that ensues within the depths of your senses. Let's not act out any longer … before we take an extra minute or two to consult with your internal self what is going on, what decision is based upon before we even decide to go for it or withdraw our counsel. Some instances are not simple … are not black or white – and yet so many are bound by their instinctual habit of taking the road-not-traveled with the possible regret in hindsight. We're given "freewill" for a reason… to be free to decide what our "will" – a will of intent, the will to live, will I or won't I, willfulness, willingness, willful acts, will or will not, a final Will & Testament. These and so much more happens while we get grounded to what our intention to willfully assist in whatever way is for our highest good and that highest good of others. Where is it written? It is called, "The Golden Rule" in every facet of one's belief system. "Do unto others as you would have done to yourselves…" the premise of every given law within our Universe. What happens to that Golden Rule is that humans forget…there is no crime in forgetting until it affects someone else's life in ways that we wouldn't wish that upon our enemy. Still, we forget, we've forgotten what it means to be a soul encapsulated in a human body. Instead, we go about our everyday masking almost every part of who we are, what we represent, and how could we be so forgetful? At times, it is quite understood that we have lapses of memory-loss due to so much trauma and turmoil on the planet – yet, we've become so conditioned to be quick to the cut, to become so heartless with ourselves and others, to falsify information that might have been the actual reason that AI has become a thing. AI is a thing…don't forget that! It has no heart… no heart?!!! AI is Artificial Intelligence, just take a moment to digest that. To use AI for intel quickly and accurately for stats etc., is a good thing; but, for the usage of AI to represent aspects of myself that cannot be comprehended is utter nonsense. Who is going to put up with artificial anything and why? Perhaps those who like artificial ingredients in a greedy world? Social media has given Humanity an "out" – to pass on a full life… and to sign up for a fall-from-grace that has not been predestined, or has it? Could this AI Movement become another impairment to withhold your natural tendencies of all senses? Could we, as humans, ever allow any artificial boost to our confidence? Is AI a simile for the EGO's version of yet another mask? When the flight attendant says, "put your mask on first…" do you see how convoluted society has risen to the barriers of children learning that the adults have to place yet another mask on for survival. However, we praise the flight attendants for assisting to "save Humanity". It is not only foolish for the adults to learn they're not smart enough to learn for themselves – unless they are not of age. At what age do you feel a child would be able to learn how to grab onto the oxygen mask for themselves? Should we reconsider the terms of in-flight rules and restrictions when most 7-8 year-adult-olds could feasibly do this on their own? Without panic? What if a parent is drinking on board the flight, possibly drunk, or, taking yet another form of medication to relax and is unable to abide by grabbing hold of the oxygen mask… then what? Yes, it could or should be up for debate, but no one thinks about these factors. What has happened is that we don't hear about it; or, did the flight attendant take care of it… without outsiders knowing? How do you know? Is it because "they" don't talk about it? How can Humanity survive if not for what matters of the Heart need to make a difference. Should our Ego meet yet another external mask who will be blamed? What does this mean? It means that in this example the egoic self says, "I don't really care about whether someone falls flat on their face, as long as it's not me." A "doggie-dog-world" except for the fact that doggies don't know better… However, when our EGO gets involved to partner up with AI in ways that Humanity did NOT sign up for, there will definitely be a war of the secular kind. A secular war of like-minded robotic people who are cast all over the Universe to dangle the carrot of misrepresentation. Huge misrepresentation of not giving a damn! Who cares if our neighbor is drowning in a pool of his own demise... leave them to figure it out? Who cares if a life of living through giving becomes a life of unforgiving those who get in our way? Where's the justice in that? Who cares if there is no justice? Who cares if what The Jetsons set out as the future now is becoming our reality? For those who do not know of The Jetsons, look it up... who wrote that script and got millions of dollars to give us a heads up that we either forgot about, didn't see it coming and/or don't know, don't care. Either way, in any given situation, what kind of perception will AI have in determining the best course of action? The only real use for anything that deems to be artificial are placing "artificial limbs" on Humans who are in need. Isn't that the exact reason for having The Golden Rule? What madman decided that the Earth plane is in need of a less in-depth lifestyle in one's life? Given the nature of the beast... is this where Humanity is going? Are we going to allow heresy to guide the future generations? Are you ok with this or abiding by a false-idol that says is God ... "follow the path of NO RETURN?" Exhibit AI. Exhibit A, is the I in the Eye of the Storm...

Are we made for this... as Billie Eilish sings, "What was I Made For?" clearly asks what God intended for me. Her voice speaks subtly to those who are now questioning this very position in life. Her generation is waking up quickly to asking this question... if even written in song form. Baby boomers have waited far too long and the IAM Movement is vastly becoming known to many. Who else but children of all ages, no matter what your age, to bear to question your clear intentions of your place in Humanity. Many singers have sung about this subject matter but what sets Billie Eilish amongst the rest is her essence of feeling. Where there is shade there is a critical artist who will disagree; and, rightfully so because they may have been purporting another side of their Ego. Most people are set into categories where Humanity will or will not "feel" what artists are putting out to the world. Many have written beautiful lyrics of the question as to their existence yet how can one say that the other is hearing the same as the other? Perception. There will be those who will throw shade on Billie Eilish singing in unison with her spiritual side what has God intended her for – and there will those who will be judgmental. Exactly why Spirit has chosen to use this as a metaphoric example of what you are thinking at this very minute. Just think about it…. We are not a Humanity of powerful examples of who and what we've been made for. Do you know? Have you taken a minute to ask that question yourself? It is about how we Feel… and how in Heaven's name can AI distinguish between one from another? What will be a crucial part of Earth's evolution is this exact matter at hand… the reality of one's happiness in being able to feel at some point of our lives we too will want the purest part of our existence to become just that, Happy. Creating your own world by perceiving what you are made of, what feelings enable one to be happy, who makes us happy, why we are not happy first and why we 'think' we must seek happiness outside of ourselves not-enough-of to blame those who are unable to make us happy; all the while, suffering in silence.

WHAT IS… LOVE?

"We live in a cynical world" as Tom Cruise said in the movie, "Jerry McGuire." a man misunderstood for his rightful place in the world while being manipulated by a society of fools. "Fool's Gold," another movie written about a man who's interpreted as a player's fool for money while searching for love. "Love Actually" seeks those couples with a plethora of events that portray the best of love and marriage while over-enacting who's fooling who. "Eat, Pray, Love" the movie that makes us think about getting married for the wrong reasons and regrets that end up for the woman to seek a new identity of self that comes with taking a year-off to "find herself." What a concept? She meets like-minded people who are also fighting off their Egos; and, finally her true north shines bright as the one fits. All of these movies listed above have one thing in common, LOVE. What is being sought is seeking you... don't place Fear in this equation, as there is NO room for Ego in a place of our truth, in our Hearts of Love. At the "heart-of-the-matter" is where we are born... our umbilical cords are cut right at the center of our navel passage; and when we cross over, our nasal passage takes its last breath. What is Love? While it seems so easy to find, it has masks of Egoic toxicity of varied kinds... yet, Love breathes-in the fragrance of Love only when it IS LOVE. The one that you seek is the ONE that IS. To uncover true love is to unmask all the facets of one's essence in a million different suits that claim to be you. To uncover truest love is to seek your own domain – either "do you make an identity nobody" OR "do you make an identity no-body?" without a body we are no-thing on Earth. No-thing is the matter while energy is soul-2-soul. Without your Ego you could not learn that you are amongst all those masks as players in a play, actors in acts that play out however and with whomever... you decide. Do you decide to act accordingly or accordingly act out? Who are the puppet-masters? Who has shown you true acts of kindness? Without ever knowing "what is love" you will not ever know thyself. *Being "BE IN GOD"*

592

Whatever lends itself to the impossible is drawn up from the top-down on Mother Earth and given to ALL. We've been given the orders from those who have seen the light yet what was once the beginning is not the end. Those who comprehend a cyclical unit structure that has been placed upon the Universe is exactly how it has been written. No man seems to find their place in any other like-minded place other than their own rightful place. These are the ebbs and flows of God's creation to allow those who already know their place in the world to fortify their rightful place without exceeding any other. Man takes a stand and carries the torch within his Heart. It is the way of the Lord that man giveth His heart to places where there are safe-havens. A safe haven merely distinguishes the places where a human feels the safest when outside influences combat one's heart strings by turning to wrongful acts of desires. We cannot say enough about how deep those heart strings truly are but a place to rest your soul is your safe haven. Can one deem to interpret the gospel from the perspective of right/wrong that has yet to be presented. We've become so engrossed in what is right or wrong instead of just living, learning and creating places that allow a human being to feel everything. What is not required by law is to not receive one's duly justice for wrongful causes which is when karma steps in. Instead, parents of the children who are responsible for a child's welfare tend to distinguish pain as a subservient monologue whose role is to extract all feelings from the equation. Feelings get in the way, "don't cry" they say it will show your vulnerability!" Don't show your true feelings, it may attract the wrong kind of people. Instead become robotic as a reality of AI that will crash-and-burn in time – but, feelings do not. Feelings are a much-needed outlet for our mind, body and soul. Unless the body isn't able to extinguish its feelings from what the mind allows or not… the mindset of the Ego will compartmentalize one's truest feelings turning one's heart to stone. What good is a cold-stoned heart? Is it to be relatable to a mindset that witnesses those who can numb their true feelings will be better off left for dead?

Can one distinguish above and/or beyond what is seen as mind over matter? The 3-Dimensional Earth plane is created to carry places of dead weight while man creates their own grave by giving into the toxicity. The righteous man continues to become that which has yet to be desired while the others bleed out from their Faith of sins. What comes after is not to be taken lightly. It is for every man to find their own way toward the light that embodies the soul. *"Light of True Light,"* as it is written…so it shall BE. A light of Freedom shines when human beings attain Freedom to believe in themselves. Those who cannot come to the table with their own Insider Beliefs will parish; and those who have gone within their own dictatorship will ascend to a Higher Consciousness. Whenever ascension is attained a level of all the five senses and beyond become one's own Bible. This is to be duly noted for those who believe the written word being The St. James Version and/or any other Christian Bible – as we grow into our own Faith, we take on the written word of newly appointed disciples of the highest order; and, each person is a reflection of those who are portrayed in the St. James Bible. The characters have changed yet the newest version of your own written word and that within unwavering Faith becomes YOU as the one in ONE Holy name. This also applies to every soul who has been driven to greatness of their own Faith and by rightful allegiance to the ONE. Therefore, every man, woman and/or child who undergoes their own darkness into the light has in-deed conquered a Jesus resemblance once they too ascend unto their own Father, in Heaven. We've all been doing the work of Heaven on Earth even though it may not always seem like it… This IS the New

World Order of the Ascension of Humanity… No one on Earth might have never fathomed that this show is going down in the History books! To date, we are at an approximate half-way point of 'weeding out' those who have ill intentions on Earth; and, getting out from a place of nowhere. The place of nowhere is one of the highest order instilling citizens of our unified countries to absorb what is only healthy for their bodies and leave the rest. Those who are still giving their bodies a run for their money… paying exorbitant monies for external vices will be a thing of the past. We know that Mother Earth is very capable of growing weed, but those who have been tainting this organic weed is who begins feeling disassociated with their lives, becoming lethargic and/or feeling out of sorts. Those who smoke weed for pain are becoming less and less motivated to do anything for themselves. These are the people who have taken it upon themselves to destroy their God-given bodies and end up in a place of no return…down the rabbit hole of vices with possible inevitability to never return. These are the reasons why so many children on Earth are under medical care from doctors needing to prescribe drugs for mental health and physical well-being. We are here to raise the vibration of this planet to a New World Order and literally call-out those who have and are still using children to fornicate, inebriate and "use" the innocent for bait and switch. All children coming down from Heaven have been given the Grace of Heaven's gate through the silver cord of their core existence; and, the dis-ease in the body is driven by those who take the bait by switching gears to allow, accept and be under the spell of evil. The spell of evil is being driven by misuse of money, power, greed, sex, drugs and everything "out there" that children are being drawn to put aside their human nature and become robotic AI's. How can a society accept casting spells to innocent children by feeding them/us all a facade of poisons? Why, more importantly, could any child be cast aside by their families for taking the bait? What implodes one child to act out-of-character becomes a very real toxic release through manipulations leading to potential suicides, overdoses and innocent bystanders who keep their mouths shut. We, a God-gifted society of children, are going to stand up, speak out and share the mass destruction with our families, friends and/or everyone who we come into contact with! This is happening right now, live-streams on TikTok, IG and almost all of social media networks. Whose fault is this? Is it the parents who ingest the same nature of the Beast? Are we going to falter as responsible parents by NOT taking the time, the effort, to sit down to evaluate ourselves? Can you truly say that you take full responsibility for the way, reason and issues that stand before you and your children? Just think about how many physical lives could have been saved if not for a parent keeping a watchful eye on their kids instead of social media absorption and manipulation. If you've been attempting to become the "cool parent trap" instead, please heed the call as to why you've stepped out of your body to recreate a monster. Who are we if not adults? Who is adulting and who is being childlike, immature by casting aside disciplining of their children for a raging party of numerous toxins. Is your child adulting? Have they become the watchful eye on Mom and/or Dad (or, whomever is supposedly in charge...)? The DD (Designated Driver)? Why is it apparent that a few of our generations of children are on some form of meds? Ask yourself this and also ask yourself why are many of God's creations coming into form with dis-ease of bodily form, ADD, ADHD, autism etc.? Is this a DNA or genetic issue, or both? Do you want to shut-out the verbal insults that others say about why your child/children are an underachiever? Could the real underachievers be those that judge us? A lack of Love in society has been built off of blaming the last generations? Or, do you know why those children who are

596

underachievers are being cast aside and have been for so long without the parents taking a closer view on the issues at hand? Do the parents of our youth require love themselves as their inability to show love? Were your parents over/underachievers themselves? Is this why you are who you are today? Did your parents show you love the same way that their parents gave them love? Do you know? Where is the thread of love in your Heritage? Has the thread been a series of unpleasant events that denied you of being loved in ways that could not be justified? Humans were sent here to bring dysfunction to the family unit so that they could clear out the unnecessary karma from generations past, present and future. In-deeds we are given freewill to show up in life by learning from our past, learning from those who raised us and how they, in turn, were raised. By passing the torch of the greatest show on Earth, we must not falter under the guises of disgraceful appearances but by delving deep into the core emotional turmoil to uncover the truth. If your grandmother was judgmental and critical in nature, that could have easily been also passed down to your mother; yet the KEY to uncovering the thread is not only to understand it by observation and counsel, but to also KNOW that we all have freewill to change the narrative. You cannot continue to blame your family, ancestors included until you face yourself in the mirror by taking into consideration the threads and cutting the ties that bind. We are all one... not done! Unravel the escapades of your ancestors and their ancestors by what it is revealed as our triggers, anger, jealousy, insecurities, and all those emotions running through you that have caused you pain. You have a choice... live in fear of love or live in self-love by working on what makes you, you.

One cannot face what is feared unless it has been taught to fear... what, other than the fear of death are you fearing? The fear of God has been given to man by man ... It is a man-made ideology typecasting man in ways that are being cast aside. Who in their right mindset could equate fear of God in any way other than what was taught? By whom was it taught? By definition, the "fear-of-God" might mean something completely different to another. That "thread" is what's necessary to observe...witnessing the thread of past reenactments and other nuances that make for a pattern of recurring events. Those are what we call triggers playing out over and over again to "show you" how not to place blame by fearing; but by witnessing what has been shown in the past, to change. A life engulfs freedom... where there are no strings attached to fearful outcomes. Fear is illness...LOVE is wellness. Whenever fear arises it breeds pain through the mind, body and soul; versus a love of self being a purification of mind, body and soul. It IS that simple. Earth was discovered in disarray for many reasons – and, since the very beginning of time has cleansed itself over and over again; until the day of redemption for all children will be felt. The redeeming soul has been given a heart of gold treasured through the omnipresent feelings of LOVE. What God has created, no man shall tear apart... similar to the vows of sacred union. No one is privy to why God has intended for man/women to learn the mystery of the Universe, only to become human to experience a lifetime of events that will give us all Love so that we too can become the greatest show on this ever-changing Earth plane called, LOVE. As the song plays out, "Live and Let Die" by Paul McCartney, Wings who so eloquently write, "when we were young and your heart was an open book, you use to say live and let live... but, in this ever-changing world in which we live in makes you give in and cry, say, "Live and Let Die." These lyrics imply that we shall not perish but have an ever-lasting life. Only the body dies... so, Live and Let Live knowing only the body dies. Do your job well and give your brother a hand, in-deeds to show your love for your fellow man. "Live & Let Live" How do you feel it, see it, breathe it, understand it…

Our Earth is coming close to understanding different cultures and races by not allowing what has been taught to override the goodness we see in others. What impaired our vision is becoming crucial to upholding a new outlook of growth in Humanity, growth in ourselves. What made us dazed and confused is the obstruction of justice in our own selves, our own vision and belief systems that we now are cutting out of our lives in order to be led to our ascension of higher consciousness. Human society has always been ever-changing in this world yet the massive upscaling is taking place in the here and now. At the present moment, people from all walks of life are researching, talking amongst themselves and family members about what is their rightful place of existence on the Earth… why they have been mesmerized into thinking they're not incapable of Love, incapable of thinking for themselves and incapable of healing their body through the natural order of Mother Earth. We, who are privy to gaining inner knowledge and truth, are leading the way for others to see…they are setting the examples. No longer have the rightful place of acceptance be that of higher ups who want to dumb us down to AI's that have no feelings. Feelings, our innate emotions are what makes us an intricate piece of human rights in taking justice into our own hands by NOT allowing others to coerce our dutiful place in this world. Thwarted into space by means of endearment is what has happened on Earth… an expression of love for human nature. There are some who seem to think they have not been given this life as a gift. What comes is what goes in/out of life and the essential need for sustenance is love, as yourself. We cannot express how this life is so very precious…until the physical life has perished, then, we surrender. And, for some there is no surrender against the forces of natural order which cause many to try to control the narrative. Instead of controlling the narrative, why not embrace life by that which it gives, in gratitude. Whenever you feel that you have a sense of calm resolve that is the Horizon of where Heaven meets Earth. This is what is called the natural order of planet Earth, Mother Earth's compassion for itself. Leave what no longer serves and embrace the service to a New World Order that only asks of you to love all, forgive all and embrace itself in all its reflection. To do this… creation will become unencumbered by fearing itself …and equally become loving itself as IS.

REGRETS…

No regrets? Or, regrets?

Where did the concept of regret begin? It all started back in the evolution of man where humans sacrificed for their families… with great regret not to have sacrificed doing things for themselves. Are we going to continue sacrificing for others or ourselves? Jesus sacrificed Himself for Humanity's sake which is much different why humans feel they need to sacrifice. It is the willful intention that causes anyone to sacrifice. Sometimes, sacrifices tend to be an extension of great love for another even when it is hidden with regrets, remorse, resentment etc. What good is sacrifice when your heart's not in it? Why sacrifice anything in life? Become your own happy moments…and live for yourself knowing that a sacrifice doesn't help others, it stumps their growth. These are the moments that we'll take with us for the duration of our lives. It's the love we gave, shared, received, became. No hidden motives or agendas… a clean slate of pure love for self and others. Have we experienced this or is the conceptual idea of sacrifice foreign to you? We live to experience life on the basis of what small sacrifices we do for others that, unknowingly, help ourselves. Find your inner sanctity to allow space for your heart to soar. When was the last time your heart soared? Has it ever? Is going with the flow of life enough? Or, does your life need chaos instead of magic? Will you seek to grasp the magic of every moment or has life been drudgery day-in-and-day-out? As the saying goes, "look at the bright side of life..." Do you? The circle of life's clock is ticking away...how many lifetimes do you feel this drudgery has been going on for? Beginning with your first kiss, look back only to find that first burst of magic. Then, try to replicate that magical feeling in other ways, creatively, lovingly, authentically. Sooner rather than later. "I've got a feeling..." sang Black-Eyed Peas will resonate with all of Humanity. An upcoming event we're looking forward to albeit; a wedding, a trip, an engagement, a good day, a new connection, a child's eyes, a dog's tail wagging, a new job, a sunrise and/or sunset, the ocean waves...absolutely anything which gives us that 'feeling!" The list goes on...if you plan ahead or plan your day why not envelop that feeling? Somewhere in your day, why not seek to find magic, even in the littlest of things; or to reinvent a new avenue of fun that jumps out to surprise you. There are many ways to add a spark of joy...it's all about gratitude. When's the last time you were grateful? Is it an everyday mantra, or, only on Thanksgiving? Aren't we living another day in gratitude, a blessing?

A LEGACY OF REGRET

Developing your skill set in whatever field of business you find your legacy is in your true purpose of being the guiding light. We're all stars that shine, so shine bright for the world to see. Releasing what no longer serves helps the evolution of our soul and depicts what our true natural course of order happens for our highest good. We've all got our crosses to bear and yet we must make sacrifices that seem to bring in a new level of unity as we draw the line of acceptance. When we end up "settling" we are saying to God that we don't fully believe we deserve better – and not that others are bad, it is that they're not on the same vibrational frequency as we are. Everyone is on a different *playing field of consciousness* and there are those who haven't even begun their journey, who are lost and still being manipulated by their Ego and those of others. Manipulation sends out feelers that say; powerless, unseen and/or unheard. Fear of being seen, however, stems from a time when being seen became too painful. Fear of being seen is a shame response – carrying the burden of shame we hide, we disappear, we avoid anything where we'd be perceived by others. To release from these chains-of-feelers many attempts to control the emotional terrain. There is power and self-respect owning your emotional state that says, no more manipulation! When we rely on our own judgment and not that of others, we take back control, becoming empowered to live the life we know we deserve. Such are those who've contained themselves, held back when they knew that 'going for it' might have given them true happiness and are attempting to rectify their reasoning for not being true to themselves. We find so many humans leaving the planet unhappy, unfulfilled, regretful, negligent of the decisions they made or didn't make. There are consequences for every decision that we make or decide not to. There are repercussions of the highest order when we say or think, "I *should have* done…said…etc." We must live with our choices and that bodes well for those who we've loved and lost. For whatever reason …be it timing, finances, maturity or whatever else is in hidden sight it is all revealed at the time we depart from our physical bodies. It's a truth-telling moment of all the events encapsulated into the feelings of, LOVE – given, received, felt, lost, or ended. A series of regretful moments where we chose to go left instead of right. We seek these moments in our day-to-day yet our Ego sometimes gets in the way. Whichever path you've chosen, know that it was the intention of your destiny. Either way, what is a life of regret when we're gone? Who will find it in their heart to heal when all is said and done? Will you give it all up for that ultimate nirvana? Or, did you just give up on life?

FORGIVENESS

When we are in a state of forgiveness, we are able to claim another higher consciousness which cannot be reinstated as anything else except what we find to be our truest self. It is not an easy feat to ascend to a higher awareness until the forgiveness has been received within and/or without. True gratefulness will take you into a state of peaceful silence that allows for those to reach out in ways that are newfound. Those people, places and/or things that extend beyond your expectations without expectations are true to their own soul's gratitude. This is the only way which humans can co-exist in light of their own gratefulness of being. A soul's journey cannot be tainted with the nonsense of Earth – insofar as what once looked good has now changed as your guiding light. A guiding light that changes and is loved no matter what is the truest soul who has attained a new level of understanding that grace has sought. Just think of all those who have yet to be forgiven throughout one's lifetime – a forgiveness of self, indeed. To forgive ourselves is to accept the errs of those crosses we've had to bear and yet we tend to encounter over and over again. What cannot be seen will show you what needs to yet be overcome, understood and sought after to obtain our peace of mind. We can either choose to give "us" another chance or treat ourselves with inner anger, frustration, disappointment and expectations that are not any others' reason to point the finger. Do what you love, live how you want, be yourself and when you "know thyself" a feeling of gratitude for everyone will surface. You will become a new person that will reintroduce you to yourself. If that is hard to understand just know that your path will be seen when the time is ready… not a moment sooner or later. How can we seek to understand that our path has been already relieved for an eternity – it is only a memory to remember. We tend to experience "deja vu" at times of trouble as it shows itself only to help us remember… The part you play in your playground-of-life will exist as you observe by witnessing what you have already gone through, who you've gone through what with and why. It may confuse you at this very moment as every human will settle into either a new self or continue to journey their path as the inevitable unfolds. This begins as you witness your soul unraveling right in front of your eyes only to become a wise human with a variety of changed behaviors, ideologies and thoughts.

What remains is how much more love one feels inside and out – who cannot forgive will turn cold to their own path blaming others. Remember this. It is no one's fault for your unhappiness, for your negativity and/or the people, places or things that have hardened your heart. We've played the "blame game" far too long until we lost ourselves in the shuffle by becoming hardened to life. All those who blame others, shout in anger, fit of gestures uncovering hidden anger, jealousy, insecurity, greed, misuse of their power all turmoil of inner poison remains. They are triggered instead of moved; they are angry instead of peaceful; they host a series of toxins, (i.e., smoking, drinking, shopping), when overdone as an escapism, an outlet for what reflects their inner unhappiness and turns it into a host of treacherous events. One fire to put out after another fire erupts and an exorbitant flow of hot lava bursts into the physical body as dis-eases. Some of those dis-eases will either take on new forms of another pain or will spread throughout one's body as other mindlessness such as; depression, negativity, loss, mental anguish, sadness etc., any other form of grieving. Sadness is deeply rooted in the ground and wants to find a sense of happiness… Experiences of grief are given to man as a way to get dirty, in sorrow, by envisioning it as the Heavens tear-up watering the ground of grief; in order to release, crying cleanses us to feel better. It's an overwhelming process of releasing that tends to be seen as a bad thing – yet those are old beliefs that need to also be released in order to feel. A world of sadness with no outlet breeds a non-emotional unfeeling society that has been taught not to feel, not to cry, not to sense, not to be human. This is the real culprit in a life unlived, in the unresolved pains of our past, in the inability to release and forgive. All forms of grief revolve around unsettled emotions that have not been resolved. Grief cannot spread unless it is not brought to the surface to be experienced by a full-term grief period. How else can we find peace-of-mind, body and soul if not aware of how deep the pain is. Suffering in misery without a space for forgiveness to experience needs to be found. Only we can save ourselves in this life. There are other external actors, players that will assist in HELPing to show you your reflection; but, it's up to you to SEE. What is unseen will show up at some point in life to choose what matters … instead of becoming invisible to what you're seeing, live your truth and walk your own path. Your heart will begin to soften with every surrender, with every walk in forgiveness, finding yourself is first. In order to be true to yourself we must stand up for our beliefs even if it hurts another; to be true to yourself we must walk our own path of truth; to

605

be true to yourself may feel like a struggle or hitting a brick wall… but, in reaching our essence truth must prevail. No matter what, where, who attempts to instill their beliefs upon you! Being strong will surface in time and your voice will be heard… no reason to shout, yell or control to seek change in another – it is about letting them be. Yelling and a quick temper is the language of Fear; being afraid causes many to hide. Insecurity and being out-of-control set the stage that it's ok to intimidate, screaming and lashing out. The more fear and threatened response, the more in the 'lizard' mode of survival brain. The more confident and secure, the more rational for seeking healthy solutions. Filling yourself with light, peace and stillness will overcome the rest. Restlessness has been invoked in those who use toxins to escape themselves, to escape what they cannot see in themselves, to escape the awareness to live a fulfilled life. At the end of our physical life and on to what remains; a purgatory of unsettled remains, unsettled resentments, unsettling feelings of those things and people who tried to help, to those who regret and find themselves saying their life was too short – a series of reasons why… they have been settling in their life will become very clear. Once this vision of truth is seen, what becomes very clear is how many people have not been able to forgive, including themselves. All forms of pain are ever-changing into different forms within the physical body and the mind. It becomes a chain-of-unresolved issues and inner grievances… contradictory to what we may believe, all of these grievances tell the individual story of inner pain and past unresolved hurts. What becomes of one's pain that begins to heal is a good cry, a sadness turns into a better realization of another's differences and the heart slowly accepts that these differences of another's pain becomes more tolerable. Slowly, we are able to see that what has been felt in others' pain is the actual pain that we too experienced at one time of our lives – how we feel in the present

606

moment reveals how we have become aware of this acceptance. To reiterate... a man who is grieving the loss of his job and is scarred by his pain becomes our witness to a time where we too have grieved a loss in the workplace. How did you feel? Did that man's grief make you mad, sad, lost, out-of-sorts? Or have you healed from losing a job knowing with acceptance that another even-better job would show up. This is a minor example as to how the reflections of others transpire into our lives to ensure that no amount of karmic insurance is due.

Remember this... it is important to change your perception by keeping your ego out of the situation; and, feel your way to a tolerable, if not more compassionate acceptance, of what is truly staring you in the face. All chaos breeds chaos even if the one you witness in others is witnessed, shared and experienced with different variables. We begin changing our perspective once we realize that this is an actual indication of either what we are still needing to heal from, or, have healed. This peace of mind becomes our ability to know we've actually healed...or, not. If we have not yet healed, we, in turn, become emotionally unavailable to set the tone of compassion for another's pain; and instead, feelings of unease/dis-ease within and/or without happens... It may take some time to fully understand your feelings as we explore the navigational system of our body. The more *"in tune"* you are with your body and what it's feeling, the closer you are to your own realization of work that is required. Without vs. within tends to show up when least expected – as what you envision on the external is a result of what is dormant on the inside. Inside out... What has come to pass will not see the light of a new day until you learn how to see clearly what is staring at your back. What seems to be so easy to do is actually very difficult. This is usually the case in life... What is looking right at you is the exact thing that needs the emphasis of your attention. We live in a Universal hologram of desires so that we can stand firmly upon this Earth knowing that externals are our reality check. All humans are privy to their own reality checks in order to envision a much better future. However, when this vision emphasizes not having enough, always wanting more, more, more…that is an internal lack. What are the signs of external wealth, desire, misuse of power and other powers of temptation that still are difficult to overcome? Who are your influencers? Are your influencers influencing you – to do what? Bad indulgences breed the same; in fact, these are the reasons why they say, "Misery loves company…" Since the beginning of time it has been witnessed over and over again how mankind/society has indulged the weak-at-heart which basically means, "weak is the heart that caves into temptation." Temptation is not the root of all evil – what is at the root is an unrooted base of belief which has not believed in itself… making itself seen as the perpetrator. What then is the difference between the temptation of the body and the temptation of the heart? Is it what the mind "thinks" it wants vs. knowing the heart has your best interest? Which hand gives out love? The right hand. Which hand receives it? The left hand. When we place our right hand with the left hand… *in God we trust, prayer*. Should one hand not wash/watch the other there is an imbalance of give and take – of what is natural to what is unnatural – to how we think we know how to give love and how to receive love on what is known as justice will be served. Injustice for all is when the right hand is not believing in the left hand… It is to have and to hold… till death do we part. Instead of doing the same old same old, we have got to understand how this regime can either harm the self or act as a gamechanger to those who are already seeing how simple life has been designed in the Universe. It's multiplication, which was the only lesson in this life on the school plane that matters. The 3,6,9 series of Cause and Effect in

Tesla's mathematical equation of the Universe multiplies in light of what the Law of Attraction does. By multiplying 3x3 which equates to 9... an example that stirs the Law of Attraction that you focus upon grows. It's that simple. To say 3,6,9 involves the Trinity and so on... of the ALL in the Spiritual realm of "As above, so below" which constitutes Heaven on Earth. If our educational system were to devise "Life Lessons" of "As Above, So Below" – the actual Laws of the Universe = this world would be more enlightened to how our internal and external workings work. Such is the simplicity of a life on this planet – what people don't understand is how simple it is. What goes without saying is the way in which society stifles humans into thinking the more complicated, convoluted and confused the better... who hasn't thought that life cannot be just simple? If so, why then is there suffering that breaks people apart, instead of what it was built for, a simplicity that belongs to those who appreciate why it was constructed simply... A simple life hosts its own confusion so why not take either route to a simple life – because it wasn't designed to do so. Once life begins it is all about wants, needs, desires; and, then the settling down, purging, letting go happens during some point in the middle of one's life only to realize how inconsequential some things that have been acquired are. Don't get me wrong here... acquiring for pleasure cannot be anything else but – but, when it is an acquiring of one's egoic negativity that breaks the bank, misusing power is what it means. Once we learn a certain adjective, called, "balance" then it is essential to note we have a clear understanding without perpetrating the egoic self as well as others egos. What has been done is already done and for those reasons we should try not to look back on the past errs of our actions. What might HELP is that whatever multiples in your life, those things bring you content, joy, peace and great moments of self-realization, it is all worth it. Someone coined the phrase, "you can't take it with you when you die" so might as well enjoy it ALL – so LIVE! Live in every space, crevasse, indoor/outdoor, utilize every piece of furniture, sing in your shower, play with all your toys, read as much as possible, listen to podcasts to learn, bring the word FUN back into every aspect of your life… as it may be our last. What people hang onto…. whatever is not used is a waste; whatever is not said is lost; wherever you go, decide; whomever you love, cherish; whichever place you land, find the goodness; ingest healthy food; drink wisely, pretend that today might just be your last. Can you honestly do these things and so many more that would make every day, "Christmas/Hanukkah" and/or "Chinese New Year" or whatever present you give to yourself. There is so much hatred, complaining, anger, hostility, unsettling emotions humans just can't let go of; and even reading this might find you sulking at your own mess… or playing the blame game. We cannot live the simple life until we, as humans, siege every moment. When was the last time you swung on a swing? When was the last time you observed the simplicity of birds in their natural habitat? When was the last time you felt so happy with joy and contentment that at that very moment, you needed and wanted for no-thing? When's the last time you embraced your loved ones a few extra minutes more? When was the last time your heart felt full of Love? Take a few moments out of your day to express your appreciation for someone's kindness; take an extra breath to sigh relief that you've been given another day on this Earth. Create a safe haven for those things that you would miss if they left your Life right at this very minute. Presence of Life is written in the veins of our bodies as the blood runs through every vessel we seek to know that the body has its own computer system. Every breath that we take… is not something humans even think about. The only time we are concerned is when, if, and who has dis-ease – then humans take notice; and, some are not

610

capable of doing so. Instilling a daily practice in your life of Gratitude for all, from ALL, in all. Soak in Life, Breath it inside with gratitude and Breath it out with gratitude. Find out what makes you happy… a sunrise, a healthy meal, the sound of the ocean, the breeze of life's breath, a song, the smells of yesterday, a handshake, a smile, a complement, a sincere friend, a trusted advisor, a confidante, family, non-family ties, a baby's eyes, a dog's tail, a tale of two soul counterparts, a love affair, a wedding, a look back to remember, boundaries, flowers bloom, wings of angels, grass roots, tree's wisdom, star-gazing, moonlight night, a warm bath, floating, ocean waves, warm sandy beaches, travel, tinted shades, road trips, blue skies, rainbows that gleam another, candle-light, home cooking, endless love, talks that last all night, snuggling, a musical piece, languages, firepits, RV trips, a toast, a mood, a ring, hands that co-create, serving others, laughter, crying, a thought, a miracle, eyes of the soul, wrinkles that are wise, grays to love by, questions of "why?" being shy, stranded, leaves falling, seasons change, lightning strikes, rumblings of earthquakes, tornado warns, warmth of Sun, reflections of Moon, traditions, change of heart, change of mind, shades of emotions, dire straits, dealbreakers, winning and losing, freedom, land, wishing wells, summer nights, a shadow, the night sky, palm trees, hammocks, vows, warm blankets, flowing hair, a lottery ticket, pocket money, investments, a portfolio, experience, listening, depths of discussion, debates, artist appreciations, favorite color, sporting events, rocks, time travel, destinations, your "go to" fav, Gregorian chanting, hymns, church, synagogue, imagination, baked goods, leftovers, a room with a view, a concert, a concerto, fur on an animal, the reflection in the window, first-morning coffee, a cold one, ice cream, milkshakes/malts, holidays, unwrapping gifts, moving, serving, giving to charity, sharing stories, learning to drive, first kiss, pregnancy, holiday lights, advice, commitment, a secret, whispers, silence.

In the eyes of our Beloved, many actions must be attended to in order for Humanity to grow… not only for the self, for the collective. If we were to utilize every obstacle as the settling of dirt to build upon our foundation we would set the groundwork for new experiences. The obstacles are intended to be there in order to set a new foundation by swiping off the old debris. Old debris comes in the form of egoic tendencies that humans hold onto for so very long, even lifetimes, a repetitive nature happens to show up and learn. It is definitely an arduous life on the Earth plane – not because the sacrifice is too great but because there is no notice of responsibility. Once we can admit our mistakes by becoming aware of why, at the core level, things have turned out this way or that way; it is in that muddled place of being lost. The egoic ID (identity) whose identification is brought to the forefront comes with certain choices and consequences to live by. We inhabit this Earth solely on the basis of our energetic force of Nature that can either be construed as a work-in-progress or a misuse of power. As with freewill, our choices construct our progress, or not; and, the ability to take notice requires a letting go "allowing" Mother Earth to exhibit how the Natural Order of how our Divine Universe brings us to the same place. When humans attempt to control the terrain, it is just a cause-for-pause (faux-pas), in order to get set by letting go. What we find, instead, is a massive traffic jam that has caused hearts to be broken, feelings to be lost, all because the foundation was built on falsity of … whatever love or unchained melody has been uncovered. We claim to love unconditionally too many loves, families, friends etc…. that claims go down the rabbit-hole. The turbulence that comes from needing to learn how you feel

612

remains to be seen by those who are on the receiving end. We "know" that "actions speak louder than words..." and that when turbulent waters rise to the surface there is an immediate reaction to the consequence of that action. Silenced by deeper issues of not accepting a harsh reality within oneself. Facing our own demons is what the shadow does best – it follows us everywhere we go; it knows us inside and out and tends to emit Fear of God into us so that our seeds cannot grow. Whenever we are not accountable for our actions, ignoring them and not holding yourself accountable, the shadow thinks it has won. In actuality, the shadow, while laughing behind your back, is using every effort of fear to enhance itself. All the while those on the receiving end are attempting to figure out what the egoic shadow of selves in another has bolstered the premises. We cannot sustain any type of relationship that is based on another's ego/shadow selves instead of trying to talk it out. The egoic behavior of others must get very grounded, deep and dirty enough to withstand the constructs of misogyny, narcissism, a disruption of greediness and every level of pain found at the core. Hence, the shadow. Embedded into the core is where one will go to find out where all the pains of our past are dormant. Not allowing people into your space for fear of the unknown, is not a crime – yet, to choose NOT to hone in on the pain is a crime of great passion. The passion for oneself to grow is required by taking into accountability our past trials and tribulations. To forego these by default is to say that you do not matter. What's the sense/cents of it all... why try to figure you out – while all along blowups are happening in every facet of one's life who is not searching. The rest of Humanity holds a place on Earth to aspire to the honesty of what core issues are to be tested and those that are not. We live in a world of deceit and manipulation that was placed upon Humanity and a place of another lie those seeps into the lives of the unaware. Those who have been unaware cannot fathom the

613

deceit that has been placed upon them. We find this abyss truly the best place to start, the void. In the rabbit hole of the void... we dig deeper than ever to realize how unscrupulous people tend to be. Pointing the finger at others is another form of not wanting to see themselves for who they truly are. We can't pretend anymore... we must take a silent vow of raw truth for ourselves... not, for others' pleasures or misconceptions of their strategies. Our weakest link is the one we are unable to see... that unforeseen link of what holds the thread in our lives cannot be broken, until it is. What figures is the notion that we come from a sacred place only to find that that place is only within the truth of our hearts. No one can make-or-break the silence if the energy has been depleted... and, this has been done. The cords get severed for good because one or both cannot sustain their truth. No discussions needed since we've been constructed to speak our peace with or without the other selves.

It is a by-product of what is yet to come and not that it will become the same thing it was... out with the old and in with the new causes us to review what is broken. The breaking of karmic ties is where we find out where we truly matter – in the light of God. No other issues can be addressed, under these circumstances, because the attitudes are a painful realization that a lie to cover up another lie will be the arrest going forward. Hence, this is where we sever ties... no man can sustain a true relationship with another until he has first faced his own truth. Leaving behind the pain becomes the place where we are unable to speak, feel, listen and be true to ourselves. We continue to placate another's behavior just by putting up with what was not our truth to begin with. That being said, we fall into the hopes and dreams of another's heart bearing access to none other than ourselves. "What goes up must come d0wn" is what has been said over these last few decades; but, while it seems to be said, the reflection of that statement incurs much. "As above, so below" and "what happens on the Earth reflects Heavenly efforts to overcome" and "any karma that needs to be dealt with will BE". Lastly, the numerical, 8 sideways, depicts the Infinity sign that deems itself. All these sayings over the years have been attempting to get our undivided attention. We pretend that all these sayings are 'out there' we listen but do not hear; or it doesn't apply; or, we're not aware yet… or, we listen yet don't receive. All sayings are bound to hit home whenever they are ready to be. No need to force anything…life just happens as we receive what is best for our highest good. Not everyone can understand what is even being said at this very moment, and it doesn't resonate…. yet. The offerings of our Heavenly family deem to be of importance when we can feel it in our hearts and souls that God has a message, that God has a plan for every one of us. Don't ignore the signs, sayings and messages from Spirit… they come to us daily, in all ways. Insofar as the overall vibe of our planet, humans are awakening every day to anew, finding more patience, understanding, not waiting for any other to make decisions for them by taking charge and empowering themselves. This is why every one of us is needed to change the vibration of the planet. Otherwise, you're not aligned and haven't got a clue… Or, if you do, you continue to question your position. No doubt we are all in a different place – that's when you know. What happens, in most cases, is that the one who has become enlightened is where the light generates itself; and, there are those who are magnetically drawn. Where there is dark there will always be a glimmer of hope, joy, peace and abundance of what one is seeking when going toward the light. That's where "the light of a new day" originated from… but humans aren't aware that this light is sacred. Even instances when we say, "Alexa, turn on the lights" this bears no implication to the actual meaning of knowing that turning on lights has a sacredness about it. God said, "Let there be light!" and, so it is. However you choose to follow your path of freewill there is the final choice, a fated one, indeed. Being more mindful "mindfulness" is an art… bringing into the essence of one's life. We tend to speak with no rhyme or reason to the Universe not being more aware of how we use our words and how we create our way forward. It is within every frequency of the tone in how we speak, the words carry the spell to Heaven and the vibration of its essence of truth. If we speak out about something or the other it is within the entire sequence of what is behind the words which are spoken being the words, the frequency of intention that harbors the act of becoming. Once we perceive how the process works perhaps more people will set the tone and choose the casting of words more carefully. We were given Spelling in our school system, weren't we? For if that wasn't enough… We learned how to spell yet teaching in the educational system, missed a crucial development of what we are learning as, "The Art of Spells" that emit out unto the Universe, BEcome. We were taught Math, Science and English etc., but "they" didn't teach us about the Tesla effects of 3,6,9 nor that Quantum Physics was inspired and derived from the Wisdom of the Spiritual world that we live in. What more can be said that the external world of the 3 Dimensional left out the crucial ingredients to become Spirit on our journey here… instead we were taught the lowest vibration is how to… manipulate power; accumulate "stuff" until that stuff becomes junk, sold on OfferUp, eBay and the likeness of such a material world. Madonna's lyrics, "Living in a Material World" apparently were not taken to Heart. Why would we be living in a world where all we came here to do is work hard by setting the tone of accumulating designer/non-designer goods only to sell them after a decade or so. What mindfulness does that bring to the actual journey of Love in our lives? Do we also cry when we cannot purchase a product? Or, is it only a tearful journey when we lose a loved one… or both? We have all been unscrupulous with regard to our buying tactics at one time or another yet what divides to conquer those toxic addictions, are those who have the funds and those who do not. Those who do have the cash flow and shop learn sooner than later that money comes and money goes – to be fruitful is a two-way street that applies with the Law of Receptivity. The Law of Receptivity expands one's own ability to be in the "know" about how we must 'shop not until we drop', but instead shop energetically so that the vibrational frequency of material wealth picks up the matching vibration – hence, gracing those who are NOT greedy but exude more wealth. The ebb-and-flow of material wealth is given to all who will not misuse their power by being greedy, or, frugal with others. No matter what happens… those who are graced with abundant wealth in their karmic tidying's have given gracefully to others. We all find greed at some point of our existence in the 3-Dimensional world but a shift happens to those who have eternal Faith of not worrying what they cannot control. What was once a bright idea about spending takes on a new flavor of giving and receiving – as in "for better or for worse." All "intentions" must hold the thread of eternal Faith … no matter what. What causes some to understand this and others don't is a "matter of believing" in the Laws of the Universe. We pretend to know what they are… yet do not believe in them with enough leverage, to help others when they are desperately in need. To give freely is one of the most compassionate acts that holds a lot of weight in the material world and also in the spirit realm. If we continue to show up by not only giving of our wealth to HELP, or, assisting to lend an ear to someone who needs to talk; to be there for someone who is ill, or has lost their job and so many other variables that occur that drive humans mad. Depression, sadness, grief and too many other emotional effects

617

of energy depletion from external sources happen; and, while that is going on where is your energetic force of nature telling you? Ask yourself, "When was the last time you reached out to assist someone in need?" be honest. It doesn't happen very much because nowadays people are so worried about giving HELP for Fear that they will be used, abused and taken for granted. Others completely ignore those who may need a HELPing hand… and, the most devastating is when for no rhyme or reason, a child takes its own life; a mother loses her baby, a friend has given up, a turn of events happens to those who did not heed the call from Spirit. How do we know? That is Eternal Faith.

No matter who comes and who goes… it's not as important as their journey in our time to clear the slate of karmic debt. Every soul will recycle until this has been attained – however long and how many lifetimes this takes, karmic debt must be slated. Forgiveness is the last payment due for all those who lost out, who gave up, who regretfully left or resentfully stayed; to those who are no longer on the Earth plane etc. dues paid. Whether or not you're in contact with people that we must forgive or not, it is a feeling that we've prayed for Forgiveness. To give it, to receive it…however it shows up does not require a one-on-one reunion…only through The Forgiveness Prayer. Conquer what you Fear most through forgiveness and learning what you were here to learn. Although the Ego does not like pleas of Forgiveness – it is exactly why when we are finally able to Forgive, it is through one's heart. There is no one bound by their ego that can find it in their heart to Forgive. Letting go of your inner pain…anger, resentment, rage, hate, jealousy, antagonistic feelings and whatever your ego wants you to hold onto will stump your evolution…remember this. Just because you feel as if you've Forgiveness doesn't mean that it holds that energy while you've done the work. We need to ensure that those being

Forgiven, including yourself, are what your heart is feeling. If a person still triggers a feeling…any kind of feeling, then, forgiveness has not yet cleared through your heart. The distinct feeling of forgiveness is; emotional peace, vulnerability and contentment by sending Love & Light through an uprise of compassion. Instead of worrying about what others are feeling, focus on getting yourselves back to a place of Love. Compassion is the LOVE that comes from above… Once this is felt for all of mankind, you will have ascended.

A long list of forgiveness comes without saying to all those who have built a wall up … and needless to say, have become the actual wall. Without forgiveness we cannot create a world without separation. Instead, the world will continue to create a conquer and divide mentality. The only place for us to escape ourselves is within…not, without. A place external to ourselves is where the actual divide separates mankind; and, the inner workings of where external deeds meet internal needs… poise no divide. In time, humans will come to understand that once you have been on the other end of the spectrum graced through forgiveness, you will then begin to understand why your right-to-forgiveness is essential. We have this long list of issues that have demanded answers but this is the exact reason why we fall into uncomfortable points of contention. This world is not built upon contentions of ill-will but a clear vision of why this happens. The mirror reflection of triggers, hate, anger, injustices, resentment, illness, dis-ease of mind and body. We can no longer expect retribution based on whatever is ailing you from the inside out. Clearly this has been a long line of experiences throughout our lives that have shown no mercy. Not being able to show mercy through the graceful art of forgiveness will not fare well to those who cannot. It is within a clear understanding that we share with you a secret mystery of the Universal language instilled in loving all of Humanity…that is, Forgiveness. The origin "to forgive, to love one another" is written in ancient history of all which has been done. Loving one another as thyself is not to be taken at face value – moreover, it is to be seen, felt, heard, expressed and lived out as a full life experience. "To thine own self be true…" comes into play when humans cannot come to terms with their own insecurities, inefficiencies and instability of what is being shown. We need to come to terms with 'in-justice for all' yet not for what injustices have been done to all. As an observer of the written word, we claim to take into account those who have been wrongly accused, but, then when the time comes to right a wrong, we are shamelessly indicative of rightful accusations. How does this make any sense to those who are the observers of a wrongful action trying to right itself? Can someone be held accountable until found guilty of the crimes committed? Or, can one be unaccounted for as guilty of crimes committed? Where is the justice in those found wrongfully committed while others get a free-pass? How can Earth allow these acts to be fair and just? While you ponder these questions, remember that it is all in your perception of what has been taught to you… or, has it? Are you experiencing levels of injustices in your own life? Who is coming to your rescue? Can you rescue yourself? In the midst of all the havoc, who has your back believing in you? There are Governors, Mayors and Heads of States where the accused of crimes committed are people who need to step down from their egos to instill justice; and there are those convicted murderers who are doing or have done time wrongfully. Who believes in a Justice system that has been duly noted of crimes of passion, murderers and/or any other alleged claims were taken into account? How can we sift through legal crimes, injustices while those who are witnessing these acts stand back to take a bow? Are these acts for us to witness and/or filter away as injustices within the Justice system? We know…. don't we? No need for us to delve deeper into the unfair nature of what was once the innocent bystander posing as such. We must claim our own beliefs, claim our rightful place in this world, claim an undaunting wavering of what has always been intended to show Humanity injustices for all. Even if there has been an alarming semblance of injustice in your lives, claim the right of power to seek forgiveness. If not, forgiveness will seek your claim-to-fame by perishing the inability to forgive others as you see yourself. "What "lies" before you is NO longer what "lies" within you as the nature of the beast continues to feed upon children. Being fed lies all of our **lives** have one-letter distinction… The letter **"v"** changes the scope of the narrative. **"V"** could imply a huge *Victory* for Humanity; or, breeds a lifelong poisonous *Venom*. It is your freewill to choose either a life of Victory or a poisonous life of Venom that has seeped through one's veins far too long. The injustice of lies that society has deemed to be their truth serum is now being exposed as a serious whiplash to those who have seen the light of a new day. Acts that have remained on Earth will be distinguished as such and under no law of penalty or perjury will be able to get very clear unless we resolve to take a new stand in our rightful justice of heart that matters… at the "heart" of the matter, justice prevails. There is no other way. Be mindful where, when and what your ego looks, sounds and feels like – this will be your clue to Q-in your own Truth. Truth feels, looks, sounds and IS a place of calm… not a calamity of events. Remember who you are, where and why you have forged to fall from a graceful state only to be forgiven and returned unscathed and graced with wings to fly. Are you 'not' cut from the same cloth as God's Love? Do you feel deserving of the Holy Grail in a Love so undeniably unwavering that no words could…nor capture its essence. Humanity must remember, recall and renew their commitment to Love… a sacred love, indeed. We're not here to unearth what is upon Earth for we are here to recapture the essence of what makes Earth its own masterpiece... An enchanting song of notes on the trees, blue as the skies in Heaven's sent, planetary alignments in tone, vibe and scent. Stars that shine brighter when seen as is, notes on the scales forging truth in the veins of leaves and a wind stronger in the strength in one's FAITH. Whoever blasphemies their art of beliefs will endure a tornado so powerful that not even crimes of passion can undo those scattered away, dust in the wind. Long ago and far away will the dust of evil NOT cleanse itself as a speck to procreate, but, as one's time on the Earth plane eternally dismissed. "For God so Loves the World..." to instill new ground rules for all humans that have vitally destroyed His children upon the Earth. There are many specks of dust that were created in order to be eternally dismissed for humans to realize how valued Love is... Some will ask what purpose does their unspoken evil-acts hold upon a purposeful life of goodness in order to change the narrative for Mother Earth's ascension? It has everything to do with change, as Humanity forges ahead humans are now privy to what has long been hidden 'behind the curtain' of darkness; and now into a new day of light. This changes everything and everything changes in Light of those who gave us their best show on Earth. Who's to say that was or is their greatest work not the main event? What IS the main event is that Mother Earth's time to change, evolve and create a new world for us ALL is NOW. All of Humanity has decided to join in witnessing Creation create a New World Order... *ALL FOR ONE, ONE FOR ALL.*

FORGIVENESS OF CIRCUMSTANCE

"To be or not to be…" in Shakespearean terms, "Lest we forget to forgive those who have been held accountable or not of what remains". How does one forgive? Or, forget? Can we put someone in a state of freezing their true feelings just because they have become a victim… Are you a victim? What is victimhood? Victimhood is where one believes that others have done various injustices that they have succumbed to believing in the worst…and, in the worst way. A victim only is a victim when the circumstances are not understood and the past behavior is not forgotten and/or not forgiven. Why do we settle comfortably numb in "victimhood" where we live to recite over again…to anyone who will listen? Victim of circumstance lends itself to over-thinking that they cannot forgive; and there is no salvaging the person who begrudged them. To assert oneself is to review all the factors of a situation; and, for the part you have played. What is a victim's role if not for being on the other end of shadow work of a low-frequency that requires their Ego to be stroked? It is also a mirror reflection of the thread that binds the victim with the perpetrator of that lesson. When, or if one comes to understand the nature of the reasons behind a guilty party that connects the dots to your ancestral lineage, then perhaps, a need for forgiveness can be overcome. This does not happen easily you see… the perpetrator is also the victim here. They have also been riddled with guilt from their family lineage for entertaining the thread of perpetrator and victim all in one life cycle. This happens for a soul to get a complete understanding of circumstances involving both sides to the story. "What will be will BE".

Walking in life must be experienced in all forms and understood in its entirety – as Jesus said, "Don't judge a man until you have walked a mile in his shoes". Romans 12:15-16

Rejoice with those who rejoice, and weep with those who weep. In essence, "Love your neighbor as yourself."

A SPIRITUAL REVOLUTION

Humans have a series of networks that assist us on Earth and one of the many places for us to join, other than a WIFI Network, is our own inner network of what has been known as our internal network system. (INS) Our internal network system, INS, gives us an inner sense of knowing. We either know what we know, or, establish our own inner guidance of what truths will fair well and what won't. Our State of Faith is what we know that gives us our strength-in-Faith the IN'S that has been with us since inception is the only network that holds any ground. The WIFI network has been built to expound the outer doings of people, places and/or things that Humanity is able to capture through visual effects, states of mind, travel to unknown places and a plethora of imagination that can be of some help or a hindrance to society. In whatever fashion these networks tend to have one thing in common… They are leading everyone to either seek an external force of what *lies* on the outer extremities vs. what our inner self-reflection network will show up as intuitive hits, downloads and signs from the Universe to reap the benefits of the journey. The common denominator is the self – to know oneself inside and out. What tends to happen though is the external self is vying for attention while the inner workings predict a natural flow of smooth sailing. How one receives it is crucial… so that both external/internal seek what is known as the, "Horizon", a balance of Yin/Yang. The resonance Force of Nature can only be felt from the *inside out*. *Within sees* itself without… "A force to be reckoned with…" is what this implies. Earth is a powerful force, a balancing act which we've all been privy to experience. One hand washes the other as the right-hand gives Love; the left-hand receives Love. ***In prayer***, the two are intertwined as ONE. That is the Natural Order of energy on the Earth – give and you shall receive. The beast, however, is where external order breeds havoc on the whole of Humanity: chaos, destruction and imbalances; in order to bring changes of perspective, inception of an Ego mindset, etc., of what we are about to receive. Whenever we are given gifts from Heaven a series of events are shown in sequential order, to those who observe miracles. These and many more heartfelt actions are from those who have been guided to learn from their lessons from a rightful place of receiving. Gifts received might look like external rewards… i.e., money, property, allowances; yet, the inner workings of Spirit go deeper than what truly matters. What internal gifts matter bring rewards… of trust, loyalty, patience, forgiveness, acceptance without assumptions, doubt of expectations and much more. Here is the difference for Humanity's sake – sacrifices to lend a helping hand where needed, give money to those in need, give to the needy and to need or want for nothing in return. Selfless acts of kindness, just because… Have you been a witness to selfless acts of kindness? Have you anonymously given of yourself" in ways that need no audience, appreciation, compensation or any other external recognition? With that being said… take a moment to recapture the face of a child on Christmas, birthdays, etc., only to witness the miracle of joy. We've forgotten what that is like because society has outdone itself in matters that shout out to those who have to acquire "stuff" in order to be happy. Overdoing, acquiring, owning, etc., of anything lends itself to take the joy out of it. Not that it doesn't 'feel good' at the time, but in time, it loses that loving feeling. There's a huge difference to what we acquire, why we acquire and how we are able to acquire it. It is the Ego that wants humans to 'give in' to the mindset of greed. If someone has the means by which to acquire that gives them a sense of self-worth, great happiness and implies to extend right-of-heart, in the natural order, then who is to criticize those actions. The only contradiction and/or verdict of judgment are those who do not have the means or good-will intent to naturally want another's happiness more than their own. This is a selfless act of kindness... For those who have been privy in relation to acquiring just because it soothes the soul, then, it goes without saying that your heart is full-filled. There are humans that acquire for other reasons, yet, the innocence of one's beauty shows through to the core of one's heart.

There comes a time where what has been acquired will dissipate for our next generation of children... but, in the meantime, any acquisition done for the benefit of self is duly noted. Those who are Ego bound have a difference of opinion and view others' ability as a reason to critique. There are many arts that humans have been given to co-create using their imagination, perfecting a signature piece that is blessed by God. Whatever your art is... generated within your heart & soul, will create miracles. This is exactly why it is of such great importance to demonstrate your place in this world, crafting a career/life-long expression-of-self from the Heart. All things that have potential to grow are seeded from our inner hearts... jobs come and go but what remains is the impressionable acts/deeds that go unnoticed. Even a smile exchanged from the heart is felt by all. Societies "claim-to-fame" has instilled a warped sense of acquired acts of Ego-driven to crash-and-burn. So many Hollywood actors have crashed and burned after so many have been exposed. Be very WARY of those who are dangling the caveat of success, power, money before you so that you fall from grace. In order to know the difference, do the hard work, from your heart, and let the rest fall into place. Due diligence falls under the category of self-improvement while 'in justice for all' does not become a justice of the peace or even a just way. Furthermore, it depicts a self-discipline that cannot be acquired through any form of government and/or external Matrix. If we were to seek justice, we would act upon the need to ensure unlawful crimes of those who have served unfair time…behind bars. What does this tell us about our Justice system? Misuse-of-power and a fight-for-one's place has NO place in court. The external place for any justice will end up in the place where no one is seeking. That place is in one's own heart… Accredited are those whose karma has not lapsed for deeds done that are above the law, but to all of those who help assist others to do the same. We applaud all of those who do their jobs with-and-for the highest good to "serve & protect" mankind. We've known many firefighters, police officers, teachers, doctors, lawyers, CEO's etc., that are given the power to lead, teach and show honorability 'represent' a goodness of character. What makes people do good is their upbringing – those who raised them, those who saved them, those who have seen them fall yet carried them home, those who cry for HELP and to all those who have served as helping hands, open hearts admitting to such compassion. There are many statesmen who had such power and attempted to beat the system, got caught and are behind bars. There are neighbors who deserve to be in the line of fire and still beating the system… There are all kinds of humans who have put their foot forward to either assist or hinder situations that are clearly out of our control. Can you claim doing the right thing lending a compassionate ear, hand, or just to physically be with someone who needs to reach out? Do you know who these people are that you've entrusted for so long… and, how long? We meet a stranger for 5-minutes who chooses to lend a helping hand; while on the other hand, we contact a loved one for help and end up falling short. Does time really matter when it comes to who, what, and where we instill our Faith? Have you ever thought of this… or, is it easier just to brush it under the rug by justifying another's bad behavior… time and time again? We are not here to judge anyone for acts of injustices yet to enlighten one's awareness of those things we deem important to our radar … or, not. We can either stay passive-aggressive or find a way out of the injustices of the world by letting go and letting God. Whatever you do choose will definitely be sorted out in *Heaven's gate*.

When we gather together, in the Eye of the Beholder, we begin to realize our soul's path. As far as our Beloved, the vision gets dimmer as one gets their frequency overwhelmed with: hunger, greed, money, power and the like. What raises our vibrational frequency is in a place where our truth steers us into our Heart. What truly matters is what our Heart feels… nothing more, nothing less. If your heart's in-it-to-win it then you have a distinct awareness. The Ego cannot override the Heart *unless* you allow the material world to control you. What bears witness to this is while you're out shopping around ask yourself, "Do I really "need" this item?" if your Heart says, not really… then, it goes without saying that your Ego will justify it to change your mind. Why this happens is crucial to our existence because it goes without saying that we always know better. Whenever we lead with the Ego, we receive instant gratification then fall into debt with regret. Why this happens is to continue to show us how deeply controlling the Ego is readily for the taking. To compromise what is already ingrained fumes of remorse, regret, resistance of despair having to get back into the rabbit hole... Self-discipline is the energetic force of Nature. Given the natural course of what Mother Nature provides is our deepest responsibility to be aware that our lives run smoother when there is no resistance. If humans were able to understand that there is no need for control. That control only exists for the Ego to show you what you're NOT in-control of ... Mother Earth is within every human's spirit embodied by a pre-programmed mathematically, scientific Hologram. It is the way existence plays out in the Natural Order of things and in-light-of that makes humans think their actions are also not preordained; so as to stop the madness of needing control. It is control that hinders our progress, not to mention, questions of the Ego. Therefore, when the Ego interferes with your decision-making it is showing you how little control you have and how easily controlled you are. The less control you have of your decisions...the more self-worth in disciplining yourself to recall a place where everything has already been done. The natural order of existence is to let life play out in whatever way it is given – and any/all decisions become your lessons. It's that extra charge on your credit card; it's a spam call; it's that last drink that drives you to black out or worse yet, an accidental incident that injures, kills others; it's that complacent version of yourself that is enabling others to make decisions for them; it's that parent who coddles their child/children; it's that parent who fails to take responsibility; it's all of these and so much more... that drives the inability to lose control. What makes life so amazing is that once you're able to connect the threads of Heritage we could actually infer to those things that actually do add-value, have a longing of existence in what matters...at the heart of those on Earth. Many more people would then be able to co-create by using, finding, exploring their innate treasures for the goodness of Humanity. The opposing energy that renders self-control when out-of-control is discipline. Buying more, acquiring stuff…not only designer labels but whatever doesn't fit into your budget is a red-flag that your Ego has taken you on a wild goose chase… Should designer items or whatever means of attraction you desire externally be done with "awareness" that would cut down our debt ratio.

In the end-of-life, what appears as the absence of those loved and lost, is a huge reunion of Heavenly LOVE embracing your essence. Those who have undergone a near-death experience (NDE) felt this type of embrace. The only part of loss in death is the human physical body… The etheric body encompasses all of our life's experiences and remains in the Astral 5D plane until such a rise-up of higher consciousness is attained. Kriyas have to also be completely open to attain the level of higher consciousness – which isn't a far cry from a Kundalini Rising. In order for all the 7-body chakras to open up, we must embrace our own Ego, that slithers throughout each chakra of the body, rising up to meet oneself – when an explosion of higher consciousness ensues. Once that is attained the physical body experiences levels of higher consciousness throughout by way of various connections with Spirit guides, Archangels, Ascended Masters etc. Very few have attained this level of Mastery, yet, it has been done and many of our lightworkers, seers and sages on the Earth plane have gained their wings. We've all been given a so-called "purpose" of assurance …lending a helping hand to others, servicing in-deeds, indeed.

What matters to some on Earth is a completely revolutionized storyline to those who KNOW doesn't matter… As a matter of fact, if you must question what is the matter you have not yet ascended. The emphasis on Earth is not only the materialistic matters; but that of the physical tangible desires; and what matters as in, "no matter what;" to, "no matter what happens…" when one gives up their need to control. What we learn is not only given to us as a "remembrance" not to seek. Once this merger happens within a soul's connection, their life review takes place; not unless you've undergone several Dark-Night of the Soul experiences that have elevated your Kundalini Rising, elevating an explosion of Higher Consciousness. Whatever Higher Consciousness has taken place, is up to Spirit to distinguish whether a further review is required. No one is exempt from not having a past-life review unless you have attained Ascension to Higher Consciousness. When we combine physical matters to matters of the heart, sensing will override what makes sense. The Ego may lead or choose to take a back seat to the Heart – for within every Heart is all that matters.

What comes around does not necessarily stick around when it comes back to double-check its prey and/or to check if it's been prayed for. We've all witnessed people, places and things that have a shelf life of years only to disappear… When karmic justice reels Her in yet another chance at what left you naked, is the ability to surrender and allow this karma to yield either a new chance or to seek what changes haven't been made in order to cut the threads that bind. Those times when you could have sworn up and down that this one is your twin flame… but ended up as a soul mate for you to learn from is by example. A twin-soul is a soul connection; yet a mate that flames the fires of desire ends up getting burned! No one truly has explained the Terms and Conditions for how people intertwine with others and why there even needs to be a so-called label of who stands for what. "One man's poison is another man's treasure…" exhibits what happens when an individual perception of another's situation is understood, rectified and/or forgiven. We are only human standing for how we have been taught, what is or is not remembered, who holds a special place in your heart and why; for this we cannot lie, so many variables to every life experience who we have lost and loved – and who we may yet still love, or not. Ariana Grande in her song, "Thank U, Next" depicts what most people desire to say but are unable to be honest... when a relationship fails do we say, "thank you" for the time spent together? Not usually... but, in hindsight we internalize a thank you for not subjecting us to anymore cruel intentions – and releasing us from moments in time that were or were not wasted time. In essence, once we understand the nature of the beast, we end up realizing it was we who are exhibiting a surrender to self upon realization of letting go of all toxic relationships. It's already been established that whatever is reaped will be sowed yet many humans do not think about the actual repercussions until it's too late.

Our value system has a plethora of depth by which people are not capable of understanding – every Lotus Flower has layers; as we also refer to peeling back the layers of an onion. There is no difference in either except the Lotus flower has been a symbol of Shiva, the other half of Shakti...representing Yin/Yang. Mother Earth has brought these two together to live life as ONE. What causes friction between the two is whose perspective is to be seen and/or heard as the two become one... the one that can perceive both sides as the whole-of-life has full understanding of a Lotus Flower. We do not need to pick a Lotus Flower, or ANY other Flower as the moment one chooses to pick (i.e., criticism, judgements, rage, anger, jealousy, pride etc.) wilts away. Casting any type of judgements and/or criticism bleeds out many thorns that do not allow for the wholeness of our Holy self. We've been known to self-loath in our own place of self; within that

632

same energy field, the energy flows toward those that it can equate to and with. Like attracts like in the Natural Divine Order of things on Earth. Similar circumstances happen to your near-and-dear circle of trustworthy friends who hold the energetic field of trust as a unified circle. If that trust is broken in any way, the energetic field becomes smaller and smaller. While on your spiritual journey, this inevitably happens because not every person will be able to join you on the same energetic frequency as you. It is NOT to say one person is higher, better or knows anything other than they are progressing by doing the inner work…nothing better than seeing progress being made; not as a divide but perhaps as an inspiration. Hope leads to many good things when we see how effortless the energy of our Universal force in Mother Nature works in tandem with the ALL. Once you gain this understanding, your questions fall by the wayside and the rest is History. What is gained in the History books is for those who believe in the adage, "History repeats itself…" Yet in what way does this happen? It only happens when humans are not responding to their own awareness for change – and their "mindset" becomes a vague interpretation of 'same ole' same ole' as the narrative. When your mind is set upon the old ways of doing things, in whatever fashion that is leading us to, either treason or treasured memories will remain a thing of the past…unless someone changes their mindset. We're not here to judge another's actions of 50 years ago, or, are we? Is the same indicted Hitler in the forefront of our democracy? Can we paint the same picture as our brothers who went before World War II so that we could stand up for Freedom of Rights? Is there any difference as to what was then and now going on in other said-countries fighting for their democracy? If so, what do you assess as your own Freedom of Rights?

Are we given any Freedom... or is this just a passing phase for those who are sheepishly too scared to speak up? What isn't going to happen is one man under any type of Justice system able to sustain an entire country of Historic episodes... what might just gain world peace, however, is if every man, woman and/or children assessed their own Right of Freedom by staying righteous to their destiny. This isn't to say that your vote does not give your country a chance to change; it just means that you elect the better of two evils... and stay in your own lane. No one seems to understand that fighting a good fight just leads to critical judgments from outsiders' perceptions which lead to havoc ensuing. People have no idea how to stay in their own lane without using their voice, why? We've all been pre-programmed to NOT stand up and fight for our own individual rights and instead get in others' business where it need not be. It's bad enough that all wars begin within a family unit, let alone an entire democracy of humans who believe their way is the right way. Who will change the right-to-vote? Will there be a place in time where AI will be the only voters in our world? Does this concern you that a robot could, would, and/or can be allowed to vote? On what basis could this possibly take a president elect? What will be a thing of the past...literally and figuratively. Who will train, teach and learn about the candidates up for elections? How will the AI demonstration take notice of a liar, thief and/or what has been done over the course of time? Will they (AI) be trained by their Chief of Staff to listen to whomever is in command? Or, will the world of human rights be a thing of the past? And, will a presidential election get erased by the governments in charge of pruning their Rights of Staff? Will AI robots be chosen by race, creed, and/or color of, what, per se? Does anyone think that an AI President will execute a new Constitution? How will this be done without using the past 50 or so years, as example? Inevitably nothing will change the demographics of political warfare unless we all stand up for our own Right of Freedom by NOT allowing such nonsense to take place. It will be a cold day in Hell, shall we say, when robots are put into a political position of power, or not?

Perhaps this will be the determining factor where it is not written in the Book of Revelations that a demonstrative AI robot will take flight into the political arena? Or is it written... As in all those still 'asleep', – is mentioned. Those who live in FEAR... Fear is what makes warfare a necessity, what makes people justify their own means to an end, what makes one even see through Ego I's of any kind... What makes the ultimate divided we stand, united we will fall, such a reality that no one person would, could and/or should rightfully allow? We are "One Nation Under God" whether you fear that, whether you believe or disbelieve, whether your fear is far too strong or whether your fear of using your voice will entrap you into becoming and not believing in a God. This is the reality going on in our world today... take notice of what is going on around your countries, other foreign lands and policies and who is barking up the wrong trees? Barking dogs claim to alert others there's danger around, or, we want attention and need to speak up; and, then there's the so-called wife, who barks orders to her husband; and, what do they all have in common with the bark on trees? *WISDOM.* Are we adhering to wise choices stating a maturity; or, are we attempting to control by barking up the wrong tree? A voice that is silent has much more power over those who speak rubbish... Can we ascertain the difference? We guarantee that you shall perish or have everlasting life, this is the truth. What is your truth? The Revelation on Earth as it is in Heaven will be.... no external forces leading you on a wild-goose chase; a community of organizations, human rights' movements and/or chosen officials who will change the way they are leading the path; and all will be shown IN truth. What will fall away … is The American Dream so as to adhere to an overall happiness and peace in the extraordinarily simple things in Life. The warfare, riots, havoc of power-hungry masses will NOT be able to control mankind any longer. This is not a prediction, it is written in The Bible as in massive demolition, destruction will take place – a clearing out and purging of assets, acquired junk etc., that will allow many to *restructure* based upon their beliefs, wants and needs, where NO external evil influencers will have a voice. This will be a long haul and in a futuristic plan that has already begun… decades of darkness being extinguished in a world of enlightenment to reign. We are not there yet, not even in the slightest… hang in there, sit back and watch the greatest show ever on Earth of a New World Order – The Golden Age. History being rewritten has arrived…

There will be more storms, another War-of-Wills, a vast number of people in power being called out over and over again, so much chaos will ensue; and it is up to each of us to gain your strength of resolve to stay in your own lane. Withholding critical judgments, sarcasm, attacks made on your so-called circle of people who are near-and-dear; and other Earthly warfare that will enrich our visions, curtailing our fear to levels that are too low to contain one's freedom and/or rightful place in this world. Be strong, be a force to reckon with and stand up for your own. Empowered! To date, we've been holding back BUT now mankind has been made aware; and, cannot be forgotten. This is what God has intended for all children… marked by, "His Will Be Done." Whatever you do or don't understand in this life will come back around in another – or through the false visions that have held you back from others who will not be joining you. What this means is that even though you have ascended into a new vision of the work that you've done on yourself, others will not be able to follow until and *only* until their work is done. We get what we deserve that each man, woman and/or child who has rightfully seen and done the work of our Lord Jesus by His sacrifice, by His compassion, by His forgiveness and the All-encompassing that which IS. Whoever stays back will undergo a new-life vision with new players who are the perfect cast of characters which will enable your sight to be found or, another goes around. We cannot take full responsibility for those who may not see what you have come to know; therefore, cast aside all your doubts of how effortless it is to be seen and to know what is needed in order to see. What we seek is seeing you at the perfect time and in perfect order. In order to cast aside what others, see as a mountain out of a molehill, by not perceiving things bigger than they are, only to find problems arise. Cast aside your anger, jealousy, resentments, inability to forgive others and follow exactly what our Lord Jesus showed up when on Earth, as Man. Being of one mind is not the same as being of ONE mind. In the lower-case scenario it deems here, on Earth; and in all upper-case scenarios, is written AS IS. We come into this life seeking ourselves; we leave this life either in self-realization or a blank space that will be written upon again. We've been here all along… What humans fail to understand is that those in Spirit are waiting for Humanity to believe in your direction, for you to question, for you to wonder… what, where, and how your life is going. Have you had any inquiries, questions and doubts that you are seeking answers? Have you asked? Have you thought of praying? Do you realize that it takes one question, one minute, one to seek THE ONE for any such guidance?

The secret is not so much that you do not ask, but that you Believe in the power of the spirit world. Humans profess that they believe and have enormous Faith yet they don't believe in themselves. One who seeks to ask questions will get their answer(s) but not unless a show-of Faith overcomes the fear of God. To hold a Fear in the Divine, Spirit world, God, Love of… the ALL is where we must begin to question ourselves. 'What goes around comes around' in a life of experiences begins by enacting sequels from one act to the next. When life experiences extract your Fears – then, you have arrived. If you are in question, seek your own guidance and/or the guidance of your spiritual angels, past-loved ones in Heaven, our Lord Jesus through prayer. This is what prayer is for… praying is asking and meditation is receiving. A meditation of receiving requires us to release control and allow whatever comes/goes in our lives… Every aspect of our lives is one-step closer to the other in getting there. Perhaps it will take many lifetimes to get out of the matrix and into the realm of awareness; and for us to realize that we are ALL of mankind. We can either accept this to be true or reject it by rehearsing with questions instead of knowing what builds wisdom. Maturity is definitely the spice of life once you connect the threads that bind to your innate Heritage. Insofar as who you've been, where you are is exactly the place that has been designed for you; and the people in your lives have been picked out for your soul's growth. We are not here to sell you a piece of land – just to show you the landscape that life has given all Humans to experience. What you do with it is completely up to your Will & Testament. There are no other gods before you nor any gods in the afterlife, except for ONE GOD that IS. Grace in God means that you have been given a new life to endure your old one to learn from… if your will-to-live overpowers your unwillingness to be yourself through the looking glass of many reflections; then a maturity cannot yet be acquired, even if desired. What will end up happening is every mirrored reflection from a past-life will endure a new mirror that will attach itself to you until you see

638

your reflection. Once a true awareness of ONE reflection is sought, there is wisdom. A willingness to *escape* those reflections will enlighten you through your journey until the light becomes you. "ONE Nation Under GOD...Indivisible with Liberty & Justice for All" in, "The Pledge of Allegiance" which is taught to children. What has happened on Earth has clearly been a deceiving promise to manipulate only to be used, abused, tortured, spit out and flushed down the rabbit hole of lies. Will you care to save yourself by clawing your way out of the Matrix to attain Freedom? Those who have cut the umbilical cord to coercion will gain their right-to- freedom by using those who have destroyed our allegiance for the betterment of mankind. Will you choose YOU? The cases of missing children's whereabouts, the sexual abuse, the coercion of funds, mind-boggling lies etc., that have been believed have now been exposed and cast out – as are those who will beg for mercy. Under the Laws of this Universe, every person who deems to follow a wrongful place of evidence to end what is good and just in this world, will fall into their own demise of the black hole. Castaways have been and are falling as we speak into a black hole where there is no salvation. We believe in the power of three (3) as; The Father, The Son, The Holy Ghost is the empowerment of the value of The Trinity. As The Trinity, we have been warned that the abundance on Earth shows up as a clear indication of everything happening in 3's; however, by common definition the 3 is known as inventor Nikola Tesla has theorized his divisibility by whatever number duplicates the power of The Trinity. Within that power of 3 is The Holy Spirit's energy which captivates our attention as miracles that evolve in the highest quotient. When Tesla's theory began to evolve the world was not only captivated but also a newly formed ideology was born. This has led to the power of 3 in aspects which surmises as 3,6,9's infinite sequences that when divided, added and/or even multiplied by these numbers a vast evolution takes place. These evolutionary number sequences remain in our everyday life as it takes on the ultimate mathematical equation from where the Universe has been built. The Universal hologram was constructed with this Theory of Energy which was held in high regard by modern physics through the study of numbers in atomic and subatomic particles. The 3 in the English alphabet is C for Christ; the 6 is the F for one's Faith; and the 9 is the I as in Identification – all of one's self. To misconstrue these as anything else would be identified as an act of a Maleficent's evil threat to the male of the Son, imposing degrees of impotency in all mankind. Designing this Universe was the threat from Lucifer's ego to all of mankind where the darkness has been attempting to rule out the light by Identification of the EGO. The Ego was put into place and is exactly why Lucifer fell from grace to show us that many will be tested; some will fail and others will ascend. There is no way in GOD's Grace that light will ever be extinguished from ALL. The light shines in darkness by imposing itself with the good that man bears witness to and for all children will survive and find themselves in God's grace… We say, "It's all good…" but a better way to say that is, "It's ALL GOD…" This Universe was not meant to be anything other than it IS… a school for humans to attain ultimate ascension. There will be many who may think they have ascended may be thought as, "bragger's rites" but for those who remain silent, have truly ascended. As with Jesus' ascension is the story of man's ascension – and, to those who will condemn their rightful seat at The Last Supper. In Leonardo DaVinci's "The Last Supper" the 3 Disciples painted together were; Judas, Peter and John. Peter seems angry and John seems faint, but Judas' face is portrayed in his shadow; losing Christ's light. Judas, the traitor, holds in his hand a bag of money from the misuse of power which he received from the chief priests who he had gone to make a bargain – an ultimate betrayal portrayed on this Earth plane. From where we are today, Earth has been having its own "War of the Roses" as society infringed upon children whose Faith has to be tested to become self-realized. This began back in the time of Adam & Eve where she was tested by Adam to pick from the Tree of Life; an apple that was tainted with all of the egoic violence, rage, anger, depressions, sadness, purging in whatever way was made possible to seek one's own Faith. We have to understand that the Ego was built for this very reason… not for another's treason. What has become of our Faith is what, why and where our soul arrives in Humanity. For Humanity's sake we are still under the guise of an Egoic structure and will remain intact for all to experience on their journey. When Jesus' followers became too insistent with their egos, Jesus knew it was a time of great change. His followers became His enemies yet the Faith of one disciple lasted throughout history… this follower is Humanity's Faith in Jesus' name, Amen. Jesus did not attempt to change His followers into believing He is or was better than any man; only guided them all who put their trust and Faith in God. Are we amongst those followers? Could there be any reason that we too are not worthy of His trust? Outbreaks of dis-ease have been cast upon Earth, as written in The Bible. Will another pandemic masterfully be sighted in order to gain more leverage/ground to those who still are in Fear? What will it take for those of great Faith lead the pack by guiding those still asleep and fearful of their lives? What is this Fear of God doing to society? Are we weak in Faith? Will those sheepishly still on the fence be granted salvation? Is the worst-case scenario a death of the physical body any more fearful than an outbreak of dis-ease that could inevitably proport humans into death, despair by not believing in themselves? "God helps those who help themselves…" Why are you not helping yourself by leaving the so-called propaganda to all those still asleep? Inevitably, human life of the physical body will end … no matter what happens, so, what are you so afraid of? Why is the Fear of societal diseases any different than the effects of drugs, sex and alcohol more deadly to the physical body which humans find more appealing? Death is the ultimate life sentence to those who have such an innate fear of dying – but that is a part of life. What then is the actual Fear and at what cost? Fear fears it-self… and without so much as a word of trust humans can't be extinct. Humanity is what breeds it-self over and over in order to allow for our ONE God to Love it-self. Man cannot be the only species who reclaims it-self as breeders of any one species – all life reclaims itself as one. "We are not here to question why; we are here to do and die…" as the Bible states and offers Humanity so many ways with which to live life knowing that it is a life lived in a physical body. To experience life on this planet is all for one and one for all – not having to worry at any moment one body will perish but have everlasting life.

For Humanity to be in full awareness knowing that once the body parishes, it too will seek to find shelter, in the all. A soul will be able to live forever as long as that soul has not been actively intentional in hurting children and all others. Mother Earth does not embrace the evil on Her planet – and the only reason She has allowed such activities to happen is to give humans another chance before they are disintegrated. Mother Earth loves all Her children just the same… and when you land here, you are given "freewill" to make better choices for yourself. Should any human destroy a child in any way – there will be mass destruction; which is happening on the planet as we speak. Those who have created a platform of a vindictive presence to control, coerce, manipulate, elusive acts of crime, passion, sex, violence, etc., abuse of any kind is not tolerated. "Leave no stone unturned…" as the Bible represents what is taking place on this Holy land. What is going on today is rewriting History … Each of us are not only living examples of this, but remember that we signed up for the task. Remember, this life is a gift, a presence of our Divine Holy land… NOT Disneyland. To every child upon this Earth, we applaud those who have assisted in the uprising of our planet – and to show our gratitude, you will see many miracles take place, wait. watch. seek. This will be the grand illusion of shows on Earth. Those who have attained awareness are a poignant energy for our Earth and will be handsomely rewarded… now and forever.

If we could take all those farewells of yesterday's moments that gifted us with lessons learned; we'd forgive our families by sending Love so that we could take on a new flight. A new Revolution begins to take flight to those who seek a truth that will enable even the smallest change to take place. This Spiritual Revolution changes the blueprint of our lives which will spearhead a paradigm shift into every life – emitting a new fragrance of burnt orange crisps. The setting Sun's fragrance holds every child's rewind of glimpses into the past – with a burst of lemon gently squeezed into the Sun of a new day. What is washed away will always be remembered within Love; and, the gentle cool breeze breathes air into our very essence. All those who leave the 'matrix of darkness' into their own awakening will live a life that will never be the same. A light shines bright for all to be guided along the footprints in the sparkling sand. We leave behind the illusions of a world built on deceptive forces that no longer have a hold on us. Exiting the tunnels of the matrix releases all past integers of the vertical files for good…once glimpses of light shine through one's inability to be manipulated, coerced, lied to etc herein is the beginning of our Individual Revolution. Those who are still in darkness of the matrix will continue to be tempted by those dangling carats that are dulled cubes of zirconia. We are living in a plastic, zirconia dragula-like entity of darkness that plays havoc on others' energy levels that are low. Those who use external vices to get high, numb themselves, paint the town red, watch, listen, sing, and co-exist in the darkness are easily swayed…to say the least. Lower vibrations whose light is dim-to-none will be the first to be allured, tested to insurmountable heightened lows. These energy vampires hit the ground flying to every human who is not coherent, mindful, attentive and aware of these dark entities. As "their" dictatorship hosts plenty of so-called seances that lift evil from down under should know not to play with power. What is convoluted is believing in who others follow… when others follow suit, the hierarchy grows into a whole new dragula. Needless to say, it may seem quite difficult to believe, but isn't that the reason that some are vibrating on higher frequencies than others?

WORLD'S COLLIDE & THE OTHER SIDE

Under the guise of yin/yang, what we hold very near and dear to our hearts in understanding the world of all its compartments on Earth will lend itself to what's being done and seen currently. Compartments of every aspect of that yin/yang energy host. A play of energy involves the yin/feminine/Moon with the yang/masculine/Sun incorporated under the vast Universe that encompasses the entire solar system…and finite stars. Under this vast world comes layers upon layers of auric energies from within the cells and physical embodiment that also blend within and without the facets making up our Universe. What people dismiss are all the elements within this Universe that pertain to all those additional emotions and clouds of thoughts which are in the ethers of our existence. What we fail to realize is that all these

644

compartments, per se, are working in tandem threading every morsel of human's existence within the existence of Life. Humans tend to take this world as face-value without inquiring where, why and how these threads can commune together in this tapestry. What is out of our control is everything that we're not seeing from a bird's eye view of external situations that coexist within us. We are Humans who coexist within a world of worlds; dimensions intertwined within dimensions; scales of windchimes that incorporate soundwaves that placate our entire solar system. It's not easy to bundle this world into one lineage of family ancestors when, in fact, all of us are connected – a world within worlds. Science meets Spirituality.

JUXTAPOSED IMPRESSIONS OF INJUSTICES

Whatever we are to impress upon in this lifetime, it comes with the need that requires juxtaposed efforts whereby one hand washes the other…and, in the likes of Charles Dickens, "All's fair in love and war." By what right do humans have the ability to choose what they deem as "fair?" Is it fair to assume anything, especially that which shaves off a lifetime of what we're all here to become? Our Heritage in Humanity, as a whole, is to know yourself as all Love and by definition that "fairness-in-war" comes ideally with a price. Perhaps what Dickens really meant by this was to seek a happy medium within your own Ego, to say that, in either case of how one chooses to live – do you choose to love, or do you find your choice of Egoic self who is at war? The lessons of this, "School of Hard Knocks" pose no threat in finding that wars are meant to shake things up to find the silver lining of Love that is threaded in every aspect of our lives. To seek out war, just for your egoic to feel better, to gain power, to show the world, to sell your soul is yet another. If you choose to be at war within yourself - as you envision war in this world, that will be your purposeful dissonance in this lifetime. A world of wars that appear on the outside is an affinity for whatever wars you're struggling internally. By definition, not for the same issues that "they" are fighting against; but for you to see the thread of an internal struggle within your life. Whether this means your hatred, anger, resentment, jealousy and/or an affluent misuse of power might be present in your world. However, if you can envision these all-out wars on the outside as separate – meaning, they do not affect your personal journey, then you have begun to understand. What Dickens imprinted in our world is that, should you choose war, you will be that war unto yourself and those matters needing to be justified must be served. Although we tend to seek justice, when it is not given, how does that make you feel? Earth is a hologram of self-inflicted pain if you allow…and, should you understand The Law of Cause & Effect, this pain will not be affecting you. For under the guise of our Heavenly guides, justice is always served as, it is the Law – and, when humans take the law into their own hands…who will wash away your misdoings? It may be difficult to understand… but as much as you want to control your destiny by serving another their pain; that is of your Ego. Under the Laws of the Universe, we have been gifted to partake in observing how God's intention for Humanity is to serve and allow what will inevitably happen in Divine timing. The Laws of the Universe are not meant to be broken – as the laws of the Earth are broken. Justice on this Earth cannot be done by humans…it is the acts of what is fair and just that is being determined, through God's Love. Whenever you seek revenge on injustices for all…that breeds a karmic tie to our Heritage that needs to be cleared and/or severed. The feeling of injustice in the world is threaded to past injustices of one's own life, or lifetimes of our past. When we "strike a cord" that triggers us to assert action…this can lead to adding more karmic debt which takes more time to render a clean slate. When we allow the injustices of the world not to affect us in a personal way; and the matters of injustices in our personal lives not to affect us, "knowing" that they will be handled, this is Faith. Our lives are in the hands of God…is another way of understanding the right hand gives while the left hand receives. In-between is an unwavering FAITH for Humanity, in prayer. What Humanity is learning the hard way is to TRUST in themselves – seen, spoken, heard, taught, for your Highest good. Empowerment for the good of Humanity is for the good of self, when one hand washes another – no matter what someone has said, done etc., it is not for us to entertain vengeful justice. A tall order, for some…yet what is being done will be duly noted on their karmic ledger. Falling from grace doesn't happen for no reason…those who are here, on the Earth have taken a huge leap of FAITH coming here to make History. Waiver as you will to your beliefs for what remains is the impression that bodes truth. Do not be pressured to follow the rules for the rules will end up being followed, no matter what. Rules of the Highest Order; and, not those of Freedom in The Declaration of Independence that is being stripped away from Humanity. The same people who signed The Declaration of Independence are the same people who are trying to take away our Freedom. John Hancock may have been the Founder of our Forefathers but he was a Freemasonry who wanted to impose his power upon the people. "We The People" are awakening to these juxtaposed Ego heads of warfare that emit decisions that are not what the people would choose. Right? Do you want your country to be under siege from a war that we know nothing or very little about – who is telling the truth about what countries are fighting for or against? What we do know is that "they" have been lying to "We The People" far too long…and, no matter whether we need to be privy of their every scandal isn't the issue, as attempting to take our Freedom. Do you realize what massive injustice that would be if our Freedom were taken by exactly those who created it for the people? The lineage of our founding Fathers is threaded in the same darkness as the man who implements rules that are broken. These are literally "sworn in" bounded by the likes of all past Presidents and all who are in that position of power. Other countries do not have these legalities yet they do emit the same impressions of darkness that are bound by cultural differences, misuse of power in other varied ways. Whatever position all "governing" agencies have in common is a misrepresentation to all of Humanity. What will come of this only "they" know... yet, staying out of the line-of-fire is highly suggested. Being empowered means to take your own life into your hands...and lead a life of peace, comfort, joy, health and happiness in LOVE. In Love of selfless acts that help to serve, in-deeds for Humanity – that gives each human a reason, a purpose to have chosen this life. Coming to grips with your truth will propel you to your evolution than to entertain warfare that not only repeats History, but warrants a finder's fee for not dabbling in darkness. That fee is a metaphor for a "get out of jail Free" card in a monopolized effort to control. Why does History repeat itself? Humanity evolves while History repeats – a polarity of need to either learn for yourself or remain lost. The mere reason that History has repeated itself time and time again is for those who are lost wandering this Earth repeating their karmic time and time again. History that repeats is there to shine the light on making changes in this lifetime and choosing you ... over the mind control that "they" have repeated. There is no difference in the threads of time – the only difference is in the suits/physical embodiment of darkness. Choose wisely.

JACOB'S LADDER

While the story of Jacob's ladder sets the tone for what Humanity perceives as their own *"Stairway to Heaven"* it lends itself many interpretations. The ladder was meant for those who have struggled with their own crosses to bear and have undergone much strife in the meantime. What was once Humanity's cross is a clear indication of what has been brought to the attention of those whose voices have been heard. We are struggling no longer to accept vindictive child abuse and those who have been victims both through their voice (let their voices be heard), and through the opinions of those who are not yet privy to let them in… All children have been rescued from the ashes… no longer victims of molestation, sex trafficking, murder, both physical and mental abuse, medicinal weed being tainted for the obsession of those who are weak, pot smoking overkill that leads to self-destruction of the brain waves … and prescribed medicines with a 6-page history of side effects no one could survive. These are just a few of the virtual realities on Earth, not to mention those coming from our AI robotic hypnosis, which will turn this place into the walking dead. What many are unaware of is that this has been preordained for those who are still asleep to wake up! This is the one and only ordination that would host a number of humans right out of their skin and onto their knees begging forgiveness for not paying more attention to what your child/children are doing in a corrupt world. If this is speaking to you directly, please find it in your heart-of-hearts to forgive yourselves and begin a new chapter in your life and the lives of your children. The children who literally chose you, each and every child has chosen their parents, (arguably or not…) to whom deep-seated trauma, lessons and a number of other incidents which cannot be discussed have happened for the good of Humanity; even though it has been viewed as ignorance. Watch what the public deems as acceptable for children's viewing in the near future. Watch Humanity take a turn for the worst before it gets better. History will indeed repeat itself, but, not in the same manner as what was… The present-day circumstances unfolding for Humanity is going to be a newly unwritten story that no human can or will be able to fathom. It will not be for the sake of Humanity as it will be in spite of, for Humanity's sake.

Where Humanity has suffered greatly under duress, she has found a newfound strength where all these uncoverings that have been exposed for the entire world to view have been getting much attention – especially after so many musicians, songwriters, actors, who have been victims themselves. What can Humanity do now? Will Humanity identify without a reasonably doubt that these torture chambers we've been witnessed to will have a greater impact on you? Seek comfort in knowing that Heaven's gates will not behold all perpetrators that have been hurt in any way… these acts that cannot be spoken of are forgivable only to those who are forgiving. For the rest of Humanity, a number of defeats have proven to be worthy of those who are undergoing their own Jacob's ladder. We've been leaning toward a massive restructuring on Earth that will allow Mother Earth to formulate by sharing Her higher consciousness to those who have been working on themselves for the sake of Humanity. These openings will allow Her to commit Her initial plan of taking no prisoners to leaving no child behind. What more could we ask for than a world of peace, prosperity and eternal Faith for all children. Before you jump for joy, however, there is one little request from the Spirit world that must be done… PRAYER. A prayer to the highest power of LOVE will be granted as long as there are Believers. Just as in the movie, "Elf" where every man, woman and child sang salutations of Joy… and for every bell that rang in, "It's A Wonderful Life". We've had plenty of time to fall from grace…now, let us pick up our hearts unto the Lord. We 'pick up' is yet another term for ascending to new vibrational frequencies in order for a New World Order. The vibrational resonance of sound will, indeed, be the new way in which healing will occur – it is "out there" already, yet, to most who are dabbling, a gift of great Faith must be had in order to heal. No matter what type of healing the body requires, it must be in good Faith. If it's not in good Faith… or, if there are doubts of any kind, one must not be subjected to feeling as though the means to an end is never-arriving; eternal Faith takes lifetimes for some. We live in a cynical world where all those who have left this planet by means of their sins of darkness, are placed upon the children. What kind of world would even remotely "allow" an energy of evil destruction upon children to incarnate? It's been said that this energy does not need to be evil again, however, one must not need-to-know all the magic going-on – yet what Spirit will say is that should you place evil on another's child that evil will be sent back to you! Beware of how you treat others… the intentions of vibration will automatically rectify themselves.

When we fall for the same ole' same ole' routine of mass destruction the world of illusion falters; and if we fix our own faults of mass corruption, destruction and self-sabotage the same routine starts to unfold as peace, harmony, success etc. With that in mind…it's no wonder why the AI robotic Space X and more are creating a world of dispassionate, complacency, a lifestyle of congruent mass destruction in partaking in what we know to be disturbed. These are the well-known facts as many who are leaving behind a stream of corner rhinestones that look much like Barbie's world… instead of the land of the free, home of the brave. Why the 3-Dimensional world was plagued with a replica of what version we'd call, "The American Dream" has posed as a very big wallet with empty pockets that have turned into plastic. In the new Barbie movie what is criticized as less-than-intelligence is geared toward a comedy of errors that leaves Ken a laughing stock while Barbie finds her own place in the world. Now the world has changed to where the masculine has been demoted and what's incremental is that feminine empowerment takes precedence. This cannot be seen as a joke, but is topping the charts with those both GenX and Millennials paying top dollar. When a film is equipped to pay top dollar for these actors to conjugate words of wisdom for the new world's generations…what message is this spitting out? Isn't it true that women in power have a say so but are still not being paid out what men are being paid? Do we still see a discrepancy in this world when it comes to power and money versus a dream house with lots of pink accessories that will end up costing parents a hefty price – and, who wins… Mattel, Inc. This is a prime example of not only Hollywood dreaming but is also a clear indication of how much women are still being devalued, instead of what the initial reaction to this movie being, a string of comedies while Barbie remains the center of attraction…with Ken's pocketbook.

What society has done is continue to place a very distinct familiarity for generations that have come after the Baby Boomers to entice them into what looks like "I'm obsessed" moments. Classical movies are a thing of the past by how a woman was still concerned in teasing the masculine with her "personal goods" to get her way – what has changed? Some may say this was meant to be a comedy of ways in which a woman lends true beauty to her man… yet, the jokes on those that fall for it. Why are we living in a Barbie world, as a Barbie girl? What is being taught to our youth is that Cinderella had to scrub floors and sing songs of being granted one night with the prince. Both women are depicted very differently…yet the common denominator is that Cinderella and Barbie end up getting their Prince/Ken. The major differences are that Cinderella's Fairy Godmother shows up answering her prayers while the Barbie doll was created with a boyfriend/friend Ken doll who when they met, she felt a strong attraction. The reason why Cinderella became the very first showcasing of the epitome love story in 1950, for girls of all ages was to establish a "true love" early on to Believe this could be possible. Barbie came shortly thereafter as a conglomerate to accent a new-love story portrayed by plastic dolls in 1959 showcasing how a girl could meet her "true love". However, both Cinderella and Barbie (who finally comes to life in 2023) get their "true love" that came with a price. Cinderella had to forgo her family of stepsisters who were extremely envious of her natural beauty; while Barbie was plastic with all the accouterments to entice her bae. Cinderella was a humble hard-working maiden that said a prayer while Barbie's world was already built on having it all. As both of these narratives cajole girls who witness, by example, the manipulations of showcasing how to get a man; but who has kept the man? Cinderella. Back in the days where a girl grows up learning values of power that are innately an attraction-getter to a man by means of cooking, cleaning, sewing, etc. while the past few decades are attributes of a liberal girl with plenty of plastic to showcase her skinny body in pink. The demographics of girls are clearly distinguished by the value of one's character and "how to get-a-man" bodes a much different narrative as "how-to-keep" a man. As the story continues, Cinderella is swept off her feet with her Prince Charming living in "true love" forever; and, Barbie runs into various snags with Ken attempting to keep him by her alluring desirable ways. What message are both of these sending to young innocent girls? Clearly a discombobulated message worth noting … the outer appearance of sexy, in all pink, heels, hair done, makeup done, convertible car, houses etc., while a humble maiden with very little to offer gets a miracle of God's grace. Now girls of all ages are wanting what they've been habitually taught as "how to get-a-man." The traditional version of a girl being taught cooking, cleaning, sewing, etc., has long been gone and the truth of the matter is that men are searching for a Cinderella…and girls believe they must attract, entice in a Barbie-girl way. What a world of difference has fallen from establishing traditional values and methods of learning – to – a fallen angel whose wings are getting cut with every popstar, actor, model wannabes…. Who can justify that now girls are tuning into social media platforms for styling hair, fashion trends, buying makeup and how-to-apply makeup, and a plethora of plastic ways which they will become much more desirable. It's not unlikely that this has not been going on way before the actual showcasing of Cinderella; but the message was quite different in those days. Girls' mothers were teaching them all the ways to be the greatest wife, mother, and taking time out from their busy day to assist their little girls to grow up getting their "true love" story. What happened though is society took the tradition out of the narrative by merging toxic desires of dysmorphia, anorexia, bleeding out pockets of money for clothes, shoes, makeup etc., that "they" reprogrammed by marketing products for power and money. This has been going on for decades… and now social media is replacing the mother (feminine) figure for reasons of no time, energy and/or placing attention on these children. What will come next? How can a society of plastic garbage be recycled to become anew?

Based upon the old version of tradition that once was seen as important to establish a relationship merged into the Liberation

Movement whereby women wanted equality on all fronts – what has actually happened is that women have taken it upon themselves to "have it all." Women today are forging ahead in matters of career power yet still a long way from obtaining equal pay. Women are attempting to establish anew in other areas of personal power yet while they are forging ahead in business, in their home life, for some, has been vacant. Massive trust is being given to the masculine to uphold some of the duties as a "stay-at-home" father while others are beating themselves to the ground with overwork. There has been a changing of the guards in the household and many men are uncertain of their duties. Rightfully so… Therefore, we have what is called, "role reversal" in some households. Taking on this role for some men has not been that easy and for others is natural. When it comes to gender differences in raising a child, the men clearly are aware of the boy-to-man changes, challenges and roles; however, the masculine role to girl gender impedes various other impositions such as… "having the talk" in some instances. It is very important to state that a woman's place can and will continue to be in two different places at one time – the differences are only when it comes to certain extremes. Some parents do have the parental power instilled as long as they are in agreement. For others this newly founded position on the father/masculine's side has yet to be determined. There are no "set rules" as parents have not been given a "Life Manual' per se… therefore, much of the parenting is and has always been a clear contention to those who do not have set down rules, discipline from their own childhood. Every child bears a different requirement of discipline and every parent has their own set of rules and standards of disciplining. What collapses is the system with which it has been built. All of Humanity has been raised in a dysfunctional family since the beginning for very good reasons. We are Earth-bound humans who are living in what you could term, "purgatory" in order to seek themselves and ascend to a higher consciousness.

THREADS OF STORIES

We get so excited when we meet new people whose storyline collaborates with ours…it's like meeting an old friend from our past, feels like those scars might actually begin to heal, it's a story-within a -story… reading between the lines and realizing we're all connected. Our stories connect us to others and others' stories connect to those others… and, all those threads of stories immigrate from our ancestral lineages of their stories…One thread of our ancestral storyline that couldn't be severed can now be severed…with hard work, discipline and vigilant patience. Everyone on Earth is working on severing parts of their Heritage so that a new frontier can be awakened. This is a common thread for all of Humanity who has been here before and knows the drill. So many souls have reincarnated upon Earth at this time to sever ties, to light the pathway and to build a New World Order. Our ancestors of many centuries past will be freed … as will every human who seeks to impart a congregation of soul-to-soul connections. Worlds will collide between our Heritage & The New World Order… Each thread that will be severed to Free our ancestral lineage will hold a special place in the heart of God. Let bygones be bygones…forgetful are those who seek to remember. Procrastinating only breeds tomorrow, yet there is no tomorrow…we only have now. Tomorrow cannot be promised to anyone so what are you waiting for? Do all those things, within reason, that make you light up, make you feel Free, give you a reason and the will to Live, love is seeking your Love…it is ALL in YOU! Let's give it another attempt to find ourselves in a different place; in a different mind that is no longer set

656

to fail; in a way forward, not backward; alone, not lonely; reserving the right to always be right; extract the tit-for-tat accountability of yourself and others; be in a place where you were once 'born Free'. Will you leave this world the same way you came? Instead of being forgetful and alone; how about remembering we're all going Home. Feeling lonely is one thing, but knowing the feeling that we're never alone is another. Our ancestors are within, all of what we know is within; everyone we talk to is a brother, mother, father, sister…from another family in time; and, to all of those strangers, acquaintances who we pass by are also from another family in time. All the different faces, places are traces of threads in another lifetime.

"No one said it would be easy… this thing called Life." quoted from so many in the course of our lifetime and the glue that holds us together, Love, actually. No other form of essence within our embodiment could ever understand this unless you have secretly hidden your feelings for so long… What comes and whatever goes is not so much the issue as is the essence of self that remains buried within our existence. We've come to learn, over time, that the truths of our vices can only be hidden for so long. This causes outbursts of pent-up emotions and earthquakes, all hidden from within. If we are all connected, threaded together as one in Humanity, why do some experience earthquakes and other locations do not? Climate and climate change definitely go hand-in-hand; yet this is seen only to the external eye of our imagination. The planetary alignments matter… science meets spirituality that involves Mother Earth's purging as external vices are merging. A purging of inner workings is happening and it couldn't happen without the compassion of Our Mother. Mother Earth and The Blessed Mother encompassing ALL Mothers on this Holy ground. There are those chasers; tornado chasers who seek out

657

natural disasters to acquire valuable information and as an adrenaline rush. What does that say about one's inner Heritage meets Nature? There are those who seek narcotics for that adrenaline rush and those who naturally seek out that vibe... yet, both very similar in Nature. The external disasters wreak havoc from the internal everyday struggles of "this thing called life." No matter what struggles we may experience, it is all the same... Hardships, fights, demons, control, anger, heartaches, jealousy and questions of the like occur when life is in session. Does Mother Earth feel everything and everyone's feelings? Yes. Imagine that! If just one human is riddled with guilt for an eternity, how do you think Mother Earth feels? Eternal guilt or eternal compassion to all who feel their own guilt as sinful as the next one. Guilty is as guilty does... so, who is the guilty party? Can we ever imagine a life without external feelings to live by and to learn from? Well.... Get ready to witness people learning to live without feelings, living as robotic as the computer that draws their attention without emotion – a world of AI robots? How does this make you feel? Or doesn't it? To draw on such emotions is to be told 'not' to cry being shouted at by a parent who was also taught not to show emotion. How else could this world survive?

What else is there if not in our emotions to navigate the terrain? Here is a short-list on how our *Emotional impact our Physical Health*:

Brain: **Stress**

Head: **Frustration**

Neck & Spine: **Tension**

Thyroid: **Mistrust**

Heart: **Stress, Fright**

Lungs: **Grief, Fear**

Digestive Tract: **Anxiety**

Liver: **Rage, Jealousy**

Adrenals: **Fight-or-Flight**

Gallbladder: **Anger**

Spleen: **Guilt**

Kidneys: **Fear, Shock**

Where would and where will Humanity go from here? Humanity comes from the word, human... What if the world became non-humans? Where would the fun be then? Who would the power go to if there is no more misuse of power to control? Who rightfully "owns" any power? Energy is still power even if it will be used for robotic reasons of excavating the human population – or – half human, half robot? Will the AI Movement attract humans into re-designing emotions to unemotional availability? Who has the emotional intelligence, then? What will humans represent in the future, say 2151, who will be in charge...of whose energy? Think again. A world of humans empowered by the Sun turned into a world of robots empowered by darkness. How could the Sun ever be eliminated? 40 days and 40 nights happened, didn't it? What occurred within those 40 days and 40 nights? How did light reappear? Are you so-called taking your power back? Or, shouldn't we? Hence, this is the only way in which the light of the world reappears... humans taking their 'innate' rightful power back to the light of their own truth and stopped listening to the darkness before dawn. With every sunset there will be a sunrise... yet it will only occur if YOU choose to empower yourselves with the path of truth. If you're not familiar with this path yet, don't hesitate to ask. Ask and you shall receive, that's power! A powerful person is one who takes others into consideration... that is unconditional love. How else will the world evolve IF not for all of Humanity to raise themselves to live a full life, to learn what will assist them to evolve and to surrender to the Heavens for the final supper of, "Know Thyself". When one becomes ONE in an unconditional Love for ALL – returning back to Mother Earth need not BE. That IS the metaphoric chapter in The Bible as inscribed in "The Last Supper" as to attain enlightenment as "Know Thyself."

The next generations are the next cohort, from the Greek alphabet; Generation Alpha and Generation Beta – born not into the old, but the start of something new. Generation Alpha/2010-2024; Generation Beta/2025-2039; Generation Gamma/2040-2054; Generation Delta/2055-2069 leading the pact as technical gurus, influencers of a Natural Order, socially ept, an overall Hierarchy of newly identified as Natural Co-Creators. To say that these up-and-coming generations will be very different is to be exact – their level of consciousness in remembering will be heightened; as will be their innate gifts. We all will be learning from these generations about the true values of believing in themselves and choosing to be empowered from the string of silver horses. Freedom will reign for all to claim!

The remnants of another day depict that we continue to struggle with each day that unfolds yet as a new day appears, why not change the narrative to "What lesson does today have for me?" For the majority of society has learned that complacency is real instead of a reenactment of a new day to learn, to grow, to serve and to survive instead of what others' want for us... and themselves. How has human existence shown up over the course of time? With repetition for a dying existence? Or, as a place to call our Home? In hindsight... everything that happens to us, for us, at us and with us... becomes us. Einstein quoted the world as, "indivisible." That which is withIN IS. Quantum physics meets biological science of what matters and is tangibly held IS NOT. We may appear to be a mere atom with molecular structure yet in no other Universe is there a biological clock that tells every atom when its time has expired.

That is the power of Love where, with every "expiration of..." a human life, it bears withIN the soulful nature of existence. Science has finally met with Spirituality - within and without... Energy cannot exist without the power of NOW in every moment of every life, we are the powers that BE. Whatever you have thought to believe = BE LEAVE - BE INTERNAL - BE ETERNAL - BE ASCENDENTS - 'BE' VIBES.... B E L I E V E "LIFE" IS... IN SPIRIT. "To BE or not to BE" in Shakespearean. We cannot endure to conquer anything external to us than to otherwise be in-the-moment of every moment of/for Life. Whatever you can perceive as being is exactly what you believe to be true. In the Bible depicted, "The Last Supper" makes me wonder... "who made the last supper?" Was it Jesus' disciples? No, they were sitting at the table with Jesus... So, what is the metaphoric meaning of "Know Thyself" as depicted in "The Last Supper?" It is a humbling experience to believe in those you have come to trust ... and have been tried and true through our entire lives, isn't this so? Humans tend to put their trust in others who may not have been so deserving of our trust. For this, a "Last Supper," is given as a "last chance" for those who have deceived us to forgo their deceit and realize the errors of deception of their own making. Every disciple whom Jesus believed to be true found themselves in their own time, in their own way. Jesus did not curse these disciples for not following Him – He forgave them and He forgave us all. Those unforgiving of others cannot be forgiving of themselves... What makes you all-mighty in not being able to forgive? A lack of forgiveness only breeds nuances of whatever is good in our lives as every person we encounter re-invent themselves for the sake of self. "What's love got to do with it?" a song back in the day sung by the late and great, "Tina Turner" who made us feel our way through this question. She vibrated that nuance of change in the question itself... "who needs a heart when a heart can be broken" reassures us that the only feeling that matters is that of the heart. Not only that but a clear distinction of why we need to feel, why we need to cry, why we need to know why... for whatever the reason, you do it for me... what's love but a second-hand emotion?" These are clear indications of why we need to feel, why our hearts need to break and why should a second-hand emotion not be the first thing we feel? What is required for humans to feel is NOT a source of life experience that we were taught; as it turns out to be second-hand to those who haven't realized that to feel is to live a life of love. It's second-hand nature's way of saying, "look to learn through another's pain..." Does this make sense? If we cannot have a sense of feeling the ebb and flow of life's trials and tribulations ... then, what else is there? Learn to endure *even* if that means by means of another's pain – even more so learning to feel through the unconditional love of it all. If not to learn from... at least to learn through life's experiences of our own hardships of pain. This is what 40 days of darkness means in The Bible... not to see another's pain as your own, vital to being human. We seek to be sought out through pains, sorrows of our days and tomorrows... without seeking within to find ourselves again.

God only knows what has befallen Humanity will rise again in Humans....

HU = Humans Unite.

Humanity unites when disaster prevails to show us what visions we seek to see. Death is not only for the dying – it is for all existing humans seeking to find themselves in a new light of day. Without a new perspective of that which is a forgiving heart in lieu of what is felt… and, in spite of what is not. The contradiction that life beholds is to bring clear sight of what is felt, why it is felt, to whom it is felt – and, if not, why? "For Whom The Bell Tolls" asks those of us who believe we stand alone in the world. There is no one else but you, the one who is seeking the ONE. In essence, this energy revisits itself in order to gain its own knowledge of what is your truth. This truth also inhibits one from furthering their understanding as many factors in one's own truth have a way of reverting back to a place when there wasn't a difference of that truth. Right and/or wrong did not exist in the beginning of time – it wasn't until the temptation to eat the apple that Adam tempted Eve with time-to-assist and return back to the natural order in a lost world of no order. The only place for your own truth has already been written in your heart but not yet perceived with your body – thereby an unknowing of knowingness.

What has already been written on Earth can be subjected to change only if the heart insists that it is for the betterment of the whole. No other type of referencing of truth needs further explanation… it is your Heart that knows. Your Ego, however, will find ways to implement a solid argument that might even have you buying into it… but, in mid-sentence a feeling of unease may come over as your senses reeling you back to your truth of Heart. Heart-to-heart conversations need no words… they feel. What does this say about the endless amounts of wasted time humans attempt to change the narrative of one's destiny/fate. Fated destiny is the only way to attain your heart's truth – there is no other; and, when you seek to understand that "going with the flow" is what is meant to be, then you will ride the waves of your written destiny – with your eyes closed and a smile as wide as the oceans. Given that "in-hindsight" we come to understand the reasons why... Foregoing evidentiary evidence otherwise is a sheer play of your egoic self. Why not take "yourself" out of the equation by seeking to play the main role in your play-full life? When the ID - identifying of the self, egoic self comes to play, it becomes a life full of chaos, action, drama, confusion etc., only to watch you squirm. Be mindful mind-full of the ways which the ego schemes as it knows you very well… it's been with you your entire existence for you to jump, drop and squeeze your way out of yourself and into a life of unresolved karma. "What karma is this?" one may ask… if your answer is to "change the narrative" and learn lessons you are on path… if not, seek your own self in the ocean of one's fated destiny. In order to believe one's own truth, humanity must suffer the pains of growing up… not your ordinary physicality of the body but the "growing up" of those things that have imparted karmic havoc in life. There is no other way than the way which children can learn, grow and find a place to be at peace. There is no other way … when it comes to finding yourself as a self-realization that comes to those who seek out their own beasts-of-burden and come to terms with this truth. Once the egoic mindset has been set free, human existence complies with a resounding "Yes!" Our egoic self-hides its truth in what is very well known as; justifying the means, keeping a mindset without changes, albeit changes for the better while shaming their own selves of the hardships, trials and tribulations, of what they did and/or did not answer the call to when inadvertently they knew it was a wake-up call. What has caused a stir in many hearts is the overridden "guilt" that they feel for not succumbing to what is very foreign as happiness. No other human who can make you happy other than yourself. Feeding your ego with guilt, shame, anxiety and stress is a cause of another concern and has no bearing on the recipient of harboring another's' issues. What is clearly not predictive of all humans is the onset of moments when hitting rock bottom ends up in the faces of those who are innocent bystanders. For those who are witness to struggling with another's egoic stress, please stand by to encounter what is really being revealed. The stresses of mankind stand out amongst the rest as a hidden agenda of feeling surrounded by problems of others, going out of their way to please as in "people pleasing" and a surge of other resources lie in hidden pain itself. Many are riddled with so much guilt that they cannot even consume what is vastly known as an innocence they've forgotten. The innocence of childhood... guilt plays havoc on all who have tried to beat the system by ignoring others and only thinking about themselves. If this guilt continues to override another's ill-mannered tempers, triggers, outbursts this too is a clear indication of what has been left behind. So many humans have been stuck in a time-warp of guilty pleasures from their past, of guilty by association, of guilty lashing out, of guilty-seeking those who are fragile and unattainable and/or unable to stick up for themselves; and, to all those who have found the one who is guilty of not thinking of anyone else, other than themselves... has much karma to pay. This is one of the most hideous crimes to all who have found themselves the "guilty party" for acts that were done to and/or for the ego – now clearly are paying a hefty price. The recipient of these karmic injustices may or may not seek to witness these undertakings yet the reality is very real, indeed. Behold, another source of contention within one's own self-worth is needing to forgive all of those people, places and/or things that have caused turmoil within... then, without. We've all been there at one lifetime or another and without the reassurance of our own Love-of-self, one is unable to find peace of mind. Their egoic mindsets have led us all to formulate a lifeline of trauma until one is able to be free. Allowing yourself to undergo the pain by realization, by acceptance and through the acts of God's Love can set the course of Freedom. Through a semblance of initial pain into forgiveness established, one will procreate over and over again on Earth with a wide arena of characters which they have not been able to forgive, accept, send light and love and ultimately release. Once we are able to stop pointing the blame at another, at all others and take full responsibility for our actions we will remain tied and bound on this planet of karmic justice. Karma must be forgiven to all and to the self… then anew will be born. *Rebirth*.

Give until it hurts, forgive all, send all your worries, stress and painful truths over to God and He will guide you to where you will be Free to be ME… Mother Earth, on Earth's Motherland where compassion reigns above all. See yourself and others in the eyes of love – given to those you Love first and bring a sense of peace unto your world in the light of a wonderful new beginning. The treacherous silence begets to hold one in captivity…until a union for peaceful new beginnings are held in sacred Love and felt for all Humanity. Go toward the light of every dark crevasse within yourself that is unable to let it go… and move on. Within the darkness is a glimmer of light, hope and a resounding showcase of strength. By all means do NOT give into the darkness that shadows your true purpose on your life's journey. A journey unlike any other that could and will cease to exist – find yourself in the wake of silence before the physical body dies and the only thing left is an unfulfilled soul who gets lost again only to find itself. Please find yourself without reserving another space on this Earth for yet another goes around. Review, recollect, re-establish and revisit all those who have jolted your peace-of-mind just so that you can gain your strength to become what you were meant.

JOURNEY TO LOVE

What has been a contention since inception is to believe that anything external will make us happy. All fabricated nonsense to inflict this upon anyone. No one person, place and/or thing can make us happy if we cannot come to believe our happiness lives within us. This Universe seems to have been constructed from the outside in…but, it is the exact opposite. The Universal truths are within each and every one of us and it is our responsibility to ourselves to find that truth. To dig deeper than ever is required, to enjoy your own company and to not feel the loneliness as anything other than capturing the fragrance of life from deep within our essence. Look forward to another day, breathe in every morsel of your existence by perceiving life as the present it is. Who does that? Those who are on their Journey of Love to achieve inner stability, great wealth-in-health and a newfound happiness for not only their own creation but also for the creations of those that have come before and for those who will come thereafter. The path to awareness is a lone trail of trepidation, an arduous self-realization, not up for discussion, contemplation…just a silent whisper in the wind. Should you breathe in life everlasting as an inner exchange for realizing that to give of yourself for the highest good of others will grow your wings to fly…eternal life shall be yours. Accomplishing what others do not value in you becomes the way of life – not imposing any desire/need to be approved. The requirements that others have wanted from you is certainly not what is necessary for you to uphold and value. It is an outsider's perception that will not matter when you value your own selves by not needing to gain

667

anyone's approval…this includes every person who has told us so. Do we dare to be our own individuals seeking no-thing else but what makes you do you that leads to pure happiness. A common ground for those who will debate the crucial aspects of what every human on Earth is doing here and why. Just be yourself and seek no one's approval but your own. Once you succumb to another's Ego you become another mask that will tether your soul adding yet another layer of "What Am I Made For…" Perception is key. The key to perception is the whereabouts of what our own mindset has or hasn't believed to be true. Whatever your personal cases of vendettas, extreme assurances of what you believe to be true and in what particular errs of others' perceptions play either a familiar role, or not, must all be taken into account. We seek others' acceptance, their word-is-solid truth, to tell us that their truth should be sought out; and, to trust in that word for these so-called perceived remembrances of what was taught and what to believe in ourselves and others. It becomes mind boggling to what is actually believed to be the truth because so many outer factors play into our mind. Why do people seek outside counsel whenever there is a decision to be made? What makes some humans *not* question their own counsel? Does this pertain to you? Think about it…. For whatever reason, humans have relied on others to dictate their decisions since inception. Could it have to do with the fact that society has, once again, placed upon us another layer with which to question our own dictatorship? Not only that… but humans have a stigma about following their own advice even when, in their heart-of-hearts, they know something to be true. It's as if humans have been avoiding themselves and entrusting others to sway their perceived opinions, decisions at every turn. Why? Does this come from childhood? Does Humanity's ability to sway trump decisions that they know to be truly harmful but nonetheless keep to themselves?

Where did society intervene in people's inability to make decisions for others but not for themselves? It's as if others are in charge of our lives… it's as if Humanity has not conquered at all… it's as if the last of Humanity standing carries an inferiority complex so deep that to find it would be one's own detriment to society. Has this happened? Where in your life have decisions been made for you? Come to think of it, where are you right now in your current life …are you angry, disappointed, unhappy that you listened to "so and so" for guidance when you know in hindsight that was not the best decision for you? Humans decided long ago that it is easier to place the blame on another/others instead of taking on responsibility for their decisions. Why? When did this begin in your life? Has it started in childhood without ever really knowing? We've all got our circle of friends whom we trust to tell us what is the best course of action – only to find out later that the advice was coming from a jealous friend. Do you realize that this occurs daily in families, friends, co-workers, businesses and a vast number of acquaintances whom we trust better than our own judgment. To ascertain this on a much deeper level requires much psychological help in determining where this began. Most definitely it has begun sometime during our being raised to believe that those in authority "know" better. Perhaps this is true in some ways but to believe it to be true with everyone who we meet is another way of saying that we have no power over our lives. External perceptions that we invite under the disguise of borrowed knowledge that others have acquired, better than us, is ludacris. In the Bible, Ludacris is a songwriter who wrote, "War with God " is a clear depiction of what Humanity has been undergoing for quite some time. In Ludacris' lyrics it is written, "the guilty will speak" to all those who fight for themselves through their Ego. What he is saying is that all those in the industry believe they are the so-called better man, outright euphemisms of the Egoic type cry out that the only way which man can survive is through their Ego and the perceptions of what others think of them. At every turn, man has been crying out for the attention of others from an Egoic place of contention of the MORE Movement that brings man down to a level of "the Devil made me do it."

What has been witnessed in the external world are those who have made a name for themselves out of what they believed in their hearts as an overriding power that they came to shout out they matter in a world of disillusionment. All courses of actions where "shout outs" to those whose Ego selves need reassurance, rest assured that's all they've wanted to conquer. So many in the Arts have been a source to reckon with because what they want is what so many are still searching for, recognition. A sense of establishing a career that places them on the map for what they believe to be true; and, we the outsiders looking into their lives either agree or not. Finding these artists our fav's or our foes. This is by far the clearest example of how Humanity has strayed from believing in themselves from a heartful place of peace instead of an angered place of injustices. They've been given a name for themselves because they did not get it in other places with people that did not give them the time of day. What causes humans to extend such outrage of anger that seeps throughout one's life? A cause for concern when we look deeper into the psyche of where this all began in our lives. To witness the outside world as an "hatred, angry world" is exactly what is going on on the "inside." Is it a crime that most artists have been handed a pot of gold by selling their soul? Could this be what the conspiracy theories are all boasting about? Where did this all come from? This MORE Movement has been around since the beginning of time on the Earth plane primarily because it comes with the matter of materialism NOT spiritualism. Why? We are on the ground floor on Earth, breeding power, money, etc., all of Egoic nature. What is to happen with Humanity is for those who seek their own counsel to follow the way of Spirit without selling your soul. Humanity must start at the ground level of the Base Chakra, that of sex, drugs and rock'n'roll to play out, find out all there is about your Ego. The Earth plane is our Ego and to free oneself of this by befriending our Ego is to seek Spiritual guidance from the heart. Once this happens, all "matters of the heart" take real precedence. It's clearly NOT easy to do… yet many are becoming enlightened to this practice of "Know Thyself." If you are, then you are starting to seek your own counsel by representing your true essence from a standpoint of your Faith. Faith vs. Fear is what the Earth plane is all about!

Remember this …. especially if you are seeking to be a part of the MORE Movement. In order to equip oneself with the trajectory of being able to separate yourself from the others, one must seek the place of their own truth upon the Earth plane. The MORE Movement is designed to establish these factors by distinguishing amongst them. We don't recognize our Egoic self until it is way past the due date of what type of decision overrides the other by seeing it for whatever it has brought. What it will bring, based upon knowing oneself will be a clear understanding with NO Fear. Sometimes we choose the other for apparent reasons that may boost our Ego up and/or feel superior to one another; however, that leads to self-sabotage. Some of the reasons why we require the Ego are apparent: gaining self-confidence, establishing a reputable underdog, salvaging ourselves in times of need, requiring to override for the betterment of Humanity and so many other reasons why. There are many apparent reasons why Humanity requires the Ego that shows up for every human in ways that establish why the shadow was innately built. In certain other cases, our Ego continues to impart many lessons for us to grow from with the ability to use our better judgment. This is where the Heart space overrides what our mind-set has been alluring us into for the better of one's life. We can either embrace this Egoic self or we can continue to allow it to override our better judgment – it is up to us utilizing our freewill. Once we have overcome, the Heart space of all decisions are used as our primary default instead…hence, Love overcomes all Fear. When the Heart is in charge all doubts, questions, fear of any kind evaporates into the ethers as abundant Love, Faith and Trust. This is Divine Love… The cataclysmic events of our lives lead us to the very place where we used to know into new avenues of acceptance showing up as going with the flow that reassures our hearts in peace. We cannot determine when this will happen for every human on the face of the Earth but typically this occurs when the student is ready to venture upon their journey inward. We cannot be required to place a timeframe on those who are becoming aware accepting that a higher consciousness is leading one's path; but you will KNOW when this is.

Divine timing happens at all times… yet to those who are not going with the flow it can be an arduous journey through "The Dark Night of the Soul." Why is our shadow work called, "The Dark Night of the Soul" it's because we must go deep within our darkness in order to find where our light is. The timing is always on point for those who have gained their flow… and, even though many are still struggling through it, when we release control, everything falls back on course. What in your life is begging you to let go of trying to control the terrain? Can you? Are you experiencing your Dark Night of the Soul?

Do you know what to expect? Once you undergo a series of happenstances in your segway of seeking your path it will become much clearer. There are basic ascension symptoms that every human undergoes in the beginning and throughout the rest of doing the inner work. This work can and does take decades and/or many lifetimes to establish the initial *Stages of Ascension*. The very first stage are people who do not vibrate on the same frequency with you and must depart your life – however that pans out. This is how you will begin to become aware that God has heard your prayers.

Below are the basic ascension symptoms, as follows:

STAGES OF ASCENSION

1. A Hopeful Meaning to Life

2. Breakdowns

3. Feeling Strange

4. Spiritual Magnet

5. Curiosity

6. Lonely Hearts

7. Recluse

8. Mother Nature

9. Questions of an Ego

10. Heightened Senses

11. Stalled Progress

12. Physical/Emotional waves

13. Am I "CRAZY?"

14. Humanities Disasters

15. Dreams vs. Reality

16. Letting Go

17. In-Deeds we Serve

18. Leap of Faith

19. The SHIFT – Spiritual Haven In FAITH, TRUST

20. ALL IS GOD. ™

Do you recognize some of these ascension stages? If so, you are officially "on path!" Many will recognize some of these symptoms as they have begun their flight… Some are still in fight-or-flight, some are still attempting to tame their desires and some are in-deep with attempting to figure out why the Ego is even necessary for our journey. Hunched tight shoulders are the external results of a fight-or-flight modality. "When the student is ready the Master appears…" Until the Master appears, many nuances will arise… such as: painful truths that the human body can no longer sustain; innocence of where we seek to exist that becomes nonexistent; failures from the errs of our ways; manipulations of the strangest; lies that befall us into false beliefs and the list goes on. We cannot conceive of the realization that distractions of all kinds tend to be an avoidance that we grew up with in childhood. Those who have no childhood memories, can't focus and/or life feels like a blur has physical remnants of tight or sore hips. This is indicative of the fact that all of our childhoods had to have certain traumas in order for us to become our highest selves. Our inner emotional issues appear as dis-ease in our external body…it is our ability to navigate that bears substance. Either in this lifetime or many others until we gain a clearer understanding of what it means to have eternal Faith. Many like to hear themselves say how "Faithful" they yet doubt life unfolding as Divine Order. What we KNOW to be true has no room for questions until it does… to question our own internal guidance is one thing – until we question why we don't have the Faith that leads to a clear truth of understanding. Every road has its turns that are

674

required in order to establish a deeper *Faith in God*. Faith in God is the ultimate Love of Self that constitutes a deep knowing. When we "know" something as true… either statistically or proven fact, there is no going back and forth usually because we aren't here to prove Science wrong. For whomever is in question of their roadless travels only remain in question in order to experience what they already know. Even going down a different path or choosing a different route is confirmation that it has to be so until you get that instinctual knowing as to why it all happened, in hindsight. So many things get clearer to us when we look back over the terrain, after the fact – this is the only time looking back to review what happened is not a detriment; but, going back to revisit the past as it is, is to our detriment. If ever going back lends itself to how we sabotaged our path this becomes a detriment at first which becomes a clear knowing. When was the last time you too made the decision to go back into a partnership only to be led into knowing exactly why, after some time has passed, why that person is no longer in your life currently. The energies are ever-changing… either we surpass what was into a higher understanding or we continue repeating until the inevitable happens. "What we resist persists" in every instance, higher understanding of what we experience on the external that reflects our inner world. Being still and knowing is easier than what it appears to be for whatever reason we already know yet the stillness must override one's mindset to what has become of you. Very few people can be 'still' and others continue to escape themselves at the very onset of seeing their own reflection. What has been a contention to find oneself becomes a series of unfortunate, yet advantageous, events where we see our own selves through the eyes of others. What energies are facing you in your life right at this very moment? Could it be attempts to find out what it is you really don't like about what you see in others as the Universal design to see yourself and what you too are not liking in you? This becomes our raw truth … to understand that what you may not accept in others is a form of what you are not accepting in yourself. You will know that Spirit is doing its job to show you your rawness in others as you will experience a pouring out of emotions – defensiveness, anger, shame, blame, disgust, animosity, jealousy and all those negative emotions that come to highlight what we need working on in our lives. Anxious thoughts are a sign that any attachment needs aren't met…the root of all anxiety is the fear/grief of losing someone. Studies have proven that once humans can defy their own gravity, they have definitely been privy to the Science that implodes with Spirit. Our spiritual path is intermingled with the natural order of Mother Earth – a scientific methodology that breeds a new Humanity. Mother Earth has been designed by the 3,6,9 Method that Nickola Tesla invented where everything in-and-of-the Earth is a Mathematical construct. We've all been given this equation for the usage of understanding the real world as it has been structured. What befalls planet Earth are those who have not educated themselves enough to know that all of the Earth plane is a gravitational pull which gives Humanity a reason not to believe. This began in early 200 BC where the Earth became what is known as, the planet of, "Hard Knocks" and underground forces had been spotted using Earth for their own purposes of knocking out this beautiful planet by overriding the scientific parts of Her beauty; and, deceiving Humanity in believing that all matter matters. Therefore, Mother Earth's people became greedy, jealous, envious to the point that a new Hierarchy was born of mass corruption… not seen, but evolved as what we would call today's conspiracy theories of madness. Whatever you may or may not believe doesn't matter on this Earth because as many already are aware the Earth plane is strictly an energetic planet that has been in trouble… until now.

676

The powers that be have allowed Humanity to become very aware, through all social media platforms, of the corruption front and center. What does matter is that now Humanity has been able to raise Her frequency elevating to new Higher Consciousness unlike ever before in the History of this planet! Everyone has now become privy and a witness to observing the hidden evil people, places and things who have attempted and been unsuccessful in hurting our planet. We thank all those negative forces for bringing social media platforms to the spotlight of the hidden because now Humanity and humans who are here to assist have all been salvaged! It's not over, however, as much of the evil forces in Nature are still being extracted never to return… it is Mother Earth's planet that will seize to allow these energies to ever enter again. The workings of Spirit do not need to reveal exactly how this has been happening but everyone on Mother Earth is opening their awareness to what is true. Much has been hidden which in certain cases is for the highest good of those humans who need not see other happenings that would torment the human mind instead of reducing the stress and anxiety of what has been going on. Social warfare is on high alert and the good news is that most of Humanity is ready to fight for peace of mind instead of an eye for an eye mentality. Awareness has given Humanity a new lifeline… so, even if you're not on the battlefields of war, just know that those are not our battles to interfere with years of animosity, but it is our right to claim those who have been tortured to death, families etc., and to claim freedom and peace through a collective prayer is all we are being asked to do. Why should we fight fire-with-fire when we know that someone and/or many will inevitably get burned? We stay on the sidelines because this is not our war to fight the enemy but to seek outside help from all of the children of God and pray. This is what being a witness does mean… not to add fuel to any fires – emitting a collective-prayer circle through social media, through friends and family to pray for all who are at war. PRAY. even if you don't so much as believe it can help others, even more so… PRAY. What comes to pass will eliminate evil energies that cannot seek to find their own peace within themselves so they go seeking wars with other countries, people and whatever ways to destroy. Keep praying for every country on this planet… "What the world needs now, is LOVE sweet LOVE."

Even when we don't hold the Faith that is required to live a truthful life path it becomes much clearer when we actually realize that we are the ones that need to see what is true for our highest good. Some add value while others fail to see what their true essence is. We've been in the dark practically our entire lives and now that external influencers have shown up sharing what is really going on this gives us the freedom of movement. At every turn Humanity is becoming more cognizant with world events, trades, wars and reptilian activity – for if it weren't for social media platforms, humans would still be in the dark. There are reasons behind why "everything happens for a reason" and now we know. Too bad there are still those who haven't 'gotten the memo' but that is only a matter of time. Our initial response is to bat an evil eye at those who are evil but to do this would be harmful only to those doing that – and those knowing that the mirror has two faces brings us back to why we do not choose to fight fire-with-fire. All the truths of one's life unravels to show what does happen, what can happen and what has happened to anyone who withstands the tests of time. We gather our wits by purging those people, places and things that have yet to find our own faults and their own inactivity to taking responsibility. When one person is hurting … if you do and/or don't realize it, that one person multiplied by Infinity is going through similar pain. When we observe this happening many say, "not my circus, not my monkeys" in order to keep themselves out of the equation; all the while, knowing that they too are using it to *escape* from their own pain. We're all threaded together on this Earth and for whatever it's worth, viewing others in pain may speak volumes to another existing pain that is repressed within you. How long can we continue watching others in pain before we realize that a sliver of their storyline has been engrained somewhere in our narrative. We sometimes do see the threat of pain people are going through and yet our pain is far too great to do the work on us. Therefore, many make it all about the pain of others and are unlikely to admit to being about them. Witnessing how this happens, listening to another's painful truth gives way to our being truthful and seeking common ground that we are all human. This thread shows up at some point in time when we're ready to see it and learn from others' pain. Not all comes front and center about us in the present time; but we develop great compassion for those who are suffering because we too have suffered. No matter what the pain and suffering is for certain people just know that at some point in our lives we too wanted to be heard, coddle led, given a hug, seen what another feels and felt what another feels etc. To escape all pain from happening, to ignore another's pain and to not choose to accept another's pain as to hurt to acknowledge is escaping oneself from healing. We know that what is being witnessed on the Earth plane – wars, suffering, deaths of our brotherhood of man, it is "we" that are witnessing but this may or may not affect you personally but it does have an effect on us …as we are one. It takes a true warrior to eventually see how much pain and suffering there is in this world and understand that it may not affect our families directly – but, we are affected because true compassion is the thread that connects all of mankind. You may say what you will … yet it is your freewill to enter into a plea of others' pain and suffering as our own. All lives matter!

All children matter! All of the pain and suffering is real! All stories need to be told, podcasted out unto the world so that those who lack clear sight and compassion will come to terms with how very real the pain/suffering of others inflicts upon the entirety of the world. This is why it is called, "world events" to hear what is happening in all parts of the world and as cheesy as it sounds, praying for world peace…collectively is what the world is in need of. Why would we not pray for peace for Mother Earth? Were we not taught to pray for others and for ourselves? Where did "prayer" go? Why has it been extracted from our day-to-day life? Did it go away when society overruled it so as not to believe, "In God We Trust?" Taking away from prayer in homes, schools and in whatever world event or close-to-home terrorism that had to happen for us to learn how society has manipulated the narrative? Who cares? Just because 911 did not happen directly to your immediate families does not mean that to those it did happen to are hurting while they still are in remembrance of their loved ones lost? When did the act of prayer become nonexistent? Did this begin in our home life where our parents and/or those who raised us chose to leave prayer out of the homelife? When did all these false pretenses of others beget to become your nuances of life-long beliefs gone wild? Is it true that the majority of society only prays for those who have been lost in 911 and other terrorist attacks upon our planet in the past few decades forgetting their own? Do you pray for those suffering from dis-ease in their bodies? Do you pray when you witness an ambulance rushing to the nearest hospital in a possible life-threatening emergency? Do we pray when someone has been taken ill? Do we pray for those who we hear about acquaintances and/or mere strangers from outside our circle who have received bad news about their health i.e., "did you hear a no-name has cancer?" What drives Humanity away? Is it fear for the inevitable? Is it too painful or not when we hear of bad news because that's all we've been exposed to? Is it fair to hold onto the adage, "Fear of God?" Why do people fear God? Is it because they have been engaging in sins of the flesh, beastly burdens and other forms of whatever evil they are ingesting only to be scared of this Judgment Day? Who wouldn't fear any form of death since it is the only thing that fears itself? The "fear of self" is the death that begins the moment we enter the Earth plane... we are dying. Why not set another type of lifestyle where we enter as the Elder and work our way back to childhood...would that be a better solution to experience life backwards in order to not fear the painful deterioration of the human body? Is that what we truly are fearing – yes, a big part of our fears are not only our bodies giving out from ill-health but the absolution of a death that takes the human body form unto the Earth. This body is by definition what the Earth is made for... we live each day feeding our bodies that which is unhealthy – all the unhealthy patterns of ourselves and our ancestral lineage where we cannot escape the "devil is in the details" we are too weak to willfully fight by being healthy – mind, body. All forms of "stress" kill. In whatever form of stress impacts our bodies it must be faced and dealt with – and, more importantly, to those who abuse their bodies for the Fun of it. What denotes stress in one's body is another's way with which abuse of the body; unhealthy eating, drinking, sex, smoking to any and all dis-eases that show up will have to be dealt with as karmic retribution. Most eating dis-orders aren't disorders – they're attempts of gaining control after a betrayal, violation and/or emotional neglect. If you witnessed fighting, betrayals within a family who did not provide emotional support, food becomes the emotional outlet. All disorders give off a sense of control where there is none... What impairs someone from moving their body is not the same as another who has fallen from grace abusing the body. Many are just stressed out from work and unable to seek solace as this form of escapism entertains stress; while others are eating healthy and seeking purification may still have hidden stress factors such as when high-bl0od pressure, diabetes and those forms of silent killers that impact the body at some point. Then, of course, there is the virus, Covid, aluminum sightings, pesticides and a plethora of plastic-wrapped unhealthy foods sold which many have not been made aware of that are affecting Humanity.

When will humans take their power back and become their own health advisors to eat healthy, work out and learn about what it takes to purify the body? Not following the "crowd" is a good start… Having bloodwork done to dive deep into your own DNA is another good start – and, following a healthy course of life will give you the freedom from a good portion of the fear that is eluding others. Ignorance is bliss or not? From karmic debt we all have the willful power to choose what our bodies can or cannot handle. Some eat because of emotions they are not able to dissect and/or contain…some eat to pass the time, and some do not eat enough to gain the proteins and veggies while others are bulimic or anorexic. We cannot stress enough the importance of awareness in purification of body and mind… this is the only stress of energy exchange we want to impose upon. What is seen may be too difficult for humans to realize that their physical body contains the energy of the Universe and must be healthy-to-be-wealthy in all aspects of our lives. Many realize but are still bashing their bodies to live up to their addictions, knowingly. There are definite repercussions to not treating your body with love, care and respect. All external additives will impair the physical body… hence, the energetic forces cannot be sustained or tampered with unless they are and dis-ease becomes the norm. Whatever contains the internal/external illnesses of our body are inflictions of pain and suffering that need healing is awareness. Fittingly are those whose ancestors had suffered their own course of dis-ease in their bodies that have filtered into the DNA of our own... this too must be addressed. Whenever we are not feeling 100% it is because somewhere within our own connectivity are blocks of energy that need healing. They say, "what's good for the goose is good for the gander" but is it? Why should any addiction be sought as a "if you can't beat 'em, join 'em" mentality? Have you ever placed yourself in that situation...knowing that you are subjecting illness upon your body? Humanity must become more aware of the variables that lead one into temptation... body and mind override.

How can we, as a society, become all-knowing if not through a deep assessment of what we are made of? Look within, seek outside counsel and find ways in which you can build up your external resources of the physical body that emulates our inner workings. This is where one's beginning journey happens for most. What, who and how are your energies being drained? Are you aware of the physical body that connects the inner workings of our past, present and what the future of awareness can do to save ourselves? Will you ascertain an honest-to-goodness future of gaining access to what is going on inside so that the external body correlates to that which is the same. "Health is wealth" of the inner meets the outer. When we seek to falter on our responsibilities, we end up wavering that which is required to go on. We continue to struggle with the masses ending up in a state of affairs that remains a concealed weapon to those who are still in the matrix. Without knowing, society has built a wall of opinions about what the matrix is all about and conspiracy theories have also been seen as a mountain of lies, judgments and opinions; but the fact remains that what is to be seen as some conspiracy theories have become actual facts to what has been hidden all along. Don't think this type of deception hasn't been around since the beginning of time… it has. The only difference is that what people think now has been tainted into pursuing what they've known all along. Hidden, ulterior motives have been a thing since Adam & Eve, since Biblical times of Sodom and Gomorrah, since the Freemasonry and that is just the tip of the iceberg. When you think that you've been outdone, you have. Whenever you feel a sense of longing for what the future will bring, or, when an Apocalypse will be arriving, it is in this way where we sacrifice ourselves for what "they" have been feeding us. Do you stay in your own lane? Can you stop listening to all the bat-shit crazies of those who live in a fear-based society? "They" want us all to be fearful, to speak out in fear, to listen to all the fads of what's to come … holding a place of all this in the name of Fear. What would happen if this wasn't the case? Could you reconsider your life in any different version? A version of only Love through what emotional independence is really all about… a standup life for only a love that enters can be really felt within. No matter what externals you're feeling right now have you settled, have you caved, have you grown apart from all those who turn up as adding value, or, a helping hand? Will you see how this sets you apart from what has been said for lifetimes…and, lifetimes ago prior to where you are now. Can you see yourself as a mirror reflection of all that is good in the world? Or, are you falling for the "divide and conquer" repertoire of what is "said" to be in your best interest. What is your narrative? Who is writing your story and what are you sinking your teeth into? The same old story is playing out in your life mainly because you are used to it and allow no areas of change to happen. The reason for this is that society has placed much of Humanity in a bubble only to dictate what is or isn't true. We are all privy to these narratives primarily because it is "out there" on social media, it's also been a dictatorship of what has been since the beginning of time and, the only difference is that now it is visibly seen in order for us to siphon out the chaff. In what world do we end up visiting a life of "free will" just to mess things up and continue to revisit the same old ground day after day? It has been constructed as such so that the main characters of our lives have a chance to change it up, level up and find a passionate new fulfilling life awaiting them. It may be easier, as it's always been done before, to continue living the lie that anger, depression, stress, unhappiness is the "new" norm but, then again this is what "they're saying" is what you want. How could we live in such a world that was built primarily on the end of times - instead of the beginning of times? Why not rewind our lives to when you can recall being happy? When was that exactly? Do you recall how it felt? Do you remember what made you happy? Was it "something" that made you happy or was it just living a childhood of innocence that purported you into happy moments. On the other hand, many of our childhood recollections have been tainted to the best of our comprehension which lends itself to all the destruction of the physical body to begin with. Or, perhaps we had a somewhat happy childhood that took a turn for the worse that has caused an overage of pain, discouragement, hate, anger, jealousy and other forms of addictive behaviors that we've been warped-in-time believing. We are the only ones on Earth that have sensed tension of the highest magnitude... Do you realize that? Or, has the stress and tension levels been so high that we cannot even attempt to disagree otherwise. So many humans have "NO IDEA" about how they're feeling because they're masking the pain with outside/external influences that they've become used to. The amount of pharmaceuticals used in the last few generations is astounding – everyone is taking meds, doing drugs of other kinds, drinking and masking their reality into a numbing

685

existence... "Comfortably Numb" as in the lyrics of the song by Pink Floyd. Was this the reason that the 60's, 70's were the ones to begin a new generation of sex, drugs and alcohol that began a generation whose majority of their children have been diagnosed with dis-ease of not only the generation of parents who were in the abyss; but, to all those kids who are now facing their parents wondering the same, or, attempting to escape in not only their parents' DNA but also to become comfortably numb. Do you think that pointing the finger at our parents will help to heal our pain? Or, do we take these drugs with our children – staying too cool for school – trying to maintain a youthful presence for our kids to look up to? Really?

When we feed our bodies in tangent with Nature, a purification begins and all flows in place. If not, it could imply time for a detox, eating healthy with few meats in your lifestyle, prayer before eating, a new cognizance of color in one's day-to-day wardrobe "Color My World" as in dressing for a healthy day, suiting up for a successful day, watching TikTok videos that are educating, learning new waves of passive incomes, asking others for help, resisting temptations, supplemental inquiries and seeking what value this has for you, narrowing your search for happiness to being happy every day and so many other co-creating ways to find yourself a peaceful place. Just when you think that you've nurtured your body it will seem as though it's not cooperating with your outer world. This is because your inner compass is at the Heart of truth; while your outer world is a matter of Ego. Feel the difference...

A LIFE OF RUIN… REBUILD

History repeats itself as a way to awaken Humanity from imploding…which is why, at this moment in time, everyone on the Earth's planet has signed up to assist in the evolution of our planet. To do so, we must utilize all the innate tools that were given to us all, by going inward to capture our true essence. What we want is to get reacquainted with ourselves and what our purpose is being here – not to reenact the destruction of a planet; but to raise the consciousness of our planet. We are the energetic force of Mother Earth and it will take arduous work and determination to seek our inner guidance. What's the payout? There is no payout…but, there is a place in Heaven for all of God's children who, no matter what, have raised their soul's consciousness that ultimately raises Humanity. What stands the test of time is our willingness to be honest and truthful with ourselves "knowing" that there is much more that meets the egoic "I" to life…that so-called American dream that once was the power surge of Humanity is now the powerful stance to uphold our gift of empowerment. The new "normal" is a redefined narrative of what power means to you… does power still mean what society has imposed as misuse of power in the blind-leading-the-blind. Or, can WE, you and me, change the trajectory from "Just an Old-Fashioned Love Song" by Three Dog Night to a "Come Together" by the trail-blazers, the Beatles. When we tie both threads of "an old-fashioned love song with come together" this becomes a beautiful masterpiece called, "GOD ONLY KNOWS!" King + Country. A LOVE that God only knows…the REAL YOU.

STATE OF MEDITATION

We live in an illusion of what we think, not of what is… if you think your world is a series of confusion, doubt, anguish, greed and the like; then, it is. Where do you find your peace? Being in a meditative state will assist you to find your way… doing laundry, washing dishes, gardening, swimming, walking, doggy love, a deep conversation, singing, and any form of relaxation of the mind is required. It's effortless…not necessarily a chore. Whatever the hardship is your wake-up call to seek yourself. What's sad is that so many have been programmed by routines of complacency that are not seen. You must give yourself a break time and time to reconnect with a simple, soulful life. If you're questioning yourself right now you are making progress… being aware is the beginning of your inner journey. Ignorance is bliss only to those who do not want the entirety of a blissful life. Without needing to know… without questions… without doubt. Sing along with songs that lift your soul to higher levels; read in silence; retreat; find yourself wherever that self is. Continue upgrading your life in ways that aren't pulling you down to their level; without having to convince yourself you're happy, without leading a useless life, find a useful cause to serve, in-deeds. What you are seeking is seeking you…

What so many humans fail to be is "self-confidence" primarily because of their DNA, their makeup, ancestral lineage, their need for perfection, their sense of alliances that bring them down and depressed – lost for so long that we tend to allow for these degradations. Habitual forms of action release no serotonin in one's system and the body becomes very familiar without needing joy, happiness, trust, in their lives. Everybody needs to be happy and yet so many are taking medications to attempt to be happy. How silly is this? There are so many natural forms of getting happy that are the simple pleasures in life, have we forgotten? Eastern culture puts IN the work yet has not been vigilant in getting balanced to allow others in. Western culture is primarily vying for attention – all matters of the Ego. Both civilizations have the polarity of yin/yang in high volume instead of synergizing – we are "out there" on both ends of the spectrum of the Horizon. The balance is where we meet at the Horizon in a time where we are attempting to seek balance in our lives without too little or too much of anything. Simply put, yet very hard to do... takes self-discipline, the highest form of Love, to give yourself. Eastern is mega chillness while Western is mega madness – even though these surrounding countries and states encompassing an entire Universe just fall short of their own progress. How can we merge yin/yang within ourselves? Learn to see yourself exactly as you are in an attempt to not live by anyone else's standards, morals, values, identify yourself as you...take it in. Breathe. When did Humanity seize to enjoy what has been given ... not needing so much more? Western civilization is the MORE Movement; Eastern civilization is the MEDITATION Movement – stop for a moment to see how outrageous this divide is...what happened and, more importantly, how can we merge united together with both in place, balanced? Every human on the face of the Earth has already received their balance...all you have to do is use it. Once again, it's about "want" vs. "need". Ask yourself if you really *need* to accumulate more stuff? Why not give yourself 20 minutes to get over it. What's enough? Heavily tainted by growing up, "not enough" and without getting to the core of the matter, the onion, humans will continue to be on the hamster wheel for the rest of our lives.

689

Our stillness is the quiet ones who don't attempt to change your mind but allow you to go through the motions for you to learn. If you're relating to this dynamic duos, it is exactly that – your devilish egoic ways convincingly exclude the angelic whispers of silent-knowing. We know what is right or wrong. It's the very cunning ways of one's Ego that knows itself better than you do. Consider waking up and always wanting more stuff every day shopping only to later sell half-or-more of what you were convinced you needed. What the Heart wants is knowing but what you need is for show. Herein lies the difference between needs and wants. We are not always able to justify the means so that's where the Ego gets involved. Not many have not had buyer's remorse and ended up selling excess and/or returning stuff they didn't need. What comes of all this accumulation? Is it fair to say that you shopped till you dropped thousands of dollars only to go into even greater debt? Isn't this a similar metaphoric example of what the United States have been doing now for decades? Borrowing money to pay off debt that isn't shown on the books, leaving the US in trillion-dollar debt? This is debt on a global scale and in our personal lives. Who is going to save you and who will save America? With so many hidden costs that humans tend to forget about, the monthly fees keep adding up… monthly apps, the cloud, phone service charges, uprising costs of groceries, insurance costs, upgrading phone costs, fees for music and downloading, internet WIFI and streaming, and so much more that people don't recall that is an automatic debt coming out of your bank account and/or credit card. What madness!!! Accruing excess is what society has taught America, from the get go… "they" get you so far stuck inside the cost of being in the matrix that getting out is almost impossible. People are contemplating moving, downsizing to those tiny homes just to cut costs; not to mention growing their own food and setting up passive income avenues of income. The world's gone crazy because Humans are allowing the matrix to control their world. Why? If the government has us so far into debt how else can Humanity gain real insight to the root cause of the problem. Aren't "they" supposed to be our dictatorship of change, of learning and growing, of teaching us? So far... What have you learned about the way the Western hemisphere has been taught? Are we to blame for their inability to be cost-effective? The spending is atrocious and it continues to get worse... who's looking? Why is it ok for our country and other countries to be paying off Peter to pay Paul? Have we not learned anything of value? Why is the US literally producing more dollar bills while everywhere in the world the dollar has lost its value? Does this make any sense...cents? A vicious cycle that has been like a whirlpool of contaminated earnings that no one knows about. Perhaps we should just keep using our 'plastic' credit cards and forgo what our credit rating scores say...since there is no way for people to get overly stressed about their spending while those in power are not earning their keep. Who's to say that a credit score matters ever... to whom it may concern: newsflash, humans are fed up and not giving a shit about whether they're in debt, whether they go bankrupt only to begin again – what really matters? Societal norms are being thrown out the window... and, why should Humanity suffer at the cost of "they're foolish spending?" We're aware of "it" happening – while other countries borrow from the IMP, America is trading their soul for other resources while misusing student government loans of kids that will probably never be able to pay them off. The list goes on.... When, what, and who can stop this madness? Soon, Humanity will be very clear in precisely pointing the finger back to the perpetrators who are stealing from us. Protesting, riots and the like might become a thing of the norm as it has in other parts of the countries... who will prevail? Can Humanity Save Herself? What can we do as a community to alleviate this misuse of power in the world at large? We can begin by NOT listening to all the FEAR-based threats of our so-called alleged fearless leaders and start just living a life that brings us joy, peace, comfort – ignoring what "they" say is the beginning of our Spiritual Revolution Movement. "Do as I say, not what I do" will be a thing of the past… who cares if the end game is bankruptcy – banks are losing money, someday loans will be extinct, social security will be gone and the only resources that Humans will have to fall back upon is Family. Why not live together as a family united in Love and members pitch in to assist? Things are going to change in deeper ways that will inevitably give value to the traditions of community, comradery, communion with like-minded value systems. There will be a new-value system that will hold us responsible, valued and provide a Love of safety, protection and guidance for our fellow man. Let's forgo what "they" have poisoned by dictating nonsensical stress that we need to stop spending while they spend billions/trillions on keeping up with the political lifestyle of the rich. Richness is about community, it's about family values that orchestrate a life of simple pleasures; and above all, a unity. What "they" have attempted to continue doing is to "divide and conquer" because "they" think we are stupid, that we believe everything on the news, in the media and whatever other crap they're literally/figuratively feeding us. Just think about this… A New World Order is vastly approaching and the shifting of perspectives of all Humanity who will become their own Masters of their domain!!! Be warned… all of what has been taught is being scrutinized and re-evaluated for us to live our own lives in whatever way WE choose! The past "normal" is for suckers… and a newborn awareness has been rebirthed upon our planet. Honesty is the new norm…truth of one's spirit will be what is worth fighting for…

People are waking up to the coercion of the darkness and are figuring it out…or, will be very soon. What values we hold near and dear to our hearts will be changing; and, for many, are changing now. Congruent to the times will factor into our life as an "all for one, one for all" attitude. The times have changed and humans are not seeking a vengeful place to be regretting but a place of peaceful resolve. At least the majority of Humanity has already begun seeing the errors of their ways. No one should be holding any grudges since this duplicitously leads to bad karmic debt. Knowing how karmic debt works is the first of many leaders who occupy space instead of leadership – as in taking their own life into accountability. Now, that's a leader… yet those who are occupying space tend to lead by their Ego by not caring and/or following up with their direct reports on their emotional value; instead of a 20% increase in profit gains. While some pretend to care, they won't hesitate targeting their direct reports as a line up for termination. This is a vague example of what does happen in Corporate America as so many employees have no idea what the so-called man behind the curtain is contemplating. There are some Corporate Executives who DO make a difference and do change their employees' lives by caring and protecting them when a reorganization is getting ready to happen. These are the authentic Executives and are far and few between the lines of fire. What happens when a family's income gets taken away and there are no back-ups for income? Who will take the time and effort to begin headhunting for those employees that live for their job and are like family to the Executives? This is just a quick example of what really happens in Corporate America which is not a far cry from the truth… but, this is just the tip of the iceberg. So many who gave their entire lives to their jobs, after 20-30 years, here today gone tomorrow. No one cares… especially those who are shelving-out their own huge bonuses and/or who end up on the golf course Friday afternoons while the hard-workers are struggling in Friday-night traffic just to get a night to eat with their families. This has been the American way since the beginning of time. When will this trajectory change? Will this New World Order be the start of something new? Perhaps. No one's working…

Since the 2020 Covid scare, people have given up and are unsettled in ways that cannot be described. Most people are trying other sources of passive income just to stay home with their families; others are not investing a lifetime of investing in a company that will have no payback as in stock options etc. When will Humanity replicate a life of change in the dictatorship of "work less" while getting paid the big bucks. Where are these jobs? Do they exist? Why not really delve into a proper lifestyle of doing what you love and not worrying how the rest will unfold. Yes, people have to pay for their essential requirements of holding up a household but at what cost? Today there are so many people not only out of work but getting ready for retirement so that they can finally do what they love. Why wait? The old adage, "do what you love and the money will follow" is absolutely true. It's a shame that people don't have a sense of real responsibilities for their own actions. We as a society get so complacent when we need to be assertive and vice-a-versa… Will Humanity be able to change the course of their destiny? Or, is it already written…

PARTING IS SUCH SWEET SORROW

The physical death surpasses our birth-day as its fragrance has yet to be fulfilled with the quest, "Where to from here?" With every breath we inhale comes a beauty to behold; and, on the exhale, it is none. Our eyes shut out what was too heavy a burden to bear; our

694

hands fold in prayer; and the realization becomes another Dimension. In a perfect stream between calmness and pain comes a stillness of mind-over-material gain. Those who are blind continue to follow the wounds of themselves and the others. From one minute to the next the past is laid to rest…and we ask, "Where do we go after here?" In the realms that we visit, beyond what the eye can see…are places we call Heaven-sent, worlds within others' hopes, dreams take flight; in the still of the night. Once we embrace the peace and serenity that it dictates, our hearts beat internally from God's good grace. Can we ever look back without turning to salt - or - shall we throw salt over the shoulder to which life begets? No looking back can add more salt to the wound; but casting salt to the wind turns upward a chin. Saltwater heals or leaves others revealed to the physical body's immunity. Immune to one's suffering or healing thereof can cause one to question their Faith from above… Will you look back with a smile or weep those memories … Has this Earth school revealed your dreams aren't real; and, on this playground of Life will you choose to Feel? Did you make new friends and acquaintances too and love everyone knowing you? Will you find a solace in the warmth of the Sun or bow your head low with shaming of The Son? This soul journey of no return, not unless you've not cleared karmic justice being bold. Mankind will leave behind a Legacy of ruin which every child will bear fruit or be bare. What will be forgotten or remembered, instead? A family of karmics to have and to heal within every heart that embraces those feels. When the fragrance of death's flowers is lying quietly in-graved with many a forgotten phrase. Can we learn to tolerate the weight of the dirt that fell from one's body suffering inertness? The accumulation of years releasing our tears, the wealth that was given becomes our Family's treason…nothing left for many or none. Nothing left to squander as we expired in such flounder…head down

695

with shame, guilt of displacement. Falling asleep … others will weep unknowingly ignorant to say that our soul's journey lives on; we'll see you again an innocent child … *Behold a smile.*

WAKE UP

Find your truth, find your place in this world, find what your purpose is, find yourself! Or, else, you will be "bought out" you'll "sell out" your imprint of classification to-serve will be revoked – and, a purgatory life of solitude will ensue. This is NOT to scare you … this IS to WAKE YOU UP. "Lead us not into temptation, but deliver us from all evil." Not according to religious beliefs…but according to your soul's contract for coming here to make a difference. Are you making a difference in your life? Are you making a difference in the life or lives of others? To guide, serve, help, maintain a semblance of compassion that only your heart can feel? If not, ask yourself why…and what is the deal? BE HONEST. "For God so LOVED the world that He gave His only Begotten Son, Jesus" to observe the atrocity of the ONE who came to really show us what suffering looks like…and even though we did not feel that pain, ask yourselves what pain feels like now. Understand that Love is the only way IN— to getting OUT of the darkness, Matrix. What comes will go…all else is irrelevant. Our souls will be what will be saved, nothing else will matter. Believe in yourselves, believe in living a fulfilled life right now…believe that you will save yourself and you will be saved. REMEMBER why you are here, ask for Angelic guidance…signs etc. it's all coming to the point where if you are curious in the least bit, pray for help…and it will come in Divine Timing. Do not listen to what others say nor do what others are doing – for that may be your very downfall. We are ONE and collectively we have joined forces that threads us all together – seen and unseen. Therefore, what you may think as, "it's not my problem" IS definitely your problem...it will become your problem if we cannot come into union to help assist those in need. When did you begin to 'look away' and ignore those who are suffering, who are in the hospital dying of dis-ease, those who are out on the street corners, those who chose to come with impairments so that we can LOVE ALL lives as they are our own. Believe us when we say... to ignore the obvious is a sin unto itself. "Unto itself..." for one to look away and say, they're fine, they're looking for a handout, they're lying, they're wanting to get more money to drink or whatever the case is ... are you assuming that you feel this way because you ended up being trained to think that way; or, do you know the bum the corner personally that you cannot spare a dollar, a cup of coffee or a kind word?

Humanity is spiritually starving and is in need of connectivity – a conversation, connections, historic stories of our Heritage, in-deeds to others and working to impact other lives, being of our natural order.

"A Life of Freedom is a luxurious life, in-deed!" ™

NEEDS & IMPROVEMENTS OF THE SELF

1. Resisting the external needs of the Ego
2. Temptations in the Devil is in the details
3. Selling your soul for drugs, sex and rock&roll
4. Lusting upon others' fortunes
5. Recurring nightmares
6. The boy that cried "wolf"
7. Evil doers on every level

8. Patterns of the karmic kind

9. Uploading social media 24/7

10. See me, feel me, touch me… senses overload!

11. Just desserts

As the great Master, Marcus Annius Verus Aurelius, quoted, "He who lives in harmony with himself lives in harmony with the Universe."

Being in harmony with yourself is similar to the old adage, "As Above, So Below" because we live in union with our ancestors posing as our Spirit Guides; our Ascended Masters who gather ancient knowledge for us to attain; and, the union of ALL our ancestral past- bleeds into the same threads of our current lives – working in tandem. What you may be *resisting* is not only of your Egoic self, but also the orchestration of ties that bind to our Heritage. What we cannot fathom are these Unions constructed as waves of remembrance realized to the self. Therefore, your soul connects with the Heavens while your sacred temple/physical body is grounded on Earth manifesting your day-to- day sacred journey. However, since Humanity has only known polarities as Science/Spirit in separation; once your "realization" awakens, that polarity becomes one.

The real luxuries that living authentically will offer the essence of *Freedom*:

1. Chill mornings

2. Choosing - Freewill

3. Deep sleep

4. Peace of mind

698

5. Calmness

6. Kindness

7. Being present

8. Being Loved

9. Being Respected

10. Long showers

11. Walks

12. Forgive

13. Breathing

14. Sharing Love

These are simple extravagances in a full-filled *Life of Purpose*.

CHILD'S PLAY

Spirit speaks… is our Heavenly Family helping us to work on what needs to be done in Heaven, as on Earth. We are souls of a physical embodiment first and foremost, and, that must be understood as the magic creations of our internal self... We have all found it to be quite helpful to not necessarily question the reasons behind the Heaven-sent of all the children; but to go with the flow. What some deem as the play-by-play of this "playground" called Life… Whenever the body stirs up dis-ease and/or any ailment(s) unbeknownst to our external mind, we become frail and worried, stressed out and unable to perform even daily activities. Because there are so many who are not aware that their body's bodies are communicating with them, so too, is Spirit. The body endures much, yet it is in the constructs of the mind that can set you Free. Our physical bodies are the navigational system that we impose by the mental dialogue. Be kind with your mind! We are one-in-the same… Few too many are unaware of their bodies because they haven't understood this concept; and, those that know their body, are ignorant of the cause. Love can be captured only in the simple things in our lives that matter… beginning with the connectivity of mind and body - and/or - body and mind. How do you phrase that? Do you say mind, body and soul? Or, Body, Mind and soul? However, you come to say it aloud is where your first focus is… either mind/body or body/mind. Crucial though… as your mind may toggle negativity leading your body astray with dis-ease; or, if you are privy to the conversation, you are free of dis-ease. Should you seek a body/mind connectivity, you may seek to figure out what ails your body, delving deep into your emotional tablet – only to find what dis-ease is causing you emotional trauma. The mind/body body/mind connect seeks to speak of our wounds, scars, and all dis-eases in our physical and/or mental balance. It bears witness to both.

Layers require being shed – they are the karmic threads of our past patterns, triggers and findings we have lived. The essence of the Mind/Body/Spirit - The Trinity embarks to restore our Faith, knowing there is always HOPE (Having Obedience Praise Eternal). To have the wherewithal of discipline in obeying through praising eternal Life. One of the highest forms of LOVE is self-discipline. Through "sound healing" as in the music of sound, vibration/tone sound-bowl healing, binaural and monaural and solfeggio beats are on the rise as Alternative Healing. UCLA Medical Center, as well as many others, have proven to heal through "Biofeedback" – still on the rise. In the silence of Mother Nature, one listens. Why have humans been given two ears and one mouth? Lest we listen more to what needs to be heard as a shoulder to cry, a baby's cry, to what a loved one needs to hear and why … Within every sunrise, hear the bird's chirping singing a lullaby – wake up and seize a new day's dawn as miracles await those who listen. Listening with bated breath is the highest form of communication – it means, you *care*. Sharing feelings through all forms of communication; speaking, the written word, and listening is The Trinity. Why do we see how everything happens in threes? When all is said and done, what is left is the Kingdom.

The dis-ease that encapsulates the Mind/Body/Soul connectivity is how vested are we in leveling up? Do we really want to become better humans, better partners, better parents? For what purpose would God intend His people not to be the highest best version of themselves? For Love. "Love Makes The World Go Round" because it is not round in Nature, but round as cyclical. The life cycles we reincarnate back to Earth for is to become evolved knowing who IS and our purpose to see the reflections in the mirror. Moving forward, Humanity is co-creating with their higher self to orchestrate a masterpiece. Play it forward – ask, what would be your highest self- would do, listen in silence, sing your own song, find your own way, play it forward, listen to your body and what it needs, broaden your horizons … ALL for the sake of LOVE.

"A Tale of Two Cities" that have not found their way… one that is infinite Love and the other limited in Fear. Where will your soul evolve that already knows? Can you place limits on the Love for a child – or – does it breed a fear-based illusion of "Wish You Were Here?" Just when you "think" your "Body Is A Wonderland" a flash of insight shows up as "Twice Bitten!"

"AS ABOVE, SO BELOW…" When we take full accountability for our lives, the Spirit world assists in getting Humanity to higher

levels of consciousness – attaining all Siddhis; successful achievements of our spiritual practice(s). A sannyasin, known in Hindu, as the "student" being guided by their Master during and in the afterlife will show itself. "When the student is ready, the Master appears…" There are phases, trials and tribulations, the Dark Night of the Soul, Kundalini Rising that happens until the Master of one's Domain as HELP is on the way… Love is Heaven-sent in Divine timing. Every child of God's will, in some lifetime, has and/or will attain a place where only Heaven exists…and all others remain our mirrors. When this happens… our Heavenly families, that of our ancestral lineage, will lead the way for us to follow. No questions asked as the sannyas who are ready to take the next step, already KNOW. As the body/mind connects, when the physical body has been alerted to bring a soul home, the process begins in the NOSE. "The nose knows…" Spirit is everywhere - residing on Earth and in higher vibrational consciousness, every facet of our fragrance-of-existence is working together to deal, heal, and feel! Whichever place you may come to think "As above, Soso below" IS, it is right in front of you, behind you, and side-to-side… sending messages of Love. You just call out my name, and you know that we'll be there… It is that simple. When you PRAY, asking for HELP, KNOW that ALL listen…. A sannyas knows God's Love is ALL LOVE, therefore, walking the path of the unknown leads you to what is known. Remember.

"I WILL RISE", song by Chris Tomlin

Rising up doesn't only mean "ascending" to a higher consciousness; it also implies the rise of a new day (Sunrise) – rise up to the occasion, rise up to applaud an achievement, rise up from your chair, rise up to climb the corporate ladder, "arisen" is in-deeds a simile of the exact. We know what we've been taught, what we've borrowed... but, do you recall what was the great fall of all? In the song, "American Pie" lyrics go as such; "Do you recall the day the music died...started singing, "bye, bye, Miss American Pie" drove my levy to the levy but the levy was gone..." Could you ever conceive a day that would, or could ever stop the music from playing? Every note in that song, along with all the music across our Universe, is built on sound vibration; that is our power, our energetic force of Nature, and that cannot EVER be extinguished. Music is all energy that soothes the soul for the Ages that came before and to the future of Ages to come... we sing, dance, breathe, inhale/exhale, and dive deeper into our heart strings and the threads that bind every human to the other. It's like a familiarity of Family members that tell a story... "Every story is at the heart of another's narrative..." Perhaps your story collides with the others, or another that gives way to every string on the heartstrings of your essence." When this happens, the entire Heritage of a communion of souls, *"REJOICE!"*

"WE PRAY" sung by Coldplay emits our connection to the Threads of Love, in GOD.

ABOUT THE AUTHOR

Athena Park is adopted from Athens, Greece – ancient ruins that run through my blood feeling the Love in my Heritage. When the Greeks built the Acropolis in the 5th Century BC, during the Golden Age; what fascinates is Earth is currently entering into the Golden Age, 2024. Threads of History intertwine past/present lending the essence of value, once again. Earth is re-establishing Her strength and fortitude while standing tall conquering all. The Temple of Athena indicative of a goddess warrior with a curiosity that exists IN me. My "treasure quest" within every breath of life experiences to have and to hold IS for my soul's growth. A self-realization.

My memories of childhood…a discovery connected to the Arts, Fashion and Sales aligning in an external life similar to that of a mind, body and soul connect. Mother Nature connects us ALL through Her art & beauty with every sunrise/sunset; suffice to say, thorns of mindlessness stem from the internal essence of our soul. Connectivity to ALL – within and without promises of a re-birth…alone, in silence. Authentic I live and the Word of His Will is what I shall do. I surrender in peace, joy, abundance and Love for IAM God's Love Eternal.

Within my story of scars, wounds and redemption of riddles seeks to be a love-seeking child who falls from grace, Earthbound. I fell to my knees many times for what I needed to seize; heard every lyric in the songs of Love that was strong; prayed for mercy to all who broke me in Faith that started my Soul to Heal in Grace. Seeking to find me, myself and I, through a series of relentless teachings that had me questioning, "Why?" Although I despaired in what was my Heir…what felt like a void became a Knowing. No questions to ask down a long-winding path I found what I was seeking within. Forgiveness to all and to me who now sees that every one of You who played a part in my Life has brought me peace. "Thank You" for all the memories we've shared, the laughter and pain, the deep love I've attained. A soulful resurrection to follow your Heart, no matter what… Listen to your heart, be mindful of what you speak while others are listening, know what you Know and make decisions for your Highest Consciousness… Our Heritage is born of Truth and Love showing itself in every place that I've lived and with every person I did part…a sacrifice. Bounded by hearts, we are awarded such gifts that breathe in Life year-after-year. Hold onto each moment that leads to the next, silence awaits us in awe of its place. This masterpiece is God's work...I AM the Muse.

705

AUTHOR OF:

~ SAY A PRAYER

~ THE EGO HAS LANDED